Using and Porting
the GNU Compiler Collection

Richard M. Stallman

Last update 28 July 1999

for gcc-2.95

For GCC Version 2.95

Published by the Free Software Foundation
59 Temple Place - Suite 330
Boston, MA 02111-1307, USA
ISBN 1-882114-38-8

Short Contents

Table of Contents

17 Target Description Macros 393

1 Compile C, C++, Objective C, or Fortran

The C, C++, and Objective C, and Fortran versions of the compiler are integrated; this is why we use the name "GNU Compiler Collection". GCC can compile programs written in C, C++, Objective C, or Fortran. The Fortran compiler is described in a separate manual.

"GCC" is a common shorthand term for the GNU Compiler Collection. This is both the most general name for the compiler, and the name used when the emphasis is on compiling C programs (as the abbreviation formerly stood for "GNU C Compiler").

When referring to C++ compilation, it is usual to call the compiler "G++". Since there is only one compiler, it is also accurate to call it "GCC" no matter what the language context; however, the term "G++" is more useful when the emphasis is on compiling C++ programs.

We use the name "GCC" to refer to the compilation system as a whole, and more specifically to the language-independent part of the compiler. For example, we refer to the optimization options as affecting the behavior of "GCC" or sometimes just "the compiler".

Front ends for other languages, such as Ada 9X, Fortran, Modula-3, and Pascal, are under development. These front-ends, like that for C++, are built in subdirectories of GCC and link to it. The result is an integrated compiler that can compile programs written in C, C++, Objective C, or any of the languages for which you have installed front ends.

In this manual, we only discuss the options for the C, Objective-C, and C++ compilers and those of the GCC core. Consult the documentation of the other front ends for the options to use when compiling programs written in other languages.

G++ is a *compiler*, not merely a preprocessor. G++ builds object code directly from your C++ program source. There is no intermediate C version of the program. (By contrast, for example, some other implementations use a program that generates a C program from your C++ source.) Avoiding an intermediate C representation of the program means that you get better object code, and better debugging information. The GNU debugger, GDB, works with this information in the object code to give you comprehensive C++ source-level editing capabilities (see section "C and C++" in *Debugging with GDB*).

2 GCC Command Options

When you invoke GCC, it normally does preprocessing, compilation, assembly and linking. The "overall options" allow you to stop this process at an intermediate stage. For example, the '-c' option says not to run the linker. Then the output consists of object files output by the assembler.

Other options are passed on to one stage of processing. Some options control the preprocessor and others the compiler itself. Yet other options control the assembler and linker; most of these are not documented here, since you rarely need to use any of them.

Most of the command line options that you can use with GCC are useful for C programs; when an option is only useful with another language (usually C++), the explanation says so explicitly. If the description for a particular option does not mention a source language, you can use that option with all supported languages.

See Section 2.3 [Compiling C++ Programs], page 13, for a summary of special options for compiling C++ programs.

The `gcc` program accepts options and file names as operands. Many options have multiletter names; therefore multiple single-letter options may *not* be grouped: '-dr' is very different from '-d -r'.

You can mix options and other arguments. For the most part, the order you use doesn't matter. Order does matter when you use several options of the same kind; for example, if you specify '-L' more than once, the directories are searched in the order specified.

Many options have long names starting with '-f' or with '-W'—for example, '-fforce-mem', '-fstrength-reduce', '-Wformat' and so on. Most of these have both positive and negative forms; the negative form of '-ffoo' would be '-fno-foo'. This manual documents only one of these two forms, whichever one is not the default.

2.1 Option Summary

Here is a summary of all the options, grouped by type. Explanations are in the following sections.

Overall Options
> See Section 2.2 [Options Controlling the Kind of Output], page 11.
>
> > -c -S -E -o *file* -pipe -v --help -x *language*

C Language Options
> See Section 2.4 [Options Controlling C Dialect], page 13.
>
> > -ansi -flang-isoc9x -fallow-single-precision -fcond-mismatch
> >
> > -fno-asm -fno-builtin -ffreestanding -fhosted
> >
> > -fsigned-bitfields -fsigned-char -funsigned-bitfields

```
-funsigned-char   -fwritable-strings -traditional
-traditional-cpp  -trigraphs
```

C++ Language Options

See Section 2.5 [Options Controlling C++ Dialect], page 18.

```
-fno-access-control  -fcheck-new  -fconserve-space  -fdollars-
in-identifiers
-fno-elide-constructors  -fexternal-templates  -ffor-scope
-fno-for-scope  -fno-gnu-keywords  -fguiding-decls  -fhandle-
signatures
-fhonor-std -fhuge-objects  -fno-implicit-templates  -finit-
priority
-fno-implement-inlines -fname-mangling-version-n
-fno-default-inline  -foperator-names  -fno-optional-diags  -
fpermissive
-frepo  -fstrict-prototype -fsquangle  -ftemplate-depth-n
-fthis-is-variable  -fvtable-thunks  -nostdinc++  -Wctor-dtor-
privacy
-Wno-deprecated -Weffc++  -Wno-non-template-friend
-Wnon-virtual-dtor  -Wold-style-cast  -Woverloaded-virtual
-Wno-pmf-conversions  -Wreorder  -Wsign-promo  -Wsynth
```

Warning Options

See Section 2.6 [Options to Request or Suppress Warnings], page 25.

```
-fsyntax-only  -pedantic  -pedantic-errors
-w  -W  -Wall  -Waggregate-return  -Wbad-function-cast
-Wcast-align  -Wcast-qual  -Wchar-subscripts  -Wcomment
-Wconversion  -Werror  -Wformat
-Wid-clash-len  -Wimplicit  -Wimplicit-int
-Wimplicit-function-declaration  -Wimport
-Werror-implicit-function-declaration  -Winline
-Wlarger-than-len  -Wlong-long
-Wmain  -Wmissing-declarations  -Wmissing-noreturn
-Wmissing-prototypes  -Wmultichar  -Wnested-externs
-Wno-import  -Wparentheses -Wpointer-arith  -Wredundant-decls
-Wreturn-type -Wshadow  -Wsign-compare  -Wstrict-prototypes
-Wswitch  -Wtraditional
-Wtrigraphs  -Wundef  -Wuninitialized  -Wunused
-Wwrite-strings  -Wunknown-pragmas
```

Debugging Options

See Section 2.7 [Options for Debugging Your Program or GCC], page 33.

```
-a  -ax  -dletters  -fdump-unnumbered -fpretend-float
-fprofile-arcs  -ftest-coverage
```

```
-g   -glevel  -gcoff   -gdwarf  -gdwarf-1  -gdwarf-1+  -gdwarf-
2
-ggdb   -gstabs   -gstabs+   -gxcoff   -gxcoff+
-p   -pg   -print-file-name=library   -print-libgcc-file-name
-print-prog-name=program   -print-search-dirs   -save-temps
```

Optimization Options

> See Section 2.8 [Options that Control Optimization], page 40.

```
-fbranch-probabilities   -foptimize-register-moves
-fcaller-saves   -fcse-follow-jumps   -fcse-skip-blocks
-fdelayed-branch   -fexpensive-optimizations
-ffast-math   -ffloat-store   -fforce-addr   -fforce-mem
-fdata-sections -ffunction-sections  -fgcse
-finline-functions -finline-limit-n -fkeep-inline-functions
-fno-default-inline  -fno-defer-pop   -fno-function-cse
-fno-inline   -fno-peephole  -fomit-frame-pointer -fregmove
-frerun-cse-after-loop  -frerun-loop-opt -fschedule-insns
-fschedule-insns2  -fstrength-reduce  -fthread-jumps
-funroll-all-loops   -funroll-loops
-fmove-all-movables  -freduce-all-givs -fstrict-aliasing
-O   -O0   -O1   -O2   -O3 -Os
```

Preprocessor Options

> See Section 2.9 [Options Controlling the Preprocessor], page 48.

```
-Aquestion(answer)   -C  -dD  -dM  -dN
-Dmacro[=defn]   -E  -H
-idirafter dir
-include file  -imacros file
-iprefix file  -iwithprefix dir
-iwithprefixbefore dir  -isystem dir -isystem-c++ dir
-M  -MD  -MM  -MMD  -MG  -nostdinc  -P  -trigraphs
-undef  -Umacro  -Wp,option
```

Assembler Option

> See Section 2.10 [Passing Options to the Assembler], page 51.

```
-Wa,option
```

Linker Options

> See Section 2.11 [Options for Linking], page 51.

```
object-file-name  -llibrary
-nostartfiles  -nodefaultlibs  -nostdlib
-s  -static  -shared  -symbolic
-Wl,option  -Xlinker option
-u symbol
```

Directory Options

> See Section 2.12 [Options for Directory Search], page 54.

-Bprefix   -Idir   -I-   -Ldir   -specs=file

Target Options
        See Section 2.13 [Target Options], page 55.

        -b machine   -V version

Machine Dependent Options
        See Section 2.14 [Hardware Models and Configurations], page 56.

        M680x0 Options
        -m68000   -m68020   -m68020-40   -m68020-60   -m68030   -m68040
        -m68060   -mcpu32 -m5200 -m68881   -mbitfield   -mc68000
        -mc68020   -mfpa -mnobitfield   -mrtd   -mshort   -msoft-float
        -malign-int

        VAX Options
        -mg   -mgnu   -munix

        SPARC Options
        -mcpu=cpu type
        -mtune=cpu type
        -mcmodel=code model
        -malign-jumps=num   -malign-loops=num
        -malign-functions=num
        -m32   -m64
        -mapp-regs   -mbroken-saverestore   -mcypress   -mepilogue
        -mflat   -mfpu   -mhard-float   -mhard-quad-float
        -mimpure-text   -mlive-g0   -mno-app-regs   -mno-epilogue
        -mno-flat   -mno-fpu   -mno-impure-text
        -mno-stack-bias   -mno-unaligned-doubles
        -msoft-float   -msoft-quad-float   -msparclite   -mstack-bias
        -msupersparc   -munaligned-doubles   -mv8

        Convex Options
        -mc1   -mc2   -mc32   -mc34   -mc38
        -margcount   -mnoargcount
        -mlong32   -mlong64
        -mvolatile-cache   -mvolatile-nocache

        AMD29K Options
        -m29000   -m29050   -mbw   -mnbw   -mdw   -mndw
        -mlarge   -mnormal   -msmall
        -mkernel-registers   -mno-reuse-arg-regs
        -mno-stack-check   -mno-storem-bug
        -mreuse-arg-regs   -msoft-float   -mstack-check
        -mstorem-bug   -muser-registers

ARM Options
```
-mapcs-frame -mno-apcs-frame
-mapcs-26 -mapcs-32
-mapcs-stack-check -mno-apcs-stack-check
-mapcs-float -mno-apcs-float
-mapcs-reentrant -mno-apcs-reentrant
-msched-prolog -mno-sched-prolog
-mlittle-endian -mbig-endian -mwords-little-endian
-mshort-load-bytes -mno-short-load-bytes -mshort-load-words
-mno-short-load-words -msoft-float -mhard-float -mfpe
-mthumb-interwork -mno-thumb-interwork
-mcpu= -march= -mfpe=
-mstructure-size-boundary=
-mbsd -mxopen -mno-symrename
-mabort-on-noreturn
-mno-sched-prolog
```

Thumb Options
```
-mtpcs-frame -mno-tpcs-frame
-mtpcs-leaf-frame -mno-tpcs-leaf-frame
-mlittle-endian  -mbig-endian
-mthumb-interwork -mno-thumb-interwork
-mstructure-size-boundary=
```

MN10200 Options
```
-mrelax
```

MN10300 Options
```
-mmult-bug
-mno-mult-bug
-mrelax
```

M32R/D Options
```
-mcode-model=model type   -msdata=sdata type
-G num
```

M88K Options
```
-m88000  -m88100  -m88110  -mbig-pic
-mcheck-zero-division  -mhandle-large-shift
-midentify-revision  -mno-check-zero-division
-mno-ocs-debug-info  -mno-ocs-frame-position
-mno-optimize-arg-area  -mno-serialize-volatile
-mno-underscores  -mocs-debug-info
```

```
-mocs-frame-position   -moptimize-arg-area
-mserialize-volatile   -mshort-data-num   -msvr3
-msvr4   -mtrap-large-shift   -muse-div-instruction
-mversion-03.00   -mwarn-passed-structs
```

RS/6000 and PowerPC Options
```
-mcpu=cpu type
-mtune=cpu type
-mpower   -mno-power   -mpower2   -mno-power2
-mpowerpc   -mno-powerpc
-mpowerpc-gpopt   -mno-powerpc-gpopt
-mpowerpc-gfxopt   -mno-powerpc-gfxopt
-mnew-mnemonics   -mno-new-mnemonics
-mfull-toc   -mminimal-toc   -mno-fop-in-toc   -mno-sum-in-toc
-maix64   -maix32   -mxl-call   -mno-xl-call   -mthreads   -mpe
-msoft-float   -mhard-float   -mmultiple   -mno-multiple
-mstring   -mno-string   -mupdate   -mno-update
-mfused-madd   -mno-fused-madd   -mbit-align   -mno-bit-align
-mstrict-align   -mno-strict-align   -mrelocatable
-mno-relocatable   -mrelocatable-lib   -mno-relocatable-lib
-mtoc   -mno-toc   -mlittle   -mlittle-endian   -mbig   -mbig-endian
-mcall-aix   -mcall-sysv   -mprototype   -mno-prototype
-msim   -mmvme   -mads   -myellowknife   -memb   -msdata
-msdata=opt   -G num
```

RT Options
```
-mcall-lib-mul   -mfp-arg-in-fpregs   -mfp-arg-in-gregs
-mfull-fp-blocks   -mhc-struct-return   -min-line-mul
-mminimum-fp-blocks   -mnohc-struct-return
```

MIPS Options
```
-mabicalls   -mcpu=cpu type   -membedded-data
-membedded-pic   -mfp32   -mfp64   -mgas   -mgp32   -mgp64
-mgpopt   -mhalf-pic   -mhard-float   -mint64   -mips1
-mips2   -mips3 -mips4 -mlong64   -mlong32 -mlong-calls
-mmemcpy   -mmips-as   -mmips-tfile   -mno-abicalls
-mno-embedded-data   -mno-embedded-pic
-mno-gpopt   -mno-long-calls
-mno-memcpy   -mno-mips-tfile   -mno-rnames   -mno-stats
-mrnames   -msoft-float
-m4650   -msingle-float   -mmad
-mstats   -EL   -EB   -G num   -nocpp
-mabi=32 -mabi=n32 -mabi=64 -mabi=eabi
```

i386 Options
```
-mcpu=cpu type
-march=cpu type
-mieee-fp  -mno-fancy-math-387
-mno-fp-ret-in-387  -msoft-float  -msvr3-shlib
-mno-wide-multiply  -mrtd  -malign-double
-mreg-alloc=list  -mregparm=num
-malign-jumps=num  -malign-loops=num
-malign-functions=num -mpreferred-stack-boundary=num
```

HPPA Options
```
-march=architecture type
-mbig-switch  -mdisable-fpregs  -mdisable-indexing
-mfast-indirect-calls  -mgas  -mjump-in-delay
-mlong-load-store  -mno-big-switch  -mno-disable-fpregs
-mno-disable-indexing  -mno-fast-indirect-calls  -mno-gas
-mno-jump-in-delay  -mno-long-load-store
-mno-portable-runtime  -mno-soft-float  -mno-space
-mno-space-regs  -msoft-float  -mpa-risc-1-0
-mpa-risc-1-1  -mpa-risc-2-0 -mportable-runtime
-mschedule=cpu type  -mspace  -mspace-regs
```

Intel 960 Options
```
-mcpu type  -masm-compat  -mclean-linkage
-mcode-align  -mcomplex-addr  -mleaf-procedures
-mic-compat  -mic2.0-compat  -mic3.0-compat
-mintel-asm  -mno-clean-linkage  -mno-code-align
-mno-complex-addr  -mno-leaf-procedures
-mno-old-align  -mno-strict-align  -mno-tail-call
-mnumerics  -mold-align  -msoft-float  -mstrict-align
-mtail-call
```

DEC Alpha Options
```
-mfp-regs  -mno-fp-regs -mno-soft-float  -msoft-float
-malpha-as -mgas
-mieee  -mieee-with-inexact  -mieee-conformant
-mfp-trap-mode=mode  -mfp-rounding-mode=mode
-mtrap-precision=mode  -mbuild-constants
-mcpu=cpu type
-mbwx -mno-bwx -mcix -mno-cix -mmax -mno-max
-mmemory-latency=time
```

Clipper Options
```
-mc300  -mc400
```

H8/300 Options

```
-mrelax  -mh -ms -mint32  -malign-300
```

SH Options

```
-m1  -m2  -m3  -m3e  -mb  -ml  -mdalign -mrelax
```

System V Options

```
-Qy  -Qn  -YP,paths  -Ym,dir
```

ARC Options

```
-EB  -EL
-mmangle-cpu  -mcpu=cpu  -mtext=text section
-mdata=data section  -mrodata=readonly data section
```

TMS320C3x/C4x Options

```
-mcpu=cpu -mbig -msmall -mregparm -mmemparm
-mfast-fix -mmpyi -mbk -mti -mdp-isr-reload
-mrpts=count  -mrptb -mdb -mloop-unsigned
-mparallel-insns -mparallel-mpy -mpreserve-float
```

V850 Options

```
-mlong-calls -mno-long-calls -mep -mno-ep
-mprolog-function -mno-prolog-function -mspace
-mtda=n -msda=n -mzda=n
-mv850 -mbig-switch
```

NS32K Options

```
-m32032 -m32332 -m32532 -m32081 -m32381 -mmult-add -mnomult-
add
-msoft-float -mrtd -mnortd -mregparam -mnoregparam -msb -mnosb
-mbitfield -mnobitfield -mhimem -mnohimem
```

Code Generation Options

See Section 2.15 [Options for Code Generation Conventions], page 108.

```
-fcall-saved-reg  -fcall-used-reg
-fexceptions -ffixed-reg  -finhibit-size-directive
-fcheck-memory-usage  -fprefix-function-name
-fno-common  -fno-ident  -fno-gnu-linker
-fpcc-struct-return  -fpic  -fPIC
-freg-struct-return  -fshared-data  -fshort-enums
-fshort-double  -fvolatile  -fvolatile-global
-fvolatile-static -fverbose-asm -fpack-struct
-fstack-check  -fargument-alias  -fargument-noalias
```

```
-fargument-noalias-global   -fleading-underscore
```

2.2 Options Controlling the Kind of Output

Compilation can involve up to four stages: preprocessing, compilation proper, assembly and linking, always in that order. The first three stages apply to an individual source file, and end by producing an object file; linking combines all the object files (those newly compiled, and those specified as input) into an executable file.

For any given input file, the file name suffix determines what kind of compilation is done:

file.c   C source code which must be preprocessed.

file.i   C source code which should not be preprocessed.

file.ii   C++ source code which should not be preprocessed.

file.m   Objective-C source code. Note that you must link with the library 'libobjc.a' to make an Objective-C program work.

file.h   C header file (not to be compiled or linked).

file.cc
file.cxx
file.cpp
file.C   C++ source code which must be preprocessed. Note that in '.cxx', the last two letters must both be literally 'x'. Likewise, '.C' refers to a literal capital C.

file.s   Assembler code.

file.S   Assembler code which must be preprocessed.

other   An object file to be fed straight into linking. Any file name with no recognized suffix is treated this way.

You can specify the input language explicitly with the '-x' option:

-x *language*
               Specify explicitly the *language* for the following input files (rather than letting the compiler choose a default based on the file name suffix). This option applies to all following input files until the next '-x' option. Possible values for *language* are:

```
c  objective-c  c++
c-header  cpp-output  c++-cpp-output
assembler  assembler-with-cpp
```

-x none   Turn off any specification of a language, so that subsequent files are handled according to their file name suffixes (as they are if '-x' has not been used at all).

If you only want some of the stages of compilation, you can use '-x' (or filename suffixes) to tell gcc where to start, and one of the options '-c', '-S', or '-E' to say where gcc is to stop. Note that some combinations (for example, '-x cpp-output -E' instruct gcc to do nothing at all.

-c
: Compile or assemble the source files, but do not link. The linking stage simply is not done. The ultimate output is in the form of an object file for each source file.

  By default, the object file name for a source file is made by replacing the suffix '.c', '.i', '.s', etc., with '.o'.

  Unrecognized input files, not requiring compilation or assembly, are ignored.

-S
: Stop after the stage of compilation proper; do not assemble. The output is in the form of an assembler code file for each non-assembler input file specified.

  By default, the assembler file name for a source file is made by replacing the suffix '.c', '.i', etc., with '.s'.

  Input files that don't require compilation are ignored.

-E
: Stop after the preprocessing stage; do not run the compiler proper. The output is in the form of preprocessed source code, which is sent to the standard output.

  Input files which don't require preprocessing are ignored.

-o file
: Place output in file *file*. This applies regardless to whatever sort of output is being produced, whether it be an executable file, an object file, an assembler file or preprocessed C code.

  Since only one output file can be specified, it does not make sense to use '-o' when compiling more than one input file, unless you are producing an executable file as output.

  If '-o' is not specified, the default is to put an executable file in 'a.out', the object file for 'source.*suffix*' in 'source.o', its assembler file in 'source.s', and all preprocessed C source on standard output.

-v
: Print (on standard error output) the commands executed to run the stages of compilation. Also print the version number of the compiler driver program and of the preprocessor and the compiler proper.

-pipe
: Use pipes rather than temporary files for communication between the various stages of compilation. This fails to work on some systems where the assembler is unable to read from a pipe; but the GNU assembler has no trouble.

--help
: Print (on the standard output) a description of the command line options understood by gcc. If the -v option is also specified

then `--help` will also be passed on to the various processes invoked by `gcc`, so that they can display the command line options they accept. If the `-W` option is also specified then command line options which have no documentation associated with them will also be displayed.

2.3 Compiling C++ Programs

C++ source files conventionally use one of the suffixes '.C', '.cc', '.cpp', '.c++', '.cp', or '.cxx'; preprocessed C++ files use the suffix '.ii'. GCC recognizes files with these names and compiles them as C++ programs even if you call the compiler the same way as for compiling C programs (usually with the name `gcc`).

However, C++ programs often require class libraries as well as a compiler that understands the C++ language—and under some circumstances, you might want to compile programs from standard input, or otherwise without a suffix that flags them as C++ programs. `g++` is a program that calls GCC with the default language set to C++, and automatically specifies linking against the C++ library. On many systems, the script `g++` is also installed with the name `c++`.

When you compile C++ programs, you may specify many of the same command-line options that you use for compiling programs in any language; or command-line options meaningful for C and related languages; or options that are meaningful only for C++ programs. See Section 2.4 [Options Controlling C Dialect], page 13, for explanations of options for languages related to C. See Section 2.5 [Options Controlling C++ Dialect], page 18, for explanations of options that are meaningful only for C++ programs.

2.4 Options Controlling C Dialect

The following options control the dialect of C (or languages derived from C, such as C++ and Objective C) that the compiler accepts:

-ansi   In C mode, support all ANSI standard C programs. In C++ mode, remove GNU extensions that conflict with ANSI C++.

            This turns off certain features of GCC that are incompatible with ANSI C (when compiling C code), or of ANSI standard C++ (when compiling C++ code), such as the `asm` and `typeof` keywords, and predefined macros such as `unix` and `vax` that identify the type of system you are using. It also enables the undesirable and rarely used ANSI trigraph feature. For the C compiler, it disables recognition of C++ style '//' comments as well as the `inline` keyword. For the C++ compiler, '-foperator-names' is enabled as well.

The alternate keywords `__asm__`, `__extension__`, `__inline__` and `__typeof__` continue to work despite '`-ansi`'. You would not want to use them in an ANSI C program, of course, but it is useful to put them in header files that might be included in compilations done with '`-ansi`'. Alternate predefined macros such as `__unix__` and `__vax__` are also available, with or without '`-ansi`'.

The '`-ansi`' option does not cause non-ANSI programs to be rejected gratuitously. For that, '`-pedantic`' is required in addition to '`-ansi`'. See Section 2.6 [Warning Options], page 25.

The macro `__STRICT_ANSI__` is predefined when the '`-ansi`' option is used. Some header files may notice this macro and refrain from declaring certain functions or defining certain macros that the ANSI standard doesn't call for; this is to avoid interfering with any programs that might use these names for other things.

The functions `alloca`, `abort`, `exit`, and `_exit` are not builtin functions when '`-ansi`' is used.

`-flang-isoc9x`

Enable support for features found in the C9X standard. In particular, enable support for the C9X `restrict` keyword.

Even when this option is not specified, you can still use some C9X features in so far as they do not conflict with previous C standards. For example, you may use `__restrict__` even when -flang-isoc9x is not specified.

`-fno-asm`   Do not recognize `asm`, `inline` or `typeof` as a keyword, so that code can use these words as identifiers. You can use the keywords `__asm__`, `__inline__` and `__typeof__` instead. '`-ansi`' implies '`-fno-asm`'.

In C++, this switch only affects the `typeof` keyword, since `asm` and `inline` are standard keywords. You may want to use the '`-fno-gnu-keywords`' flag instead, as it also disables the other, C++-specific, extension keywords such as `headof`.

`-fno-builtin`

Don't recognize builtin functions that do not begin with '`__builtin_`' as prefix. Currently, the functions affected include `abort`, `abs`, `alloca`, `cos`, `exit`, `fabs`, `ffs`, `labs`, `memcmp`, `memcpy`, `sin`, `sqrt`, `strcmp`, `strcpy`, and `strlen`.

GCC normally generates special code to handle certain builtin functions more efficiently; for instance, calls to `alloca` may become single instructions that adjust the stack directly, and calls to `memcpy` may become inline copy loops. The resulting code is often both smaller and faster, but since the function calls no longer appear as such, you cannot set a breakpoint on those calls, nor can you change the behavior of the functions by linking with a different library.

The '-ansi' option prevents `alloca` and `ffs` from being builtin functions, since these functions do not have an ANSI standard meaning.

-fhosted

Assert that compilation takes place in a hosted environment. This implies '-fbuiltin'. A hosted environment is one in which the entire standard library is available, and in which `main` has a return type of `int`. Examples are nearly everything except a kernel. This is equivalent to '-fno-freestanding'.

-ffreestanding

Assert that compilation takes place in a freestanding environment. This implies '-fno-builtin'. A freestanding environment is one in which the standard library may not exist, and program startup may not necessarily be at `main`. The most obvious example is an OS kernel. This is equivalent to '-fno-hosted'.

-trigraphs

Support ANSI C trigraphs. You don't want to know about this brain-damage. The '-ansi' option implies '-trigraphs'.

-traditional

Attempt to support some aspects of traditional C compilers. Specifically:

- All `extern` declarations take effect globally even if they are written inside of a function definition. This includes implicit declarations of functions.

- The newer keywords `typeof`, `inline`, `signed`, `const` and `volatile` are not recognized. (You can still use the alternative keywords such as `__typeof__`, `__inline__`, and so on.)

- Comparisons between pointers and integers are always allowed.

- Integer types `unsigned short` and `unsigned char` promote to `unsigned int`.

- Out-of-range floating point literals are not an error.

- Certain constructs which ANSI regards as a single invalid preprocessing number, such as '0xe-0xd', are treated as expressions instead.

- String "constants" are not necessarily constant; they are stored in writable space, and identical looking constants are allocated separately. (This is the same as the effect of '-fwritable-strings'.)

- All automatic variables not declared `register` are preserved by `longjmp`. Ordinarily, GNU C follows ANSI C: automatic variables not declared `volatile` may be clobbered.

- The character escape sequences '\x' and '\a' evaluate as the literal characters 'x' and 'a' respectively. Without '-traditional', '\x' is a prefix for the hexadecimal representation of a character, and '\a' produces a bell.

You may wish to use '-fno-builtin' as well as '-traditional' if your program uses names that are normally GNU C builtin functions for other purposes of its own.

You cannot use '-traditional' if you include any header files that rely on ANSI C features. Some vendors are starting to ship systems with ANSI C header files and you cannot use '-traditional' on such systems to compile files that include any system headers.

The '-traditional' option also enables '-traditional-cpp', which is described next.

-traditional-cpp

Attempt to support some aspects of traditional C preprocessors. Specifically:

- Comments convert to nothing at all, rather than to a space. This allows traditional token concatenation.

- In a preprocessing directive, the '#' symbol must appear as the first character of a line.

- Macro arguments are recognized within string constants in a macro definition (and their values are stringified, though without additional quote marks, when they appear in such a context). The preprocessor always considers a string constant to end at a newline.

- The predefined macro `__STDC__` is not defined when you use '-traditional', but `__GNUC__` is (since the GNU extensions which `__GNUC__` indicates are not affected by '-traditional'). If you need to write header files that work differently depending on whether '-traditional' is in use, by testing both of these predefined macros you can distinguish four situations: GNU C, traditional GNU C, other ANSI C compilers, and other old C compilers. The predefined macro `__STDC_VERSION__` is also not defined when you use '-traditional'. See section "Standard Predefined Macros" in *The C Preprocessor*, for more discussion of these and other predefined macros.

- The preprocessor considers a string constant to end at a newline (unless the newline is escaped with '\'). (Without

'-traditional', string constants can contain the newline character as typed.)

-fcond-mismatch

Allow conditional expressions with mismatched types in the second and third arguments. The value of such an expression is void.

-funsigned-char

Let the type `char` be unsigned, like `unsigned char`.

Each kind of machine has a default for what `char` should be. It is either like `unsigned char` by default or like `signed char` by default.

Ideally, a portable program should always use `signed char` or `unsigned char` when it depends on the signedness of an object. But many programs have been written to use plain `char` and expect it to be signed, or expect it to be unsigned, depending on the machines they were written for. This option, and its inverse, let you make such a program work with the opposite default.

The type `char` is always a distinct type from each of `signed char` or `unsigned char`, even though its behavior is always just like one of those two.

-fsigned-char

Let the type `char` be signed, like `signed char`.

Note that this is equivalent to '-fno-unsigned-char', which is the negative form of '-funsigned-char'. Likewise, the option '-fno-signed-char' is equivalent to '-funsigned-char'.

You may wish to use '-fno-builtin' as well as '-traditional' if your program uses names that are normally GNU C builtin functions for other purposes of its own.

You cannot use '-traditional' if you include any header files that rely on ANSI C features. Some vendors are starting to ship systems with ANSI C header files and you cannot use '-traditional' on such systems to compile files that include any system headers.

-fsigned-bitfields
-funsigned-bitfields
-fno-signed-bitfields
-fno-unsigned-bitfields

These options control whether a bitfield is signed or unsigned, when the declaration does not use either `signed` or `unsigned`. By default, such a bitfield is signed, because this is consistent: the basic integer types such as `int` are signed types.

However, when '-traditional' is used, bitfields are all unsigned no matter what.

-fwritable-strings

Store string constants in the writable data segment and don't uniquize them. This is for compatibility with old programs which assume they can write into string constants. The option '-traditional' also has this effect.

Writing into string constants is a very bad idea; "constants" should be constant.

-fallow-single-precision

Do not promote single precision math operations to double precision, even when compiling with '-traditional'.

Traditional K&R C promotes all floating point operations to double precision, regardless of the sizes of the operands. On the architecture for which you are compiling, single precision may be faster than double precision. If you must use '-traditional', but want to use single precision operations when the operands are single precision, use this option. This option has no effect when compiling with ANSI or GNU C conventions (the default).

2.5 Options Controlling C++ Dialect

This section describes the command-line options that are only meaningful for C++ programs; but you can also use most of the GNU compiler options regardless of what language your program is in. For example, you might compile a file firstClass.C like this:

```
g++ -g -frepo -O -c firstClass.C
```

In this example, only '-frepo' is an option meant only for C++ programs; you can use the other options with any language supported by GCC.

Here is a list of options that are *only* for compiling C++ programs:

-fno-access-control

Turn off all access checking. This switch is mainly useful for working around bugs in the access control code.

-fcheck-new

Check that the pointer returned by operator new is non-null before attempting to modify the storage allocated. The current Working Paper requires that operator new never return a null pointer, so this check is normally unnecessary.

An alternative to using this option is to specify that your operator new does not throw any exceptions; if you declare it 'throw()', g++ will check the return value. See also 'new (nothrow)'.

`-fconserve-space`

> Put uninitialized or runtime-initialized global variables into the common segment, as C does. This saves space in the executable at the cost of not diagnosing duplicate definitions. If you compile with this flag and your program mysteriously crashes after `main()` has completed, you may have an object that is being destroyed twice because two definitions were merged.
>
> This option is no longer useful on most targets, now that support has been added for putting variables into BSS without making them common.

`-fdollars-in-identifiers`

> Accept '`$`' in identifiers. You can also explicitly prohibit use of '`$`' with the option '`-fno-dollars-in-identifiers`'. (GNU C allows '`$`' by default on most target systems, but there are a few exceptions.) Traditional C allowed the character '`$`' to form part of identifiers. However, ANSI C and C++ forbid '`$`' in identifiers.

`-fno-elide-constructors`

> The C++ standard allows an implementation to omit creating a temporary which is only used to initialize another object of the same type. Specifying this option disables that optimization, and forces g++ to call the copy constructor in all cases.

`-fexternal-templates`

> Cause template instantiations to obey '`#pragma interface`' and '`implementation`'; template instances are emitted or not according to the location of the template definition. See Section 5.5 [Template Instantiation], page 211, for more information.
>
> This option is deprecated.

`-falt-external-templates`

> Similar to -fexternal-templates, but template instances are emitted or not according to the place where they are first instantiated. See Section 5.5 [Template Instantiation], page 211, for more information.
>
> This option is deprecated.

`-ffor-scope`
`-fno-for-scope`

> If -ffor-scope is specified, the scope of variables declared in a *for-init-statement* is limited to the '`for`' loop itself, as specified by the draft C++ standard. If -fno-for-scope is specified, the scope of variables declared in a *for-init-statement* extends to the end of the enclosing scope, as was the case in old versions of gcc, and other (traditional) implementations of C++.

The default if neither flag is given to follow the standard, but to allow and give a warning for old-style code that would otherwise be invalid, or have different behavior.

`-fno-gnu-keywords`

Do not recognize `classof`, `headof`, `signature`, `sigof` or `typeof` as a keyword, so that code can use these words as identifiers. You can use the keywords `__classof__`, `__headof__`, `__signature__`, `__sigof__`, and `__typeof__` instead. '-ansi' implies '-fno-gnu-keywords'.

`-fguiding-decls`

Treat a function declaration with the same type as a potential function template instantiation as though it declares that instantiation, not a normal function. If a definition is given for the function later in the translation unit (or another translation unit if the target supports weak symbols), that definition will be used; otherwise the template will be instantiated. This behavior reflects the C++ language prior to September 1996, when guiding declarations were removed.

This option implies '-fname-mangling-version-0', and will not work with other name mangling versions. Like all options that change the ABI, all C++ code, *including libgcc.a* must be built with the same setting of this option.

`-fhandle-signatures`

Recognize the `signature` and `sigof` keywords for specifying abstract types. The default ('-fno-handle-signatures') is not to recognize them. See Section 5.7 [C++ Signatures], page 215.

`-fhonor-std`

Treat the `namespace std` as a namespace, instead of ignoring it. For compatibility with earlier versions of g++, the compiler will, by default, ignore `namespace-declarations`, `using-declarations`, `using-directives`, and `namespace-names`, if they involve `std`.

`-fhuge-objects`

Support virtual function calls for objects that exceed the size representable by a 'short int'. Users should not use this flag by default; if you need to use it, the compiler will tell you so.

This flag is not useful when compiling with -fvtable-thunks.

Like all options that change the ABI, all C++ code, *including libgcc* must be built with the same setting of this option.

`-fno-implicit-templates`

Never emit code for non-inline templates which are instantiated implicitly (i.e. by use); only emit code for explicit instantiations. See Section 5.5 [Template Instantiation], page 211, for more information.

`-fno-implicit-inline-templates`

Don't emit code for implicit instantiations of inline templates, either. The default is to handle inlines differently so that compiles with and without optimization will need the same set of explicit instantiations.

`-finit-priority`

Support '`__attribute__ ((init_priority (n)))`' for controlling the order of initialization of file-scope objects. On ELF targets, this requires GNU ld 2.10 or later.

`-fno-implement-inlines`

To save space, do not emit out-of-line copies of inline functions controlled by '`#pragma implementation`'. This will cause linker errors if these functions are not inlined everywhere they are called.

`-fname-mangling-version-`*n*

Control the way in which names are mangled. Version 0 is compatible with versions of g++ before 2.8. Version 1 is the default. Version 1 will allow correct mangling of function templates. For example, version 0 mangling does not mangle foo<int, double> and foo<int, char> given this declaration:

```
template <class T, class U> void foo(T t);
```

Like all options that change the ABI, all C++ code, *including libgcc* must be built with the same setting of this option.

`-foperator-names`

Recognize the operator name keywords **and**, **bitand**, **bitor**, **compl**, **not**, **or** and **xor** as synonyms for the symbols they refer to. '`-ansi`' implies '`-foperator-names`'.

`-fno-optional-diags`

Disable diagnostics that the standard says a compiler does not need to issue. Currently, the only such diagnostic issued by g++ is the one for a name having multiple meanings within a class.

`-fpermissive`

Downgrade messages about nonconformant code from errors to warnings. By default, g++ effectively sets '`-pedantic-errors`' without '`-pedantic`'; this option reverses that. This behavior and this option are superceded by '`-pedantic`', which works as it does for GNU C.

`-frepo`   Enable automatic template instantiation. This option also implies '`-fno-implicit-templates`'. See Section 5.5 [Template Instantiation], page 211, for more information.

`-fno-rtti`
> Disable generation of the information used by C++ runtime type identification features ('`dynamic_cast`' and '`typeid`'). If you don't use those parts of the language (or exception handling, which uses '`dynamic_cast`' internally), you can save some space by using this flag.

`-fstrict-prototype`
> Within an '`extern "C"`' linkage specification, treat a function declaration with no arguments, such as '`int foo ();`', as declaring the function to take no arguments. Normally, such a declaration means that the function `foo` can take any combination of arguments, as in C. '`-pedantic`' implies '`-fstrict-prototype`' unless overridden with '`-fno-strict-prototype`'.
>
> Specifying this option will also suppress implicit declarations of functions.
>
> This flag no longer affects declarations with C++ linkage.

`-fsquangle`
`-fno-squangle`
> '`-fsquangle`' will enable a compressed form of name mangling for identifiers. In particular, it helps to shorten very long names by recognizing types and class names which occur more than once, replacing them with special short ID codes. This option also requires any C++ libraries being used to be compiled with this option as well. The compiler has this disabled (the equivalent of '`-fno-squangle`') by default.
>
> Like all options that change the ABI, all C++ code, *including libgcc.a* must be built with the same setting of this option.

`-ftemplate-depth-`*n*
> Set the maximum instantiation depth for template classes to *n*. A limit on the template instantiation depth is needed to detect endless recursions during template class instantiation. ANSI/ISO C++ conforming programs must not rely on a maximum depth greater than 17.

`-fthis-is-variable`
> Permit assignment to `this`. The incorporation of user-defined free store management into C++ has made assignment to '`this`' an anachronism. Therefore, by default it is invalid to assign to `this` within a class member function; that is, GNU C++ treats '`this`' in a member function of class X as a non-lvalue of type '`X *`'. However, for backwards compatibility, you can make it valid with '`-fthis-is-variable`'.

`-fvtable-thunks`
> Use '`thunks`' to implement the virtual function dispatch table ('`vtable`'). The traditional (cfront-style) approach to imple-

menting vtables was to store a pointer to the function and two offsets for adjusting the 'this' pointer at the call site. Newer implementations store a single pointer to a 'thunk' function which does any necessary adjustment and then calls the target function.

This option also enables a heuristic for controlling emission of vtables; if a class has any non-inline virtual functions, the vtable will be emitted in the translation unit containing the first one of those.

Like all options that change the ABI, all C++ code, *including libgcc.a* must be built with the same setting of this option.

`-nostdinc++`

Do not search for header files in the standard directories specific to C++, but do still search the other standard directories. (This option is used when building the C++ library.)

In addition, these optimization, warning, and code generation options have meanings only for C++ programs:

`-fno-default-inline`

Do not assume 'inline' for functions defined inside a class scope. See Section 2.8 [Options That Control Optimization], page 40. Note that these functions will have linkage like inline functions; they just won't be inlined by default.

`-Wctor-dtor-privacy (C++ only)`

Warn when a class seems unusable, because all the constructors or destructors in a class are private and the class has no friends or public static member functions.

`-Wnon-virtual-dtor (C++ only)`

Warn when a class declares a non-virtual destructor that should probably be virtual, because it looks like the class will be used polymorphically.

`-Wreorder (C++ only)`

Warn when the order of member initializers given in the code does not match the order in which they must be executed. For instance:

```
struct A {
  int i;
  int j;
  A(): j (0), i (1) { }
};
```

Here the compiler will warn that the member initializers for 'i' and 'j' will be rearranged to match the declaration order of the members.

The following '-W...' options are not affected by '-Wall'.

-Weffc++ (C++ only)
> Warn about violations of various style guidelines from Scott
> Meyers' *Effective C++* books. If you use this option, you should
> be aware that the standard library headers do not obey all of
> these guidelines; you can use 'grep -v' to filter out those warn-
> ings.

-Wno-deprecated (C++ only)
> Do not warn about usage of deprecated features. See Sec-
> tion 4.40 [Deprecated Features], page 206.

-Wno-non-template-friend (C++ only)
> Disable warnings when non-templatized friend functions are de-
> clared within a template. With the advent of explicit template
> specification support in g++, if the name of the friend is an
> unqualified-id (ie, 'friend foo(int)'), the C++ language spec-
> ification demands that the friend declare or define an ordinary,
> nontemplate function. (Section 14.5.3). Before g++ implemented
> explicit specification, unqualified-ids could be interpreted as a
> particular specialization of a templatized function. Because this
> non-conforming behavior is no longer the default behavior for
> g++, '-Wnon-template-friend' allows the compiler to check ex-
> isting code for potential trouble spots, and is on by default.
> This new compiler behavior can also be turned off with the flag
> '-fguiding-decls', which activates the older, non-specification
> compiler code, or with '-Wno-non-template-friend' which
> keeps the conformant compiler code but disables the helpful
> warning.

-Wold-style-cast (C++ only)
> Warn if an old-style (C-style) cast is used within a C++ program.
> The new-style casts ('static_cast', 'reinterpret_cast', and
> 'const_cast') are less vulnerable to unintended effects.

-Woverloaded-virtual (C++ only)
> Warn when a derived class function declaration may be an error
> in defining a virtual function. In a derived class, the definitions
> of virtual functions must match the type signature of a virtual
> function declared in the base class. With this option, the com-
> piler warns when you define a function with the same name as a
> virtual function, but with a type signature that does not match
> any declarations from the base class.

-Wno-pmf-conversions (C++ only)
> Disable the diagnostic for converting a bound pointer to member
> function to a plain pointer.

-Wsign-promo (C++ only)
>   Warn when overload resolution chooses a promotion from un-
>   signed or enumeral type to a signed type over a conversion to an
>   unsigned type of the same size. Previous versions of g++ would
>   try to preserve unsignedness, but the standard mandates the
>   current behavior.

-Wsynth (C++ only)
>   Warn when g++'s synthesis behavior does not match that of
>   cfront. For instance:

```
struct A {
  operator int ();
  A& operator = (int);
};

main ()
{
  A a,b;
  a = b;
}
```

>   In this example, g++ will synthesize a default 'A& operator =
>   (const A&);', while cfront will use the user-defined 'operator
>   ='.

2.6 Options to Request or Suppress Warnings

Warnings are diagnostic messages that report constructions which are not inherently erroneous but which are risky or suggest there may have been an error.

You can request many specific warnings with options beginning '-W', for example '-Wimplicit' to request warnings on implicit declarations. Each of these specific warning options also has a negative form beginning '-Wno-' to turn off warnings; for example, '-Wno-implicit'. This manual lists only one of the two forms, whichever is not the default.

These options control the amount and kinds of warnings produced by GCC:

-fsyntax-only
>   Check the code for syntax errors, but don't do anything beyond
>   that.

-pedantic
>   Issue all the warnings demanded by strict ANSI C and ISO C++;
>   reject all programs that use forbidden extensions.

>   Valid ANSI C and ISO C++ programs should compile prop-
>   erly with or without this option (though a rare few will require

'-ansi'). However, without this option, certain GNU extensions and traditional C and C++ features are supported as well. With this option, they are rejected.

'-pedantic' does not cause warning messages for use of the alternate keywords whose names begin and end with '__'. Pedantic warnings are also disabled in the expression that follows _ _extension__. However, only system header files should use these escape routes; application programs should avoid them. See Section 4.35 [Alternate Keywords], page 202.

This option is not intended to be *useful*; it exists only to satisfy pedants who would otherwise claim that GCC fails to support the ANSI standard.

Some users try to use '-pedantic' to check programs for strict ANSI C conformance. They soon find that it does not do quite what they want: it finds some non-ANSI practices, but not all— only those for which ANSI C *requires* a diagnostic.

A feature to report any failure to conform to ANSI C might be useful in some instances, but would require considerable additional work and would be quite different from '-pedantic'. We don't have plans to support such a feature in the near future.

-pedantic-errors
          Like '-pedantic', except that errors are produced rather than warnings.

-w   Inhibit all warning messages.

-Wno-import
          Inhibit warning messages about the use of '#import'.

-Wchar-subscripts
          Warn if an array subscript has type char. This is a common cause of error, as programmers often forget that this type is signed on some machines.

-Wcomment
          Warn whenever a comment-start sequence '/*' appears in a '/*' comment, or whenever a Backslash-Newline appears in a '//' comment.

-Wformat   Check calls to printf and scanf, etc., to make sure that the arguments supplied have types appropriate to the format string specified.

-Wimplicit-int
          Warn when a declaration does not specify a type.

```
-Wimplicit-function-declaration
-Werror-implicit-function-declaration
```
Give a warning (or error) whenever a function is used before being declared.

`-Wimplicit`

Same as '`-Wimplicit-int`' and '`-Wimplicit-function-`' '`declaration`'.

`-Wmain` Warn if the type of 'main' is suspicious. 'main' should be a function with external linkage, returning int, taking either zero arguments, two, or three arguments of appropriate types.

`-Wmultichar`

Warn if a multicharacter constant ("`'FOOF'`") is used. Usually they indicate a typo in the user's code, as they have implementation-defined values, and should not be used in portable code.

`-Wparentheses`

Warn if parentheses are omitted in certain contexts, such as when there is an assignment in a context where a truth value is expected, or when operators are nested whose precedence people often get confused about.

Also warn about constructions where there may be confusion to which **if** statement an **else** branch belongs. Here is an example of such a case:

```
{
  if (a)
    if (b)
      foo ();
  else
    bar ();
}
```

In C, every **else** branch belongs to the innermost possible **if** statement, which in this example is **if (b)**. This is often not what the programmer expected, as illustrated in the above example by indentation the programmer chose. When there is the potential for this confusion, GNU C will issue a warning when this flag is specified. To eliminate the warning, add explicit braces around the innermost **if** statement so there is no way the **else** could belong to the enclosing **if**. The resulting code would look like this:

```
{
  if (a)
    {
      if (b)
```

```
        foo ();
      else
        bar ();
    }
  }
```

-Wreturn-type
> Warn whenever a function is defined with a return-type that
> defaults to int. Also warn about any return statement with no
> return-value in a function whose return-type is not void.

-Wswitch   Warn whenever a switch statement has an index of enumeral
> type and lacks a case for one or more of the named codes of
> that enumeration. (The presence of a default label prevents
> this warning.) case labels outside the enumeration range also
> provoke warnings when this option is used.

-Wtrigraphs
> Warn if any trigraphs are encountered (assuming they are en-
> abled).

-Wunused   Warn whenever a variable is unused aside from its declaration,
> whenever a function is declared static but never defined, when-
> ever a label is declared but not used, and whenever a statement
> computes a result that is explicitly not used.
>
> In order to get a warning about an unused function parameter,
> you must specify both '-W' and '-Wunused'.
>
> To suppress this warning for an expression, simply cast it to void.
> For unused variables, parameters and labels, use the 'unused'
> attribute (see Section 4.29 [Variable Attributes], page 185).

-Wuninitialized
> An automatic variable is used without first being initialized.
>
> These warnings are possible only in optimizing compilation, be-
> cause they require data flow information that is computed only
> when optimizing. If you don't specify '-O', you simply won't get
> these warnings.
>
> These warnings occur only for variables that are candidates for
> register allocation. Therefore, they do not occur for a variable
> that is declared volatile, or whose address is taken, or whose
> size is other than 1, 2, 4 or 8 bytes. Also, they do not occur for
> structures, unions or arrays, even when they are in registers.
>
> Note that there may be no warning about a variable that is used
> only to compute a value that itself is never used, because such
> computations may be deleted by data flow analysis before the
> warnings are printed.
>
> These warnings are made optional because GCC is not smart
> enough to see all the reasons why the code might be correct

despite appearing to have an error. Here is one example of how this can happen:

```
{
  int x;
  switch (y)
    {
    case 1: x = 1;
      break;
    case 2: x = 4;
      break;
    case 3: x = 5;
    }
  foo (x);
}
```

If the value of y is always 1, 2 or 3, then x is always initialized, but GCC doesn't know this. Here is another common case:

```
{
  int save_y;
  if (change_y) save_y = y, y = new_y;
  ...
  if (change_y) y = save_y;
}
```

This has no bug because `save_y` is used only if it is set.

Some spurious warnings can be avoided if you declare all the functions you use that never return as `noreturn`. See Section 4.23 [Function Attributes], page 177.

-Wunknown-pragmas

Warn when a #pragma directive is encountered which is not understood by GCC. If this command line option is used, warnings will even be issued for unknown pragmas in system header files. This is not the case if the warnings were only enabled by the '-Wall' command line option.

-Wall   All of the above '-W' options combined. This enables all the warnings about constructions that some users consider questionable, and that are easy to avoid (or modify to prevent the warning), even in conjunction with macros.

The following '-W...' options are not implied by '-Wall'. Some of them warn about constructions that users generally do not consider questionable, but which occasionally you might wish to check for; others warn about constructions that are necessary or hard to avoid in some cases, and there is no simple way to modify the code to suppress the warning.

-W   Print extra warning messages for these events:

- A nonvolatile automatic variable might be changed by a call to `longjmp`. These warnings as well are possible only in optimizing compilation.

  The compiler sees only the calls to `setjmp`. It cannot know where `longjmp` will be called; in fact, a signal handler could call it at any point in the code. As a result, you may get a warning even when there is in fact no problem because `longjmp` cannot in fact be called at the place which would cause a problem.

- A function can return either with or without a value. (Falling off the end of the function body is considered returning without a value.) For example, this function would evoke such a warning:

  ```
  foo (a)
  {
    if (a > 0)
      return a;
  }
  ```

- An expression-statement or the left-hand side of a comma expression contains no side effects. To suppress the warning, cast the unused expression to void. For example, an expression such as 'x[i,j]' will cause a warning, but 'x[(void)i,j]' will not.

- An unsigned value is compared against zero with '<' or '<='.

- A comparison like 'x<=y<=z' appears; this is equivalent to '(x<=y ? 1 : 0) <= z', which is a different interpretation from that of ordinary mathematical notation.

- Storage-class specifiers like `static` are not the first things in a declaration. According to the C Standard, this usage is obsolescent.

- If '-Wall' or '-Wunused' is also specified, warn about unused arguments.

- A comparison between signed and unsigned values could produce an incorrect result when the signed value is converted to unsigned.
  (But don't warn if '-Wno-sign-compare' is also specified.)

- An aggregate has a partly bracketed initializer. For example, the following code would evoke such a warning, because braces are missing around the initializer for `x.h`:

  ```
  struct s { int f, g; };
  struct t { struct s h; int i; };
  struct t x = { 1, 2, 3 };
  ```

- An aggregate has an initializer which does not initialize all members. For example, the following code would cause such a warning, because `x.h` would be implicitly initialized to zero:

  ```
  struct s { int f, g, h; };
  struct s x = { 3, 4 };
  ```

`-Wtraditional`
> Warn about certain constructs that behave differently in traditional and ANSI C.
>
> - Macro arguments occurring within string constants in the macro body. These would substitute the argument in traditional C, but are part of the constant in ANSI C.
> - A function declared external in one block and then used after the end of the block.
> - A `switch` statement has an operand of type `long`.
> - A non-`static` function declaration follows a `static` one. This construct is not accepted by some traditional C compilers.

`-Wundef`   Warn if an undefined identifier is evaluated in an '`#if`' directive.

`-Wshadow`   Warn whenever a local variable shadows another local variable.

`-Wid-clash-`*len*
> Warn whenever two distinct identifiers match in the first *len* characters. This may help you prepare a program that will compile with certain obsolete, brain-damaged compilers.

`-Wlarger-than-`*len*
> Warn whenever an object of larger than *len* bytes is defined.

`-Wpointer-arith`
> Warn about anything that depends on the "size of" a function type or of `void`. GNU C assigns these types a size of 1, for convenience in calculations with `void *` pointers and pointers to functions.

`-Wbad-function-cast`
> Warn whenever a function call is cast to a non-matching type. For example, warn if `int malloc()` is cast to `anything *`.

`-Wcast-qual`
> Warn whenever a pointer is cast so as to remove a type qualifier from the target type. For example, warn if a `const char *` is cast to an ordinary `char *`.

`-Wcast-align`
> Warn whenever a pointer is cast such that the required alignment of the target is increased. For example, warn if a `char`

    * is cast to an `int` * on machines where integers can only be
accessed at two- or four-byte boundaries.

`-Wwrite-strings`
    Give string constants the type `const char [`*length*`]` so that copy-
ing the address of one into a non-`const char` * pointer will get
a warning. These warnings will help you find at compile time
code that can try to write into a string constant, but only if you
have been very careful about using `const` in declarations and
prototypes. Otherwise, it will just be a nuisance; this is why we
did not make '`-Wall`' request these warnings.

`-Wconversion`
    Warn if a prototype causes a type conversion that is different
from what would happen to the same argument in the absence of
a prototype. This includes conversions of fixed point to floating
and vice versa, and conversions changing the width or signedness
of a fixed point argument except when the same as the default
promotion.

    Also, warn if a negative integer constant expression is implicitly
converted to an unsigned type. For example, warn about the
assignment `x = -1` if `x` is unsigned. But do not warn about
explicit casts like (`unsigned`) `-1`.

`-Wsign-compare`
    Warn when a comparison between signed and unsigned values
could produce an incorrect result when the signed value is converted to unsigned. This warning is also enabled by '`-W`'; to
get the other warnings of '`-W`' without this warning, use '`-W
-Wno-sign-compare`'.

`-Waggregate-return`
    Warn if any functions that return structures or unions are de-
fined or called. (In languages where you can return an array,
this also elicits a warning.)

`-Wstrict-prototypes`
    Warn if a function is declared or defined without specifying the
argument types. (An old-style function definition is permitted
without a warning if preceded by a declaration which specifies
the argument types.)

`-Wmissing-prototypes`
    Warn if a global function is defined without a previous prototype
declaration. This warning is issued even if the definition itself
provides a prototype. The aim is to detect global functions that
fail to be declared in header files.

`-Wmissing-declarations`

> Warn if a global function is defined without a previous declaration. Do so even if the definition itself provides a prototype. Use this option to detect global functions that are not declared in header files.

`-Wmissing-noreturn`

> Warn about functions which might be candidates for attribute `noreturn`. Note these are only possible candidates, not absolute ones. Care should be taken to manually verify functions actually do not ever return before adding the `noreturn` attribute, otherwise subtle code generation bugs could be introduced.

`-Wredundant-decls`

> Warn if anything is declared more than once in the same scope, even in cases where multiple declaration is valid and changes nothing.

`-Wnested-externs`

> Warn if an `extern` declaration is encountered within an function.

`-Winline`   Warn if a function can not be inlined, and either it was declared as inline, or else the '`-finline-functions`' option was given.

`-Wlong-long`

> Warn if '`long long`' type is used. This is default. To inhibit the warning messages, use '`-Wno-long-long`'. Flags '`-Wlong-long`' and '`-Wno-long-long`' are taken into account only when '`-pedantic`' flag is used.

`-Werror`   Make all warnings into errors.

2.7 Options for Debugging Your Program or GCC

GCC has various special options that are used for debugging either your program or GCC:

`-g`   Produce debugging information in the operating system's native format (stabs, COFF, XCOFF, or DWARF). GDB can work with this debugging information.

> On most systems that use stabs format, '`-g`' enables use of extra debugging information that only GDB can use; this extra information makes debugging work better in GDB but will probably make other debuggers crash or refuse to read the program. If you want to control for certain whether to generate the extra information, use '`-gstabs+`', '`-gstabs`', '`-gxcoff+`', '`-gxcoff`', '`-gdwarf-1+`', or '`-gdwarf-1`' (see below).

> Unlike most other C compilers, GCC allows you to use '`-g`' with '`-O`'. The shortcuts taken by optimized code may occasionally

produce surprising results: some variables you declared may not exist at all; flow of control may briefly move where you did not expect it; some statements may not be executed because they compute constant results or their values were already at hand; some statements may execute in different places because they were moved out of loops.

Nevertheless it proves possible to debug optimized output. This makes it reasonable to use the optimizer for programs that might have bugs.

The following options are useful when GCC is generated with the capability for more than one debugging format.

-ggdb   Produce debugging information for use by GDB. This means to use the most expressive format available (DWARF 2, stabs, or the native format if neither of those are supported), including GDB extensions if at all possible.

-gstabs   Produce debugging information in stabs format (if that is supported), without GDB extensions. This is the format used by DBX on most BSD systems. On MIPS, Alpha and System V Release 4 systems this option produces stabs debugging output which is not understood by DBX or SDB. On System V Release 4 systems this option requires the GNU assembler.

-gstabs+   Produce debugging information in stabs format (if that is supported), using GNU extensions understood only by the GNU debugger (GDB). The use of these extensions is likely to make other debuggers crash or refuse to read the program.

-gcoff   Produce debugging information in COFF format (if that is supported). This is the format used by SDB on most System V systems prior to System V Release 4.

-gxcoff   Produce debugging information in XCOFF format (if that is supported). This is the format used by the DBX debugger on IBM RS/6000 systems.

-gxcoff+   Produce debugging information in XCOFF format (if that is supported), using GNU extensions understood only by the GNU debugger (GDB). The use of these extensions is likely to make other debuggers crash or refuse to read the program, and may cause assemblers other than the GNU assembler (GAS) to fail with an error.

-gdwarf   Produce debugging information in DWARF version 1 format (if that is supported). This is the format used by SDB on most System V Release 4 systems.

-gdwarf+   Produce debugging information in DWARF version 1 format (if that is supported), using GNU extensions understood only by the GNU debugger (GDB). The use of these extensions is likely to make other debuggers crash or refuse to read the program.

`-gdwarf-2`

Produce debugging information in DWARF version 2 format (if that is supported). This is the format used by DBX on IRIX 6.

`-g`*level*
`-ggdb`*level*
`-gstabs`*level*
`-gcoff`*level*
`-gxcoff`*level*
`-gdwarf`*level*
`-gdwarf-2`*level*

Request debugging information and also use *level* to specify how much information. The default level is 2.

Level 1 produces minimal information, enough for making backtraces in parts of the program that you don't plan to debug. This includes descriptions of functions and external variables, but no information about local variables and no line numbers.

Level 3 includes extra information, such as all the macro definitions present in the program. Some debuggers support macro expansion when you use '`-g3`'.

`-p`   Generate extra code to write profile information suitable for the analysis program `prof`. You must use this option when compiling the source files you want data about, and you must also use it when linking.

`-pg`   Generate extra code to write profile information suitable for the analysis program `gprof`. You must use this option when compiling the source files you want data about, and you must also use it when linking.

`-a`   Generate extra code to write profile information for basic blocks, which will record the number of times each basic block is executed, the basic block start address, and the function name containing the basic block. If '`-g`' is used, the line number and filename of the start of the basic block will also be recorded. If not overridden by the machine description, the default action is to append to the text file '`bb.out`'.

This data could be analyzed by a program like `tcov`. Note, however, that the format of the data is not what `tcov` expects. Eventually GNU `gprof` should be extended to process this data.

`-Q`   Makes the compiler print out each function name as it is compiled, and print some statistics about each pass when it finishes.

`-ax`   Generate extra code to profile basic blocks. Your executable will produce output that is a superset of that produced when '`-a`'

is used. Additional output is the source and target address of
the basic blocks where a jump takes place, the number of times
a jump is executed, and (optionally) the complete sequence of
basic blocks being executed. The output is appended to file
'bb.out'.

You can examine different profiling aspects without recompilation. Your executable will read a list of function names from file
'bb.in'. Profiling starts when a function on the list is entered
and stops when that invocation is exited. To exclude a function
from profiling, prefix its name with '-'. If a function name is
not unique, you can disambiguate it by writing it in the form
'/path/filename.d:functionname'. Your executable will write
the available paths and filenames in file 'bb.out'.

Several function names have a special meaning:

__bb_jumps__

> Write source, target and frequency of jumps to file
> 'bb.out'.

__bb_hidecall__

> Exclude function calls from frequency count.

__bb_showret__

> Include function returns in frequency count.

__bb_trace__

> Write the sequence of basic blocks executed to file
> 'bbtrace.gz'. The file will be compressed using the
> program 'gzip', which must exist in your PATH. On
> systems without the 'popen' function, the file will be
> named 'bbtrace' and will not be compressed. **Pro-
> filing for even a few seconds on these systems will
> produce a very large file.** Note: __bb_hidecall__
> and __bb_showret__ will not affect the sequence
> written to 'bbtrace.gz'.

Here's a short example using different profiling parameters in
file 'bb.in'. Assume function foo consists of basic blocks 1 and
2 and is called twice from block 3 of function main. After the
calls, block 3 transfers control to block 4 of main.

With __bb_trace__ and main contained in file 'bb.in', the following sequence of blocks is written to file 'bbtrace.gz': 0 3 1 2
1 2 4. The return from block 2 to block 3 is not shown, because
the return is to a point inside the block and not to the top. The
block address 0 always indicates, that control is transferred to
the trace from somewhere outside the observed functions. With
'-foo' added to 'bb.in', the blocks of function foo are removed
from the trace, so only 0 3 4 remains.

With `__bb_jumps__` and `main` contained in file 'bb.in', jump frequencies will be written to file 'bb.out'. The frequencies are obtained by constructing a trace of blocks and incrementing a counter for every neighbouring pair of blocks in the trace. The trace 0 3 1 2 1 2 4 displays the following frequencies:

```
Jump from block 0x0 to block 0x3 executed 1 time(s)
Jump from block 0x3 to block 0x1 executed 1 time(s)
Jump from block 0x1 to block 0x2 executed 2 time(s)
Jump from block 0x2 to block 0x1 executed 1 time(s)
Jump from block 0x2 to block 0x4 executed 1 time(s)
```

With `__bb_hidecall__`, control transfer due to call instructions is removed from the trace, that is the trace is cut into three parts: 0 3 4, 0 1 2 and 0 1 2. With `__bb_showret__`, control transfer due to return instructions is added to the trace. The trace becomes: 0 3 1 2 3 1 2 3 4. Note, that this trace is not the same, as the sequence written to 'bbtrace.gz'. It is solely used for counting jump frequencies.

-fprofile-arcs

Instrument *arcs* during compilation. For each function of your program, GCC creates a program flow graph, then finds a spanning tree for the graph. Only arcs that are not on the spanning tree have to be instrumented: the compiler adds code to count the number of times that these arcs are executed. When an arc is the only exit or only entrance to a block, the instrumentation code can be added to the block; otherwise, a new basic block must be created to hold the instrumentation code.

Since not every arc in the program must be instrumented, programs compiled with this option run faster than programs compiled with '-a', which adds instrumentation code to every basic block in the program. The tradeoff: since `gcov` does not have execution counts for all branches, it must start with the execution counts for the instrumented branches, and then iterate over the program flow graph until the entire graph has been solved. Hence, `gcov` runs a little more slowly than a program which uses information from '-a'.

'-fprofile-arcs' also makes it possible to estimate branch probabilities, and to calculate basic block execution counts. In general, basic block execution counts do not give enough information to estimate all branch probabilities. When the compiled program exits, it saves the arc execution counts to a file called '*sourcename*.da'. Use the compiler option '-fbranch-probabilities' (see Section 2.8 [Options that Control Optimization], page 40) when recompiling, to optimize using estimated branch probabilities.

-ftest-coverage
> Create data files for the gcov code-coverage utility (see Chapter 6 [gcov: a GCC Test Coverage Program], page 217). The data file names begin with the name of your source file:

> *sourcename*.bb
>> A mapping from basic blocks to line numbers, which gcov uses to associate basic block execution counts with line numbers.

> *sourcename*.bbg
>> A list of all arcs in the program flow graph. This allows gcov to reconstruct the program flow graph, so that it can compute all basic block and arc execution counts from the information in the *sourcename*.da file (this last file is the output from '-fprofile-arcs').

-Q   Makes the compiler print out each function name as it is compiled, and print some statistics about each pass when it finishes.

-d*letters*   Says to make debugging dumps during compilation at times specified by *letters*. This is used for debugging the compiler. The file names for most of the dumps are made by appending a word to the source file name (e.g. 'foo.c.rtl' or 'foo.c.jump'). Here are the possible letters for use in *letters*, and their meanings:

> 'b'   Dump after computing branch probabilities, to 'file.bp'.

> 'c'   Dump after instruction combination, to the file 'file.combine'.

> 'd'   Dump after delayed branch scheduling, to 'file.dbr'.

> 'D'   Dump all macro definitions, at the end of preprocessing, in addition to normal output.

> 'r'   Dump after RTL generation, to 'file.rtl'.

> 'j'   Dump after first jump optimization, to 'file.jump'.

> 'F'   Dump after purging ADDRESSOF, to 'file.addressof'.

> 'f'   Dump after flow analysis, to 'file.flow'.

> 'g'   Dump after global register allocation, to 'file.greg'.

> 'G'   Dump after GCSE, to 'file.gcse'.

> 'j'   Dump after first jump optimization, to 'file.jump'.

'J'   Dump after last jump optimization, to 'file.jump2'.

'k'   Dump after conversion from registers to stack, to
              'file.stack'.

'l'   Dump after local register allocation, to 'file.lreg'.

'L'   Dump after loop optimization, to 'file.loop'.

'M'   Dump after performing the machine dependent re-
              organisation pass, to 'file.mach'.

'N'   Dump after the register move pass, to 'file.regmove'.

'r'   Dump after RTL generation, to 'file.rtl'.

'R'   Dump after the second instruction scheduling pass,
              to 'file.sched2'.

's'   Dump after CSE (including the jump optimization
              that sometimes follows CSE), to 'file.cse'.

'S'   Dump after the first instruction scheduling pass, to
              'file.sched'.

't'   Dump after the second CSE pass (including the
              jump optimization that sometimes follows CSE), to
              'file.cse2'.

'a'   Produce all the dumps listed above.

'm'   Print statistics on memory usage, at the end of the
              run, to standard error.

'p'   Annotate the assembler output with a comment in-
              dicating which pattern and alternative was used.
              The length of each instruction is also printed.

'x'   Just generate RTL for a function instead of compil-
              ing it. Usually used with 'r'.

'y'   Dump debugging information during parsing, to
              standard error.

'A'   Annotate the assembler output with miscellaneous
              debugging information.

-fdump-unnumbered
              When doing debugging dumps (see -d option above), suppress
              instruction numbers and line number note output. This makes
              it more feasible to use diff on debugging dumps for compiler in-
              vokations with different options, in particular with and without
              -g.

`-fpretend-float`

> When running a cross-compiler, pretend that the target machine uses the same floating point format as the host machine. This causes incorrect output of the actual floating constants, but the actual instruction sequence will probably be the same as GCC would make when running on the target machine.

`-save-temps`

> Store the usual "temporary" intermediate files permanently; place them in the current directory and name them based on the source file. Thus, compiling 'foo.c' with '-c -save-temps' would produce files 'foo.i' and 'foo.s', as well as 'foo.o'.

`-print-file-name=`*library*

> Print the full absolute name of the library file *library* that would be used when linking—and don't do anything else. With this option, GCC does not compile or link anything; it just prints the file name.

`-print-prog-name=`*program*

> Like '-print-file-name', but searches for a program such as 'cpp'.

`-print-libgcc-file-name`

> Same as '-print-file-name=libgcc.a'.
>
> This is useful when you use '-nostdlib' or '-nodefaultlibs' but you do want to link with 'libgcc.a'. You can do
>
>   `gcc -nostdlib` *files*... `'gcc -print-libgcc-file-name'`

`-print-search-dirs`

> Print the name of the configured installation directory and a list of program and library directories gcc will search—and don't do anything else.
>
> This is useful when gcc prints the error message 'installation problem, cannot exec cpp: No such file or directory'. To resolve this you either need to put 'cpp' and the other compiler components where gcc expects to find them, or you can set the environment variable `GCC_EXEC_PREFIX` to the directory where you installed them. Don't forget the trailing '/'. See Section 2.16 [Environment Variables], page 114.

2.8 Options That Control Optimization

These options control various sorts of optimizations:

`-O`
`-O1`
> Optimize. Optimizing compilation takes somewhat more time, and a lot more memory for a large function.

Without '-O', the compiler's goal is to reduce the cost of compilation and to make debugging produce the expected results. Statements are independent: if you stop the program with a breakpoint between statements, you can then assign a new value to any variable or change the program counter to any other statement in the function and get exactly the results you would expect from the source code.

Without '-O', the compiler only allocates variables declared **register** in registers. The resulting compiled code is a little worse than produced by PCC without '-O'.

With '-O', the compiler tries to reduce code size and execution time.

When you specify '-O', the compiler turns on '-fthread-jumps' and '-fdefer-pop' on all machines. The compiler turns on '-fdelayed-branch' on machines that have delay slots, and '-fomit-frame-pointer' on machines that can support debugging even without a frame pointer. On some machines the compiler also turns on other flags.

-O2   Optimize even more. GCC performs nearly all supported optimizations that do not involve a space-speed tradeoff. The compiler does not perform loop unrolling or function inlining when you specify '-O2'. As compared to '-O', this option increases both compilation time and the performance of the generated code.

           '-O2' turns on all optional optimizations except for loop unrolling and function inlining. It also turns on the '-fforce-mem' option on all machines and frame pointer elimination on machines where doing so does not interfere with debugging.

-O3   Optimize yet more. '-O3' turns on all optimizations specified by '-O2' and also turns on the '**inline-functions**' option.

-O0   Do not optimize.

-Os   Optimize for size. '-Os' enables all '-O2' optimizations that do not typically increase code size. It also performs further optimizations designed to reduce code size.

           If you use multiple '-O' options, with or without level numbers, the last such option is the one that is effective.

Options of the form '-f*flag*' specify machine-independent flags. Most flags have both positive and negative forms; the negative form of '-ffoo' would be '-fno-foo'. In the table below, only one of the forms is listed— the one which is not the default. You can figure out the other form by either removing 'no-' or adding it.

`-ffloat-store`

> Do not store floating point variables in registers, and inhibit other options that might change whether a floating point value is taken from a register or memory.
>
> This option prevents undesirable excess precision on machines such as the 68000 where the floating registers (of the 68881) keep more precision than a **double** is supposed to have. Similarly for the x86 architecture. For most programs, the excess precision does only good, but a few programs rely on the precise definition of IEEE floating point. Use '`-ffloat-store`' for such programs, after modifying them to store all pertinent intermediate computations into variables.

`-fno-default-inline`

> Do not make member functions inline by default merely because they are defined inside the class scope (C++ only). Otherwise, when you specify '`-O`', member functions defined inside class scope are compiled inline by default; i.e., you don't need to add '`inline`' in front of the member function name.

`-fno-defer-pop`

> Always pop the arguments to each function call as soon as that function returns. For machines which must pop arguments after a function call, the compiler normally lets arguments accumulate on the stack for several function calls and pops them all at once.

`-fforce-mem`

> Force memory operands to be copied into registers before doing arithmetic on them. This produces better code by making all memory references potential common subexpressions. When they are not common subexpressions, instruction combination should eliminate the separate register-load. The '`-O2`' option turns on this option.

`-fforce-addr`

> Force memory address constants to be copied into registers before doing arithmetic on them. This may produce better code just as '`-fforce-mem`' may.

`-fomit-frame-pointer`

> Don't keep the frame pointer in a register for functions that don't need one. This avoids the instructions to save, set up and restore frame pointers; it also makes an extra register available in many functions. **It also makes debugging impossible on some machines.**
>
> On some machines, such as the Vax, this flag has no effect, because the standard calling sequence automatically handles the frame pointer and nothing is saved by pretending it doesn't exist. The machine-description macro `FRAME_POINTER_REQUIRED`

controls whether a target machine supports this flag. See Section 17.5 [Registers], page 413.

-fno-inline

Don't pay attention to the `inline` keyword. Normally this option is used to keep the compiler from expanding any functions inline. Note that if you are not optimizing, no functions can be expanded inline.

-finline-functions

Integrate all simple functions into their callers. The compiler heuristically decides which functions are simple enough to be worth integrating in this way.

If all calls to a given function are integrated, and the function is declared `static`, then the function is normally not output as assembler code in its own right.

-finline-limit-*n*

By default, gcc limits the size of functions that can be inlined. This flag allows the control of this limit for functions that are explicitly marked as inline (ie marked with the inline keyword or defined within the class definition in c++). *n* is the size of functions that can be inlined in number of pseudo instructions (not counting parameter handling). The default value of n is 10000. Increasing this value can result in more inlined code at the cost of compilation time and memory consumption. Decreasing usually makes the compilation faster and less code will be inlined (which presumably means slower programs). This option is particularly useful for programs that use inlining heavily such as those based on recursive templates with c++.

Note: pseudo instruction represents, in this particular context, an abstract measurement of function's size. In no way, it represents a count of assembly instructions and as such its exact meaning might change from one release to an another.

-fkeep-inline-functions

Even if all calls to a given function are integrated, and the function is declared `static`, nevertheless output a separate run-time callable version of the function. This switch does not affect `extern inline` functions.

-fkeep-static-consts

Emit variables declared `static const` when optimization isn't turned on, even if the variables aren't referenced.

GCC enables this option by default. If you want to force the compiler to check if the variable was referenced, regardless of whether or not optimization is turned on, use the '-fno-keep-static-consts' option.

-fno-function-cse
:   Do not put function addresses in registers; make each instruction that calls a constant function contain the function's address explicitly.

    This option results in less efficient code, but some strange hacks that alter the assembler output may be confused by the optimizations performed when this option is not used.

-ffast-math
:   This option allows GCC to violate some ANSI or IEEE rules and/or specifications in the interest of optimizing code for speed. For example, it allows the compiler to assume arguments to the sqrt function are non-negative numbers and that no floating-point values are NaNs.

    This option should never be turned on by any '-O' option since it can result in incorrect output for programs which depend on an exact implementation of IEEE or ANSI rules/specifications for math functions.

The following options control specific optimizations. The '-O2' option turns on all of these optimizations except '-funroll-loops' and '-funroll-all-loops'. On most machines, the '-O' option turns on the '-fthread-jumps' and '-fdelayed-branch' options, but specific machines may handle it differently.

You can use the following flags in the rare cases when "fine-tuning" of optimizations to be performed is desired.

-fstrength-reduce
:   Perform the optimizations of loop strength reduction and elimination of iteration variables.

-fthread-jumps
:   Perform optimizations where we check to see if a jump branches to a location where another comparison subsumed by the first is found. If so, the first branch is redirected to either the destination of the second branch or a point immediately following it, depending on whether the condition is known to be true or false.

-fcse-follow-jumps
:   In common subexpression elimination, scan through jump instructions when the target of the jump is not reached by any other path. For example, when CSE encounters an if statement with an else clause, CSE will follow the jump when the condition tested is false.

-fcse-skip-blocks
:   This is similar to '-fcse-follow-jumps', but causes CSE to follow jumps which conditionally skip over blocks. When

CSE encounters a simple `if` statement with no else clause, '-fcse-skip-blocks' causes CSE to follow the jump around the body of the `if`.

-frerun-cse-after-loop

Re-run common subexpression elimination after loop optimizations has been performed.

-frerun-loop-opt

Run the loop optimizer twice.

-fgcse   Perform a global common subexpression elimination pass. This pass also performs global constant and copy propagation.

-fexpensive-optimizations

Perform a number of minor optimizations that are relatively expensive.

-foptimize-register-moves
-fregmove

Attempt to reassign register numbers in move instructions and as operands of other simple instructions in order to maximize the amount of register tying. This is especially helpful on machines with two-operand instructions. GCC enables this optimization by default with '-O2' or higher.

Note -fregmove and -foptimize-register-moves are the same optimization.

-fdelayed-branch

If supported for the target machine, attempt to reorder instructions to exploit instruction slots available after delayed branch instructions.

-fschedule-insns

If supported for the target machine, attempt to reorder instructions to eliminate execution stalls due to required data being unavailable. This helps machines that have slow floating point or memory load instructions by allowing other instructions to be issued until the result of the load or floating point instruction is required.

-fschedule-insns2

Similar to '-fschedule-insns', but requests an additional pass of instruction scheduling after register allocation has been done. This is especially useful on machines with a relatively small number of registers and where memory load instructions take more than one cycle.

-ffunction-sections
-fdata-sections

Place each function or data item into its own section in the output file if the target supports arbitrary sections. The name of the function or the name of the data item determines the section's name in the output file.

Use these options on systems where the linker can perform optimizations to improve locality of reference in the instruction space. HPPA processors running HP-UX and Sparc processors running Solaris 2 have linkers with such optimizations. Other systems using the ELF object format as well as AIX may have these optimizations in the future.

Only use these options when there are significant benefits from doing so. When you specify these options, the assembler and linker will create larger object and executable files and will also be slower. You will not be able to use gprof on all systems if you specify this option and you may have problems with debugging if you specify both this option and '-g'.

-fcaller-saves

Enable values to be allocated in registers that will be clobbered by function calls, by emitting extra instructions to save and restore the registers around such calls. Such allocation is done only when it seems to result in better code than would otherwise be produced.

This option is always enabled by default on certain machines, usually those which have no call-preserved registers to use instead.

For all machines, optimization level 2 and higher enables this flag by default.

-funroll-loops

Perform the optimization of loop unrolling. This is only done for loops whose number of iterations can be determined at compile time or run time. '-funroll-loops' implies both '-fstrength-reduce' and '-frerun-cse-after-loop'.

-funroll-all-loops

Perform the optimization of loop unrolling. This is done for all loops and usually makes programs run more slowly. '-funroll-all-loops' implies '-fstrength-reduce' as well as '-frerun-cse-after-loop'.

-fmove-all-movables

Forces all invariant computations in loops to be moved outside the loop.

-freduce-all-givs

Forces all general-induction variables in loops to be strength-reduced.

Note: When compiling programs written in Fortran, '-fmove-all-movables' and '-freduce-all-givs' are enabled by default when you use the optimizer.

These options may generate better or worse code; results are highly dependent on the structure of loops within the source code.

These two options are intended to be removed someday, once they have helped determine the efficacy of various approaches to improving loop optimizations.

Please let us (gcc@gcc.gnu.org and fortran@gnu.org) know how use of these options affects the performance of your production code. We're very interested in code that runs *slower* when these options are *enabled*.

-fno-peephole

Disable any machine-specific peephole optimizations.

-fbranch-probabilities

After running a program compiled with '-fprofile-arcs' (see Section 2.7 [Options for Debugging Your Program or gcc], page 33), you can compile it a second time using '-fbranch-probabilities', to improve optimizations based on guessing the path a branch might take.

With '-fbranch-probabilities', GCC puts a 'REG_EXEC_COUNT' note on the first instruction of each basic block, and a 'REG_BR_PROB' note on each 'JUMP_INSN' and 'CALL_INSN'. These can be used to improve optimization. Currently, they are only used in one place: in 'reorg.c', instead of guessing which path a branch is mostly to take, the 'REG_BR_PROB' values are used to exactly determine which path is taken more often.

-fstrict-aliasing

Allows the compiler to assume the strictest aliasing rules applicable to the language being compiled. For C (and C++), this activates optimizations based on the type of expressions. In particular, an object of one type is assumed never to reside at the same address as an object of a different type, unless the types are almost the same. For example, an **unsigned int** can alias an **int**, but not a **void*** or a **double**. A character type may alias any other type.

Pay special attention to code like this:

```
union a_union {
  int i;
  double d;
};
```

```
int f() {
  a_union t;
  t.d = 3.0;
  return t.i;
}
```

The practice of reading from a different union member than the one most recently written to (called "type-punning") is common. Even with '-fstrict-aliasing', type-punning is allowed, provided the memory is accessed through the union type. So, the code above will work as expected. However, this code might not:

```
int f() {
  a_union t;
  int* ip;
  t.d = 3.0;
  ip = &t.i;
  return *ip;
}
```

Every language that wishes to perform language-specific alias analysis should define a function that computes, given an `tree` node, an alias set for the node. Nodes in different alias sets are not allowed to alias. For an example, see the C front-end function `c_get_alias_set`.

2.9 Options Controlling the Preprocessor

These options control the C preprocessor, which is run on each C source file before actual compilation.

If you use the '-E' option, nothing is done except preprocessing. Some of these options make sense only together with '-E' because they cause the preprocessor output to be unsuitable for actual compilation.

-include *file*

> Process *file* as input before processing the regular input file. In effect, the contents of *file* are compiled first. Any '-D' and '-U' options on the command line are always processed before '-include *file*', regardless of the order in which they are written. All the '-include' and '-imacros' options are processed in the order in which they are written.

-imacros *file*

> Process *file* as input, discarding the resulting output, before processing the regular input file. Because the output generated from *file* is discarded, the only effect of '-imacros *file*' is to make the macros defined in *file* available for use in the main input.

Any '-D' and '-U' options on the command line are always processed before '-imacros file', regardless of the order in which they are written. All the '-include' and '-imacros' options are processed in the order in which they are written.

-idirafter *dir*

Add the directory *dir* to the second include path. The directories on the second include path are searched when a header file is not found in any of the directories in the main include path (the one that '-I' adds to).

-iprefix *prefix*

Specify *prefix* as the prefix for subsequent '-iwithprefix' options.

-iwithprefix *dir*

Add a directory to the second include path. The directory's name is made by concatenating *prefix* and *dir*, where *prefix* was specified previously with '-iprefix'. If you have not specified a prefix yet, the directory containing the installed passes of the compiler is used as the default.

-iwithprefixbefore *dir*

Add a directory to the main include path. The directory's name is made by concatenating *prefix* and *dir*, as in the case of '-iwithprefix'.

-isystem *dir*

Add a directory to the beginning of the second include path, marking it as a system directory, so that it gets the same special treatment as is applied to the standard system directories.

-nostdinc

Do not search the standard system directories for header files. Only the directories you have specified with '-I' options (and the current directory, if appropriate) are searched. See Section 2.12 [Directory Options], page 54, for information on '-I'.

By using both '-nostdinc' and '-I-', you can limit the include-file search path to only those directories you specify explicitly.

-undef   Do not predefine any nonstandard macros. (Including architecture flags).

-E   Run only the C preprocessor. Preprocess all the C source files specified and output the results to standard output or to the specified output file.

-C   Tell the preprocessor not to discard comments. Used with the '-E' option.

-P   Tell the preprocessor not to generate '#line' directives. Used with the '-E' option.

-M   Tell the preprocessor to output a rule suitable for `make` describ-
                ing the dependencies of each object file. For each source file, the
                preprocessor outputs one `make`-rule whose target is the object
                file name for that source file and whose dependencies are all the
                `#include` header files it uses. This rule may be a single line
                or may be continued with '\'-newline if it is long. The list of
                rules is printed on standard output instead of the preprocessed
                C program.

                '-M' implies '-E'.

                Another way to specify output of a `make` rule is by setting the
                environment variable `DEPENDENCIES_OUTPUT` (see Section 2.16
                [Environment Variables], page 114).

-MM   Like '-M' but the output mentions only the user header files
                included with '`#include "`*file*`"`'. System header files included
                with '`#include <`*file*`>`' are omitted.

-MD   Like '-M' but the dependency information is written to a file
                made by replacing ".c" with ".d" at the end of the input file
                names. This is in addition to compiling the file as specified—
                '-MD' does not inhibit ordinary compilation the way '-M' does.

                In Mach, you can use the utility `md` to merge multiple depen-
                dency files into a single dependency file suitable for using with
                the '`make`' command.

-MMD   Like '-MD' except mention only user header files, not system
                header files.

-MG   Treat missing header files as generated files and assume they
                live in the same directory as the source file. If you specify '-MG',
                you must also specify either '-M' or '-MM'. '-MG' is not supported
                with '-MD' or '-MMD'.

-H   Print the name of each header file used, in addition to other
                normal activities.

-A*question*(*answer*)
                Assert the answer *answer* for *question*, in case it is tested with
                a preprocessing conditional such as '`#if #`*question*`(`*answer*`)`'.
                '-A-' disables the standard assertions that normally describe
                the target machine.

-D*macro*   Define macro *macro* with the string '1' as its definition.

-D*macro*=*defn*
                Define macro *macro* as *defn*. All instances of '-D' on the com-
                mand line are processed before any '-U' options.

-U*macro*   Undefine macro *macro*. '-U' options are evaluated after all '-D'
                options, but before any '-`include`' and '-`imacros`' options.

-dM   Tell the preprocessor to output only a list of the macro defini-
            tions that are in effect at the end of preprocessing. Used with
            the '-E' option.

-dD   Tell the preprocessing to pass all macro definitions into the out-
            put, in their proper sequence in the rest of the output.

-dN   Like '-dD' except that the macro arguments and contents are
            omitted. Only '#define *name*' is included in the output.

-trigraphs
            Support ANSI C trigraphs. The '-ansi' option also has this
            effect.

-Wp,*option*
            Pass *option* as an option to the preprocessor. If *option* contains
            commas, it is split into multiple options at the commas.

2.10 Passing Options to the Assembler

You can pass options to the assembler.

-Wa,*option*
            Pass *option* as an option to the assembler. If *option* contains
            commas, it is split into multiple options at the commas.

2.11 Options for Linking

These options come into play when the compiler links object files into an
executable output file. They are meaningless if the compiler is not doing a
link step.

object-file-name
            A file name that does not end in a special recognized suffix is
            considered to name an object file or library. (Object files are
            distinguished from libraries by the linker according to the file
            contents.) If linking is done, these object files are used as input
            to the linker.

-c
-S
-E   If any of these options is used, then the linker is not run, and ob-
            ject file names should not be used as arguments. See Section 2.2
            [Overall Options], page 11.

-l*library* Search the library named *library* when linking.

            It makes a difference where in the command you write this op-
            tion; the linker searches processes libraries and object files in
            the order they are specified. Thus, 'foo.o -lz bar.o' searches

library 'z' after file 'foo.o' but before 'bar.o'. If 'bar.o' refers
to functions in 'z', those functions may not be loaded.

The linker searches a standard list of directories for the library,
which is actually a file named 'lib*library*.a'. The linker then
uses this file as if it had been specified precisely by name.

The directories searched include several standard system directories plus any that you specify with '-L'.

Normally the files found this way are library files—archive files
whose members are object files. The linker handles an archive
file by scanning through it for members which define symbols
that have so far been referenced but not defined. But if the file
that is found is an ordinary object file, it is linked in the usual
fashion. The only difference between using an '-l' option and
specifying a file name is that '-l' surrounds *library* with 'lib'
and '.a' and searches several directories.

-lobjc   You need this special case of the '-l' option in order to link an
            Objective C program.

-nostartfiles
            Do not use the standard system startup files when linking. The
            standard system libraries are used normally, unless -nostdlib
            or -nodefaultlibs is used.

-nodefaultlibs
            Do not use the standard system libraries when linking. Only the
            libraries you specify will be passed to the linker. The standard
            startup files are used normally, unless -nostartfiles is used.
            The compiler may generate calls to memcmp, memset, and mem-
            cpy for System V (and ANSI C) environments or to bcopy and
            bzero for BSD environments. These entries are usually resolved
            by entries in libc. These entry points should be supplied through
            some other mechanism when this option is specified.

-nostdlib
            Do not use the standard system startup files or libraries when
            linking. No startup files and only the libraries you specify will
            be passed to the linker. The compiler may generate calls to
            memcmp, memset, and memcpy for System V (and ANSI C) en-
            vironments or to bcopy and bzero for BSD environments. These
            entries are usually resolved by entries in libc. These entry points
            should be supplied through some other mechanism when this op-
            tion is specified.

            One of the standard libraries bypassed by '-nostdlib' and
            '-nodefaultlibs' is 'libgcc.a', a library of internal subrou-
            tines that GCC uses to overcome shortcomings of particular
            machines, or special needs for some languages. (See Chapter 13

[Interfacing to GCC Output], page 271, for more discussion of
'`libgcc.a`'.) In most cases, you need '`libgcc.a`' even when you
want to avoid other standard libraries. In other words, when
you specify '`-nostdlib`' or '`-nodefaultlibs`' you should usually
specify '`-lgcc`' as well. This ensures that you have no unresolved
references to internal GCC library subroutines. (For example,
'`__main`', used to ensure C++ constructors will be called; see
Section 3.7 [`collect2`], page 158.)

`-s`   Remove all symbol table and relocation information from the
            executable.

`-static`   On systems that support dynamic linking, this prevents linking
            with the shared libraries. On other systems, this option has no
            effect.

`-shared`   Produce a shared object which can then be linked with other
            objects to form an executable. Not all systems support this op-
            tion. You must also specify '`-fpic`' or '`-fPIC`' on some systems
            when you specify this option.

`-symbolic`
            Bind references to global symbols when building a shared object.
            Warn about any unresolved references (unless overridden by the
            link editor option '`-Xlinker -z -Xlinker defs`'). Only a few
            systems support this option.

`-Xlinker` *option*
            Pass *option* as an option to the linker. You can use this to supply
            system-specific linker options which GCC does not know how to
            recognize.

            If you want to pass an option that takes an argument, you must
            use '`-Xlinker`' twice, once for the option and once for the argu-
            ment. For example, to pass '`-assert definitions`', you must
            write '`-Xlinker -assert -Xlinker definitions`'. It does not
            work to write '`-Xlinker "-assert definitions"`', because this
            passes the entire string as a single argument, which is not what
            the linker expects.

`-Wl,`*option*
            Pass *option* as an option to the linker. If *option* contains com-
            mas, it is split into multiple options at the commas.

`-u` *symbol*   Pretend the symbol *symbol* is undefined, to force linking of li-
            brary modules to define it. You can use '`-u`' multiple times with
            different symbols to force loading of additional library modules.

2.12 Options for Directory Search

These options specify directories to search for header files, for libraries and for parts of the compiler:

-I*dir* Add the directory *dir* to the head of the list of directories to be searched for header files. This can be used to override a system header file, substituting your own version, since these directories are searched before the system header file directories. If you use more than one '-I' option, the directories are scanned in left-to-right order; the standard system directories come after.

-I-   Any directories you specify with '-I' options before the '-I-' option are searched only for the case of '#include "*file*"'; they are not searched for '#include <*file*>'.

If additional directories are specified with '-I' options after the '-I-', these directories are searched for all '#include' directives. (Ordinarily *all* '-I' directories are used this way.)

In addition, the '-I-' option inhibits the use of the current directory (where the current input file came from) as the first search directory for '#include "*file*"'. There is no way to override this effect of '-I-'. With '-I.' you can specify searching the directory which was current when the compiler was invoked. That is not exactly the same as what the preprocessor does by default, but it is often satisfactory.

'-I-' does not inhibit the use of the standard system directories for header files. Thus, '-I-' and '-nostdinc' are independent.

-L*dir* Add directory *dir* to the list of directories to be searched for '-l'.

-B*prefix* This option specifies where to find the executables, libraries, include files, and data files of the compiler itself.

The compiler driver program runs one or more of the subprograms 'cpp', 'cc1', 'as' and 'ld'. It tries *prefix* as a prefix for each program it tries to run, both with and without '*machine/version/*' (see Section 2.13 [Target Options], page 55).

For each subprogram to be run, the compiler driver first tries the '-B' prefix, if any. If that name is not found, or if '-B' was not specified, the driver tries two standard prefixes, which are '/usr/lib/gcc/' and '/usr/local/lib/gcc-lib/'. If neither of those results in a file name that is found, the unmodified program name is searched for using the directories specified in your 'PATH' environment variable.

'-B' prefixes that effectively specify directory names also apply to libraries in the linker, because the compiler translates these

options into '-L' options for the linker. They also apply to includes files in the preprocessor, because the compiler translates
these options into '-isystem' options for the preprocessor. In
this case, the compiler appends 'include' to the prefix.

The run-time support file 'libgcc.a' can also be searched for
using the '-B' prefix, if needed. If it is not found there, the two
standard prefixes above are tried, and that is all. The file is left
out of the link if it is not found by those means.

Another way to specify a prefix much like the '-B' prefix is to use
the environment variable GCC_EXEC_PREFIX. See Section 2.16
[Environment Variables], page 114.

-specs=file

Process file after the compiler reads in the standard 'specs' file,
in order to override the defaults that the 'gcc' driver program
uses when determining what switches to pass to 'cc1', 'cc1plus',
'as', 'ld', etc. More than one '-specs='file can be specified on
the command line, and they are processed in order, from left to
right.

2.13 Specifying Target Machine and Compiler Version

By default, GCC compiles code for the same type of machine that you
are using. However, it can also be installed as a cross-compiler, to compile
for some other type of machine. In fact, several different configurations of
GCC, for different target machines, can be installed side by side. Then you
specify which one to use with the '-b' option.

In addition, older and newer versions of GCC can be installed side by
side. One of them (probably the newest) will be the default, but you may
sometimes wish to use another.

-b machine

The argument machine specifies the target machine for compilation. This is useful when you have installed GCC as a cross-
compiler.

The value to use for machine is the same as was specified as
the machine type when configuring GCC as a cross-compiler.
For example, if a cross-compiler was configured with 'configure
i386v', meaning to compile for an 80386 running System V, then
you would specify '-b i386v' to run that cross compiler.

When you do not specify '-b', it normally means to compile for
the same type of machine that you are using.

-V version   The argument version specifies which version of GCC to run.
This is useful when multiple versions are installed. For example,
version might be '2.0', meaning to run GCC version 2.0.

The default version, when you do not specify '-V', is the last version of GCC that you installed.

The '-b' and '-V' options actually work by controlling part of the file name used for the executable files and libraries used for compilation. A given version of GCC, for a given target machine, is normally kept in the directory '/usr/local/lib/gcc-lib/*machine*/*version*'.

Thus, sites can customize the effect of '-b' or '-V' either by changing the names of these directories or adding alternate names (or symbolic links). If in directory '/usr/local/lib/gcc-lib/' the file '80386' is a link to the file 'i386v', then '-b 80386' becomes an alias for '-b i386v'.

In one respect, the '-b' or '-V' do not completely change to a different compiler: the top-level driver program gcc that you originally invoked continues to run and invoke the other executables (preprocessor, compiler per se, assembler and linker) that do the real work. However, since no real work is done in the driver program, it usually does not matter that the driver program in use is not the one for the specified target and version.

The only way that the driver program depends on the target machine is in the parsing and handling of special machine-specific options. However, this is controlled by a file which is found, along with the other executables, in the directory for the specified version and target machine. As a result, a single installed driver program adapts to any specified target machine and compiler version.

The driver program executable does control one significant thing, however: the default version and target machine. Therefore, you can install different instances of the driver program, compiled for different targets or versions, under different names.

For example, if the driver for version 2.0 is installed as ogcc and that for version 2.1 is installed as gcc, then the command gcc will use version 2.1 by default, while ogcc will use 2.0 by default. However, you can choose either version with either command with the '-V' option.

2.14 Hardware Models and Configurations

Earlier we discussed the standard option '-b' which chooses among different installed compilers for completely different target machines, such as Vax vs. 68000 vs. 80386.

In addition, each of these target machine types can have its own special options, starting with '-m', to choose among various hardware models or configurations—for example, 68010 vs 68020, floating coprocessor or none. A single installed version of the compiler can compile for any model or configuration, according to the options specified.

Some configurations of the compiler also support additional special options, usually for compatibility with other compilers on the same platform.

These options are defined by the macro **TARGET_SWITCHES** in the machine description. The default for the options is also defined by that macro, which enables you to change the defaults.

2.14.1 M680x0 Options

These are the '-m' options defined for the 68000 series. The default values for these options depends on which style of 68000 was selected when the compiler was configured; the defaults for the most common choices are given below.

-m68000
-mc68000   Generate output for a 68000. This is the default when the compiler is configured for 68000-based systems.

Use this option for microcontrollers with a 68000 or EC000 core, including the 68008, 68302, 68306, 68307, 68322, 68328 and 68356.

-m68020
-mc68020   Generate output for a 68020. This is the default when the compiler is configured for 68020-based systems.

-m68881   Generate output containing 68881 instructions for floating point. This is the default for most 68020 systems unless '-nfp' was specified when the compiler was configured.

-m68030   Generate output for a 68030. This is the default when the compiler is configured for 68030-based systems.

-m68040   Generate output for a 68040. This is the default when the compiler is configured for 68040-based systems.

This option inhibits the use of 68881/68882 instructions that have to be emulated by software on the 68040. Use this option if your 68040 does not have code to emulate those instructions.

-m68060   Generate output for a 68060. This is the default when the compiler is configured for 68060-based systems.

This option inhibits the use of 68020 and 68881/68882 instructions that have to be emulated by software on the 68060. Use this option if your 68060 does not have code to emulate those instructions.

-mcpu32   Generate output for a CPU32. This is the default when the compiler is configured for CPU32-based systems.

Use this option for microcontrollers with a CPU32 or CPU32+ core, including the 68330, 68331, 68332, 68333, 68334, 68336, 68340, 68341, 68349 and 68360.

-m5200   Generate output for a 520X "coldfire" family cpu. This is the default when the compiler is configured for 520X-based systems.

Use this option for microcontroller with a 5200 core, including the MCF5202, MCF5203, MCF5204 and MCF5202.

-m68020-40

Generate output for a 68040, without using any of the new instructions. This results in code which can run relatively efficiently on either a 68020/68881 or a 68030 or a 68040. The generated code does use the 68881 instructions that are emulated on the 68040.

-m68020-60

Generate output for a 68060, without using any of the new instructions. This results in code which can run relatively efficiently on either a 68020/68881 or a 68030 or a 68040. The generated code does use the 68881 instructions that are emulated on the 68060.

-mfpa   Generate output containing Sun FPA instructions for floating point.

-msoft-float

Generate output containing library calls for floating point. **Warning:** the requisite libraries are not available for all m68k targets. Normally the facilities of the machine's usual C compiler are used, but this can't be done directly in cross-compilation. You must make your own arrangements to provide suitable library functions for cross-compilation. The embedded targets 'm68k-*-aout' and 'm68k-*-coff' do provide software floating point support.

-mshort   Consider type `int` to be 16 bits wide, like `short int`.

-mnobitfield

Do not use the bit-field instructions. The '-m68000', '-mcpu32' and '-m5200' options imply '-mnobitfield'.

-mbitfield

Do use the bit-field instructions. The '-m68020' option implies '-mbitfield'. This is the default if you use a configuration designed for a 68020.

-mrtd   Use a different function-calling convention, in which functions that take a fixed number of arguments return with the `rtd` instruction, which pops their arguments while returning. This saves one instruction in the caller since there is no need to pop the arguments there.

This calling convention is incompatible with the one normally used on Unix, so you cannot use it if you need to call libraries compiled with the Unix compiler.

Also, you must provide function prototypes for all functions that take variable numbers of arguments (including `printf`); otherwise incorrect code will be generated for calls to those functions.

In addition, seriously incorrect code will result if you call a function with too many arguments. (Normally, extra arguments are harmlessly ignored.)

The `rtd` instruction is supported by the 68010, 68020, 68030, 68040, 68060 and CPU32 processors, but not by the 68000 or 5200.

`-malign-int`
`-mno-align-int`

Control whether GCC aligns `int`, `long`, `long long`, `float`, `double`, and `long double` variables on a 32-bit boundary ('`-malign-int`') or a 16-bit boundary ('`-mno-align-int`'). Aligning variables on 32-bit boundaries produces code that runs somewhat faster on processors with 32-bit busses at the expense of more memory.

Warning: if you use the '`-malign-int`' switch, GCC will align structures containing the above types differently than most published application binary interface specifications for the m68k.

2.14.2 VAX Options

These '`-m`' options are defined for the Vax:

`-munix`   Do not output certain jump instructions (`aobleq` and so on) that the Unix assembler for the Vax cannot handle across long ranges.

`-mgnu`   Do output those jump instructions, on the assumption that you will assemble with the GNU assembler.

`-mg`   Output code for g-format floating point numbers instead of d-format.

2.14.3 SPARC Options

These '`-m`' switches are supported on the SPARC:

`-mno-app-regs`
`-mapp-regs`

Specify '`-mapp-regs`' to generate output using the global registers 2 through 4, which the SPARC SVR4 ABI reserves for applications. This is the default.

To be fully SVR4 ABI compliant at the cost of some performance loss, specify '`-mno-app-regs`'. You should compile libraries and system software with this option.

`-mfpu`
`-mhard-float`

>   Generate output containing floating point instructions. This is
>   the default.

`-mno-fpu`
`-msoft-float`

>   Generate output containing library calls for floating point.
>   **Warning:** the requisite libraries are not available for all SPARC
>   targets. Normally the facilities of the machine's usual C compiler
>   are used, but this cannot be done directly in cross-compilation.
>   You must make your own arrangements to provide suitable li-
>   brary functions for cross-compilation. The embedded targets
>   'sparc-*-aout' and 'sparclite-*-*' do provide software float-
>   ing point support.
>
>   '-msoft-float' changes the calling convention in the output file;
>   therefore, it is only useful if you compile *all* of a program with
>   this option. In particular, you need to compile 'libgcc.a', the
>   library that comes with GCC, with '-msoft-float' in order for
>   this to work.

`-mhard-quad-float`

>   Generate output containing quad-word (long double) floating
>   point instructions.

`-msoft-quad-float`

>   Generate output containing library calls for quad-word (long
>   double) floating point instructions. The functions called are
>   those specified in the SPARC ABI. This is the default.
>
>   As of this writing, there are no sparc implementations that have
>   hardware support for the quad-word floating point instructions.
>   They all invoke a trap handler for one of these instructions,
>   and then the trap handler emulates the effect of the instruction.
>   Because of the trap handler overhead, this is much slower than
>   calling the ABI library routines. Thus the '-msoft-quad-float'
>   option is the default.

`-mno-epilogue`
`-mepilogue`

>   With '-mepilogue' (the default), the compiler always emits code
>   for function exit at the end of each function. Any function exit
>   in the middle of the function (such as a return statement in C)
>   will generate a jump to the exit code at the end of the function.
>   With '-mno-epilogue', the compiler tries to emit exit code in-
>   line at every function exit.

`-mno-flat`
`-mflat`   With '-mflat', the compiler does not generate save/restore in-
>   structions and will use a "flat" or single register window calling

convention. This model uses %i7 as the frame pointer and is compatible with the normal register window model. Code from either may be intermixed. The local registers and the input registers (0-5) are still treated as "call saved" registers and will be saved on the stack as necessary.

With '-mno-flat' (the default), the compiler emits save/restore instructions (except for leaf functions) and is the normal mode of operation.

-mno-unaligned-doubles
-munaligned-doubles

Assume that doubles have 8 byte alignment. This is the default.

With '-munaligned-doubles', GCC assumes that doubles have 8 byte alignment only if they are contained in another type, or if they have an absolute address. Otherwise, it assumes they have 4 byte alignment. Specifying this option avoids some rare compatibility problems with code generated by other compilers. It is not the default because it results in a performance loss, especially for floating point code.

-mv8
-msparclite

These two options select variations on the SPARC architecture.

By default (unless specifically configured for the Fujitsu SPARClite), GCC generates code for the v7 variant of the SPARC architecture.

'-mv8' will give you SPARC v8 code. The only difference from v7 code is that the compiler emits the integer multiply and integer divide instructions which exist in SPARC v8 but not in SPARC v7.

'-msparclite' will give you SPARClite code. This adds the integer multiply, integer divide step and scan (ffs) instructions which exist in SPARClite but not in SPARC v7.

These options are deprecated and will be deleted in a future GCC release. They have been replaced with '-mcpu=xxx'.

-mcypress
-msupersparc

These two options select the processor for which the code is optimised.

With '-mcypress' (the default), the compiler optimizes code for the Cypress CY7C602 chip, as used in the SparcStation/SparcServer 3xx series. This is also appropriate for the older SparcStation 1, 2, IPX etc.

With '-msupersparc' the compiler optimizes code for the Super-Sparc cpu, as used in the SparcStation 10, 1000 and 2000 series. This flag also enables use of the full SPARC v8 instruction set.

These options are deprecated and will be deleted in a future GCC release. They have been replaced with '-mcpu=xxx'.

-mcpu=*cpu_type*

Set the instruction set, register set, and instruction scheduling parameters for machine type *cpu_type*. Supported values for *cpu_type* are 'v7', 'cypress', 'v8', 'supersparc', 'sparclite', 'hypersparc', 'sparclite86x', 'f930', 'f934', 'sparclet', 'tsc701', 'v9', and 'ultrasparc'.

Default instruction scheduling parameters are used for values that select an architecture and not an implementation. These are 'v7', 'v8', 'sparclite', 'sparclet', 'v9'.

Here is a list of each supported architecture and their supported implementations.

v7:	cypress
v8:	supersparc, hypersparc
sparclite:	f930, f934, sparclite86x
sparclet:	tsc701
v9:	ultrasparc

-mtune=*cpu_type*

Set the instruction scheduling parameters for machine type *cpu_type*, but do not set the instruction set or register set that the option '-mcpu='*cpu_type* would.

The same values for '-mcpu='*cpu_type* are used for '-mtune=' *cpu_type*, though the only useful values are those that select a particular cpu implementation: 'cypress', 'supersparc', 'hypersparc', 'f930', 'f934', 'sparclite86x', 'tsc701', 'ultrasparc'.

-malign-loops=*num*

Align loops to a 2 raised to a *num* byte boundary. If '-malign-loops' is not specified, the default is 2.

-malign-jumps=*num*

Align instructions that are only jumped to to a 2 raised to a *num* byte boundary. If '-malign-jumps' is not specified, the default is 2.

-malign-functions=*num*

Align the start of functions to a 2 raised to *num* byte boundary. If '-malign-functions' is not specified, the default is 2 if compiling for 32 bit sparc, and 5 if compiling for 64 bit sparc.

These '-m' switches are supported in addition to the above on the SPAR-CLET processor.

`-mlittle-endian`

> Generate code for a processor running in little-endian mode.

`-mlive-g0`

> Treat register %g0 as a normal register. GCC will continue to clobber it as necessary but will not assume it always reads as 0.

`-mbroken-saverestore`

> Generate code that does not use non-trivial forms of the **save** and **restore** instructions. Early versions of the SPARCLET processor do not correctly handle **save** and **restore** instructions used with arguments. They correctly handle them used without arguments. A **save** instruction used without arguments increments the current window pointer but does not allocate a new stack frame. It is assumed that the window overflow trap handler will properly handle this case as will interrupt handlers.

These '-m' switches are supported in addition to the above on SPARC V9 processors in 64 bit environments.

`-mlittle-endian`

> Generate code for a processor running in little-endian mode.

`-m32`
`-m64`   Generate code for a 32 bit or 64 bit environment. The 32 bit environment sets int, long and pointer to 32 bits. The 64 bit environment sets int to 32 bits and long and pointer to 64 bits.

`-mcmodel=medlow`

> Generate code for the Medium/Low code model: the program must be linked in the low 32 bits of the address space. Pointers are 64 bits. Programs can be statically or dynamically linked.

`-mcmodel=medmid`

> Generate code for the Medium/Middle code model: the program must be linked in the low 44 bits of the address space, the text segment must be less than 2G bytes, and data segment must be within 2G of the text segment. Pointers are 64 bits.

`-mcmodel=medany`

> Generate code for the Medium/Anywhere code model: the program may be linked anywhere in the address space, the text segment must be less than 2G bytes, and data segment must be within 2G of the text segment. Pointers are 64 bits.

`-mcmodel=embmedany`

> Generate code for the Medium/Anywhere code model for embedded systems: assume a 32 bit text and a 32 bit data segment, both starting anywhere (determined at link time). Register %g4 points to the base of the data segment. Pointers still 64 bits. Programs are statically linked, PIC is not supported.

`-mstack-bias`
`-mno-stack-bias`

> With '`-mstack-bias`', GCC assumes that the stack pointer, and frame pointer if present, are offset by -2047 which must be added back when making stack frame references. Otherwise, assume no such offset is present.

2.14.4 Convex Options

These '`-m`' options are defined for Convex:

`-mc1`   Generate output for C1. The code will run on any Convex machine. The preprocessor symbol `__convex__c1__` is defined.

`-mc2`   Generate output for C2. Uses instructions not available on C1. Scheduling and other optimizations are chosen for max performance on C2. The preprocessor symbol `__convex_c2__` is defined.

`-mc32`   Generate output for C32xx. Uses instructions not available on C1. Scheduling and other optimizations are chosen for max performance on C32. The preprocessor symbol `__convex_c32__` is defined.

`-mc34`   Generate output for C34xx. Uses instructions not available on C1. Scheduling and other optimizations are chosen for max performance on C34. The preprocessor symbol `__convex_c34__` is defined.

`-mc38`   Generate output for C38xx. Uses instructions not available on C1. Scheduling and other optimizations are chosen for max performance on C38. The preprocessor symbol `__convex_c38__` is defined.

`-margcount`

> Generate code which puts an argument count in the word preceding each argument list. This is compatible with regular CC, and a few programs may need the argument count word. GDB and other source-level debuggers do not need it; this info is in the symbol table.

`-mnoargcount`

> Omit the argument count word. This is the default.

`-mvolatile-cache`

> Allow volatile references to be cached. This is the default.

`-mvolatile-nocache`

> Volatile references bypass the data cache, going all the way to memory. This is only needed for multi-processor code that does not use standard synchronization instructions. Making non-volatile references to volatile locations will not necessarily work.

-mlong32   Type long is 32 bits, the same as type int. This is the default.

-mlong64   Type long is 64 bits, the same as type long long. This option is useless, because no library support exists for it.

2.14.5 AMD29K Options

These '-m' options are defined for the AMD Am29000:

-mdw   Generate code that assumes the DW bit is set, i.e., that byte and halfword operations are directly supported by the hardware. This is the default.

-mndw   Generate code that assumes the DW bit is not set.

-mbw   Generate code that assumes the system supports byte and halfword write operations. This is the default.

-mnbw   Generate code that assumes the systems does not support byte and halfword write operations. '-mnbw' implies '-mndw'.

-msmall   Use a small memory model that assumes that all function addresses are either within a single 256 KB segment or at an absolute address of less than 256k. This allows the `call` instruction to be used instead of a `const`, `consth`, `calli` sequence.

-mnormal Use the normal memory model: Generate `call` instructions only when calling functions in the same file and `calli` instructions otherwise. This works if each file occupies less than 256 KB but allows the entire executable to be larger than 256 KB. This is the default.

-mlarge   Always use `calli` instructions. Specify this option if you expect a single file to compile into more than 256 KB of code.

-m29050   Generate code for the Am29050.

-m29000   Generate code for the Am29000. This is the default.

-mkernel-registers
          Generate references to registers `gr64-gr95` instead of to registers `gr96-gr127`. This option can be used when compiling kernel code that wants a set of global registers disjoint from that used by user-mode code.

          Note that when this option is used, register names in '-f' flags must use the normal, user-mode, names.

-muser-registers
          Use the normal set of global registers, `gr96-gr127`. This is the default.

`-mstack-check`
`-mno-stack-check`

> Insert (or do not insert) a call to `__msp_check` after each stack adjustment. This is often used for kernel code.

`-mstorem-bug`
`-mno-storem-bug`

> '`-mstorem-bug`' handles 29k processors which cannot handle the separation of a mtsrim insn and a storem instruction (most 29000 chips to date, but not the 29050).

`-mno-reuse-arg-regs`
`-mreuse-arg-regs`

> '`-mno-reuse-arg-regs`' tells the compiler to only use incoming argument registers for copying out arguments. This helps detect calling a function with fewer arguments than it was declared with.

`-mno-impure-text`
`-mimpure-text`

> '`-mimpure-text`', used in addition to '`-shared`', tells the compiler to not pass '`-assert pure-text`' to the linker when linking a shared object.

`-msoft-float`

> Generate output containing library calls for floating point. **Warning:** the requisite libraries are not part of GCC. Normally the facilities of the machine's usual C compiler are used, but this can't be done directly in cross-compilation. You must make your own arrangements to provide suitable library functions for cross-compilation.

`-mno-multm`

> Do not generate multm or multmu instructions. This is useful for some embedded systems which do not have trap handlers for these instructions.

2.14.6 ARM Options

These '`-m`' options are defined for Advanced RISC Machines (ARM) architectures:

`-mapcs-frame`

> Generate a stack frame that is compliant with the ARM Procedure Call Standard for all functions, even if this is not strictly necessary for correct execution of the code. Specifying '`-fomit-frame-pointer`' with this option will cause the stack frames not to be generated for leaf functions. The default is '`-mno-apcs-frame`'.

-mapcs   This is a synonym for '-mapcs-frame'.

-mapcs-26

Generate code for a processor running with a 26-bit program
counter, and conforming to the function calling standards for
the APCS 26-bit option. This option replaces the '-m2' and
'-m3' options of previous releases of the compiler.

-mapcs-32

Generate code for a processor running with a 32-bit program
counter, and conforming to the function calling standards for
the APCS 32-bit option. This option replaces the '-m6' option
of previous releases of the compiler.

-mapcs-stack-check

Generate code to check the amount of stack space available upon
entry to every function (that actually uses some stack space).
If there is insufficient space available then either the function
'__rt_stkovf_split_small' or '__rt_stkovf_split_big' will
be called, depending upon the amount of stack space required.
The run time system is required to provide these functions. The
default is '-mno-apcs-stack-check', since this produces smaller
code.

-mapcs-float

Pass floating point arguments using the float point registers.
This is one of the variants of the APCS. This option is reccom-
mended if the target hardware has a floating point unit or if a
lot of floating point arithmetic is going to be performed by the
code. The default is '-mno-apcs-float', since integer only code
is slightly increased in size if '-mapcs-float' is used.

-mapcs-reentrant

Generate reentrant, position independent code. This is the
equivalent to specifying the '-fpic' option. The default is
'-mno-apcs-reentrant'.

-mthumb-interwork

Generate code which supports calling between the ARM and
THUMB instruction sets. Without this option the two instruction sets cannot be reliably used inside one program. The default
is '-mno-thumb-interwork', since slightly larger code is generated when '-mthumb-interwork' is specified.

-mno-sched-prolog

Prevent the reordering of instructions in the function prolog,
or the merging of those instruction with the instructions in the
function's body. This means that all functions will start with a
recognisable set of instructions (or in fact one of a chioce from
a small set of different function prologues), and this information

can be used to locate the start if functions inside an executable piece of code. The default is '`-msched-prolog`'.

`-mhard-float`

Generate output containing floating point instructions. This is the default.

`-msoft-float`

Generate output containing library calls for floating point. **Warning:** the requisite libraries are not available for all ARM targets. Normally the facilities of the machine's usual C compiler are used, but this cannot be done directly in cross-compilation. You must make your own arrangements to provide suitable library functions for cross-compilation.

'`-msoft-float`' changes the calling convention in the output file; therefore, it is only useful if you compile *all* of a program with this option. In particular, you need to compile '`libgcc.a`', the library that comes with GCC, with '`-msoft-float`' in order for this to work.

`-mlittle-endian`

Generate code for a processor running in little-endian mode. This is the default for all standard configurations.

`-mbig-endian`

Generate code for a processor running in big-endian mode; the default is to compile code for a little-endian processor.

`-mwords-little-endian`

This option only applies when generating code for big-endian processors. Generate code for a little-endian word order but a big-endian byte order. That is, a byte order of the form '`32107654`'. Note: this option should only be used if you require compatibility with code for big-endian ARM processors generated by versions of the compiler prior to 2.8.

`-mshort-load-bytes`

Do not try to load half-words (eg '`short`'s) by loading a word from an unaligned address. For some targets the MMU is configured to trap unaligned loads; use this option to generate code that is safe in these environments.

`-mno-short-load-bytes`

Use unaligned word loads to load half-words (eg '`short`'s). This option produces more efficient code, but the MMU is sometimes configured to trap these instructions.

`-mshort-load-words`

This is a synonym for the '`-mno-short-load-bytes`'.

-mno-short-load-words
> This is a synonym for the '-mshort-load-bytes'.

-mbsd
> This option only applies to RISC iX. Emulate the native BSD-mode compiler. This is the default if '-ansi' is not specified.

-mxopen
> This option only applies to RISC iX. Emulate the native X/Open-mode compiler.

-mno-symrename
> This option only applies to RISC iX. Do not run the assembler post-processor, 'symrename', after code has been assembled. Normally it is necessary to modify some of the standard symbols in preparation for linking with the RISC iX C library; this option suppresses this pass. The post-processor is never run when the compiler is built for cross-compilation.

-mcpu=<name>
-mtune=<name>
> This specifies the name of the target ARM processor. GCC uses this name to determine what kind of instructions it can use when generating assembly code. Permissable names are: arm2, arm250, arm3, arm6, arm60, arm600, arm610, arm620, arm7, arm7m, arm7d, arm7dm, arm7di, arm7dmi, arm70, arm700, arm700i, arm710, arm710c, arm7100, arm7500, arm7500fe, arm7tdmi, arm8, strongarm, strongarm110, strongarm1100, arm8, arm810, arm9, arm9tdmi. '-mtune=' is a synonym for '-mcpue=' to support older versions of GCC.

-march=<name>
> This specifies the name of the target ARM architecture. GCC uses this name to determine what kind of instructions it can use when generating assembly code. This option can be used in conjunction with or instead of the '-mcpu=' option. Permissable names are: armv2, armv2a, armv3, armv3m, armv4, armv4t

-mfpe=<number>
-mfp=<number>
> This specifes the version of the floating point emulation available on the target. Permissable values are 2 and 3. '-mfp=' is a synonym for '-mfpe=' to support older versions of GCC.

-mstructure-size-boundary=<n>
> The size of all structures and unions will be rounded up to a multiple of the number of bits set by this option. Permissable values are 8 and 32. The default value varies for different toolchains. For the COFF targeted toolchain the default value is 8. Specifying the larger number can produced faster, more efficient code, but can also increase the size of the program. The two values are potentially incompatible. Code compiled with one value cannot

necessarily expect to work with code or libraries compiled with
the other value, if they exchange information using structures
or unions. Programmers are encouraged to use the 32 value as
future versions of the toolchain may default to this value.

`-mabort-on-noreturn`

Generate a call to the function abort at the end of a noreturn
function. It will be executed if the function tries to return.

2.14.7 Thumb Options

`-mthumb-interwork`

Generate code which supports calling between the THUMB and
ARM instruction sets. Without this option the two instruction
sets cannot be reliably used inside one program. The default
is '`-mno-thumb-interwork`', since slightly smaller code is generated with this option.

`-mtpcs-frame`

Generate a stack frame that is compliant with the Thumb Procedure Call Standard for all non-leaf functions. (A leaf function
is one that does not call any other functions). The default is
'`-mno-apcs-frame`'.

`-mtpcs-leaf-frame`

Generate a stack frame that is compliant with the Thumb Procedure Call Standard for all leaf functions. (A leaf function
is one that does not call any other functions). The default is
'`-mno-apcs-leaf-frame`'.

`-mlittle-endian`

Generate code for a processor running in little-endian mode.
This is the default for all standard configurations.

`-mbig-endian`

Generate code for a processor running in big-endian mode.

`-mstructure-size-boundary=<n>`

The size of all structures and unions will be rounded up to a multiple of the number of bits set by this option. Permissable values
are 8 and 32. The default value varies for different toolchains.
For the COFF targeted toolchain the default value is 8. Specifying the larger number can produced faster, more efficient code,
but can also increase the size of the program. The two values are
potentially incompatible. Code compiled with one value cannot
necessarily expect to work with code or libraries compiled with
the other value, if they exchange information using structures
or unions. Programmers are encouraged to use the 32 value as
future versions of the toolchain may default to this value.

2.14.8 MN10200 Options

These '-m' options are defined for Matsushita MN10200 architectures:

-mrelax Indicate to the linker that it should perform a relaxation optimization pass to shorten branches, calls and absolute memory addresses. This option only has an effect when used on the command line for the final link step.

     This option makes symbolic debugging impossible.

2.14.9 MN10300 Options

These '-m' options are defined for Matsushita MN10300 architectures:

-mmult-bug

     Generate code to avoid bugs in the multiply instructions for the MN10300 processors. This is the default.

-mno-mult-bug

     Do not generate code to avoid bugs in the multiply instructions for the MN10300 processors.

-mrelax Indicate to the linker that it should perform a relaxation optimization pass to shorten branches, calls and absolute memory addresses. This option only has an effect when used on the command line for the final link step.

     This option makes symbolic debugging impossible.

2.14.10 M32R/D Options

These '-m' options are defined for Mitsubishi M32R/D architectures:

-mcode-model=small

     Assume all objects live in the lower 16MB of memory (so that their addresses can be loaded with the ld24 instruction), and assume all subroutines are reachable with the bl instruction. This is the default.

     The addressability of a particular object can be set with the model attribute.

-mcode-model=medium

     Assume objects may be anywhere in the 32 bit address space (the compiler will generate seth/add3 instructions to load their addresses), and assume all subroutines are reachable with the bl instruction.

-mcode-model=large

     Assume objects may be anywhere in the 32 bit address space (the compiler will generate seth/add3 instructions to load their addresses), and assume subroutines may not be reachable with the `bl` instruction (the compiler will generate the much slower `seth/add3/jl` instruction sequence).

`-msdata=none`

Disable use of the small data area. Variables will be put into one of '`.data`', '`bss`', or '`.rodata`' (unless the `section` attribute has been specified). This is the default.

The small data area consists of sections '`.sdata`' and '`.sbss`'. Objects may be explicitly put in the small data area with the `section` attribute using one of these sections.

`-msdata=sdata`

Put small global and static data in the small data area, but do not generate special code to reference them.

`-msdata=use`

Put small global and static data in the small data area, and generate special instructions to reference them.

`-G num`   Put global and static objects less than or equal to *num* bytes into the small data or bss sections instead of the normal data or bss sections. The default value of *num* is 8. The '`-msdata`' option must be set to one of '`sdata`' or '`use`' for this option to have any effect.

All modules should be compiled with the same '`-G num`' value. Compiling with different values of *num* may or may not work; if it doesn't the linker will give an error message - incorrect code will not be generated.

2.14.11 M88K Options

These '`-m`' options are defined for Motorola 88k architectures:

`-m88000`   Generate code that works well on both the m88100 and the m88110.

`-m88100`   Generate code that works best for the m88100, but that also runs on the m88110.

`-m88110`   Generate code that works best for the m88110, and may not run on the m88100.

`-mbig-pic`

Obsolete option to be removed from the next revision. Use '`-fPIC`'.

`-midentify-revision`

Include an `ident` directive in the assembler output recording the source file name, compiler name and version, timestamp, and compilation flags used.

`-mno-underscores`

> In assembler output, emit symbol names without adding an underscore character at the beginning of each name. The default is to use an underscore as prefix on each name.

`-mocs-debug-info`
`-mno-ocs-debug-info`

> Include (or omit) additional debugging information (about registers used in each stack frame) as specified in the 88open Object Compatibility Standard, "OCS". This extra information allows debugging of code that has had the frame pointer eliminated. The default for DG/UX, SVr4, and Delta 88 SVr3.2 is to include this information; other 88k configurations omit this information by default.

`-mocs-frame-position`

> When emitting COFF debugging information for automatic variables and parameters stored on the stack, use the offset from the canonical frame address, which is the stack pointer (register 31) on entry to the function. The DG/UX, SVr4, Delta88 SVr3.2, and BCS configurations use '`-mocs-frame-position`'; other 88k configurations have the default '`-mno-ocs-frame-position`'.

`-mno-ocs-frame-position`

> When emitting COFF debugging information for automatic variables and parameters stored on the stack, use the offset from the frame pointer register (register 30). When this option is in effect, the frame pointer is not eliminated when debugging information is selected by the -g switch.

`-moptimize-arg-area`
`-mno-optimize-arg-area`

> Control how function arguments are stored in stack frames. '`-moptimize-arg-area`' saves space by optimizing them, but this conflicts with the 88open specifications. The opposite alternative, '`-mno-optimize-arg-area`', agrees with 88open standards. By default GCC does not optimize the argument area.

`-mshort-data-`*num*

> Generate smaller data references by making them relative to `r0`, which allows loading a value using a single instruction (rather than the usual two). You control which data references are affected by specifying *num* with this option. For example, if you specify '`-mshort-data-512`', then the data references affected are those involving displacements of less than 512 bytes. '`-mshort-data-`*num*' is not effective for *num* greater than 64k.

`-mserialize-volatile`
`-mno-serialize-volatile`

> Do, or don't, generate code to guarantee sequential consistency of volatile memory references. By default, consistency is guaranteed.
>
> The order of memory references made by the MC88110 processor does not always match the order of the instructions requesting those references. In particular, a load instruction may execute before a preceding store instruction. Such reordering violates sequential consistency of volatile memory references, when there are multiple processors. When consistency must be guaranteed, GNU C generates special instructions, as needed, to force execution in the proper order.
>
> The MC88100 processor does not reorder memory references and so always provides sequential consistency. However, by default, GNU C generates the special instructions to guarantee consistency even when you use '`-m88100`', so that the code may be run on an MC88110 processor. If you intend to run your code only on the MC88100 processor, you may use '`-mno-serialize-volatile`'.
>
> The extra code generated to guarantee consistency may affect the performance of your application. If you know that you can safely forgo this guarantee, you may use '`-mno-serialize-volatile`'.

`-msvr4`
`-msvr3`

> Turn on ('`-msvr4`') or off ('`-msvr3`') compiler extensions related to System V release 4 (SVr4). This controls the following:
>
> 1. Which variant of the assembler syntax to emit.
>
> 2. '`-msvr4`' makes the C preprocessor recognize '`#pragma weak`' that is used on System V release 4.
>
> 3. '`-msvr4`' makes GCC issue additional declaration directives used in SVr4.
>
> '`-msvr4`' is the default for the m88k-motorola-sysv4 and m88k-dg-dgux m88k configurations. '`-msvr3`' is the default for all other m88k configurations.

`-mversion-03.00`

> This option is obsolete, and is ignored.

`-mno-check-zero-division`
`-mcheck-zero-division`

> Do, or don't, generate code to guarantee that integer division by zero will be detected. By default, detection is guaranteed.
>
> Some models of the MC88100 processor fail to trap upon integer division by zero under certain conditions. By default, when

compiling code that might be run on such a processor, GNU C generates code that explicitly checks for zero-valued divisors and traps with exception number 503 when one is detected. Use of mno-check-zero-division suppresses such checking for code generated to run on an MC88100 processor.

GNU C assumes that the MC88110 processor correctly detects all instances of integer division by zero. When '-m88110' is specified, both '-mcheck-zero-division' and '-mno-check-zero-division' are ignored, and no explicit checks for zero-valued divisors are generated.

-muse-div-instruction

Use the div instruction for signed integer division on the MC88100 processor. By default, the div instruction is not used.

On the MC88100 processor the signed integer division instruction div) traps to the operating system on a negative operand. The operating system transparently completes the operation, but at a large cost in execution time. By default, when compiling code that might be run on an MC88100 processor, GNU C emulates signed integer division using the unsigned integer division instruction divu), thereby avoiding the large penalty of a trap to the operating system. Such emulation has its own, smaller, execution cost in both time and space. To the extent that your code's important signed integer division operations are performed on two nonnegative operands, it may be desirable to use the div instruction directly.

On the MC88110 processor the div instruction (also known as the divs instruction) processes negative operands without trapping to the operating system. When '-m88110' is specified, '-muse-div-instruction' is ignored, and the div instruction is used for signed integer division.

Note that the result of dividing INT_MIN by -1 is undefined. In particular, the behavior of such a division with and without '-muse-div-instruction' may differ.

-mtrap-large-shift
-mhandle-large-shift

Include code to detect bit-shifts of more than 31 bits; respectively, trap such shifts or emit code to handle them properly. By default GCC makes no special provision for large bit shifts.

-mwarn-passed-structs

Warn when a function passes a struct as an argument or result. Structure-passing conventions have changed during the evolution of the C language, and are often the source of portability problems. By default, GCC issues no such warning.

2.14.12 IBM RS/6000 and PowerPC Options

These '-m' options are defined for the IBM RS/6000 and PowerPC:

```
-mpower
-mno-power
-mpower2
-mno-power2
-mpowerpc
-mno-powerpc
-mpowerpc-gpopt
-mno-powerpc-gpopt
-mpowerpc-gfxopt
-mno-powerpc-gfxopt
-mpowerpc64
-mno-powerpc64
```

> GCC supports two related instruction set architectures for the RS/6000 and PowerPC. The *POWER* instruction set are those instructions supported by the 'rios' chip set used in the original RS/6000 systems and the *PowerPC* instruction set is the architecture of the Motorola MPC5xx, MPC6xx, MPC8xx microprocessors, and the IBM 4xx microprocessors.
>
> Neither architecture is a subset of the other. However there is a large common subset of instructions supported by both. An MQ register is included in processors supporting the POWER architecture.
>
> You use these options to specify which instructions are available on the processor you are using. The default value of these options is determined when configuring GCC. Specifying the '-mcpu=*cpu_type*' overrides the specification of these options. We recommend you use the '-mcpu=*cpu_type*' option rather than the options listed above.
>
> The '-mpower' option allows GCC to generate instructions that are found only in the POWER architecture and to use the MQ register. Specifying '-mpower2' implies '-power' and also allows GCC to generate instructions that are present in the POWER2 architecture but not the original POWER architecture.
>
> The '-mpowerpc' option allows GCC to generate instructions that are found only in the 32-bit subset of the PowerPC architecture. Specifying '-mpowerpc-gpopt' implies '-mpowerpc' and also allows GCC to use the optional PowerPC architecture instructions in the General Purpose group, including floating-point square root. Specifying '-mpowerpc-gfxopt' implies '-mpowerpc' and also allows GCC to use the optional PowerPC architecture instructions in the Graphics group, including floating-point select.

The '-mpowerpc64' option allows GCC to generate the additional 64-bit instructions that are found in the full PowerPC64 architecture and to treat GPRs as 64-bit, doubleword quantities. GCC defaults to '-mno-powerpc64'.

If you specify both '-mno-power' and '-mno-powerpc', GCC will use only the instructions in the common subset of both architectures plus some special AIX common-mode calls, and will not use the MQ register. Specifying both '-mpower' and '-mpowerpc' permits GCC to use any instruction from either architecture and to allow use of the MQ register; specify this for the Motorola MPC601.

-mnew-mnemonics
-mold-mnemonics

Select which mnemonics to use in the generated assembler code. '-mnew-mnemonics' requests output that uses the assembler mnemonics defined for the PowerPC architecture, while '-mold-mnemonics' requests the assembler mnemonics defined for the POWER architecture. Instructions defined in only one architecture have only one mnemonic; GCC uses that mnemonic irrespective of which of these options is specified.

GCC defaults to the mnemonics appropriate for the architecture in use. Specifying '-mcpu=cpu_type' sometimes overrides the value of these option. Unless you are building a cross-compiler, you should normally not specify either '-mnew-mnemonics' or '-mold-mnemonics', but should instead accept the default.

-mcpu=cpu_type

Set architecture type, register usage, choice of mnemonics, and instruction scheduling parameters for machine type cpu_type. Supported values for cpu_type are 'rs6000', 'rios1', 'rios2', 'rsc', '601', '602', '603', '603e', '604', '604e', '620', '740', '750', 'power', 'power2', 'powerpc', '403', '505', '801', '821', '823', and '860' and 'common'. '-mcpu=power', '-mcpu=power2', and '-mcpu=powerpc' specify generic POWER, POWER2 and pure PowerPC (i.e., not MPC601) architecture machine types, with an appropriate, generic processor model assumed for scheduling purposes.

Specifying any of the following options: '-mcpu=rios1', '-mcpu=rios2', '-mcpu=rsc', '-mcpu=power', or '-mcpu=power2' enables the '-mpower' option and disables the '-mpowerpc' option; '-mcpu=601' enables both the '-mpower' and '-mpowerpc' options. All of '-mcpu=602', '-mcpu=603', '-mcpu=603e', '-mcpu=604', '-mcpu=620', enable the '-mpowerpc' option and disable the '-mpower' option. Exactly similarly, all of '-mcpu=403', '-mcpu=505', '-mcpu=821', '-mcpu=860' and

'-mcpu=powerpc' enable the '-mpowerpc' option and disable the '-mpower' option. '-mcpu=common' disables both the '-mpower' and '-mpowerpc' options.

AIX versions 4 or greater selects '-mcpu=common' by default, so that code will operate on all members of the RS/6000 and PowerPC families. In that case, GCC will use only the instructions in the common subset of both architectures plus some special AIX common-mode calls, and will not use the MQ register. GCC assumes a generic processor model for scheduling purposes.

Specifying any of the options '-mcpu=rios1', '-mcpu=rios2', '-mcpu=rsc', '-mcpu=power', or '-mcpu=power2' also disables the 'new-mnemonics' option. Specifying '-mcpu=601', '-mcpu=602', '-mcpu=603', '-mcpu=603e', '-mcpu=604', '620', '403', or '-mcpu=powerpc' also enables the 'new-mnemonics' option.

Specifying '-mcpu=403', '-mcpu=821', or '-mcpu=860' also enables the '-msoft-float' option.

-mtune=*cpu_type*

Set the instruction scheduling parameters for machine type *cpu_type*, but do not set the architecture type, register usage, choice of mnemonics like '-mcpu='*cpu_type* would. The same values for *cpu_type* are used for '-mtune='*cpu_type* as for '-mcpu='*cpu_type*. The '-mtune='*cpu_type* option overrides the '-mcpu='*cpu_type* option in terms of instruction scheduling parameters.

-mfull-toc
-mno-fp-in-toc
-mno-sum-in-toc
-mminimal-toc

Modify generation of the TOC (Table Of Contents), which is created for every executable file. The '-mfull-toc' option is selected by default. In that case, GCC will allocate at least one TOC entry for each unique non-automatic variable reference in your program. GCC will also place floating-point constants in the TOC. However, only 16,384 entries are available in the TOC.

If you receive a linker error message that saying you have overflowed the available TOC space, you can reduce the amount of TOC space used with the '-mno-fp-in-toc' and '-mno-sum-in-toc' options. '-mno-fp-in-toc' prevents GCC from putting floating-point constants in the TOC and '-mno-sum-in-toc' forces GCC to generate code to calculate the sum of an address and a constant at run-time instead of putting that sum into the TOC. You may specify one or both of these options. Each causes GCC to produce very slightly slower and larger code at the expense of conserving TOC space.

If you still run out of space in the TOC even when you specify both of these options, specify '-mminimal-toc' instead. This option causes GCC to make only one TOC entry for every file. When you specify this option, GCC will produce code that is slower and larger but which uses extremely little TOC space. You may wish to use this option only on files that contain less frequently executed code.

-maix64
-maix32
Enable AIX 64-bit ABI and calling convention: 64-bit pointers, 64-bit **long** type, and the infrastructure needed to support them. Specifying '-maix64' implies '-mpowerpc64' and '-mpowerpc', while '-maix32' disables the 64-bit ABI and implies '-mno-powerpc64'. GCC defaults to '-maix32'.

-mxl-call
-mno-xl-call
On AIX, pass floating-point arguments to prototyped functions beyond the register save area (RSA) on the stack in addition to argument FPRs. The AIX calling convention was extended but not initially documented to handle an obscure K&R C case of calling a function that takes the address of its arguments with fewer arguments than declared. AIX XL compilers access floating point arguments which do not fit in the RSA from the stack when a subroutine is compiled without optimization. Because always storing floating-point arguments on the stack is inefficient and rarely needed, this option is not enabled by default and only is necessary when calling subroutines compiled by AIX XL compilers without optimization.

-mthreads
Support *AIX Threads*. Link an application written to use *pthreads* with special libraries and startup code to enable the application to run.

-mpe
Support *IBM RS/6000 SP Parallel Environment* (PE). Link an application written to use message passing with special startup code to enable the application to run. The system must have PE installed in the standard location ('/usr/lpp/ppe.poe/'), or the 'specs' file must be overridden with the '-specs=' option to specify the appropriate directory location. The Parallel Environment does not support threads, so the '-mpe' option and the '-mthreads' option are incompatible.

`-msoft-float`
`-mhard-float`

> Generate code that does not use (uses) the floating-point register set. Software floating point emulation is provided if you use the '`-msoft-float`' option, and pass the option to GCC when linking.

`-mmultiple`
`-mno-multiple`

> Generate code that uses (does not use) the load multiple word instructions and the store multiple word instructions. These instructions are generated by default on POWER systems, and not generated on PowerPC systems. Do not use '`-mmultiple`' on little endian PowerPC systems, since those instructions do not work when the processor is in little endian mode. The exceptions are PPC740 and PPC750 which permit the instructions usage in little endian mode.

`-mstring`
`-mno-string`

> Generate code that uses (does not use) the load string instructions and the store string word instructions to save multiple registers and do small block moves. These instructions are generated by default on POWER systems, and not generated on PowerPC systems. Do not use '`-mstring`' on little endian PowerPC systems, since those instructions do not work when the processor is in little endian mode. The exceptions are PPC740 and PPC750 which permit the instructions usage in little endian mode.

`-mupdate`
`-mno-update`

> Generate code that uses (does not use) the load or store instructions that update the base register to the address of the calculated memory location. These instructions are generated by default. If you use '`-mno-update`', there is a small window between the time that the stack pointer is updated and the address of the previous frame is stored, which means code that walks the stack frame across interrupts or signals may get corrupted data.

`-mfused-madd`
`-mno-fused-madd`

> Generate code that uses (does not use) the floating point multiply and accumulate instructions. These instructions are generated by default if hardware floating is used.

`-mno-bit-align`

`-mbit-align`

> On System V.4 and embedded PowerPC systems do not (do) force structures and unions that contain bit fields to be aligned to the base type of the bit field.
>
> For example, by default a structure containing nothing but 8 `unsigned` bitfields of length 1 would be aligned to a 4 byte boundary and have a size of 4 bytes. By using '`-mno-bit-align`', the structure would be aligned to a 1 byte boundary and be one byte in size.

`-mno-strict-align`

`-mstrict-align`

> On System V.4 and embedded PowerPC systems do not (do) assume that unaligned memory references will be handled by the system.

`-mrelocatable`

`-mno-relocatable`

> On embedded PowerPC systems generate code that allows (does not allow) the program to be relocated to a different address at runtime. If you use '`-mrelocatable`' on any module, all objects linked together must be compiled with '`-mrelocatable`' or '`-mrelocatable-lib`'.

`-mrelocatable-lib`

`-mno-relocatable-lib`

> On embedded PowerPC systems generate code that allows (does not allow) the program to be relocated to a different address at runtime. Modules compiled with '`-mrelocatable-lib`' can be linked with either modules compiled without '`-mrelocatable`' and '`-mrelocatable-lib`' or with modules compiled with the '`-mrelocatable`' options.

`-mno-toc`

`-mtoc` On System V.4 and embedded PowerPC systems do not (do) assume that register 2 contains a pointer to a global area pointing to the addresses used in the program.

`-mlittle`

`-mlittle-endian`

> On System V.4 and embedded PowerPC systems compile code for the processor in little endian mode. The '`-mlittle-endian`' option is the same as '`-mlittle`'.

`-mbig`

`-mbig-endian`

> On System V.4 and embedded PowerPC systems compile code for the processor in big endian mode. The '`-mbig-endian`' option is the same as '`-mbig`'.

`-mcall-sysv`

> On System V.4 and embedded PowerPC systems compile code using calling conventions that adheres to the March 1995 draft of the System V Application Binary Interface, PowerPC processor supplement. This is the default unless you configured GCC using 'powerpc-*-eabiaix'.

`-mcall-sysv-eabi`

> Specify both '-mcall-sysv' and '-meabi' options.

`-mcall-sysv-noeabi`

> Specify both '-mcall-sysv' and '-mno-eabi' options.

`-mcall-aix`

> On System V.4 and embedded PowerPC systems compile code using calling conventions that are similar to those used on AIX. This is the default if you configured GCC using 'powerpc-*-eabiaix'.

`-mcall-solaris`

> On System V.4 and embedded PowerPC systems compile code for the Solaris operating system.

`-mcall-linux`

> On System V.4 and embedded PowerPC systems compile code for the Linux-based GNU system.

`-mprototype`
`-mno-prototype`

> On System V.4 and embedded PowerPC systems assume that all calls to variable argument functions are properly prototyped. Otherwise, the compiler must insert an instruction before every non prototyped call to set or clear bit 6 of the condition code register (CR) to indicate whether floating point values were passed in the floating point registers in case the function takes a variable arguments. With '-mprototype', only calls to prototyped variable argument functions will set or clear the bit.

`-msim`

> On embedded PowerPC systems, assume that the startup module is called 'sim-crt0.o' and that the standard C libraries are 'libsim.a' and 'libc.a'. This is the default for 'powerpc-*-eabisim'. configurations.

`-mmvme`

> On embedded PowerPC systems, assume that the startup module is called 'crt0.o' and the standard C libraries are 'libmvme.a' and 'libc.a'.

`-mads`

> On embedded PowerPC systems, assume that the startup module is called 'crt0.o' and the standard C libraries are 'libads.a' and 'libc.a'.

-myellowknife
On embedded PowerPC systems, assume that the startup module is called '`crt0.o`' and the standard C libraries are '`libyk.a`' and '`libc.a`'.

-memb
On embedded PowerPC systems, set the *PPC_EMB* bit in the ELF flags header to indicate that '`eabi`' extended relocations are used.

-meabi
-mno-eabi
On System V.4 and embedded PowerPC systems do (do not) adhere to the Embedded Applications Binary Interface (eabi) which is a set of modifications to the System V.4 specifications. Selecting -meabi means that the stack is aligned to an 8 byte boundary, a function __eabi is called to from main to set up the eabi environment, and the '-msdata' option can use both r2 and r13 to point to two separate small data areas. Selecting -mno-eabi means that the stack is aligned to a 16 byte boundary, do not call an initialization function from main, and the '-msdata' option will only use r13 to point to a single small data area. The '-meabi' option is on by default if you configured GCC using one of the '`powerpc*-*-eabi*`' options.

-msdata=eabi
On System V.4 and embedded PowerPC systems, put small initialized const global and static data in the '.sdata2' section, which is pointed to by register r2. Put small initialized non-const global and static data in the '.sdata' section, which is pointed to by register r13. Put small uninitialized global and static data in the '.sbss' section, which is adjacent to the '.sdata' section. The '-msdata=eabi' option is incompatible with the '-mrelocatable' option. The '-msdata=eabi' option also sets the '-memb' option.

-msdata=sysv
On System V.4 and embedded PowerPC systems, put small global and static data in the '.sdata' section, which is pointed to by register r13. Put small uninitialized global and static data in the '.sbss' section, which is adjacent to the '.sdata' section. The '-msdata=sysv' option is incompatible with the '-mrelocatable' option.

-msdata=default
-msdata
On System V.4 and embedded PowerPC systems, if '-meabi' is used, compile code the same as '-msdata=eabi', otherwise compile code the same as '-msdata=sysv'.

-msdata-data

> On System V.4 and embedded PowerPC systems, put small
> global and static data in the '.sdata' section. Put small unini-
> tialized global and static data in the '.sbss' section. Do not use
> register r13 to address small data however. This is the default
> behavior unless other '-msdata' options are used.

-msdata=none
-mno-sdata

> On embedded PowerPC systems, put all initialized global and
> static data in the '.data' section, and all uninitialized data in
> the '.bss' section.

-G num

> On embedded PowerPC systems, put global and static items less
> than or equal to *num* bytes into the small data or bss sections
> instead of the normal data or bss section. By default, *num* is 8.
> The '-G *num*' switch is also passed to the linker. All modules
> should be compiled with the same '-G *num*' value.

-mregnames
-mno-regnames

> On System V.4 and embedded PowerPC systems do (do not)
> emit register names in the assembly language output using sym-
> bolic forms.

2.14.13 IBM RT Options

These '-m' options are defined for the IBM RT PC:

-min-line-mul

> Use an in-line code sequence for integer multiplies. This is the
> default.

-mcall-lib-mul

> Call lmul$$ for integer multiples.

-mfull-fp-blocks

> Generate full-size floating point data blocks, including the min-
> imum amount of scratch space recommended by IBM. This is
> the default.

-mminimum-fp-blocks

> Do not include extra scratch space in floating point data blocks.
> This results in smaller code, but slower execution, since scratch
> space must be allocated dynamically.

-mfp-arg-in-fpregs

> Use a calling sequence incompatible with the IBM calling con-
> vention in which floating point arguments are passed in floating
> point registers. Note that varargs.h and stdargs.h will not
> work with floating point operands if this option is specified.

-mfp-arg-in-gregs
>   Use the normal calling convention for floating point arguments.
>   This is the default.

-mhc-struct-return
>   Return structures of more than one word in memory, rather than
>   in a register. This provides compatibility with the MetaWare
>   HighC (hc) compiler. Use the option '-fpcc-struct-return'
>   for compatibility with the Portable C Compiler (pcc).

-mnohc-struct-return
>   Return some structures of more than one word in registers, when
>   convenient. This is the default. For compatibility with the IBM-
>   supplied compilers, use the option '-fpcc-struct-return' or
>   the option '-mhc-struct-return'.

2.14.14 MIPS Options

These '-m' options are defined for the MIPS family of computers:

-mcpu=*cpu type*
>   Assume the defaults for the machine type *cpu type* when
>   scheduling instructions. The choices for *cpu type* are 'r2000',
>   'r3000', 'r3900', 'r4000', 'r4100', 'r4300', 'r4400', 'r4600',
>   'r4650', 'r5000', 'r6000', 'r8000', and 'orion'. Additionally,
>   the 'r2000', 'r3000', 'r4000', 'r5000', and 'r6000' can be ab-
>   breviated as 'r2k' (or 'r2K'), 'r3k', etc. While picking a specific
>   *cpu type* will schedule things appropriately for that particular
>   chip, the compiler will not generate any code that does not meet
>   level 1 of the MIPS ISA (instruction set architecture) without a
>   '-mipsX' or '-mabi' switch being used.

-mips1   Issue instructions from level 1 of the MIPS ISA. This is the
>   default. 'r3000' is the default *cpu type* at this ISA level.

-mips2   Issue instructions from level 2 of the MIPS ISA (branch likely,
>   square root instructions). 'r6000' is the default *cpu type* at this
>   ISA level.

-mips3   Issue instructions from level 3 of the MIPS ISA (64 bit instruc-
>   tions). 'r4000' is the default *cpu type* at this ISA level.

-mips4   Issue instructions from level 4 of the MIPS ISA (conditional
>   move, prefetch, enhanced FPU instructions). 'r8000' is the de-
>   fault *cpu type* at this ISA level.

-mfp32   Assume that 32 32-bit floating point registers are available. This
>   is the default.

-mfp64   Assume that 32 64-bit floating point registers are available. This
>   is the default when the '-mips3' option is used.

-mgp32   Assume that 32 32-bit general purpose registers are available. This is the default.

-mgp64   Assume that 32 64-bit general purpose registers are available. This is the default when the '-mips3' option is used.

-mint64   Force int and long types to be 64 bits wide. See '-mlong32' for an explanation of the default, and the width of pointers.

-mlong64   Force long types to be 64 bits wide. See '-mlong32' for an explanation of the default, and the width of pointers.

-mlong32   Force long, int, and pointer types to be 32 bits wide.

            If none of '-mlong32', '-mlong64', or '-mint64' are set, the size of ints, longs, and pointers depends on the ABI and ISA choosen. For '-mabi=32', and '-mabi=n32', ints and longs are 32 bits wide. For '-mabi=64', ints are 32 bits, and longs are 64 bits wide. For '-mabi=eabi' and either '-mips1' or '-mips2', ints and longs are 32 bits wide. For '-mabi=eabi' and higher ISAs, ints are 32 bits, and longs are 64 bits wide. The width of pointer types is the smaller of the width of longs or the width of general purpose registers (which in turn depends on the ISA).

-mabi=32
-mabi=o64
-mabi=n32
-mabi=64
-mabi=eabi

            Generate code for the indicated ABI. The default instruction level is '-mips1' for '32', '-mips3' for 'n32', and '-mips4' otherwise. Conversely, with '-mips1' or '-mips2', the default ABI is '32'; otherwise, the default ABI is '64'.

-mmips-as

            Generate code for the MIPS assembler, and invoke 'mips-tfile' to add normal debug information. This is the default for all platforms except for the OSF/1 reference platform, using the OSF/rose object format. If the either of the '-gstabs' or '-gstabs+' switches are used, the 'mips-tfile' program will encapsulate the stabs within MIPS ECOFF.

-mgas   Generate code for the GNU assembler. This is the default on the OSF/1 reference platform, using the OSF/rose object format. Also, this is the default if the configure option '--with-gnu-as' is used.

-msplit-addresses
-mno-split-addresses

            Generate code to load the high and low parts of address constants separately. This allows gcc to optimize away redundant loads of the high order bits of addresses. This optimization requires GNU as and GNU ld. This optimization is enabled by default for some embedded targets where GNU as and GNU ld are standard.

`-mrnames`
`-mno-rnames`

The '`-mrnames`' switch says to output code using the MIPS software names for the registers, instead of the hardware names (ie, *a0* instead of *$4*). The only known assembler that supports this option is the Algorithmics assembler.

`-mgpopt`
`-mno-gpopt`

The '`-mgpopt`' switch says to write all of the data declarations before the instructions in the text section, this allows the MIPS assembler to generate one word memory references instead of using two words for short global or static data items. This is on by default if optimization is selected.

`-mstats`
`-mno-stats`

For each non-inline function processed, the '`-mstats`' switch causes the compiler to emit one line to the standard error file to print statistics about the program (number of registers saved, stack size, etc.).

`-mmemcpy`
`-mno-memcpy`

The '`-mmemcpy`' switch makes all block moves call the appropriate string function ('`memcpy`' or '`bcopy`') instead of possibly generating inline code.

`-mmips-tfile`
`-mno-mips-tfile`

The '`-mno-mips-tfile`' switch causes the compiler not postprocess the object file with the '`mips-tfile`' program, after the MIPS assembler has generated it to add debug support. If '`mips-tfile`' is not run, then no local variables will be available to the debugger. In addition, '`stage2`' and '`stage3`' objects will have the temporary file names passed to the assembler embedded in the object file, which means the objects will not compare the same. The '`-mno-mips-tfile`' switch should only be used when there are bugs in the '`mips-tfile`' program that prevents compilation.

`-msoft-float`

Generate output containing library calls for floating point. **Warning:** the requisite libraries are not part of GCC. Normally the facilities of the machine's usual C compiler are used, but this can't be done directly in cross-compilation. You must make your own arrangements to provide suitable library functions for cross-compilation.

`-mhard-float`

Generate output containing floating point instructions. This is the default if you use the unmodified sources.

`-mabicalls`
`-mno-abicalls`

Emit (or do not emit) the pseudo operations '`.abicalls`', '`.cpload`', and '`.cprestore`' that some System V.4 ports use for position independent code.

`-mlong-calls`
`-mno-long-calls`

Do all calls with the '`JALR`' instruction, which requires loading up a function's address into a register before the call. You need to use this switch, if you call outside of the current 512 megabyte segment to functions that are not through pointers.

`-mhalf-pic`
`-mno-half-pic`

Put pointers to extern references into the data section and load them up, rather than put the references in the text section.

`-membedded-pic`
`-mno-embedded-pic`

Generate PIC code suitable for some embedded systems. All calls are made using PC relative address, and all data is addressed using the $gp register. No more than 65536 bytes of global data may be used. This requires GNU as and GNU ld which do most of the work. This currently only works on targets which use ECOFF; it does not work with ELF.

`-membedded-data`
`-mno-embedded-data`

Allocate variables to the read-only data section first if possible, then next in the small data section if possible, otherwise in data. This gives slightly slower code than the default, but reduces the amount of RAM required when executing, and thus may be preferred for some embedded systems.

`-msingle-float`
`-mdouble-float`

The '`-msingle-float`' switch tells gcc to assume that the floating point coprocessor only supports single precision operations, as on the '`r4650`' chip. The '`-mdouble-float`' switch permits gcc to use double precision operations. This is the default.

`-mmad`
`-mno-mad`   Permit use of the 'mad', 'madu' and 'mul' instructions, as on the 'r4650' chip.

`-m4650`   Turns on '-msingle-float', '-mmad', and, at least for now, '-mcpu=r4650'.

`-mips16`
`-mno-mips16`
   Enable 16-bit instructions.

`-mentry`   Use the entry and exit pseudo ops. This option can only be used with '-mips16'.

`-EL`   Compile code for the processor in little endian mode. The requisite libraries are assumed to exist.

`-EB`   Compile code for the processor in big endian mode. The requisite libraries are assumed to exist.

`-G num`   Put global and static items less than or equal to *num* bytes into the small data or bss sections instead of the normal data or bss section. This allows the assembler to emit one word memory reference instructions based on the global pointer (*gp* or *$28*), instead of the normal two words used. By default, *num* is 8 when the MIPS assembler is used, and 0 when the GNU assembler is used. The '-G num' switch is also passed to the assembler and linker. All modules should be compiled with the same '-G num' value.

`-nocpp`   Tell the MIPS assembler to not run its preprocessor over user assembler files (with a '.s' suffix) when assembling them.

These options are defined by the macro `TARGET_SWITCHES` in the machine description. The default for the options is also defined by that macro, which enables you to change the defaults.

2.14.15 Intel 386 Options

These '-m' options are defined for the i386 family of computers:

`-mcpu=`*cpu type*
   Assume the defaults for the machine type *cpu type* when scheduling instructions. The choices for *cpu type* are:

'i386'   'i486'   'i586'   'i686'
'pentium'   'pentiumpro' 'k6'

While picking a specific *cpu type* will schedule things appropriately for that particular chip, the compiler will not generate any code that does not run on the i386 without the '-march=*cpu type*' option being used. 'i586' is equivalent to 'pentium' and 'i686' is equivalent to 'pentiumpro'. 'k6' is the AMD chip as opposed to the Intel ones.

-march=*cpu type*

Generate instructions for the machine type *cpu type*. The choices for *cpu type* are the same as for '-mcpu'. Moreover, specifying '-march=*cpu type*' implies '-mcpu=*cpu type*'.

-m386
-m486
-mpentium
-mpentiumpro

Synonyms for -mcpu=i386, -mcpu=i486, -mcpu=pentium, and -mcpu=pentiumpro respectively. These synonyms are deprecated.

-mieee-fp
-mno-ieee-fp

Control whether or not the compiler uses IEEE floating point comparisons. These handle correctly the case where the result of a comparison is unordered.

-msoft-float

Generate output containing library calls for floating point. **Warning:** the requisite libraries are not part of GCC. Normally the facilities of the machine's usual C compiler are used, but this can't be done directly in cross-compilation. You must make your own arrangements to provide suitable library functions for cross-compilation.

On machines where a function returns floating point results in the 80387 register stack, some floating point opcodes may be emitted even if '-msoft-float' is used.

-mno-fp-ret-in-387

Do not use the FPU registers for return values of functions.

The usual calling convention has functions return values of types **float** and **double** in an FPU register, even if there is no FPU. The idea is that the operating system should emulate an FPU.

The option '-mno-fp-ret-in-387' causes such values to be returned in ordinary CPU registers instead.

-mno-fancy-math-387

Some 387 emulators do not support the **sin**, **cos** and **sqrt** instructions for the 387. Specify this option to avoid generating those instructions. This option is the default on FreeBSD. As of revision 2.6.1, these instructions are not generated unless you also use the '-ffast-math' switch.

`-malign-double`
`-mno-align-double`

>   Control whether GCC aligns `double`, `long double`, and `long`
>   `long` variables on a two word boundary or a one word boundary.
>   Aligning `double` variables on a two word boundary will produce
>   code that runs somewhat faster on a 'Pentium' at the expense
>   of more memory.
>
>   **Warning:** if you use the '-malign-double' switch, structures
>   containing the above types will be aligned differently than the
>   published application binary interface specifications for the 386.

`-msvr3-shlib`
`-mno-svr3-shlib`

>   Control whether GCC places uninitialized locals into `bss` or
>   `data`. '-msvr3-shlib' places these locals into `bss`. These op-
>   tions are meaningful only on System V Release 3.

`-mno-wide-multiply`
`-mwide-multiply`

>   Control whether GCC uses the `mul` and `imul` that produce 64
>   bit results in `eax:edx` from 32 bit operands to do `long long`
>   multiplies and 32-bit division by constants.

`-mrtd`   Use a different function-calling convention, in which functions
>   that take a fixed number of arguments return with the `ret num`
>   instruction, which pops their arguments while returning. This
>   saves one instruction in the caller since there is no need to pop
>   the arguments there.
>
>   You can specify that an individual function is called with this
>   calling sequence with the function attribute 'stdcall'. You can
>   also override the '-mrtd' option by using the function attribute
>   'cdecl'. See Section 4.23 [Function Attributes], page 177.
>
>   **Warning:** this calling convention is incompatible with the one
>   normally used on Unix, so you cannot use it if you need to call
>   libraries compiled with the Unix compiler.
>
>   Also, you must provide function prototypes for all functions that
>   take variable numbers of arguments (including `printf`); other-
>   wise incorrect code will be generated for calls to those functions.
>
>   In addition, seriously incorrect code will result if you call a func-
>   tion with too many arguments. (Normally, extra arguments are
>   harmlessly ignored.)

`-mreg-alloc=`*regs*

>   Control the default allocation order of integer registers. The
>   string *regs* is a series of letters specifying a register. The sup-
>   ported letters are: `a` allocate EAX; `b` allocate EBX; `c` allocate
>   ECX; `d` allocate EDX; `S` allocate ESI; `D` allocate EDI; `B` allocate
>   EBP.

`-mregparm=`*num*

> Control how many registers are used to pass integer arguments.
> By default, no registers are used to pass arguments, and at most
> 3 registers can be used. You can control this behavior for a
> specific function by using the function attribute '`regparm`'. See
> Section 4.23 [Function Attributes], page 177.
>
> **Warning:** if you use this switch, and *num* is nonzero, then you
> must build all modules with the same value, including any li-
> braries. This includes the system libraries and startup modules.

`-malign-loops=`*num*

> Align loops to a 2 raised to a *num* byte boundary. If
> '`-malign-loops`' is not specified, the default is 2 unless gas
> 2.8 (or later) is being used in which case the default is to align
> the loop on a 16 byte boundary if it is less than 8 bytes away.

`-malign-jumps=`*num*

> Align instructions that are only jumped to to a 2 raised to a *num*
> byte boundary. If '`-malign-jumps`' is not specified, the default
> is 2 if optimizing for a 386, and 4 if optimizing for a 486 unless
> gas 2.8 (or later) is being used in which case the default is to
> align the instruction on a 16 byte boundary if it is less than 8
> bytes away.

`-malign-functions=`*num*

> Align the start of functions to a 2 raised to *num* byte bound-
> ary. If '`-malign-functions`' is not specified, the default is 2 if
> optimizing for a 386, and 4 if optimizing for a 486.

`-mpreferred-stack-boundary=`*num*

> Attempt to keep the stack boundary aligned to a 2 raised to
> *num* byte boundary. If '`-mpreferred-stack-boundary`' is not
> specified, the default is 4 (16 bytes or 128 bits).
>
> The stack is required to be aligned on a 4 byte boundary.
> On Pentium and PentiumPro, `double` and `long double` values
> should be aligned to an 8 byte boundary (see '`-malign-double`')
> or suffer significant run time performance penalties. On Pentium
> III, the Streaming SIMD Extention (SSE) data type `__m128` suf-
> fers similar penalties if it is not 16 byte aligned.
>
> To ensure proper alignment of this values on the stack, the stack
> boundary must be as aligned as that required by any value stored
> on the stack. Further, every function must be generated such
> that it keeps the stack aligned. Thus calling a function compiled
> with a higher preferred stack boundary from a function compiled
> with a lower preferred stack boundary will most likely misalign
> the stack. It is recommended that libraries that use callbacks
> always use the default setting.

This extra alignment does consume extra stack space. Code
that is sensitive to stack space usage, such as embedded systems
and operating system kernels, may want to reduce the preferred
alignment to '-mpreferred-stack-boundary=2'.

2.14.16 HPPA Options

These '-m' options are defined for the HPPA family of computers:

`-march=`*architecture type*

Generate code for the specified architecture. The choices for
architecture type are '1.0' for PA 1.0, '1.1' for PA 1.1, and '2.0'
for PA 2.0 processors. Refer to '/usr/lib/sched.models' on an
HP-UX system to determine the proper architecture option for
your machine. Code compiled for lower numbered architectures
will run on higher numbered architectures, but not the other
way around.

PA 2.0 support currently requires gas snapshot 19990413 or
later. The next release of binutils (current is 2.9.1) will probably
contain PA 2.0 support.

`-mpa-risc-1-0`
`-mpa-risc-1-1`
`-mpa-risc-2-0`

Synonyms for -march=1.0, -march=1.1, and -march=2.0 respectively.

`-mbig-switch`

Generate code suitable for big switch tables. Use this option only
if the assembler/linker complain about out of range branches
within a switch table.

`-mjump-in-delay`

Fill delay slots of function calls with unconditional jump instructions by modifying the return pointer for the function call to be
the target of the conditional jump.

`-mdisable-fpregs`

Prevent floating point registers from being used in any manner.
This is necessary for compiling kernels which perform lazy context switching of floating point registers. If you use this option
and attempt to perform floating point operations, the compiler
will abort.

`-mdisable-indexing`

Prevent the compiler from using indexing address modes. This
avoids some rather obscure problems when compiling MIG generated code under MACH.

`-mno-space-regs`
>   Generate code that assumes the target has no space registers.
>   This allows GCC to generate faster indirect calls and use un-
>   scaled index address modes.
>
>   Such code is suitable for level 0 PA systems and kernels.

`-mfast-indirect-calls`
>   Generate code that assumes calls never cross space boundaries.
>   This allows GCC to emit code which performs faster indirect
>   calls.
>
>   This option will not work in the presense of shared libraries or
>   nested functions.

`-mspace`   Optimize for space rather than execution time. Currently this
>   only enables out of line function prologues and epilogues. This
>   option is incompatible with PIC code generation and profiling.

`-mlong-load-store`
>   Generate 3-instruction load and store sequences as sometimes
>   required by the HP-UX 10 linker. This is equivalent to the '+k'
>   option to the HP compilers.

`-mportable-runtime`
>   Use the portable calling conventions proposed by HP for ELF
>   systems.

`-mgas`   Enable the use of assembler directives only GAS understands.

`-mschedule=`*cpu type*
>   Schedule code according to the constraints for the machine type
>   *cpu type*. The choices for *cpu type* are '700' '7100', '7100LC',
>   '7200', and '8000'. Refer to '`/usr/lib/sched.models`' on an
>   HP-UX system to determine the proper scheduling option for
>   your machine.

`-mlinker-opt`
>   Enable the optimization pass in the HPUX linker. Note this
>   makes symbolic debugging impossible. It also triggers a bug in
>   the HPUX 8 and HPUX 9 linkers in which they give bogus error
>   messages when linking some programs.

`-msoft-float`
>   Generate output containing library calls for floating point.
>   **Warning:** the requisite libraries are not available for all HPPA
>   targets. Normally the facilities of the machine's usual C compiler
>   are used, but this cannot be done directly in cross-compilation.
>   You must make your own arrangements to provide suitable li-
>   brary functions for cross-compilation. The embedded target
>   '`hppa1.1-*-pro`' does provide software floating point support.

'`-msoft-float`' changes the calling convention in the output file; therefore, it is only useful if you compile *all* of a program with this option. In particular, you need to compile '`libgcc.a`', the library that comes with GCC, with '`-msoft-float`' in order for this to work.

2.14.17 Intel 960 Options

These '`-m`' options are defined for the Intel 960 implementations:

`-m`*cpu type*

> Assume the defaults for the machine type *cpu type* for some of the other options, including instruction scheduling, floating point support, and addressing modes. The choices for *cpu type* are '`ka`', '`kb`', '`mc`', '`ca`', '`cf`', '`sa`', and '`sb`'. The default is '`kb`'.

`-mnumerics`
`-msoft-float`

> The '`-mnumerics`' option indicates that the processor does support floating-point instructions. The '`-msoft-float`' option indicates that floating-point support should not be assumed.

`-mleaf-procedures`
`-mno-leaf-procedures`

> Do (or do not) attempt to alter leaf procedures to be callable with the `bal` instruction as well as `call`. This will result in more efficient code for explicit calls when the `bal` instruction can be substituted by the assembler or linker, but less efficient code in other cases, such as calls via function pointers, or using a linker that doesn't support this optimization.

`-mtail-call`
`-mno-tail-call`

> Do (or do not) make additional attempts (beyond those of the machine-independent portions of the compiler) to optimize tail-recursive calls into branches. You may not want to do this because the detection of cases where this is not valid is not totally complete. The default is '`-mno-tail-call`'.

`-mcomplex-addr`
`-mno-complex-addr`

> Assume (or do not assume) that the use of a complex addressing mode is a win on this implementation of the i960. Complex addressing modes may not be worthwhile on the K-series, but they definitely are on the C-series. The default is currently '`-mcomplex-addr`' for all processors except the CB and CC.

-mcode-align
-mno-code-align

> Align code to 8-byte boundaries for faster fetching (or don't bother). Currently turned on by default for C-series implementations only.

-mic-compat
-mic2.0-compat
-mic3.0-compat

> Enable compatibility with iC960 v2.0 or v3.0.

-masm-compat
-mintel-asm

> Enable compatibility with the iC960 assembler.

-mstrict-align
-mno-strict-align

> Do not permit (do permit) unaligned accesses.

-mold-align

> Enable structure-alignment compatibility with Intel's gcc release version 1.3 (based on gcc 1.37). This option implies '-mstrict-align'.

-mlong-double-64

> Implement type 'long double' as 64-bit floating point numbers. Without the option 'long double' is implemented by 80-bit floating point numbers. The only reason we have it because there is no 128-bit 'long double' support in 'fp-bit.c' yet. So it is only useful for people using soft-float targets. Otherwise, we should recommend against use of it.

2.14.18 DEC Alpha Options

These '-m' options are defined for the DEC Alpha implementations:

-mno-soft-float
-msoft-float

> Use (do not use) the hardware floating-point instructions for floating-point operations. When -msoft-float is specified, functions in 'libgcc1.c' will be used to perform floating-point operations. Unless they are replaced by routines that emulate the floating-point operations, or compiled in such a way as to call such emulations routines, these routines will issue floating-point operations. If you are compiling for an Alpha without floating-point operations, you must ensure that the library is built so as not to call them.
>
> Note that Alpha implementations without floating-point operations are required to have floating-point registers.

`-mfp-reg`
`-mno-fp-regs`

Generate code that uses (does not use) the floating-point register set. `-mno-fp-regs` implies `-msoft-float`. If the floating-point register set is not used, floating point operands are passed in integer registers as if they were integers and floating-point results are passed in $0 instead of $f0. This is a non-standard calling sequence, so any function with a floating-point argument or return value called by code compiled with `-mno-fp-regs` must also be compiled with that option.

A typical use of this option is building a kernel that does not use, and hence need not save and restore, any floating-point registers.

`-mieee`   The Alpha architecture implements floating-point hardware optimized for maximum performance. It is mostly compliant with the IEEE floating point standard. However, for full compliance, software assistance is required. This option generates code fully IEEE compliant code *except* that the *inexact flag* is not maintained (see below). If this option is turned on, the CPP macro `_IEEE_FP` is defined during compilation. The option is a shorthand for: '`-D_IEEE_FP -mfp-trap-mode=su -mtrap-precision=i -mieee-conformant`'. The resulting code is less efficient but is able to correctly support denormalized numbers and exceptional IEEE values such as not-a-number and plus/minus infinity. Other Alpha compilers call this option `-ieee_with_no_inexact`.

`-mieee-with-inexact`

This is like '`-mieee`' except the generated code also maintains the IEEE *inexact flag*. Turning on this option causes the generated code to implement fully-compliant IEEE math. The option is a shorthand for '`-D_IEEE_FP -D_IEEE_FP_INEXACT`' plus the three following: '`-mieee-conformant`', '`-mfp-trap-mode=sui`', and '`-mtrap-precision=i`'. On some Alpha implementations the resulting code may execute significantly slower than the code generated by default. Since there is very little code that depends on the *inexact flag*, you should normally not specify this option. Other Alpha compilers call this option '`-ieee_with_inexact`'.

`-mfp-trap-mode=`*trap mode*

This option controls what floating-point related traps are enabled. Other Alpha compilers call this option '`-fptm `'*trap mode*. The trap mode can be set to one of four values:

'n'   This is the default (normal) setting. The only traps that are enabled are the ones that cannot be disabled in software (e.g., division by zero trap).

'u'   In addition to the traps enabled by 'n', underflow
                 traps are enabled as well.

'su'   Like 'su', but the instructions are marked to be
                 safe for software completion (see Alpha architecture
                 manual for details).

'sui'   Like 'su', but inexact traps are enabled as well.

-mfp-rounding-mode=*rounding mode*
        Selects the IEEE rounding mode. Other Alpha compilers call
        this option '-fprm '*rounding mode*. The *rounding mode* can be
        one of:

'n'   Normal IEEE rounding mode. Floating point num-
                 bers are rounded towards the nearest machine num-
                 ber or towards the even machine number in case of
                 a tie.

'm'   Round towards minus infinity.

'c'   Chopped rounding mode. Floating point numbers
                 are rounded towards zero.

'd'   Dynamic rounding mode. A field in the floating
                 point control register (*fpcr*, see Alpha architecture
                 reference manual) controls the rounding mode in ef-
                 fect. The C library initializes this register for round-
                 ing towards plus infinity. Thus, unless your program
                 modifies the *fpcr*, 'd' corresponds to round towards
                 plus infinity.

-mtrap-precision=*trap precision*
        In the Alpha architecture, floating point traps are imprecise.
        This means without software assistance it is impossible to re-
        cover from a floating trap and program execution normally needs
        to be terminated. GCC can generate code that can assist operat-
        ing system trap handlers in determining the exact location that
        caused a floating point trap. Depending on the requirements of
        an application, different levels of precisions can be selected:

'p'   Program precision. This option is the default and
                 means a trap handler can only identify which pro-
                 gram caused a floating point exception.

'f'   Function precision. The trap handler can determine
                 the function that caused a floating point exception.

'i'   Instruction precision. The trap handler can deter-
                 mine the exact instruction that caused a floating
                 point exception.

Other Alpha compilers provide the equivalent options called '-scope_safe' and '-resumption_safe'.

`-mieee-conformant`

This option marks the generated code as IEEE conformant. You must not use this option unless you also specify '-mtrap-precision=i' and either '-mfp-trap-mode=su' or '-mfp-trap-mode=sui'. Its only effect is to emit the line '.eflag 48' in the function prologue of the generated assembly file. Under DEC Unix, this has the effect that IEEE-conformant math library routines will be linked in.

`-mbuild-constants`

Normally GCC examines a 32- or 64-bit integer constant to see if it can construct it from smaller constants in two or three instructions. If it cannot, it will output the constant as a literal and generate code to load it from the data segment at runtime.

Use this option to require GCC to construct *all* integer constants using code, even if it takes more instructions (the maximum is six).

You would typically use this option to build a shared library dynamic loader. Itself a shared library, it must relocate itself in memory before it can find the variables and constants in its own data segment.

`-malpha-as`
`-mgas`   Select whether to generate code to be assembled by the vendor-supplied assembler ('-malpha-as') or by the GNU assembler '-mgas'.

`-mbwx`
`-mno-bwx`
`-mcix`
`-mno-cix`
`-mmax`
`-mno-max`   Indicate whether GCC should generate code to use the optional BWX, CIX, and MAX instruction sets. The default is to use the instruction sets supported by the CPU type specified via '-mcpu=' option or that of the CPU on which GCC was built if none was specified.

`-mcpu=`*cpu_type*

Set the instruction set, register set, and instruction scheduling parameters for machine type *cpu_type*. You can specify either the 'EV' style name or the corresponding chip number. GCC supports scheduling parameters for the EV4 and EV5 family of processors and will choose the default values for the instruction set from the processor you specify. If you do not specify a processor type, GCC will default to the processor on which the compiler was built.

Supported values for *cpu_type* are

'ev4'
'21064'   Schedules as an EV4 and has no instruction set extensions.

'ev5'
'21164'   Schedules as an EV5 and has no instruction set extensions.

'ev56'
'21164a'   Schedules as an EV5 and supports the BWX extension.

'pca56'
'21164pc'
'21164PC'   Schedules as an EV5 and supports the BWX and MAX extensions.

'ev6'
'21264'   Schedules as an EV5 (until Digital releases the scheduling parameters for the EV6) and supports the BWX, CIX, and MAX extensions.

-mmemory-latency=*time*

Sets the latency the scheduler should assume for typical memory references as seen by the application. This number is highly dependant on the memory access patterns used by the application and the size of the external cache on the machine.

Valid options for *time* are

'*number*'   A decimal number representing clock cycles.

'L1'
'L2'
'L3'
'main'   The compiler contains estimates of the number of clock cycles for "typical" EV4 & EV5 hardware for the Level 1, 2 & 3 caches (also called Dcache, Scache, and Bcache), as well as to main memory. Note that L3 is only valid for EV5.

2.14.19 Clipper Options

These '-m' options are defined for the Clipper implementations:

-mc300   Produce code for a C300 Clipper processor. This is the default.

-mc400   Produce code for a C400 Clipper processor i.e. use floating point registers f8..f15.

2.14.20 H8/300 Options

These '-m' options are defined for the H8/300 implementations:

-mrelax   Shorten some address references at link time, when possible; uses the linker option '-relax'. See section "ld and the H8/300" in *Using ld*, for a fuller description.

-mh   Generate code for the H8/300H.

-ms   Generate code for the H8/S.

-mint32   Make int data 32 bits by default.

-malign-300

On the h8/300h, use the same alignment rules as for the h8/300. The default for the h8/300h is to align longs and floats on 4 byte boundaries. '-malign-300' causes them to be aligned on 2 byte boundaries. This option has no effect on the h8/300.

2.14.21 SH Options

These '-m' options are defined for the SH implementations:

-m1   Generate code for the SH1.

-m2   Generate code for the SH2.

-m3   Generate code for the SH3.

-m3e   Generate code for the SH3e.

-mb   Compile code for the processor in big endian mode.

-ml   Compile code for the processor in little endian mode.

-mdalign   Align doubles at 64 bit boundaries. Note that this changes the calling conventions, and thus some functions from the standard C library will not work unless you recompile it first with -mdalign.

-mrelax   Shorten some address references at link time, when possible; uses the linker option '-relax'.

2.14.22 Options for System V

These additional options are available on System V Release 4 for compatibility with other compilers on those systems:

-G   Create a shared object. It is recommended that '-symbolic' or '-shared' be used instead.

-Qy   Identify the versions of each tool used by the compiler, in a .ident assembler directive in the output.

-Qn   Refrain from adding .ident directives to the output file (this is
             the default).

-YP,*dirs*   Search the directories *dirs*, and no others, for libraries specified
             with '-l'.

-Ym,*dir*   Look in the directory *dir* to find the M4 preprocessor. The
             assembler uses this option.

2.14.23 TMS320C3x/C4x Options

These '-m' options are defined for TMS320C3x/C4x implementations:

-mcpu=*cpu_type*

             Set the instruction set, register set, and instruction scheduling
             parameters for machine type *cpu_type*. Supported values for
             cpu_type are 'c30', 'c31', 'c32', 'c40', and 'c44'. The default is
             'c40' to generate code for the TMS320C40.

-mbig-memory

-mbig

-msmall-memory

-msmall   Generates code for the big or small memory model. The small
             memory model assumed that all data fits into one 64K word
             page. At run-time the data page (DP) register must be set to
             point to the 64K page containing the .bss and .data program
             sections. The big memory model is the default and requires
             reloading of the DP register for every direct memory access.

-mbk

-mno-bk   Allow (disallow) allocation of general integer operands into the
             block count register BK.

-mdb

-mno-db   Enable (disable) generation of code using decrement and branch,
             DBcond(D), instructions. This is enabled by default for the
             C4x. To be on the safe side, this is disabled for the C3x, since
             the maximum iteration count on the C3x is $2^23 + 1$ (but who
             iterates loops more than 2^23 times on the C3x?). Note that
             GCC will try to reverse a loop so that it can utilise the decrement
             and branch instruction, but will give up if there is more than
             one memory reference in the loop. Thus a loop where the loop
             counter is decremented can generate slightly more efficient code,
             in cases where the RPTB instruction cannot be utilised.

-mdp-isr-reload

-mparanoid

             Force the DP register to be saved on entry to an interrupt ser-
             vice routine (ISR), reloaded to point to the data section, and

restored on exit from the ISR. This should not be required unless someone has violated the small memory model by modifying the DP register, say within an object library.

-mmpyi
-mno-mpyi

> For the C3x use the 24-bit MPYI instruction for integer multiplies instead of a library call to guarantee 32-bit results. Note that if one of the operands is a constant, then the multiplication will be performed using shifts and adds. If the -mmpyi option is not specified for the C3x, then squaring operations are performed inline instead of a library call.

-mfast-fix
-mno-fast-fix

> The C3x/C4x FIX instruction to convert a floating point value to an integer value chooses the nearest integer less than or equal to the floating point value rather than to the nearest integer. Thus if the floating point number is negative, the result will be incorrectly truncated an additional code is necessary to detect and correct this case. This option can be used to disable generation of the additional code required to correct the result.

-mrptb
-mno-rptb

> Enable (disable) generation of repeat block sequences using the RPTB instruction for zero overhead looping. The RPTB construct is only used for innermost loops that do not call functions or jump across the loop boundaries. There is no advantage having nested RPTB loops due to the overhead required to save and restore the RC, RS, and RE registers. This is enabled by default with -O2.

-mrpts=*count*
-mno-rpts

> Enable (disable) the use of the single instruction repeat instruction RPTS. If a repeat block contains a single instruction, and the loop count can be guaranteed to be less than the value *count*, GCC will emit a RPTS instruction instead of a RPTB. If no value is specified, then a RPTS will be emitted even if the loop count cannot be determined at compile time. Note that the repeated instruction following RPTS does not have to be reloaded from memory each iteration, thus freeing up the CPU buses for oeprands. However, since interrupts are blocked by this instruction, it is disabled by default.

-mloop-unsigned
-mno-loop-unsigned

> The maximum iteration count when using RPTS and RPTB
> (and DB on the C40) is 2^31 + 1 since these instructions test
> if the iteration count is negative to terminate the loop. If the
> iteration count is unsigned there is a possibility than the 2^31
> + 1 maximum iteration count may be exceeded. This switch
> allows an unsigned iteration count.

-mti

> Try to emit an assembler syntax that the TI assembler (asm30)
> is happy with. This also enforces compatibility with the API
> employed by the TI C3x C compiler. For example, long doubles
> are passed as structures rather than in floating point registers.

-mregparm
-mmemparm

> Generate code that uses registers (stack) for passing arguments
> to functions. By default, arguments are passed in registers where
> possible rather than by pushing arguments on to the stack.

-mparallel-insns
-mno-parallel-insns

> Allow the generation of parallel instructions. This is enabled by
> default with -O2.

-mparallel-mpy
-mno-parallel-mpy

> Allow the generation of MPY||ADD and MPY||SUB parallel
> instructions, provided -mparallel-insns is also specified. These
> instructions have tight register constraints which can pessimize
> the code generation of large functions.

2.14.24 V850 Options

These '-m' options are defined for V850 implementations:

-mlong-calls
-mno-long-calls

> Treat all calls as being far away (near). If calls are assumed to
> be far away, the compiler will always load the functions address
> up into a register, and call indirect through the pointer.

-mno-ep
-mep

> Do not optimize (do optimize) basic blocks that use the same
> index pointer 4 or more times to copy pointer into the ep register,
> and use the shorter sld and sst instructions. The '-mep' option
> is on by default if you optimize.

`-mno-prolog-function`
`-mprolog-function`

Do not use (do use) external functions to save and restore registers at the prolog and epilog of a function. The external functions are slower, but use less code space if more than one function saves the same number of registers. The '`-mprolog-function`' option is on by default if you optimize.

`-mspace`   Try to make the code as small as possible. At present, this just turns on the '`-mep`' and '`-mprolog-function`' options.

`-mtda=`*n*   Put static or global variables whose size is *n* bytes or less into the tiny data area that register **ep** points to. The tiny data area can hold up to 256 bytes in total (128 bytes for byte references).

`-msda=`*n*   Put static or global variables whose size is *n* bytes or less into the small data area that register **gp** points to. The small data area can hold up to 64 kilobytes.

`-mzda=`*n*   Put static or global variables whose size is *n* bytes or less into the first 32 kilobytes of memory.

`-mv850`   Specify that the target processor is the V850.

`-mbig-switch`

Generate code suitable for big switch tables. Use this option only if the assembler/linker complain about out of range branches within a switch table.

2.14.25 ARC Options

These options are defined for ARC implementations:

`-EL`   Compile code for little endian mode. This is the default.

`-EB`   Compile code for big endian mode.

`-mmangle-cpu`

Prepend the name of the cpu to all public symbol names. In multiple-processor systems, there are many ARC variants with different instruction and register set characteristics. This flag prevents code compiled for one cpu to be linked with code compiled for another. No facility exists for handling variants that are "almost identical". This is an all or nothing option.

`-mcpu=`*cpu*

Compile code for ARC variant *cpu*. Which variants are supported depend on the configuration. All variants support '`-mcpu=base`', this is the default.

-mtext=*text section*
-mdata=*data section*
-mrodata=*readonly data section*
>   Put functions, data, and readonly data in *text section*, *data
>   section*, and *readonly data section* respectively by default. This
>   can be overridden with the `section` attribute. See Section 4.29
>   [Variable Attributes], page 185.

2.14.26 NS32K Options

These are the '-m' options defined for the 32000 series. The default values
for these options depends on which style of 32000 was selected when the
compiler was configured; the defaults for the most common choices are given
below.

-m32032
-m32032   Generate output for a 32032. This is the default when the com-
>   piler is configured for 32032 and 32016 based systems.

-m32332
-m32332   Generate output for a 32332. This is the default when the com-
>   piler is configured for 32332-based systems.

-m32532
-m32532   Generate output for a 32532. This is the default when the com-
>   piler is configured for 32532-based systems.

-m32081   Generate output containing 32081 instructions for floating point.
>   This is the default for all systems.

-m32381   Generate output containing 32381 instructions for floating point.
>   This also implies '-m32081'. The 32381 is only compatible with
>   the 32332 and 32532 cpus. This is the default for the pc532-
>   netbsd configuration.

-mmulti-add
>   Try and generate multiply-add floating point instructions `polyF`
>   and `dotF`. This option is only available if the '-m32381' op-
>   tion is in effect. Using these instructions requires changes to
>   to register allocation which generally has a negative impact on
>   performance. This option should only be enabled when compil-
>   ing code particularly likely to make heavy use of multiply-add
>   instructions.

-mnomulti-add
>   Do not try and generate multiply-add floating point instructions
>   `polyF` and `dotF`. This is the default on all platforms.

-msoft-float
>   Generate output containing library calls for floating point.
>   **Warning:** the requisite libraries may not be available.

`-mnobitfield`

> Do not use the bit-field instructions. On some machines it is faster to use shifting and masking operations. This is the default for the pc532.

`-mbitfield`

> Do use the bit-field instructions. This is the default for all platforms except the pc532.

`-mrtd`   Use a different function-calling convention, in which functions that take a fixed number of arguments return pop their arguments on return with the `ret` instruction.

> This calling convention is incompatible with the one normally used on Unix, so you cannot use it if you need to call libraries compiled with the Unix compiler.

> Also, you must provide function prototypes for all functions that take variable numbers of arguments (including `printf`); otherwise incorrect code will be generated for calls to those functions.

> In addition, seriously incorrect code will result if you call a function with too many arguments. (Normally, extra arguments are harmlessly ignored.)

> This option takes its name from the 680x0 `rtd` instruction.

`-mregparam`

> Use a different function-calling convention where the first two arguments are passed in registers.

> This calling convention is incompatible with the one normally used on Unix, so you cannot use it if you need to call libraries compiled with the Unix compiler.

`-mnoregparam`

> Do not pass any arguments in registers. This is the default for all targets.

`-msb`   It is OK to use the sb as an index register which is always loaded with zero. This is the default for the pc532-netbsd target.

`-mnosb`   The sb register is not available for use or has not been initialized to zero by the run time system. This is the default for all targets except the pc532-netbsd. It is also implied whenever '`-mhimem`' or '`-fpic`' is set.

`-mhimem` Many ns32000 series addressing modes use displacements of up to 512MB. If an address is above 512MB then displacements from zero can not be used. This option causes code to be generated which can be loaded above 512MB. This may be useful for operating systems or ROM code.

-mnohimem
> Assume code will be loaded in the first 512MB of virtual address space. This is the default for all platforms.

2.15 Options for Code Generation Conventions

These machine-independent options control the interface conventions used in code generation.

Most of them have both positive and negative forms; the negative form of '-ffoo' would be '-fno-foo'. In the table below, only one of the forms is listed—the one which is not the default. You can figure out the other form by either removing 'no-' or adding it.

-fexceptions
> Enable exception handling. Generates extra code needed to propagate exceptions. For some targets, this implies generation of frame unwind information for all functions. This can produce significant data size overhead, although it does not affect execution. If you do not specify this option, it is enabled by default for languages like C++ which normally require exception handling, and disabled for languages like C that do not normally require it. However, when compiling C code that needs to interoperate properly with exception handlers written in C++, you may need to enable this option. You may also wish to disable this option is you are compiling older C++ programs that don't use exception handling.

-fpcc-struct-return
> Return "short" `struct` and `union` values in memory like longer ones, rather than in registers. This convention is less efficient, but it has the advantage of allowing intercallability between GCC-compiled files and files compiled with other compilers.
>
> The precise convention for returning structures in memory depends on the target configuration macros.
>
> Short structures and unions are those whose size and alignment match that of some integer type.

-freg-struct-return
> Use the convention that `struct` and `union` values are returned in registers when possible. This is more efficient for small structures than '-fpcc-struct-return'.
>
> If you specify neither '-fpcc-struct-return' nor its contrary '-freg-struct-return', GCC defaults to whichever convention is standard for the target. If there is no standard convention, GCC defaults to '-fpcc-struct-return', except on targets where GCC is the principal compiler. In those cases, we

can choose the standard, and we chose the more efficient register
return alternative.

`-fshort-enums`

Allocate to an `enum` type only as many bytes as it needs for the
declared range of possible values. Specifically, the `enum` type
will be equivalent to the smallest integer type which has enough
room.

`-fshort-double`

Use the same size for `double` as for `float`.

`-fshared-data`

Requests that the data and non-`const` variables of this compilation be shared data rather than private data. The distinction
makes sense only on certain operating systems, where shared
data is shared between processes running the same program,
while private data exists in one copy per process.

`-fno-common`

Allocate even uninitialized global variables in the bss section of
the object file, rather than generating them as common blocks.
This has the effect that if the same variable is declared (without
`extern`) in two different compilations, you will get an error when
you link them. The only reason this might be useful is if you
wish to verify that the program will work on other systems which
always work this way.

`-fno-ident`

Ignore the '`#ident`' directive.

`-fno-gnu-linker`

Do not output global initializations (such as C++ constructors
and destructors) in the form used by the GNU linker (on systems
where the GNU linker is the standard method of handling them).
Use this option when you want to use a non-GNU linker, which
also requires using the `collect2` program to make sure the system linker includes constructors and destructors. (`collect2` is
included in the GCC distribution.) For systems which *must* use
`collect2`, the compiler driver `gcc` is configured to do this automatically.

`-finhibit-size-directive`

Don't output a `.size` assembler directive, or anything else that
would cause trouble if the function is split in the middle, and
the two halves are placed at locations far apart in memory. This
option is used when compiling '`crtstuff.c`'; you should not
need to use it for anything else.

-fverbose-asm

> Put extra commentary information in the generated assembly code to make it more readable. This option is generally only of use to those who actually need to read the generated assembly code (perhaps while debugging the compiler itself).
>
> '-fno-verbose-asm', the default, causes the extra information to be omitted and is useful when comparing two assembler files.

-fvolatile

> Consider all memory references through pointers to be volatile.

-fvolatile-global

> Consider all memory references to extern and global data items to be volatile. GCC does not consider static data items to be volatile because of this switch.

-fvolatile-static

> Consider all memory references to static data to be volatile.

-fpic
> Generate position-independent code (PIC) suitable for use in a shared library, if supported for the target machine. Such code accesses all constant addresses through a global offset table (GOT). The dynamic loader resolves the GOT entries when the program starts (the dynamic loader is not part of GCC; it is part of the operating system). If the GOT size for the linked executable exceeds a machine-specific maximum size, you get an error message from the linker indicating that '-fpic' does not work; in that case, recompile with '-fPIC' instead. (These maximums are 16k on the m88k, 8k on the Sparc, and 32k on the m68k and RS/6000. The 386 has no such limit.)
>
> Position-independent code requires special support, and therefore works only on certain machines. For the 386, GCC supports PIC for System V but not for the Sun 386i. Code generated for the IBM RS/6000 is always position-independent.

-fPIC
> If supported for the target machine, emit position-independent code, suitable for dynamic linking and avoiding any limit on the size of the global offset table. This option makes a difference on the m68k, m88k, and the Sparc.
>
> Position-independent code requires special support, and therefore works only on certain machines.

-ffixed-*reg*

> Treat the register named *reg* as a fixed register; generated code should never refer to it (except perhaps as a stack pointer, frame pointer or in some other fixed role).
>
> *reg* must be the name of a register. The register names accepted are machine-specific and are defined in the **REGISTER_NAMES** macro in the machine description macro file.

This flag does not have a negative form, because it specifies a three-way choice.

`-fcall-used-`*reg*

Treat the register named *reg* as an allocable register that is clobbered by function calls. It may be allocated for temporaries or variables that do not live across a call. Functions compiled this way will not save and restore the register *reg*.

It is an error to used this flag with the frame pointer or stack pointer. Use of this flag for other registers that have fixed pervasive roles in the machine's execution model will produce disastrous results.

This flag does not have a negative form, because it specifies a three-way choice.

`-fcall-saved-`*reg*

Treat the register named *reg* as an allocable register saved by functions. It may be allocated even for temporaries or variables that live across a call. Functions compiled this way will save and restore the register *reg* if they use it.

It is an error to used this flag with the frame pointer or stack pointer. Use of this flag for other registers that have fixed pervasive roles in the machine's execution model will produce disastrous results.

A different sort of disaster will result from the use of this flag for a register in which function values may be returned.

This flag does not have a negative form, because it specifies a three-way choice.

`-fpack-struct`

Pack all structure members together without holes. Usually you would not want to use this option, since it makes the code suboptimal, and the offsets of structure members won't agree with system libraries.

`-fcheck-memory-usage`

Generate extra code to check each memory access. GCC will generate code that is suitable for a detector of bad memory accesses such as 'Checker'.

Normally, you should compile all, or none, of your code with this option.

If you do mix code compiled with and without this option, you must ensure that all code that has side effects and that is called by code compiled with this option is, itself, compiled with this option. If you do not, you might get erroneous messages from the detector.

If you use functions from a library that have side-effects (such as **read**), you might not be able to recompile the library and specify this option. In that case, you can enable the '-fprefix-function-name' option, which requests GCC to encapsulate your code and make other functions look as if they were compiled with '-fcheck-memory-usage'. This is done by calling "stubs", which are provided by the detector. If you cannot find or build stubs for every function you call, you might have to specify '-fcheck-memory-usage' without '-fprefix-function-name'.

If you specify this option, you can not use the **asm** or **__asm__** keywords in functions with memory checking enabled. The compiler cannot understand what the **asm** statement will do, and therefore cannot generate the appropriate code, so it is rejected. However, the function attribute **no_check_memory_usage** will disable memory checking within a function, and **asm** statements can be put inside such functions. Inline expansion of a non-checked function within a checked function is permitted; the inline function's memory accesses won't be checked, but the rest will.

If you move your **asm** statements to non-checked inline functions, but they do access memory, you can add calls to the support code in your inline function, to indicate any reads, writes, or copies being done. These calls would be similar to those done in the stubs described above.

-fprefix-function-name

Request GCC to add a prefix to the symbols generated for function names. GCC adds a prefix to the names of functions defined as well as functions called. Code compiled with this option and code compiled without the option can't be linked together, unless stubs are used.

If you compile the following code with '-fprefix-function-name'

```
extern void bar (int);
void
foo (int a)
{
  return bar (a + 5);
}
```

GCC will compile the code as if it was written:

```
extern void prefix_bar (int);
void
prefix_foo (int a)
{
  return prefix_bar (a + 5);
```

```
}
```
This option is designed to be used with '-fcheck-memory-usage'.

-finstrument-functions

Generate instrumentation calls for entry and exit to functions. Just after function entry and just before function exit, the following profiling functions will be called with the address of the current function and its call site. (On some platforms, __builtin_return_address does not work beyond the current function, so the call site information may not be available to the profiling functions otherwise.)

```
void __cyg_profile_func_enter (void *this_fn, void *call_site);
void __cyg_profile_func_exit  (void *this_fn, void *call_site);
```

The first argument is the address of the start of the current function, which may be looked up exactly in the symbol table.

This instrumentation is also done for functions expanded inline in other functions. The profiling calls will indicate where, conceptually, the inline function is entered and exited. This means that addressable versions of such functions must be available. If all your uses of a function are expanded inline, this may mean an additional expansion of code size. If you use 'extern inline' in your C code, an addressable version of such functions must be provided. (This is normally the case anyways, but if you get lucky and the optimizer always expands the functions inline, you might have gotten away without providing static copies.)

A function may be given the attribute no_instrument_function, in which case this instrumentation will not be done. This can be used, for example, for the profiling functions listed above, high-priority interrupt routines, and any functions from which the profiling functions cannot safely be called (perhaps signal handlers, if the profiling routines generate output or allocate memory).

-fstack-check

Generate code to verify that you do not go beyond the boundary of the stack. You should specify this flag if you are running in an environment with multiple threads, but only rarely need to specify it in a single-threaded environment since stack overflow is automatically detected on nearly all systems if there is only one stack.

-fargument-alias
-fargument-noalias
-fargument-noalias-global

Specify the possible relationships among parameters and between parameters and global data.

'-fargument-alias' specifies that arguments (parameters) may alias each other and may alias global storage.
'-fargument-noalias' specifies that arguments do not alias each other, but may alias global storage. '-fargument-noalias-global' specifies that arguments do not alias each other and do not alias global storage.

Each language will automatically use whatever option is required by the language standard. You should not need to use these options yourself.

-fleading-underscore
> This option and its counterpart, -fno-leading-underscore, forcibly change the way C symbols are represented in the object file. One use is to help link with legacy assembly code.
>
> Be warned that you should know what you are doing when invoking this option, and that not all targets provide complete support for it.

2.16 Environment Variables Affecting GCC

This section describes several environment variables that affect how GCC operates. Some of them work by specifying directories or prefixes to use when searching for various kinds of files. Some are used to specify other aspects of the compilation environment.

Note that you can also specify places to search using options such as '-B', '-I' and '-L' (see Section 2.12 [Directory Options], page 54). These take precedence over places specified using environment variables, which in turn take precedence over those specified by the configuration of GCC. See Section 17.1 [Driver], page 393.

LANG
LC_CTYPE
LC_MESSAGES
LC_ALL
> These environment variables control the way that GCC uses localization information that allow GCC to work with different national conventions. GCC inspects the locale categories LC_CTYPE and LC_MESSAGES if it has been configured to do so. These locale categories can be set to any value supported by your installation. A typical value is 'en_UK' for English in the United Kingdom.
>
> The LC_CTYPE environment variable specifies character classification. GCC uses it to determine the character boundaries in a string; this is needed for some multibyte encodings that contain quote and escape characters that would otherwise be interpreted as a string end or escape.

The `LC_MESSAGES` environment variable specifies the language to use in diagnostic messages.

If the `LC_ALL` environment variable is set, it overrides the value of `LC_CTYPE` and `LC_MESSAGES`; otherwise, `LC_CTYPE` and `LC_MESSAGES` default to the value of the `LANG` environment variable. If none of these variables are set, GCC defaults to traditional C English behavior.

TMPDIR   If `TMPDIR` is set, it specifies the directory to use for temporary files. GCC uses temporary files to hold the output of one stage of compilation which is to be used as input to the next stage: for example, the output of the preprocessor, which is the input to the compiler proper.

GCC_EXEC_PREFIX

If `GCC_EXEC_PREFIX` is set, it specifies a prefix to use in the names of the subprograms executed by the compiler. No slash is added when this prefix is combined with the name of a subprogram, but you can specify a prefix that ends with a slash if you wish.

If GCC cannot find the subprogram using the specified prefix, it tries looking in the usual places for the subprogram.

The default value of `GCC_EXEC_PREFIX` is '*prefix*/lib/gcc-lib/' where *prefix* is the value of **prefix** when you ran the 'configure' script.

Other prefixes specified with '-B' take precedence over this prefix.

This prefix is also used for finding files such as 'crt0.o' that are used for linking.

In addition, the prefix is used in an unusual way in finding the directories to search for header files. For each of the standard directories whose name normally begins with '/usr/local/lib/gcc-lib' (more precisely, with the value of `GCC_INCLUDE_DIR`), GCC tries replacing that beginning with the specified prefix to produce an alternate directory name. Thus, with '-Bfoo/', GCC will search 'foo/bar' where it would normally search '/usr/local/lib/bar'. These alternate directories are searched first; the standard directories come next.

COMPILER_PATH

The value of `COMPILER_PATH` is a colon-separated list of directories, much like `PATH`. GCC tries the directories thus specified when searching for subprograms, if it can't find the subprograms using `GCC_EXEC_PREFIX`.

LIBRARY_PATH

>The value of LIBRARY_PATH is a colon-separated list of directories, much like PATH. When configured as a native compiler, GCC tries the directories thus specified when searching for special linker files, if it can't find them using GCC_EXEC_PREFIX. Linking using GCC also uses these directories when searching for ordinary libraries for the '-l' option (but directories specified with '-L' come first).

C_INCLUDE_PATH
CPLUS_INCLUDE_PATH
OBJC_INCLUDE_PATH

>These environment variables pertain to particular languages. Each variable's value is a colon-separated list of directories, much like PATH. When GCC searches for header files, it tries the directories listed in the variable for the language you are using, after the directories specified with '-I' but before the standard header file directories.

DEPENDENCIES_OUTPUT

>If this variable is set, its value specifies how to output dependencies for Make based on the header files processed by the compiler. This output looks much like the output from the '-M' option (see Section 2.9 [Preprocessor Options], page 48), but it goes to a separate file, and is in addition to the usual results of compilation.

>The value of DEPENDENCIES_OUTPUT can be just a file name, in which case the Make rules are written to that file, guessing the target name from the source file name. Or the value can have the form 'file target', in which case the rules are written to file file using target as the target name.

LANG

>This variable is used to pass locale information to the compiler. One way in which this information is used is to determine the character set to be used when character literals, string literals and comments are parsed in C and C++. When the compiler is configured to allow multibyte characters, the following values for LANG are recognized:

>>C-JIS   Recognize JIS characters.

>>C-SJIS   Recognize SJIS characters.

>>C-EUCJP   Recognize EUCJP characters.

>If LANG is not defined, or if it has some other value, then the compiler will use mblen and mbtowc as defined by the default locale to recognize and translate multibyte characters.

2.17 Running Protoize

The program **protoize** is an optional part of GNU C. You can use it to add prototypes to a program, thus converting the program to ANSI C in one respect. The companion program **unprotoize** does the reverse: it removes argument types from any prototypes that are found.

When you run these programs, you must specify a set of source files as command line arguments. The conversion programs start out by compiling these files to see what functions they define. The information gathered about a file *foo* is saved in a file named '*foo*.X'.

After scanning comes actual conversion. The specified files are all eligible to be converted; any files they include (whether sources or just headers) are eligible as well.

But not all the eligible files are converted. By default, **protoize** and **unprotoize** convert only source and header files in the current directory. You can specify additional directories whose files should be converted with the '-d *directory*' option. You can also specify particular files to exclude with the '-x *file*' option. A file is converted if it is eligible, its directory name matches one of the specified directory names, and its name within the directory has not been excluded.

Basic conversion with **protoize** consists of rewriting most function definitions and function declarations to specify the types of the arguments. The only ones not rewritten are those for varargs functions.

protoize optionally inserts prototype declarations at the beginning of the source file, to make them available for any calls that precede the function's definition. Or it can insert prototype declarations with block scope in the blocks where undeclared functions are called.

Basic conversion with **unprotoize** consists of rewriting most function declarations to remove any argument types, and rewriting function definitions to the old-style pre-ANSI form.

Both conversion programs print a warning for any function declaration or definition that they can't convert. You can suppress these warnings with '-q'.

The output from **protoize** or **unprotoize** replaces the original source file. The original file is renamed to a name ending with '.save'. If the '.save' file already exists, then the source file is simply discarded.

protoize and **unprotoize** both depend on GCC itself to scan the program and collect information about the functions it uses. So neither of these programs will work until GCC is installed.

Here is a table of the options you can use with **protoize** and **unprotoize**. Each option works with both programs unless otherwise stated.

-B *directory*

> Look for the file 'SYSCALLS.c.X' in *directory*, instead of the usual directory (normally '/usr/local/lib'). This file contains

prototype information about standard system functions. This option applies only to `protoize`.

-c *compilation-options*

Use *compilation-options* as the options when running `gcc` to produce the '.X' files. The special option '-aux-info' is always passed in addition, to tell `gcc` to write a '.X' file.

Note that the compilation options must be given as a single argument to `protoize` or `unprotoize`. If you want to specify several `gcc` options, you must quote the entire set of compilation options to make them a single word in the shell.

There are certain `gcc` arguments that you cannot use, because they would produce the wrong kind of output. These include '-g', '-O', '-c', '-S', and '-o' If you include these in the *compilation-options*, they are ignored.

-C   Rename files to end in '.C' instead of '.c'. This is convenient if you are converting a C program to C++. This option applies only to `protoize`.

-g   Add explicit global declarations. This means inserting explicit declarations at the beginning of each source file for each function that is called in the file and was not declared. These declarations precede the first function definition that contains a call to an undeclared function. This option applies only to `protoize`.

-i *string*   Indent old-style parameter declarations with the string *string*. This option applies only to `protoize`.

`unprotoize` converts prototyped function definitions to old-style function definitions, where the arguments are declared between the argument list and the initial '{'. By default, `unprotoize` uses five spaces as the indentation. If you want to indent with just one space instead, use '-i " "'.

-k   Keep the '.X' files. Normally, they are deleted after conversion is finished.

-l   Add explicit local declarations. `protoize` with '-l' inserts a prototype declaration for each function in each block which calls the function without any declaration. This option applies only to `protoize`.

-n   Make no real changes. This mode just prints information about the conversions that would have been done without '-n'.

-N   Make no '.save' files. The original files are simply deleted. Use this option with caution.

-p *program*

Use the program *program* as the compiler. Normally, the name 'gcc' is used.

-q   Work quietly. Most warnings are suppressed.

-v   Print the version number, just like '-v' for gcc.

If you need special compiler options to compile one of your program's source files, then you should generate that file's '.X' file specially, by running gcc on that source file with the appropriate options and the option '-aux-info'. Then run protoize on the entire set of files. protoize will use the existing '.X' file because it is newer than the source file. For example:

```
gcc -Dfoo=bar file1.c -aux-info
protoize *.c
```

You need to include the special files along with the rest in the protoize command, even though their '.X' files already exist, because otherwise they won't get converted.

See Section 7.11 [Protoize Caveats], page 244, for more information on how to use protoize successfully.

Note most of this information is out of date and superceded by the EGCS install procedures. It is provided for historical reference only.

3 Installing GNU CC

Here is the procedure for installing GNU CC on a GNU or Unix system. See Section 3.6 [VMS Install], page 155, for VMS systems. In this section we assume you compile in the same directory that contains the source files; see Section 3.3 [Other Dir], page 148, to find out how to compile in a separate directory on Unix systems.

You cannot install GNU C by itself on MSDOS; it will not compile under any MSDOS compiler except itself. You need to get the complete compilation package DJGPP, which includes binaries as well as sources, and includes all the necessary compilation tools and libraries.

1. If you have built GNU CC previously in the same directory for a different target machine, do 'make distclean' to delete all files that might be invalid. One of the files this deletes is 'Makefile'; if 'make distclean' complains that 'Makefile' does not exist, it probably means that the directory is already suitably clean.

2. On a System V release 4 system, make sure '/usr/bin' precedes '/usr/ucb' in PATH. The cc command in '/usr/ucb' uses libraries which have bugs.

3. Make sure the Bison parser generator is installed. (This is unnecessary if the Bison output files 'c-parse.c' and 'cexp.c' are more recent than 'c-parse.y' and 'cexp.y' and you do not plan to change the '.y' files.)

   Bison versions older than Sept 8, 1988 will produce incorrect output for 'c-parse.c'.

4. If you have chosen a configuration for GNU CC which requires other GNU tools (such as GAS or the GNU linker) instead of the standard system tools, install the required tools in the build directory under the names 'as', 'ld' or whatever is appropriate. This will enable the compiler to find the proper tools for compilation of the program 'enquire'.

   Alternatively, you can do subsequent compilation using a value of the PATH environment variable such that the necessary GNU tools come before the standard system tools.

5. Specify the host, build and target machine configurations. You do this when you run the 'configure' script.

   The *build* machine is the system which you are using, the *host* machine is the system where you want to run the resulting compiler (normally the build machine), and the *target* machine is the system for which you want the compiler to generate code.

   If you are building a compiler to produce code for the machine it runs on (a native compiler), you normally do not need to specify any operands to 'configure'; it will try to guess the type of machine you are on and use that as the build, host and target machines. So you don't need to specify a configuration when building a native compiler unless 'configure' cannot figure out what your configuration is or guesses wrong.

In those cases, specify the build machine's *configuration name* with the '--host' option; the host and target will default to be the same as the host machine. (If you are building a cross-compiler, see Section 3.4 [Cross-Compiler], page 149.)

Here is an example:

```
./configure --host=sparc-sun-sunos4.1
```

A configuration name may be canonical or it may be more or less abbreviated.

A canonical configuration name has three parts, separated by dashes. It looks like this: '*cpu-company-system*'. (The three parts may themselves contain dashes; 'configure' can figure out which dashes serve which purpose.) For example, 'm68k-sun-sunos4.1' specifies a Sun 3.

You can also replace parts of the configuration by nicknames or aliases. For example, 'sun3' stands for 'm68k-sun', so 'sun3-sunos4.1' is another way to specify a Sun 3. You can also use simply 'sun3-sunos', since the version of SunOS is assumed by default to be version 4.

You can specify a version number after any of the system types, and some of the CPU types. In most cases, the version is irrelevant, and will be ignored. So you might as well specify the version if you know it.

See Section 3.2 [Configurations], page 131, for a list of supported configuration names and notes on many of the configurations. You should check the notes in that section before proceeding any further with the installation of GNU CC.

6. When running configure, you may also need to specify certain additional options that describe variant hardware and software configurations. These are '--with-gnu-as', '--with-gnu-ld', '--with-stabs' and '--nfp'.

'--with-gnu-as'

If you will use GNU CC with the GNU assembler (GAS), you should declare this by using the '--with-gnu-as' option when you run 'configure'.

Using this option does not install GAS. It only modifies the output of GNU CC to work with GAS. Building and installing GAS is up to you.

Conversely, if you *do not* wish to use GAS and do not specify '--with-gnu-as' when building GNU CC, it is up to you to make sure that GAS is not installed. GNU CC searches for a program named as in various directories; if the program it finds is GAS, then it runs GAS. If you are not sure where GNU CC finds the assembler it is using, try specifying '-v' when you run it.

The systems where it makes a difference whether you use GAS are
'hppa1.0-*any-any*', 'hppa1.1-*any-any*', 'i386-*any*-sysv', 'i386-*any*-isc',
'i860-*any*-bsd', 'm68k-bull-sysv',
'm68k-hp-hpux', 'm68k-sony-bsd',
'm68k-altos-sysv', 'm68000-hp-hpux',
'm68000-att-sysv', '*any*-lynx-lynxos', and 'mips-*any*').
On any other system, '--with-gnu-as' has no effect.

On the systems listed above (except for the HP-PA, for ISC on the 386, and for 'mips-sgi-irix5.*'), if you use GAS, you should also use the GNU linker (and specify '--with-gnu-ld').

'--with-gnu-ld'

Specify the option '--with-gnu-ld' if you plan to use the GNU linker with GNU CC.

This option does not cause the GNU linker to be installed; it just modifies the behavior of GNU CC to work with the GNU linker.

'--with-stabs'

On MIPS based systems and on Alphas, you must specify whether you want GNU CC to create the normal ECOFF debugging format, or to use BSD-style stabs passed through the ECOFF symbol table. The normal ECOFF debug format cannot fully handle languages other than C. BSD stabs format can handle other languages, but it only works with the GNU debugger GDB.

Normally, GNU CC uses the ECOFF debugging format by default; if you prefer BSD stabs, specify '--with-stabs' when you configure GNU CC.

No matter which default you choose when you configure GNU CC, the user can use the '-gcoff' and '-gstabs+' options to specify explicitly the debug format for a particular compilation.

'--with-stabs' is meaningful on the ISC system on the 386, also, if '--with-gas' is used. It selects use of stabs debugging information embedded in COFF output. This kind of debugging information supports C++ well; ordinary COFF debugging information does not.

'--with-stabs' is also meaningful on 386 systems running SVR4. It selects use of stabs debugging information embedded in ELF output. The C++ compiler currently (2.6.0) does not support the DWARF debugging information normally used on 386 SVR4 platforms; stabs provide a workable alternative. This requires gas and gdb, as the normal SVR4 tools can not generate or interpret stabs.

'--nfp'   On certain systems, you must specify whether the machine has a floating point unit. These systems include 'm68k-sun-sunos*n*' and 'm68k-isi-bsd'. On any other system, '--nfp' currently has no effect, though perhaps there are other systems where it could usefully make a difference.

'--enable-haifa'
'--disable-haifa'
            Use '--enable-haifa' to enable use of an experimental instruction scheduler (from IBM Haifa). This may or may not produce better code. Some targets on which it is known to be a win enable it by default; use '--disable-haifa' to disable it in these cases. configure will print out whether the Haifa scheduler is enabled when it is run.

'--enable-threads=*type*'
            Certain systems, notably Linux-based GNU systems, can't be relied on to supply a threads facility for the Objective C runtime and so will default to single-threaded runtime. They may, however, have a library threads implementation available, in which case threads can be enabled with this option by supplying a suitable *type*, probably 'posix'. The possibilities for *type* are 'single', 'posix', 'win32', 'solaris', 'irix' and 'mach'.

'--enable-checking'
            When you specify this option, the compiler is built to perform checking of tree node types when referencing fields of that node. This does not change the generated code, but adds error checking within the compiler. This will slow down the compiler and may only work properly if you are building the compiler with GNU C.

            The 'configure' script searches subdirectories of the source directory for other compilers that are to be integrated into GNU CC. The GNU compiler for C++, called G++ is in a subdirectory named 'cp'. 'configure' inserts rules into 'Makefile' to build all of those compilers.

            Here we spell out what files will be set up by configure. Normally you need not be concerned with these files.

            • A file named 'config.h' is created that contains a '#include' of the top-level config file for the machine you will run the compiler on (see Chapter 18 [Config], page 523). This file is responsible for defining information about the host machine. It includes 'tm.h'.

The top-level config file is located in the subdirectory
'config'. Its name is always 'xm-*something*.h'; usually
'xm-*machine*.h', but there are some exceptions.

If your system does not support symbolic links,
you might want to set up 'config.h' to contain a
'#include' command which refers to the appropriate
file.

- A file named 'tconfig.h' is created which includes the
  top-level config file for your target machine. This is
  used for compiling certain programs to run on that machine.

- A file named 'tm.h' is created which includes the
  machine-description macro file for your target machine.
  It should be in the subdirectory 'config' and its name
  is often '*machine*.h'.

'--enable-nls'
'--disable-nls'
     The '--enable-nls' option enables Native Language Sup-
     port (NLS), which lets GCC output diagnostics in languages
     other than American English. No translations are avail-
     able yet, so the main users of this option now are those
     translating GCC's diagnostics who want to test their work.
     Once translations become available, Native Language Sup-
     port will become enabled by default. The '--disable-nls'
     option disables NLS.

'--with-included-gettext'
     If NLS is enabled, the GCC build procedure normally at-
     tempts to use the host's gettext libraries, and falls back on
     GCC's copy of the GNU gettext library only if the host
     libraries do not suffice. The '--with-included-gettext'
     option causes the build procedure to prefer its copy of GNU
     gettext.

'--with-catgets'
     If NLS is enabled, and if the host lacks gettext but has
     the inferior catgets interface, the GCC build procedure
     normally ignores catgets and instead uses GCC's copy of
     the GNU gettext library. The '--with-catgets' option
     causes the build procedure to use the host's catgets in this
     situation.

7. In certain cases, you should specify certain other options when you run
   configure.

   - The standard directory for installing GNU CC is '/usr/local/lib'.
     If you want to install its files somewhere else, specify '--prefix=*dir*'

when you run 'configure'. Here *dir* is a directory name to use instead of '/usr/local' for all purposes with one exception: the directory '/usr/local/include' is searched for header files no matter where you install the compiler. To override this name, use the --with-local-prefix option below. The directory you specify need not exist, but its parent directory must exist.

- Specify '--with-local-prefix=*dir*' if you want the compiler to search directory '*dir*/include' for locally installed header files *instead* of '/usr/local/include'.

You should specify '--with-local-prefix' **only** if your site has a different convention (not '/usr/local') for where to put site-specific files.

The default value for '--with-local-prefix' is '/usr/local' regardless of the value of '--prefix'. Specifying '--prefix' has no effect on which directory GNU CC searches for local header files. This may seem counterintuitive, but actually it is logical.

The purpose of '--prefix' is to specify where to *install GNU CC*. The local header files in '/usr/local/include'—if you put any in that directory—are not part of GNU CC. They are part of other programs—perhaps many others. (GNU CC installs its own header files in another directory which is based on the '--prefix' value.)

Do not specify '/usr' as the '--with-local-prefix'! The directory you use for '--with-local-prefix' **must not** contain any of the system's standard header files. If it did contain them, certain programs would be miscompiled (including GNU Emacs, on certain targets), because this would override and nullify the header file corrections made by the fixincludes script.

Indications are that people who use this option use it based on mistaken ideas of what it is for. People use it as if it specified where to install part of GNU CC. Perhaps they make this assumption because installing GNU CC creates the directory.

8. Build the compiler. Just type 'make LANGUAGES=c' in the compiler directory.

'LANGUAGES=c' specifies that only the C compiler should be compiled. The makefile normally builds compilers for all the supported languages; currently, C, C++ and Objective C. However, C is the only language that is sure to work when you build with other non-GNU C compilers. In addition, building anything but C at this stage is a waste of time.

In general, you can specify the languages to build by typing the argument 'LANGUAGES="*list*"', where *list* is one or more words from the list 'c', 'c++', and 'objective-c'. If you have any additional GNU compilers as subdirectories of the GNU CC source directory, you may also specify their names in this list.

Ignore any warnings you may see about "statement not reached" in 'insn-emit.c'; they are normal. Also, warnings about "unknown escape sequence" are normal in 'genopinit.c' and perhaps some other files. Likewise, you should ignore warnings about "constant is so large that it is unsigned" in 'insn-emit.c' and 'insn-recog.c', a warning about a comparison always being zero in 'enquire.o', and warnings about shift counts exceeding type widths in 'cexp.y'. Any other compilation errors may represent bugs in the port to your machine or operating system, and should be investigated and reported (see Chapter 8 [Bugs], page 251).

Some compilers fail to compile GNU CC because they have bugs or limitations. For example, the Microsoft compiler is said to run out of macro space. Some Ultrix compilers run out of expression space; then you need to break up the statement where the problem happens.

9. If you are building a cross-compiler, stop here. See Section 3.4 [Cross-Compiler], page 149.

10. Move the first-stage object files and executables into a subdirectory with this command:

    make stage1

The files are moved into a subdirectory named 'stage1'. Once installation is complete, you may wish to delete these files with rm -r stage1.

11. If you have chosen a configuration for GNU CC which requires other GNU tools (such as GAS or the GNU linker) instead of the standard system tools, install the required tools in the 'stage1' subdirectory under the names 'as', 'ld' or whatever is appropriate. This will enable the stage 1 compiler to find the proper tools in the following stage.

Alternatively, you can do subsequent compilation using a value of the PATH environment variable such that the necessary GNU tools come before the standard system tools.

12. Recompile the compiler with itself, with this command:

    make CC="stage1/xgcc -Bstage1/" CFLAGS="-g -O2"

This is called making the stage 2 compiler.

The command shown above builds compilers for all the supported languages. If you don't want them all, you can specify the languages to build by typing the argument 'LANGUAGES="list"'. list should contain one or more words from the list 'c', 'c++', 'objective-c', and 'proto'. Separate the words with spaces. 'proto' stands for the programs protoize and unprotoize; they are not a separate language, but you use LANGUAGES to enable or disable their installation.

If you are going to build the stage 3 compiler, then you might want to build only the C language in stage 2.

Once you have built the stage 2 compiler, if you are short of disk space, you can delete the subdirectory 'stage1'.

On a 68000 or 68020 system lacking floating point hardware, unless you have selected a 'tm.h' file that expects by default that there is no such hardware, do this instead:

```
make CC="stage1/xgcc -Bstage1/" CFLAGS="-g -O2 -msoft-float"
```

13. If you wish to test the compiler by compiling it with itself one more time, install any other necessary GNU tools (such as GAS or the GNU linker) in the 'stage2' subdirectory as you did in the 'stage1' subdirectory, then do this:

```
make stage2
make CC="stage2/xgcc -Bstage2/" CFLAGS="-g -O2"
```

This is called making the stage 3 compiler. Aside from the '-B' option, the compiler options should be the same as when you made the stage 2 compiler. But the LANGUAGES option need not be the same. The command shown above builds compilers for all the supported languages; if you don't want them all, you can specify the languages to build by typing the argument 'LANGUAGES="*list*"', as described above.

If you do not have to install any additional GNU tools, you may use the command

```
make bootstrap LANGUAGES=language-list BOOT_CFLAGS=option-list
```

instead of making 'stage1', 'stage2', and performing the two compiler builds.

14. Compare the latest object files with the stage 2 object files—they ought to be identical, aside from time stamps (if any).

On some systems, meaningful comparison of object files is impossible; they always appear "different." This is currently true on Solaris and some systems that use ELF object file format. On some versions of Irix on SGI machines and DEC Unix (OSF/1) on Alpha systems, you will not be able to compare the files without specifying '-save-temps'; see the description of individual systems above to see if you get comparison failures. You may have similar problems on other systems.

Use this command to compare the files:

```
make compare
```

This will mention any object files that differ between stage 2 and stage 3. Any difference, no matter how innocuous, indicates that the stage 2 compiler has compiled GNU CC incorrectly, and is therefore a potentially serious bug which you should investigate and report (see Chapter 8 [Bugs], page 251).

If your system does not put time stamps in the object files, then this is a faster way to compare them (using the Bourne shell):

```
for file in *.o; do
cmp $file stage2/$file
done
```

If you have built the compiler with the '-mno-mips-tfile' option on MIPS machines, you will not be able to compare the files.

15. Install the compiler driver, the compiler's passes and run-time support with 'make install'. Use the same value for CC, CFLAGS and LANGUAGES that you used when compiling the files that are being installed. One reason this is necessary is that some versions of Make have bugs and recompile files gratuitously when you do this step. If you use the same variable values, those files will be recompiled properly.

For example, if you have built the stage 2 compiler, you can use the following command:

```
make install CC="stage2/xgcc -Bstage2/" CFLAGS="-g -O" LANGUAGES="list"
```

This copies the files 'cc1', 'cpp' and 'libgcc.a' to files 'cc1', 'cpp' and 'libgcc.a' in the directory '/usr/local/lib/gcc-lib/*target*/*version*', which is where the compiler driver program looks for them. Here *target* is the canonicalized form of target machine type specified when you ran 'configure', and *version* is the version number of GNU CC. This naming scheme permits various versions and/or cross-compilers to coexist. It also copies the executables for compilers for other languages (e.g., 'cc1plus' for C++) to the same directory.

This also copies the driver program 'xgcc' into '/usr/local/bin/gcc', so that it appears in typical execution search paths. It also copies 'gcc.1' into '/usr/local/man/man1' and info pages into '/usr/local/info'.

On some systems, this command causes recompilation of some files. This is usually due to bugs in make. You should either ignore this problem, or use GNU Make.

Warning: there is a bug in alloca in the Sun library. To avoid this bug, be sure to install the executables of GNU CC that were compiled by GNU CC. (That is, the executables from stage 2 or 3, not stage 1.) They use alloca as a built-in function and never the one in the library.

(It is usually better to install GNU CC executables from stage 2 or 3, since they usually run faster than the ones compiled with some other compiler.)

16. If you're going to use C++, you need to install the C++ runtime library. This includes all I/O functionality, special class libraries, etc.

The standard C++ runtime library for GNU CC is called 'libstdc++'. An obsolescent library 'libg++' may also be available, but it's necessary only for older software that hasn't been converted yet; if you don't know whether you need 'libg++' then you probably don't need it.

Here's one way to build and install 'libstdc++' for GNU CC:

- Build and install GNU CC, so that invoking 'gcc' obtains the GNU CC that was just built.

- Obtain a copy of a compatible 'libstdc++' distribution. For example, the 'libstdc++-2.8.0.tar.gz' distribution should be compatible with GCC 2.8.0. GCC distributors normally distribute 'libstdc++' as well.
- Set the 'CXX' environment variable to 'gcc' while running the 'libstdc++' distribution's 'configure' command. Use the same 'configure' options that you used when you invoked GCC's 'configure' command.
- Invoke 'make' to build the C++ runtime.
- Invoke 'make install' to install the C++ runtime.

To summarize, after building and installing GNU CC, invoke the following shell commands in the topmost directory of the C++ library distribution. For *configure-options*, use the same options that you used to configure GNU CC.

```
$ CXX=gcc ./configure configure-options
$ make
$ make install
```

17. GNU CC includes a runtime library for Objective-C because it is an integral part of the language. You can find the files associated with the library in the subdirectory 'objc'. The GNU Objective-C Runtime Library requires header files for the target's C library in order to be compiled,and also requires the header files for the target's thread library if you want thread support. See Section 3.4.5 [Cross-Compilers and Header Files], page 153, for discussion about header files issues for cross-compilation.

When you run 'configure', it picks the appropriate Objective-C thread implementation file for the target platform. In some situations, you may wish to choose a different back-end as some platforms support multiple thread implementations or you may wish to disable thread support completely. You do this by specifying a value for the *OBJC_THREAD_FILE* makefile variable on the command line when you run make, for example:

```
make CC="stage2/xgcc -Bstage2/" CFLAGS="-g -O2" OBJC_THREAD_FILE=thr-
single
```

Below is a list of the currently available back-ends.

- thr-single Disable thread support, should work for all platforms.
- thr-decosf1 DEC OSF/1 thread support.
- thr-irix SGI IRIX thread support.
- thr-mach Generic MACH thread support, known to work on NEXTSTEP.
- thr-os2 IBM OS/2 thread support.
- thr-posix Generix POSIX thread support.
- thr-pthreads PCThreads on Linux-based GNU systems.

- thr-solaris SUN Solaris thread support.
- thr-win32 Microsoft Win32 API thread support.

3.1 Files Created by `configure`

Here we spell out what files will be set up by `configure`. Normally you need not be concerned with these files.

- A file named 'config.h' is created that contains a '#include' of the top-level config file for the machine you will run the compiler on (see Chapter 18 [Config], page 523). This file is responsible for defining information about the host machine. It includes 'tm.h'.

  The top-level config file is located in the subdirectory 'config'. Its name is always 'xm-*something*.h'; usually 'xm-*machine*.h', but there are some exceptions.

  If your system does not support symbolic links, you might want to set up 'config.h' to contain a '#include' command which refers to the appropriate file.

- A file named 'tconfig.h' is created which includes the top-level config file for your target machine. This is used for compiling certain programs to run on that machine.

- A file named 'tm.h' is created which includes the machine-description macro file for your target machine. It should be in the subdirectory 'config' and its name is often '*machine*.h'.

- The command file 'configure' also constructs the file 'Makefile' by adding some text to the template file 'Makefile.in'. The additional text comes from files in the 'config' directory, named 't-*target*' and 'x-*host*'. If these files do not exist, it means nothing needs to be added for a given target or host.

3.2 Configurations Supported by GNU CC

Here are the possible CPU types:

1750a, a29k, alpha, arm, c*n*, clipper, dsp16xx, elxsi, h8300, hppa1.0, hppa1.1, i370, i386, i486, i586, i860, i960, m32r, m68000, m68k, m88k, mips, mipsel, mips64, mips64el, ns32k, powerpc, powerpcle, pyramid, romp, rs6000, sh, sparc, sparclite, sparc64, vax, we32k.

Here are the recognized company names. As you can see, customary abbreviations are used rather than the longer official names.

acorn, alliant, altos, apollo, apple, att, bull, cbm, convergent, convex, crds, dec, dg, dolphin, elxsi, encore, harris, hitachi, hp, ibm, intergraph, isi, mips, motorola, ncr, next, ns, omron, plexus, sequent, sgi, sony, sun, tti, unicom, wrs.

The company name is meaningful only to disambiguate when the rest of the information supplied is insufficient. You can omit it, writing just 'cpu-system', if it is not needed. For example, 'vax-ultrix4.2' is equivalent to 'vax-dec-ultrix4.2'.

Here is a list of system types:

> 386bsd, aix, acis, amigaos, aos, aout, aux, bosx, bsd, clix, coff, ctix, cxux, dgux, dynix, ebmon, ecoff, elf, esix, freebsd, hms, genix, gnu, linux-gnu, hiux, hpux, iris, irix, isc, luna, lynxos, mach, minix, msdos, mvs, netbsd, newsos, nindy, ns, osf, osfrose, ptx, riscix, riscos, rtu, sco, sim, solaris, sunos, sym, sysv, udi, ultrix, unicos, uniplus, unos, vms, vsta, vxworks, winnt, xenix.

You can omit the system type; then 'configure' guesses the operating system from the CPU and company.

You can add a version number to the system type; this may or may not make a difference. For example, you can write 'bsd4.3' or 'bsd4.4' to distinguish versions of BSD. In practice, the version number is most needed for 'sysv3' and 'sysv4', which are often treated differently.

If you specify an impossible combination such as 'i860-dg-vms', then you may get an error message from 'configure', or it may ignore part of the information and do the best it can with the rest. 'configure' always prints the canonical name for the alternative that it used. GNU CC does not support all possible alternatives.

Often a particular model of machine has a name. Many machine names are recognized as aliases for CPU/company combinations. Thus, the machine name 'sun3', mentioned above, is an alias for 'm68k-sun'. Sometimes we accept a company name as a machine name, when the name is popularly used for a particular machine. Here is a table of the known machine names:

> 3300, 3b1, 3bn, 7300, altos3068, altos, apollo68, att-7300, balance, convex-cn, crds, decstation-3100, decstation, delta, encore, fx2800, gmicro, hp7nn, hp8nn, hp9k2nn, hp9k3nn, hp9k7nn, hp9k8nn, iris4d, iris, isi68, m3230, magnum, merlin, miniframe, mmax, news-3600, news800, news, next, pbd, pc532, pmax, powerpc, powerpcle, ps2, risc-news, rtpc, sun2, sun386i, sun386, sun3, sun4, symmetry, tower-32, tower.

Remember that a machine name specifies both the cpu type and the company name. If you want to install your own homemade configuration files, you can use 'local' as the company name to access them. If you use configuration 'cpu-local', the configuration name without the cpu prefix is used to form the configuration file names.

Thus, if you specify 'm68k-local', configuration uses files 'm68k.md', 'local.h', 'm68k.c', 'xm-local.h', 't-local', and 'x-local', all in the directory 'config/m68k'.

Here is a list of configurations that have special treatment or special things you must know:

'1750a-*-*'

> MIL-STD-1750A processors.
>
> The MIL-STD-1750A cross configuration produces output for as1750, an assembler/linker available under the GNU Public License for the 1750A. as1750 can be obtained at *ftp://ftp.fta-berlin.de/pub/crossgcc/1750gals/*. A similarly licensed simulator for the 1750A is available from same address.
>
> You should ignore a fatal error during the building of libgcc (libgcc is not yet implemented for the 1750A.)
>
> The as1750 assembler requires the file 'ms1750.inc', which is found in the directory 'config/1750a'.
>
> GNU CC produced the same sections as the Fairchild F9450 C Compiler, namely:
>
> Normal   The program code section.
>
> Static   The read/write (RAM) data section.
>
> Konst   The read-only (ROM) constants section.
>
> Init   Initialization section (code to copy KREL to SREL).
>
> The smallest addressable unit is 16 bits (BITS_PER_UNIT is 16). This means that type 'char' is represented with a 16-bit word per character. The 1750A's "Load/Store Upper/Lower Byte" instructions are not used by GNU CC.

'alpha-*-osf1'

> Systems using processors that implement the DEC Alpha architecture and are running the DEC Unix (OSF/1) operating system, for example the DEC Alpha AXP systems.CC.)
>
> GNU CC writes a '.verstamp' directive to the assembler output file unless it is built as a cross-compiler. It gets the version to use from the system header file '/usr/include/stamp.h'. If you install a new version of DEC Unix, you should rebuild GCC to pick up the new version stamp.
>
> Note that since the Alpha is a 64-bit architecture, cross-compilers from 32-bit machines will not generate code as efficient as that generated when the compiler is running on a 64-bit machine because many optimizations that depend on being able to represent a word on the target in an integral value on the host cannot be performed. Building cross-compilers on the Alpha for 32-bit machines has only been tested in a few cases and may not work properly.
>
> make compare may fail on old versions of DEC Unix unless you add '-save-temps' to CFLAGS. On these systems, the name

of the assembler input file is stored in the object file, and that makes comparison fail if it differs between the `stage1` and `stage2` compilations. The option '`-save-temps`' forces a fixed name to be used for the assembler input file, instead of a randomly chosen name in '`/tmp`'. Do not add '`-save-temps`' unless the comparisons fail without that option. If you add '`-save-temps`', you will have to manually delete the '`.i`' and '`.s`' files after each series of compilations.

GNU CC now supports both the native (ECOFF) debugging format used by DBX and GDB and an encapsulated STABS format for use only with GDB. See the discussion of the '`--with-stabs`' option of '`configure`' above for more information on these formats and how to select them.

There is a bug in DEC's assembler that produces incorrect line numbers for ECOFF format when the '`.align`' directive is used. To work around this problem, GNU CC will not emit such alignment directives while writing ECOFF format debugging information even if optimization is being performed. Unfortunately, this has the very undesirable side-effect that code addresses when '`-O`' is specified are different depending on whether or not '`-g`' is also specified.

To avoid this behavior, specify '`-gstabs+`' and use GDB instead of DBX. DEC is now aware of this problem with the assembler and hopes to provide a fix shortly.

'`arc-*-elf`'

         Argonaut ARC processor. This configuration is intended for embedded systems.

'`arm-*-aout`'

         Advanced RISC Machines ARM-family processors. These are often used in embedded applications. There are no standard Unix configurations. This configuration corresponds to the basic instruction sequences and will produce '`a.out`' format object modules.

         You may need to make a variant of the file '`arm.h`' for your particular configuration.

'`arm-*-linuxaout`'

         Any of the ARM family processors running the Linux-based GNU system with the '`a.out`' binary format (ELF is not yet supported). You must use version 2.8.1.0.7 or later of the GNU/Linux binutils, which you can download from '`sunsite.unc.edu:/pub/Linux/GCC`' and other mirror sites for Linux-based GNU systems.

'arm-*-riscix'
> The ARM2 or ARM3 processor running RISC iX, Acorn's port
> of BSD Unix. If you are running a version of RISC iX prior to 1.2
> then you must specify the version number during configuration.
> Note that the assembler shipped with RISC iX does not support
> stabs debugging information; a new version of the assembler,
> with stabs support included, is now available from Acorn and
> via ftp 'ftp.acorn.com:/pub/riscix/as+xterm.tar.Z'. To
> enable stabs debugging, pass '--with-gnu-as' to configure.
>
> You will need to install GNU 'sed' before you can run configure.

'a29k'
> AMD Am29k-family processors. These are normally used in
> embedded applications. There are no standard Unix configura-
> tions. This configuration corresponds to AMD's standard calling
> sequence and binary interface and is compatible with other 29k
> tools.
>
> You may need to make a variant of the file 'a29k.h' for your
> particular configuration.

'a29k-*-bsd'
> AMD Am29050 used in a system running a variant of BSD Unix.

'decstation-*'
> MIPS-based DECstations can support three different person-
> alities: Ultrix, DEC OSF/1, and OSF/rose. (Alpha-based
> DECstation products have a configuration name beginning with
> 'alpha-dec'.) To configure GCC for these platforms use the
> following configurations:
>
> 'decstation-ultrix'
> > Ultrix configuration.
>
> 'decstation-osf1'
> > Dec's version of OSF/1.
>
> 'decstation-osfrose'
> > Open Software Foundation reference port of OSF/1
> > which uses the OSF/rose object file format instead
> > of ECOFF. Normally, you would not select this con-
> > figuration.
>
> The MIPS C compiler needs to be told to increase its table size
> for switch statements with the '-Wf,-XNg1500' option in order to
> compile 'cp/parse.c'. If you use the '-O2' optimization option,
> you also need to use '-Olimit 3000'. Both of these options are
> automatically generated in the 'Makefile' that the shell script
> 'configure' builds. If you override the CC make variable and
> use the MIPS compilers, you may need to add '-Wf,-XNg1500
> -Olimit 3000'.

`'elxsi-elxsi-bsd'`

> The Elxsi's C compiler has known limitations that prevent it from compiling GNU C. Please contact `mrs@cygnus.com` for more details.

`'dsp16xx'`   A port to the AT&T DSP1610 family of processors.

`'h8300-*-*'`

> Hitachi H8/300 series of processors.
>
> The calling convention and structure layout has changed in release 2.6. All code must be recompiled. The calling convention now passes the first three arguments in function calls in registers. Structures are no longer a multiple of 2 bytes.

`'hppa*-*-*'`

> There are several variants of the HP-PA processor which run a variety of operating systems. GNU CC must be configured to use the correct processor type and operating system, or GNU CC will not function correctly. The easiest way to handle this problem is to *not* specify a target when configuring GNU CC, the `'configure'` script will try to automatically determine the right processor type and operating system.
>
> `'-g'` does not work on HP-UX, since that system uses a peculiar debugging format which GNU CC does not know about. However, `'-g'` will work if you also use GAS and GDB in conjunction with GCC. We highly recommend using GAS for all HP-PA configurations.
>
> You should be using GAS-2.6 (or later) along with GDB-4.16 (or later). These can be retrieved from all the traditional GNU ftp archive sites.
>
> On some versions of HP-UX, you will need to install GNU `'sed'`.
>
> You will need to be install GAS into a directory before /bin, /usr/bin, and /usr/ccs/bin in your search path. You should install GAS before you build GNU CC.
>
> To enable debugging, you must configure GNU CC with the `'--with-gnu-as'` option before building.

`'i370-*-*'`

> This port is very preliminary and has many known bugs. We hope to have a higher-quality port for this machine soon.

`'i386-*-linux-gnuoldld'`

> Use this configuration to generate `'a.out'` binaries on Linux-based GNU systems if you do not have gas/binutils version 2.5.2 or later installed. This is an obsolete configuration.

'i386-*-linux-gnuaout'

> Use this configuration to generate 'a.out' binaries on Linux-
> based GNU systems. This configuration is being superseded.
> You must use gas/binutils version 2.5.2 or later.

'i386-*-linux-gnu'

> Use this configuration to generate ELF binaries on Linux-based
> GNU systems. You must use gas/binutils version 2.5.2 or later.

'i386-*-sco'

> Compilation with RCC is recommended. Also, it may be a good
> idea to link with GNU malloc instead of the malloc that comes
> with the system.

'i386-*-sco3.2v4'

> Use this configuration for SCO release 3.2 version 4.

'i386-*-sco3.2v5*'

> Use this for the SCO OpenServer Release family including 5.0.0,
> 5.0.2, 5.0.4, 5.0.5, Internet FastStart 1.0, and Internet FastStart
> 1.1.
>
> GNU CC can generate COFF binaries if you specify '-mcoff'
> or ELF binaries, the default. A full 'make bootstrap' is recom-
> mended so that an ELF compiler that builds ELF is generated.
>
> You must have TLS597 from ftp://ftp.sco.com/TLS installed
> for ELF C++ binaries to work correctly on releases before 5.0.4.
>
> The native SCO assembler that is provided with the OS at no
> charge is normally required. If, however, you must be able to
> use the GNU assembler (perhaps you have complex asms) you
> must configure this package '--with-gnu-as'. To do this, install
> (cp or symlink) gcc/as to your copy of the GNU assembler. You
> must use a recent version of GNU binutils; version 2.9.1 seems to
> work well. If you select this option, you will be unable to build
> COFF images. Trying to do so will result in non-obvious failures.
> In general, the "–with-gnu-as" option isn't as well tested as the
> native assembler.
>
> *NOTE:* If you are building C++, you must follow the in-
> structions about invoking 'make bootstrap' because the native
> OpenServer compiler may build a 'cc1plus' that will not cor-
> rectly parse many valid C++ programs. You must do a 'make
> bootstrap' if you are building with the native compiler.

'i386-*-isc'

> It may be a good idea to link with GNU malloc instead of the
> malloc that comes with the system.
>
> In ISC version 4.1, 'sed' core dumps when building 'deduced.h'.
> Use the version of 'sed' from version 4.0.

'i386-*-esix'

> It may be good idea to link with GNU malloc instead of the malloc that comes with the system.

'i386-ibm-aix'

> You need to use GAS version 2.1 or later, and LD from GNU binutils version 2.2 or later.

'i386-sequent-bsd'

> Go to the Berkeley universe before compiling.

'i386-sequent-ptx1*'
'i386-sequent-ptx2*'

> You must install GNU 'sed' before running 'configure'.

'i386-sun-sunos4'

> You may find that you need another version of GNU CC to begin bootstrapping with, since the current version when built with the system's own compiler seems to get an infinite loop compiling part of 'libgcc2.c'. GNU CC version 2 compiled with GNU CC (any version) seems not to have this problem.

> See Section 3.5 [Sun Install], page 154, for information on installing GNU CC on Sun systems.

'i[345]86-*-winnt3.5'

> This version requires a GAS that has not yet been released. Until it is, you can get a prebuilt binary version via anonymous ftp from 'cs.washington.edu:pub/gnat' or 'cs.nyu.edu:pub/gnat'. You must also use the Microsoft header files from the Windows NT 3.5 SDK. Find these on the CDROM in the '/mstools/h' directory dated 9/4/94. You must use a fixed version of Microsoft linker made especially for NT 3.5, which is also is available on the NT 3.5 SDK CDROM. If you do not have this linker, can you also use the linker from Visual C/C++ 1.0 or 2.0.

> Installing GNU CC for NT builds a wrapper linker, called 'ld.exe', which mimics the behaviour of Unix 'ld' in the specification of libraries ('-L' and '-l'). 'ld.exe' looks for both Unix and Microsoft named libraries. For example, if you specify '-lfoo', 'ld.exe' will look first for 'libfoo.a' and then for 'foo.lib'.

> You may install GNU CC for Windows NT in one of two ways, depending on whether or not you have a Unix-like shell and various Unix-like utilities.

> 1. If you do not have a Unix-like shell and few Unix-like utilities, you will use a DOS style batch script called 'configure.bat'. Invoke it as configure winnt from an MSDOS console window or from the program manager

dialog box. 'configure.bat' assumes you have already installed and have in your path a Unix-like 'sed' program which is used to create a working 'Makefile' from 'Makefile.in'.

'Makefile' uses the Microsoft Nmake program maintenance utility and the Visual C/C++ V8.00 compiler to build GNU CC. You need only have the utilities 'sed' and 'touch' to use this installation method, which only automatically builds the compiler itself. You must then examine what 'fixinc.winnt' does, edit the header files by hand and build 'libgcc.a' manually.

2. The second type of installation assumes you are running a Unix-like shell, have a complete suite of Unix-like utilities in your path, and have a previous version of GNU CC already installed, either through building it via the above installation method or acquiring a pre-built binary. In this case, use the 'configure' script in the normal fashion.

'i860-intel-osf1'

This is the Paragon. If you have version 1.0 of the operating system, see Section 7.2 [Installation Problems], page 223, for special things you need to do to compensate for peculiarities in the system.

'*-lynx-lynxos'

LynxOS 2.2 and earlier comes with GNU CC 1.x already installed as '/bin/gcc'. You should compile with this instead of '/bin/cc'. You can tell GNU CC to use the GNU assembler and linker, by specifying '--with-gnu-as --with-gnu-ld' when configuring. These will produce COFF format object files and executables; otherwise GNU CC will use the installed tools, which produce 'a.out' format executables.

'm32r-*-elf'

Mitsubishi M32R processor. This configuration is intended for embedded systems.

'm68000-hp-bsd'

HP 9000 series 200 running BSD. Note that the C compiler that comes with this system cannot compile GNU CC; contact law@cygnus.com to get binaries of GNU CC for bootstrapping.

'm68k-altos'

Altos 3068. You must use the GNU assembler, linker and debugger. Also, you must fix a kernel bug. Details in the file 'README.ALTOS'.

'm68k-apple-aux'

Apple Macintosh running A/UX. You may configure GCC to use
either the system assembler and linker or the GNU assembler
and linker. You should use the GNU configuration if you can,
especially if you also want to use GNU C++. You enabled that
configuration with + the '--with-gnu-as' and '--with-gnu-ld'
options to `configure`.

Note the C compiler that comes with this system cannot compile
GNU CC. You can find binaries of GNU CC for bootstrapping
on `jagubox.gsfc.nasa.gov`. You will also a patched version of
'/bin/ld' there that raises some of the arbitrary limits found in
the original.

'm68k-att-sysv'

AT&T 3b1, a.k.a. 7300 PC. Special procedures are needed to
compile GNU CC with this machine's standard C compiler, due
to bugs in that compiler. You can bootstrap it more easily with
previous versions of GNU CC if you have them.

Installing GNU CC on the 3b1 is difficult if you do not already
have GNU CC running, due to bugs in the installed C compiler.
However, the following procedure might work. We are unable to
test it.

1. Comment out the '#include "config.h"' line near the
   start of 'cccp.c' and do 'make cpp'. This makes a preliminary version of GNU cpp.

2. Save the old '/lib/cpp' and copy the preliminary GNU cpp
   to that file name.

3. Undo your change in 'cccp.c', or reinstall the original version, and do 'make cpp' again.

4. Copy this final version of GNU cpp into '/lib/cpp'.

5. Replace every occurrence of `obstack_free` in the file
   'tree.c' with `_obstack_free`.

6. Run `make` to get the first-stage GNU CC.

7. Reinstall the original version of '/lib/cpp'.

8. Now you can compile GNU CC with itself and install it in
   the normal fashion.

'm68k-bull-sysv'

Bull DPX/2 series 200 and 300 with BOS-2.00.45 up to BOS-
2.01. GNU CC works either with native assembler or GNU
assembler. You can use GNU assembler with native coff generation by providing '--with-gnu-as' to the configure script
or use GNU assembler with dbx-in-coff encapsulation by providing '--with-gnu-as --stabs'. For any problem with native

assembler or for availability of the DPX/2 port of GAS, contact `F.Pierresteguy@frcl.bull.fr`.

'm68k-crds-unox'

Use '`configure unos`' for building on Unos.

The Unos assembler is named `casm` instead of `as`. For some strange reason linking '`/bin/as`' to '`/bin/casm`' changes the behavior, and does not work. So, when installing GNU CC, you should install the following script as '`as`' in the subdirectory where the passes of GCC are installed:

```
#!/bin/sh
casm $*
```

The default Unos library is named '`libunos.a`' instead of '`libc.a`'. To allow GNU CC to function, either change all references to '`-lc`' in '`gcc.c`' to '`-lunos`' or link '`/lib/libc.a`' to '`/lib/libunos.a`'.

When compiling GNU CC with the standard compiler, to overcome bugs in the support of `alloca`, do not use '`-O`' when making stage 2. Then use the stage 2 compiler with '`-O`' to make the stage 3 compiler. This compiler will have the same characteristics as the usual stage 2 compiler on other systems. Use it to make a stage 4 compiler and compare that with stage 3 to verify proper compilation.

(Perhaps simply defining `ALLOCA` in '`x-crds`' as described in the comments there will make the above paragraph superfluous. Please inform us of whether this works.)

Unos uses memory segmentation instead of demand paging, so you will need a lot of memory. 5 Mb is barely enough if no other tasks are running. If linking '`cc1`' fails, try putting the object files into a library and linking from that library.

'm68k-hp-hpux'

HP 9000 series 300 or 400 running HP-UX. HP-UX version 8.0 has a bug in the assembler that prevents compilation of GNU CC. To fix it, get patch PHCO_4484 from HP.

In addition, if you wish to use gas '`--with-gnu-as`' you must use gas version 2.1 or later, and you must use the GNU linker version 2.1 or later. Earlier versions of gas relied upon a program which converted the gas output into the native HP-UX format, but that program has not been kept up to date. gdb does not understand that native HP-UX format, so you must use gas if you wish to use gdb.

'm68k-sun'

> Sun 3. We do not provide a configuration file to use the Sun FPA by default, because programs that establish signal handlers for floating point traps inherently cannot work with the FPA.
>
> See Section 3.5 [Sun Install], page 154, for information on installing GNU CC on Sun systems.

'm88k-*-svr3'

> Motorola m88k running the AT&T/Unisoft/Motorola V.3 reference port. These systems tend to use the Green Hills C, revision 1.8.5, as the standard C compiler. There are apparently bugs in this compiler that result in object files differences between stage 2 and stage 3. If this happens, make the stage 4 compiler and compare it to the stage 3 compiler. If the stage 3 and stage 4 object files are identical, this suggests you encountered a problem with the standard C compiler; the stage 3 and 4 compilers may be usable.
>
> It is best, however, to use an older version of GNU CC for bootstrapping if you have one.

'm88k-*-dgux'

> Motorola m88k running DG/UX. To build 88open BCS native or cross compilers on DG/UX, specify the configuration name as 'm88k-*-dguxbcs' and build in the 88open BCS software development environment. To build ELF native or cross compilers on DG/UX, specify 'm88k-*-dgux' and build in the DG/UX ELF development environment. You set the software development environment by issuing 'sde-target' command and specifying either 'm88kbcs' or 'm88kdguxelf' as the operand.
>
> If you do not specify a configuration name, 'configure' guesses the configuration based on the current software development environment.

'm88k-tektronix-sysv3'

> Tektronix XD88 running UTekV 3.2e. Do not turn on optimization while building stage1 if you bootstrap with the buggy Green Hills compiler. Also, The bundled LAI System V NFS is buggy so if you build in an NFS mounted directory, start from a fresh reboot, or avoid NFS all together. Otherwise you may have trouble getting clean comparisons between stages.

'mips-mips-bsd'

> MIPS machines running the MIPS operating system in BSD mode. It's possible that some old versions of the system lack the functions memcpy, memcmp, and memset. If your system lacks these, you must remove or undo the definition of TARGET_MEM_FUNCTIONS in 'mips-bsd.h'.

The MIPS C compiler needs to be told to increase its table size for switch statements with the '-Wf,-XNg1500' option in order to compile 'cp/parse.c'. If you use the '-O2' optimization option, you also need to use '-Olimit 3000'. Both of these options are automatically generated in the 'Makefile' that the shell script 'configure' builds. If you override the CC make variable and use the MIPS compilers, you may need to add '-Wf,-XNg1500 -Olimit 3000'.

'mips-mips-riscos*'

The MIPS C compiler needs to be told to increase its table size for switch statements with the '-Wf,-XNg1500' option in order to compile 'cp/parse.c'. If you use the '-O2' optimization option, you also need to use '-Olimit 3000'. Both of these options are automatically generated in the 'Makefile' that the shell script 'configure' builds. If you override the CC make variable and use the MIPS compilers, you may need to add '-Wf,-XNg1500 -Olimit 3000'.

MIPS computers running RISC-OS can support four different personalities: default, BSD 4.3, System V.3, and System V.4 (older versions of RISC-OS don't support V.4). To configure GCC for these platforms use the following configurations:

'mips-mips-riscosrev'

Default configuration for RISC-OS, revision **rev**.

'mips-mips-riscosrevbsd'

BSD 4.3 configuration for RISC-OS, revision **rev**.

'mips-mips-riscosrevsysv4'

System V.4 configuration for RISC-OS, revision **rev**.

'mips-mips-riscosrevsysv'

System V.3 configuration for RISC-OS, revision **rev**.

The revision **rev** mentioned above is the revision of RISC-OS to use. You must reconfigure GCC when going from a RISC-OS revision 4 to RISC-OS revision 5. This has the effect of avoiding a linker bug (see Section 7.2 [Installation Problems], page 223, for more details).

'mips-sgi-*'

In order to compile GCC on an SGI running IRIX 4, the "c.hdr.lib" option must be installed from the CD-ROM supplied from Silicon Graphics. This is found on the 2nd CD in release 4.0.1.

In order to compile GCC on an SGI running IRIX 5, the "compiler_dev.hdr" subsystem must be installed from the IDO CD-ROM supplied by Silicon Graphics.

`make compare` may fail on version 5 of IRIX unless you add '`-save-temps`' to `CFLAGS`. On these systems, the name of the assembler input file is stored in the object file, and that makes comparison fail if it differs between the `stage1` and `stage2` compilations. The option '`-save-temps`' forces a fixed name to be used for the assembler input file, instead of a randomly chosen name in '`/tmp`'. Do not add '`-save-temps`' unless the comparisons fail without that option. If you do you '`-save-temps`', you will have to manually delete the '`.i`' and '`.s`' files after each series of compilations.

The MIPS C compiler needs to be told to increase its table size for switch statements with the '`-Wf,-XNg1500`' option in order to compile '`cp/parse.c`'. If you use the '`-O2`' optimization option, you also need to use '`-Olimit 3000`'. Both of these options are automatically generated in the '`Makefile`' that the shell script '`configure`' builds. If you override the `CC` make variable and use the MIPS compilers, you may need to add '`-Wf,-XNg1500 -Olimit 3000`'.

On Irix version 4.0.5F, and perhaps on some other versions as well, there is an assembler bug that reorders instructions incorrectly. To work around it, specify the target configuration '`mips-sgi-irix4loser`'. This configuration inhibits assembler optimization.

In a compiler configured with target '`mips-sgi-irix4`', you can turn off assembler optimization by using the '`-noasmopt`' option. This compiler option passes the option '`-O0`' to the assembler, to inhibit reordering.

The '`-noasmopt`' option can be useful for testing whether a problem is due to erroneous assembler reordering. Even if a problem does not go away with '`-noasmopt`', it may still be due to assembler reordering—perhaps GNU CC itself was miscompiled as a result.

To enable debugging under Irix 5, you must use GNU as 2.5 or later, and use the '`--with-gnu-as`' configure option when configuring gcc. GNU as is distributed as part of the binutils package.

'`mips-sony-sysv`'

Sony MIPS NEWS. This works in NEWSOS 5.0.1, but not in 5.0.2 (which uses ELF instead of COFF). Support for 5.0.2 will probably be provided soon by volunteers. In particular, the linker does not like the code generated by GCC when shared libraries are linked in.

'ns32k-encore'

Encore ns32000 system. Encore systems are supported only under BSD.

'ns32k-*-genix'

National Semiconductor ns32000 system. Genix has bugs in `alloca` and `malloc`; you must get the compiled versions of these from GNU Emacs.

'ns32k-sequent'

Go to the Berkeley universe before compiling.

'ns32k-utek'

UTEK ns32000 system ("merlin"). The C compiler that comes with this system cannot compile GNU CC; contact 'tektronix!reed!mason' to get binaries of GNU CC for bootstrapping.

'romp-*-aos'
'romp-*-mach'

The only operating systems supported for the IBM RT PC are AOS and MACH. GNU CC does not support AIX running on the RT. We recommend you compile GNU CC with an earlier version of itself; if you compile GNU CC with `hc`, the Metaware compiler, it will work, but you will get mismatches between the stage 2 and stage 3 compilers in various files. These errors are minor differences in some floating-point constants and can be safely ignored; the stage 3 compiler is correct.

'rs6000-*-aix'
'powerpc-*-aix'

Various early versions of each release of the IBM XLC compiler will not bootstrap GNU CC. Symptoms include differences between the stage2 and stage3 object files, and errors when compiling 'libgcc.a' or 'enquire'. Known problematic releases include: xlc-1.2.1.8, xlc-1.3.0.0 (distributed with AIX 3.2.5), and xlc-1.3.0.19. Both xlc-1.2.1.28 and xlc-1.3.0.24 (PTF 432238) are known to produce working versions of GNU CC, but most other recent releases correctly bootstrap GNU CC.

Release 4.3.0 of AIX and ones prior to AIX 3.2.4 include a version of the IBM assembler which does not accept debugging directives: assembler updates are available as PTFs. Also, if you are using AIX 3.2.5 or greater and the GNU assembler, you must have a version modified after October 16th, 1995 in order for the GNU C compiler to build. See the file 'README.RS6000' for more details on any of these problems.

GNU CC does not yet support the 64-bit PowerPC instructions.

Objective C does not work on this architecture because it makes assumptions that are incompatible with the calling conventions.

AIX on the RS/6000 provides support (NLS) for environments outside of the United States. Compilers and assemblers use NLS to support locale-specific representations of various objects including floating-point numbers ("." vs "," for separating decimal fractions). There have been problems reported where the library linked with GNU CC does not produce the same floating-point formats that the assembler accepts. If you have this problem, set the LANG environment variable to "C" or "En_US".

Due to changes in the way that GNU CC invokes the binder (linker) for AIX 4.1, you may now receive warnings of duplicate symbols from the link step that were not reported before. The assembly files generated by GNU CC for AIX have always included multiple symbol definitions for certain global variable and function declarations in the original program. The warnings should not prevent the linker from producing a correct library or runnable executable.

By default, AIX 4.1 produces code that can be used on either Power or PowerPC processors.

You can specify a default version for the '-mcpu='*cpu_type* switch by using the configure option '--with-cpu-'*cpu_type*.

'powerpc-*-elf'
'powerpc-*-sysv4'

>PowerPC system in big endian mode, running System V.4.

>You can specify a default version for the '-mcpu='*cpu_type* switch by using the configure option '--with-cpu-'*cpu_type*.

'powerpc-*-linux-gnu'

>PowerPC system in big endian mode, running the Linux-based GNU system.

>You can specify a default version for the '-mcpu='*cpu_type* switch by using the configure option '--with-cpu-'*cpu_type*.

'powerpc-*-eabiaix'

>Embedded PowerPC system in big endian mode with -mcall-aix selected as the default.

>You can specify a default version for the '-mcpu='*cpu_type* switch by using the configure option '--with-cpu-'*cpu_type*.

'powerpc-*-eabisim'

>Embedded PowerPC system in big endian mode for use in running under the PSIM simulator.

>You can specify a default version for the '-mcpu='*cpu_type* switch by using the configure option '--with-cpu-'*cpu_type*.

'powerpc-*-eabi'

> Embedded PowerPC system in big endian mode.
>
> You can specify a default version for the '-mcpu='*cpu_type* switch by using the configure option '--with-cpu-'*cpu_type*.

'powerpcle-*-elf'
'powerpcle-*-sysv4'

> PowerPC system in little endian mode, running System V.4.
>
> You can specify a default version for the '-mcpu='*cpu_type* switch by using the configure option '--with-cpu-'*cpu_type*.

'powerpcle-*-solaris2*'

> PowerPC system in little endian mode, running Solaris 2.5.1 or higher.
>
> You can specify a default version for the '-mcpu='*cpu_type* switch by using the configure option '--with-cpu-'*cpu_type*. Beta versions of the Sun 4.0 compiler do not seem to be able to build GNU CC correctly. There are also problems with the host assembler and linker that are fixed by using the GNU versions of these tools.

'powerpcle-*-eabisim'

> Embedded PowerPC system in little endian mode for use in running under the PSIM simulator.

'powerpcle-*-eabi'

> Embedded PowerPC system in little endian mode.
>
> You can specify a default version for the '-mcpu='*cpu_type* switch by using the configure option '--with-cpu-'*cpu_type*.

'powerpcle-*-winnt'
'powerpcle-*-pe'

> PowerPC system in little endian mode running Windows NT.
>
> You can specify a default version for the '-mcpu='*cpu_type* switch by using the configure option '--with-cpu-'*cpu_type*.

'vax-dec-ultrix'

> Don't try compiling with Vax C (vcc). It produces incorrect code in some cases (for example, when alloca is used).
>
> Meanwhile, compiling 'cp/parse.c' with pcc does not work because of an internal table size limitation in that compiler. To avoid this problem, compile just the GNU C compiler first, and use it to recompile building all the languages that you want to run.

'sparc-sun-*'

> See Section 3.5 [Sun Install], page 154, for information on installing GNU CC on Sun systems.

'vax-dec-vms'
> See Section 3.6 [VMS Install], page 155, for details on how to
> install GNU CC on VMS.

'we32k-*-*'
> These computers are also known as the 3b2, 3b5, 3b20 and other
> similar names. (However, the 3b1 is actually a 68000; see Sec-
> tion 3.2 [Configurations], page 131.)
>
> Don't use '-g' when compiling with the system's compiler. The
> system's linker seems to be unable to handle such a large pro-
> gram with debugging information.
>
> The system's compiler runs out of capacity when compiling
> 'stmt.c' in GNU CC. You can work around this by building
> 'cpp' in GNU CC first, then use that instead of the system's
> preprocessor with the system's C compiler to compile 'stmt.c'.
> Here is how:
>
> ```
> mv /lib/cpp /lib/cpp.att
> cp cpp /lib/cpp.gnu
> echo '/lib/cpp.gnu -traditional ${1+"$@"}' > /lib/cpp
> chmod +x /lib/cpp
> ```
>
> The system's compiler produces bad code for some of the GNU
> CC optimization files. So you must build the stage 2 compiler
> without optimization. Then build a stage 3 compiler with opti-
> mization. That executable should work. Here are the necessary
> commands:
>
> ```
> make LANGUAGES=c CC=stage1/xgcc CFLAGS="-Bstage1/ -g"
> make stage2
> make CC=stage2/xgcc CFLAGS="-Bstage2/ -g -O"
> ```
>
> You may need to raise the ULIMIT setting to build a C++ com-
> piler, as the file 'cc1plus' is larger than one megabyte.

3.3 Compilation in a Separate Directory

If you wish to build the object files and executables in a directory other
than the one containing the source files, here is what you must do differently:

1. Make sure you have a version of Make that supports the VPATH feature.
   (GNU Make supports it, as do Make versions on most BSD systems.)

2. If you have ever run 'configure' in the source directory, you must undo
   the configuration. Do this by running:

   ```
   make distclean
   ```

3. Go to the directory in which you want to build the compiler before
   running 'configure':

   ```
   mkdir gcc-sun3
   ```

```
cd gcc-sun3
```
On systems that do not support symbolic links, this directory must be on the same file system as the source code directory.

4. Specify where to find 'configure' when you run it:
   ```
   ../gcc/configure ...
   ```
   This also tells configure where to find the compiler sources; configure takes the directory from the file name that was used to invoke it. But if you want to be sure, you can specify the source directory with the '--srcdir' option, like this:
   ```
   ../gcc/configure --srcdir=../gcc other options
   ```
   The directory you specify with '--srcdir' need not be the same as the one that configure is found in.

Now, you can run make in that directory. You need not repeat the configuration steps shown above, when ordinary source files change. You must, however, run configure again when the configuration files change, if your system does not support symbolic links.

3.4 Building and Installing a Cross-Compiler

GNU CC can function as a cross-compiler for many machines, but not all.

- Cross-compilers for the Mips as target using the Mips assembler currently do not work, because the auxiliary programs 'mips-tdump.c' and 'mips-tfile.c' can't be compiled on anything but a Mips. It does work to cross compile for a Mips if you use the GNU assembler and linker.

- Cross-compilers between machines with different floating point formats have not all been made to work. GNU CC now has a floating point emulator with which these can work, but each target machine description needs to be updated to take advantage of it.

- Cross-compilation between machines of different word sizes is somewhat problematic and sometimes does not work.

Since GNU CC generates assembler code, you probably need a cross-assembler that GNU CC can run, in order to produce object files. If you want to link on other than the target machine, you need a cross-linker as well. You also need header files and libraries suitable for the target machine that you can install on the host machine.

3.4.1 Steps of Cross-Compilation

To compile and run a program using a cross-compiler involves several steps:

- Run the cross-compiler on the host machine to produce assembler files for the target machine. This requires header files for the target machine.

- Assemble the files produced by the cross-compiler. You can do this either with an assembler on the target machine, or with a cross-assembler on the host machine.

- Link those files to make an executable. You can do this either with a linker on the target machine, or with a cross-linker on the host machine. Whichever machine you use, you need libraries and certain startup files (typically 'crt....o') for the target machine.

It is most convenient to do all of these steps on the same host machine, since then you can do it all with a single invocation of GNU CC. This requires a suitable cross-assembler and cross-linker. For some targets, the GNU assembler and linker are available.

3.4.2 Configuring a Cross-Compiler

To build GNU CC as a cross-compiler, you start out by running 'configure'. Use the '--target=*target*' to specify the target type. If 'configure' was unable to correctly identify the system you are running on, also specify the '--build=*build*' option. For example, here is how to configure for a cross-compiler that produces code for an HP 68030 system running BSD on a system that 'configure' can correctly identify:

```
./configure --target=m68k-hp-bsd4.3
```

3.4.3 Tools and Libraries for a Cross-Compiler

If you have a cross-assembler and cross-linker available, you should install them now. Put them in the directory '/usr/local/*target*/bin'. Here is a table of the tools you should put in this directory:

'as'   This should be the cross-assembler.

'ld'   This should be the cross-linker.

'ar'   This should be the cross-archiver: a program which can manipulate archive files (linker libraries) in the target machine's format.

'ranlib'   This should be a program to construct a symbol table in an archive file.

The installation of GNU CC will find these programs in that directory, and copy or link them to the proper place to for the cross-compiler to find them when run later.

The easiest way to provide these files is to build the Binutils package and GAS. Configure them with the same '--host' and '--target' options that you use for configuring GNU CC, then build and install them. They install their executables automatically into the proper directory. Alas, they do not support all the targets that GNU CC supports.

If you want to install libraries to use with the cross-compiler, such as a standard C library, put them in the directory '/usr/local/*target*/lib'; installation of GNU CC copies all the files in that subdirectory into the proper place for GNU CC to find them and link with them. Here's an example of copying some libraries from a target machine:

```
ftp target-machine
lcd /usr/local/target/lib
cd /lib
get libc.a
cd /usr/lib
get libg.a
get libm.a
quit
```

The precise set of libraries you'll need, and their locations on the target machine, vary depending on its operating system.

Many targets require "start files" such as 'crt0.o' and 'crtn.o' which are linked into each executable; these too should be placed in '/usr/local/*target*/lib'. There may be several alternatives for 'crt0.o', for use with profiling or other compilation options. Check your target's definition of STARTFILE_SPEC to find out what start files it uses. Here's an example of copying these files from a target machine:

```
ftp target-machine
lcd /usr/local/target/lib
prompt
cd /lib
mget *crt*.o
cd /usr/lib
mget *crt*.o
quit
```

3.4.4 'libgcc.a' and Cross-Compilers

Code compiled by GNU CC uses certain runtime support functions implicitly. Some of these functions can be compiled successfully with GNU CC itself, but a few cannot be. These problem functions are in the source file 'libgcc1.c'; the library made from them is called 'libgcc1.a'.

When you build a native compiler, these functions are compiled with some other compiler–the one that you use for bootstrapping GNU CC. Presumably it knows how to open code these operations, or else knows how to call the run-time emulation facilities that the machine comes with. But this approach doesn't work for building a cross-compiler. The compiler that you use for building knows about the host system, not the target system.

So, when you build a cross-compiler you have to supply a suitable library 'libgcc1.a' that does the job it is expected to do.

To compile 'libgcc1.c' with the cross-compiler itself does not work. The functions in this file are supposed to implement arithmetic operations that GNU CC does not know how to open code for your target machine. If these functions are compiled with GNU CC itself, they will compile into infinite recursion.

On any given target, most of these functions are not needed. If GNU CC can open code an arithmetic operation, it will not call these functions to perform the operation. It is possible that on your target machine, none of these functions is needed. If so, you can supply an empty library as 'libgcc1.a'.

Many targets need library support only for multiplication and division. If you are linking with a library that contains functions for multiplication and division, you can tell GNU CC to call them directly by defining the macros MULSI3_LIBCALL, and the like. These macros need to be defined in the target description macro file. For some targets, they are defined already. This may be sufficient to avoid the need for libgcc1.a; if so, you can supply an empty library.

Some targets do not have floating point instructions; they need other functions in 'libgcc1.a', which do floating arithmetic. Recent versions of GNU CC have a file which emulates floating point. With a certain amount of work, you should be able to construct a floating point emulator that can be used as 'libgcc1.a'. Perhaps future versions will contain code to do this automatically and conveniently. That depends on whether someone wants to implement it.

Some embedded targets come with all the necessary 'libgcc1.a' routines written in C or assembler. These targets build 'libgcc1.a' automatically and you do not need to do anything special for them. Other embedded targets do not need any 'libgcc1.a' routines since all the necessary operations are supported by the hardware.

If your target system has another C compiler, you can configure GNU CC as a native compiler on that machine, build just 'libgcc1.a' with 'make libgcc1.a' on that machine, and use the resulting file with the cross-compiler. To do this, execute the following on the target machine:

```
cd target-build-dir
./configure --host=sparc --target=sun3
make libgcc1.a
```

And then this on the host machine:

```
ftp target-machine
binary
cd target-build-dir
get libgcc1.a
quit
```

Another way to provide the functions you need in 'libgcc1.a' is to define the appropriate perform_... macros for those functions. If these definitions do not use the C arithmetic operators that they are meant to implement, you should be able to compile them with the cross-compiler you are building. (If these definitions already exist for your target file, then you are all set.)

To build 'libgcc1.a' using the perform macros, use 'LIBGCC1=libgcc1.a OLDCC=./xgcc' when building the compiler. Otherwise, you should place your replacement library under the name 'libgcc1.a' in the directory in which you will build the cross-compiler, before you run make.

3.4.5 Cross-Compilers and Header Files

If you are cross-compiling a standalone program or a program for an embedded system, then you may not need any header files except the few that are part of GNU CC (and those of your program). However, if you intend to link your program with a standard C library such as 'libc.a', then you probably need to compile with the header files that go with the library you use.

The GNU C compiler does not come with these files, because (1) they are system-specific, and (2) they belong in a C library, not in a compiler.

If the GNU C library supports your target machine, then you can get the header files from there (assuming you actually use the GNU library when you link your program).

If your target machine comes with a C compiler, it probably comes with suitable header files also. If you make these files accessible from the host machine, the cross-compiler can use them also.

Otherwise, you're on your own in finding header files to use when cross-compiling.

When you have found suitable header files, put them in the directory '/usr/local/*target*/include', before building the cross compiler. Then installation will run fixincludes properly and install the corrected versions of the header files where the compiler will use them.

Provide the header files before you build the cross-compiler, because the build stage actually runs the cross-compiler to produce parts of 'libgcc.a'. (These are the parts that *can* be compiled with GNU CC.) Some of them need suitable header files.

Here's an example showing how to copy the header files from a target machine. On the target machine, do this:

```
(cd /usr/include; tar cf - .) > tarfile
```

Then, on the host machine, do this:

```
ftp target-machine
lcd /usr/local/target/include
get tarfile
quit
tar xf tarfile
```

3.4.6 Actually Building the Cross-Compiler

Now you can proceed just as for compiling a single-machine compiler through the step of building stage 1. If you have not provided some sort of 'libgcc1.a', then compilation will give up at the point where it needs that file, printing a suitable error message. If you do provide 'libgcc1.a', then building the compiler will automatically compile and link a test program called 'libgcc1-test'; if you get errors in the linking, it means that not all of the necessary routines in 'libgcc1.a' are available.

You must provide the header file 'float.h'. One way to do this is to compile 'enquire' and run it on your target machine. The job of 'enquire' is to run on the target machine and figure out by experiment the nature of its floating point representation. 'enquire' records its findings in the header file 'float.h'. If you can't produce this file by running 'enquire' on the target machine, then you will need to come up with a suitable 'float.h' in some other way (or else, avoid using it in your programs).

Do not try to build stage 2 for a cross-compiler. It doesn't work to rebuild GNU CC as a cross-compiler using the cross-compiler, because that would produce a program that runs on the target machine, not on the host. For example, if you compile a 386-to-68030 cross-compiler with itself, the result will not be right either for the 386 (because it was compiled into 68030 code) or for the 68030 (because it was configured for a 386 as the host). If you want to compile GNU CC into 68030 code, whether you compile it on a 68030 or with a cross-compiler on a 386, you must specify a 68030 as the host when you configure it.

To install the cross-compiler, use 'make install', as usual.

3.5 Installing GNU CC on the Sun

On Solaris, do not use the linker or other tools in '/usr/ucb' to build GNU CC. Use /usr/ccs/bin.

If the assembler reports 'Error: misaligned data' when bootstrapping, you are probably using an obsolete version of the GNU assembler. Upgrade to the latest version of GNU binutils, or use the Solaris assembler.

Make sure the environment variable FLOAT_OPTION is not set when you compile 'libgcc.a'. If this option were set to f68881 when 'libgcc.a' is compiled, the resulting code would demand to be linked with a special startup file and would not link properly without special pains.

There is a bug in alloca in certain versions of the Sun library. To avoid this bug, install the binaries of GNU CC that were compiled by GNU CC. They use alloca as a built-in function and never the one in the library.

Some versions of the Sun compiler crash when compiling GNU CC. The problem is a segmentation fault in cpp. This problem seems to be due to the bulk of data in the environment variables. You may be able to avoid it by using the following command to compile GNU CC with Sun CC:

```
make CC="TERMCAP=x OBJS=x LIBFUNCS=x STAGESTUFF=x cc"
```

SunOS 4.1.3 and 4.1.3_U1 have bugs that can cause intermittent core dumps when compiling GNU CC. A common symptom is an internal compiler error which does not recur if you run it again. To fix the problem, install Sun recommended patch 100726 (for SunOS 4.1.3) or 101508 (for SunOS 4.1.3_U1), or upgrade to a later SunOS release.

3.6 Installing GNU CC on VMS

The VMS version of GNU CC is distributed in a backup saveset containing both source code and precompiled binaries.

To install the 'gcc' command so you can use the compiler easily, in the same manner as you use the VMS C compiler, you must install the VMS CLD file for GNU CC as follows:

1. Define the VMS logical names 'GNU_CC' and 'GNU_CC_INCLUDE' to point to the directories where the GNU CC executables ('gcc-cpp.exe', 'gcc-cc1.exe', etc.) and the C include files are kept respectively. This should be done with the commands:

   ```
   $ assign /system /translation=concealed -
     disk:[gcc.] gnu_cc
   $ assign /system /translation=concealed -
     disk:[gcc.include.] gnu_cc_include
   ```

   with the appropriate disk and directory names. These commands can be placed in your system startup file so they will be executed whenever the machine is rebooted. You may, if you choose, do this via the 'GCC_INSTALL.COM' script in the '[GCC]' directory.

2. Install the 'GCC' command with the command line:

   ```
   $ set command /table=sys$common:[syslib]dcltables -
     /output=sys$common:[syslib]dcltables gnu_cc:[000000]gcc
   $ install replace sys$common:[syslib]dcltables
   ```

3. To install the help file, do the following:

   ```
   $ library/help sys$library:helplib.hlb gcc.hlp
   ```

   Now you can invoke the compiler with a command like 'gcc /verbose file.c', which is equivalent to the command 'gcc -v -c file.c' in Unix.

If you wish to use GNU C++ you must first install GNU CC, and then perform the following steps:

1. Define the VMS logical name 'GNU_GXX_INCLUDE' to point to the directory where the preprocessor will search for the C++ header files. This can be done with the command:

   ```
   $ assign /system /translation=concealed -
     disk:[gcc.gxx_include.] gnu_gxx_include
   ```

with the appropriate disk and directory name. If you are going to be using a C++ runtime library, this is where its install procedure will install its header files.

2. Obtain the file 'gcc-cc1plus.exe', and place this in the same directory that 'gcc-cc1.exe' is kept.

The GNU C++ compiler can be invoked with a command like 'gcc /plus /verbose file.cc', which is equivalent to the command 'g++ -v -c file.cc' in Unix.

We try to put corresponding binaries and sources on the VMS distribution tape. But sometimes the binaries will be from an older version than the sources, because we don't always have time to update them. (Use the '/version' option to determine the version number of the binaries and compare it with the source file 'version.c' to tell whether this is so.) In this case, you should use the binaries you get to recompile the sources. If you must recompile, here is how:

1. Execute the command procedure 'vmsconfig.com' to set up the files 'tm.h', 'config.h', 'aux-output.c', and 'md.', and to create files 'tconfig.h' and 'hconfig.h'. This procedure also creates several linker option files used by 'make-cc1.com' and a data file used by 'make-l2.com'.

   ```
   $ @vmsconfig.com
   ```

2. Setup the logical names and command tables as defined above. In addition, define the VMS logical name 'GNU_BISON' to point at the to the directories where the Bison executable is kept. This should be done with the command:

   ```
   $ assign /system /translation=concealed -
     disk:[bison.] gnu_bison
   ```

   You may, if you choose, use the 'INSTALL_BISON.COM' script in the '[BISON]' directory.

3. Install the 'BISON' command with the command line:

   ```
   $ set command /table=sys$common:[syslib]dcltables -
   /output=sys$common:[syslib]dcltables -
   gnu_bison:[000000]bison
   $ install replace sys$common:[syslib]dcltables
   ```

4. Type '@make-gcc' to recompile everything (alternatively, submit the file 'make-gcc.com' to a batch queue). If you wish to build the GNU C++ compiler as well as the GNU CC compiler, you must first edit 'make-gcc.com' and follow the instructions that appear in the comments.

5. In order to use GCC, you need a library of functions which GCC compiled code will call to perform certain tasks, and these functions are defined in the file 'libgcc2.c'. To compile this you should use

the command procedure 'make-12.com', which will generate the library 'libgcc2.olb'. 'libgcc2.olb' should be built using the compiler built from the same distribution that 'libgcc2.c' came from, and 'make-gcc.com' will automatically do all of this for you.

To install the library, use the following commands:

```
$ library gnu_cc:[000000]gcclib/delete=(new,eprintf)
$ library gnu_cc:[000000]gcclib/delete=L_*
$ library libgcc2/extract=*/output=libgcc2.obj
$ library gnu_cc:[000000]gcclib libgcc2.obj
```

The first command simply removes old modules that will be replaced with modules from 'libgcc2' under different module names. The modules **new** and **eprintf** may not actually be present in your 'gcclib.olb'—if the VMS librarian complains about those modules not being present, simply ignore the message and continue on with the next command. The second command removes the modules that came from the previous version of the library 'libgcc2.c'.

Whenever you update the compiler on your system, you should also update the library with the above procedure.

6. You may wish to build GCC in such a way that no files are written to the directory where the source files reside. An example would be the when the source files are on a read-only disk. In these cases, execute the following DCL commands (substituting your actual path names):

```
$ assign dua0:[gcc.build_dir.]/translation=concealed, -
         dua1:[gcc.source_dir.]/translation=concealed  gcc_build
$ set default gcc_build:[000000]
```

where the directory 'dua1:[gcc.source_dir]' contains the source code, and the directory 'dua0:[gcc.build_dir]' is meant to contain all of the generated object files and executables. Once you have done this, you can proceed building GCC as described above. (Keep in mind that 'gcc_build' is a rooted logical name, and thus the device names in each element of the search list must be an actual physical device name rather than another rooted logical name).

7. **If you are building GNU CC with a previous version of GNU CC, you also should check to see that you have the newest version of the assembler**. In particular, GNU CC version 2 treats global constant variables slightly differently from GNU CC version 1, and GAS version 1.38.1 does not have the patches required to work with GCC version 2. If you use GAS 1.38.1, then **extern const** variables will not have the read-only bit set, and the linker will generate warning messages about mismatched psect attributes for these variables. These warning messages are merely a nuisance, and can safely be ignored.

If you are compiling with a version of GNU CC older than 1.33, specify '/DEFINE=("inline=")' as an option in all the compilations. This requires editing all the **gcc** commands in 'make-cc1.com'. (The older versions had problems supporting `inline`.) Once you have a working 1.33 or newer GNU CC, you can change this file back.

8. If you want to build GNU CC with the VAX C compiler, you will need to make minor changes in 'make-cccp.com' and 'make-cc1.com' to choose alternate definitions of `CC`, `CFLAGS`, and `LIBS`. See comments in those files. However, you must also have a working version of the GNU assembler (GNU as, aka GAS) as it is used as the back-end for GNU CC to produce binary object modules and is not included in the GNU CC sources. GAS is also needed to compile 'libgcc2' in order to build 'gcclib' (see above); 'make-l2.com' expects to be able to find it operational in 'gnu_cc:[000000]gnu-as.exe'.

To use GNU CC on VMS, you need the VMS driver programs 'gcc.exe', 'gcc.com', and 'gcc.cld'. They are distributed with the VMS binaries ('gcc-vms') rather than the GNU CC sources. GAS is also included in 'gcc-vms', as is Bison.

Once you have successfully built GNU CC with VAX C, you should use the resulting compiler to rebuild itself. Before doing this, be sure to restore the `CC`, `CFLAGS`, and `LIBS` definitions in 'make-cccp.com' and 'make-cc1.com'. The second generation compiler will be able to take advantage of many optimizations that must be suppressed when building with other compilers.

Under previous versions of GNU CC, the generated code would occasionally give strange results when linked with the sharable 'VAXCRTL' library. Now this should work.

Even with this version, however, GNU CC itself should not be linked with the sharable 'VAXCRTL'. The version of `qsort` in 'VAXCRTL' has a bug (known to be present in VMS versions V4.6 through V5.5) which causes the compiler to fail.

The executables are generated by 'make-cc1.com' and 'make-cccp.com' use the object library version of 'VAXCRTL' in order to make use of the `qsort` routine in 'gcclib.olb'. If you wish to link the compiler executables with the shareable image version of 'VAXCRTL', you should edit the file 'tm.h' (created by 'vmsconfig.com') to define the macro `QSORT_WORKAROUND`.

`QSORT_WORKAROUND` is always defined when GNU CC is compiled with VAX C, to avoid a problem in case 'gcclib.olb' is not yet available.

3.7 `collect2`

GNU CC uses a utility called `collect2` on nearly all systems to arrange to call various initialization functions at start time.

The program `collect2` works by linking the program once and looking through the linker output file for symbols with particular names indicating they are constructor functions. If it finds any, it creates a new temporary

'.c' file containing a table of them, compiles it, and links the program a second time including that file.

The actual calls to the constructors are carried out by a subroutine called `__main`, which is called (automatically) at the beginning of the body of `main` (provided `main` was compiled with GNU CC). Calling `__main` is necessary, even when compiling C code, to allow linking C and C++ object code together. (If you use '`-nostdlib`', you get an unresolved reference to `__main`, since it's defined in the standard GCC library. Include '`-lgcc`' at the end of your compiler command line to resolve this reference.)

The program `collect2` is installed as `ld` in the directory where the passes of the compiler are installed. When `collect2` needs to find the *real* `ld`, it tries the following file names:

- '`real-ld`' in the directories listed in the compiler's search directories.
- '`real-ld`' in the directories listed in the environment variable `PATH`.
- The file specified in the `REAL_LD_FILE_NAME` configuration macro, if specified.
- '`ld`' in the compiler's search directories, except that `collect2` will not execute itself recursively.
- '`ld`' in `PATH`.

"The compiler's search directories" means all the directories where `gcc` searches for passes of the compiler. This includes directories that you specify with '`-B`'.

Cross-compilers search a little differently:

- '`real-ld`' in the compiler's search directories.
- '*target*-`real-ld`' in `PATH`.
- The file specified in the `REAL_LD_FILE_NAME` configuration macro, if specified.
- '`ld`' in the compiler's search directories.
- '*target*-`ld`' in `PATH`.

`collect2` explicitly avoids running `ld` using the file name under which `collect2` itself was invoked. In fact, it remembers up a list of such names—in case one copy of `collect2` finds another copy (or version) of `collect2` installed as `ld` in a second place in the search path.

`collect2` searches for the utilities `nm` and `strip` using the same algorithm as above for `ld`.

3.8 Standard Header File Directories

`GCC_INCLUDE_DIR` means the same thing for native and cross. It is where GNU CC stores its private include files, and also where GNU CC stores the fixed include files. A cross compiled GNU CC runs `fixincludes` on the header files in '`$(tooldir)/include`'. (If the cross compilation header files need to be fixed, they must be installed before GNU CC is built. If the cross compilation header files are already suitable for ANSI C and GNU CC, nothing special need be done).

GPLUSPLUS_INCLUDE_DIR means the same thing for native and cross. It is where g++ looks first for header files. The C++ library installs only target independent header files in that directory.

LOCAL_INCLUDE_DIR is used only for a native compiler. It is normally '/usr/local/include'. GNU CC searches this directory so that users can install header files in '/usr/local/include'.

CROSS_INCLUDE_DIR is used only for a cross compiler. GNU CC doesn't install anything there.

TOOL_INCLUDE_DIR is used for both native and cross compilers. It is the place for other packages to install header files that GNU CC will use. For a cross-compiler, this is the equivalent of '/usr/include'. When you build a cross-compiler, fixincludes processes any header files in this directory.

4 Extensions to the C Language Family

GNU C provides several language features not found in ANSI standard
C. (The '-pedantic' option directs GNU CC to print a warning message if
any of these features is used.) To test for the availability of these features
in conditional compilation, check for a predefined macro __GNUC__, which is
always defined under GNU CC.

These extensions are available in C and Objective C. Most of them are
also available in C++. See Chapter 5 [Extensions to the C++ Language],
page 207, for extensions that apply *only* to C++.

4.1 Statements and Declarations in Expressions

A compound statement enclosed in parentheses may appear as an expression in GNU C. This allows you to use loops, switches, and local variables
within an expression.

Recall that a compound statement is a sequence of statements surrounded
by braces; in this construct, parentheses go around the braces. For example:

```
({ int y = foo (); int z;
   if (y > 0) z = y;
   else z = - y;
   z; })
```

is a valid (though slightly more complex than necessary) expression for the
absolute value of foo ().

The last thing in the compound statement should be an expression followed by a semicolon; the value of this subexpression serves as the value of
the entire construct. (If you use some other kind of statement last within
the braces, the construct has type **void**, and thus effectively no value.)

This feature is especially useful in making macro definitions "safe" (so
that they evaluate each operand exactly once). For example, the "maximum"
function is commonly defined as a macro in standard C as follows:

```
#define max(a,b) ((a) > (b) ? (a) : (b))
```

But this definition computes either *a* or *b* twice, with bad results if the
operand has side effects. In GNU C, if you know the type of the operands
(here let's assume **int**), you can define the macro safely as follows:

```
#define maxint(a,b) \
    ({int _a = (a), _b = (b); _a > _b ? _a : _b; })
```

Embedded statements are not allowed in constant expressions, such as
the value of an enumeration constant, the width of a bit field, or the initial
value of a static variable.

If you don't know the type of the operand, you can still do this, but you
must use **typeof** (see Section 4.7 [Typeof], page 167) or type naming (see
Section 4.6 [Naming Types], page 166).

4.2 Locally Declared Labels

Each statement expression is a scope in which *local labels* can be declared. A local label is simply an identifier; you can jump to it with an ordinary `goto` statement, but only from within the statement expression it belongs to.

A local label declaration looks like this:

　　`__label__` *label*;

or

　　`__label__` *label1*, *label2*, `...`;

Local label declarations must come at the beginning of the statement expression, right after the '`({`', before any ordinary declarations.

The label declaration defines the label *name*, but does not define the label itself. You must do this in the usual way, with *label*:, within the statements of the statement expression.

The local label feature is useful because statement expressions are often used in macros. If the macro contains nested loops, a `goto` can be useful for breaking out of them. However, an ordinary label whose scope is the whole function cannot be used: if the macro can be expanded several times in one function, the label will be multiply defined in that function. A local label avoids this problem. For example:

```
#define SEARCH(array, target)                       \
({                                                   \
  __label__ found;                                   \
  typeof (target) _SEARCH_target = (target);         \
  typeof (*(array)) *_SEARCH_array = (array);        \
  int i, j;                                          \
  int value;                                         \
  for (i = 0; i < max; i++)                          \
    for (j = 0; j < max; j++)                        \
      if (_SEARCH_array[i][j] == _SEARCH_target)     \
        { value = i; goto found; }                   \
  value = -1;                                        \
 found:                                              \
  value;                                             \
})
```

4.3 Labels as Values

You can get the address of a label defined in the current function (or a containing function) with the unary operator '`&&`'. The value has type `void *`. This value is a constant and can be used wherever a constant of that type is valid. For example:

```
void *ptr;
...
ptr = &&foo;
```

To use these values, you need to be able to jump to one. This is done with the computed goto statement[1], goto *exp;. For example,

```
goto *ptr;
```

Any expression of type void * is allowed.

One way of using these constants is in initializing a static array that will serve as a jump table:

```
static void *array[] = { &&foo, &&bar, &&hack };
```

Then you can select a label with indexing, like this:

```
goto *array[i];
```

Note that this does not check whether the subscript is in bounds—array indexing in C never does that.

Such an array of label values serves a purpose much like that of the switch statement. The switch statement is cleaner, so use that rather than an array unless the problem does not fit a switch statement very well.

Another use of label values is in an interpreter for threaded code. The labels within the interpreter function can be stored in the threaded code for super-fast dispatching.

You can use this mechanism to jump to code in a different function. If you do that, totally unpredictable things will happen. The best way to avoid this is to store the label address only in automatic variables and never pass it as an argument.

4.4 Nested Functions

A *nested function* is a function defined inside another function. (Nested functions are not supported for GNU C++.) The nested function's name is local to the block where it is defined. For example, here we define a nested function named square, and call it twice:

```
foo (double a, double b)
{
  double square (double z) { return z * z; }

  return square (a) + square (b);
}
```

The nested function can access all the variables of the containing function that are visible at the point of its definition. This is called *lexical scoping*.

---

[1] The analogous feature in Fortran is called an assigned goto, but that name seems inappropriate in C, where one can do more than simply store label addresses in label variables.

For example, here we show a nested function which uses an inherited variable named `offset`:

```
bar (int *array, int offset, int size)
{
  int access (int *array, int index)
    { return array[index + offset]; }
  int i;
  ...
  for (i = 0; i < size; i++)
    ... access (array, i) ...
}
```

Nested function definitions are permitted within functions in the places where variable definitions are allowed; that is, in any block, before the first statement in the block.

It is possible to call the nested function from outside the scope of its name by storing its address or passing the address to another function:

```
hack (int *array, int size)
{
  void store (int index, int value)
    { array[index] = value; }

  intermediate (store, size);
}
```

Here, the function `intermediate` receives the address of `store` as an argument. If `intermediate` calls `store`, the arguments given to `store` are used to store into `array`. But this technique works only so long as the containing function (`hack`, in this example) does not exit.

If you try to call the nested function through its address after the containing function has exited, all hell will break loose. If you try to call it after a containing scope level has exited, and if it refers to some of the variables that are no longer in scope, you may be lucky, but it's not wise to take the risk. If, however, the nested function does not refer to anything that has gone out of scope, you should be safe.

GNU CC implements taking the address of a nested function using a technique called *trampolines*. A paper describing them is available as 'http://master.debian.org/~karlheg/Usenix88-lexic.pdf'.

A nested function can jump to a label inherited from a containing function, provided the label was explicitly declared in the containing function (see Section 4.2 [Local Labels], page 162). Such a jump returns instantly to the containing function, exiting the nested function which did the `goto` and any intermediate functions as well. Here is an example:

```
bar (int *array, int offset, int size)
{
  __label__ failure;
  int access (int *array, int index)
    {
      if (index > size)
        goto failure;
      return array[index + offset];
    }
  int i;
  ...
  for (i = 0; i < size; i++)
    ... access (array, i) ...
  ...
  return 0;

 /* Control comes here from access
    if it detects an error.   */
 failure:
  return -1;
}
```

A nested function always has internal linkage. Declaring one with **extern** is erroneous. If you need to declare the nested function before its definition, use **auto** (which is otherwise meaningless for function declarations).

```
bar (int *array, int offset, int size)
{
  __label__ failure;
  auto int access (int *, int);
  ...
  int access (int *array, int index)
    {
      if (index > size)
        goto failure;
      return array[index + offset];
    }
  ...
}
```

4.5 Constructing Function Calls

Using the built-in functions described below, you can record the arguments a function received, and call another function with the same arguments, without knowing the number or types of the arguments.

You can also record the return value of that function call, and later return that value, without knowing what data type the function tried to return (as long as your caller expects that data type).

`__builtin_apply_args ()`

> This built-in function returns a pointer of type `void *` to data describing how to perform a call with the same arguments as were passed to the current function.
>
> The function saves the arg pointer register, structure value address, and all registers that might be used to pass arguments to a function into a block of memory allocated on the stack. Then it returns the address of that block.

`__builtin_apply (`*function*`, `*arguments*`, `*size*`)`

> This built-in function invokes *function* (type `void (*)()`) with a copy of the parameters described by *arguments* (type `void *`) and *size* (type `int`).
>
> The value of *arguments* should be the value returned by `__builtin_apply_args`. The argument *size* specifies the size of the stack argument data, in bytes.
>
> This function returns a pointer of type `void *` to data describing how to return whatever value was returned by *function*. The data is saved in a block of memory allocated on the stack.
>
> It is not always simple to compute the proper value for *size*. The value is used by `__builtin_apply` to compute the amount of data that should be pushed on the stack and copied from the incoming argument area.

`__builtin_return (`*result*`)`

> This built-in function returns the value described by *result* from the containing function. You should specify, for *result*, a value returned by `__builtin_apply`.

4.6 Naming an Expression's Type

You can give a name to the type of an expression using a `typedef` declaration with an initializer. Here is how to define *name* as a type name for the type of *exp*:

```
typedef name = exp;
```

This is useful in conjunction with the statements-within-expressions feature. Here is how the two together can be used to define a safe "maximum" macro that operates on any arithmetic type:

```
#define max(a,b) \
  ({typedef _ta = (a), _tb = (b);  \
    _ta _a = (a); _tb _b = (b);     \
```

```
_a > _b ? _a : _b; })
```

The reason for using names that start with underscores for the local variables is to avoid conflicts with variable names that occur within the expressions that are substituted for a and b. Eventually we hope to design a new form of declaration syntax that allows you to declare variables whose scopes start only after their initializers; this will be a more reliable way to prevent such conflicts.

4.7 Referring to a Type with `typeof`

Another way to refer to the type of an expression is with `typeof`. The syntax of using of this keyword looks like `sizeof`, but the construct acts semantically like a type name defined with `typedef`.

There are two ways of writing the argument to `typeof`: with an expression or with a type. Here is an example with an expression:

```
typeof (x[0](1))
```

This assumes that x is an array of functions; the type described is that of the values of the functions.

Here is an example with a typename as the argument:

```
typeof (int *)
```

Here the type described is that of pointers to `int`.

If you are writing a header file that must work when included in ANSI C programs, write `__typeof__` instead of `typeof`. See Section 4.35 [Alternate Keywords], page 202.

A `typeof`-construct can be used anywhere a typedef name could be used. For example, you can use it in a declaration, in a cast, or inside of `sizeof` or `typeof`.

- This declares y with the type of what x points to.

    ```
    typeof (*x) y;
    ```

- This declares y as an array of such values.

    ```
    typeof (*x) y[4];
    ```

- This declares y as an array of pointers to characters:

    ```
    typeof (typeof (char *)[4]) y;
    ```

    It is equivalent to the following traditional C declaration:

    ```
    char *y[4];
    ```

To see the meaning of the declaration using `typeof`, and why it might be a useful way to write, let's rewrite it with these macros:

```
#define pointer(T)  typeof(T *)
#define array(T, N) typeof(T [N])
```

Now the declaration can be rewritten this way:

```
array (pointer (char), 4) y;
```
Thus, `array (pointer (char), 4)` is the type of arrays of 4 pointers to char.

4.8 Generalized Lvalues

Compound expressions, conditional expressions and casts are allowed as lvalues provided their operands are lvalues. This means that you can take their addresses or store values into them.

Standard C++ allows compound expressions and conditional expressions as lvalues, and permits casts to reference type, so use of this extension is deprecated for C++ code.

For example, a compound expression can be assigned, provided the last expression in the sequence is an lvalue. These two expressions are equivalent:

```
(a, b) += 5
a, (b += 5)
```

Similarly, the address of the compound expression can be taken. These two expressions are equivalent:

```
&(a, b)
a, &b
```

A conditional expression is a valid lvalue if its type is not void and the true and false branches are both valid lvalues. For example, these two expressions are equivalent:

```
(a ? b : c) = 5
(a ? b = 5 : (c = 5))
```

A cast is a valid lvalue if its operand is an lvalue. A simple assignment whose left-hand side is a cast works by converting the right-hand side first to the specified type, then to the type of the inner left-hand side expression. After this is stored, the value is converted back to the specified type to become the value of the assignment. Thus, if `a` has type `char *`, the following two expressions are equivalent:

```
(int)a = 5
(int)(a = (char *)(int)5)
```

An assignment-with-arithmetic operation such as '+=' applied to a cast performs the arithmetic using the type resulting from the cast, and then continues as in the previous case. Therefore, these two expressions are equivalent:

```
(int)a += 5
(int)(a = (char *)(int) ((int)a + 5))
```

You cannot take the address of an lvalue cast, because the use of its address would not work out coherently. Suppose that `&(int)f` were permitted, where `f` has type `float`. Then the following statement would try to store an integer bit-pattern where a floating point number belongs:

```
*&(int)f = 1;
```

This is quite different from what `(int)f = 1` would do—that would convert 1 to floating point and store it. Rather than cause this inconsistency, we think it is better to prohibit use of '&' on a cast.

If you really do want an `int *` pointer with the address of `f`, you can simply write `(int *)&f`.

4.9 Conditionals with Omitted Operands

The middle operand in a conditional expression may be omitted. Then if the first operand is nonzero, its value is the value of the conditional expression.

Therefore, the expression

```
x ? : y
```

has the value of `x` if that is nonzero; otherwise, the value of `y`.

This example is perfectly equivalent to

```
x ? x : y
```

In this simple case, the ability to omit the middle operand is not especially useful. When it becomes useful is when the first operand does, or may (if it is a macro argument), contain a side effect. Then repeating the operand in the middle would perform the side effect twice. Omitting the middle operand uses the value already computed without the undesirable effects of recomputing it.

4.10 Double-Word Integers

GNU C supports data types for integers that are twice as long as `int`. Simply write `long long int` for a signed integer, or `unsigned long long int` for an unsigned integer. To make an integer constant of type `long long int`, add the suffix LL to the integer. To make an integer constant of type `unsigned long long int`, add the suffix ULL to the integer.

You can use these types in arithmetic like any other integer types. Addition, subtraction, and bitwise boolean operations on these types are opencoded on all types of machines. Multiplication is open-coded if the machine supports fullword-to-doubleword a widening multiply instruction. Division and shifts are open-coded only on machines that provide special support. The operations that are not open-coded use special library routines that come with GNU CC.

There may be pitfalls when you use `long long` types for function arguments, unless you declare function prototypes. If a function expects type `int` for its argument, and you pass a value of type `long long int`, confusion will result because the caller and the subroutine will disagree about the number of bytes for the argument. Likewise, if the function expects **long**

`long int` and you pass `int`. The best way to avoid such problems is to use prototypes.

4.11 Complex Numbers

GNU C supports complex data types. You can declare both complex integer types and complex floating types, using the keyword `__complex__`.

For example, '`__complex__ double x;`' declares `x` as a variable whose real part and imaginary part are both of type `double`. '`__complex__ short int y;`' declares `y` to have real and imaginary parts of type `short int`; this is not likely to be useful, but it shows that the set of complex types is complete.

To write a constant with a complex data type, use the suffix 'i' or 'j' (either one; they are equivalent). For example, `2.5fi` has type `__complex__ float` and `3i` has type `__complex__ int`. Such a constant always has a pure imaginary value, but you can form any complex value you like by adding one to a real constant.

To extract the real part of a complex-valued expression *exp*, write `__real__` *exp*. Likewise, use `__imag__` to extract the imaginary part.

The operator '~' performs complex conjugation when used on a value with a complex type.

GNU CC can allocate complex automatic variables in a noncontiguous fashion; it's even possible for the real part to be in a register while the imaginary part is on the stack (or vice-versa). None of the supported debugging info formats has a way to represent noncontiguous allocation like this, so GNU CC describes a noncontiguous complex variable as if it were two separate variables of noncomplex type. If the variable's actual name is `foo`, the two fictitious variables are named `foo$real` and `foo$imag`. You can examine and set these two fictitious variables with your debugger.

A future version of GDB will know how to recognize such pairs and treat them as a single variable with a complex type.

4.12 Hex Floats

GNU CC recognizes floating-point numbers written not only in the usual decimal notation, such as `1.55e1`, but also numbers such as `0x1.fp3` written in hexadecimal format. In that format the `0x` hex introducer and the `p` or `P` exponent field are mandatory. The exponent is a decimal number that indicates the power of 2 by which the significand part will be multiplied. Thus `0x1.f` is 1 15/16, `p3` multiplies it by 8, and the value of `0x1.fp3` is the same as `1.55e1`.

Unlike for floating-point numbers in the decimal notation the exponent is always required in the hexadecimal notation. Otherwise the compiler would not be able to resolve the ambiguity of, e.g., `0x1.f`. This could mean `1.0f` or 1.9375 since f is also the extension for floating-point constants of type float.

4.13 Arrays of Length Zero

Zero-length arrays are allowed in GNU C. They are very useful as the last element of a structure which is really a header for a variable-length object:

```
struct line {
  int length;
  char contents[0];
};

{
  struct line *thisline = (struct line *)
    malloc (sizeof (struct line) + this_length);
  thisline->length = this_length;
}
```

In standard C, you would have to give contents a length of 1, which means either you waste space or complicate the argument to malloc.

4.14 Arrays of Variable Length

Variable-length automatic arrays are allowed in GNU C. These arrays are declared like any other automatic arrays, but with a length that is not a constant expression. The storage is allocated at the point of declaration and deallocated when the brace-level is exited. For example:

```
FILE *
concat_fopen (char *s1, char *s2, char *mode)
{
  char str[strlen (s1) + strlen (s2) + 1];
  strcpy (str, s1);
  strcat (str, s2);
  return fopen (str, mode);
}
```

Jumping or breaking out of the scope of the array name deallocates the storage. Jumping into the scope is not allowed; you get an error message for it.

You can use the function alloca to get an effect much like variable-length arrays. The function alloca is available in many other C implementations (but not in all). On the other hand, variable-length arrays are more elegant.

There are other differences between these two methods. Space allocated with alloca exists until the containing *function* returns. The space for a variable-length array is deallocated as soon as the array name's scope ends.

(If you use both variable-length arrays and `alloca` in the same function, deallocation of a variable-length array will also deallocate anything more recently allocated with `alloca`.)

You can also use variable-length arrays as arguments to functions:

```
struct entry
tester (int len, char data[len][len])
{
  ...
}
```

The length of an array is computed once when the storage is allocated and is remembered for the scope of the array in case you access it with `sizeof`.

If you want to pass the array first and the length afterward, you can use a forward declaration in the parameter list—another GNU extension.

```
struct entry
tester (int len; char data[len][len], int len)
{
  ...
}
```

The 'int len' before the semicolon is a *parameter forward declaration*, and it serves the purpose of making the name `len` known when the declaration of `data` is parsed.

You can write any number of such parameter forward declarations in the parameter list. They can be separated by commas or semicolons, but the last one must end with a semicolon, which is followed by the "real" parameter declarations. Each forward declaration must match a "real" declaration in parameter name and data type.

4.15 Macros with Variable Numbers of Arguments

In GNU C, a macro can accept a variable number of arguments, much as a function can. The syntax for defining the macro looks much like that used for a function. Here is an example:

```
#define eprintf(format, args...)  \
  fprintf (stderr, format , ## args)
```

Here `args` is a *rest argument*: it takes in zero or more arguments, as many as the call contains. All of them plus the commas between them form the value of `args`, which is substituted into the macro body where `args` is used. Thus, we have this expansion:

```
eprintf ("%s:%d: ", input_file_name, line_number)
↦
  fprintf (stderr, "%s:%d: " , input_file_name, line_number)
```

Note that the comma after the string constant comes from the definition of `eprintf`, whereas the last comma comes from the value of `args`.

The reason for using '##' is to handle the case when `args` matches no arguments at all. In this case, `args` has an empty value. In this case, the second comma in the definition becomes an embarrassment: if it got through to the expansion of the macro, we would get something like this:

```
fprintf (stderr, "success!\n" , )
```

which is invalid C syntax. '##' gets rid of the comma, so we get the following instead:

```
fprintf (stderr, "success!\n")
```

This is a special feature of the GNU C preprocessor: '##' before a rest argument that is empty discards the preceding sequence of non-whitespace characters from the macro definition. (If another macro argument precedes, none of it is discarded.)

It might be better to discard the last preprocessor token instead of the last preceding sequence of non-whitespace characters; in fact, we may someday change this feature to do so. We advise you to write the macro definition so that the preceding sequence of non-whitespace characters is just a single token, so that the meaning will not change if we change the definition of this feature.

4.16 Non-Lvalue Arrays May Have Subscripts

Subscripting is allowed on arrays that are not lvalues, even though the unary '&' operator is not. For example, this is valid in GNU C though not valid in other C dialects:

```
struct foo {int a[4];};

struct foo f();

bar (int index)
{
  return f().a[index];
}
```

4.17 Arithmetic on `void`- and Function-Pointers

In GNU C, addition and subtraction operations are supported on pointers to `void` and on pointers to functions. This is done by treating the size of a `void` or of a function as 1.

A consequence of this is that `sizeof` is also allowed on `void` and on function types, and returns 1.

The option '-Wpointer-arith' requests a warning if these extensions are used.

4.18 Non-Constant Initializers

As in standard C++, the elements of an aggregate initializer for an automatic variable are not required to be constant expressions in GNU C. Here is an example of an initializer with run-time varying elements:

```
foo (float f, float g)
{
  float beat_freqs[2] = { f-g, f+g };
  ...
}
```

4.19 Constructor Expressions

GNU C supports constructor expressions. A constructor looks like a cast containing an initializer. Its value is an object of the type specified in the cast, containing the elements specified in the initializer.

Usually, the specified type is a structure. Assume that **struct foo** and **structure** are declared as shown:

```
struct foo {int a; char b[2];} structure;
```

Here is an example of constructing a **struct foo** with a constructor:

```
structure = ((struct foo) {x + y, 'a', 0});
```

This is equivalent to writing the following:

```
{
  struct foo temp = {x + y, 'a', 0};
  structure = temp;
}
```

You can also construct an array. If all the elements of the constructor are (made up of) simple constant expressions, suitable for use in initializers, then the constructor is an lvalue and can be coerced to a pointer to its first element, as shown here:

```
char **foo = (char *[]) { "x", "y", "z" };
```

Array constructors whose elements are not simple constants are not very useful, because the constructor is not an lvalue. There are only two valid ways to use it: to subscript it, or initialize an array variable with it. The former is probably slower than a **switch** statement, while the latter does the same thing an ordinary C initializer would do. Here is an example of subscripting an array constructor:

```
output = ((int[]) { 2, x, 28 }) [input];
```

Constructor expressions for scalar types and union types are is also allowed, but then the constructor expression is equivalent to a cast.

4.20 Labeled Elements in Initializers

Standard C requires the elements of an initializer to appear in a fixed order, the same as the order of the elements in the array or structure being initialized.

In GNU C you can give the elements in any order, specifying the array indices or structure field names they apply to. This extension is not implemented in GNU C++.

To specify an array index, write '[index]' or '[index] =' before the element value. For example,

```
int a[6] = { [4] 29, [2] = 15 };
```

is equivalent to

```
int a[6] = { 0, 0, 15, 0, 29, 0 };
```

The index values must be constant expressions, even if the array being initialized is automatic.

To initialize a range of elements to the same value, write '[first ... last] = value'. For example,

```
int widths[] = { [0 ... 9] = 1, [10 ... 99] = 2, [100] = 3 };
```

Note that the length of the array is the highest value specified plus one.

In a structure initializer, specify the name of a field to initialize with 'fieldname:' before the element value. For example, given the following structure,

```
struct point { int x, y; };
```

the following initialization

```
struct point p = { y: yvalue, x: xvalue };
```

is equivalent to

```
struct point p = { xvalue, yvalue };
```

Another syntax which has the same meaning is '.fieldname ='., as shown here:

```
struct point p = { .y = yvalue, .x = xvalue };
```

You can also use an element label (with either the colon syntax or the period-equal syntax) when initializing a union, to specify which element of the union should be used. For example,

```
union foo { int i; double d; };
```

```
union foo f = { d: 4 };
```

will convert 4 to a **double** to store it in the union using the second element. By contrast, casting 4 to type **union foo** would store it into the union as the integer **i**, since it is an integer. (See Section 4.22 [Cast to Union], page 176.)

You can combine this technique of naming elements with ordinary C initialization of successive elements. Each initializer element that does not

have a label applies to the next consecutive element of the array or structure.
For example,

```
int a[6] = { [1] = v1, v2, [4] = v4 };
```

is equivalent to

```
int a[6] = { 0, v1, v2, 0, v4, 0 };
```

Labeling the elements of an array initializer is especially useful when the
indices are characters or belong to an **enum** type. For example:

```
int whitespace[256]
  = { [' '] = 1, ['\t'] = 1, ['\h'] = 1,
      ['\f'] = 1, ['\n'] = 1, ['\r'] = 1 };
```

4.21 Case Ranges

You can specify a range of consecutive values in a single **case** label, like
this:

```
case low ... high:
```

This has the same effect as the proper number of individual **case** labels, one
for each integer value from *low* to *high*, inclusive.

This feature is especially useful for ranges of ASCII character codes:

```
case 'A' ... 'Z':
```

Be careful: Write spaces around the . . ., for otherwise it may be parsed
wrong when you use it with integer values. For example, write this:

```
case 1 ... 5:
```

rather than this:

```
case 1...5:
```

4.22 Cast to a Union Type

A cast to union type is similar to other casts, except that the type specified is a union type. You can specify the type either with **union** *tag* or with
a typedef name. A cast to union is actually a constructor though, not a
cast, and hence does not yield an lvalue like normal casts. (See Section 4.19
[Constructors], page 174.)

The types that may be cast to the union type are those of the members
of the union. Thus, given the following union and variables:

```
union foo { int i; double d; };
int x;
double y;
```

both **x** and **y** can be cast to type **union** foo.

Using the cast as the right-hand side of an assignment to a variable of
union type is equivalent to storing in a member of the union:

```
union foo u;
...
u = (union foo) x   ≡   u.i = x
u = (union foo) y   ≡   u.d = y
```

You can also use the union cast as a function argument:

```
void hack (union foo);
...
hack ((union foo) x);
```

4.23 Declaring Attributes of Functions

In GNU C, you declare certain things about functions called in your program which help the compiler optimize function calls and check your code more carefully.

The keyword `__attribute__` allows you to specify special attributes when making a declaration. This keyword is followed by an attribute specification inside double parentheses. Nine attributes, `noreturn`, `const`, `format`, `no_instrument_function`, `section`, `constructor`, `destructor`, `unused` and `weak` are currently defined for functions. Other attributes, including `section` are supported for variables declarations (see Section 4.29 [Variable Attributes], page 185) and for types (see Section 4.30 [Type Attributes], page 189).

You may also specify attributes with '`__`' preceding and following each keyword. This allows you to use them in header files without being concerned about a possible macro of the same name. For example, you may use `__noreturn__` instead of `noreturn`.

noreturn   A few standard library functions, such as `abort` and `exit`, cannot return. GNU CC knows this automatically. Some programs define their own functions that never return. You can declare them `noreturn` to tell the compiler this fact. For example,

```
void fatal () __attribute__ ((noreturn));

void
fatal (...)
{
  ... /* Print error message. */ ...
    exit (1);
}
```

The `noreturn` keyword tells the compiler to assume that `fatal` cannot return. It can then optimize without regard to what would happen if `fatal` ever did return. This makes slightly better code. More importantly, it helps avoid spurious warnings of uninitialized variables.

Do not assume that registers saved by the calling function are restored before calling the `noreturn` function.

It does not make sense for a `noreturn` function to have a return type other than `void`.

The attribute `noreturn` is not implemented in GNU C versions earlier than 2.5. An alternative way to declare that a function does not return, which works in the current version and in some older versions, is as follows:

```
typedef void voidfn ();


volatile voidfn fatal;
```

`const`   Many functions do not examine any values except their arguments, and have no effects except the return value. Such a function can be subject to common subexpression elimination and loop optimization just as an arithmetic operator would be. These functions should be declared with the attribute `const`. For example,

```
int square (int) __attribute__ ((const));
```

says that the hypothetical function `square` is safe to call fewer times than the program says.

The attribute `const` is not implemented in GNU C versions earlier than 2.5. An alternative way to declare that a function has no side effects, which works in the current version and in some older versions, is as follows:

```
typedef int intfn ();


extern const intfn square;
```

This approach does not work in GNU C++ from 2.6.0 on, since the language specifies that the 'const' must be attached to the return value.

Note that a function that has pointer arguments and examines the data pointed to must *not* be declared `const`. Likewise, a function that calls a non-`const` function usually must not be `const`. It does not make sense for a `const` function to return `void`.

`format` (*archetype*, *string-index*, *first-to-check*)

The `format` attribute specifies that a function takes `printf`, `scanf`, or `strftime` style arguments which should be type-checked against a format string. For example, the declaration:

```
extern int
my_printf (void *my_object, const char *my_format, ...)
        __attribute__ ((format (printf, 2, 3)));
```

causes the compiler to check the arguments in calls to `my_printf` for consistency with the `printf` style format string argument `my_format`.

The parameter *archetype* determines how the format string is interpreted, and should be either `printf`, `scanf`, or `strftime`. The parameter *string-index* specifies which argument is the format string argument (starting from 1), while *first-to-check* is the number of the first argument to check against the format string. For functions where the arguments are not available to be checked (such as `vprintf`), specify the third parameter as zero. In this case the compiler only checks the format string for consistency.

In the example above, the format string (`my_format`) is the second argument of the function `my_print`, and the arguments to check start with the third argument, so the correct parameters for the format attribute are 2 and 3.

The `format` attribute allows you to identify your own functions which take format strings as arguments, so that GNU CC can check the calls to these functions for errors. The compiler always checks formats for the ANSI library functions `printf`, `fprintf`, `sprintf`, `scanf`, `fscanf`, `sscanf`, `strftime`, `vprintf`, `vfprintf` and `vsprintf` whenever such warnings are requested (using '`-Wformat`'), so there is no need to modify the header file '`stdio.h`'.

`format_arg` (*string-index*)

The `format_arg` attribute specifies that a function takes `printf` or `scanf` style arguments, modifies it (for example, to translate it into another language), and passes it to a `printf` or `scanf` style function. For example, the declaration:

```
extern char *
my_dgettext (char *my_domain, const char *my_format)
        __attribute__ ((format_arg (2)));
```

causes the compiler to check the arguments in calls to `my_dgettext` whose result is passed to a `printf`, `scanf`, or `strftime` type function for consistency with the `printf` style format string argument `my_format`.

The parameter *string-index* specifies which argument is the format string argument (starting from 1).

The `format-arg` attribute allows you to identify your own functions which modify format strings, so that GNU CC can check the calls to `printf`, `scanf`, or `strftime` function whose operands are a call to one of your own function. The compiler always treats `gettext`, `dgettext`, and `dcgettext` in this manner.

`no_instrument_function`

> If '-finstrument-functions' is given, profiling function calls will be generated at entry and exit of most user-compiled functions. Functions with this attribute will not be so instrumented.

`section ("section-name")`

> Normally, the compiler places the code it generates in the **text** section. Sometimes, however, you need additional sections, or you need certain particular functions to appear in special sections. The **section** attribute specifies that a function lives in a particular section. For example, the declaration:
>
> ```
> extern void foobar (void) __attribute__ ((section ("bar")));
> ```
>
> puts the function **foobar** in the **bar** section.
>
> Some file formats do not support arbitrary sections so the **section** attribute is not available on all platforms. If you need to map the entire contents of a module to a particular section, consider using the facilities of the linker instead.

`constructor`
`destructor`

> The **constructor** attribute causes the function to be called automatically before execution enters **main ()**. Similarly, the **destructor** attribute causes the function to be called automatically after **main ()** has completed or **exit ()** has been called. Functions with these attributes are useful for initializing data that will be used implicitly during the execution of the program.
>
> These attributes are not currently implemented for Objective C.

`unused`
> This attribute, attached to a function, means that the function is meant to be possibly unused. GNU CC will not produce a warning for this function. GNU C++ does not currently support this attribute as definitions without parameters are valid in C++.

`weak`
> The **weak** attribute causes the declaration to be emitted as a weak symbol rather than a global. This is primarily useful in defining library functions which can be overridden in user code, though it can also be used with non-function declarations. Weak symbols are supported for ELF targets, and also for a.out targets when using the GNU assembler and linker.

`alias ("target")`

> The **alias** attribute causes the declaration to be emitted as an alias for another symbol, which must be specified. For instance,
>
> ```
> void __f () { /* do something */; }
> void f () __attribute__ ((weak, alias ("__f")));
> ```
>
> declares 'f' to be a weak alias for '__f'. In C++, the mangled name for the target must be used.

Not all target machines support this attribute.

no_check_memory_usage

If '-fcheck-memory-usage' is given, calls to support routines will be generated before most memory accesses, to permit support code to record usage and detect uses of uninitialized or unallocated storage. Since the compiler cannot handle them properly, asm statements are not allowed. Declaring a function with this attribute disables the memory checking code for that function, permitting the use of asm statements without requiring separate compilation with different options, and allowing you to write support routines of your own if you wish, without getting infinite recursion if they get compiled with this option.

regparm (*number*)

On the Intel 386, the regparm attribute causes the compiler to pass up to *number* integer arguments in registers *EAX*, *EDX*, and *ECX* instead of on the stack. Functions that take a variable number of arguments will continue to be passed all of their arguments on the stack.

stdcall   On the Intel 386, the stdcall attribute causes the compiler to assume that the called function will pop off the stack space used to pass arguments, unless it takes a variable number of arguments.

The PowerPC compiler for Windows NT currently ignores the stdcall attribute.

cdecl   On the Intel 386, the cdecl attribute causes the compiler to assume that the calling function will pop off the stack space used to pass arguments. This is useful to override the effects of the '-mrtd' switch.

The PowerPC compiler for Windows NT currently ignores the cdecl attribute.

longcall   On the RS/6000 and PowerPC, the longcall attribute causes the compiler to always call the function via a pointer, so that functions which reside further than 64 megabytes (67,108,864 bytes) from the current location can be called.

dllimport

On the PowerPC running Windows NT, the dllimport attribute causes the compiler to call the function via a global pointer to the function pointer that is set up by the Windows NT dll library. The pointer name is formed by combining __imp_ and the function name.

dllexport

On the PowerPC running Windows NT, the dllexport attribute causes the compiler to provide a global pointer to the function pointer, so that it can be called with the `dllimport` attribute. The pointer name is formed by combining `__imp_` and the function name.

`exception` (*except-func* [, *except-arg*])

On the PowerPC running Windows NT, the `exception` attribute causes the compiler to modify the structured exception table entry it emits for the declared function. The string or identifier *except-func* is placed in the third entry of the structured exception table. It represents a function, which is called by the exception handling mechanism if an exception occurs. If it was specified, the string or identifier *except-arg* is placed in the fourth entry of the structured exception table.

`function_vector`

Use this option on the H8/300 and H8/300H to indicate that the specified function should be called through the function vector. Calling a function through the function vector will reduce code size, however; the function vector has a limited size (maximum 128 entries on the H8/300 and 64 entries on the H8/300H) and shares space with the interrupt vector.

You must use GAS and GLD from GNU binutils version 2.7 or later for this option to work correctly.

`interrupt_handler`

Use this option on the H8/300 and H8/300H to indicate that the specified function is an interrupt handler. The compiler will generate function entry and exit sequences suitable for use in an interrupt handler when this attribute is present.

`eightbit_data`

Use this option on the H8/300 and H8/300H to indicate that the specified variable should be placed into the eight bit data section. The compiler will generate more efficient code for certain operations on data in the eight bit data area. Note the eight bit data area is limited to 256 bytes of data.

You must use GAS and GLD from GNU binutils version 2.7 or later for this option to work correctly.

`tiny_data`

Use this option on the H8/300H to indicate that the specified variable should be placed into the tiny data section. The compiler will generate more efficient code for loads and stores on data in the tiny data section. Note the tiny data area is limited to slightly under 32kbytes of data.

`interrupt`

Use this option on the M32R/D to indicate that the specified function is an interrupt handler. The compiler will generate function entry and exit sequences suitable for use in an interrupt handler when this attribute is present.

`model` (*model-name*)

Use this attribute on the M32R/D to set the addressability of an object, and the code generated for a function. The identifier *model-name* is one of `small`, `medium`, or `large`, representing each of the code models.

Small model objects live in the lower 16MB of memory (so that their addresses can be loaded with the `ld24` instruction), and are callable with the `bl` instruction.

Medium model objects may live anywhere in the 32 bit address space (the compiler will generate `seth/add3` instructions to load their addresses), and are callable with the `bl` instruction.

Large model objects may live anywhere in the 32 bit address space (the compiler will generate `seth/add3` instructions to load their addresses), and may not be reachable with the `bl` instruction (the compiler will generate the much slower `seth/add3/jl` instruction sequence).

You can specify multiple attributes in a declaration by separating them by commas within the double parentheses or by immediately following an attribute declaration with another attribute declaration.

Some people object to the `__attribute__` feature, suggesting that ANSI C's `#pragma` should be used instead. There are two reasons for not doing this.

1. It is impossible to generate `#pragma` commands from a macro.
2. There is no telling what the same `#pragma` might mean in another compiler.

These two reasons apply to almost any application that might be proposed for `#pragma`. It is basically a mistake to use `#pragma` for *anything*.

4.24 Prototypes and Old-Style Function Definitions

GNU C extends ANSI C to allow a function prototype to override a later old-style non-prototype definition. Consider the following example:

```
/* Use prototypes unless the compiler is old-fashioned.  */
#ifdef __STDC__
#define P(x) x
#else
#define P(x) ()
#endif
```

```
/* Prototype function declaration.  */
int isroot P((uid_t));

/* Old-style function definition.  */
int
isroot (x)    /* ??? lossage here ??? */
    uid_t x;
{
  return x == 0;
}
```

Suppose the type `uid_t` happens to be `short`. ANSI C does not allow this example, because subword arguments in old-style non-prototype definitions are promoted. Therefore in this example the function definition's argument is really an `int`, which does not match the prototype argument type of `short`.

This restriction of ANSI C makes it hard to write code that is portable to traditional C compilers, because the programmer does not know whether the `uid_t` type is `short`, `int`, or `long`. Therefore, in cases like these GNU C allows a prototype to override a later old-style definition. More precisely, in GNU C, a function prototype argument type overrides the argument type specified by a later old-style definition if the former type is the same as the latter type before promotion. Thus in GNU C the above example is equivalent to the following:

```
int isroot (uid_t);

int
isroot (uid_t x)
{
  return x == 0;
}
```

GNU C++ does not support old-style function definitions, so this extension is irrelevant.

4.25 C++ Style Comments

In GNU C, you may use C++ style comments, which start with '`//`' and continue until the end of the line. Many other C implementations allow such comments, and they are likely to be in a future C standard. However, C++ style comments are not recognized if you specify '`-ansi`' or '`-traditional`', since they are incompatible with traditional constructs like `dividend//*comment*/divisor`.

4.26 Dollar Signs in Identifier Names

In GNU C, you may normally use dollar signs in identifier names. This is because many traditional C implementations allow such identifiers. However, dollar signs in identifiers are not supported on a few target machines, typically because the target assembler does not allow them.

4.27 The Character (ESC) in Constants

You can use the sequence '\e' in a string or character constant to stand for the ASCII character (ESC).

4.28 Inquiring on Alignment of Types or Variables

The keyword `__alignof__` allows you to inquire about how an object is aligned, or the minimum alignment usually required by a type. Its syntax is just like `sizeof`.

For example, if the target machine requires a `double` value to be aligned on an 8-byte boundary, then `__alignof__` (double) is 8. This is true on many RISC machines. On more traditional machine designs, `__alignof__` (double) is 4 or even 2.

Some machines never actually require alignment; they allow reference to any data type even at an odd addresses. For these machines, `__alignof__` reports the *recommended* alignment of a type.

When the operand of `__alignof__` is an lvalue rather than a type, the value is the largest alignment that the lvalue is known to have. It may have this alignment as a result of its data type, or because it is part of a structure and inherits alignment from that structure. For example, after this declaration:

```
struct foo { int x; char y; } foo1;
```

the value of `__alignof__` (foo1.y) is probably 2 or 4, the same as `__alignof__` (int), even though the data type of `foo1.y` does not itself demand any alignment.

A related feature which lets you specify the alignment of an object is `__attribute__` ((aligned (*alignment*))); see the following section.

4.29 Specifying Attributes of Variables

The keyword `__attribute__` allows you to specify special attributes of variables or structure fields. This keyword is followed by an attribute specification inside double parentheses. Eight attributes are currently defined for variables: `aligned`, `mode`, `nocommon`, `packed`, `section`, `transparent_union`, `unused`, and `weak`. Other attributes are available for functions (see

Section 4.23 [Function Attributes], page 177) and for types (see Section 4.30 [Type Attributes], page 189).

You may also specify attributes with '__' preceding and following each keyword. This allows you to use them in header files without being concerned about a possible macro of the same name. For example, you may use __ aligned__ instead of aligned.

aligned (*alignment*)

This attribute specifies a minimum alignment for the variable or structure field, measured in bytes. For example, the declaration:

```
int x __attribute__ ((aligned (16))) = 0;
```

causes the compiler to allocate the global variable x on a 16-byte boundary. On a 68040, this could be used in conjunction with an asm expression to access the move16 instruction which requires 16-byte aligned operands.

You can also specify the alignment of structure fields. For example, to create a double-word aligned int pair, you could write:

```
struct foo { int x[2] __attribute__ ((aligned (8))); };
```

This is an alternative to creating a union with a double member that forces the union to be double-word aligned.

It is not possible to specify the alignment of functions; the alignment of functions is determined by the machine's requirements and cannot be changed. You cannot specify alignment for a typedef name because such a name is just an alias, not a distinct type.

As in the preceding examples, you can explicitly specify the alignment (in bytes) that you wish the compiler to use for a given variable or structure field. Alternatively, you can leave out the alignment factor and just ask the compiler to align a variable or field to the maximum useful alignment for the target machine you are compiling for. For example, you could write:

```
short array[3] __attribute__ ((aligned));
```

Whenever you leave out the alignment factor in an aligned attribute specification, the compiler automatically sets the alignment for the declared variable or field to the largest alignment which is ever used for any data type on the target machine you are compiling for. Doing this can often make copy operations more efficient, because the compiler can use whatever instructions copy the biggest chunks of memory when performing copies to or from the variables or fields that you have aligned this way.

The aligned attribute can only increase the alignment; but you can decrease it by specifying packed as well. See below.

Note that the effectiveness of aligned attributes may be limited by inherent limitations in your linker. On many systems, the linker is only able to arrange for variables to be aligned up to a certain maximum alignment. (For some linkers, the maximum supported alignment may be very very small.) If your linker is only able to align variables up to a maximum of 8 byte alignment, then specifying `aligned(16)` in an `__attribute__` will still only provide you with 8 byte alignment. See your linker documentation for further information.

mode (*mode*)

> This attribute specifies the data type for the declaration—whichever type corresponds to the mode *mode*. This in effect lets you request an integer or floating point type according to its width.
>
> You may also specify a mode of '`byte`' or '`__byte__`' to indicate the mode corresponding to a one-byte integer, '`word`' or '`__word__`' for the mode of a one-word integer, and '`pointer`' or '`__pointer__`' for the mode used to represent pointers.

nocommon

> This attribute specifies requests GNU CC not to place a variable "common" but instead to allocate space for it directly. If you specify the '`-fno-common`' flag, GNU CC will do this for all variables.
>
> Specifying the `nocommon` attribute for a variable provides an initialization of zeros. A variable may only be initialized in one source file.

packed

> The `packed` attribute specifies that a variable or structure field should have the smallest possible alignment—one byte for a variable, and one bit for a field, unless you specify a larger value with the `aligned` attribute.
>
> Here is a structure in which the field `x` is packed, so that it immediately follows `a`:
>
> ```
> struct foo
> {
>   char a;
>   int x[2] __attribute__ ((packed));
> };
> ```

section ("section-name")

> Normally, the compiler places the objects it generates in sections like `data` and `bss`. Sometimes, however, you need additional sections, or you need certain particular variables to appear in special sections, for example to map to special hardware. The `section` attribute specifies that a variable (or function) lives in a particular section. For example, this small program uses several specific section names:
>
> ```
> struct duart a __attribute__ ((section ("DUART_A"))) = { 0 };
> ```

```
struct duart b __attribute__ ((section ("DUART_B"))) = { 0 };
char stack[10000] __attribute__ ((section ("STACK"))) = { 0 };
int init_data __attribute__ ((section ("INITDATA"))) = 0;

main()
{
  /* Initialize stack pointer */
  init_sp (stack + sizeof (stack));

  /* Initialize initialized data */
  memcpy (&init_data, &data, &edata - &data);

  /* Turn on the serial ports */
  init_duart (&a);
  init_duart (&b);
}
```

Use the `section` attribute with an *initialized* definition of a *global* variable, as shown in the example. GNU CC issues a warning and otherwise ignores the `section` attribute in uninitialized variable declarations.

You may only use the `section` attribute with a fully initialized global definition because of the way linkers work. The linker requires each object be defined once, with the exception that uninitialized variables tentatively go in the `common` (or `bss`) section and can be multiply "defined". You can force a variable to be initialized with the '-fno-common' flag or the `nocommon` attribute.

Some file formats do not support arbitrary sections so the `section` attribute is not available on all platforms. If you need to map the entire contents of a module to a particular section, consider using the facilities of the linker instead.

`transparent_union`

This attribute, attached to a function parameter which is a union, means that the corresponding argument may have the type of any union member, but the argument is passed as if its type were that of the first union member. For more details see See Section 4.30 [Type Attributes], page 189. You can also use this attribute on a `typedef` for a union data type; then it applies to all function parameters with that type.

`unused`
This attribute, attached to a variable, means that the variable is meant to be possibly unused. GNU CC will not produce a warning for this variable.

`weak`
The `weak` attribute is described in See Section 4.23 [Function Attributes], page 177.

`model (`*model-name*`)`

> Use this attribute on the M32R/D to set the addressability of an object. The identifier *model-name* is one of `small`, `medium`, or `large`, representing each of the code models.

> Small model objects live in the lower 16MB of memory (so that their addresses can be loaded with the `ld24` instruction).

> Medium and large model objects may live anywhere in the 32 bit address space (the compiler will generate `seth/add3` instructions to load their addresses).

To specify multiple attributes, separate them by commas within the double parentheses: for example, '`__attribute__ ((aligned (16), packed))`'.

4.30 Specifying Attributes of Types

The keyword `__attribute__` allows you to specify special attributes of `struct` and `union` types when you define such types. This keyword is followed by an attribute specification inside double parentheses. Three attributes are currently defined for types: `aligned`, `packed`, and `transparent_union`. Other attributes are defined for functions (see Section 4.23 [Function Attributes], page 177) and for variables (see Section 4.29 [Variable Attributes], page 185).

You may also specify any one of these attributes with '`__`' preceding and following its keyword. This allows you to use these attributes in header files without being concerned about a possible macro of the same name. For example, you may use `__aligned__` instead of `aligned`.

You may specify the `aligned` and `transparent_union` attributes either in a `typedef` declaration or just past the closing curly brace of a complete enum, struct or union type *definition* and the `packed` attribute only past the closing brace of a definition.

You may also specify attributes between the enum, struct or union tag and the name of the type rather than after the closing brace.

`aligned (`*alignment*`)`

> This attribute specifies a minimum alignment (in bytes) for variables of the specified type. For example, the declarations:

> ```
> struct S { short f[3]; } __attribute__ ((aligned (8)));
> typedef int more_aligned_int __attribute__ ((aligned (8)));
> ```

> force the compiler to insure (as far as it can) that each variable whose type is `struct S` or `more_aligned_int` will be allocated and aligned *at least* on a 8-byte boundary. On a Sparc, having all variables of type `struct S` aligned to 8-byte boundaries allows the compiler to use the `ldd` and `std` (doubleword load and store) instructions when copying one variable of type `struct S` to another, thus improving run-time efficiency.

Note that the alignment of any given **struct** or **union** type is required by the ANSI C standard to be at least a perfect multiple of the lowest common multiple of the alignments of all of the members of the **struct** or **union** in question. This means that you *can* effectively adjust the alignment of a **struct** or **union** type by attaching an **aligned** attribute to any one of the members of such a type, but the notation illustrated in the example above is a more obvious, intuitive, and readable way to request the compiler to adjust the alignment of an entire **struct** or **union** type.

As in the preceding example, you can explicitly specify the alignment (in bytes) that you wish the compiler to use for a given **struct** or **union** type. Alternatively, you can leave out the alignment factor and just ask the compiler to align a type to the maximum useful alignment for the target machine you are compiling for. For example, you could write:

```
struct S { short f[3]; } __attribute__ ((aligned));
```

Whenever you leave out the alignment factor in an **aligned** attribute specification, the compiler automatically sets the alignment for the type to the largest alignment which is ever used for any data type on the target machine you are compiling for. Doing this can often make copy operations more efficient, because the compiler can use whatever instructions copy the biggest chunks of memory when performing copies to or from the variables which have types that you have aligned this way.

In the example above, if the size of each **short** is 2 bytes, then the size of the entire **struct S** type is 6 bytes. The smallest power of two which is greater than or equal to that is 8, so the compiler sets the alignment for the entire **struct S** type to 8 bytes.

Note that although you can ask the compiler to select a time-efficient alignment for a given type and then declare only individual stand-alone objects of that type, the compiler's ability to select a time-efficient alignment is primarily useful only when you plan to create arrays of variables having the relevant (efficiently aligned) type. If you declare or use arrays of variables of an efficiently-aligned type, then it is likely that your program will also be doing pointer arithmetic (or subscripting, which amounts to the same thing) on pointers to the relevant type, and the code that the compiler generates for these pointer arithmetic operations will often be more efficient for efficiently-aligned types than for other types.

The **aligned** attribute can only increase the alignment; but you can decrease it by specifying **packed** as well. See below.

Note that the effectiveness of **aligned** attributes may be limited by inherent limitations in your linker. On many systems, the linker is only able to arrange for variables to be aligned up to a certain maximum alignment. (For some linkers, the maximum supported alignment may be very very small.) If your linker is only able to align variables up to a maximum of 8 byte alignment, then specifying **aligned(16)** in an **__attribute__** will still only provide you with 8 byte alignment. See your linker documentation for further information.

packed

This attribute, attached to an **enum**, **struct**, or **union** type definition, specified that the minimum required memory be used to represent the type.

Specifying this attribute for **struct** and **union** types is equivalent to specifying the **packed** attribute on each of the structure or union members. Specifying the '**-fshort-enums**' flag on the line is equivalent to specifying the **packed** attribute on all **enum** definitions.

You may only specify this attribute after a closing curly brace on an **enum** definition, not in a **typedef** declaration, unless that declaration also contains the definition of the **enum**.

transparent_union

This attribute, attached to a **union** type definition, indicates that any function parameter having that union type causes calls to that function to be treated in a special way.

First, the argument corresponding to a transparent union type can be of any type in the union; no cast is required. Also, if the union contains a pointer type, the corresponding argument can be a null pointer constant or a void pointer expression; and if the union contains a void pointer type, the corresponding argument can be any pointer expression. If the union member type is a pointer, qualifiers like **const** on the referenced type must be respected, just as with normal pointer conversions.

Second, the argument is passed to the function using the calling conventions of first member of the transparent union, not the calling conventions of the union itself. All members of the union must have the same machine representation; this is necessary for this argument passing to work properly.

Transparent unions are designed for library functions that have multiple interfaces for compatibility reasons. For example, suppose the **wait** function must accept either a value of type **int *** to comply with Posix, or a value of type **union wait *** to comply with the 4.1BSD interface. If **wait**'s parameter were **void ***, **wait** would accept both kinds of arguments, but it would also accept any other pointer type and this would make argument type checking less useful. Instead, `<sys/wait.h>` might define the interface as follows:

```
typedef union
  {
    int *__ip;
    union wait *__up;
  } wait_status_ptr_t __attribute__ ((__transparent_union__));
```

```
pid_t wait (wait_status_ptr_t);
```

This interface allows either `int *` or `union wait *` arguments to be passed, using the `int *` calling convention. The program can call `wait` with arguments of either type:

```
int w1 () { int w; return wait (&w); }
int w2 () { union wait w; return wait (&w); }
```

With this interface, `wait`'s implementation might look like this:

```
pid_t wait (wait_status_ptr_t p)
{
  return waitpid (-1, p.__ip, 0);
}
```

unused   When attached to a type (including a `union` or a `struct`), this attribute means that variables of that type are meant to appear possibly unused. GNU CC will not produce a warning for any variables of that type, even if the variable appears to do nothing. This is often the case with lock or thread classes, which are usually defined and then not referenced, but contain constructors and destructors that have nontrivial bookkeeping functions.

To specify multiple attributes, separate them by commas within the double parentheses: for example, '`__attribute__ ((aligned (16), packed))`'.

4.31 An Inline Function is As Fast As a Macro

By declaring a function `inline`, you can direct GNU CC to integrate that function's code into the code for its callers. This makes execution faster by eliminating the function-call overhead; in addition, if any of the actual argument values are constant, their known values may permit simplifications at compile time so that not all of the inline function's code needs to be included. The effect on code size is less predictable; object code may be larger or smaller with function inlining, depending on the particular case. Inlining of functions is an optimization and it really "works" only in optimizing compilation. If you don't use '`-O`', no function is really inline.

To declare a function inline, use the `inline` keyword in its declaration, like this:

```
inline int
inc (int *a)
{
  (*a)++;
}
```

(If you are writing a header file to be included in ANSI C programs, write `__inline__` instead of `inline`. See Section 4.35 [Alternate Keywords], page 202.) You can also make all "simple enough" functions inline with the option '`-finline-functions`'.

Note that certain usages in a function definition can make it unsuitable for inline substitution. Among these usages are: use of varargs, use of alloca, use of variable sized data types (see Section 4.14 [Variable Length], page 171), use of computed goto (see Section 4.3 [Labels as Values], page 162), use of nonlocal goto, and nested functions (see Section 4.4 [Nested Functions], page 163). Using '`-Winline`' will warn when a function marked `inline` could not be substituted, and will give the reason for the failure.

Note that in C and Objective C, unlike C++, the `inline` keyword does not affect the linkage of the function.

GNU CC automatically inlines member functions defined within the class body of C++ programs even if they are not explicitly declared `inline`. (You can override this with '`-fno-default-inline`'; see Section 2.5 [Options Controlling C++ Dialect], page 18.)

When a function is both inline and `static`, if all calls to the function are integrated into the caller, and the function's address is never used, then the function's own assembler code is never referenced. In this case, GNU CC does not actually output assembler code for the function, unless you specify the option '`-fkeep-inline-functions`'. Some calls cannot be integrated for various reasons (in particular, calls that precede the function's definition cannot be integrated, and neither can recursive calls within the definition). If there is a nonintegrated call, then the function is compiled to assembler code as usual. The function must also be compiled as usual if the program refers to its address, because that can't be inlined.

When an inline function is not `static`, then the compiler must assume that there may be calls from other source files; since a global symbol can be defined only once in any program, the function must not be defined in the other source files, so the calls therein cannot be integrated. Therefore, a non-`static` inline function is always compiled on its own in the usual fashion.

If you specify both `inline` and `extern` in the function definition, then the definition is used only for inlining. In no case is the function compiled on its own, not even if you refer to its address explicitly. Such an address becomes an external reference, as if you had only declared the function, and had not defined it.

This combination of `inline` and `extern` has almost the effect of a macro. The way to use it is to put a function definition in a header file with these keywords, and put another copy of the definition (lacking `inline` and `extern`) in a library file. The definition in the header file will cause most calls to the function to be inlined. If any uses of the function remain, they will refer to the single copy in the library.

GNU C does not inline any functions when not optimizing. It is not clear whether it is better to inline or not, in this case, but we found that a correct implementation when not optimizing was difficult. So we did the easy thing, and turned it off.

4.32 Assembler Instructions with C Expression Operands

In an assembler instruction using `asm`, you can specify the operands of the instruction using C expressions. This means you need not guess which registers or memory locations will contain the data you want to use.

You must specify an assembler instruction template much like what appears in a machine description, plus an operand constraint string for each operand.

For example, here is how to use the 68881's `fsinx` instruction:

```
asm ("fsinx %1,%0" : "=f" (result) : "f" (angle));
```

Here `angle` is the C expression for the input operand while `result` is that of the output operand. Each has '`"f"`' as its operand constraint, saying that a floating point register is required. The '`=`' in '`=f`' indicates that the operand is an output; all output operands' constraints must use '`=`'. The constraints use the same language used in the machine description (see Section 16.6 [Constraints], page 337).

Each operand is described by an operand-constraint string followed by the C expression in parentheses. A colon separates the assembler template from the first output operand and another separates the last output operand from the first input, if any. Commas separate the operands within each group. The total number of operands is limited to ten or to the maximum number of operands in any instruction pattern in the machine description, whichever is greater.

If there are no output operands but there are input operands, you must place two consecutive colons surrounding the place where the output operands would go.

Output operand expressions must be lvalues; the compiler can check this. The input operands need not be lvalues. The compiler cannot check whether the operands have data types that are reasonable for the instruction being executed. It does not parse the assembler instruction template and does not know what it means or even whether it is valid assembler input. The extended `asm` feature is most often used for machine instructions the compiler itself does not know exist. If the output expression cannot be directly addressed (for example, it is a bit field), your constraint must allow a register. In that case, GNU CC will use the register as the output of the `asm`, and then store that register into the output.

The ordinary output operands must be write-only; GNU CC will assume that the values in these operands before the instruction are dead and need not be generated. Extended asm supports input-output or read-write operands. Use the constraint character '+' to indicate such an operand and list it with the output operands.

When the constraints for the read-write operand (or the operand in which only some of the bits are to be changed) allows a register, you may, as an alternative, logically split its function into two separate operands, one input operand and one write-only output operand. The connection between them is expressed by constraints which say they need to be in the same location when the instruction executes. You can use the same C expression for both operands, or different expressions. For example, here we write the (fictitious) 'combine' instruction with `bar` as its read-only source operand and `foo` as its read-write destination:

```
asm ("combine %2,%0" : "=r" (foo) : "0" (foo), "g" (bar));
```

The constraint '"0"' for operand 1 says that it must occupy the same location as operand 0. A digit in constraint is allowed only in an input operand and it must refer to an output operand.

Only a digit in the constraint can guarantee that one operand will be in the same place as another. The mere fact that `foo` is the value of both operands is not enough to guarantee that they will be in the same place in the generated assembler code. The following would not work reliably:

```
asm ("combine %2,%0" : "=r" (foo) : "r" (foo), "g" (bar));
```

Various optimizations or reloading could cause operands 0 and 1 to be in different registers; GNU CC knows no reason not to do so. For example, the compiler might find a copy of the value of `foo` in one register and use it for operand 1, but generate the output operand 0 in a different register (copying it afterward to `foo`'s own address). Of course, since the register for operand 1 is not even mentioned in the assembler code, the result will not work, but GNU CC can't tell that.

Some instructions clobber specific hard registers. To describe this, write a third colon after the input operands, followed by the names of the clobbered hard registers (given as strings). Here is a realistic example for the VAX:

```
asm volatile ("movc3 %0,%1,%2"
              : /* no outputs */
              : "g" (from), "g" (to), "g" (count)
              : "r0", "r1", "r2", "r3", "r4", "r5");
```

It is an error for a clobber description to overlap an input or output operand (for example, an operand describing a register class with one member, mentioned in the clobber list). Most notably, it is invalid to describe that an input operand is modified, but unused as output. It has to be specified as an input and output operand anyway. Note that if there are only unused output operands, you will then also need to specify `volatile` for the `asm` construct, as described below.

If you refer to a particular hardware register from the assembler code, you will probably have to list the register after the third colon to tell the compiler the register's value is modified. In some assemblers, the register names begin with '%'; to produce one '%' in the assembler code, you must write '%%' in the input.

If your assembler instruction can alter the condition code register, add 'cc' to the list of clobbered registers. GNU CC on some machines represents the condition codes as a specific hardware register; 'cc' serves to name this register. On other machines, the condition code is handled differently, and specifying 'cc' has no effect. But it is valid no matter what the machine.

If your assembler instruction modifies memory in an unpredictable fashion, add 'memory' to the list of clobbered registers. This will cause GNU CC to not keep memory values cached in registers across the assembler instruction.

You can put multiple assembler instructions together in a single `asm` template, separated either with newlines (written as '\n') or with semicolons if the assembler allows such semicolons. The GNU assembler allows semicolons and most Unix assemblers seem to do so. The input operands are guaranteed not to use any of the clobbered registers, and neither will the output operands' addresses, so you can read and write the clobbered registers as many times as you like. Here is an example of multiple instructions in a template; it assumes the subroutine _foo accepts arguments in registers 9 and 10:

```
asm ("movl %0,r9;movl %1,r10;call _foo"
     : /* no outputs */
     : "g" (from), "g" (to)
     : "r9", "r10");
```

Unless an output operand has the '&' constraint modifier, GNU CC may allocate it in the same register as an unrelated input operand, on the assumption the inputs are consumed before the outputs are produced. This assumption may be false if the assembler code actually consists of more than one instruction. In such a case, use '&' for each output operand that may not overlap an input. See Section 16.6.4 [Modifiers], page 343.

If you want to test the condition code produced by an assembler instruction, you must include a branch and a label in the `asm` construct, as follows:

```
asm ("clr %0;frob %1;beq 0f;mov #1,%0;0:"
     : "g" (result)
     : "g" (input));
```

This assumes your assembler supports local labels, as the GNU assembler and most Unix assemblers do.

Speaking of labels, jumps from one `asm` to another are not supported. The compiler's optimizers do not know about these jumps, and therefore they cannot take account of them when deciding how to optimize.

Usually the most convenient way to use these `asm` instructions is to encapsulate them in macros that look like functions. For example,

```
#define sin(x)           \
({ double __value, __arg = (x);     \
    asm ("fsinx %1,%0": "=f" (__value): "f" (__arg));  \
    __value; })
```

Here the variable `__arg` is used to make sure that the instruction operates on a proper `double` value, and to accept only those arguments x which can convert automatically to a `double`.

Another way to make sure the instruction operates on the correct data type is to use a cast in the `asm`. This is different from using a variable `__arg` in that it converts more different types. For example, if the desired type were `int`, casting the argument to `int` would accept a pointer with no complaint, while assigning the argument to an `int` variable named `__arg` would warn about using a pointer unless the caller explicitly casts it.

If an `asm` has output operands, GNU CC assumes for optimization purposes the instruction has no side effects except to change the output operands. This does not mean instructions with a side effect cannot be used, but you must be careful, because the compiler may eliminate them if the output operands aren't used, or move them out of loops, or replace two with one if they constitute a common subexpression. Also, if your instruction does have a side effect on a variable that otherwise appears not to change, the old value of the variable may be reused later if it happens to be found in a register.

You can prevent an `asm` instruction from being deleted, moved significantly, or combined, by writing the keyword `volatile` after the `asm`. For example:

```
#define get_and_set_priority(new)  \
({ int __old; \
    asm volatile ("get_and_set_priority %0, %1": "=g" (__old) :\
    "g" (new));  __old; })
```

If you write an `asm` instruction with no outputs, GNU CC will know the instruction has side-effects and will not delete the instruction or move it outside of loops. If the side-effects of your instruction are not purely external, but will affect variables in your program in ways other than reading the inputs and clobbering the specified registers or memory, you should write the `volatile` keyword to prevent future versions of GNU CC from moving the instruction around within a core region.

An `asm` instruction without any operands or clobbers (and "old style" `asm`) will not be deleted or moved significantly, regardless, unless it is unreachable, the same wasy as if you had written a `volatile` keyword.

Note that even a volatile `asm` instruction can be moved in ways that appear insignificant to the compiler, such as across jump instructions. You can't expect a sequence of volatile `asm` instructions to remain perfectly consecutive. If you want consecutive output, use a single `asm`.

It is a natural idea to look for a way to give access to the condition code left by the assembler instruction. However, when we attempted to implement this, we found no way to make it work reliably. The problem is that output operands might need reloading, which would result in additional following "store" instructions. On most machines, these instructions would alter the condition code before there was time to test it. This problem doesn't arise for ordinary "test" and "compare" instructions because they don't have any output operands.

If you are writing a header file that should be includable in ANSI C programs, write `__asm__` instead of `asm`. See Section 4.35 [Alternate Keywords], page 202.

4.32.1 i386 floating point asm operands

There are several rules on the usage of stack-like regs in asm_operands insns. These rules apply only to the operands that are stack-like regs:

1. Given a set of input regs that die in an asm_operands, it is necessary to know which are implicitly popped by the asm, and which must be explicitly popped by gcc.

   An input reg that is implicitly popped by the asm must be explicitly clobbered, unless it is constrained to match an output operand.

2. For any input reg that is implicitly popped by an asm, it is necessary to know how to adjust the stack to compensate for the pop. If any non-popped input is closer to the top of the reg-stack than the implicitly popped reg, it would not be possible to know what the stack looked like — it's not clear how the rest of the stack "slides up".

   All implicitly popped input regs must be closer to the top of the reg-stack than any input that is not implicitly popped.

   It is possible that if an input dies in an insn, reload might use the input reg for an output reload. Consider this example:

   ```
   asm ("foo" : "=t" (a) : "f" (b));
   ```

   This asm says that input B is not popped by the asm, and that the asm pushes a result onto the reg-stack, ie, the stack is one deeper after the asm than it was before. But, it is possible that reload will think that it can use the same reg for both the input and the output, if input B dies in this insn.

   If any input operand uses the `f` constraint, all output reg constraints must use the `&` earlyclobber.

   The asm above would be written as

```
asm ("foo" : "=&t" (a) : "f" (b));
```

3. Some operands need to be in particular places on the stack. All output operands fall in this category — there is no other way to know which regs the outputs appear in unless the user indicates this in the constraints.

   Output operands must specifically indicate which reg an output appears in after an asm. =f is not allowed: the operand constraints must select a class with a single reg.

4. Output operands may not be "inserted" between existing stack regs. Since no 387 opcode uses a read/write operand, all output operands are dead before the asm_operands, and are pushed by the asm_operands. It makes no sense to push anywhere but the top of the reg-stack.

   Output operands must start at the top of the reg-stack: output operands may not "skip" a reg.

5. Some asm statements may need extra stack space for internal calculations. This can be guaranteed by clobbering stack registers unrelated to the inputs and outputs.

Here are a couple of reasonable asms to want to write. This asm takes one input, which is internally popped, and produces two outputs.

```
asm ("fsincos" : "=t" (cos), "=u" (sin) : "0" (inp));
```

This asm takes two inputs, which are popped by the `fyl2xp1` opcode, and replaces them with one output. The user must code the `st(1)` clobber for reg-stack.c to know that `fyl2xp1` pops both inputs.

```
asm ("fyl2xp1" : "=t" (result) : "0" (x), "u" (y) : "st(1)");
```

4.33 Controlling Names Used in Assembler Code

You can specify the name to be used in the assembler code for a C function or variable by writing the `asm` (or `__asm__`) keyword after the declarator as follows:

```
int foo asm ("myfoo") = 2;
```

This specifies that the name to be used for the variable `foo` in the assembler code should be 'myfoo' rather than the usual '_foo'.

On systems where an underscore is normally prepended to the name of a C function or variable, this feature allows you to define names for the linker that do not start with an underscore.

You cannot use `asm` in this way in a function *definition*; but you can get the same effect by writing a declaration for the function before its definition and putting `asm` there, like this:

```
extern func () asm ("FUNC");

func (x, y)
     int x, y;
```

...

It is up to you to make sure that the assembler names you choose do not conflict with any other assembler symbols. Also, you must not use a register name; that would produce completely invalid assembler code. GNU CC does not as yet have the ability to store static variables in registers. Perhaps that will be added.

4.34 Variables in Specified Registers

GNU C allows you to put a few global variables into specified hardware registers. You can also specify the register in which an ordinary register variable should be allocated.

- Global register variables reserve registers throughout the program. This may be useful in programs such as programming language interpreters which have a couple of global variables that are accessed very often.

- Local register variables in specific registers do not reserve the registers. The compiler's data flow analysis is capable of determining where the specified registers contain live values, and where they are available for other uses. Stores into local register variables may be deleted when they appear to be dead according to dataflow analysis. References to local register variables may be deleted or moved or simplified.

  These local variables are sometimes convenient for use with the extended asm feature (see Section 4.32 [Extended Asm], page 194), if you want to write one output of the assembler instruction directly into a particular register. (This will work provided the register you specify fits the constraints specified for that operand in the asm.)

4.34.1 Defining Global Register Variables

You can define a global register variable in GNU C like this:

```
register int *foo asm ("a5");
```

Here a5 is the name of the register which should be used. Choose a register which is normally saved and restored by function calls on your machine, so that library routines will not clobber it.

Naturally the register name is cpu-dependent, so you would need to conditionalize your program according to cpu type. The register a5 would be a good choice on a 68000 for a variable of pointer type. On machines with register windows, be sure to choose a "global" register that is not affected magically by the function call mechanism.

In addition, operating systems on one type of cpu may differ in how they name the registers; then you would need additional conditionals. For example, some 68000 operating systems call this register %a5.

Eventually there may be a way of asking the compiler to choose a register automatically, but first we need to figure out how it should choose and how to enable you to guide the choice. No solution is evident.

Defining a global register variable in a certain register reserves that register entirely for this use, at least within the current compilation. The register will not be allocated for any other purpose in the functions in the current compilation. The register will not be saved and restored by these functions. Stores into this register are never deleted even if they would appear to be dead, but references may be deleted or moved or simplified.

It is not safe to access the global register variables from signal handlers, or from more than one thread of control, because the system library routines may temporarily use the register for other things (unless you recompile them specially for the task at hand).

It is not safe for one function that uses a global register variable to call another such function **foo** by way of a third function **lose** that was compiled without knowledge of this variable (i.e. in a different source file in which the variable wasn't declared). This is because **lose** might save the register and put some other value there. For example, you can't expect a global register variable to be available in the comparison-function that you pass to **qsort**, since **qsort** might have put something else in that register. (If you are prepared to recompile **qsort** with the same global register variable, you can solve this problem.)

If you want to recompile **qsort** or other source files which do not actually use your global register variable, so that they will not use that register for any other purpose, then it suffices to specify the compiler option '**-ffixed-***reg*'. You need not actually add a global register declaration to their source code.

A function which can alter the value of a global register variable cannot safely be called from a function compiled without this variable, because it could clobber the value the caller expects to find there on return. Therefore, the function which is the entry point into the part of the program that uses the global register variable must explicitly save and restore the value which belongs to its caller.

On most machines, **longjmp** will restore to each global register variable the value it had at the time of the **setjmp**. On some machines, however, **longjmp** will not change the value of global register variables. To be portable, the function that called **setjmp** should make other arrangements to save the values of the global register variables, and to restore them in a **longjmp**. This way, the same thing will happen regardless of what **longjmp** does.

All global register variable declarations must precede all function definitions. If such a declaration could appear after function definitions, the declaration would be too late to prevent the register from being used for other purposes in the preceding functions.

Global register variables may not have initial values, because an executable file has no means to supply initial contents for a register.

On the Sparc, there are reports that g3 ... g7 are suitable registers, but certain library functions, such as `getwd`, as well as the subroutines for division and remainder, modify g3 and g4. g1 and g2 are local temporaries.

On the 68000, a2 ... a5 should be suitable, as should d2 ... d7. Of course, it will not do to use more than a few of those.

4.34.2 Specifying Registers for Local Variables

You can define a local register variable with a specified register like this:

```
register int *foo asm ("a5");
```

Here `a5` is the name of the register which should be used. Note that this is the same syntax used for defining global register variables, but for a local variable it would appear within a function.

Naturally the register name is cpu-dependent, but this is not a problem, since specific registers are most often useful with explicit assembler instructions (see Section 4.32 [Extended Asm], page 194). Both of these things generally require that you conditionalize your program according to cpu type.

In addition, operating systems on one type of cpu may differ in how they name the registers; then you would need additional conditionals. For example, some 68000 operating systems call this register `%a5`.

Defining such a register variable does not reserve the register; it remains available for other uses in places where flow control determines the variable's value is not live. However, these registers are made unavailable for use in the reload pass; excessive use of this feature leaves the compiler too few available registers to compile certain functions.

This option does not guarantee that GNU CC will generate code that has this variable in the register you specify at all times. You may not code an explicit reference to this register in an `asm` statement and assume it will always refer to this variable.

Stores into local register variables may be deleted when they appear to be dead according to dataflow analysis. References to local register variables may be deleted or moved or simplified.

4.35 Alternate Keywords

The option '`-traditional`' disables certain keywords; '`-ansi`' disables certain others. This causes trouble when you want to use GNU C extensions, or ANSI C features, in a general-purpose header file that should be usable by all programs, including ANSI C programs and traditional ones. The keywords `asm`, `typeof` and `inline` cannot be used since they won't work in a program compiled with '`-ansi`', while the keywords `const`, `volatile`, `signed`, `typeof` and `inline` won't work in a program compiled with '`-traditional`'.

The way to solve these problems is to put '__' at the beginning and end of each problematical keyword. For example, use __asm__ instead of asm, __const__ instead of const, and __inline__ instead of inline.

Other C compilers won't accept these alternative keywords; if you want to compile with another compiler, you can define the alternate keywords as macros to replace them with the customary keywords. It looks like this:

```
#ifndef __GNUC__
#define __asm__ asm
#endif
```

'-pedantic' causes warnings for many GNU C extensions. You can prevent such warnings within one expression by writing __extension__ before the expression. __extension__ has no effect aside from this.

4.36 Incomplete enum Types

You can define an enum tag without specifying its possible values. This results in an incomplete type, much like what you get if you write struct foo without describing the elements. A later declaration which does specify the possible values completes the type.

You can't allocate variables or storage using the type while it is incomplete. However, you can work with pointers to that type.

This extension may not be very useful, but it makes the handling of enum more consistent with the way struct and union are handled.

This extension is not supported by GNU C++.

4.37 Function Names as Strings

GNU CC predefines two string variables to be the name of the current function. The variable __FUNCTION__ is the name of the function as it appears in the source. The variable __PRETTY_FUNCTION__ is the name of the function pretty printed in a language specific fashion.

These names are always the same in a C function, but in a C++ function they may be different. For example, this program:

```
extern "C" {
extern int printf (char *, ...);
}

class a {
 public:
  sub (int i)
    {
      printf ("__FUNCTION__ = %s\n", __FUNCTION__);
      printf ("__PRETTY_FUNCTION__ = %s\n", __PRETTY_FUNCTION__);
```

```
        }
    };

    int
    main (void)
    {
      a ax;
      ax.sub (0);
      return 0;
    }
```

gives this output:

```
    __FUNCTION__ = sub
    __PRETTY_FUNCTION__ = int  a::sub (int)
```

These names are not macros: they are predefined string variables. For example, '#ifdef __FUNCTION__' does not have any special meaning inside a function, since the preprocessor does not do anything special with the identifier __FUNCTION__.

4.38 Getting the Return or Frame Address of a Function

These functions may be used to get information about the callers of a function.

__builtin_return_address (*level*)

> This function returns the return address of the current function, or of one of its callers. The *level* argument is number of frames to scan up the call stack. A value of 0 yields the return address of the current function, a value of 1 yields the return address of the caller of the current function, and so forth.
>
> The *level* argument must be a constant integer.
>
> On some machines it may be impossible to determine the return address of any function other than the current one; in such cases, or when the top of the stack has been reached, this function will return 0.
>
> This function should only be used with a non-zero argument for debugging purposes.

__builtin_frame_address (*level*)

> This function is similar to __builtin_return_address, but it returns the address of the function frame rather than the return address of the function. Calling __builtin_frame_address with a value of 0 yields the frame address of the current function, a value of 1 yields the frame address of the caller of the current function, and so forth.

The frame is the area on the stack which holds local variables and saved registers. The frame address is normally the address of the first word pushed on to the stack by the function. However, the exact definition depends upon the processor and the calling convention. If the processor has a dedicated frame pointer register, and the function has a frame, then `__builtin_frame_address` will return the value of the frame pointer register.

The caveats that apply to `__builtin_return_address` apply to this function as well.

4.39 Other built-in functions provided by GNU CC

GNU CC provides a large number of built-in functions other than the ones mentioned above. Some of these are for internal use in the processing of exceptions or variable-length argument lists and will not be documented here because they may change from time to time; we do not recommend general use of these functions.

The remaining functions are provided for optimization purposes.

GNU CC includes builtin versions of many of the functions in the standard C library. These will always be treated as having the same meaning as the C library function even if you specify the '`-fno-builtin`' (see Section 2.4 [C Dialect Options], page 13) option. These functions correspond to the C library functions `alloca`, `ffs`, `abs`, `fabsf`, `fabs`, `fabsl`, `labs`, `memcpy`, `memcmp`, `strcmp`, `strcpy`, `strlen`, `sqrtf`, `sqrt`, `sqrtl`, `sinf`, `sin`, `sinl`, `cosf`, `cos`, and `cosl`.

You can use the builtin function `__builtin_constant_p` to determine if a value is known to be constant at compile-time and hence that GNU CC can perform constant-folding on expressions involving that value. The argument of the function is the value to test. The function returns the integer 1 if the argument is known to be a compile-time constant and 0 if it is not known to be a compile-time constant. A return of 0 does not indicate that the value is *not* a constant, but merely that GNU CC cannot prove it is a constant with the specified value of the '`-O`' option.

You would typically use this function in an embedded application where memory was a critical resource. If you have some complex calculation, you may want it to be folded if it involves constants, but need to call a function if it does not. For example:

```
#define Scale_Value(X)  \
    (__builtin_constant_p (X) ? ((X) * SCALE + OFFSET) : Scale (X))
```

You may use this builtin function in either a macro or an inline function. However, if you use it in an inlined function and pass an argument of the function as the argument to the builtin, GNU CC will never return 1 when you call the inline function with a string constant or constructor expression (see Section 4.19 [Constructors], page 174) and will not return 1 when you pass a constant numeric value to the inline function unless you specify the '-O' option.

4.40 Deprecated Features

In the past, the GNU C++ compiler was extended to experiment with new features, at a time when the C++ language was still evolving. Now that the C++ standard is complete, some of those features are superceded by superior alternatives. Using the old features might cause a warning in some cases that the feature will be dropped in the future. In other cases, the feature might be gone already.

While the list below is not exhaustive, it documents some of the options that are now deprecated:

-fthis-is-variable

> In early versions of C++, assignment to this could be used to implement application-defined memory allocation. Now, allocation functions ('operator new') are the standard-conforming way to achieve the same effect.

-fexternal-templates
-falt-external-templates

> These are two of the many ways for g++ to implement template instantiation. See Section 5.5 [Template Instantiation], page 211. The C++ standard clearly defines how template definitions have to be organized across implementation units. g++ has an implicit instantiation mechanism that should work just fine for standard-conforming code.

5 Extensions to the C++ Language

The GNU compiler provides these extensions to the C++ language (and you can also use most of the C language extensions in your C++ programs). If you want to write code that checks whether these features are available, you can test for the GNU compiler the same way as for C programs: check for a predefined macro `__GNUC__`. You can also use `__GNUG__` to test specifically for GNU C++ (see section "Standard Predefined Macros" in *The C Preprocessor*).

5.1 Named Return Values in C++

GNU C++ extends the function-definition syntax to allow you to specify a name for the result of a function outside the body of the definition, in C++ programs:

```
type
functionname (args) return resultname;
{
   ...
   body
   ...
}
```

You can use this feature to avoid an extra constructor call when a function result has a class type. For example, consider a function `m`, declared as 'X v = m ();', whose result is of class `X`:

```
X
m ()
{
   X b;
   b.a = 23;
   return b;
}
```

Although `m` appears to have no arguments, in fact it has one implicit argument: the address of the return value. At invocation, the address of enough space to hold `v` is sent in as the implicit argument. Then `b` is constructed and its `a` field is set to the value 23. Finally, a copy constructor (a constructor of the form 'X(X&)') is applied to `b`, with the (implicit) return value location as the target, so that `v` is now bound to the return value.

But this is wasteful. The local `b` is declared just to hold something that will be copied right out. While a compiler that combined an "elision" algorithm with interprocedural data flow analysis could conceivably eliminate all of this, it is much more practical to allow you to assist the compiler in generating efficient code by manipulating the return value explicitly, thus avoiding the local variable and copy constructor altogether.

Using the extended GNU C++ function-definition syntax, you can avoid the temporary allocation and copying by naming **r** as your return value at the outset, and assigning to its **a** field directly:

```
X
m () return r;
{
   r.a = 23;
}
```

The declaration of **r** is a standard, proper declaration, whose effects are executed **before** any of the body of **m**.

Functions of this type impose no additional restrictions; in particular, you can execute **return** statements, or return implicitly by reaching the end of the function body ("falling off the edge"). Cases like

```
X
m () return r (23);
{
   return;
}
```

(or even 'X m () return r (23); { }') are unambiguous, since the return value **r** has been initialized in either case. The following code may be hard to read, but also works predictably:

```
X
m () return r;
{
   X b;
   return b;
}
```

The return value slot denoted by **r** is initialized at the outset, but the statement 'return b;' overrides this value. The compiler deals with this by destroying **r** (calling the destructor if there is one, or doing nothing if there is not), and then reinitializing **r** with **b**.

This extension is provided primarily to help people who use overloaded operators, where there is a great need to control not just the arguments, but the return values of functions. For classes where the copy constructor incurs a heavy performance penalty (especially in the common case where there is a quick default constructor), this is a major savings. The disadvantage of this extension is that you do not control when the default constructor for the return value is called: it is always called at the beginning.

5.2 Minimum and Maximum Operators in C++

It is very convenient to have operators which return the "minimum" or the "maximum" of two arguments. In GNU C++ (but not in GNU C),

a <? b   is the *minimum*, returning the smaller of the numeric values *a*
          and *b*;

a >? b   is the *maximum*, returning the larger of the numeric values *a*
          and *b*.

These operations are not primitive in ordinary C++, since you can use
a macro to return the minimum of two things in C++, as in the following
example.

```
#define MIN(X,Y) ((X) < (Y) ? : (X) : (Y))
```

You might then use 'int min = MIN (i, j);' to set *min* to the minimum
value of variables *i* and *j*.

However, side effects in X or Y may cause unintended behavior. For example, MIN (i++, j++) will fail, incrementing the smaller counter twice. A
GNU C extension allows you to write safe macros that avoid this kind of
problem (see Section 4.6 [Naming an Expression's Type], page 166). However, writing MIN and MAX as macros also forces you to use function-call
notation for a fundamental arithmetic operation. Using GNU C++ extensions, you can write 'int min = i <? j;' instead.

Since <? and >? are built into the compiler, they properly handle expressions with side-effects; 'int min = i++ <? j++;' works correctly.

5.3 `goto` and Destructors in GNU C++

In C++ programs, you can safely use the `goto` statement. When you
use it to exit a block which contains aggregates requiring destructors, the
destructors will run before the `goto` transfers control.

The compiler still forbids using `goto` to *enter* a scope that requires constructors.

5.4 Declarations and Definitions in One Header

C++ object definitions can be quite complex. In principle, your source
code will need two kinds of things for each object that you use across more
than one source file. First, you need an *interface* specification, describing its
structure with type declarations and function prototypes. Second, you need
the *implementation* itself. It can be tedious to maintain a separate interface
description in a header file, in parallel to the actual implementation. It is
also dangerous, since separate interface and implementation definitions may
not remain parallel.

With GNU C++, you can use a single header file for both purposes.

Warning: The mechanism to specify this is in transition. For the
nonce, you must use one of two `#pragma` commands; in a future
release of GNU C++, an alternative mechanism will make these
`#pragma` commands unnecessary.

The header file contains the full definitions, but is marked with '#pragma interface' in the source code. This allows the compiler to use the header file only as an interface specification when ordinary source files incorporate it with #include. In the single source file where the full implementation belongs, you can use either a naming convention or '#pragma implementation' to indicate this alternate use of the header file.

#pragma interface
#pragma interface "*subdir/objects*.h"

> Use this directive in *header files* that define object classes, to save space in most of the object files that use those classes. Normally, local copies of certain information (backup copies of inline member functions, debugging information, and the internal tables that implement virtual functions) must be kept in each object file that includes class definitions. You can use this pragma to avoid such duplication. When a header file containing '#pragma interface' is included in a compilation, this auxiliary information will not be generated (unless the main input source file itself uses '#pragma implementation'). Instead, the object files will contain references to be resolved at link time.

> The second form of this directive is useful for the case where you have multiple headers with the same name in different directories. If you use this form, you must specify the same string to '#pragma implementation'.

#pragma implementation
#pragma implementation "*objects*.h"

> Use this pragma in a *main input file*, when you want full output from included header files to be generated (and made globally visible). The included header file, in turn, should use '#pragma interface'. Backup copies of inline member functions, debugging information, and the internal tables used to implement virtual functions are all generated in implementation files.

> If you use '#pragma implementation' with no argument, it applies to an include file with the same basename[1] as your source file. For example, in 'allclass.cc', giving just '#pragma implementation' by itself is equivalent to '#pragma implementation "allclass.h"'.

> In versions of GNU C++ prior to 2.6.0 'allclass.h' was treated as an implementation file whenever you would include it from 'allclass.cc' even if you never specified '#pragma implementation'. This was deemed to be more trouble than it was worth, however, and disabled.

---

[1] A file's *basename* was the name stripped of all leading path information and of trailing suffixes, such as '.h' or '.C' or '.cc'.

If you use an explicit '#pragma implementation', it must appear in your source file *before* you include the affected header files.

Use the string argument if you want a single implementation file to include code from multiple header files. (You must also use '#include' to include the header file; '#pragma implementation' only specifies how to use the file—it doesn't actually include it.)

There is no way to split up the contents of a single header file into multiple implementation files.

'#pragma implementation' and '#pragma interface' also have an effect on function inlining.

If you define a class in a header file marked with '#pragma interface', the effect on a function defined in that class is similar to an explicit extern declaration—the compiler emits no code at all to define an independent version of the function. Its definition is used only for inlining with its callers.

Conversely, when you include the same header file in a main source file that declares it as '#pragma implementation', the compiler emits code for the function itself; this defines a version of the function that can be found via pointers (or by callers compiled without inlining). If all calls to the function can be inlined, you can avoid emitting the function by compiling with '-fno-implement-inlines'. If any calls were not inlined, you will get linker errors.

5.5 Where's the Template?

C++ templates are the first language feature to require more intelligence from the environment than one usually finds on a UNIX system. Somehow the compiler and linker have to make sure that each template instance occurs exactly once in the executable if it is needed, and not at all otherwise. There are two basic approaches to this problem, which I will refer to as the Borland model and the Cfront model.

Borland model

Borland C++ solved the template instantiation problem by adding the code equivalent of common blocks to their linker; the compiler emits template instances in each translation unit that uses them, and the linker collapses them together. The advantage of this model is that the linker only has to consider the object files themselves; there is no external complexity to worry about. This disadvantage is that compilation time is increased because the template code is being compiled repeatedly. Code written for this model tends to include definitions of all templates in the header file, since they must be seen to be instantiated.

Cfront model

> The AT&T C++ translator, Cfront, solved the template instantiation problem by creating the notion of a template repository, an automatically maintained place where template instances are stored. A more modern version of the repository works as follows: As individual object files are built, the compiler places any template definitions and instantiations encountered in the repository. At link time, the link wrapper adds in the objects in the repository and compiles any needed instances that were not previously emitted. The advantages of this model are more optimal compilation speed and the ability to use the system linker; to implement the Borland model a compiler vendor also needs to replace the linker. The disadvantages are vastly increased complexity, and thus potential for error; for some code this can be just as transparent, but in practice it can been very difficult to build multiple programs in one directory and one program in multiple directories. Code written for this model tends to separate definitions of non-inline member templates into a separate file, which should be compiled separately.

When used with GNU ld version 2.8 or later on an ELF system such as Linux/GNU or Solaris 2, or on Microsoft Windows, g++ supports the Borland model. On other systems, g++ implements neither automatic model.

A future version of g++ will support a hybrid model whereby the compiler will emit any instantiations for which the template definition is included in the compile, and store template definitions and instantiation context information into the object file for the rest. The link wrapper will extract that information as necessary and invoke the compiler to produce the remaining instantiations. The linker will then combine duplicate instantiations.

In the mean time, you have the following options for dealing with template instantiations:

1. Compile your template-using code with '-frepo'. The compiler will generate files with the extension '.rpo' listing all of the template instantiations used in the corresponding object files which could be instantiated there; the link wrapper, 'collect2', will then update the '.rpo' files to tell the compiler where to place those instantiations and rebuild any affected object files. The link-time overhead is negligible after the first pass, as the compiler will continue to place the instantiations in the same files.

   This is your best option for application code written for the Borland model, as it will just work. Code written for the Cfront model will need to be modified so that the template definitions are available at one or more points of instantiation; usually this is as simple as adding `#include <tmethods.cc>` to the end of each template header.

   For library code, if you want the library to provide all of the template instantiations it needs, just try to link all of its object files together;

the link will fail, but cause the instantiations to be generated as a side effect. Be warned, however, that this may cause conflicts if multiple libraries try to provide the same instantiations. For greater control, use explicit instantiation as described in the next option.

2. Compile your code with '-fno-implicit-templates' to disable the implicit generation of template instances, and explicitly instantiate all the ones you use. This approach requires more knowledge of exactly which instances you need than do the others, but it's less mysterious and allows greater control. You can scatter the explicit instantiations throughout your program, perhaps putting them in the translation units where the instances are used or the translation units that define the templates themselves; you can put all of the explicit instantiations you need into one big file; or you can create small files like

```
#include "Foo.h"
#include "Foo.cc"

template class Foo<int>;
template ostream& operator <<
                (ostream&, const Foo<int>&);
```

for each of the instances you need, and create a template instantiation library from those.

If you are using Cfront-model code, you can probably get away with not using '-fno-implicit-templates' when compiling files that don't '#include' the member template definitions.

If you use one big file to do the instantiations, you may want to compile it without '-fno-implicit-templates' so you get all of the instances required by your explicit instantiations (but not by any other files) without having to specify them as well.

g++ has extended the template instantiation syntax outlined in the Working Paper to allow forward declaration of explicit instantiations and instantiation of the compiler support data for a template class (i.e. the vtable) without instantiating any of its members:

```
extern template int max (int, int);
inline template class Foo<int>;
```

3. Do nothing. Pretend g++ does implement automatic instantiation management. Code written for the Borland model will work fine, but each translation unit will contain instances of each of the templates it uses. In a large program, this can lead to an unacceptable amount of code duplication.

4. Add '#pragma interface' to all files containing template definitions. For each of these files, add '#pragma implementation "filename"' to the top of some '.C' file which '#include's it. Then compile everything with '-fexternal-templates'. The templates will then only be expanded in the translation unit which implements them (i.e. has a '#pragma

implementation' line for the file where they live); all other files will use
external references. If you're lucky, everything should work properly.
If you get undefined symbol errors, you need to make sure that each
template instance which is used in the program is used in the file which
implements that template. If you don't have any use for a particular
instance in that file, you can just instantiate it explicitly, using the
syntax from the latest C++ working paper:

```
template class A<int>;
template ostream& operator << (ostream&, const A<int>&);
```

This strategy will work with code written for either model. If you
are using code written for the Cfront model, the file containing a class
template and the file containing its member templates should be implemented in the same translation unit.

A slight variation on this approach is to instead use the flag
'-falt-external-templates'; this flag causes template instances to
be emitted in the translation unit that implements the header where
they are first instantiated, rather than the one which implements the
file where the templates are defined. This header must be the same in
all translation units, or things are likely to break.

See Section 5.4 [Declarations and Definitions in One Header], page 209,
for more discussion of these pragmas.

5.6 Extracting the function pointer from a bound pointer to member function

In C++, pointer to member functions (PMFs) are implemented using a
wide pointer of sorts to handle all the possible call mechanisms; the PMF
needs to store information about how to adjust the 'this' pointer, and if
the function pointed to is virtual, where to find the vtable, and where in the
vtable to look for the member function. If you are using PMFs in an inner
loop, you should really reconsider that decision. If that is not an option,
you can extract the pointer to the function that would be called for a given
object/PMF pair and call it directly inside the inner loop, to save a bit of
time.

Note that you will still be paying the penalty for the call through a function pointer; on most modern architectures, such a call defeats the branch
prediction features of the CPU. This is also true of normal virtual function
calls.

The syntax for this extension is

```
extern A a;
extern int (A::*fp)();
typedef int (*fptr)(A *);

fptr p = (fptr)(a.*fp);
```

You must specify '`-Wno-pmf-conversions`' to use this extension.

5.7 Type Abstraction using Signatures

In GNU C++, you can use the keyword `signature` to define a completely abstract class interface as a datatype. You can connect this abstraction with actual classes using signature pointers. If you want to use signatures, run the GNU compiler with the '`-fhandle-signatures`' command-line option. (With this option, the compiler reserves a second keyword `sigof` as well, for a future extension.)

Roughly, signatures are type abstractions or interfaces of classes. Some other languages have similar facilities. C++ signatures are related to ML's signatures, Haskell's type classes, definition modules in Modula-2, interface modules in Modula-3, abstract types in Emerald, type modules in Trellis/Owl, categories in Scratchpad II, and types in POOL-I. For a more detailed discussion of signatures, see *Signatures: A Language Extension for Improving Type Abstraction and Subtype Polymorphism in C++* by Gerald Baumgartner and Vincent F. Russo (Tech report CSD–TR–95–051, Dept. of Computer Sciences, Purdue University, August 1995, a slightly improved version appeared in *Software—Practice & Experience*, **25**(8), pp. 863–889, August 1995). You can get the tech report by anonymous FTP from `ftp.cs.purdue.edu` in '`pub/gb/Signature-design.ps.gz`'.

Syntactically, a signature declaration is a collection of member function declarations and nested type declarations. For example, this signature declaration defines a new abstract type `S` with member functions '`int foo ()`' and '`int bar (int)`':

```
signature S
{
  int foo ();
  int bar (int);
};
```

Since signature types do not include implementation definitions, you cannot write an instance of a signature directly. Instead, you can define a pointer to any class that contains the required interfaces as a *signature pointer*. Such a class *implements* the signature type.

To use a class as an implementation of `S`, you must ensure that the class has public member functions '`int foo ()`' and '`int bar (int)`'. The class can have other member functions as well, public or not; as long as it offers what's declared in the signature, it is suitable as an implementation of that signature type.

For example, suppose that `C` is a class that meets the requirements of signature `S` (`C` *conforms to* `S`). Then

```
C obj;
S * p = &obj;
```

defines a signature pointer `p` and initializes it to point to an object of type
`C`. The member function call 'int i = p->foo ();' executes 'obj.foo ()'.

Abstract virtual classes provide somewhat similar facilities in standard
C++. There are two main advantages to using signatures instead:

1. Subtyping becomes independent from inheritance. A class or signature
   type `T` is a subtype of a signature type `S` independent of any inheritance
   hierarchy as long as all the member functions declared in `S` are also
   found in `T`. So you can define a subtype hierarchy that is completely
   independent from any inheritance (implementation) hierarchy, instead
   of being forced to use types that mirror the class inheritance hierarchy.

2. Signatures allow you to work with existing class hierarchies as implementations of a signature type. If those class hierarchies are only available in compiled form, you're out of luck with abstract virtual classes,
   since an abstract virtual class cannot be retrofitted on top of existing
   class hierarchies. So you would be required to write interface classes as
   subtypes of the abstract virtual class.

There is one more detail about signatures. A signature declaration can
contain member function *definitions* as well as member function declarations. A signature member function with a full definition is called a *default
implementation*; classes need not contain that particular interface in order
to conform. For example, a class `C` can conform to the signature

```
signature T
{
  int f (int);
  int f0 () { return f (0); };
};
```

whether or not `C` implements the member function 'int f0 ()'. If you define
`C::f0`, that definition takes precedence; otherwise, the default implementation `S::f0` applies.

6 gcov: a Test Coverage Program

gcov is a tool you can use in conjunction with GNU CC to test code coverage in your programs.

This chapter describes version 1.5 of gcov.

6.1 Introduction to gcov

gcov is a test coverage program. Use it in concert with GNU CC to analyze your programs to help create more efficient, faster running code. You can use gcov as a profiling tool to help discover where your optimization efforts will best affect your code. You can also use gcov along with the other profiling tool, gprof, to assess which parts of your code use the greatest amount of computing time.

Profiling tools help you analyze your code's performance. Using a profiler such as gcov or gprof, you can find out some basic performance statistics, such as:

- how often each line of code executes
- what lines of code are actually executed
- how much computing time each section of code uses

Once you know these things about how your code works when compiled, you can look at each module to see which modules should be optimized. gcov helps you determine where to work on optimization.

Software developers also use coverage testing in concert with testsuites, to make sure software is actually good enough for a release. Testsuites can verify that a program works as expected; a coverage program tests to see how much of the program is exercised by the testsuite. Developers can then determine what kinds of test cases need to be added to the testsuites to create both better testing and a better final product.

You should compile your code without optimization if you plan to use gcov because the optimization, by combining some lines of code into one function, may not give you as much information as you need to look for 'hot spots' where the code is using a great deal of computer time. Likewise, because gcov accumulates statistics by line (at the lowest resolution), it works best with a programming style that places only one statement on each line. If you use complicated macros that expand to loops or to other control structures, the statistics are less helpful—they only report on the line where the macro call appears. If your complex macros behave like functions, you can replace them with inline functions to solve this problem.

gcov creates a logfile called 'sourcefile.gcov' which indicates how many times each line of a source file 'sourcefile.c' has executed. You can use these logfiles along with gprof to aid in fine-tuning the performance of your programs. gprof gives timing information you can use along with the information you get from gcov.

gcov works only on code compiled with GNU CC. It is not compatible with any other profiling or test coverage mechanism.

6.2 Invoking gcov

gcov [-b] [-v] [-n] [-l] [-f] [-o directory] *sourcefile*

-b   Write branch frequencies to the output file, and write branch summary info to the standard output. This option allows you to see how often each branch in your program was taken.

-v   Display the gcov version number (on the standard error stream).

-n   Do not create the gcov output file.

-l   Create long file names for included source files. For example, if the header file 'x.h' contains code, and was included in the file 'a.c', then running gcov on the file 'a.c' will produce an output file called 'a.c.x.h.gcov' instead of 'x.h.gcov'. This can be useful if 'x.h' is included in multiple source files.

-f   Output summaries for each function in addition to the file level summary.

-o   The directory where the object files live. Gcov will search for .bb, .bbg, and .da files in this directory.

When using gcov, you must first compile your program with two special GNU CC options: '-fprofile-arcs -ftest-coverage'. This tells the compiler to generate additional information needed by gcov (basically a flow graph of the program) and also includes additional code in the object files for generating the extra profiling information needed by gcov. These additional files are placed in the directory where the source code is located.

Running the program will cause profile output to be generated. For each source file compiled with -fprofile-arcs, an accompanying .da file will be placed in the source directory.

Running gcov with your program's source file names as arguments will now produce a listing of the code along with frequency of execution for each line. For example, if your program is called 'tmp.c', this is what you see when you use the basic gcov facility:

```
$ gcc -fprofile-arcs -ftest-coverage tmp.c
$ a.out
$ gcov tmp.c
 87.50% of 8 source lines executed in file tmp.c
Creating tmp.c.gcov.
```

The file 'tmp.c.gcov' contains output from gcov. Here is a sample:

```
                main()
                {
```

```
         1        int i, total;

         1        total = 0;

        11        for (i = 0; i < 10; i++)
        10            total += i;

         1        if (total != 45)
    ######            printf ("Failure\n");
                  else
         1            printf ("Success\n");
         1    }
```

When you use the '-b' option, your output looks like this:

```
$ gcov -b tmp.c
 87.50% of 8 source lines executed in file tmp.c
 80.00% of 5 branches executed in file tmp.c
 80.00% of 5 branches taken at least once in file tmp.c
 50.00% of 2 calls executed in file tmp.c
Creating tmp.c.gcov.
```

Here is a sample of a resulting 'tmp.c.gcov' file:

```
                  main()
                  {
         1        int i, total;

         1        total = 0;

        11        for (i = 0; i < 10; i++)
branch 0 taken = 91%
branch 1 taken = 100%
branch 2 taken = 100%
        10            total += i;

         1        if (total != 45)
branch 0 taken = 100%
    ######            printf ("Failure\n");
call 0 never executed
branch 1 never executed
                  else
         1            printf ("Success\n");
call 0 returns = 100%
         1    }
```

For each basic block, a line is printed after the last line of the basic block describing the branch or call that ends the basic block. There can be multiple branches and calls listed for a single source line if there are multiple basic blocks that end on that line. In this case, the branches and calls are each given a number. There is no simple way to map these branches and calls back to source constructs. In general, though, the lowest numbered branch or call will correspond to the leftmost construct on the source line.

For a branch, if it was executed at least once, then a percentage indicating the number of times the branch was taken divided by the number of times the branch was executed will be printed. Otherwise, the message "never executed" is printed.

For a call, if it was executed at least once, then a percentage indicating the number of times the call returned divided by the number of times the call was executed will be printed. This will usually be 100%, but may be less for functions call `exit` or `longjmp`, and thus may not return everytime they are called.

The execution counts are cumulative. If the example program were executed again without removing the `.da` file, the count for the number of times each line in the source was executed would be added to the results of the previous run(s). This is potentially useful in several ways. For example, it could be used to accumulate data over a number of program runs as part of a test verification suite, or to provide more accurate long-term information over a large number of program runs.

The data in the `.da` files is saved immediately before the program exits. For each source file compiled with -fprofile-arcs, the profiling code first attempts to read in an existing `.da` file; if the file doesn't match the executable (differing number of basic block counts) it will ignore the contents of the file. It then adds in the new execution counts and finally writes the data to the file.

6.3 Using gcov with GCC Optimization

If you plan to use `gcov` to help optimize your code, you must first compile your program with two special GNU CC options: '-fprofile-arcs -ftest-coverage'. Aside from that, you can use any other GNU CC options; but if you want to prove that every single line in your program was executed, you should not compile with optimization at the same time. On some machines the optimizer can eliminate some simple code lines by combining them with other lines. For example, code like this:

```
if (a != b)
   c = 1;
else
   c = 0;
```

can be compiled into one instruction on some machines. In this case, there is no way for `gcov` to calculate separate execution counts for each line because there isn't separate code for each line. Hence the `gcov` output looks like this if you compiled the program with optimization:

```
100   if (a != b)
100     c = 1;
100   else
100     c = 0;
```

The output shows that this block of code, combined by optimization, executed 100 times. In one sense this result is correct, because there was only one instruction representing all four of these lines. However, the output does not indicate how many times the result was 0 and how many times the result was 1.

6.4 Brief description of `gcov` data files

`gcov` uses three files for doing profiling. The names of these files are derived from the original *source* file by substituting the file suffix with either `.bb`, `.bbg`, or `.da`. All of these files are placed in the same directory as the source file, and contain data stored in a platform-independent method.

The `.bb` and `.bbg` files are generated when the source file is compiled with the GNU CC '`-ftest-coverage`' option. The `.bb` file contains a list of source files (including headers), functions within those files, and line numbers corresponding to each basic block in the source file.

The `.bb` file format consists of several lists of 4-byte integers which correspond to the line numbers of each basic block in the file. Each list is terminated by a line number of 0. A line number of -1 is used to designate that the source file name (padded to a 4-byte boundary and followed by another -1) follows. In addition, a line number of -2 is used to designate that the name of a function (also padded to a 4-byte boundary and followed by a -2) follows.

The `.bbg` file is used to reconstruct the program flow graph for the source file. It contains a list of the program flow arcs (possible branches taken from one basic block to another) for each function which, in combination with the `.bb` file, enables gcov to reconstruct the program flow.

In the `.bbg` file, the format is:

```
number of basic blocks for function #0 (4-byte number)
total number of arcs for function #0 (4-byte number)
count of arcs in basic block #0 (4-byte number)
destination basic block of arc #0 (4-byte number)
flag bits (4-byte number)
destination basic block of arc #1 (4-byte number)
flag bits (4-byte number)
...
destination basic block of arc #N (4-byte number)
flag bits (4-byte number)
```

```
count of arcs in basic block #1 (4-byte number)
destination basic block of arc #0 (4-byte number)
flag bits (4-byte number)
    ...
```

A -1 (stored as a 4-byte number) is used to separate each function's list of basic blocks, and to verify that the file has been read correctly.

The .da file is generated when a program containing object files built with the GNU CC '-fprofile-arcs' option is executed. A separate .da file is created for each source file compiled with this option, and the name of the .da file is stored as an absolute pathname in the resulting object file. This path name is derived from the source file name by substituting a .da suffix.

The format of the .da file is fairly simple. The first 8-byte number is the number of counts in the file, followed by the counts (stored as 8-byte numbers). Each count corresponds to the number of times each arc in the program is executed. The counts are cumulative; each time the program is executed, it attemps to combine the existing .da files with the new counts for this invocation of the program. It ignores the contents of any .da files whose number of arcs doesn't correspond to the current program, and merely overwrites them instead.

All three of these files use the functions in gcov-io.h to store integers; the functions in this header provide a machine-independent mechanism for storing and retrieving data from a stream.

7 Known Causes of Trouble with GCC

This section describes known problems that affect users of GCC. Most of these are not GCC bugs per se—if they were, we would fix them. But the result for a user may be like the result of a bug.

Some of these problems are due to bugs in other software, some are missing features that are too much work to add, and some are places where people's opinions differ as to what is best.

7.1 Actual Bugs We Haven't Fixed Yet

- The `fixincludes` script interacts badly with automounters; if the directory of system header files is automounted, it tends to be unmounted while `fixincludes` is running. This would seem to be a bug in the automounter. We don't know any good way to work around it.

- The `fixproto` script will sometimes add prototypes for the `sigsetjmp` and `siglongjmp` functions that reference the `jmp_buf` type before that type is defined. To work around this, edit the offending file and place the typedef in front of the prototypes.

- There are several obscure case of mis-using struct, union, and enum tags that are not detected as errors by the compiler.

- When '`-pedantic-errors`' is specified, GCC will incorrectly give an error message when a function name is specified in an expression involving the comma operator.

- Loop unrolling doesn't work properly for certain C++ programs. This is a bug in the C++ front end. It sometimes emits incorrect debug info, and the loop unrolling code is unable to recover from this error.

7.2 Installation Problems

This is a list of problems (and some apparent problems which don't really mean anything is wrong) that show up during installation of GNU CC.

- On certain systems, defining certain environment variables such as `CC` can interfere with the functioning of `make`.

- If you encounter seemingly strange errors when trying to build the compiler in a directory other than the source directory, it could be because you have previously configured the compiler in the source directory. Make sure you have done all the necessary preparations. See Section 3.3 [Other Dir], page 148.

- If you build GCC on a BSD system using a directory stored in a System V file system, problems may occur in running `fixincludes` if the System V file system doesn't support symbolic links. These problems result in a failure to fix the declaration of `size_t` in '`sys/types.h`'. If you find that `size_t` is a signed type and that type mismatches occur, this could be the cause.

The solution is not to use such a directory for building GCC.

- In previous versions of GCC, the `gcc` driver program looked for `as` and `ld` in various places; for example, in files beginning with '/usr/local/lib/gcc-'. GCC version 2 looks for them in the directory '/usr/local/lib/gcc-lib/*target*/*version*'.

  Thus, to use a version of `as` or `ld` that is not the system default, for example `gas` or GNU `ld`, you must put them in that directory (or make links to them from that directory).

- Some commands executed when making the compiler may fail (return a non-zero status) and be ignored by `make`. These failures, which are often due to files that were not found, are expected, and can safely be ignored.

- It is normal to have warnings in compiling certain files about unreachable code and about enumeration type clashes. These files' names begin with 'insn-'. Also, 'real.c' may get some warnings that you can ignore.

- Sometimes `make` recompiles parts of the compiler when installing the compiler. In one case, this was traced down to a bug in `make`. Either ignore the problem or switch to GNU Make.

- If you have installed a program known as purify, you may find that it causes errors while linking `enquire`, which is part of building GCC. The fix is to get rid of the file `real-ld` which purify installs—so that GCC won't try to use it.

- On GNU/Linux SLS 1.01, there is a problem with 'libc.a': it does not contain the obstack functions. However, GCC assumes that the obstack functions are in 'libc.a' when it is the GNU C library. To work around this problem, change the `__GNU_LIBRARY__` conditional around line 31 to '#if 1'.

- On some 386 systems, building the compiler never finishes because `enquire` hangs due to a hardware problem in the motherboard—it reports floating point exceptions to the kernel incorrectly. You can install GCC except for 'float.h' by patching out the command to run `enquire`. You may also be able to fix the problem for real by getting a replacement motherboard. This problem was observed in Revision E of the Micronics motherboard, and is fixed in Revision F. It has also been observed in the MYLEX MXA-33 motherboard.

  If you encounter this problem, you may also want to consider removing the FPU from the socket during the compilation. Alternatively, if you are running SCO Unix, you can reboot and force the FPU to be ignored. To do this, type 'hd(40)unix auto ignorefpu'.

- On some 386 systems, GCC crashes trying to compile 'enquire.c'. This happens on machines that don't have a 387 FPU chip. On 386 machines, the system kernel is supposed to emulate the 387 when you don't have one. The crash is due to a bug in the emulator.

One of these systems is the Unix from Interactive Systems: 386/ix. On this system, an alternate emulator is provided, and it does work. To use it, execute this command as super-user:

```
ln /etc/emulator.rel1 /etc/emulator
```

and then reboot the system. (The default emulator file remains present under the name 'emulator.dflt'.)

Try using '/etc/emulator.att', if you have such a problem on the SCO system.

Another system which has this problem is Esix. We don't know whether it has an alternate emulator that works.

On NetBSD 0.8, a similar problem manifests itself as these error messages:

```
enquire.c: In function 'fprop':
enquire.c:2328: floating overflow
```

- On SCO systems, when compiling GCC with the system's compiler, do not use '-O'. Some versions of the system's compiler miscompile GCC with '-O'.

- Sometimes on a Sun 4 you may observe a crash in the program genflags or genoutput while building GCC. This is said to be due to a bug in sh. You can probably get around it by running genflags or genoutput manually and then retrying the make.

- On Solaris 2, executables of GCC version 2.0.2 are commonly available, but they have a bug that shows up when compiling current versions of GCC: undefined symbol errors occur during assembly if you use '-g'.

  The solution is to compile the current version of GCC without '-g'. That makes a working compiler which you can use to recompile with '-g'.

- Solaris 2 comes with a number of optional OS packages. Some of these packages are needed to use GCC fully. If you did not install all optional packages when installing Solaris, you will need to verify that the packages that GCC needs are installed.

  To check whether an optional package is installed, use the pkginfo command. To add an optional package, use the pkgadd command. For further details, see the Solaris documentation.

  For Solaris 2.0 and 2.1, GCC needs six packages: 'SUNWarc', 'SUNWbtool', 'SUNWesu', 'SUNWhea', 'SUNWlibm', and 'SUNWtoo'.

  For Solaris 2.2, GCC needs an additional seventh package: 'SUNWsprot'.

- On Solaris 2, trying to use the linker and other tools in '/usr/ucb' to install GCC has been observed to cause trouble. For example, the linker may hang indefinitely. The fix is to remove '/usr/ucb' from your PATH.

- If you use the 1.31 version of the MIPS assembler (such as was shipped with Ultrix 3.1), you will need to use the -fno-delayed-branch switch when optimizing floating point code. Otherwise, the assembler will complain when the GCC compiler fills a branch delay slot with a floating point instruction, such as `add.d`.

- If on a MIPS system you get an error message saying "does not have gp sections for all it's [sic] sectons [sic]", don't worry about it. This happens whenever you use GAS with the MIPS linker, but there is not really anything wrong, and it is okay to use the output file. You can stop such warnings by installing the GNU linker.

  It would be nice to extend GAS to produce the gp tables, but they are optional, and there should not be a warning about their absence.

- In Ultrix 4.0 on the MIPS machine, 'stdio.h' does not work with GNU CC at all unless it has been fixed with `fixincludes`. This causes problems in building GCC. Once GCC is installed, the problems go away.

  To work around this problem, when making the stage 1 compiler, specify this option to Make:

  ```
  GCC_FOR_TARGET="./xgcc -B./ -I./include"
  ```

  When making stage 2 and stage 3, specify this option:

  ```
  CFLAGS="-g -I./include"
  ```

- Users have reported some problems with version 2.0 of the MIPS compiler tools that were shipped with Ultrix 4.1. Version 2.10 which came with Ultrix 4.2 seems to work fine.

  Users have also reported some problems with version 2.20 of the MIPS compiler tools that were shipped with RISC/os 4.x. The earlier version 2.11 seems to work fine.

- Some versions of the MIPS linker will issue an assertion failure when linking code that uses `alloca` against shared libraries on RISC-OS 5.0, and DEC's OSF/1 systems. This is a bug in the linker, that is supposed to be fixed in future revisions. To protect against this, GCC passes '-non_shared' to the linker unless you pass an explicit '-shared' or '-call_shared' switch.

- On System V release 3, you may get this error message while linking:

  ```
  ld fatal: failed to write symbol name something
    in strings table for file whatever
  ```

  This probably indicates that the disk is full or your ULIMIT won't allow the file to be as large as it needs to be.

  This problem can also result because the kernel parameter MAXUMEM is too small. If so, you must regenerate the kernel and make the value much larger. The default value is reported to be 1024; a value of 32768 is said to work. Smaller values may also work.

- On System V, if you get an error like this,

```
/usr/local/lib/bison.simple: In function 'yyparse':
/usr/local/lib/bison.simple:625: virtual memory exhausted
```
that too indicates a problem with disk space, ULIMIT, or `MAXUMEM`.

- Current GCC versions probably do not work on version 2 of the NeXT operating system.

- On NeXTStep 3.0, the Objective C compiler does not work, due, apparently, to a kernel bug that it happens to trigger. This problem does not happen on 3.1.

- On the Tower models 4n0 and 6n0, by default a process is not allowed to have more than one megabyte of memory. GCC cannot compile itself (or many other programs) with '`-O`' in that much memory.

  To solve this problem, reconfigure the kernel adding the following line to the configuration file:

  ```
  MAXUMEM = 4096
  ```

- On HP 9000 series 300 or 400 running HP-UX release 8.0, there is a bug in the assembler that must be fixed before GCC can be built. This bug manifests itself during the first stage of compilation, while building '`libgcc2.a`':

  ```
  _floatdisf
  cc1: warning: '-g' option not supported on this version of GCC
  cc1: warning: '-g1' option not supported on this version of GCC
  ./xgcc: Internal compiler error: program as got fatal signal 11
  ```

  A patched version of the assembler is available by anonymous ftp from `altdorf.ai.mit.edu` as the file '`archive/cph/hpux-8.0-assembler`'. If you have HP software support, the patch can also be obtained directly from HP, as described in the following note:

  > This is the patched assembler, to patch SR#1653-010439, where the assembler aborts on floating point constants.

  > The bug is not really in the assembler, but in the shared library version of the function "cvtnum(3c)". The bug on "cvtnum(3c)" is SR#4701-078451. Anyway, the attached assembler uses the archive library version of "cvtnum(3c)" and thus does not exhibit the bug.

  This patch is also known as PHCO_4484.

- On HP-UX version 8.05, but not on 8.07 or more recent versions, the `fixproto` shell script triggers a bug in the system shell. If you encounter this problem, upgrade your operating system or use BASH (the GNU shell) to run `fixproto`.

- Some versions of the Pyramid C compiler are reported to be unable to compile GCC. You must use an older version of GCC for bootstrapping. One indication of this problem is if you get a crash when GCC compiles the function `muldi3` in file '`libgcc2.c`'.

You may be able to succeed by getting GCC version 1, installing it, and using it to compile GCC version 2. The bug in the Pyramid C compiler does not seem to affect GCC version 1.

- There may be similar problems on System V Release 3.1 on 386 systems.
- On the Intel Paragon (an i860 machine), if you are using operating system version 1.0, you will get warnings or errors about redefinition of `va_arg` when you build GCC.

  If this happens, then you need to link most programs with the library 'iclib.a'. You must also modify 'stdio.h' as follows: before the lines

  ```
  #if     defined(__i860__) && !defined(_VA_LIST)
  #include <va_list.h>
  ```

  insert the line

  ```
  #if __PGC__
  ```

  and after the lines

  ```
  extern int  vprintf(const char *, va_list );
  extern int  vsprintf(char *, const char *, va_list );
  #endif
  ```

  insert the line

  ```
  #endif /* __PGC__ */
  ```

  These problems don't exist in operating system version 1.1.

- On the Altos 3068, programs compiled with GCC won't work unless you fix a kernel bug. This happens using system versions V.2.2 1.0gT1 and V.2.2 1.0e and perhaps later versions as well. See the file 'README.ALTOS'.
- You will get several sorts of compilation and linking errors on the we32k if you don't follow the special instructions. See Section 3.2 [Configurations], page 131.
- A bug in the HP-UX 8.05 (and earlier) shell will cause the fixproto program to report an error of the form:

  ```
  ./fixproto: sh internal 1K buffer overflow
  ```

  To fix this, change the first line of the fixproto script to look like:

  ```
  #!/bin/ksh
  ```

7.3 Cross-Compiler Problems

You may run into problems with cross compilation on certain machines, for several reasons.

- Cross compilation can run into trouble for certain machines because some target machines' assemblers require floating point numbers to be written as *integer* constants in certain contexts.

The compiler writes these integer constants by examining the floating point value as an integer and printing that integer, because this is simple to write and independent of the details of the floating point representation. But this does not work if the compiler is running on a different machine with an incompatible floating point format, or even a different byte-ordering.

In addition, correct constant folding of floating point values requires representing them in the target machine's format. (The C standard does not quite require this, but in practice it is the only way to win.)

It is now possible to overcome these problems by defining macros such as `REAL_VALUE_TYPE`. But doing so is a substantial amount of work for each target machine. See Section 17.18 [Cross-compilation], page 508.

- At present, the program 'mips-tfile' which adds debug support to object files on MIPS systems does not work in a cross compile environment.

7.4 Interoperation

This section lists various difficulties encountered in using GNU C or GNU C++ together with other compilers or with the assemblers, linkers, libraries and debuggers on certain systems.

- Objective C does not work on the RS/6000.
- GNU C++ does not do name mangling in the same way as other C++ compilers. This means that object files compiled with one compiler cannot be used with another.

  This effect is intentional, to protect you from more subtle problems. Compilers differ as to many internal details of C++ implementation, including: how class instances are laid out, how multiple inheritance is implemented, and how virtual function calls are handled. If the name encoding were made the same, your programs would link against libraries provided from other compilers—but the programs would then crash when run. Incompatible libraries are then detected at link time, rather than at run time.

- Older GDB versions sometimes fail to read the output of GCC version 2. If you have trouble, get GDB version 4.4 or later.
- DBX rejects some files produced by GCC, though it accepts similar constructs in output from PCC. Until someone can supply a coherent description of what is valid DBX input and what is not, there is nothing I can do about these problems. You are on your own.
- The GNU assembler (GAS) does not support PIC. To generate PIC code, you must use some other assembler, such as '/bin/as'.
- On some BSD systems, including some versions of Ultrix, use of profiling causes static variable destructors (currently used only in C++) not to be run.

- Use of '-I/usr/include' may cause trouble.

  Many systems come with header files that won't work with GCC unless corrected by `fixincludes`. The corrected header files go in a new directory; GCC searches this directory before '/usr/include'. If you use '-I/usr/include', this tells GCC to search '/usr/include' earlier on, before the corrected headers. The result is that you get the uncorrected header files.

  Instead, you should use these options (when compiling C programs):

  > -I/usr/local/lib/gcc-lib/*target*/*version*/include -I/usr/include

  For C++ programs, GCC also uses a special directory that defines C++ interfaces to standard C subroutines. This directory is meant to be searched *before* other standard include directories, so that it takes precedence. If you are compiling C++ programs and specifying include directories explicitly, use this option first, then the two options above:

  > -I/usr/local/lib/g++-include

- On some SGI systems, when you use '-lgl_s' as an option, it gets translated magically to '-lgl_s -lX11_s -lc_s'. Naturally, this does not happen when you use GCC. You must specify all three options explicitly.

- On a Sparc, GCC aligns all values of type `double` on an 8-byte boundary, and it expects every `double` to be so aligned. The Sun compiler usually gives `double` values 8-byte alignment, with one exception: function arguments of type `double` may not be aligned.

  As a result, if a function compiled with Sun CC takes the address of an argument of type `double` and passes this pointer of type `double *` to a function compiled with GCC, dereferencing the pointer may cause a fatal signal.

  One way to solve this problem is to compile your entire program with GNU CC. Another solution is to modify the function that is compiled with Sun CC to copy the argument into a local variable; local variables are always properly aligned. A third solution is to modify the function that uses the pointer to dereference it via the following function `access_double` instead of directly with '*':

```
inline double
access_double (double *unaligned_ptr)
{
  union d2i { double d; int i[2]; };

  union d2i *p = (union d2i *) unaligned_ptr;
  union d2i u;

  u.i[0] = p->i[0];
  u.i[1] = p->i[1];
```

```
    return u.d;
}
```

Storing into the pointer can be done likewise with the same union.

- On Solaris, the `malloc` function in the 'libmalloc.a' library may allocate memory that is only 4 byte aligned. Since GCC on the Sparc assumes that doubles are 8 byte aligned, this may result in a fatal signal if doubles are stored in memory allocated by the 'libmalloc.a' library.

  The solution is to not use the 'libmalloc.a' library. Use instead `malloc` and related functions from 'libc.a'; they do not have this problem.

- Sun forgot to include a static version of 'libdl.a' with some versions of SunOS (mainly 4.1). This results in undefined symbols when linking static binaries (that is, if you use '-static'). If you see undefined symbols _dlclose, _dlsym or _dlopen when linking, compile and link against the file 'mit/util/misc/dlsym.c' from the MIT version of X windows.

- The 128-bit long double format that the Sparc port supports currently works by using the architecturally defined quad-word floating point instructions. Since there is no hardware that supports these instructions they must be emulated by the operating system. Long doubles do not work in Sun OS versions 4.0.3 and earlier, because the kernel emulator uses an obsolete and incompatible format. Long doubles do not work in Sun OS version 4.1.1 due to a problem in a Sun library. Long doubles do work on Sun OS versions 4.1.2 and higher, but GCC does not enable them by default. Long doubles appear to work in Sun OS 5.x (Solaris 2.x).

- On HP-UX version 9.01 on the HP PA, the HP compiler `cc` does not compile GCC correctly. We do not yet know why. However, GCC compiled on earlier HP-UX versions works properly on HP-UX 9.01 and can compile itself properly on 9.01.

- On the HP PA machine, ADB sometimes fails to work on functions compiled with GCC. Specifically, it fails to work on functions that use `alloca` or variable-size arrays. This is because GCC doesn't generate HP-UX unwind descriptors for such functions. It may even be impossible to generate them.

- Debugging ('-g') is not supported on the HP PA machine, unless you use the preliminary GNU tools (see Chapter 3 [Installation], page 121).

- Taking the address of a label may generate errors from the HP-UX PA assembler. GAS for the PA does not have this problem.

- Using floating point parameters for indirect calls to static functions will not work when using the HP assembler. There simply is no way for GCC to specify what registers hold arguments for static functions when using the HP assembler. GAS for the PA does not have this problem.

- In extremely rare cases involving some very large functions you may receive errors from the HP linker complaining about an out of bounds unconditional branch offset. This used to occur more often in previous versions of GCC, but is now exceptionally rare. If you should run into it, you can work around by making your function smaller.

- GCC compiled code sometimes emits warnings from the HP-UX assembler of the form:

  ```
  (warning) Use of GR3 when
    frame >= 8192 may cause conflict.
  ```

  These warnings are harmless and can be safely ignored.

- The current version of the assembler ('/bin/as') for the RS/6000 has certain problems that prevent the '-g' option in GCC from working. Note that 'Makefile.in' uses '-g' by default when compiling 'libgcc2.c'.

  IBM has produced a fixed version of the assembler. The upgraded assembler unfortunately was not included in any of the AIX 3.2 update PTF releases (3.2.2, 3.2.3, or 3.2.3e). Users of AIX 3.1 should request PTF U403044 from IBM and users of AIX 3.2 should request PTF U416277. See the file 'README.RS6000' for more details on these updates.

  You can test for the presense of a fixed assembler by using the command

  ```
  as -u < /dev/null
  ```

  If the command exits normally, the assembler fix already is installed. If the assembler complains that "-u" is an unknown flag, you need to order the fix.

- On the IBM RS/6000, compiling code of the form

  ```
  extern int foo;
  ```

  ```
  ... foo ...
  ```

  ```
  static int foo;
  ```

  will cause the linker to report an undefined symbol foo. Although this behavior differs from most other systems, it is not a bug because redefining an extern variable as static is undefined in ANSI C.

- AIX on the RS/6000 provides support (NLS) for environments outside of the United States. Compilers and assemblers use NLS to support locale-specific representations of various objects including floating-point numbers ("." vs "," for separating decimal fractions). There have been problems reported where the library linked with GCC does not produce the same floating-point formats that the assembler accepts. If you have this problem, set the LANG environment variable to "C" or "En_US".

- Even if you specify '-fdollars-in-identifiers', you cannot successfully use '$' in identifiers on the RS/6000 due a restriction in the IBM assembler. GAS supports these identifiers.

- On the RS/6000, XLC version 1.3.0.0 will miscompile 'jump.c'. XLC version 1.3.0.1 or later fixes this problem. You can obtain XLC-1.3.0.2 by requesting PTF 421749 from IBM.

- There is an assembler bug in versions of DG/UX prior to 5.4.2.01 that occurs when the 'fldcr' instruction is used. GCC uses 'fldcr' on the 88100 to serialize volatile memory references. Use the option '-mno-serialize-volatile' if your version of the assembler has this bug.

- On VMS, GAS versions 1.38.1 and earlier may cause spurious warning messages from the linker. These warning messages complain of mismatched psect attributes. You can ignore them. See Section 3.6 [VMS Install], page 155.

- On NewsOS version 3, if you include both of the files 'stddef.h' and 'sys/types.h', you get an error because there are two typedefs of size_t. You should change 'sys/types.h' by adding these lines around the definition of size_t:

  ```
  #ifndef _SIZE_T
  #define _SIZE_T
  actual typedef here
  #endif
  ```

- On the Alliant, the system's own convention for returning structures and unions is unusual, and is not compatible with GCC no matter what options are used.

- On the IBM RT PC, the MetaWare HighC compiler (hc) uses a different convention for structure and union returning. Use the option '-mhc-struct-return' to tell GCC to use a convention compatible with it.

- On Ultrix, the Fortran compiler expects registers 2 through 5 to be saved by function calls. However, the C compiler uses conventions compatible with BSD Unix: registers 2 through 5 may be clobbered by function calls.

  GCC uses the same convention as the Ultrix C compiler. You can use these options to produce code compatible with the Fortran compiler:

  ```
  -fcall-saved-r2 -fcall-saved-r3 -fcall-saved-r4 -fcall-saved-r5
  ```

- On the WE32k, you may find that programs compiled with GCC do not work with the standard shared C library. You may need to link with the ordinary C compiler. If you do so, you must specify the following options:

  ```
  -L/usr/local/lib/gcc-lib/we32k-att-sysv/2.8.1 -lgcc -lc_s
  ```

The first specifies where to find the library 'libgcc.a' specified with
the '-lgcc' option.

GCC does linking by invoking ld, just as cc does, and there is no reason
why it *should* matter which compilation program you use to invoke ld.
If someone tracks this problem down, it can probably be fixed easily.

- On the Alpha, you may get assembler errors about invalid syntax as a
  result of floating point constants. This is due to a bug in the C library
  functions ecvt, fcvt and gcvt. Given valid floating point numbers,
  they sometimes print 'NaN'.

- On Irix 4.0.5F (and perhaps in some other versions), an assembler bug
  sometimes reorders instructions incorrectly when optimization is turned
  on. If you think this may be happening to you, try using the GNU
  assembler; GAS version 2.1 supports ECOFF on Irix.

  Or use the '-noasmopt' option when you compile GCC with itself, and
  then again when you compile your program. (This is a temporary kludge
  to turn off assembler optimization on Irix.) If this proves to be what you
  need, edit the assembler spec in the file 'specs' so that it unconditionally
  passes '-O0' to the assembler, and never passes '-O2' or '-O3'.

7.5 Problems Compiling Certain Programs

Certain programs have problems compiling.

- Parse errors may occur compiling X11 on a Decstation running Ultrix 4.2 because of problems in DEC's versions of the X11 header
  files 'X11/Xlib.h' and 'X11/Xutil.h'. People recommend adding
  '-I/usr/include/mit' to use the MIT versions of the header files, using
  the '-traditional' switch to turn off ANSI C, or fixing the header files
  by adding this:

  ```
  #ifdef __STDC__
  #define NeedFunctionPrototypes 0
  #endif
  ```

- If you have trouble compiling Perl on a SunOS 4 system, it may be
  because Perl specifies '-I/usr/ucbinclude'. This accesses the unfixed
  header files. Perl specifies the options

  ```
  -traditional -Dvolatile=__volatile__
  -I/usr/include/sun -I/usr/ucbinclude
  -fpcc-struct-return
  ```

  most of which are unnecessary with GCC 2.4.5 and newer versions. You can make a properly working Perl by setting ccflags to
  '-fwritable-strings' (implied by the '-traditional' in the original
  options) and cppflags to empty in 'config.sh', then typing './doSH;
  make depend; make'.

- On various 386 Unix systems derived from System V, including SCO, ISC, and ESIX, you may get error messages about running out of virtual memory while compiling certain programs.

  You can prevent this problem by linking GCC with the GNU malloc (which thus replaces the malloc that comes with the system). GNU malloc is available as a separate package, and also in the file 'src/gmalloc.c' in the GNU Emacs 19 distribution.

  If you have installed GNU malloc as a separate library package, use this option when you relink GCC:

  ```
  MALLOC=/usr/local/lib/libgmalloc.a
  ```

  Alternatively, if you have compiled 'gmalloc.c' from Emacs 19, copy the object file to 'gmalloc.o' and use this option when you relink GCC:

  ```
  MALLOC=gmalloc.o
  ```

7.6 Incompatibilities of GCC

There are several noteworthy incompatibilities between GNU C and most existing (non-ANSI) versions of C. The '-traditional' option eliminates many of these incompatibilities, *but not all*, by telling GNU C to behave like the other C compilers.

- GCC normally makes string constants read-only. If several identical-looking string constants are used, GCC stores only one copy of the string.

  One consequence is that you cannot call `mktemp` with a string constant argument. The function `mktemp` always alters the string its argument points to.

  Another consequence is that `sscanf` does not work on some systems when passed a string constant as its format control string or input. This is because `sscanf` incorrectly tries to write into the string constant. Likewise `fscanf` and `scanf`.

  The best solution to these problems is to change the program to use `char`-array variables with initialization strings for these purposes instead of string constants. But if this is not possible, you can use the '-fwritable-strings' flag, which directs GCC to handle string constants the same way most C compilers do. '-traditional' also has this effect, among others.

- `-2147483648` is positive.

  This is because 2147483648 cannot fit in the type `int`, so (following the ANSI C rules) its data type is `unsigned long int`. Negating this value yields 2147483648 again.

- GCC does not substitute macro arguments when they appear inside of string constants. For example, the following macro in GCC

```
#define foo(a) "a"
```
will produce output `"a"` regardless of what the argument *a* is.

The '-traditional' option directs GCC to handle such cases (among others) in the old-fashioned (non-ANSI) fashion.

- When you use `setjmp` and `longjmp`, the only automatic variables guaranteed to remain valid are those declared `volatile`. This is a consequence of automatic register allocation. Consider this function:

```
jmp_buf j;

foo ()
{
  int a, b;

  a = fun1 ();
  if (setjmp (j))
    return a;

  a = fun2 ();
  /* longjmp (j) may occur in fun3. */
  return a + fun3 ();
}
```

Here `a` may or may not be restored to its first value when the `longjmp` occurs. If `a` is allocated in a register, then its first value is restored; otherwise, it keeps the last value stored in it.

If you use the '-W' option with the '-O' option, you will get a warning when GCC thinks such a problem might be possible.

The '-traditional' option directs GNU C to put variables in the stack by default, rather than in registers, in functions that call `setjmp`. This results in the behavior found in traditional C compilers.

- Programs that use preprocessing directives in the middle of macro arguments do not work with GCC. For example, a program like this will not work:

```
foobar (
#define luser
        hack)
```

ANSI C does not permit such a construct. It would make sense to support it when '-traditional' is used, but it is too much work to implement.

- Declarations of external variables and functions within a block apply only to the block containing the declaration. In other words, they have the same scope as any other declaration in the same place.

In some other C compilers, a `extern` declaration affects all the rest of the file even if it happens within a block.

The '-traditional' option directs GNU C to treat all **extern** declarations as global, like traditional compilers.

- In traditional C, you can combine **long**, etc., with a typedef name, as shown here:

```
typedef int foo;
typedef long foo bar;
```

In ANSI C, this is not allowed: **long** and other type modifiers require an explicit **int**. Because this criterion is expressed by Bison grammar rules rather than C code, the '-traditional' flag cannot alter it.

- PCC allows typedef names to be used as function parameters. The difficulty described immediately above applies here too.

- PCC allows whitespace in the middle of compound assignment operators such as '+='. GCC, following the ANSI standard, does not allow this. The difficulty described immediately above applies here too.

- GCC complains about unterminated character constants inside of preprocessing conditionals that fail. Some programs have English comments enclosed in conditionals that are guaranteed to fail; if these comments contain apostrophes, GCC will probably report an error. For example, this code would produce an error:

```
#if 0
You can't expect this to work.
#endif
```

The best solution to such a problem is to put the text into an actual C comment delimited by '/*...*/'. However, '-traditional' suppresses these error messages.

- Many user programs contain the declaration '**long time ();**'. In the past, the system header files on many systems did not actually declare **time**, so it did not matter what type your program declared it to return. But in systems with ANSI C headers, **time** is declared to return **time_t**, and if that is not the same as **long**, then '**long time ();**' is erroneous.

  The solution is to change your program to use **time_t** as the return type of **time**.

- When compiling functions that return **float**, PCC converts it to a double. GCC actually returns a **float**. If you are concerned with PCC compatibility, you should declare your functions to return **double**; you might as well say what you mean.

- When compiling functions that return structures or unions, GCC output code normally uses a method different from that used on most versions of Unix. As a result, code compiled with GCC cannot call a structure-returning function compiled with PCC, and vice versa.

  The method used by GCC is as follows: a structure or union which is 1, 2, 4 or 8 bytes long is returned like a scalar. A structure or union with any other size is stored into an address supplied by the caller (usually in a special, fixed register, but on some machines it is passed on the stack). The machine-description macros `STRUCT_VALUE` and `STRUCT_INCOMING_VALUE` tell GCC where to pass this address.

By contrast, PCC on most target machines returns structures and unions of any size by copying the data into an area of static storage, and then returning the address of that storage as if it were a pointer value. The caller must copy the data from that memory area to the place where the value is wanted. GCC does not use this method because it is slower and nonreentrant.

On some newer machines, PCC uses a reentrant convention for all structure and union returning. GCC on most of these machines uses a compatible convention when returning structures and unions in memory, but still returns small structures and unions in registers.

You can tell GCC to use a compatible convention for all structure and union returning with the option '`-fpcc-struct-return`'.

- GNU C complains about program fragments such as '`0x74ae-0x4000`' which appear to be two hexadecimal constants separated by the minus operator. Actually, this string is a single *preprocessing token*. Each such token must correspond to one token in C. Since this does not, GNU C prints an error message. Although it may appear obvious that what is meant is an operator and two values, the ANSI C standard specifically requires that this be treated as erroneous.

  A *preprocessing token* is a *preprocessing number* if it begins with a digit and is followed by letters, underscores, digits, periods and '`e+`', '`e-`', '`E+`', or '`E-`' character sequences.

  To make the above program fragment valid, place whitespace in front of the minus sign. This whitespace will end the preprocessing number.

7.7 Fixed Header Files

GCC needs to install corrected versions of some system header files. This is because most target systems have some header files that won't work with GCC unless they are changed. Some have bugs, some are incompatible with ANSI C, and some depend on special features of other compilers.

Installing GCC automatically creates and installs the fixed header files, by running a program called `fixincludes` (or for certain targets an alternative such as `fixinc.svr4`). Normally, you don't need to pay attention to this. But there are cases where it doesn't do the right thing automatically.

- If you update the system's header files, such as by installing a new system version, the fixed header files of GCC are not automatically updated. The easiest way to update them is to reinstall GCC. (If you want to be clever, look in the makefile and you can find a shortcut.)
- On some systems, in particular SunOS 4, header file directories contain machine-specific symbolic links in certain places. This makes it possible

to share most of the header files among hosts running the same version of SunOS 4 on different machine models.

The programs that fix the header files do not understand this special way of using symbolic links; therefore, the directory of fixed header files is good only for the machine model used to build it.

In SunOS 4, only programs that look inside the kernel will notice the difference between machine models. Therefore, for most purposes, you need not be concerned about this.

It is possible to make separate sets of fixed header files for the different machine models, and arrange a structure of symbolic links so as to use the proper set, but you'll have to do this by hand.

- On Lynxos, GCC by default does not fix the header files. This is because bugs in the shell cause the `fixincludes` script to fail.

This means you will encounter problems due to bugs in the system header files. It may be no comfort that they aren't GCC's fault, but it does mean that there's nothing for us to do about them.

7.8 Standard Libraries

GCC by itself attempts to be what the ISO/ANSI C standard calls a *conforming freestanding implementation*. This means all ANSI C language features are available, as well as the contents of 'float.h', 'limits.h', 'stdarg.h', and 'stddef.h'. The rest of the C library is supplied by the vendor of the operating system. If that C library doesn't conform to the C standards, then your programs might get warnings (especially when using '-Wall') that you don't expect.

For example, the `sprintf` function on SunOS 4.1.3 returns `char *` while the C standard says that `sprintf` returns an `int`. The `fixincludes` program could make the prototype for this function match the Standard, but that would be wrong, since the function will still return `char *`.

If you need a Standard compliant library, then you need to find one, as GCC does not provide one. The GNU C library (called `glibc`) has been ported to a number of operating systems, and provides ANSI/ISO, POSIX, BSD and SystemV compatibility. You could also ask your operating system vendor if newer libraries are available.

7.9 Disappointments and Misunderstandings

These problems are perhaps regrettable, but we don't know any practical way around them.

- Certain local variables aren't recognized by debuggers when you compile with optimization.

This occurs because sometimes GCC optimizes the variable out of existence. There is no way to tell the debugger how to compute the value such a variable "would have had", and it is not clear that would be desirable anyway. So GCC simply does not mention the eliminated variable when it writes debugging information.

You have to expect a certain amount of disagreement between the executable and your source code, when you use optimization.

- Users often think it is a bug when GCC reports an error for code like this:

```
int foo (struct mumble *);

struct mumble { ... };

int foo (struct mumble *x)
{ ... }
```

This code really is erroneous, because the scope of struct mumble in the prototype is limited to the argument list containing it. It does not refer to the struct mumble defined with file scope immediately below—they are two unrelated types with similar names in different scopes.

But in the definition of foo, the file-scope type is used because that is available to be inherited. Thus, the definition and the prototype do not match, and you get an error.

This behavior may seem silly, but it's what the ANSI standard specifies. It is easy enough for you to make your code work by moving the definition of struct mumble above the prototype. It's not worth being incompatible with ANSI C just to avoid an error for the example shown above.

- Accesses to bitfields even in volatile objects works by accessing larger objects, such as a byte or a word. You cannot rely on what size of object is accessed in order to read or write the bitfield; it may even vary for a given bitfield according to the precise usage.

If you care about controlling the amount of memory that is accessed, use volatile but do not use bitfields.

- GCC comes with shell scripts to fix certain known problems in system header files. They install corrected copies of various header files in a special directory where only GCC will normally look for them. The scripts adapt to various systems by searching all the system header files for the problem cases that we know about.

If new system header files are installed, nothing automatically arranges to update the corrected header files. You will have to reinstall GCC to fix the new header files. More specifically, go to the build directory and delete the files 'stmp-fixinc' and 'stmp-headers', and the subdirectory include; then do 'make install' again.

- On 68000 and x86 systems, for instance, you can get paradoxical results if you test the precise values of floating point numbers. For example, you can find that a floating point value which is not a NaN is not equal to itself. This results from the fact that the floating point registers hold a few more bits of precision than fit in a `double` in memory. Compiled code moves values between memory and floating point registers at its convenience, and moving them into memory truncates them.

You can partially avoid this problem by using the '`-ffloat-store`' option (see Section 2.8 [Optimize Options], page 40).

- On the MIPS, variable argument functions using '`varargs.h`' cannot have a floating point value for the first argument. The reason for this is that in the absence of a prototype in scope, if the first argument is a floating point, it is passed in a floating point register, rather than an integer register.

  If the code is rewritten to use the ANSI standard '`stdarg.h`' method of variable arguments, and the prototype is in scope at the time of the call, everything will work fine.

- On the H8/300 and H8/300H, variable argument functions must be implemented using the ANSI standard '`stdarg.h`' method of variable arguments. Furthermore, calls to functions using '`stdarg.h`' variable arguments must have a prototype for the called function in scope at the time of the call.

7.10 Common Misunderstandings with GNU C++

C++ is a complex language and an evolving one, and its standard definition (the ISO C++ standard) was only recently completed. As a result, your C++ compiler may occasionally surprise you, even when its behavior is correct. This section discusses some areas that frequently give rise to questions of this sort.

7.10.1 Declare *and* Define Static Members

When a class has static data members, it is not enough to *declare* the static member; you must also *define* it. For example:

```
class Foo
{
  ...
  void method();
  static int bar;
};
```

This declaration only establishes that the class `Foo` has an `int` named `Foo::bar`, and a member function named `Foo::method`. But you still need to define *both* `method` and `bar` elsewhere. According to the draft ANSI standard, you must supply an initializer in one (and only one) source file, such as:

```
int Foo::bar = 0;
```

Other C++ compilers may not correctly implement the standard behavior. As a result, when you switch to g++ from one of these compilers, you may discover that a program that appeared to work correctly in fact does not conform to the standard: g++ reports as undefined symbols any static data members that lack definitions.

7.10.2 Temporaries May Vanish Before You Expect

It is dangerous to use pointers or references to *portions* of a temporary object. The compiler may very well delete the object before you expect it to, leaving a pointer to garbage. The most common place where this problem crops up is in classes like string classes, especially ones that define a conversion function to type **char *** or **const char *** – which is one reason why the standard **string** class requires you to call the **c_str** member function. However, any class that returns a pointer to some internal structure is potentially subject to this problem.

For example, a program may use a function **strfunc** that returns **string** objects, and another function **charfunc** that operates on pointers to **char**:

```
string strfunc ();
void charfunc (const char *);

void
f ()
{
  const char *p = strfunc().c_str();
  ...
  charfunc (p);
  ...
  charfunc (p);
}
```

In this situation, it may seem reasonable to save a pointer to the C string returned by the **c_str** member function and use that rather than call **c_str** repeatedly. However, the temporary string created by the call to **strfunc** is destroyed after **p** is initialized, at which point **p** is left pointing to freed memory.

Code like this may run successfully under some other compilers, particularly obsolete cfront-based compilers that delete temporaries along with normal local variables. However, the GNU C++ behavior is standard-conforming, so if your program depends on late destruction of temporaries it is not portable.

The safe way to write such code is to give the temporary a name, which forces it to remain until the end of the scope of the name. For example:

```
string& tmp = strfunc ();
```

```
charfunc (tmp.c_str ());
```

7.10.3 Implicit Copy-Assignment for Virtual Bases

When a base class is virtual, only one subobject of the base class belongs to each full object. Also, the constructors and destructors are invoked only once, and called from the most-derived class. However, such objects behave unspecified when being assigned. For example:

```
struct Base{
  char *name;
  Base(char *n) : name(strdup(n)){}
  Base& operator= (const Base& other){
   free (name);
   name = strdup (other.name);
  }
};

struct A:virtual Base{
  int val;
  A():Base("A"){}
};

struct B:virtual Base{
  int bval;
  B():Base("B"){}
};

struct Derived:public A, public B{
  Derived():Base("Derived"){}
};

void func(Derived &d1, Derived &d2)
{
  d1 = d2;
}
```

The C++ standard specifies that 'Base::Base' is only called once when constructing or copy-constructing a Derived object. It is unspecified whether 'Base::operator=' is called more than once when the implicit copy-assignment for Derived objects is invoked (as it is inside 'func' in the example).

g++ implements the "intuitive" algorithm for copy-assignment: assign all direct bases, then assign all members. In that algorithm, the virtual base subobject can be encountered many times. In the example, copying proceeds in the following order: 'val', 'name' (via strdup), 'bval', and 'name' again.

If application code relies on copy-assignment, a user-defined copy-assignment operator removes any uncertainties. With such an operator, the application can define whether and how the virtual base subobject is assigned.

7.11 Caveats of using `protoize`

The conversion programs `protoize` and `unprotoize` can sometimes change a source file in a way that won't work unless you rearrange it.

- `protoize` can insert references to a type name or type tag before the definition, or in a file where they are not defined.

  If this happens, compiler error messages should show you where the new references are, so fixing the file by hand is straightforward.

- There are some C constructs which `protoize` cannot figure out. For example, it can't determine argument types for declaring a pointer-to-function variable; this you must do by hand. `protoize` inserts a comment containing '???' each time it finds such a variable; so you can find all such variables by searching for this string. ANSI C does not require declaring the argument types of pointer-to-function types.

- Using `unprotoize` can easily introduce bugs. If the program relied on prototypes to bring about conversion of arguments, these conversions will not take place in the program without prototypes. One case in which you can be sure `unprotoize` is safe is when you are removing prototypes that were made with `protoize`; if the program worked before without any prototypes, it will work again without them.

  You can find all the places where this problem might occur by compiling the program with the '`-Wconversion`' option. It prints a warning whenever an argument is converted.

- Both conversion programs can be confused if there are macro calls in and around the text to be converted. In other words, the standard syntax for a declaration or definition must not result from expanding a macro. This problem is inherent in the design of C and cannot be fixed. If only a few functions have confusing macro calls, you can easily convert them manually.

- `protoize` cannot get the argument types for a function whose definition was not actually compiled due to preprocessing conditionals. When this happens, `protoize` changes nothing in regard to such a function. `protoize` tries to detect such instances and warn about them.

  You can generally work around this problem by using `protoize` step by step, each time specifying a different set of '`-D`' options for compilation, until all of the functions have been converted. There is no automatic way to verify that you have got them all, however.

- Confusion may result if there is an occasion to convert a function declaration or definition in a region of source code where there is more than one formal parameter list present. Thus, attempts to convert code containing multiple (conditionally compiled) versions of a single function header (in the same vicinity) may not produce the desired (or expected) results.

If you plan on converting source files which contain such code, it is recommended that you first make sure that each conditionally compiled region of source code which contains an alternative function header also contains at least one additional follower token (past the final right parenthesis of the function header). This should circumvent the problem.

- `unprotoize` can become confused when trying to convert a function definition or declaration which contains a declaration for a pointer-to-function formal argument which has the same name as the function being defined or declared. We recommend you avoid such choices of formal parameter names.

- You might also want to correct some of the indentation by hand and break long lines. (The conversion programs don't write lines longer than eighty characters in any case.)

7.12 Certain Changes We Don't Want to Make

This section lists changes that people frequently request, but which we do not make because we think GCC is better without them.

- Checking the number and type of arguments to a function which has an old-fashioned definition and no prototype.

  Such a feature would work only occasionally—only for calls that appear in the same file as the called function, following the definition. The only way to check all calls reliably is to add a prototype for the function. But adding a prototype eliminates the motivation for this feature. So the feature is not worthwhile.

- Warning about using an expression whose type is signed as a shift count.

  Shift count operands are probably signed more often than unsigned. Warning about this would cause far more annoyance than good.

- Warning about assigning a signed value to an unsigned variable.

  Such assignments must be very common; warning about them would cause more annoyance than good.

- Warning about unreachable code.

  It's very common to have unreachable code in machine-generated programs. For example, this happens normally in some files of GNU C itself.

- Warning when a non-void function value is ignored.

  Coming as I do from a Lisp background, I balk at the idea that there is something dangerous about discarding a value. There are functions that return values which some callers may find useful; it makes no sense to clutter the program with a cast to **void** whenever the value isn't useful.

- Assuming (for optimization) that the address of an external symbol is never zero.

  This assumption is false on certain systems when '**#pragma weak**' is used.

- Making '**-fshort-enums**' the default.

  This would cause storage layout to be incompatible with most other C compilers. And it doesn't seem very important, given that you can get the same result in other ways. The case where it matters most is when the enumeration-valued object is inside a structure, and in that case you can specify a field width explicitly.

- Making bitfields unsigned by default on particular machines where "the ABI standard" says to do so.

  The ANSI C standard leaves it up to the implementation whether a bitfield declared plain **int** is signed or not. This in effect creates two alternative dialects of C.

  The GNU C compiler supports both dialects; you can specify the signed dialect with '**-fsigned-bitfields**' and the unsigned dialect with '**-funsigned-bitfields**'. However, this leaves open the question of which dialect to use by default.

  Currently, the preferred dialect makes plain bitfields signed, because this is simplest. Since **int** is the same as **signed int** in every other context, it is cleanest for them to be the same in bitfields as well.

  Some computer manufacturers have published Application Binary Interface standards which specify that plain bitfields should be unsigned. It is a mistake, however, to say anything about this issue in an ABI. This is because the handling of plain bitfields distinguishes two dialects of C. Both dialects are meaningful on every type of machine. Whether a particular object file was compiled using signed bitfields or unsigned is of no concern to other object files, even if they access the same bitfields in the same data structures.

  A given program is written in one or the other of these two dialects. The program stands a chance to work on most any machine if it is compiled with the proper dialect. It is unlikely to work at all if compiled with the wrong dialect.

  Many users appreciate the GNU C compiler because it provides an environment that is uniform across machines. These users would be inconvenienced if the compiler treated plain bitfields differently on certain machines.

  Occasionally users write programs intended only for a particular machine type. On these occasions, the users would benefit if the GNU C compiler were to support by default the same dialect as the other compilers on that machine. But such applications are rare. And users writing a program to run on more than one type of machine cannot possibly benefit from this kind of compatibility.

This is why GCC does and will treat plain bitfields in the same fashion on all types of machines (by default).

There are some arguments for making bitfields unsigned by default on all machines. If, for example, this becomes a universal de facto standard, it would make sense for GCC to go along with it. This is something to be considered in the future.

(Of course, users strongly concerned about portability should indicate explicitly in each bitfield whether it is signed or not. In this way, they write programs which have the same meaning in both C dialects.)

- Undefining `__STDC__` when '-ansi' is not used.

  Currently, GCC defines `__STDC__` as long as you don't use '-traditional'. This provides good results in practice.

  Programmers normally use conditionals on `__STDC__` to ask whether it is safe to use certain features of ANSI C, such as function prototypes or ANSI token concatenation. Since plain 'gcc' supports all the features of ANSI C, the correct answer to these questions is "yes".

  Some users try to use `__STDC__` to check for the availability of certain library facilities. This is actually incorrect usage in an ANSI C program, because the ANSI C standard says that a conforming freestanding implementation should define `__STDC__` even though it does not have the library facilities. 'gcc -ansi -pedantic' is a conforming freestanding implementation, and it is therefore required to define `__STDC__`, even though it does not come with an ANSI C library.

  Sometimes people say that defining `__STDC__` in a compiler that does not completely conform to the ANSI C standard somehow violates the standard. This is illogical. The standard is a standard for compilers that claim to support ANSI C, such as 'gcc -ansi'—not for other compilers such as plain 'gcc'. Whatever the ANSI C standard says is relevant to the design of plain 'gcc' without '-ansi' only for pragmatic reasons, not as a requirement.

  GCC normally defines `__STDC__` to be 1, and in addition defines `__STRICT_ANSI__` if you specify the '-ansi' option. On some hosts, system include files use a different convention, where `__STDC__` is normally 0, but is 1 if the user specifies strict conformance to the C Standard. GCC follows the host convention when processing system include files, but when processing user files it follows the usual GNU C convention.

- Undefining `__STDC__` in C++.

  Programs written to compile with C++-to-C translators get the value of `__STDC__` that goes with the C compiler that is subsequently used. These programs must test `__STDC__` to determine what kind of C preprocessor that compiler uses: whether they should concatenate tokens in the ANSI C fashion or in the traditional fashion.

These programs work properly with GNU C++ if `__STDC__` is defined. They would not work otherwise.

In addition, many header files are written to provide prototypes in ANSI C but not in traditional C. Many of these header files can work without change in C++ provided `__STDC__` is defined. If `__STDC__` is not defined, they will all fail, and will all need to be changed to test explicitly for C++ as well.

- Deleting "empty" loops.

  Historically, GCC has not deleted "empty" loops under the assumption that the most likely reason you would put one in a program is to have a delay, so deleting them will not make real programs run any faster.

  However, the rationale here is that optimization of a nonempty loop cannot produce an empty one, which holds for C but is not always the case for C++.

  Moreover, with '`-funroll-loops`' small "empty" loops are already removed, so the current behavior is both sub-optimal and inconsistent and will change in the future.

- Making side effects happen in the same order as in some other compiler.

  It is never safe to depend on the order of evaluation of side effects. For example, a function call like this may very well behave differently from one compiler to another:

  ```
  void func (int, int);

  int i = 2;
  func (i++, i++);
  ```

  There is no guarantee (in either the C or the C++ standard language definitions) that the increments will be evaluated in any particular order. Either increment might happen first. `func` might get the arguments '2, 3', or it might get '3, 2', or even '2, 2'.

- Not allowing structures with volatile fields in registers.

  Strictly speaking, there is no prohibition in the ANSI C standard against allowing structures with volatile fields in registers, but it does not seem to make any sense and is probably not what you wanted to do. So the compiler will give an error message in this case.

7.13 Warning Messages and Error Messages

The GNU compiler can produce two kinds of diagnostics: errors and warnings. Each kind has a different purpose:

Errors report problems that make it impossible to compile your program. GCC reports errors with the source file name and line number where the problem is apparent.

Warnings report other unusual conditions in your code that *may* indicate a problem, although compilation can (and does) proceed. Warning messages also report the source file name and line number, but include the text '`warning:`' to distinguish them from error messages.

Warnings may indicate danger points where you should check to make sure that your program really does what you intend; or the use of obsolete features; or the use of nonstandard features of GNU C or C++. Many warnings are issued only if you ask for them, with one of the '`-W`' options (for instance, '`-Wall`' requests a variety of useful warnings).

GCC always tries to compile your program if possible; it never gratuitously rejects a program whose meaning is clear merely because (for instance) it fails to conform to a standard. In some cases, however, the C and C++ standards specify that certain extensions are forbidden, and a diagnostic *must* be issued by a conforming compiler. The '`-pedantic`' option tells GCC to issue warnings in such cases; '`-pedantic-errors`' says to make them errors instead. This does not mean that *all* non-ANSI constructs get warnings or errors.

See Section 2.6 [Options to Request or Suppress Warnings], page 25, for more detail on these and related command-line options.

8 Reporting Bugs

Your bug reports play an essential role in making GCC reliable.

When you encounter a problem, the first thing to do is to see if it is already known. See Chapter 7 [Trouble], page 223. If it isn't known, then you should report the problem.

Reporting a bug may help you by bringing a solution to your problem, or it may not. (If it does not, look in the service directory; see Chapter 9 [Service], page 259.) In any case, the principal function of a bug report is to help the entire community by making the next version of GCC work better. Bug reports are your contribution to the maintenance of GCC.

Since the maintainers are very overloaded, we cannot respond to every bug report. However, if the bug has not been fixed, we are likely to send you a patch and ask you to tell us whether it works.

In order for a bug report to serve its purpose, you must include the information that makes for fixing the bug.

8.1 Have You Found a Bug?

If you are not sure whether you have found a bug, here are some guidelines:

- If the compiler gets a fatal signal, for any input whatever, that is a compiler bug. Reliable compilers never crash.

- If the compiler produces invalid assembly code, for any input whatever (except an **asm** statement), that is a compiler bug, unless the compiler reports errors (not just warnings) which would ordinarily prevent the assembler from being run.

- If the compiler produces valid assembly code that does not correctly execute the input source code, that is a compiler bug.

  However, you must double-check to make sure, because you may have run into an incompatibility between GNU C and traditional C (see Section 7.6 [Incompatibilities], page 235). These incompatibilities might be considered bugs, but they are inescapable consequences of valuable features.

  Or you may have a program whose behavior is undefined, which happened by chance to give the desired results with another C or C++ compiler.

  For example, in many nonoptimizing compilers, you can write 'x;' at the end of a function instead of 'return x;', with the same results. But the value of the function is undefined if **return** is omitted; it is not a bug when GCC produces different results.

  Problems often result from expressions with two increment operators, as in f (*p++, *p++). Your previous compiler might have interpreted that expression the way you intended; GCC might interpret it another way. Neither compiler is wrong. The bug is in your code.

After you have localized the error to a single source line, it should be easy to check for these things. If your program is correct and well defined, you have found a compiler bug.

- If the compiler produces an error message for valid input, that is a compiler bug.

- If the compiler does not produce an error message for invalid input, that is a compiler bug. However, you should note that your idea of "invalid input" might be my idea of "an extension" or "support for traditional practice".

- If you are an experienced user of C or C++ (or Fortran or Objective-C) compilers, your suggestions for improvement of GCC are welcome in any case.

8.2 Where to Report Bugs

Send bug reports for the GNU Compiler Collection to 'gcc-bugs@gcc.gnu.org'. In accordance with the GNU-wide convention, in which bug reports for tool "foo" are sent to 'bug-foo@gnu.org', the address 'bug-gcc@gnu.org' may also be used; it will forward to the address given above.

Please see '<URL:http://www.gnu.org/software/gcc/faq.html#bugreport>' for bug reporting instructions before you post a bug report.

Often people think of posting bug reports to the newsgroup instead of mailing them. This appears to work, but it has one problem which can be crucial: a newsgroup posting does not contain a mail path back to the sender. Thus, if maintainers need more information, they may be unable to reach you. For this reason, you should always send bug reports by mail to the proper mailing list.

As a last resort, send bug reports on paper to:

```
GNU Compiler Bugs
Free Software Foundation
59 Temple Place - Suite 330
Boston, MA 02111-1307, USA
```

8.3 How to Report Bugs

You may find additional and/or more up-to-date instructions at '<URL:http://www.gnu.org/software/gcc/faq.html#bugreport>'.

The fundamental principle of reporting bugs usefully is this: **report all the facts**. If you are not sure whether to state a fact or leave it out, state it!

Often people omit facts because they think they know what causes the problem and they conclude that some details don't matter. Thus, you might assume that the name of the variable you use in an example does not matter. Well, probably it doesn't, but one cannot be sure. Perhaps the bug is a stray memory reference which happens to fetch from the location where that name is stored in memory; perhaps, if the name were different, the contents of that location would fool the compiler into doing the right thing despite the bug. Play it safe and give a specific, complete example. That is the easiest thing for you to do, and the most helpful.

Keep in mind that the purpose of a bug report is to enable someone to fix the bug if it is not known. It isn't very important what happens if the bug is already known. Therefore, always write your bug reports on the assumption that the bug is not known.

Sometimes people give a few sketchy facts and ask, "Does this ring a bell?" This cannot help us fix a bug, so it is basically useless. We respond by asking for enough details to enable us to investigate. You might as well expedite matters by sending them to begin with.

Try to make your bug report self-contained. If we have to ask you for more information, it is best if you include all the previous information in your response, as well as the information that was missing.

Please report each bug in a separate message. This makes it easier for us to track which bugs have been fixed and to forward your bugs reports to the appropriate maintainer.

To enable someone to investigate the bug, you should include all these things:

- The version of GCC. You can get this by running it with the '-v' option.

  Without this, we won't know whether there is any point in looking for the bug in the current version of GCC.

- A complete input file that will reproduce the bug. If the bug is in the C preprocessor, send a source file and any header files that it requires. If the bug is in the compiler proper ('cc1'), send the preprocessor output generated by adding '-save-temps' to the compilation command (see Section 2.7 [Debugging Options], page 33). When you do this, use the same '-I', '-D' or '-U' options that you used in actual compilation. Then send the *input*.i or *input*.ii files generated.

  A single statement is not enough of an example. In order to compile it, it must be embedded in a complete file of compiler input; and the bug might depend on the details of how this is done.

  Without a real example one can compile, all anyone can do about your bug report is wish you luck. It would be futile to try to guess how to provoke the bug. For example, bugs in register allocation and reloading frequently depend on every little detail of the function they happen in.

  Even if the input file that fails comes from a GNU program, you should still send the complete test case. Don't ask the GCC maintainers to do the extra work of obtaining the program in question—they are all overworked as it is. Also, the problem may depend on what is in the header files on your system; it is unreliable for the GCC maintainers to try the problem with the header files available to them. By sending CPP output, you can eliminate this source of uncertainty and save us a certain percentage of wild goose chases.

- The command arguments you gave GCC to compile that example and observe the bug. For example, did you use '-O'? To guarantee you won't omit something important, list all the options.

  If we were to try to guess the arguments, we would probably guess wrong and then we would not encounter the bug.

- The type of machine you are using, and the operating system name and version number.

- The operands you gave to the `configure` command when you installed the compiler.

- A complete list of any modifications you have made to the compiler source. (We don't promise to investigate the bug unless it happens in an unmodified compiler. But if you've made modifications and don't tell us, then you are sending us on a wild goose chase.)

  Be precise about these changes. A description in English is not enough—send a context diff for them.

  Adding files of your own (such as a machine description for a machine we don't support) is a modification of the compiler source.

- Details of any other deviations from the standard procedure for installing GCC.

- A description of what behavior you observe that you believe is incorrect. For example, "The compiler gets a fatal signal," or, "The assembler instruction at line 208 in the output is incorrect."

  Of course, if the bug is that the compiler gets a fatal signal, then one can't miss it. But if the bug is incorrect output, the maintainer might not notice unless it is glaringly wrong. None of us has time to study all the assembler code from a 50-line C program just on the chance that one instruction might be wrong. We need *you* to do this part!

  Even if the problem you experience is a fatal signal, you should still say so explicitly. Suppose something strange is going on, such as, your copy of the compiler is out of synch, or you have encountered a bug in the C library on your system. (This has happened!) Your copy might crash and the copy here would not. If you *said* to expect a crash, then when the compiler here fails to crash, we would know that the bug was not happening. If you don't say to expect a crash, then we would not know whether the bug was happening. We would not be able to draw any conclusion from our observations.

  If the problem is a diagnostic when compiling GCC with some other compiler, say whether it is a warning or an error.

Often the observed symptom is incorrect output when your program is run. Sad to say, this is not enough information unless the program is short and simple. None of us has time to study a large program to figure out how it would work if compiled correctly, much less which line of it was compiled wrong. So you will have to do that. Tell us which source line it is, and what incorrect result happens when that line is executed. A person who understands the program can find this as easily as finding a bug in the program itself.

- If you send examples of assembler code output from GCC, please use '-g' when you make them. The debugging information includes source line numbers which are essential for correlating the output with the input.

- If you wish to mention something in the GCC source, refer to it by context, not by line number.

  The line numbers in the development sources don't match those in your sources. Your line numbers would convey no useful information to the maintainers.

- Additional information from a debugger might enable someone to find a problem on a machine which he does not have available. However, you need to think when you collect this information if you want it to have any chance of being useful.

  For example, many people send just a backtrace, but that is never useful by itself. A simple backtrace with arguments conveys little about GCC because the compiler is largely data-driven; the same functions are called over and over for different RTL insns, doing different things depending on the details of the insn.

  Most of the arguments listed in the backtrace are useless because they are pointers to RTL list structure. The numeric values of the pointers, which the debugger prints in the backtrace, have no significance whatever; all that matters is the contents of the objects they point to (and most of the contents are other such pointers).

  In addition, most compiler passes consist of one or more loops that scan the RTL insn sequence. The most vital piece of information about such a loop—which insn it has reached—is usually in a local variable, not in an argument.

  What you need to provide in addition to a backtrace are the values of the local variables for several stack frames up. When a local variable or an argument is an RTX, first print its value and then use the GDB command `pr` to print the RTL expression that it points to. (If GDB doesn't run on your machine, use your debugger to call the function `debug_rtx` with the RTX as an argument.) In general, whenever a variable is a pointer, its value is no use without the data it points to.

Here are some things that are not necessary:

- A description of the envelope of the bug.

  Often people who encounter a bug spend a lot of time investigating which changes to the input file will make the bug go away and which changes will not affect it.

  This is often time consuming and not very useful, because the way we will find the bug is by running a single example under the debugger with breakpoints, not by pure deduction from a series of examples. You might as well save your time for something else.

  Of course, if you can find a simpler example to report *instead* of the original one, that is a convenience. Errors in the output will be easier to spot, running under the debugger will take less time, etc. Most GCC bugs involve just one function, so the most straightforward way to simplify an example is to delete all the function definitions except the one where the bug occurs. Those earlier in the file may be replaced by external declarations if the crucial function depends on them. (Exception: inline functions may affect compilation of functions defined later in the file.)

  However, simplification is not vital; if you don't want to do this, report the bug anyway and send the entire test case you used.

- In particular, some people insert conditionals '`#ifdef BUG`' around a statement which, if removed, makes the bug not happen. These are just clutter; we won't pay any attention to them anyway. Besides, you should send us cpp output, and that can't have conditionals.

- A patch for the bug.

  A patch for the bug is useful if it is a good one. But don't omit the necessary information, such as the test case, on the assumption that a patch is all we need. We might see problems with your patch and decide to fix the problem another way, or we might not understand it at all.

  Sometimes with a program as complicated as GCC it is very hard to construct an example that will make the program follow a certain path through the code. If you don't send the example, we won't be able to construct one, so we won't be able to verify that the bug is fixed.

  And if we can't understand what bug you are trying to fix, or why your patch should be an improvement, we won't install it. A test case will help us to understand.

  See Section 8.4 [Sending Patches], page 257, for guidelines on how to make it easy for us to understand and install your patches.

- A guess about what the bug is or what it depends on.

  Such guesses are usually wrong. Even I can't guess right about such things without first using the debugger to find the facts.

- A core dump file.

We have no way of examining a core dump for your type of machine unless we have an identical system—and if we do have one, we should be able to reproduce the crash ourselves.

8.4 Sending Patches for GCC

If you would like to write bug fixes or improvements for the GNU C compiler, that is very helpful. Send suggested fixes to the patches mailing list, `gcc-patches@gcc.gnu.org`.

Please follow these guidelines so we can study your patches efficiently. If you don't follow these guidelines, your information might still be useful, but using it will take extra work. Maintaining GNU C is a lot of work in the best of circumstances, and we can't keep up unless you do your best to help.

- Send an explanation with your changes of what problem they fix or what improvement they bring about. For a bug fix, just include a copy of the bug report, and explain why the change fixes the bug.

  (Referring to a bug report is not as good as including it, because then we will have to look it up, and we have probably already deleted it if we've already fixed the bug.)

- Always include a proper bug report for the problem you think you have fixed. We need to convince ourselves that the change is right before installing it. Even if it is right, we might have trouble judging it if we don't have a way to reproduce the problem.

- Include all the comments that are appropriate to help people reading the source in the future understand why this change was needed.

- Don't mix together changes made for different reasons. Send them *individually*.

  If you make two changes for separate reasons, then we might not want to install them both. We might want to install just one. If you send them all jumbled together in a single set of diffs, we have to do extra work to disentangle them—to figure out which parts of the change serve which purpose. If we don't have time for this, we might have to ignore your changes entirely.

  If you send each change as soon as you have written it, with its own explanation, then the two changes never get tangled up, and we can consider each one properly without any extra work to disentangle them.

  Ideally, each change you send should be impossible to subdivide into parts that we might want to consider separately, because each of its parts gets its motivation from the other parts.

- Send each change as soon as that change is finished. Sometimes people think they are helping us by accumulating many changes to send them all together. As explained above, this is absolutely the worst thing you could do.

Since you should send each change separately, you might as well send it right away. That gives us the option of installing it immediately if it is important.

- Use 'diff -c' to make your diffs. Diffs without context are hard for us to install reliably. More than that, they make it hard for us to study the diffs to decide whether we want to install them. Unidiff format is better than contextless diffs, but not as easy to read as '-c' format.

  If you have GNU diff, use 'diff -cp', which shows the name of the function that each change occurs in.

- Write the change log entries for your changes. We get lots of changes, and we don't have time to do all the change log writing ourselves.

  Read the 'ChangeLog' file to see what sorts of information to put in, and to learn the style that we use. The purpose of the change log is to show people where to find what was changed. So you need to be specific about what functions you changed; in large functions, it's often helpful to indicate where within the function the change was.

  On the other hand, once you have shown people where to find the change, you need not explain its purpose. Thus, if you add a new function, all you need to say about it is that it is new. If you feel that the purpose needs explaining, it probably does—but the explanation will be much more useful if you put it in comments in the code.

  If you would like your name to appear in the header line for who made the change, send us the header line.

- When you write the fix, keep in mind that we can't install a change that would break other systems.

  People often suggest fixing a problem by changing machine-independent files such as 'toplev.c' to do something special that a particular system needs. Sometimes it is totally obvious that such changes would break GCC for almost all users. We can't possibly make a change like that. At best it might tell us how to write another patch that would solve the problem acceptably.

  Sometimes people send fixes that *might* be an improvement in general—but it is hard to be sure of this. It's hard to install such changes because we have to study them very carefully. Of course, a good explanation of the reasoning by which you concluded the change was correct can help convince us.

  The safest changes are changes to the configuration files for a particular machine. These are safe because they can't create new bugs on other machines.

  Please help us keep up with the workload by designing the patch in a form that is good to install.

9 How To Get Help with GCC

If you need help installing, using or changing GCC, there are two ways to find it:

- Send a message to a suitable network mailing list. First try `gcc-bugs@gcc.gnu.org` or `bug-gcc@gnu.org`, and if that brings no response, try `gcc@gcc.gnu.org`.

- Look in the service directory for someone who might help you for a fee. The service directory is found in the file named '`SERVICE`' in the GCC distribution.

10 Contributing to GCC Development

If you would like to help pretest GCC releases to assure they work well, or if you would like to work on improving GCC, please contact the maintainers at `gcc@gcc.gnu.org`. A pretester should be willing to try to investigate bugs as well as report them.

If you'd like to work on improvements, please ask for suggested projects or suggest your own ideas. If you have already written an improvement, please tell us about it. If you have not yet started work, it is useful to contact `gcc@gcc.gnu.org` before you start; the maintainers may be able to suggest ways to make your extension fit in better with the rest of GCC and with other development plans.

11 Using GCC on VMS

Here is how to use GCC on VMS.

11.1 Include Files and VMS

Due to the differences between the filesystems of Unix and VMS, GCC attempts to translate file names in '#include' into names that VMS will understand. The basic strategy is to prepend a prefix to the specification of the include file, convert the whole filename to a VMS filename, and then try to open the file. GCC tries various prefixes one by one until one of them succeeds:

1. The first prefix is the 'GNU_CC_INCLUDE:' logical name: this is where GNU C header files are traditionally stored. If you wish to store header files in non-standard locations, then you can assign the logical 'GNU_CC_INCLUDE' to be a search list, where each element of the list is suitable for use with a rooted logical.

2. The next prefix tried is 'SYS$SYSROOT:[SYSLIB.]'. This is where VAX-C header files are traditionally stored.

3. If the include file specification by itself is a valid VMS filename, the preprocessor then uses this name with no prefix in an attempt to open the include file.

4. If the file specification is not a valid VMS filename (i.e. does not contain a device or a directory specifier, and contains a '/' character), the preprocessor tries to convert it from Unix syntax to VMS syntax.

   Conversion works like this: the first directory name becomes a device, and the rest of the directories are converted into VMS-format directory names. For example, the name 'X11/foobar.h' is translated to 'X11:[000000]foobar.h' or 'X11:foobar.h', whichever one can be opened. This strategy allows you to assign a logical name to point to the actual location of the header files.

5. If none of these strategies succeeds, the '#include' fails.

Include directives of the form:

```
#include foobar
```

are a common source of incompatibility between VAX-C and GCC. VAX-C treats this much like a standard #include <foobar.h> directive. That is incompatible with the ANSI C behavior implemented by GCC: to expand the name foobar as a macro. Macro expansion should eventually yield one of the two standard formats for #include:

```
#include "file"
#include <file>
```

If you have this problem, the best solution is to modify the source to convert the #include directives to one of the two standard forms. That will work with either compiler. If you want a quick and dirty fix, define the file names as macros with the proper expansion, like this:

```
#define stdio <stdio.h>
```

This will work, as long as the name doesn't conflict with anything else in the program.

Another source of incompatibility is that VAX-C assumes that:

```
#include "foobar"
```

is actually asking for the file 'foobar.h'. GCC does not make this assumption, and instead takes what you ask for literally; it tries to read the file 'foobar'. The best way to avoid this problem is to always specify the desired file extension in your include directives.

GCC for VMS is distributed with a set of include files that is sufficient to compile most general purpose programs. Even though the GCC distribution does not contain header files to define constants and structures for some VMS system-specific functions, there is no reason why you cannot use GCC with any of these functions. You first may have to generate or create header files, either by using the public domain utility UNSDL (which can be found on a DECUS tape), or by extracting the relevant modules from one of the system macro libraries, and using an editor to construct a C header file.

A #include file name cannot contain a DECNET node name. The preprocessor reports an I/O error if you attempt to use a node name, whether explicitly, or implicitly via a logical name.

11.2 Global Declarations and VMS

GCC does not provide the globalref, globaldef and globalvalue keywords of VAX-C. You can get the same effect with an obscure feature of GAS, the GNU assembler. (This requires GAS version 1.39 or later.) The following macros allow you to use this feature in a fairly natural way:

```
#ifdef __GNUC__
#define GLOBALREF(TYPE,NAME)                               \
  TYPE NAME                                                \
  asm ("_$$PsectAttributes_GLOBALSYMBOL$$" #NAME)
#define GLOBALDEF(TYPE,NAME,VALUE)                         \
  TYPE NAME                                                \
  asm ("_$$PsectAttributes_GLOBALSYMBOL$$" #NAME) \
    = VALUE
#define GLOBALVALUEREF(TYPE,NAME)                          \
  const TYPE NAME[1]                                       \
  asm ("_$$PsectAttributes_GLOBALVALUE$$" #NAME)
#define GLOBALVALUEDEF(TYPE,NAME,VALUE)                    \
  const TYPE NAME[1]                                       \
  asm ("_$$PsectAttributes_GLOBALVALUE$$" #NAME) \
```

```
     = {VALUE}
#else
#define GLOBALREF(TYPE,NAME) \
   globalref TYPE NAME
#define GLOBALDEF(TYPE,NAME,VALUE) \
   globaldef TYPE NAME = VALUE
#define GLOBALVALUEDEF(TYPE,NAME,VALUE) \
   globalvalue TYPE NAME = VALUE
#define GLOBALVALUEREF(TYPE,NAME) \
   globalvalue TYPE NAME
#endif
```

(The `_$$PsectAttributes_GLOBALSYMBOL` prefix at the start of the name is
removed by the assembler, after it has modified the attributes of the symbol).
These macros are provided in the VMS binaries distribution in a header file
'GNU_HACKS.H'. An example of the usage is:

```
GLOBALREF (int, ijk);
GLOBALDEF (int, jkl, 0);
```

The macros **GLOBALREF** and **GLOBALDEF** cannot be used straightforwardly
for arrays, since there is no way to insert the array dimension into the declaration at the right place. However, you can declare an array with these
macros if you first define a typedef for the array type, like this:

```
typedef int intvector[10];
GLOBALREF (intvector, foo);
```

Array and structure initializers will also break the macros; you can define
the initializer to be a macro of its own, or you can expand the **GLOBALDEF**
macro by hand. You may find a case where you wish to use the **GLOBALDEF**
macro with a large array, but you are not interested in explicitly initializing
each element of the array. In such cases you can use an initializer like: {0,},
which will initialize the entire array to 0.

A shortcoming of this implementation is that a variable declared with
GLOBALVALUEREF or **GLOBALVALUEDEF** is always an array. For example, the
declaration:

```
GLOBALVALUEREF(int, ijk);
```

declares the variable **ijk** as an array of type **int [1]**. This is done because
a globalvalue is actually a constant; its "value" is what the linker would
normally consider an address. That is not how an integer value works in
C, but it is how an array works. So treating the symbol as an array name
gives consistent results—with the exception that the value seems to have the
wrong type. **Don't try to access an element of the array.** It doesn't have any
elements. The array "address" may not be the address of actual storage.

The fact that the symbol is an array may lead to warnings where the
variable is used. Insert type casts to avoid the warnings. Here is an example;
it takes advantage of the ANSI C feature allowing macros that expand to
use the same name as the macro itself.

```
GLOBALVALUEREF (int, ss$_normal);
GLOBALVALUEDEF (int, xyzzy,123);
#ifdef __GNUC__
#define ss$_normal ((int) ss$_normal)
#define xyzzy ((int) xyzzy)
#endif
```

Don't use `globaldef` or `globalref` with a variable whose type is an enumeration type; this is not implemented. Instead, make the variable an integer, and use a `globalvaluedef` for each of the enumeration values. An example of this would be:

```
#ifdef __GNUC__
GLOBALDEF (int, color, 0);
GLOBALVALUEDEF (int, RED, 0);
GLOBALVALUEDEF (int, BLUE, 1);
GLOBALVALUEDEF (int, GREEN, 3);
#else
enum globaldef color {RED, BLUE, GREEN = 3};
#endif
```

11.3 Other VMS Issues

GCC automatically arranges for `main` to return 1 by default if you fail to specify an explicit return value. This will be interpreted by VMS as a status code indicating a normal successful completion. Version 1 of GCC did not provide this default.

GCC on VMS works only with the GNU assembler, GAS. You need version 1.37 or later of GAS in order to produce value debugging information for the VMS debugger. Use the ordinary VMS linker with the object files produced by GAS.

Under previous versions of GCC, the generated code would occasionally give strange results when linked to the sharable 'VAXCRTL' library. Now this should work.

A caveat for use of `const` global variables: the `const` modifier must be specified in every external declaration of the variable in all of the source files that use that variable. Otherwise the linker will issue warnings about conflicting attributes for the variable. Your program will still work despite the warnings, but the variable will be placed in writable storage.

Although the VMS linker does distinguish between upper and lower case letters in global symbols, most VMS compilers convert all such symbols into upper case and most run-time library routines also have upper case names. To be able to reliably call such routines, GCC (by means of the assembler GAS) converts global symbols into upper case like other VMS compilers. However, since the usual practice in C is to distinguish case, GCC (via GAS) tries to preserve usual C behavior by augmenting each name that is not all lower case. This means truncating the name to at most 23 characters and then adding more characters at the end which encode the case pattern of those 23. Names which contain at least one dollar sign are an exception; they are converted directly into upper case without augmentation.

Name augmentation yields bad results for programs that use precompiled libraries (such as Xlib) which were generated by another compiler. You can use the compiler option '/NOCASE_HACK' to inhibit augmentation; it makes external C functions and variables case-independent as is usual on VMS. Alternatively, you could write all references to the functions and variables in such libraries using lower case; this will work on VMS, but is not portable to other systems. The compiler option '/NAMES' also provides control over global name handling.

Function and variable names are handled somewhat differently with GNU C++. The GNU C++ compiler performs *name mangling* on function names, which means that it adds information to the function name to describe the data types of the arguments that the function takes. One result of this is that the name of a function can become very long. Since the VMS linker only recognizes the first 31 characters in a name, special action is taken to ensure that each function and variable has a unique name that can be represented in 31 characters.

If the name (plus a name augmentation, if required) is less than 32 characters in length, then no special action is performed. If the name is longer than 31 characters, the assembler (GAS) will generate a hash string based upon the function name, truncate the function name to 23 characters, and append the hash string to the truncated name. If the '/VERBOSE' compiler option is used, the assembler will print both the full and truncated names of each symbol that is truncated.

The '/NOCASE_HACK' compiler option should not be used when you are compiling programs that use libg++. libg++ has several instances of objects (i.e. `Filebuf` and `filebuf`) which become indistinguishable in a case-insensitive environment. This leads to cases where you need to inhibit augmentation selectively (if you were using libg++ and Xlib in the same program, for example). There is no special feature for doing this, but you can get the result by defining a macro for each mixed case symbol for which you wish to inhibit augmentation. The macro should expand into the lower case equivalent of itself. For example:

```
#define StuDlyCapS studlycaps
```

These macro definitions can be placed in a header file to minimize the number of changes to your source code.

12 GCC and Portability

The main goal of GCC was to make a good, fast compiler for machines in the class that the GNU system aims to run on: 32-bit machines that address 8-bit bytes and have several general registers. Elegance, theoretical power and simplicity are only secondary.

GCC gets most of the information about the target machine from a machine description which gives an algebraic formula for each of the machine's instructions. This is a very clean way to describe the target. But when the compiler needs information that is difficult to express in this fashion, I have not hesitated to define an ad-hoc parameter to the machine description. The purpose of portability is to reduce the total work needed on the compiler; it was not of interest for its own sake.

GCC does not contain machine dependent code, but it does contain code that depends on machine parameters such as endianness (whether the most significant byte has the highest or lowest address of the bytes in a word) and the availability of autoincrement addressing. In the RTL-generation pass, it is often necessary to have multiple strategies for generating code for a particular kind of syntax tree, strategies that are usable for different combinations of parameters. Often I have not tried to address all possible cases, but only the common ones or only the ones that I have encountered. As a result, a new target may require additional strategies. You will know if this happens because the compiler will call **abort**. Fortunately, the new strategies can be added in a machine-independent fashion, and will affect only the target machines that need them.

13 Interfacing to GCC Output

GCC is normally configured to use the same function calling convention normally in use on the target system. This is done with the machine-description macros described (see Chapter 17 [Target Macros], page 393).

However, returning of structure and union values is done differently on some target machines. As a result, functions compiled with PCC returning such types cannot be called from code compiled with GCC, and vice versa. This does not cause trouble often because few Unix library routines return structures or unions.

GCC code returns structures and unions that are 1, 2, 4 or 8 bytes long in the same registers used for `int` or `double` return values. (GCC typically allocates variables of such types in registers also.) Structures and unions of other sizes are returned by storing them into an address passed by the caller (usually in a register). The machine-description macros `STRUCT_VALUE` and `STRUCT_INCOMING_VALUE` tell GCC where to pass this address.

By contrast, PCC on most target machines returns structures and unions of any size by copying the data into an area of static storage, and then returning the address of that storage as if it were a pointer value. The caller must copy the data from that memory area to the place where the value is wanted. This is slower than the method used by GCC, and fails to be reentrant.

On some target machines, such as RISC machines and the 80386, the standard system convention is to pass to the subroutine the address of where to return the value. On these machines, GCC has been configured to be compatible with the standard compiler, when this method is used. It may not be compatible for structures of 1, 2, 4 or 8 bytes.

GCC uses the system's standard convention for passing arguments. On some machines, the first few arguments are passed in registers; in others, all are passed on the stack. It would be possible to use registers for argument passing on any machine, and this would probably result in a significant speedup. But the result would be complete incompatibility with code that follows the standard convention. So this change is practical only if you are switching to GCC as the sole C compiler for the system. We may implement register argument passing on certain machines once we have a complete GNU system so that we can compile the libraries with GCC.

On some machines (particularly the Sparc), certain types of arguments are passed "by invisible reference". This means that the value is stored in memory, and the address of the memory location is passed to the subroutine.

If you use `longjmp`, beware of automatic variables. ANSI C says that automatic variables that are not declared `volatile` have undefined values after a `longjmp`. And this is all GCC promises to do, because it is very difficult to restore register variables correctly, and one of GCC's features is that it can put variables in registers without your asking it to.

If you want a variable to be unaltered by `longjmp`, and you don't want to write `volatile` because old C compilers don't accept it, just take the address of the variable. If a variable's address is ever taken, even if just to compute it and ignore it, then the variable cannot go in a register:

```
{
    int careful;
    &careful;
    ...
}
```

Code compiled with GCC may call certain library routines. Most of them handle arithmetic for which there are no instructions. This includes multiply and divide on some machines, and floating point operations on any machine for which floating point support is disabled with '-msoft-float'. Some standard parts of the C library, such as `bcopy` or `memcpy`, are also called automatically. The usual function call interface is used for calling the library routines.

These library routines should be defined in the library 'libgcc.a', which GCC automatically searches whenever it links a program. On machines that have multiply and divide instructions, if hardware floating point is in use, normally 'libgcc.a' is not needed, but it is searched just in case.

Each arithmetic function is defined in 'libgcc1.c' to use the corresponding C arithmetic operator. As long as the file is compiled with another C compiler, which supports all the C arithmetic operators, this file will work portably. However, 'libgcc1.c' does not work if compiled with GCC, because each arithmetic function would compile into a call to itself!

14 Passes and Files of the Compiler

The overall control structure of the compiler is in 'toplev.c'. This file is responsible for initialization, decoding arguments, opening and closing files, and sequencing the passes.

The parsing pass is invoked only once, to parse the entire input. The RTL intermediate code for a function is generated as the function is parsed, a statement at a time. Each statement is read in as a syntax tree and then converted to RTL; then the storage for the tree for the statement is reclaimed. Storage for types (and the expressions for their sizes), declarations, and a representation of the binding contours and how they nest, remain until the function is finished being compiled; these are all needed to output the debugging information.

Each time the parsing pass reads a complete function definition or top-level declaration, it calls either the function `rest_of_compilation`, or the function `rest_of_decl_compilation` in 'toplev.c', which are responsible for all further processing necessary, ending with output of the assembler language. All other compiler passes run, in sequence, within `rest_of_compilation`. When that function returns from compiling a function definition, the storage used for that function definition's compilation is entirely freed, unless it is an inline function (see Section 4.31 [An Inline Function is As Fast As a Macro], page 192).

Here is a list of all the passes of the compiler and their source files. Also included is a description of where debugging dumps can be requested with '-d' options.

- Parsing. This pass reads the entire text of a function definition, constructing partial syntax trees. This and RTL generation are no longer truly separate passes (formerly they were), but it is easier to think of them as separate.

  The tree representation does not entirely follow C syntax, because it is intended to support other languages as well.

  Language-specific data type analysis is also done in this pass, and every tree node that represents an expression has a data type attached. Variables are represented as declaration nodes.

  Constant folding and some arithmetic simplifications are also done during this pass.

  The language-independent source files for parsing are 'stor-layout.c', 'fold-const.c', and 'tree.c'. There are also header files 'tree.h' and 'tree.def' which define the format of the tree representation.

  The source files to parse C are 'c-parse.in', 'c-decl.c', 'c-typeck.c', 'c-aux-info.c', 'c-convert.c', and 'c-lang.c' along with header files 'c-lex.h', and 'c-tree.h'.

  The source files for parsing C++ are 'cp-parse.y', 'cp-class.c', 'cp-cvt.c', 'cp-decl.c', 'cp-decl2.c', 'cp-dem.c', 'cp-except.c', 'cp-expr.c', 'cp-init.c', 'cp-lex.c', 'cp-method.c', 'cp-ptree.c', 'cp-search.c', 'cp-tree.c', 'cp-type2.c', and 'cp-typeck.c', along with header files 'cp-tree.def', 'cp-tree.h', and 'cp-decl.h'.

The special source files for parsing Objective C are 'objc-parse.y', 'objc-actions.c', 'objc-tree.def', and 'objc-actions.h'. Certain C-specific files are used for this as well.

The file 'c-common.c' is also used for all of the above languages.

- RTL generation. This is the conversion of syntax tree into RTL code. It is actually done statement-by-statement during parsing, but for most purposes it can be thought of as a separate pass.

  This is where the bulk of target-parameter-dependent code is found, since often it is necessary for strategies to apply only when certain standard kinds of instructions are available. The purpose of named instruction patterns is to provide this information to the RTL generation pass.

  Optimization is done in this pass for if-conditions that are comparisons, boolean operations or conditional expressions. Tail recursion is detected at this time also. Decisions are made about how best to arrange loops and how to output switch statements.

  The source files for RTL generation include 'stmt.c', 'calls.c', 'expr.c', 'explow.c', 'expmed.c', 'function.c', 'optabs.c' and 'emit-rtl.c'. Also, the file 'insn-emit.c', generated from the machine description by the program genemit, is used in this pass. The header file 'expr.h' is used for communication within this pass.

  The header files 'insn-flags.h' and 'insn-codes.h', generated from the machine description by the programs genflags and gencodes, tell this pass which standard names are available for use and which patterns correspond to them.

  Aside from debugging information output, none of the following passes refers to the tree structure representation of the function (only part of which is saved).

  The decision of whether the function can and should be expanded inline in its subsequent callers is made at the end of rtl generation. The function must meet certain criteria, currently related to the size of the function and the types and number of parameters it has. Note that this function may contain loops, recursive calls to itself (tail-recursive functions can be inlined!), gotos, in short, all constructs supported by GCC. The file 'integrate.c' contains the code to save a function's rtl for later inlining and to inline that rtl when the function is called. The header file 'integrate.h' is also used for this purpose.

  The option '-dr' causes a debugging dump of the RTL code after this pass. This dump file's name is made by appending '.rtl' to the input file name.

- Jump optimization. This pass simplifies jumps to the following instruction, jumps across jumps, and jumps to jumps. It deletes unreferenced labels and unreachable code, except that unreachable code that contains a loop is not recognized as unreachable in this pass. (Such loops are deleted later in the basic block analysis.) It also converts some code originally written with jumps into sequences of instructions that directly set values from the results of comparisons, if the machine has such instructions.

  Jump optimization is performed two or three times. The first time is immediately following RTL generation. The second time is after CSE, but only if CSE says repeated jump optimization is needed. The last time is right before the final pass. That time, cross-jumping and deletion of no-op move instructions are done together with the optimizations described above.

  The source file of this pass is 'jump.c'.

  The option '-dj' causes a debugging dump of the RTL code after this pass is run for the first time. This dump file's name is made by appending '.jump' to the input file name.

- Register scan. This pass finds the first and last use of each register, as a guide for common subexpression elimination. Its source is in 'regclass.c'.

- Jump threading. This pass detects a condition jump that branches to an identical or inverse test. Such jumps can be 'threaded' through the second conditional test. The source code for this pass is in 'jump.c'. This optimization is only performed if '-fthread-jumps' is enabled.

- Common subexpression elimination. This pass also does constant propagation. Its source file is 'cse.c'. If constant propagation causes conditional jumps to become unconditional or to become no-ops, jump optimization is run again when CSE is finished.

  The option '-ds' causes a debugging dump of the RTL code after this pass. This dump file's name is made by appending '.cse' to the input file name.

- Global common subexpression elimination. This pass performs GCSE using Morel-Renvoise Partial Redundancy Elimination, with the exception that it does not try to move invariants out of loops - that is left to the loop optimization pass. This pass also performs global constant and copy propagation.

  The source file for this pass is gcse.c.

  The option '-dG' causes a debugging dump of the RTL code after this pass. This dump file's name is made by appending '.gcse' to the input file name.

- Loop optimization. This pass moves constant expressions out of loops, and optionally does strength-reduction and loop unrolling as well. Its source files are 'loop.c' and 'unroll.c', plus the header 'loop.h' used for communication between them. Loop unrolling uses some functions in 'integrate.c' and the header 'integrate.h'.

The option '-dL' causes a debugging dump of the RTL code after this pass. This dump file's name is made by appending '.loop' to the input file name.

- If '-frerun-cse-after-loop' was enabled, a second common subexpression elimination pass is performed after the loop optimization pass. Jump threading is also done again at this time if it was specified.

  The option '-dt' causes a debugging dump of the RTL code after this pass. This dump file's name is made by appending '.cse2' to the input file name.

- Stupid register allocation is performed at this point in a nonoptimizing compilation. It does a little data flow analysis as well. When stupid register allocation is in use, the next pass executed is the reloading pass; the others in between are skipped. The source file is 'stupid.c'.

- Data flow analysis ('flow.c'). This pass divides the program into basic blocks (and in the process deletes unreachable loops); then it computes which pseudo-registers are live at each point in the program, and makes the first instruction that uses a value point at the instruction that computed the value.

  This pass also deletes computations whose results are never used, and combines memory references with add or subtract instructions to make autoincrement or autodecrement addressing.

  The option '-df' causes a debugging dump of the RTL code after this pass. This dump file's name is made by appending '.flow' to the input file name. If stupid register allocation is in use, this dump file reflects the full results of such allocation.

- Instruction combination ('combine.c'). This pass attempts to combine groups of two or three instructions that are related by data flow into single instructions. It combines the RTL expressions for the instructions by substitution, simplifies the result using algebra, and then attempts to match the result against the machine description.

  The option '-dc' causes a debugging dump of the RTL code after this pass. This dump file's name is made by appending '.combine' to the input file name.

- Register movement ('regmove.c'). This pass looks for cases where matching constraints would force an instruction to need a reload, and this reload would be a register to register move. It them attempts to change the registers used by the instruction to avoid the move instruction.

  The option '-dN' causes a debugging dump of the RTL code after this pass. This dump file's name is made by appending '.regmove' to the input file name.

- Instruction scheduling ('`sched.c`'). This pass looks for instructions whose output will not be available by the time that it is used in subsequent instructions. (Memory loads and floating point instructions often have this behavior on RISC machines). It re-orders instructions within a basic block to try to separate the definition and use of items that otherwise would cause pipeline stalls.

  Instruction scheduling is performed twice. The first time is immediately after instruction combination and the second is immediately after reload.

  The option '`-dS`' causes a debugging dump of the RTL code after this pass is run for the first time. The dump file's name is made by appending '`.sched`' to the input file name.

- Register class preferencing. The RTL code is scanned to find out which register class is best for each pseudo register. The source file is '`regclass.c`'.

- Local register allocation ('`local-alloc.c`'). This pass allocates hard registers to pseudo registers that are used only within one basic block. Because the basic block is linear, it can use fast and powerful techniques to do a very good job.

  The option '`-dl`' causes a debugging dump of the RTL code after this pass. This dump file's name is made by appending '`.lreg`' to the input file name.

- Global register allocation ('`global.c`'). This pass allocates hard registers for the remaining pseudo registers (those whose life spans are not contained in one basic block).

- Reloading. This pass renumbers pseudo registers with the hardware registers numbers they were allocated. Pseudo registers that did not get hard registers are replaced with stack slots. Then it finds instructions that are invalid because a value has failed to end up in a register, or has ended up in a register of the wrong kind. It fixes up these instructions by reloading the problematical values temporarily into registers. Additional instructions are generated to do the copying.

  The reload pass also optionally eliminates the frame pointer and inserts instructions to save and restore call-clobbered registers around calls.

  Source files are '`reload.c`' and '`reload1.c`', plus the header '`reload.h`' used for communication between them.

  The option '`-dg`' causes a debugging dump of the RTL code after this pass. This dump file's name is made by appending '`.greg`' to the input file name.

- Instruction scheduling is repeated here to try to avoid pipeline stalls due to memory loads generated for spilled pseudo registers.

  The option '`-dR`' causes a debugging dump of the RTL code after this pass. This dump file's name is made by appending '`.sched2`' to the input file name.

- Jump optimization is repeated, this time including cross-jumping and deletion of no-op move instructions.

  The option '-dJ' causes a debugging dump of the RTL code after this pass. This dump file's name is made by appending '.jump2' to the input file name.

- Delayed branch scheduling. This optional pass attempts to find instructions that can go into the delay slots of other instructions, usually jumps and calls. The source file name is 'reorg.c'.

  The option '-dd' causes a debugging dump of the RTL code after this pass. This dump file's name is made by appending '.dbr' to the input file name.

- Conversion from usage of some hard registers to usage of a register stack may be done at this point. Currently, this is supported only for the floating-point registers of the Intel 80387 coprocessor. The source file name is 'reg-stack.c'.

  The options '-dk' causes a debugging dump of the RTL code after this pass. This dump file's name is made by appending '.stack' to the input file name.

- Final. This pass outputs the assembler code for the function. It is also responsible for identifying spurious test and compare instructions. Machine-specific peephole optimizations are performed at the same time. The function entry and exit sequences are generated directly as assembler code in this pass; they never exist as RTL.

  The source files are 'final.c' plus 'insn-output.c'; the latter is generated automatically from the machine description by the tool 'genoutput'. The header file 'conditions.h' is used for communication between these files.

- Debugging information output. This is run after final because it must output the stack slot offsets for pseudo registers that did not get hard registers. Source files are 'dbxout.c' for DBX symbol table format, 'sdbout.c' for SDB symbol table format, and 'dwarfout.c' for DWARF symbol table format.

Some additional files are used by all or many passes:

- Every pass uses 'machmode.def' and 'machmode.h' which define the machine modes.

- Several passes use 'real.h', which defines the default representation of floating point constants and how to operate on them.

- All the passes that work with RTL use the header files 'rtl.h' and 'rtl.def', and subroutines in file 'rtl.c'. The tools gen* also use these files to read and work with the machine description RTL.

- Several passes refer to the header file 'insn-config.h' which contains a few parameters (C macro definitions) generated automatically from the machine description RTL by the tool genconfig.

- Several passes use the instruction recognizer, which consists of 'recog.c' and 'recog.h', plus the files 'insn-recog.c' and 'insn-extract.c' that are generated automatically from the machine description by the tools 'genrecog' and 'genextract'.

- Several passes use the header files 'regs.h' which defines the information recorded about pseudo register usage, and 'basic-block.h' which defines the information recorded about basic blocks.

- 'hard-reg-set.h' defines the type HARD_REG_SET, a bit-vector with a bit for each hard register, and some macros to manipulate it. This type is just int if the machine has few enough hard registers; otherwise it is an array of int and some of the macros expand into loops.

- Several passes use instruction attributes. A definition of the attributes defined for a particular machine is in file 'insn-attr.h', which is generated from the machine description by the program 'genattr'. The file 'insn-attrtab.c' contains subroutines to obtain the attribute values for insns. It is generated from the machine description by the program 'genattrtab'.

15 RTL Representation

Most of the work of the compiler is done on an intermediate representation called register transfer language. In this language, the instructions to be output are described, pretty much one by one, in an algebraic form that describes what the instruction does.

RTL is inspired by Lisp lists. It has both an internal form, made up of structures that point at other structures, and a textual form that is used in the machine description and in printed debugging dumps. The textual form uses nested parentheses to indicate the pointers in the internal form.

15.1 RTL Object Types

RTL uses five kinds of objects: expressions, integers, wide integers, strings and vectors. Expressions are the most important ones. An RTL expression ("RTX", for short) is a C structure, but it is usually referred to with a pointer; a type that is given the typedef name `rtx`.

An integer is simply an `int`; their written form uses decimal digits. A wide integer is an integral object whose type is `HOST_WIDE_INT` (see Chapter 18 [Config], page 523); their written form uses decimal digits.

A string is a sequence of characters. In core it is represented as a `char *` in usual C fashion, and it is written in C syntax as well. However, strings in RTL may never be null. If you write an empty string in a machine description, it is represented in core as a null pointer rather than as a pointer to a null character. In certain contexts, these null pointers instead of strings are valid. Within RTL code, strings are most commonly found inside `symbol_ref` expressions, but they appear in other contexts in the RTL expressions that make up machine descriptions.

A vector contains an arbitrary number of pointers to expressions. The number of elements in the vector is explicitly present in the vector. The written form of a vector consists of square brackets ('[...]') surrounding the elements, in sequence and with whitespace separating them. Vectors of length zero are not created; null pointers are used instead.

Expressions are classified by *expression codes* (also called RTX codes). The expression code is a name defined in 'rtl.def', which is also (in upper case) a C enumeration constant. The possible expression codes and their meanings are machine-independent. The code of an RTX can be extracted with the macro `GET_CODE` (*x*) and altered with `PUT_CODE` (*x*, *newcode*).

The expression code determines how many operands the expression contains, and what kinds of objects they are. In RTL, unlike Lisp, you cannot tell by looking at an operand what kind of object it is. Instead, you must know from its context—from the expression code of the containing expression. For example, in an expression of code `subreg`, the first operand is to be regarded as an expression and the second operand as an integer. In an expression of code `plus`, there are two operands, both of which are to be regarded as expressions. In a `symbol_ref` expression, there is one operand, which is to be regarded as a string.

Expressions are written as parentheses containing the name of the expression type, its flags and machine mode if any, and then the operands of the expression (separated by spaces).

Expression code names in the 'md' file are written in lower case, but when they appear in C code they are written in upper case. In this manual, they are shown as follows: `const_int`.

In a few contexts a null pointer is valid where an expression is normally wanted. The written form of this is `(nil)`.

15.2 RTL Classes and Formats

The various expression codes are divided into several *classes*, which are represented by single characters. You can determine the class of an RTX code with the macro `GET_RTX_CLASS` (*code*). Currently, 'rtx.def' defines these classes:

o
: An RTX code that represents an actual object, such as a register (`REG`) or a memory location (`MEM`, `SYMBOL_REF`). Constants and basic transforms on objects (`ADDRESSOF`, `HIGH`, `LO_SUM`) are also included. Note that `SUBREG` and `STRICT_LOW_PART` are not in this class, but in class `x`.

<
: An RTX code for a comparison, such as `NE` or `LT`.

1
: An RTX code for a unary arithmetic operation, such as `NEG`, `NOT`, or `ABS`. This category also includes value extension (sign or zero) and conversions between integer and floating point.

c
: An RTX code for a commutative binary operation, such as `PLUS` or `AND`. `NE` and `EQ` are comparisons, so they have class `<`.

2
: An RTX code for a non-commutative binary operation, such as `MINUS`, `DIV`, or `ASHIFTRT`.

b
: An RTX code for a bitfield operation. Currently only `ZERO_EXTRACT` and `SIGN_EXTRACT`. These have three inputs and are lvalues (so they can be used for insertion as well). See Section 15.10 [Bit Fields], page 304.

3
: An RTX code for other three input operations. Currently only `IF_THEN_ELSE`.

i
: An RTX code for an entire instruction: `INSN`, `JUMP_INSN`, and `CALL_INSN`. See Section 15.16 [Insns], page 314.

m
: An RTX code for something that matches in insns, such as `MATCH_DUP`. These only occur in machine descriptions.

x   All other RTX codes. This category includes the remaining
               codes used only in machine descriptions (DEFINE_*, etc.). It also
               includes all the codes describing side effects (SET, USE, CLOBBER,
               etc.) and the non-insns that may appear on an insn chain, such
               as NOTE, BARRIER, and CODE_LABEL.

For each expression type 'rtl.def' specifies the number of contained
objects and their kinds, with four possibilities: 'e' for expression (actually a
pointer to an expression), 'i' for integer, 'w' for wide integer, 's' for string,
and 'E' for vector of expressions. The sequence of letters for an expression
code is called its *format*. For example, the format of subreg is 'ei'.

A few other format characters are used occasionally:

u   'u' is equivalent to 'e' except that it is printed differently in
               debugging dumps. It is used for pointers to insns.

n   'n' is equivalent to 'i' except that it is printed differently in
               debugging dumps. It is used for the line number or code number
               of a note insn.

S   'S' indicates a string which is optional. In the RTL objects in
               core, 'S' is equivalent to 's', but when the object is read, from
               an 'md' file, the string value of this operand may be omitted. An
               omitted string is taken to be the null string.

V   'V' indicates a vector which is optional. In the RTL objects in
               core, 'V' is equivalent to 'E', but when the object is read from an
               'md' file, the vector value of this operand may be omitted. An
               omitted vector is effectively the same as a vector of no elements.

0   '0' means a slot whose contents do not fit any normal category.
               '0' slots are not printed at all in dumps, and are often used in
               special ways by small parts of the compiler.

There are macros to get the number of operands and the format of an
expression code:

GET_RTX_LENGTH (*code*)
               Number of operands of an RTX of code *code*.

GET_RTX_FORMAT (*code*)
               The format of an RTX of code *code*, as a C string.

Some classes of RTX codes always have the same format. For example,
it is safe to assume that all comparison operations have format ee.

1   All codes of this class have format e.

<
c
2   All codes of these classes have format ee.

b
3   All codes of these classes have format **eee**.

i   All codes of this class have formats that begin with **iuueiee**. See
                     Section 15.16 [Insns], page 314. Note that not all RTL objects
                     linked onto an insn chain are of class **i**.

o
m
x   You can make no assumptions about the format of these codes.

15.3 Access to Operands

Operands of expressions are accessed using the macros **XEXP**, **XINT**, **XWINT**
and **XSTR**. Each of these macros takes two arguments: an expression-pointer
(RTX) and an operand number (counting from zero). Thus,

    XEXP (x, 2)

accesses operand 2 of expression x, as an expression.

    XINT (x, 2)

accesses the same operand as an integer. **XSTR**, used in the same fashion,
would access it as a string.

Any operand can be accessed as an integer, as an expression or as a
string. You must choose the correct method of access for the kind of value
actually stored in the operand. You would do this based on the expression
code of the containing expression. That is also how you would know how
many operands there are.

For example, if x is a **subreg** expression, you know that it has two
operands which can be correctly accessed as **XEXP (x, 0)** and **XINT (x,
1)**. If you did **XINT (x, 0)**, you would get the address of the expression
operand but cast as an integer; that might occasionally be useful, but it
would be cleaner to write **(int) XEXP (x, 0)**. **XEXP (x, 1)** would also compile without error, and would return the second, integer operand cast as an
expression pointer, which would probably result in a crash when accessed.
Nothing stops you from writing **XEXP (x, 28)** either, but this will access
memory past the end of the expression with unpredictable results.

Access to operands which are vectors is more complicated. You can use
the macro **XVEC** to get the vector-pointer itself, or the macros **XVECEXP** and
XVECLEN to access the elements and length of a vector.

XVEC (*exp*, *idx*)
                     Access the vector-pointer which is operand number *idx* in *exp*.

XVECLEN (*exp*, *idx*)
                     Access the length (number of elements) in the vector which is
                     in operand number *idx* in *exp*. This value is an **int**.

XVECEXP (*exp*, *idx*, *eltnum*)

> Access element number *eltnum* in the vector which is in operand number *idx* in *exp*. This value is an RTX.
>
> It is up to you to make sure that *eltnum* is not negative and is less than XVECLEN (*exp*, *idx*).

All the macros defined in this section expand into lvalues and therefore can be used to assign the operands, lengths and vector elements as well as to access them.

15.4 Flags in an RTL Expression

RTL expressions contain several flags (one-bit bitfields) and other values that are used in certain types of expression. Most often they are accessed with the following macros:

MEM_VOLATILE_P (*x*)

> In mem expressions, nonzero for volatile memory references. Stored in the volatil field and printed as '/v'.

MEM_IN_STRUCT_P (*x*)

> In mem expressions, nonzero for reference to an entire structure, union or array, or to a component of one. Zero for references to a scalar variable or through a pointer to a scalar. Stored in the in_struct field and printed as '/s'. If both this flag and MEM_SCALAR_P are clear, then we don't know whether this MEM is in a structure or not. Both flags should never be simultaneously set.

MEM_SCALAR_P (*x*)

> In mem expressions, nonzero for reference to a scalar known not to be a member of a structure, union, or array. Zero for such references and for indirections through pointers, even pointers pointing to scalar types. If both this flag and MEM_STRUCT_P are clear, then we don't know whether this MEM is in a structure or not. Both flags should never be simultaneously set.

MEM_ALIAS_SET (*x*)

> In mem expressions, the alias set to which *x* belongs. If zero, *x* is not in any alias set, and may alias anything. If nonzero, *x* may only alias objects in the same alias set. This value is set (in a language-specific manner) by the front-end. This field is not a bit-field; it is in an integer, found as the second argument to the mem.

REG_LOOP_TEST_P

> In reg expressions, nonzero if this register's entire life is contained in the exit test code for some loop. Stored in the in_struct field and printed as '/s'.

REG_USERVAR_P (*x*)

> In a **reg**, nonzero if it corresponds to a variable present in the user's source code. Zero for temporaries generated internally by the compiler. Stored in the **volatil** field and printed as '/v'.

REG_FUNCTION_VALUE_P (*x*)

> Nonzero in a **reg** if it is the place in which this function's value is going to be returned. (This happens only in a hard register.) Stored in the **integrated** field and printed as '/i'.

> The same hard register may be used also for collecting the values of functions called by this one, but REG_FUNCTION_VALUE_P is zero in this kind of use.

SUBREG_PROMOTED_VAR_P

> Nonzero in a **subreg** if it was made when accessing an object that was promoted to a wider mode in accord with the PROMOTED_MODE machine description macro (see Section 17.3 [Storage Layout], page 403). In this case, the mode of the **subreg** is the declared mode of the object and the mode of SUBREG_REG is the mode of the register that holds the object. Promoted variables are always either sign- or zero-extended to the wider mode on every assignment. Stored in the **in_struct** field and printed as '/s'.

SUBREG_PROMOTED_UNSIGNED_P

> Nonzero in a **subreg** that has SUBREG_PROMOTED_VAR_P nonzero if the object being referenced is kept zero-extended and zero if it is kept sign-extended. Stored in the **unchanging** field and printed as '/u'.

RTX_UNCHANGING_P (*x*)

> Nonzero in a **reg** or **mem** if the value is not changed. (This flag is not set for memory references via pointers to constants. Such pointers only guarantee that the object will not be changed explicitly by the current function. The object might be changed by other functions or by aliasing.) Stored in the **unchanging** field and printed as '/u'.

RTX_INTEGRATED_P (*insn*)

> Nonzero in an insn if it resulted from an in-line function call. Stored in the **integrated** field and printed as '/i'.

RTX_FRAME_RELATED_P (*x*)

> Nonzero in an insn or expression which is part of a function prologue and sets the stack pointer, sets the frame pointer, or saves a register. This flag is required for exception handling support on targets with RTL prologues.

SYMBOL_REF_USED (*x*)

> In a `symbol_ref`, indicates that *x* has been used. This is normally only used to ensure that *x* is only declared external once. Stored in the **used** field.

SYMBOL_REF_FLAG (*x*)

> In a `symbol_ref`, this is used as a flag for machine-specific purposes. Stored in the **volatil** field and printed as '/v'.

LABEL_OUTSIDE_LOOP_P

> In `label_ref` expressions, nonzero if this is a reference to a label that is outside the innermost loop containing the reference to the label. Stored in the **in_struct** field and printed as '/s'.

INSN_DELETED_P (*insn*)

> In an insn, nonzero if the insn has been deleted. Stored in the **volatil** field and printed as '/v'.

INSN_ANNULLED_BRANCH_P (*insn*)

> In an **insn** in the delay slot of a branch insn, indicates that an annulling branch should be used. See the discussion under **sequence** below. Stored in the **unchanging** field and printed as '/u'.

INSN_FROM_TARGET_P (*insn*)

> In an **insn** in a delay slot of a branch, indicates that the insn is from the target of the branch. If the branch insn has INSN_ANNULLED_BRANCH_P set, this insn will only be executed if the branch is taken. For annulled branches with INSN_FROM_TARGET_P clear, the insn will be executed only if the branch is not taken. When INSN_ANNULLED_BRANCH_P is not set, this insn will always be executed. Stored in the **in_struct** field and printed as '/s'.

CONSTANT_POOL_ADDRESS_P (*x*)

> Nonzero in a `symbol_ref` if it refers to part of the current function's "constants pool". These are addresses close to the beginning of the function, and GNU CC assumes they can be addressed directly (perhaps with the help of base registers). Stored in the **unchanging** field and printed as '/u'.

CONST_CALL_P (*x*)

> In a `call_insn`, indicates that the insn represents a call to a const function. Stored in the **unchanging** field and printed as '/u'.

LABEL_PRESERVE_P (*x*)

> In a `code_label`, indicates that the label can never be deleted. Labels referenced by a non-local goto will have this bit set. Stored in the **in_struct** field and printed as '/s'.

SCHED_GROUP_P (*insn*)

During instruction scheduling, in an insn, indicates that the previous insn must be scheduled together with this insn. This is used to ensure that certain groups of instructions will not be split up by the instruction scheduling pass, for example, use insns before a `call_insn` may not be separated from the `call_insn`. Stored in the `in_struct` field and printed as '`/s`'.

These are the fields which the above macros refer to:

used

Normally, this flag is used only momentarily, at the end of RTL generation for a function, to count the number of times an expression appears in insns. Expressions that appear more than once are copied, according to the rules for shared structure (see Section 15.18 [Sharing], page 324).

In a `symbol_ref`, it indicates that an external declaration for the symbol has already been written.

In a `reg`, it is used by the leaf register renumbering code to ensure that each register is only renumbered once.

volatil

This flag is used in `mem`, `symbol_ref` and `reg` expressions and in insns. In RTL dump files, it is printed as '`/v`'.

In a `mem` expression, it is 1 if the memory reference is volatile. Volatile memory references may not be deleted, reordered or combined.

In a `symbol_ref` expression, it is used for machine-specific purposes.

In a `reg` expression, it is 1 if the value is a user-level variable. 0 indicates an internal compiler temporary.

In an insn, 1 means the insn has been deleted.

in_struct

In `mem` expressions, it is 1 if the memory datum referred to is all or part of a structure or array; 0 if it is (or might be) a scalar variable. A reference through a C pointer has 0 because the pointer might point to a scalar variable. This information allows the compiler to determine something about possible cases of aliasing.

In an insn in the delay slot of a branch, 1 means that this insn is from the target of the branch.

During instruction scheduling, in an insn, 1 means that this insn must be scheduled as part of a group together with the previous insn.

In `reg` expressions, it is 1 if the register has its entire life contained within the test expression of some loop.

In `subreg` expressions, 1 means that the `subreg` is accessing an object that has had its mode promoted from a wider mode.

In `label_ref` expressions, 1 means that the referenced label is outside the innermost loop containing the insn in which the `label_ref` was found.

In `code_label` expressions, it is 1 if the label may never be deleted. This is used for labels which are the target of non-local gotos.

In an RTL dump, this flag is represented as '/s'.

unchanging

In `reg` and `mem` expressions, 1 means that the value of the expression never changes.

In `subreg` expressions, it is 1 if the `subreg` references an unsigned object whose mode has been promoted to a wider mode.

In an insn, 1 means that this is an annulling branch.

In a `symbol_ref` expression, 1 means that this symbol addresses something in the per-function constants pool.

In a `call_insn`, 1 means that this instruction is a call to a const function.

In an RTL dump, this flag is represented as '/u'.

integrated

In some kinds of expressions, including insns, this flag means the rtl was produced by procedure integration.

In a `reg` expression, this flag indicates the register containing the value to be returned by the current function. On machines that pass parameters in registers, the same register number may be used for parameters as well, but this flag is not set on such uses.

15.5 Machine Modes

A machine mode describes a size of data object and the representation used for it. In the C code, machine modes are represented by an enumeration type, `enum machine_mode`, defined in 'machmode.def'. Each RTL expression has room for a machine mode and so do certain kinds of tree expressions (declarations and types, to be precise).

In debugging dumps and machine descriptions, the machine mode of an RTL expression is written after the expression code with a colon to separate them. The letters 'mode' which appear at the end of each machine mode name are omitted. For example, `(reg:SI 38)` is a `reg` expression with machine mode SImode. If the mode is VOIDmode, it is not written at all.

Here is a table of machine modes. The term "byte" below refers to an object of `BITS_PER_UNIT` bits (see Section 17.3 [Storage Layout], page 403).

QImode   "Quarter-Integer" mode represents a single byte treated as an integer.

HImode   "Half-Integer" mode represents a two-byte integer.

PSImode   "Partial Single Integer" mode represents an integer which occupies four bytes but which doesn't really use all four. On some machines, this is the right mode to use for pointers.

SImode   "Single Integer" mode represents a four-byte integer.

PDImode   "Partial Double Integer" mode represents an integer which occupies eight bytes but which doesn't really use all eight. On some machines, this is the right mode to use for certain pointers.

DImode   "Double Integer" mode represents an eight-byte integer.

TImode   "Tetra Integer" (?) mode represents a sixteen-byte integer.

SFmode   "Single Floating" mode represents a single-precision (four byte) floating point number.

DFmode   "Double Floating" mode represents a double-precision (eight byte) floating point number.

XFmode   "Extended Floating" mode represents a triple-precision (twelve byte) floating point number. This mode is used for IEEE extended floating point. On some systems not all bits within these bytes will actually be used.

TFmode   "Tetra Floating" mode represents a quadruple-precision (sixteen byte) floating point number.

CCmode   "Condition Code" mode represents the value of a condition code, which is a machine-specific set of bits used to represent the result of a comparison operation. Other machine-specific modes may also be used for the condition code. These modes are not used on machines that use cc0 (see see Section 17.12 [Condition Code], page 466).

BLKmode   "Block" mode represents values that are aggregates to which none of the other modes apply. In RTL, only memory references can have this mode, and only if they appear in string-move or vector instructions. On machines which have no such instructions, BLKmode will not appear in RTL.

VOIDmode Void mode means the absence of a mode or an unspecified mode. For example, RTL expressions of code const_int have mode VOIDmode because they can be taken to have whatever mode the context requires. In debugging dumps of RTL, VOIDmode is expressed by the absence of any mode.

SCmode, DCmode, XCmode, TCmode
>   These modes stand for a complex number represented as a pair
>   of floating point values. The floating point values are in SFmode,
>   DFmode, XFmode, and TFmode, respectively.

CQImode, CHImode, CSImode, CDImode, CTImode, COImode
>   These modes stand for a complex number represented as a pair
>   of integer values. The integer values are in QImode, HImode,
>   SImode, DImode, TImode, and OImode, respectively.

The machine description defines Pmode as a C macro which expands into the machine mode used for addresses. Normally this is the mode whose size is BITS_PER_WORD, SImode on 32-bit machines.

The only modes which a machine description *must* support are QImode, and the modes corresponding to BITS_PER_WORD, FLOAT_TYPE_SIZE and DOUBLE_TYPE_SIZE. The compiler will attempt to use DImode for 8-byte structures and unions, but this can be prevented by overriding the definition of MAX_FIXED_MODE_SIZE. Alternatively, you can have the compiler use TImode for 16-byte structures and unions. Likewise, you can arrange for the C type short int to avoid using HImode.

Very few explicit references to machine modes remain in the compiler and these few references will soon be removed. Instead, the machine modes are divided into mode classes. These are represented by the enumeration type enum mode_class defined in 'machmode.h'. The possible mode classes are:

MODE_INT   Integer modes. By default these are QImode, HImode, SImode,
>   DImode, and TImode.

MODE_PARTIAL_INT
>   The "partial integer" modes, PSImode and PDImode.

MODE_FLOAT
>   floating point modes. By default these are SFmode, DFmode,
>   XFmode and TFmode.

MODE_COMPLEX_INT
>   Complex integer modes. (These are not currently implemented).

MODE_COMPLEX_FLOAT
>   Complex floating point modes. By default these are SCmode,
>   DCmode, XCmode, and TCmode.

MODE_FUNCTION
>   Algol or Pascal function variables including a static chain.
>   (These are not currently implemented).

MODE_CC   Modes representing condition code values. These are CCmode
>   plus any modes listed in the EXTRA_CC_MODES macro. See Sec-
>   tion 16.10 [Jump Patterns], page 367, also see Section 17.12
>   [Condition Code], page 466.

MODE_RANDOM

> This is a catchall mode class for modes which don't fit into the above classes. Currently VOIDmode and BLKmode are in MODE_RANDOM.

Here are some C macros that relate to machine modes:

GET_MODE (*x*)

> Returns the machine mode of the RTX *x*.

PUT_MODE (*x*, *newmode*)

> Alters the machine mode of the RTX *x* to be *newmode*.

NUM_MACHINE_MODES

> Stands for the number of machine modes available on the target machine. This is one greater than the largest numeric value of any machine mode.

GET_MODE_NAME (*m*)

> Returns the name of mode *m* as a string.

GET_MODE_CLASS (*m*)

> Returns the mode class of mode *m*.

GET_MODE_WIDER_MODE (*m*)

> Returns the next wider natural mode. For example, the expression GET_MODE_WIDER_MODE (QImode) returns HImode.

GET_MODE_SIZE (*m*)

> Returns the size in bytes of a datum of mode *m*.

GET_MODE_BITSIZE (*m*)

> Returns the size in bits of a datum of mode *m*.

GET_MODE_MASK (*m*)

> Returns a bitmask containing 1 for all bits in a word that fit within mode *m*. This macro can only be used for modes whose bitsize is less than or equal to HOST_BITS_PER_INT.

GET_MODE_ALIGNMENT (*m*))

> Return the required alignment, in bits, for an object of mode *m*.

GET_MODE_UNIT_SIZE (*m*)

> Returns the size in bytes of the subunits of a datum of mode *m*. This is the same as GET_MODE_SIZE except in the case of complex modes. For them, the unit size is the size of the real or imaginary part.

GET_MODE_NUNITS (*m*)

> Returns the number of units contained in a mode, i.e., GET_MODE_SIZE divided by GET_MODE_UNIT_SIZE.

GET_CLASS_NARROWEST_MODE (*c*)

> Returns the narrowest mode in mode class *c*.

The global variables `byte_mode` and `word_mode` contain modes whose classes are `MODE_INT` and whose bitsizes are either `BITS_PER_UNIT` or `BITS_PER_WORD`, respectively. On 32-bit machines, these are `QImode` and `SImode`, respectively.

15.6 Constant Expression Types

The simplest RTL expressions are those that represent constant values.

(`const_int` *i*)

> This type of expression represents the integer value *i*. *i* is customarily accessed with the macro `INTVAL` as in `INTVAL` (*exp*), which is equivalent to `XWINT` (*exp*, 0).
>
> There is only one expression object for the integer value zero; it is the value of the variable `const0_rtx`. Likewise, the only expression for integer value one is found in `const1_rtx`, the only expression for integer value two is found in `const2_rtx`, and the only expression for integer value negative one is found in `constm1_rtx`. Any attempt to create an expression of code `const_int` and value zero, one, two or negative one will return `const0_rtx`, `const1_rtx`, `const2_rtx` or `constm1_rtx` as appropriate.
>
> Similarly, there is only one object for the integer whose value is `STORE_FLAG_VALUE`. It is found in `const_true_rtx`. If `STORE_FLAG_VALUE` is one, `const_true_rtx` and `const1_rtx` will point to the same object. If `STORE_FLAG_VALUE` is -1, `const_true_rtx` and `constm1_rtx` will point to the same object.

(`const_double`:*m addr i0 i1* ...)

> Represents either a floating-point constant of mode *m* or an integer constant too large to fit into `HOST_BITS_PER_WIDE_INT` bits but small enough to fit within twice that number of bits (GNU CC does not provide a mechanism to represent even larger constants). In the latter case, *m* will be `VOIDmode`.
>
> *addr* is used to contain the `mem` expression that corresponds to the location in memory that at which the constant can be found. If it has not been allocated a memory location, but is on the chain of all `const_double` expressions in this compilation (maintained using an undisplayed field), *addr* contains `const0_rtx`. If it is not on the chain, *addr* contains `cc0_rtx`. *addr* is customarily accessed with the macro `CONST_DOUBLE_MEM` and the chain field via `CONST_DOUBLE_CHAIN`.
>
> If *m* is `VOIDmode`, the bits of the value are stored in *i0* and *i1*. *i0* is customarily accessed with the macro `CONST_DOUBLE_LOW` and *i1* with `CONST_DOUBLE_HIGH`.

If the constant is floating point (regardless of its precision), then the number of integers used to store the value depends on the size of `REAL_VALUE_TYPE` (see Section 17.18 [Cross-compilation], page 508). The integers represent a floating point number, but not precisely in the target machine's or host machine's floating point format. To convert them to the precise bit pattern used by the target machine, use the macro `REAL_VALUE_TO_TARGET_DOUBLE` and friends (see Section 17.16.2 [Data Output], page 480).

The macro `CONST0_RTX` (*mode*) refers to an expression with value 0 in mode *mode*. If mode *mode* is of mode class `MODE_INT`, it returns `const0_rtx`. Otherwise, it returns a `CONST_DOUBLE` expression in mode *mode*. Similarly, the macro `CONST1_RTX` (*mode*) refers to an expression with value 1 in mode *mode* and similarly for `CONST2_RTX`.

(`const_string` *str*)

Represents a constant string with value *str*. Currently this is used only for insn attributes (see Section 16.15 [Insn Attributes], page 380) since constant strings in C are placed in memory.

(`symbol_ref`:*mode symbol*)

Represents the value of an assembler label for data. *symbol* is a string that describes the name of the assembler label. If it starts with a '`*`', the label is the rest of *symbol* not including the '`*`'. Otherwise, the label is *symbol*, usually prefixed with '`_`'.

The `symbol_ref` contains a mode, which is usually `Pmode`. Usually that is the only mode for which a symbol is directly valid.

(`label_ref` *label*)

Represents the value of an assembler label for code. It contains one operand, an expression, which must be a `code_label` that appears in the instruction sequence to identify the place where the label should go.

The reason for using a distinct expression type for code label references is so that jump optimization can distinguish them.

(`const`:*m exp*)

Represents a constant that is the result of an assembly-time arithmetic computation. The operand, *exp*, is an expression that contains only constants (`const_int`, `symbol_ref` and `label_ref` expressions) combined with `plus` and `minus`. However, not all combinations are valid, since the assembler cannot do arbitrary arithmetic on relocatable symbols.

m should be `Pmode`.

(`high:`*m exp*)

>   Represents the high-order bits of *exp*, usually a `symbol_ref`.
>   The number of bits is machine-dependent and is normally the
>   number of bits specified in an instruction that initializes the
>   high order bits of a register. It is used with `lo_sum` to represent
>   the typical two-instruction sequence used in RISC machines to
>   reference a global memory location.
>
>   *m* should be `Pmode`.

15.7 Registers and Memory

Here are the RTL expression types for describing access to machine registers and to main memory.

(`reg:`*m n*)

>   For small values of the integer *n* (those that are less than `FIRST_`
>   `PSEUDO_REGISTER`), this stands for a reference to machine reg-
>   ister number *n*: a *hard register*. For larger values of *n*, it stands
>   for a temporary value or *pseudo register*. The compiler's strat-
>   egy is to generate code assuming an unlimited number of such
>   pseudo registers, and later convert them into hard registers or
>   into memory references.
>
>   *m* is the machine mode of the reference. It is necessary because
>   machines can generally refer to each register in more than one
>   mode. For example, a register may contain a full word but there
>   may be instructions to refer to it as a half word or as a single
>   byte, as well as instructions to refer to it as a floating point
>   number of various precisions.
>
>   Even for a register that the machine can access in only one mode,
>   the mode must always be specified.
>
>   The symbol `FIRST_PSEUDO_REGISTER` is defined by the machine
>   description, since the number of hard registers on the machine is
>   an invariant characteristic of the machine. Note, however, that
>   not all of the machine registers must be general registers. All
>   the machine registers that can be used for storage of data are
>   given hard register numbers, even those that can be used only
>   in certain instructions or can hold only certain types of data.
>
>   A hard register may be accessed in various modes throughout
>   one function, but each pseudo register is given a natural mode
>   and is accessed only in that mode. When it is necessary to
>   describe an access to a pseudo register using a nonnatural mode,
>   a `subreg` expression is used.
>
>   A `reg` expression with a machine mode that specifies more than
>   one word of data may actually stand for several consecutive reg-
>   isters. If in addition the register number specifies a hardware

register, then it actually represents several consecutive hardware registers starting with the specified one.

Each pseudo register number used in a function's RTL code is represented by a unique `reg` expression.

Some pseudo register numbers, those within the range of `FIRST_VIRTUAL_REGISTER` to `LAST_VIRTUAL_REGISTER` only appear during the RTL generation phase and are eliminated before the optimization phases. These represent locations in the stack frame that cannot be determined until RTL generation for the function has been completed. The following virtual register numbers are defined:

`VIRTUAL_INCOMING_ARGS_REGNUM`

> This points to the first word of the incoming arguments passed on the stack. Normally these arguments are placed there by the caller, but the callee may have pushed some arguments that were previously passed in registers.

> When RTL generation is complete, this virtual register is replaced by the sum of the register given by `ARG_POINTER_REGNUM` and the value of `FIRST_PARM_OFFSET`.

`VIRTUAL_STACK_VARS_REGNUM`

> If `FRAME_GROWS_DOWNWARD` is defined, this points to immediately above the first variable on the stack. Otherwise, it points to the first variable on the stack.

> `VIRTUAL_STACK_VARS_REGNUM` is replaced with the sum of the register given by `FRAME_POINTER_REGNUM` and the value `STARTING_FRAME_OFFSET`.

`VIRTUAL_STACK_DYNAMIC_REGNUM`

> This points to the location of dynamically allocated memory on the stack immediately after the stack pointer has been adjusted by the amount of memory desired.

> This virtual register is replaced by the sum of the register given by `STACK_POINTER_REGNUM` and the value `STACK_DYNAMIC_OFFSET`.

`VIRTUAL_OUTGOING_ARGS_REGNUM`

> This points to the location in the stack at which outgoing arguments should be written when the stack is pre-pushed (arguments pushed using push insns should always use `STACK_POINTER_REGNUM`).

> This virtual register is replaced by the sum of the register given by STACK_POINTER_REGNUM and the value STACK_POINTER_OFFSET.

(subreg:*m* *reg* *wordnum*)

> subreg expressions are used to refer to a register in a machine mode other than its natural one, or to refer to one register of a multi-word reg that actually refers to several registers.
>
> Each pseudo-register has a natural mode. If it is necessary to operate on it in a different mode—for example, to perform a fullword move instruction on a pseudo-register that contains a single byte—the pseudo-register must be enclosed in a subreg. In such a case, *wordnum* is zero.
>
> Usually *m* is at least as narrow as the mode of *reg*, in which case it is restricting consideration to only the bits of *reg* that are in *m*.
>
> Sometimes *m* is wider than the mode of *reg*. These subreg expressions are often called *paradoxical*. They are used in cases where we want to refer to an object in a wider mode but do not care what value the additional bits have. The reload pass ensures that paradoxical references are only made to hard registers.
>
> The other use of subreg is to extract the individual registers of a multi-register value. Machine modes such as DImode and TImode can indicate values longer than a word, values which usually require two or more consecutive registers. To access one of the registers, use a subreg with mode SImode and a *wordnum* that says which register.
>
> Storing in a non-paradoxical subreg has undefined results for bits belonging to the same word as the subreg. This laxity makes it easier to generate efficient code for such instructions. To represent an instruction that preserves all the bits outside of those in the subreg, use strict_low_part around the subreg.
>
> The compilation parameter WORDS_BIG_ENDIAN, if set to 1, says that word number zero is the most significant part; otherwise, it is the least significant part.
>
> On a few targets, FLOAT_WORDS_BIG_ENDIAN disagrees with WORDS_BIG_ENDIAN. However, most parts of the compiler treat floating point values as if they had the same endianness as integer values. This works because they handle them solely as a collection of integer values, with no particular numerical value. Only real.c and the runtime libraries care about FLOAT_WORDS_BIG_ENDIAN.
>
> Between the combiner pass and the reload pass, it is possible to have a paradoxical subreg which contains a mem instead of a

reg as its first operand. After the reload pass, it is also possible to have a non-paradoxical subreg which contains a mem; this usually occurs when the mem is a stack slot which replaced a pseudo register.

Note that it is not valid to access a DFmode value in SFmode using a subreg. On some machines the most significant part of a DFmode value does not have the same format as a single-precision floating value.

It is also not valid to access a single word of a multi-word value in a hard register when less registers can hold the value than would be expected from its size. For example, some 32-bit machines have floating-point registers that can hold an entire DFmode value. If register 10 were such a register (subreg:SI (reg:DF 10) 1) would be invalid because there is no way to convert that reference to a single machine register. The reload pass prevents subreg expressions such as these from being formed.

The first operand of a subreg expression is customarily accessed with the SUBREG_REG macro and the second operand is customarily accessed with the SUBREG_WORD macro.

(scratch:m)

This represents a scratch register that will be required for the execution of a single instruction and not used subsequently. It is converted into a reg by either the local register allocator or the reload pass.

scratch is usually present inside a clobber operation (see Section 15.13 [Side Effects], page 307).

(cc0)   This refers to the machine's condition code register. It has no operands and may not have a machine mode. There are two ways to use it:

- To stand for a complete set of condition code flags. This is best on most machines, where each comparison sets the entire series of flags.

  With this technique, (cc0) may be validly used in only two contexts: as the destination of an assignment (in test and compare instructions) and in comparison operators comparing against zero (const_int with value zero; that is to say, const0_rtx).

- To stand for a single flag that is the result of a single condition. This is useful on machines that have only a single flag bit, and in which comparison instructions must specify the condition to test.

  With this technique, (cc0) may be validly used in only two contexts: as the destination of an assignment (in test and compare instructions) where the source is a comparison operator, and as the first operand of `if_then_else` (in a conditional branch).

There is only one expression object of code `cc0`; it is the value of the variable `cc0_rtx`. Any attempt to create an expression of code `cc0` will return `cc0_rtx`.

Instructions can set the condition code implicitly. On many machines, nearly all instructions set the condition code based on the value that they compute or store. It is not necessary to record these actions explicitly in the RTL because the machine description includes a prescription for recognizing the instructions that do so (by means of the macro `NOTICE_UPDATE_CC`). See Section 17.12 [Condition Code], page 466. Only instructions whose sole purpose is to set the condition code, and instructions that use the condition code, need mention (`cc0`).

On some machines, the condition code register is given a register number and a `reg` is used instead of (`cc0`). This is usually the preferable approach if only a small subset of instructions modify the condition code. Other machines store condition codes in general registers; in such cases a pseudo register should be used.

Some machines, such as the Sparc and RS/6000, have two sets of arithmetic instructions, one that sets and one that does not set the condition code. This is best handled by normally generating the instruction that does not set the condition code, and making a pattern that both performs the arithmetic and sets the condition code register (which would not be (`cc0`) in this case). For examples, search for 'addcc' and 'andcc' in 'sparc.md'.

(pc)   This represents the machine's program counter. It has no operands and may not have a machine mode. (`pc`) may be validly used only in certain specific contexts in jump instructions.

There is only one expression object of code `pc`; it is the value of the variable `pc_rtx`. Any attempt to create an expression of code `pc` will return `pc_rtx`.

All instructions that do not jump alter the program counter implicitly by incrementing it, but there is no need to mention this in the RTL.

(mem: *m addr*)

This RTX represents a reference to main memory at an address represented by the expression *addr*. *m* specifies how large a unit of memory is accessed.

(`addressof`:*m reg*)

> This RTX represents a request for the address of register *reg*. Its mode is always `Pmode`. If there are any `addressof` expressions left in the function after CSE, *reg* is forced into the stack and the `addressof` expression is replaced with a `plus` expression for the address of its stack slot.

15.8 RTL Expressions for Arithmetic

Unless otherwise specified, all the operands of arithmetic expressions must be valid for mode *m*. An operand is valid for mode *m* if it has mode *m*, or if it is a `const_int` or `const_double` and *m* is a mode of class `MODE_INT`.

For commutative binary operations, constants should be placed in the second operand.

(`plus`:*m x y*)

> Represents the sum of the values represented by *x* and *y* carried out in machine mode *m*.

(`lo_sum`:*m x y*)

> Like `plus`, except that it represents that sum of *x* and the low-order bits of *y*. The number of low order bits is machine-dependent but is normally the number of bits in a `Pmode` item minus the number of bits set by the `high` code (see Section 15.6 [Constants], page 293).
>
> *m* should be `Pmode`.

(`minus`:*m x y*)

> Like `plus` but represents subtraction.

(`compare`:*m x y*)

> Represents the result of subtracting *y* from *x* for purposes of comparison. The result is computed without overflow, as if with infinite precision.
>
> Of course, machines can't really subtract with infinite precision. However, they can pretend to do so when only the sign of the result will be used, which is the case when the result is stored in the condition code. And that is the only way this kind of expression may validly be used: as a value to be stored in the condition codes.
>
> The mode *m* is not related to the modes of *x* and *y*, but instead is the mode of the condition code value. If (`cc0`) is used, it is `VOIDmode`. Otherwise it is some mode in class `MODE_CC`, often `CCmode`. See Section 17.12 [Condition Code], page 466.
>
> Normally, *x* and *y* must have the same mode. Otherwise, `compare` is valid only if the mode of *x* is in class `MODE_INT` and

y is a `const_int` or `const_double` with mode `VOIDmode`. The mode of x determines what mode the comparison is to be done in; thus it must not be `VOIDmode`.

If one of the operands is a constant, it should be placed in the second operand and the comparison code adjusted as appropriate.

A `compare` specifying two `VOIDmode` constants is not valid since there is no way to know in what mode the comparison is to be performed; the comparison must either be folded during the compilation or the first operand must be loaded into a register while its mode is still known.

(neg:m x)

Represents the negation (subtraction from zero) of the value represented by x, carried out in mode m.

(mult:m x y)

Represents the signed product of the values represented by x and y carried out in machine mode m.

Some machines support a multiplication that generates a product wider than the operands. Write the pattern for this as

(mult:m (sign_extend:m x) (sign_extend:m y))

where m is wider than the modes of x and y, which need not be the same.

Write patterns for unsigned widening multiplication similarly using `zero_extend`.

(div:m x y)

Represents the quotient in signed division of x by y, carried out in machine mode m. If m is a floating point mode, it represents the exact quotient; otherwise, the integerized quotient.

Some machines have division instructions in which the operands and quotient widths are not all the same; you should represent such instructions using `truncate` and `sign_extend` as in,

(truncate:$m1$ (div:$m2$ x (sign_extend:$m2$ y)))

(udiv:m x y)

Like `div` but represents unsigned division.

(mod:m x y)
(umod:m x y)

Like `div` and `udiv` but represent the remainder instead of the quotient.

(smin:m x y)
(smax:m x y)

Represents the smaller (for `smin`) or larger (for `smax`) of x and y, interpreted as signed integers in mode m.

`(umin:`*m x y*`)`
`(umax:`*m x y*`)`

> Like `smin` and `smax`, but the values are interpreted as unsigned integers.

`(not:`*m x*`)`

> Represents the bitwise complement of the value represented by *x*, carried out in mode *m*, which must be a fixed-point machine mode.

`(and:`*m x y*`)`

> Represents the bitwise logical-and of the values represented by *x* and *y*, carried out in machine mode *m*, which must be a fixed-point machine mode.

`(ior:`*m x y*`)`

> Represents the bitwise inclusive-or of the values represented by *x* and *y*, carried out in machine mode *m*, which must be a fixed-point mode.

`(xor:`*m x y*`)`

> Represents the bitwise exclusive-or of the values represented by *x* and *y*, carried out in machine mode *m*, which must be a fixed-point mode.

`(ashift:`*m x c*`)`

> Represents the result of arithmetically shifting *x* left by *c* places. *x* have mode *m*, a fixed-point machine mode. *c* be a fixed-point mode or be a constant with mode `VOIDmode`; which mode is determined by the mode called for in the machine description entry for the left-shift instruction. For example, on the Vax, the mode of *c* is `QImode` regardless of *m*.

`(lshiftrt:`*m x c*`)`
`(ashiftrt:`*m x c*`)`

> Like `ashift` but for right shift. Unlike the case for left shift, these two operations are distinct.

`(rotate:`*m x c*`)`
`(rotatert:`*m x c*`)`

> Similar but represent left and right rotate. If *c* is a constant, use `rotate`.

`(abs:`*m x*`)`

> Represents the absolute value of *x*, computed in mode *m*.

`(sqrt:`*m x*`)`

> Represents the square root of *x*, computed in mode *m*. Most often *m* will be a floating point mode.

(ffs:*m* x)

> Represents one plus the index of the least significant 1-bit in x, represented as an integer of mode *m*. (The value is zero if x is zero.) The mode of x need not be *m*; depending on the target machine, various mode combinations may be valid.

15.9 Comparison Operations

Comparison operators test a relation on two operands and are considered to represent a machine-dependent nonzero value described by, but not necessarily equal to, `STORE_FLAG_VALUE` (see Section 17.19 [Misc], page 511) if the relation holds, or zero if it does not. The mode of the comparison operation is independent of the mode of the data being compared. If the comparison operation is being tested (e.g., the first operand of an `if_then_else`), the mode must be `VOIDmode`. If the comparison operation is producing data to be stored in some variable, the mode must be in class `MODE_INT`. All comparison operations producing data must use the same mode, which is machine-specific.

There are two ways that comparison operations may be used. The comparison operators may be used to compare the condition codes (`cc0`) against zero, as in `(eq (cc0) (const_int 0))`. Such a construct actually refers to the result of the preceding instruction in which the condition codes were set. The instructing setting the condition code must be adjacent to the instruction using the condition code; only **note** insns may separate them.

Alternatively, a comparison operation may directly compare two data objects. The mode of the comparison is determined by the operands; they must both be valid for a common machine mode. A comparison with both operands constant would be invalid as the machine mode could not be deduced from it, but such a comparison should never exist in RTL due to constant folding.

In the example above, if (`cc0`) were last set to (`compare` x y), the comparison operation is identical to (`eq` x y). Usually only one style of comparisons is supported on a particular machine, but the combine pass will try to merge the operations to produce the **eq** shown in case it exists in the context of the particular insn involved.

Inequality comparisons come in two flavors, signed and unsigned. Thus, there are distinct expression codes **gt** and **gtu** for signed and unsigned greater-than. These can produce different results for the same pair of integer values: for example, 1 is signed greater-than -1 but not unsigned greater-than, because -1 when regarded as unsigned is actually `0xffffffff` which is greater than 1.

The signed comparisons are also used for floating point values. Floating point comparisons are distinguished by the machine modes of the operands.

(eq:*m x y*)

> 1 if the values represented by *x* and *y* are equal, otherwise 0.

(ne:*m x y*)

> 1 if the values represented by *x* and *y* are not equal, otherwise 0.

(gt:*m x y*)

> 1 if the *x* is greater than *y*. If they are fixed-point, the comparison is done in a signed sense.

(gtu:*m x y*)

> Like gt but does unsigned comparison, on fixed-point numbers only.

(lt:*m x y*)
(ltu:*m x y*)

> Like gt and gtu but test for "less than".

(ge:*m x y*)
(geu:*m x y*)

> Like gt and gtu but test for "greater than or equal".

(le:*m x y*)
(leu:*m x y*)

> Like gt and gtu but test for "less than or equal".

(if_then_else *cond then else*)

> This is not a comparison operation but is listed here because it is always used in conjunction with a comparison operation. To be precise, *cond* is a comparison expression. This expression represents a choice, according to *cond*, between the value represented by *then* and the one represented by *else*.
>
> On most machines, if_then_else expressions are valid only to express conditional jumps.

(cond [*test1 value1 test2 value2* ...] *default*)

> Similar to if_then_else, but more general. Each of *test1*, *test2*, ... is performed in turn. The result of this expression is the *value* corresponding to the first non-zero test, or *default* if none of the tests are non-zero expressions.
>
> This is currently not valid for instruction patterns and is supported only for insn attributes. See Section 16.15 [Insn Attributes], page 380.

15.10 Bit Fields

Special expression codes exist to represent bitfield instructions. These types of expressions are lvalues in RTL; they may appear on the left side of an assignment, indicating insertion of a value into the specified bit field.

(sign_extract:*m* *loc* *size* *pos*)

>   This represents a reference to a sign-extended bit field contained or starting in *loc* (a memory or register reference). The bit field is *size* bits wide and starts at bit *pos*. The compilation option BITS_BIG_ENDIAN says which end of the memory unit *pos* counts from.
>
>   If *loc* is in memory, its mode must be a single-byte integer mode. If *loc* is in a register, the mode to use is specified by the operand of the insv or extv pattern (see Section 16.7 [Standard Names], page 350) and is usually a full-word integer mode, which is the default if none is specified.
>
>   The mode of *pos* is machine-specific and is also specified in the insv or extv pattern.
>
>   The mode *m* is the same as the mode that would be used for *loc* if it were a register.

(zero_extract:*m* *loc* *size* *pos*)

>   Like sign_extract but refers to an unsigned or zero-extended bit field. The same sequence of bits are extracted, but they are filled to an entire word with zeros instead of by sign-extension.

15.11 Conversions

All conversions between machine modes must be represented by explicit conversion operations. For example, an expression which is the sum of a byte and a full word cannot be written as (plus:SI (reg:QI 34) (reg:SI 80)) because the plus operation requires two operands of the same machine mode. Therefore, the byte-sized operand is enclosed in a conversion operation, as in

>   (plus:SI (sign_extend:SI (reg:QI 34)) (reg:SI 80))

The conversion operation is not a mere placeholder, because there may be more than one way of converting from a given starting mode to the desired final mode. The conversion operation code says how to do it.

For all conversion operations, *x* must not be VOIDmode because the mode in which to do the conversion would not be known. The conversion must either be done at compile-time or *x* must be placed into a register.

(sign_extend:*m* *x*)

>   Represents the result of sign-extending the value *x* to machine mode *m*. *m* must be a fixed-point mode and *x* a fixed-point value of a mode narrower than *m*.

(zero_extend:*m* *x*)

>   Represents the result of zero-extending the value *x* to machine mode *m*. *m* must be a fixed-point mode and *x* a fixed-point value of a mode narrower than *m*.

(float_extend:*m x*)
> Represents the result of extending the value *x* to machine mode *m*. *m* must be a floating point mode and *x* a floating point value of a mode narrower than *m*.

(truncate:*m x*)
> Represents the result of truncating the value *x* to machine mode *m*. *m* must be a fixed-point mode and *x* a fixed-point value of a mode wider than *m*.

(float_truncate:*m x*)
> Represents the result of truncating the value *x* to machine mode *m*. *m* must be a floating point mode and *x* a floating point value of a mode wider than *m*.

(float:*m x*)
> Represents the result of converting fixed point value *x*, regarded as signed, to floating point mode *m*.

(unsigned_float:*m x*)
> Represents the result of converting fixed point value *x*, regarded as unsigned, to floating point mode *m*.

(fix:*m x*)
> When *m* is a fixed point mode, represents the result of converting floating point value *x* to mode *m*, regarded as signed. How rounding is done is not specified, so this operation may be used validly in compiling C code only for integer-valued operands.

(unsigned_fix:*m x*)
> Represents the result of converting floating point value *x* to fixed point mode *m*, regarded as unsigned. How rounding is done is not specified.

(fix:*m x*)
> When *m* is a floating point mode, represents the result of converting floating point value *x* (valid for mode *m*) to an integer, still represented in floating point mode *m*, by rounding towards zero.

15.12 Declarations

Declaration expression codes do not represent arithmetic operations but rather state assertions about their operands.

(strict_low_part (subreg:*m* (reg:*n r*) 0))
> This expression code is used in only one context: as the destination operand of a **set** expression. In addition, the operand of this expression must be a non-paradoxical **subreg** expression.

The presence of `strict_low_part` says that the part of the register which is meaningful in mode *n*, but is not part of mode *m*, is not to be altered. Normally, an assignment to such a subreg is allowed to have undefined effects on the rest of the register when *m* is less than a word.

15.13 Side Effect Expressions

The expression codes described so far represent values, not actions. But machine instructions never produce values; they are meaningful only for their side effects on the state of the machine. Special expression codes are used to represent side effects.

The body of an instruction is always one of these side effect codes; the codes described above, which represent values, appear only as the operands of these.

(set *lval* *x*)

Represents the action of storing the value of *x* into the place represented by *lval*. *lval* must be an expression representing a place that can be stored in: `reg` (or `subreg` or `strict_low_part`), `mem`, `pc` or `cc0`.

If *lval* is a `reg`, `subreg` or `mem`, it has a machine mode; then *x* must be valid for that mode.

If *lval* is a `reg` whose machine mode is less than the full width of the register, then it means that the part of the register specified by the machine mode is given the specified value and the rest of the register receives an undefined value. Likewise, if *lval* is a `subreg` whose machine mode is narrower than the mode of the register, the rest of the register can be changed in an undefined way.

If *lval* is a `strict_low_part` of a `subreg`, then the part of the register specified by the machine mode of the `subreg` is given the value *x* and the rest of the register is not changed.

If *lval* is (`cc0`), it has no machine mode, and *x* may be either a `compare` expression or a value that may have any mode. The latter case represents a "test" instruction. The expression (set (cc0) (reg:*m* *n*)) is equivalent to (set (cc0) (compare (reg:*m* *n*) (const_int 0))). Use the former expression to save space during the compilation.

If *lval* is (`pc`), we have a jump instruction, and the possibilities for *x* are very limited. It may be a `label_ref` expression (unconditional jump). It may be an `if_then_else` (conditional jump), in which case either the second or the third operand must be (`pc`) (for the case which does not jump) and the other of the two must be a `label_ref` (for the case which does jump). *x* may also be a `mem` or (`plus:SI` (`pc`) *y*), where *y* may be a `reg` or a `mem`; these unusual patterns are used to represent jumps through branch tables.

If *lval* is neither (`cc0`) nor (`pc`), the mode of *lval* must not be `VOIDmode` and the mode of *x* must be valid for the mode of *lval*.

lval is customarily accessed with the `SET_DEST` macro and *x* with the `SET_SRC` macro.

(`return`)   As the sole expression in a pattern, represents a return from the current function, on machines where this can be done with one instruction, such as Vaxes. On machines where a multi-instruction "epilogue" must be executed in order to return from the function, returning is done by jumping to a label which precedes the epilogue, and the `return` expression code is never used.

Inside an `if_then_else` expression, represents the value to be placed in `pc` to return to the caller.

Note that an insn pattern of (`return`) is logically equivalent to (`set` (`pc`) (`return`)), but the latter form is never used.

(`call` *function nargs*)

Represents a function call. *function* is a `mem` expression whose address is the address of the function to be called. *nargs* is an expression which can be used for two purposes: on some machines it represents the number of bytes of stack argument; on others, it represents the number of argument registers.

Each machine has a standard machine mode which *function* must have. The machine description defines macro `FUNCTION_MODE` to expand into the requisite mode name. The purpose of this mode is to specify what kind of addressing is allowed, on machines where the allowed kinds of addressing depend on the machine mode being addressed.

(`clobber` *x*)

Represents the storing or possible storing of an unpredictable, undescribed value into *x*, which must be a `reg`, `scratch` or `mem` expression.

One place this is used is in string instructions that store standard values into particular hard registers. It may not be worth the trouble to describe the values that are stored, but it is essential to inform the compiler that the registers will be altered, lest it attempt to keep data in them across the string instruction.

If *x* is (`mem:BLK` (`const_int 0`)), it means that all memory locations must be presumed clobbered.

Note that the machine description classifies certain hard registers as "call-clobbered". All function call instructions are assumed by default to clobber these registers, so there is no need to use `clobber` expressions to indicate this fact. Also, each function call is assumed to have the potential to alter any memory location, unless the function is declared `const`.

If the last group of expressions in a `parallel` are each a `clobber` expression whose arguments are `reg` or `match_scratch` (see Section 16.3 [RTL Template], page 328) expressions, the combiner phase can add the appropriate `clobber` expressions to an insn it has constructed when doing so will cause a pattern to be matched.

This feature can be used, for example, on a machine that whose multiply and add instructions don't use an MQ register but which has an add-accumulate instruction that does clobber the MQ register. Similarly, a combined instruction might require a temporary register while the constituent instructions might not.

When a `clobber` expression for a register appears inside a `parallel` with other side effects, the register allocator guarantees that the register is unoccupied both before and after that insn. However, the reload phase may allocate a register used for one of the inputs unless the '`&`' constraint is specified for the selected alternative (see Section 16.6.4 [Modifiers], page 343). You can clobber either a specific hard register, a pseudo register, or a `scratch` expression; in the latter two cases, GNU CC will allocate a hard register that is available there for use as a temporary.

For instructions that require a temporary register, you should use `scratch` instead of a pseudo-register because this will allow the combiner phase to add the `clobber` when required. You do this by coding (`clobber` (`match_scratch` ...)). If you do clobber a pseudo register, use one which appears nowhere else—generate a new one each time. Otherwise, you may confuse CSE.

There is one other known use for clobbering a pseudo register in a `parallel`: when one of the input operands of the insn is also clobbered by the insn. In this case, using the same pseudo register in the clobber and elsewhere in the insn produces the expected results.

(`use` x)   Represents the use of the value of x. It indicates that the value in x at this point in the program is needed, even though it may not be apparent why this is so. Therefore, the compiler will not attempt to delete previous instructions whose only effect is to store a value in x. x must be a `reg` expression.

During the reload phase, an insn that has a `use` as pattern can carry a reg_equal note. These `use` insns will be deleted before the reload phase exits.

During the delayed branch scheduling phase, *x* may be an insn. This indicates that *x* previously was located at this place in the code and its data dependencies need to be taken into account. These `use` insns will be deleted before the delayed branch scheduling phase exits.

`(parallel [`*x0 x1* `...])`

Represents several side effects performed in parallel. The square brackets stand for a vector; the operand of `parallel` is a vector of expressions. *x0*, *x1* and so on are individual side effect expressions—expressions of code `set`, `call`, `return`, `clobber` or `use`.

"In parallel" means that first all the values used in the individual side-effects are computed, and second all the actual side-effects are performed. For example,

```
(parallel [(set (reg:SI 1) (mem:SI (reg:SI 1)))
           (set (mem:SI (reg:SI 1)) (reg:SI 1))])
```

says unambiguously that the values of hard register 1 and the memory location addressed by it are interchanged. In both places where `(reg:SI 1)` appears as a memory address it refers to the value in register 1 *before* the execution of the insn.

It follows that it is *incorrect* to use `parallel` and expect the result of one `set` to be available for the next one. For example, people sometimes attempt to represent a jump-if-zero instruction this way:

```
(parallel [(set (cc0) (reg:SI 34))
           (set (pc) (if_then_else
                        (eq (cc0) (const_int 0))
                        (label_ref ...)
                        (pc)))])
```

But this is incorrect, because it says that the jump condition depends on the condition code value *before* this instruction, not on the new value that is set by this instruction.

Peephole optimization, which takes place together with final assembly code output, can produce insns whose patterns consist of a `parallel` whose elements are the operands needed to output the resulting assembler code—often `reg`, `mem` or constant expressions. This would not be well-formed RTL at any other stage in compilation, but it is ok then because no further optimization remains to be done. However, the definition of the macro `NOTICE_UPDATE_CC`, if any, must deal with such insns if you define any peephole optimizations.

(sequence [*insns* ...])

> Represents a sequence of insns. Each of the *insns* that appears
> in the vector is suitable for appearing in the chain of insns, so it
> must be an `insn`, `jump_insn`, `call_insn`, `code_label`, `barrier`
> or `note`.
>
> A `sequence` RTX is never placed in an actual insn during RTL
> generation. It represents the sequence of insns that result from
> a `define_expand` *before* those insns are passed to `emit_insn`
> to insert them in the chain of insns. When actually inserted,
> the individual sub-insns are separated out and the `sequence` is
> forgotten.
>
> After delay-slot scheduling is completed, an insn and all the
> insns that reside in its delay slots are grouped together into a
> `sequence`. The insn requiring the delay slot is the first insn in
> the vector; subsequent insns are to be placed in the delay slot.
>
> `INSN_ANNULLED_BRANCH_P` is set on an insn in a delay slot to
> indicate that a branch insn should be used that will conditionally
> annul the effect of the insns in the delay slots. In such a case,
> `INSN_FROM_TARGET_P` indicates that the insn is from the target
> of the branch and should be executed only if the branch is taken;
> otherwise the insn should be executed only if the branch is not
> taken. See Section 16.15.7 [Delay Slots], page 388.

These expression codes appear in place of a side effect, as the body of
an insn, though strictly speaking they do not always describe side effects as
such:

(asm_input *s*)

> Represents literal assembler code as described by the string *s*.

(unspec [*operands* ...] *index*)
(unspec_volatile [*operands* ...] *index*)

> Represents a machine-specific operation on *operands*. *index*
> selects between multiple machine-specific operations. `unspec_`
> `volatile` is used for volatile operations and operations that may
> trap; `unspec` is used for other operations.
>
> These codes may appear inside a `pattern` of an insn, inside a
> `parallel`, or inside an expression.

(addr_vec:*m* [*lr0 lr1* ...])

> Represents a table of jump addresses. The vector elements *lr0*,
> etc., are `label_ref` expressions. The mode *m* specifies how
> much space is given to each address; normally *m* would be `Pmode`.

(addr_diff_vec:*m base* [*lr0 lr1* ...] *min max flags*)

> Represents a table of jump addresses expressed as offsets from
> *base*. The vector elements *lr0*, etc., are `label_ref` expressions

and so is *base*. The mode *m* specifies how much space is given to each address-difference. *min* and *max* are set up by branch shortening and hold a label with a minimum and a maximum address, respectively. *flags* indicates the relative position of *base*, *min* and *max* to the cointaining insn and of *min* and *max* to *base*. See rtl.def for details.

15.14 Embedded Side-Effects on Addresses

Six special side-effect expression codes appear as memory addresses.

(pre_dec:*m x*)

Represents the side effect of decrementing *x* by a standard amount and represents also the value that *x* has after being decremented. *x* must be a `reg` or `mem`, but most machines allow only a `reg`. *m* must be the machine mode for pointers on the machine in use. The amount *x* is decremented by is the length in bytes of the machine mode of the containing memory reference of which this expression serves as the address. Here is an example of its use:

        (mem:DF (pre_dec:SI (reg:SI 39)))

This says to decrement pseudo register 39 by the length of a `DFmode` value and use the result to address a `DFmode` value.

(pre_inc:*m x*)

Similar, but specifies incrementing *x* instead of decrementing it.

(post_dec:*m x*)

Represents the same side effect as `pre_dec` but a different value. The value represented here is the value *x* has *before* being decremented.

(post_inc:*m x*)

Similar, but specifies incrementing *x* instead of decrementing it.

(post_modify:*m x y*)

Represents the side effect of setting *x* to *y* and represents *x* before *x* is modified. *x* must be a `reg` or `mem`, but most machines allow only a `reg`. *m* must be the machine mode for pointers on the machine in use. The amount *x* is decremented by is the length in bytes of the machine mode of the containing memory reference of which this expression serves as the address. Note that this is not currently implemented.

The expression *y* must be one of three forms:

            (plus:*m x z*), (minus:*m x z*), or (plus:*m x i*),

where *z* is an index register and *i* is a constant.

Here is an example of its use:

```
(mem:SF (post_modify:SI (reg:SI 42) (plus (reg:SI 42) \
       (reg:SI 48)))))
```

This says to modify pseudo register 42 by adding the contents
of pseudo register 48 to it, after the use of whatever 42 points
to.

(pre_modify:*m* x *expr*)
> Similar except side effects happen before the use.

These embedded side effect expressions must be used with care. Instruction patterns may not use them. Until the 'flow' pass of the compiler, they
may occur only to represent pushes onto the stack. The 'flow' pass finds
cases where registers are incremented or decremented in one instruction and
used as an address shortly before or after; these cases are then transformed
to use pre- or post-increment or -decrement.

If a register used as the operand of these expressions is used in another
address in an insn, the original value of the register is used. Uses of the register outside of an address are not permitted within the same insn as a use in
an embedded side effect expression because such insns behave differently on
different machines and hence must be treated as ambiguous and disallowed.

An instruction that can be represented with an embedded side effect could
also be represented using **parallel** containing an additional **set** to describe
how the address register is altered. This is not done because machines that
allow these operations at all typically allow them wherever a memory address
is called for. Describing them as additional parallel stores would require
doubling the number of entries in the machine description.

15.15 Assembler Instructions as Expressions

The RTX code `asm_operands` represents a value produced by a user-
specified assembler instruction. It is used to represent an **asm** statement
with arguments. An **asm** statement with a single output operand, like this:

```
asm ("foo %1,%2,%0" : "=a" (outputvar) : "g" (x + y), "di" (*z));
```

is represented using a single `asm_operands` RTX which represents the value
that is stored in `outputvar`:

```
(set rtx-for-outputvar
     (asm_operands "foo %1,%2,%0" "a" 0
                   [rtx-for-addition-result rtx-for-*z]
                   [(asm_input:m1 "g")
                    (asm_input:m2 "di")]))
```

Here the operands of the `asm_operands` RTX are the assembler template
string, the output-operand's constraint, the index-number of the output
operand among the output operands specified, a vector of input operand
RTX's, and a vector of input-operand modes and constraints. The mode *m1*
is the mode of the sum x+y; *m2* is that of *z.

When an `asm` statement has multiple output values, its insn has several such `set` RTX's inside of a `parallel`. Each `set` contains a `asm_operands`; all of these share the same assembler template and vectors, but each contains the constraint for the respective output operand. They are also distinguished by the output-operand index number, which is 0, 1, ... for successive output operands.

15.16 Insns

The RTL representation of the code for a function is a doubly-linked chain of objects called *insns*. Insns are expressions with special codes that are used for no other purpose. Some insns are actual instructions; others represent dispatch tables for `switch` statements; others represent labels to jump to or various sorts of declarative information.

In addition to its own specific data, each insn must have a unique id-number that distinguishes it from all other insns in the current function (after delayed branch scheduling, copies of an insn with the same id-number may be present in multiple places in a function, but these copies will always be identical and will only appear inside a `sequence`), and chain pointers to the preceding and following insns. These three fields occupy the same position in every insn, independent of the expression code of the insn. They could be accessed with `XEXP` and `XINT`, but instead three special macros are always used:

INSN_UID (*i*)
> Accesses the unique id of insn *i*.

PREV_INSN (*i*)
> Accesses the chain pointer to the insn preceding *i*. If *i* is the first insn, this is a null pointer.

NEXT_INSN (*i*)
> Accesses the chain pointer to the insn following *i*. If *i* is the last insn, this is a null pointer.

The first insn in the chain is obtained by calling `get_insns`; the last insn is the result of calling `get_last_insn`. Within the chain delimited by these insns, the `NEXT_INSN` and `PREV_INSN` pointers must always correspond: if *insn* is not the first insn,

>   NEXT_INSN (PREV_INSN (*insn*)) == *insn*

is always true and if *insn* is not the last insn,

>   PREV_INSN (NEXT_INSN (*insn*)) == *insn*

is always true.

After delay slot scheduling, some of the insns in the chain might be `sequence` expressions, which contain a vector of insns. The value of `NEXT_INSN` in all but the last of these insns is the next insn in the vector; the value of `NEXT_INSN` of the last insn in the vector is the same as the value of `NEXT_INSN` for the `sequence` in which it is contained. Similar rules apply for `PREV_INSN`.

This means that the above invariants are not necessarily true for insns inside `sequence` expressions. Specifically, if *insn* is the first insn in a `sequence`, `NEXT_INSN (PREV_INSN (`*insn*`))` is the insn containing the `sequence` expression, as is the value of `PREV_INSN (NEXT_INSN (`*insn*`))` is *insn* is the last insn in the `sequence` expression. You can use these expressions to find the containing `sequence` expression.

Every insn has one of the following six expression codes:

insn
: The expression code `insn` is used for instructions that do not jump and do not do function calls. `sequence` expressions are always contained in insns with code `insn` even if one of those insns should jump or do function calls.

  Insns with code `insn` have four additional fields beyond the three mandatory ones listed above. These four are described in a table below.

jump_insn
: The expression code `jump_insn` is used for instructions that may jump (or, more generally, may contain `label_ref` expressions). If there is an instruction to return from the current function, it is recorded as a `jump_insn`.

  `jump_insn` insns have the same extra fields as `insn` insns, accessed in the same way and in addition contain a field `JUMP_LABEL` which is defined once jump optimization has completed.

  For simple conditional and unconditional jumps, this field contains the `code_label` to which this insn will (possibly conditionally) branch. In a more complex jump, `JUMP_LABEL` records one of the labels that the insn refers to; the only way to find the others is to scan the entire body of the insn.

  Return insns count as jumps, but since they do not refer to any labels, they have zero in the `JUMP_LABEL` field.

call_insn
: The expression code `call_insn` is used for instructions that may do function calls. It is important to distinguish these instructions because they imply that certain registers and memory locations may be altered unpredictably.

  `call_insn` insns have the same extra fields as `insn` insns, accessed in the same way and in addition contain a field `CALL_INSN_FUNCTION_USAGE`, which contains a list (chain of `expr_list` expressions) containing `use` and `clobber` expressions that denote hard registers used or clobbered by the called function. A register specified in a `clobber` in this list is modified *after* the execution of the `call_insn`, while a register in a `clobber` in the body of the `call_insn` is clobbered before the insn completes execution. `clobber` expressions in this list augment registers specified in `CALL_USED_REGISTERS` (see Section 17.5.1 [Register Basics], page 414).

`code_label`

A `code_label` insn represents a label that a jump insn can jump to. It contains two special fields of data in addition to the three standard ones. `CODE_LABEL_NUMBER` is used to hold the *label number*, a number that identifies this label uniquely among all the labels in the compilation (not just in the current function). Ultimately, the label is represented in the assembler output as an assembler label, usually of the form 'L*n*' where *n* is the label number.

When a `code_label` appears in an RTL expression, it normally appears within a `label_ref` which represents the address of the label, as a number.

The field `LABEL_NUSES` is only defined once the jump optimization phase is completed and contains the number of times this label is referenced in the current function.

`barrier`   Barriers are placed in the instruction stream when control cannot flow past them. They are placed after unconditional jump instructions to indicate that the jumps are unconditional and after calls to `volatile` functions, which do not return (e.g., `exit`). They contain no information beyond the three standard fields.

`note`   `note` insns are used to represent additional debugging and declarative information. They contain two nonstandard fields, an integer which is accessed with the macro `NOTE_LINE_NUMBER` and a string accessed with `NOTE_SOURCE_FILE`.

If `NOTE_LINE_NUMBER` is positive, the note represents the position of a source line and `NOTE_SOURCE_FILE` is the source file name that the line came from. These notes control generation of line number data in the assembler output.

Otherwise, `NOTE_LINE_NUMBER` is not really a line number but a code with one of the following values (and `NOTE_SOURCE_FILE` must contain a null pointer):

`NOTE_INSN_DELETED`

Such a note is completely ignorable. Some passes of the compiler delete insns by altering them into notes of this kind.

NOTE_INSN_BLOCK_BEG
NOTE_INSN_BLOCK_END

> These types of notes indicate the position of the beginning and end of a level of scoping of variable names. They control the output of debugging information.

NOTE_INSN_EH_REGION_BEG
NOTE_INSN_EH_REGION_END

> These types of notes indicate the position of the beginning and end of a level of scoping for exception handling. NOTE_BLOCK_NUMBER identifies which CODE_LABEL is associated with the given region.

NOTE_INSN_LOOP_BEG
NOTE_INSN_LOOP_END

> These types of notes indicate the position of the beginning and end of a **while** or **for** loop. They enable the loop optimizer to find loops quickly.

NOTE_INSN_LOOP_CONT

> Appears at the place in a loop that **continue** statements jump to.

NOTE_INSN_LOOP_VTOP

> This note indicates the place in a loop where the exit test begins for those loops in which the exit test has been duplicated. This position becomes another virtual start of the loop when considering loop invariants.

NOTE_INSN_FUNCTION_END

> Appears near the end of the function body, just before the label that **return** statements jump to (on machine where a single instruction does not suffice for returning). This note may be deleted by jump optimization.

NOTE_INSN_SETJMP

> Appears following each call to **setjmp** or a related function.

These codes are printed symbolically when they appear in debugging dumps.

The machine mode of an insn is normally **VOIDmode**, but some phases use the mode for various purposes.

The common subexpression elimination pass sets the mode of an insn to **QImode** when it is the first insn in a block that has already been processed.

The second Haifa scheduling pass, for targets that can multiple issue, sets the mode of an insn to `TImode` when it is believed that the instruction begins an issue group. That is, when the instruction cannot issue simultaneously with the previous. This may be relied on by later passes, in particular machine-dependant reorg.

Here is a table of the extra fields of `insn`, `jump_insn` and `call_insn` insns:

PATTERN (*i*)

An expression for the side effect performed by this insn. This must be one of the following codes: `set`, `call`, `use`, `clobber`, `return`, `asm_input`, `asm_output`, `addr_vec`, `addr_diff_vec`, `trap_if`, `unspec`, `unspec_volatile`, `parallel`, or `sequence`. If it is a `parallel`, each element of the `parallel` must be one these codes, except that `parallel` expressions cannot be nested and `addr_vec` and `addr_diff_vec` are not permitted inside a `parallel` expression.

INSN_CODE (*i*)

An integer that says which pattern in the machine description matches this insn, or -1 if the matching has not yet been attempted.

Such matching is never attempted and this field remains -1 on an insn whose pattern consists of a single `use`, `clobber`, `asm_input`, `addr_vec` or `addr_diff_vec` expression.

Matching is also never attempted on insns that result from an `asm` statement. These contain at least one `asm_operands` expression. The function `asm_noperands` returns a non-negative value for such insns.

In the debugging output, this field is printed as a number followed by a symbolic representation that locates the pattern in the 'md' file as some small positive or negative offset from a named pattern.

LOG_LINKS (*i*)

A list (chain of `insn_list` expressions) giving information about dependencies between instructions within a basic block. Neither a jump nor a label may come between the related insns.

REG_NOTES (*i*)

A list (chain of `expr_list` and `insn_list` expressions) giving miscellaneous information about the insn. It is often information pertaining to the registers used in this insn.

The `LOG_LINKS` field of an insn is a chain of `insn_list` expressions. Each of these has two operands: the first is an insn, and the second is another `insn_list` expression (the next one in the chain). The last `insn_list` in the chain has a null pointer as second operand. The significant thing about the chain is which insns appear in it (as first operands of `insn_list` expressions). Their order is not significant.

This list is originally set up by the flow analysis pass; it is a null pointer until then. Flow only adds links for those data dependencies which can be used for instruction combination. For each insn, the flow analysis pass adds a link to insns which store into registers values that are used for the first time in this insn. The instruction scheduling pass adds extra links so that every dependence will be represented. Links represent data dependencies, antidependencies and output dependencies; the machine mode of the link distinguishes these three types: antidependencies have mode `REG_DEP_ANTI`, output dependencies have mode `REG_DEP_OUTPUT`, and data dependencies have mode `VOIDmode`.

The `REG_NOTES` field of an insn is a chain similar to the `LOG_LINKS` field but it includes `expr_list` expressions in addition to `insn_list` expressions. There are several kinds of register notes, which are distinguished by the machine mode, which in a register note is really understood as being an `enum reg_note`. The first operand *op* of the note is data whose meaning depends on the kind of note.

The macro `REG_NOTE_KIND` (*x*) returns the kind of register note. Its counterpart, the macro `PUT_REG_NOTE_KIND` (*x, newkind*) sets the register note type of *x* to be *newkind*.

Register notes are of three classes: They may say something about an input to an insn, they may say something about an output of an insn, or they may create a linkage between two insns. There are also a set of values that are only used in `LOG_LINKS`.

These register notes annotate inputs to an insn:

REG_DEAD   The value in *op* dies in this insn; that is to say, altering the value immediately after this insn would not affect the future behavior of the program.

> This does not necessarily mean that the register *op* has no useful value after this insn since it may also be an output of the insn. In such a case, however, a `REG_DEAD` note would be redundant and is usually not present until after the reload pass, but no code relies on this fact.

REG_INC   The register *op* is incremented (or decremented; at this level there is no distinction) by an embedded side effect inside this insn. This means it appears in a `post_inc`, `pre_inc`, `post_dec` or `pre_dec` expression.

REG_NONNEG

> The register *op* is known to have a nonnegative value when this insn is reached. This is used so that decrement and branch until zero instructions, such as the m68k dbra, can be matched.

The `REG_NONNEG` note is added to insns only if the machine description has a 'decrement_and_branch_until_zero' pattern.

REG_NO_CONFLICT

This insn does not cause a conflict between *op* and the item being set by this insn even though it might appear that it does. In other words, if the destination register and *op* could otherwise be assigned the same register, this insn does not prevent that assignment.

Insns with this note are usually part of a block that begins with a `clobber` insn specifying a multi-word pseudo register (which will be the output of the block), a group of insns that each set one word of the value and have the `REG_NO_CONFLICT` note attached, and a final insn that copies the output to itself with an attached `REG_EQUAL` note giving the expression being computed. This block is encapsulated with `REG_LIBCALL` and `REG_RETVAL` notes on the first and last insns, respectively.

REG_LABEL

This insn uses *op*, a `code_label`, but is not a `jump_insn`. The presence of this note allows jump optimization to be aware that *op* is, in fact, being used.

The following notes describe attributes of outputs of an insn:

REG_EQUIV
REG_EQUAL

This note is only valid on an insn that sets only one register and indicates that that register will be equal to *op* at run time; the scope of this equivalence differs between the two types of notes. The value which the insn explicitly copies into the register may look different from *op*, but they will be equal at run time. If the output of the single `set` is a `strict_low_part` expression, the note refers to the register that is contained in `SUBREG_REG` of the `subreg` expression.

For `REG_EQUIV`, the register is equivalent to *op* throughout the entire function, and could validly be replaced in all its occurrences by *op*. ("Validly" here refers to the data flow of the program; simple replacement may make some insns invalid.) For example, when a constant is loaded into a register that is never assigned any other value, this kind of note is used.

When a parameter is copied into a pseudo-register at entry to a function, a note of this kind records that the register is equivalent to the stack slot where the parameter was passed. Although in this case the register may be set by other insns, it is still valid to replace the register by the stack slot throughout the function.

A `REG_EQUIV` note is also used on an instruction which copies a register parameter into a pseudo-register at entry to a function, if there is a stack slot where that parameter could be stored. Although other insns may set the pseudo-register, it is valid for the compiler to replace the pseudo-register by stack slot throughout the function, provided the compiler ensures that the stack slot is properly initialized by making the replacement in the initial copy instruction as well. This is used on machines for which the calling convention allocates stack space for register parameters. See `REG_PARM_STACK_SPACE` in Section 17.7.5 [Stack Arguments], page 435.

In the case of `REG_EQUAL`, the register that is set by this insn will be equal to *op* at run time at the end of this insn but not necessarily elsewhere in the function. In this case, *op* is typically an arithmetic expression. For example, when a sequence of insns such as a library call is used to perform an arithmetic operation, this kind of note is attached to the insn that produces or copies the final value.

These two notes are used in different ways by the compiler passes. `REG_EQUAL` is used by passes prior to register allocation (such as common subexpression elimination and loop optimization) to tell them how to think of that value. `REG_EQUIV` notes are used by register allocation to indicate that there is an available substitute expression (either a constant or a `mem` expression for the location of a parameter on the stack) that may be used in place of a register if insufficient registers are available.

Except for stack homes for parameters, which are indicated by a `REG_EQUIV` note and are not useful to the early optimization passes and pseudo registers that are equivalent to a memory location throughout there entire life, which is not detected until later in the compilation, all equivalences are initially indicated by an attached `REG_EQUAL` note. In the early stages of register allocation, a `REG_EQUAL` note is changed into a `REG_EQUIV` note if *op* is a constant and the insn represents the only set of its destination register.

Thus, compiler passes prior to register allocation need only check for `REG_EQUAL` notes and passes subsequent to register allocation need only check for `REG_EQUIV` notes.

`REG_UNUSED`

The register *op* being set by this insn will not be used in a subsequent insn. This differs from a `REG_DEAD` note, which indicates that the value in an input will not be used subsequently. These two notes are independent; both may be present for the same register.

REG_WAS_0
> The single output of this insn contained zero before this insn. *op* is the insn that set it to zero. You can rely on this note if it is present and *op* has not been deleted or turned into a `note`; its absence implies nothing.

These notes describe linkages between insns. They occur in pairs: one insn has one of a pair of notes that points to a second insn, which has the inverse note pointing back to the first insn.

REG_RETVAL
> This insn copies the value of a multi-insn sequence (for example, a library call), and *op* is the first insn of the sequence (for a library call, the first insn that was generated to set up the arguments for the library call).

> Loop optimization uses this note to treat such a sequence as a single operation for code motion purposes and flow analysis uses this note to delete such sequences whose results are dead.

> A `REG_EQUAL` note will also usually be attached to this insn to provide the expression being computed by the sequence.

> These notes will be deleted after reload, since they are no longer accurate or useful.

REG_LIBCALL
> This is the inverse of `REG_RETVAL`: it is placed on the first insn of a multi-insn sequence, and it points to the last one.

> These notes are deleted after reload, since they are no longer useful or accurate.

REG_CC_SETTER
REG_CC_USER
> On machines that use `cc0`, the insns which set and use `cc0` set and use `cc0` are adjacent. However, when branch delay slot filling is done, this may no longer be true. In this case a `REG_CC_USER` note will be placed on the insn setting `cc0` to point to the insn using `cc0` and a `REG_CC_SETTER` note will be placed on the insn using `cc0` to point to the insn setting `cc0`.

These values are only used in the `LOG_LINKS` field, and indicate the type of dependency that each link represents. Links which indicate a data dependence (a read after write dependence) do not use any code, they simply have mode `VOIDmode`, and are printed without any descriptive text.

REG_DEP_ANTI
> This indicates an anti dependence (a write after read dependence).

REG_DEP_OUTPUT

> This indicates an output dependence (a write after write dependence).

These notes describe information gathered from gcov profile data. They are stored in the REG_NOTES field of an insn as an expr_list.

REG_EXEC_COUNT

> This is used to indicate the number of times a basic block was executed according to the profile data. The note is attached to the first insn in the basic block.

REG_BR_PROB

> This is used to specify the ratio of branches to non-branches of a branch insn according to the profile data. The value is stored as a value between 0 and REG_BR_PROB_BASE; larger values indicate a higher probability that the branch will be taken.

REG_BR_PRED

> These notes are found in JUMP insns after delayed branch scheduling has taken place. They indicate both the direction and the likelyhood of the JUMP. The format is a bitmask of ATTR_FLAG_* values.

REG_FRAME_RELATED_EXPR

> This is used on an RTX_FRAME_RELATED_P insn wherein the attached expression is used in place of the actual insn pattern. This is done in cases where the pattern is either complex or misleading.

For convenience, the machine mode in an insn_list or expr_list is printed using these symbolic codes in debugging dumps.

The only difference between the expression codes insn_list and expr_list is that the first operand of an insn_list is assumed to be an insn and is printed in debugging dumps as the insn's unique id; the first operand of an expr_list is printed in the ordinary way as an expression.

15.17 RTL Representation of Function-Call Insns

Insns that call subroutines have the RTL expression code call_insn. These insns must satisfy special rules, and their bodies must use a special RTL expression code, call.

A call expression has two operands, as follows:

(call (mem:*fm* *addr*) *nbytes*)

Here *nbytes* is an operand that represents the number of bytes of argument data being passed to the subroutine, *fm* is a machine mode (which must equal as the definition of the FUNCTION_MODE macro in the machine description) and *addr* represents the address of the subroutine.

For a subroutine that returns no value, the `call` expression as shown above is the entire body of the insn, except that the insn might also contain `use` or `clobber` expressions.

For a subroutine that returns a value whose mode is not `BLKmode`, the value is returned in a hard register. If this register's number is r, then the body of the call insn looks like this:

```
(set (reg:m r)
     (call (mem:fm addr) nbytes))
```

This RTL expression makes it clear (to the optimizer passes) that the appropriate register receives a useful value in this insn.

When a subroutine returns a `BLKmode` value, it is handled by passing to the subroutine the address of a place to store the value. So the call insn itself does not "return" any value, and it has the same RTL form as a call that returns nothing.

On some machines, the call instruction itself clobbers some register, for example to contain the return address. `call_insn` insns on these machines should have a body which is a **parallel** that contains both the `call` expression and `clobber` expressions that indicate which registers are destroyed. Similarly, if the call instruction requires some register other than the stack pointer that is not explicitly mentioned it its RTL, a `use` subexpression should mention that register.

Functions that are called are assumed to modify all registers listed in the configuration macro `CALL_USED_REGISTERS` (see Section 17.5.1 [Register Basics], page 414) and, with the exception of `const` functions and library calls, to modify all of memory.

Insns containing just `use` expressions directly precede the `call_insn` insn to indicate which registers contain inputs to the function. Similarly, if registers other than those in `CALL_USED_REGISTERS` are clobbered by the called function, insns containing a single `clobber` follow immediately after the call to indicate which registers.

15.18 Structure Sharing Assumptions

The compiler assumes that certain kinds of RTL expressions are unique; there do not exist two distinct objects representing the same value. In other cases, it makes an opposite assumption: that no RTL expression object of a certain kind appears in more than one place in the containing structure.

These assumptions refer to a single function; except for the RTL objects that describe global variables and external functions, and a few standard objects such as small integer constants, no RTL objects are common to two functions.

- Each pseudo-register has only a single `reg` object to represent it, and therefore only a single machine mode.

- For any symbolic label, there is only one **symbol_ref** object referring to it.

- There is only one **const_int** expression with value 0, only one with value 1, and only one with value -1. Some other integer values are also stored uniquely.

- There is only one **pc** expression.

- There is only one **cc0** expression.

- There is only one **const_double** expression with value 0 for each floating point mode. Likewise for values 1 and 2.

- No **label_ref** or **scratch** appears in more than one place in the RTL structure; in other words, it is safe to do a tree-walk of all the insns in the function and assume that each time a **label_ref** or **scratch** is seen it is distinct from all others that are seen.

- Only one **mem** object is normally created for each static variable or stack slot, so these objects are frequently shared in all the places they appear. However, separate but equal objects for these variables are occasionally made.

- When a single **asm** statement has multiple output operands, a distinct **asm_operands** expression is made for each output operand. However, these all share the vector which contains the sequence of input operands. This sharing is used later on to test whether two **asm_operands** expressions come from the same statement, so all optimizations must carefully preserve the sharing if they copy the vector at all.

- No RTL object appears in more than one place in the RTL structure except as described above. Many passes of the compiler rely on this by assuming that they can modify RTL objects in place without unwanted side-effects on other insns.

- During initial RTL generation, shared structure is freely introduced. After all the RTL for a function has been generated, all shared structure is copied by **unshare_all_rtl** in 'emit-rtl.c', after which the above rules are guaranteed to be followed.

- During the combiner pass, shared structure within an insn can exist temporarily. However, the shared structure is copied before the combiner is finished with the insn. This is done by calling **copy_rtx_if_shared**, which is a subroutine of **unshare_all_rtl**.

15.19 Reading RTL

To read an RTL object from a file, call **read_rtx**. It takes one argument, a stdio stream, and returns a single RTL object.

Reading RTL from a file is very slow. This is not currently a problem since reading RTL occurs only as part of building the compiler.

People frequently have the idea of using RTL stored as text in a file as an interface between a language front end and the bulk of GNU CC. This idea is not feasible.

GNU CC was designed to use RTL internally only. Correct RTL for a given program is very dependent on the particular target machine. And the RTL does not contain all the information about the program.

The proper way to interface GNU CC to a new language front end is with the "tree" data structure. There is no manual for this data structure, but it is described in the files 'tree.h' and 'tree.def'.

16 Machine Descriptions

A machine description has two parts: a file of instruction patterns ('.md' file) and a C header file of macro definitions.

The '.md' file for a target machine contains a pattern for each instruction that the target machine supports (or at least each instruction that is worth telling the compiler about). It may also contain comments. A semicolon causes the rest of the line to be a comment, unless the semicolon is inside a quoted string.

See the next chapter for information on the C header file.

16.1 Everything about Instruction Patterns

Each instruction pattern contains an incomplete RTL expression, with pieces to be filled in later, operand constraints that restrict how the pieces can be filled in, and an output pattern or C code to generate the assembler output, all wrapped up in a `define_insn` expression.

A `define_insn` is an RTL expression containing four or five operands:

1. An optional name. The presence of a name indicate that this instruction pattern can perform a certain standard job for the RTL-generation pass of the compiler. This pass knows certain names and will use the instruction patterns with those names, if the names are defined in the machine description.

   The absence of a name is indicated by writing an empty string where the name should go. Nameless instruction patterns are never used for generating RTL code, but they may permit several simpler insns to be combined later on.

   Names that are not thus known and used in RTL-generation have no effect; they are equivalent to no name at all.

2. The *RTL template* (see Section 16.3 [RTL Template], page 328) is a vector of incomplete RTL expressions which show what the instruction should look like. It is incomplete because it may contain `match_operand`, `match_operator`, and `match_dup` expressions that stand for operands of the instruction.

   If the vector has only one element, that element is the template for the instruction pattern. If the vector has multiple elements, then the instruction pattern is a `parallel` expression containing the elements described.

3. A condition. This is a string which contains a C expression that is the final test to decide whether an insn body matches this pattern.

   For a named pattern, the condition (if present) may not depend on the data in the insn being matched, but only on the target-machine-type flags. The compiler needs to test these conditions during initialization in order to learn exactly which named instructions are available in a particular run.

For nameless patterns, the condition is applied only when matching an individual insn, and only after the insn has matched the pattern's recognition template. The insn's operands may be found in the vector `operands`.

4. The *output template*: a string that says how to output matching insns as assembler code. '%' in this string specifies where to substitute the value of an operand. See Section 16.4 [Output Template], page 334.

   When simple substitution isn't general enough, you can specify a piece of C code to compute the output. See Section 16.5 [Output Statement], page 335.

5. Optionally, a vector containing the values of attributes for insns matching this pattern. See Section 16.15 [Insn Attributes], page 380.

16.2 Example of `define_insn`

Here is an actual example of an instruction pattern, for the 68000/68020.

```
(define_insn "tstsi"
  [(set (cc0)
        (match_operand:SI 0 "general_operand" "rm"))]
  ""
  "*
{ if (TARGET_68020 || ! ADDRESS_REG_P (operands[0]))
    return \"tstl %0\";
  return \"cmpl #0,%0\"; }")
```

This is an instruction that sets the condition codes based on the value of a general operand. It has no condition, so any insn whose RTL description has the form shown may be handled according to this pattern. The name 'tstsi' means "test a SImode value" and tells the RTL generation pass that, when it is necessary to test such a value, an insn to do so can be constructed using this pattern.

The output control string is a piece of C code which chooses which output template to return based on the kind of operand and the specific type of CPU for which code is being generated.

'"rm"' is an operand constraint. Its meaning is explained below.

16.3 RTL Template

The RTL template is used to define which insns match the particular pattern and how to find their operands. For named patterns, the RTL template also says how to construct an insn from specified operands.

Construction involves substituting specified operands into a copy of the template. Matching involves determining the values that serve as the operands in the insn being matched. Both of these activities are controlled by special expression types that direct matching and substitution of the operands.

(`match_operand:`*m* *n* *predicate* *constraint*)

> This expression is a placeholder for operand number *n* of the insn. When constructing an insn, operand number *n* will be substituted at this point. When matching an insn, whatever appears at this position in the insn will be taken as operand number *n*; but it must satisfy *predicate* or this instruction pattern will not match at all.

> Operand numbers must be chosen consecutively counting from zero in each instruction pattern. There may be only one `match_operand` expression in the pattern for each operand number. Usually operands are numbered in the order of appearance in `match_operand` expressions. In the case of a `define_expand`, any operand numbers used only in `match_dup` expressions have higher values than all other operand numbers.

> *predicate* is a string that is the name of a C function that accepts two arguments, an expression and a machine mode. During matching, the function will be called with the putative operand as the expression and *m* as the mode argument (if *m* is not specified, `VOIDmode` will be used, which normally causes *predicate* to accept any mode). If it returns zero, this instruction pattern fails to match. *predicate* may be an empty string; then it means no test is to be done on the operand, so anything which occurs in this position is valid.

> Most of the time, *predicate* will reject modes other than *m*—but not always. For example, the predicate `address_operand` uses *m* as the mode of memory ref that the address should be valid for. Many predicates accept `const_int` nodes even though their mode is `VOIDmode`.

> *constraint* controls reloading and the choice of the best register class to use for a value, as explained later (see Section 16.6 [Constraints], page 337).

> People are often unclear on the difference between the constraint and the predicate. The predicate helps decide whether a given insn matches the pattern. The constraint plays no role in this decision; instead, it controls various decisions in the case of an insn which does match.

> On CISC machines, the most common *predicate* is `"general_operand"`. This function checks that the putative operand is either a constant, a register or a memory reference, and that it is valid for mode *m*.

For an operand that must be a register, *predicate* should be
`"register_operand"`. Using `"general_operand"` would be
valid, since the reload pass would copy any non-register operands
through registers, but this would make GNU CC do extra work,
it would prevent invariant operands (such as constant) from being removed from loops, and it would prevent the register allocator from doing the best possible job. On RISC machines, it is
usually most efficient to allow *predicate* to accept only objects
that the constraints allow.

For an operand that must be a constant, you must be sure to
either use `"immediate_operand"` for *predicate*, or make the instruction pattern's extra condition require a constant, or both.
You cannot expect the constraints to do this work! If the constraints allow only constants, but the predicate allows something
else, the compiler will crash when that case arises.

(`match_scratch:`*m n constraint*)

> This expression is also a placeholder for operand number *n* and
> indicates that operand must be a `scratch` or `reg` expression.
>
> When matching patterns, this is equivalent to
>
>> (`match_operand:`*m n* `"scratch_operand"` *pred*)
>
> but, when generating RTL, it produces a (`scratch:`*m*) expres-
> sion.
>
> If the last few expressions in a `parallel` are `clobber` expressions
> whose operands are either a hard register or `match_scratch`,
> the combiner can add or delete them when necessary. See Sec-
> tion 15.13 [Side Effects], page 307.

(`match_dup` *n*)

> This expression is also a placeholder for operand number *n*. It is
> used when the operand needs to appear more than once in the
> insn.
>
> In construction, `match_dup` acts just like `match_operand`: the
> operand is substituted into the insn being constructed. But
> in matching, `match_dup` behaves differently. It assumes that
> operand number *n* has already been determined by a `match_operand` appearing earlier in the recognition template, and it
> matches only an identical-looking expression.

(`match_operator:`*m n predicate* [*operands*...])

> This pattern is a kind of placeholder for a variable RTL expres-
> sion code.
>
> When constructing an insn, it stands for an RTL expression
> whose expression code is taken from that of operand *n*, and
> whose operands are constructed from the patterns *operands*.

When matching an expression, it matches an expression if the function *predicate* returns nonzero on that expression *and* the patterns *operands* match the operands of the expression.

Suppose that the function `commutative_operator` is defined as follows, to match any expression whose operator is one of the commutative arithmetic operators of RTL and whose mode is *mode*:

```
int
commutative_operator (x, mode)
     rtx x;
     enum machine_mode mode;
{
  enum rtx_code code = GET_CODE (x);
  if (GET_MODE (x) != mode)
    return 0;
  return (GET_RTX_CLASS (code) == 'c'
          || code == EQ || code == NE);
}
```

Then the following pattern will match any RTL expression consisting of a commutative operator applied to two general operands:

```
(match_operator:SI 3 "commutative_operator"
 [(match_operand:SI 1 "general_operand" "g")
  (match_operand:SI 2 "general_operand" "g")])
```

Here the vector [*operands*...] contains two patterns because the expressions to be matched all contain two operands.

When this pattern does match, the two operands of the commutative operator are recorded as operands 1 and 2 of the insn. (This is done by the two instances of `match_operand`.) Operand 3 of the insn will be the entire commutative expression: use `GET_CODE (operands[3])` to see which commutative operator was used.

The machine mode *m* of `match_operator` works like that of `match_operand`: it is passed as the second argument to the predicate function, and that function is solely responsible for deciding whether the expression to be matched "has" that mode.

When constructing an insn, argument 3 of the gen-function will specify the operation (i.e. the expression code) for the expression to be made. It should be an RTL expression, whose expression code is copied into a new expression whose operands are arguments 1 and 2 of the gen-function. The subexpressions of argument 3 are not used; only its expression code matters.

When `match_operator` is used in a pattern for matching an insn, it usually best if the operand number of the `match_operator` is higher than that of the actual operands of the insn. This improves register allocation because the register allocator often looks at operands 1 and 2 of insns to see if it can do register tying.

There is no way to specify constraints in `match_operator`. The operand of the insn which corresponds to the `match_operator` never has any constraints because it is never reloaded as a whole. However, if parts of its *operands* are matched by `match_operand` patterns, those parts may have constraints of their own.

(`match_op_dup:`*m* *n*[*operands*...])

Like `match_dup`, except that it applies to operators instead of operands. When constructing an insn, operand number *n* will be substituted at this point. But in matching, `match_op_dup` behaves differently. It assumes that operand number *n* has already been determined by a `match_operator` appearing earlier in the recognition template, and it matches only an identical-looking expression.

(`match_parallel` *n* *predicate* [*subpat*...])

This pattern is a placeholder for an insn that consists of a `parallel` expression with a variable number of elements. This expression should only appear at the top level of an insn pattern.

When constructing an insn, operand number *n* will be substituted at this point. When matching an insn, it matches if the body of the insn is a `parallel` expression with at least as many elements as the vector of *subpat* expressions in the `match_parallel`, if each *subpat* matches the corresponding element of the `parallel`, *and* the function *predicate* returns nonzero on the `parallel` that is the body of the insn. It is the responsibility of the predicate to validate elements of the `parallel` beyond those listed in the `match_parallel`.

A typical use of `match_parallel` is to match load and store multiple expressions, which can contain a variable number of elements in a `parallel`. For example,

```
(define_insn ""
  [(match_parallel 0 "load_multiple_operation"
     [(set (match_operand:SI 1 "gpc_reg_operand" "=r")
           (match_operand:SI 2 "memory_operand" "m"))
      (use (reg:SI 179))
      (clobber (reg:SI 179))])]
  ""
  "loadm 0,0,%1,%2")
```

This example comes from 'a29k.md'. The function `load_multiple_operations` is defined in 'a29k.c' and checks that subsequent elements in the `parallel` are the same as the `set`

in the pattern, except that they are referencing subsequent registers and memory locations.

An insn that matches this pattern might look like:

```
(parallel
 [(set (reg:SI 20) (mem:SI (reg:SI 100)))
  (use (reg:SI 179))
  (clobber (reg:SI 179))
  (set (reg:SI 21)
       (mem:SI (plus:SI (reg:SI 100)
                        (const_int 4))))
  (set (reg:SI 22)
       (mem:SI (plus:SI (reg:SI 100)
                        (const_int 8))))])
```

(match_par_dup *n* [*subpat*...])

> Like `match_op_dup`, but for `match_parallel` instead of `match_operator`.

(match_insn *predicate*)

> Match a complete insn. Unlike the other `match_*` recognizers, `match_insn` does not take an operand number.
>
> The machine mode *m* of `match_insn` works like that of `match_operand`: it is passed as the second argument to the predicate function, and that function is solely responsible for deciding whether the expression to be matched "has" that mode.

(match_insn2 *n predicate*)

> Match a complete insn.
>
> The machine mode *m* of `match_insn2` works like that of `match_operand`: it is passed as the second argument to the predicate function, and that function is solely responsible for deciding whether the expression to be matched "has" that mode.

(address (match_operand:*m n* "address_operand" ""))

> This complex of expressions is a placeholder for an operand number *n* in a "load address" instruction: an operand which specifies a memory location in the usual way, but for which the actual operand value used is the address of the location, not the contents of the location.
>
> `address` expressions never appear in RTL code, only in machine descriptions. And they are used only in machine descriptions that do not use the operand constraint feature. When operand constraints are in use, the letter 'p' in the constraint serves this purpose.
>
> *m* is the machine mode of the *memory location being addressed*, not the machine mode of the address itself. That mode is always the same on a given target machine (it is `Pmode`, which

normally is `SImode`), so there is no point in mentioning it; thus, no machine mode is written in the `address` expression. If some day support is added for machines in which addresses of different kinds of objects appear differently or are used differently (such as the PDP-10), different formats would perhaps need different machine modes and these modes might be written in the `address` expression.

16.4 Output Templates and Operand Substitution

The *output template* is a string which specifies how to output the assembler code for an instruction pattern. Most of the template is a fixed string which is output literally. The character '%' is used to specify where to substitute an operand; it can also be used to identify places where different variants of the assembler require different syntax.

In the simplest case, a '%' followed by a digit *n* says to output operand *n* at that point in the string.

'%' followed by a letter and a digit says to output an operand in an alternate fashion. Four letters have standard, built-in meanings described below. The machine description macro `PRINT_OPERAND` can define additional letters with nonstandard meanings.

'%c*digit*' can be used to substitute an operand that is a constant value without the syntax that normally indicates an immediate operand.

'%n*digit*' is like '%c*digit*' except that the value of the constant is negated before printing.

'%a*digit*' can be used to substitute an operand as if it were a memory reference, with the actual operand treated as the address. This may be useful when outputting a "load address" instruction, because often the assembler syntax for such an instruction requires you to write the operand as if it were a memory reference.

'%l*digit*' is used to substitute a `label_ref` into a jump instruction.

'%=' outputs a number which is unique to each instruction in the entire compilation. This is useful for making local labels to be referred to more than once in a single template that generates multiple assembler instructions.

'%' followed by a punctuation character specifies a substitution that does not use an operand. Only one case is standard: '%%' outputs a '%' into the assembler code. Other nonstandard cases can be defined in the `PRINT_OPERAND` macro. You must also define which punctuation characters are valid with the `PRINT_OPERAND_PUNCT_VALID_P` macro.

The template may generate multiple assembler instructions. Write the text for the instructions, with '\;' between them.

When the RTL contains two operands which are required by constraint to match each other, the output template must refer only to the lower-numbered operand. Matching operands are not always identical, and the rest of the compiler arranges to put the proper RTL expression for printing into the lower-numbered operand.

One use of nonstandard letters or punctuation following '%' is to distinguish between different assembler languages for the same machine; for example, Motorola syntax versus MIT syntax for the 68000. Motorola syntax requires periods in most opcode names, while MIT syntax does not. For example, the opcode 'movel' in MIT syntax is 'move.l' in Motorola syntax. The same file of patterns is used for both kinds of output syntax, but the character sequence '%.' is used in each place where Motorola syntax wants a period. The PRINT_OPERAND macro for Motorola syntax defines the sequence to output a period; the macro for MIT syntax defines it to do nothing.

As a special case, a template consisting of the single character # instructs the compiler to first split the insn, and then output the resulting instructions separately. This helps eliminate redundancy in the output templates. If you have a define_insn that needs to emit multiple assembler instructions, and there is an matching define_split already defined, then you can simply use # as the output template instead of writing an output template that emits the multiple assembler instructions.

If the macro ASSEMBLER_DIALECT is defined, you can use construct of the form '{option0|option1|option2}' in the templates. These describe multiple variants of assembler language syntax. See Section 17.16.7 [Instruction Output], page 494.

16.5 C Statements for Assembler Output

Often a single fixed template string cannot produce correct and efficient assembler code for all the cases that are recognized by a single instruction pattern. For example, the opcodes may depend on the kinds of operands; or some unfortunate combinations of operands may require extra machine instructions.

If the output control string starts with a '@', then it is actually a series of templates, each on a separate line. (Blank lines and leading spaces and tabs are ignored.) The templates correspond to the pattern's constraint alternatives (see Section 16.6.2 [Multi-Alternative], page 342). For example, if a target machine has a two-address add instruction 'addr' to add into a register and another 'addm' to add a register to memory, you might write this pattern:

```
(define_insn "addsi3"
  [(set (match_operand:SI 0 "general_operand" "=r,m")
        (plus:SI (match_operand:SI 1 "general_operand" "0,0")
                 (match_operand:SI 2 "general_operand" "g,r")))]
  ""
  "@
   addr %2,%0
```

```
addm %2,%0")
```

If the output control string starts with a '*', then it is not an output template but rather a piece of C program that should compute a template. It should execute a **return** statement to return the template-string you want. Most such templates use C string literals, which require doublequote characters to delimit them. To include these doublequote characters in the string, prefix each one with '\'.

The operands may be found in the array **operands**, whose C data type is **rtx []**.

It is very common to select different ways of generating assembler code based on whether an immediate operand is within a certain range. Be careful when doing this, because the result of **INTVAL** is an integer on the host machine. If the host machine has more bits in an **int** than the target machine has in the mode in which the constant will be used, then some of the bits you get from **INTVAL** will be superfluous. For proper results, you must carefully disregard the values of those bits.

It is possible to output an assembler instruction and then go on to output or compute more of them, using the subroutine **output_asm_insn**. This receives two arguments: a template-string and a vector of operands. The vector may be **operands**, or it may be another array of **rtx** that you declare locally and initialize yourself.

When an insn pattern has multiple alternatives in its constraints, often the appearance of the assembler code is determined mostly by which alternative was matched. When this is so, the C code can test the variable **which_alternative**, which is the ordinal number of the alternative that was actually satisfied (0 for the first, 1 for the second alternative, etc.).

For example, suppose there are two opcodes for storing zero, 'clrreg' for registers and 'clrmem' for memory locations. Here is how a pattern could use **which_alternative** to choose between them:

```
(define_insn ""
  [(set (match_operand:SI 0 "general_operand" "=r,m")
        (const_int 0))]
  ""
  "*
  return (which_alternative == 0
          ? \"clrreg %0\" : \"clrmem %0\");
  ")
```

The example above, where the assembler code to generate was *solely* determined by the alternative, could also have been specified as follows, having the output control string start with a '@':

```
(define_insn ""
  [(set (match_operand:SI 0 "general_operand" "=r,m")
        (const_int 0))]
  ""
  "@
  clrreg %0
  clrmem %0")
```

16.6 Operand Constraints

Each `match_operand` in an instruction pattern can specify a constraint for the type of operands allowed. Constraints can say whether an operand may be in a register, and which kinds of register; whether the operand can be a memory reference, and which kinds of address; whether the operand may be an immediate constant, and which possible values it may have. Constraints can also require two operands to match.

16.6.1 Simple Constraints

The simplest kind of constraint is a string full of letters, each of which describes one kind of operand that is permitted. Here are the letters that are allowed:

'm'   A memory operand is allowed, with any kind of address that the machine supports in general.

'o'   A memory operand is allowed, but only if the address is *offsettable*. This means that adding a small integer (actually, the width in bytes of the operand, as determined by its machine mode) may be added to the address and the result is also a valid memory address.

           For example, an address which is constant is offsettable; so is an address that is the sum of a register and a constant (as long as a slightly larger constant is also within the range of address-offsets supported by the machine); but an autoincrement or autodecrement address is not offsettable. More complicated indirect/indexed addresses may or may not be offsettable depending on the other addressing modes that the machine supports.

           Note that in an output operand which can be matched by another operand, the constraint letter 'o' is valid only when accompanied by both '<' (if the target machine has predecrement addressing) and '>' (if the target machine has preincrement addressing).

'V'   A memory operand that is not offsettable. In other words, anything that would fit the 'm' constraint but not the 'o' constraint.

'<'   A memory operand with autodecrement addressing (either pre-decrement or postdecrement) is allowed.

'>'   A memory operand with autoincrement addressing (either preincrement or postincrement) is allowed.

'r'   A register operand is allowed provided that it is in a general register.

'd', 'a', 'f', . . .

Other letters can be defined in machine-dependent fashion to stand for particular classes of registers. 'd', 'a' and 'f' are defined on the 68000/68020 to stand for data, address and floating point registers.

'i'   An immediate integer operand (one with constant value) is allowed. This includes symbolic constants whose values will be known only at assembly time.

'n'   An immediate integer operand with a known numeric value is allowed. Many systems cannot support assembly-time constants for operands less than a word wide. Constraints for these operands should use 'n' rather than 'i'.

'I', 'J', 'K', . . . 'P'

Other letters in the range 'I' through 'P' may be defined in a machine-dependent fashion to permit immediate integer operands with explicit integer values in specified ranges. For example, on the 68000, 'I' is defined to stand for the range of values 1 to 8. This is the range permitted as a shift count in the shift instructions.

'E'   An immediate floating operand (expression code `const_double`) is allowed, but only if the target floating point format is the same as that of the host machine (on which the compiler is running).

'F'   An immediate floating operand (expression code `const_double`) is allowed.

'G', 'H'   'G' and 'H' may be defined in a machine-dependent fashion to permit immediate floating operands in particular ranges of values.

's'   An immediate integer operand whose value is not an explicit integer is allowed.

This might appear strange; if an insn allows a constant operand with a value not known at compile time, it certainly must allow any known value. So why use 's' instead of 'i'? Sometimes it allows better code to be generated.

For example, on the 68000 in a fullword instruction it is possible to use an immediate operand; but if the immediate value is between -128 and 127, better code results from loading the value into a register and using the register. This is because the load into the register can be done with a 'moveq' instruction. We arrange for this to happen by defining the letter 'K' to mean "any integer outside the range -128 to 127", and then specifying 'Ks' in the operand constraints.

'g'   Any register, memory or immediate integer operand is allowed, except for registers that are not general registers.

'X'   Any operand whatsoever is allowed, even if it does not satisfy `general_operand`. This is normally used in the constraint of a `match_scratch` when certain alternatives will not actually require a scratch register.

'0', '1', '2', ... '9'

An operand that matches the specified operand number is allowed. If a digit is used together with letters within the same alternative, the digit should come last.

This is called a *matching constraint* and what it really means is that the assembler has only a single operand that fills two roles considered separate in the RTL insn. For example, an add insn has two input operands and one output operand in the RTL, but on most CISC machines an add instruction really has only two operands, one of them an input-output operand:

    addl #35,r12

Matching constraints are used in these circumstances. More precisely, the two operands that match must include one input-only operand and one output-only operand. Moreover, the digit must be a smaller number than the number of the operand that uses it in the constraint.

For operands to match in a particular case usually means that they are identical-looking RTL expressions. But in a few special cases specific kinds of dissimilarity are allowed. For example, `*x` as an input operand will match `*x++` as an output operand. For proper results in such cases, the output template should always use the output-operand's number when printing the operand.

'p'   An operand that is a valid memory address is allowed. This is for "load address" and "push address" instructions.

'p' in the constraint must be accompanied by `address_operand` as the predicate in the `match_operand`. This predicate interprets the mode specified in the `match_operand` as the mode of the memory reference for which the address would be valid.

'Q', 'R', 'S', ... 'U'

Letters in the range 'Q' through 'U' may be defined in a machine-dependent fashion to stand for arbitrary operand types. The

machine description macro `EXTRA_CONSTRAINT` is passed the
operand as its first argument and the constraint letter as its
second operand.

A typical use for this would be to distinguish certain types of
memory references that affect other insn operands.

Do not define these constraint letters to accept register references (`reg`); the reload pass does not expect this and would not
handle it properly.

In order to have valid assembler code, each operand must satisfy its constraint. But a failure to do so does not prevent the pattern from applying
to an insn. Instead, it directs the compiler to modify the code so that the
constraint will be satisfied. Usually this is done by copying an operand into
a register.

Contrast, therefore, the two instruction patterns that follow:

```
(define_insn ""
  [(set (match_operand:SI 0 "general_operand" "=r")
        (plus:SI (match_dup 0)
                 (match_operand:SI 1 "general_operand" "r")))]
  ""
  "...")
```

which has two operands, one of which must appear in two places, and

```
(define_insn ""
  [(set (match_operand:SI 0 "general_operand" "=r")
        (plus:SI (match_operand:SI 1 "general_operand" "0")
                 (match_operand:SI 2 "general_operand" "r")))]
  ""
  "...")
```

which has three operands, two of which are required by a constraint to be
identical. If we are considering an insn of the form

```
(insn n prev next
  (set (reg:SI 3)
       (plus:SI (reg:SI 6) (reg:SI 109)))
  ...)
```

the first pattern would not apply at all, because this insn does not contain
two identical subexpressions in the right place. The pattern would say,
"That does not look like an add instruction; try other patterns." The second
pattern would say, "Yes, that's an add instruction, but there is something
wrong with it." It would direct the reload pass of the compiler to generate
additional insns to make the constraint true. The results might look like
this:

```
(insn n2 prev n
  (set (reg:SI 3) (reg:SI 6))
  ...)
```

```
(insn n n2 next
  (set (reg:SI 3)
       (plus:SI (reg:SI 3) (reg:SI 109)))
  ...)
```

It is up to you to make sure that each operand, in each pattern, has constraints that can handle any RTL expression that could be present for that operand. (When multiple alternatives are in use, each pattern must, for each possible combination of operand expressions, have at least one alternative which can handle that combination of operands.) The constraints don't need to *allow* any possible operand—when this is the case, they do not constrain—but they must at least point the way to reloading any possible operand so that it will fit.

- If the constraint accepts whatever operands the predicate permits, there is no problem: reloading is never necessary for this operand.

  For example, an operand whose constraints permit everything except registers is safe provided its predicate rejects registers.

  An operand whose predicate accepts only constant values is safe provided its constraints include the letter 'i'. If any possible constant value is accepted, then nothing less than 'i' will do; if the predicate is more selective, then the constraints may also be more selective.

- Any operand expression can be reloaded by copying it into a register. So if an operand's constraints allow some kind of register, it is certain to be safe. It need not permit all classes of registers; the compiler knows how to copy a register into another register of the proper class in order to make an instruction valid.

- A nonoffsettable memory reference can be reloaded by copying the address into a register. So if the constraint uses the letter 'o', all memory references are taken care of.

- A constant operand can be reloaded by allocating space in memory to hold it as preinitialized data. Then the memory reference can be used in place of the constant. So if the constraint uses the letters 'o' or 'm', constant operands are not a problem.

- If the constraint permits a constant and a pseudo register used in an insn was not allocated to a hard register and is equivalent to a constant, the register will be replaced with the constant. If the predicate does not permit a constant and the insn is re-recognized for some reason, the compiler will crash. Thus the predicate must always recognize any objects allowed by the constraint.

If the operand's predicate can recognize registers, but the constraint does not permit them, it can make the compiler crash. When this operand happens to be a register, the reload pass will be stymied, because it does not know how to copy a register temporarily into memory.

If the predicate accepts a unary operator, the constraint applies to the operand. For example, the MIPS processor at ISA level 3 supports an instruction which adds two registers in SImode to produce a DImode result, but only if the registers are correctly sign extended. This predicate for the input operands accepts a sign_extend of an SImode register. Write the constraint to indicate the type of register that is required for the operand of the sign_extend.

16.6.2 Multiple Alternative Constraints

Sometimes a single instruction has multiple alternative sets of possible operands. For example, on the 68000, a logical-or instruction can combine register or an immediate value into memory, or it can combine any kind of operand into a register; but it cannot combine one memory location into another.

These constraints are represented as multiple alternatives. An alternative can be described by a series of letters for each operand. The overall constraint for an operand is made from the letters for this operand from the first alternative, a comma, the letters for this operand from the second alternative, a comma, and so on until the last alternative. Here is how it is done for fullword logical-or on the 68000:

```
(define_insn "iorsi3"
  [(set (match_operand:SI 0 "general_operand" "=m,d")
        (ior:SI (match_operand:SI 1 "general_operand" "%0,0")
                (match_operand:SI 2 "general_operand" "dKs,dmKs")))]
  ...)
```

The first alternative has 'm' (memory) for operand 0, '0' for operand 1 (meaning it must match operand 0), and 'dKs' for operand 2. The second alternative has 'd' (data register) for operand 0, '0' for operand 1, and 'dmKs' for operand 2. The '=' and '%' in the constraints apply to all the alternatives; their meaning is explained in the next section (see Section 16.6.3 [Class Preferences], page 343).

If all the operands fit any one alternative, the instruction is valid. Otherwise, for each alternative, the compiler counts how many instructions must be added to copy the operands so that that alternative applies. The alternative requiring the least copying is chosen. If two alternatives need the same amount of copying, the one that comes first is chosen. These choices can be altered with the '?' and '!' characters:

?   Disparage slightly the alternative that the '?' appears in, as a choice when no alternative applies exactly. The compiler regards this alternative as one unit more costly for each '?' that appears in it.

!   ✱   Disparage severely the alternative that the '!' appears in. This
               alternative can still be used if it fits without reloading, but if
               reloading is needed, some other alternative will be used.

When an insn pattern has multiple alternatives in its constraints, often
the appearance of the assembler code is determined mostly by which alternative was matched. When this is so, the C code for writing the assembler
code can use the variable `which_alternative`, which is the ordinal number
of the alternative that was actually satisfied (0 for the first, 1 for the second
alternative, etc.). See Section 16.5 [Output Statement], page 335.

16.6.3 Register Class Preferences

The operand constraints have another function: they enable the compiler
to decide which kind of hardware register a pseudo register is best allocated
to. The compiler examines the constraints that apply to the insns that use
the pseudo register, looking for the machine-dependent letters such as 'd' and
'a' that specify classes of registers. The pseudo register is put in whichever
class gets the most "votes". The constraint letters 'g' and 'r' also vote:
they vote in favor of a general register. The machine description says which
registers are considered general.

Of course, on some machines all registers are equivalent, and no register
classes are defined. Then none of this complexity is relevant.

16.6.4 Constraint Modifier Characters

Here are constraint modifier characters.

'='   Means that this operand is write-only for this instruction: the
            previous value is discarded and replaced by output data.

'+'   Means that this operand is both read and written by the in-
            struction.

            When the compiler fixes up the operands to satisfy the con-
            straints, it needs to know which operands are inputs to the in-
            struction and which are outputs from it. '=' identifies an output;
            '+' identifies an operand that is both input and output; all other
            operands are assumed to be input only.

'&'   Means (in a particular alternative) that this operand is an *ear-
            lyclobber* operand, which is modified before the instruction is
            finished using the input operands. Therefore, this operand may
            not lie in a register that is used as an input operand or as part
            of any memory address.

            '&' applies only to the alternative in which it is written. In
            constraints with multiple alternatives, sometimes one alternative
            requires '&' while others do not. See, for example, the '`movdf`'
            insn of the 68000.

An input operand can be tied to an earlyclobber operand if its only use as an input occurs before the early result is written. Adding alternatives of this form often allows GCC to produce better code when only some of the inputs can be affected by the earlyclobber. See, for example, the 'mulsi3' insn of the ARM.

'&' does not obviate the need to write '='.

'%' Declares the instruction to be commutative for this operand and the following operand. This means that the compiler may interchange the two operands if that is the cheapest way to make all operands fit the constraints. This is often used in patterns for addition instructions that really have only two operands: the result must go in one of the arguments. Here for example, is how the 68000 halfword-add instruction is defined:

```
(define_insn "addhi3"
  [(set (match_operand:HI 0 "general_operand" "=m,r")
      (plus:HI (match_operand:HI 1 "general_operand" "%0,0")
               (match_operand:HI 2 "general_operand" "di,g")))]
  ...)
```

'#' Says that all following characters, up to the next comma, are to be ignored as a constraint. They are significant only for choosing register preferences.

'*' Says that the following character should be ignored when choosing register preferences. '*' has no effect on the meaning of the constraint as a constraint, and no effect on reloading.

Here is an example: the 68000 has an instruction to sign-extend a halfword in a data register, and can also sign-extend a value by copying it into an address register. While either kind of register is acceptable, the constraints on an address-register destination are less strict, so it is best if register allocation makes an address register its goal. Therefore, '*' is used so that the 'd' constraint letter (for data register) is ignored when computing register preferences.

```
(define_insn "extendhisi2"
  [(set (match_operand:SI 0 "general_operand" "=*d,a")
      (sign_extend:SI
        (match_operand:HI 1 "general_operand" "0,g")))]
  ...)
```

16.6.5 Constraints for Particular Machines

Whenever possible, you should use the general-purpose constraint letters in asm arguments, since they will convey meaning more readily to people reading your code. Failing that, use the constraint letters that usually have very similar meanings across architectures. The most commonly used constraints are 'm' and 'r' (for memory and general-purpose registers respectively; see Section 16.6.1 [Simple Constraints], page 337), and 'I', usually the letter indicating the most common immediate-constant format.

For each machine architecture, the 'config/*machine*.h' file defines additional constraints. These constraints are used by the compiler itself for instruction generation, as well as for asm statements; therefore, some of the constraints are not particularly interesting for asm. The constraints are defined through these macros:

REG_CLASS_FROM_LETTER
: Register class constraints (usually lower case).

CONST_OK_FOR_LETTER_P
: Immediate constant constraints, for non-floating point constants of word size or smaller precision (usually upper case).

CONST_DOUBLE_OK_FOR_LETTER_P
: Immediate constant constraints, for all floating point constants and for constants of greater than word size precision (usually upper case).

EXTRA_CONSTRAINT
: Special cases of registers or memory. This macro is not required, and is only defined for some machines.

Inspecting these macro definitions in the compiler source for your machine is the best way to be certain you have the right constraints. However, here is a summary of the machine-dependent constraints available on some particular machines.

ARM family—'arm.h'

f	Floating-point register
F	One of the floating-point constants 0.0, 0.5, 1.0, 2.0, 3.0, 4.0, 5.0 or 10.0
G	Floating-point constant that would satisfy the constraint 'F' if it were negated
I	Integer that is valid as an immediate operand in a data processing instruction. That is, an integer in the range 0 to 255 rotated by a multiple of 2
J	Integer in the range -4095 to 4095
K	Integer that satisfies constraint 'I' when inverted (ones complement)
L	Integer that satisfies constraint 'I' when negated (twos complement)
M	Integer in the range 0 to 32

Q	A memory reference where the exact address is in a single register ("m" is preferable for **asm** statements)
R	An item in the constant pool
S	A symbol in the text segment of the current file

AMD 29000 family — 'a29k.h'

l	Local register 0
b	Byte Pointer ('BP') register
q	'Q' register
h	Special purpose register
A	First accumulator register
a	Other accumulator register
f	Floating point register
I	Constant greater than 0, less than 0x100
J	Constant greater than 0, less than 0x10000
K	Constant whose high 24 bits are on (1)
L	16 bit constant whose high 8 bits are on (1)
M	32 bit constant whose high 16 bits are on (1)
N	32 bit negative constant that fits in 8 bits
O	The constant 0x80000000 or, on the 29050, any 32 bit constant whose low 16 bits are 0.
P	16 bit negative constant that fits in 8 bits
G	
H	A floating point constant (in **asm** statements, use the machine independent 'E' or 'F' instead)

IBM RS6000 — 'rs6000.h'

b	Address base register
f	Floating point register
h	'MQ', 'CTR', or 'LINK' register
q	'MQ' register
c	'CTR' register
l	'LINK' register
x	'CR' register (condition register) number 0
y	'CR' register (condition register)

z	'FPMEM' stack memory for FPR-GPR transfers
I	Signed 16 bit constant
J	Constant whose low 16 bits are 0
K	Constant whose high 16 bits are 0
L	Constant suitable as a mask operand
M	Constant larger than 31
N	Exact power of 2
O	Zero
P	Constant whose negation is a signed 16 bit constant
G	Floating point constant that can be loaded into a register with one instruction per word
Q	Memory operand that is an offset from a register ('m' is preferable for asm statements)
R	AIX TOC entry
S	Constant suitable as a 64-bit mask operand
U	System V Release 4 small data area reference

Intel 386—`i386.h`

q	'a', b, c, or d register
A	'a', or d register (for 64-bit ints)
f	Floating point register
t	First (top of stack) floating point register
u	Second floating point register
a	'a' register
b	'b' register
c	'c' register
d	'd' register
D	'di' register
S	'si' register
I	Constant in range 0 to 31 (for 32 bit shifts)
J	Constant in range 0 to 63 (for 64 bit shifts)
K	'0xff'
L	'0xffff'

M	0, 1, 2, or 3 (shifts for `lea` instruction)
N	Constant in range 0 to 255 (for `out` instruction)
G	Standard 80387 floating point constant

Intel 960—'`i960.h`'

f	Floating point register (`fp0` to `fp3`)
l	Local register (`r0` to `r15`)
b	Global register (`g0` to `g15`)
d	Any local or global register
I	Integers from 0 to 31
J	0
K	Integers from -31 to 0
G	Floating point 0
H	Floating point 1

MIPS—'`mips.h`'

d	General-purpose integer register
f	Floating-point register (if available)
h	'Hi' register
l	'Lo' register
x	'Hi' or 'Lo' register
y	General-purpose integer register
z	Floating-point status register
I	Signed 16 bit constant (for arithmetic instructions)
J	Zero
K	Zero-extended 16-bit constant (for logic instructions)
L	Constant with low 16 bits zero (can be loaded with `lui`)
M	32 bit constant which requires two instructions to load (a constant which is not 'I', 'K', or 'L')
N	Negative 16 bit constant
O	Exact power of two
P	Positive 16 bit constant

G	Floating point zero
Q	Memory reference that can be loaded with more than one instruction ('m' is preferable for **asm** statements)
R	Memory reference that can be loaded with one instruction ('m' is preferable for **asm** statements)
S	Memory reference in external OSF/rose PIC format ('m' is preferable for **asm** statements)

Motorola 680x0— `m68k.h`

a	Address register
d	Data register
f	68881 floating-point register, if available
x	Sun FPA (floating-point) register, if available
y	First 16 Sun FPA registers, if available
I	Integer in the range 1 to 8
J	16 bit signed number
K	Signed number whose magnitude is greater than 0x80
L	Integer in the range -8 to -1
M	Signed number whose magnitude is greater than 0x100
G	Floating point constant that is not a 68881 constant
H	Floating point constant that can be used by Sun FPA

SPARC— `sparc.h`

f	Floating-point register that can hold 32 or 64 bit values.
e	Floating-point register that can hold 64 or 128 bit values.
I	Signed 13 bit constant
J	Zero
K	32 bit constant with the low 12 bits clear (a constant that can be loaded with the **sethi** instruction)
G	Floating-point zero

H	Signed 13 bit constant, sign-extended to 32 or 64 bits
Q	Memory reference that can be loaded with one instruction ('m' is more appropriate for **asm** statements)
S	Constant, or memory address
T	Memory address aligned to an 8-byte boundary
U	Even register

16.6.6 Not Using Constraints

Some machines are so clean that operand constraints are not required. For example, on the Vax, an operand valid in one context is valid in any other context. On such a machine, every operand constraint would be 'g', excepting only operands of "load address" instructions which are written as if they referred to a memory location's contents but actual refer to its address. They would have constraint 'p'.

For such machines, instead of writing 'g' and 'p' for all the constraints, you can choose to write a description with empty constraints. Then you write '""' for the constraint in every **match_operand**. Address operands are identified by writing an **address** expression around the **match_operand**, not by their constraints.

When the machine description has just empty constraints, certain parts of compilation are skipped, making the compiler faster. However, few machines actually do not need constraints; all machine descriptions now in existence use constraints.

16.7 Standard Pattern Names For Generation

Here is a table of the instruction names that are meaningful in the RTL generation pass of the compiler. Giving one of these names to an instruction pattern tells the RTL generation pass that it can use the pattern to accomplish a certain task.

'mov*m*'   Here *m* stands for a two-letter machine mode name, in lower case. This instruction pattern moves data with that machine mode from operand 1 to operand 0. For example, 'movsi' moves full-word data.

    If operand 0 is a **subreg** with mode *m* of a register whose own mode is wider than *m*, the effect of this instruction is to store the specified value in the part of the register that corresponds to mode *m*. The effect on the rest of the register is undefined.

This class of patterns is special in several ways. First of all, each of these names *must* be defined, because there is no other way to copy a datum from one place to another.

Second, these patterns are not used solely in the RTL generation pass. Even the reload pass can generate move insns to copy values from stack slots into temporary registers. When it does so, one of the operands is a hard register and the other is an operand that can need to be reloaded into a register.

Therefore, when given such a pair of operands, the pattern must generate RTL which needs no reloading and needs no temporary registers—no registers other than the operands. For example, if you support the pattern with a **define_expand**, then in such a case the **define_expand** mustn't call **force_reg** or any other such function which might generate new pseudo registers.

This requirement exists even for subword modes on a RISC machine where fetching those modes from memory normally requires several insns and some temporary registers. Look in 'spur.md' to see how the requirement can be satisfied.

During reload a memory reference with an invalid address may be passed as an operand. Such an address will be replaced with a valid address later in the reload pass. In this case, nothing may be done with the address except to use it as it stands. If it is copied, it will not be replaced with a valid address. No attempt should be made to make such an address into a valid address and no routine (such as **change_address**) that will do so may be called. Note that **general_operand** will fail when applied to such an address.

The global variable **reload_in_progress** (which must be explicitly declared if required) can be used to determine whether such special handling is required.

The variety of operands that have reloads depends on the rest of the machine description, but typically on a RISC machine these can only be pseudo registers that did not get hard registers, while on other machines explicit memory references will get optional reloads.

If a scratch register is required to move an object to or from memory, it can be allocated using **gen_reg_rtx** prior to life analysis.

If there are cases needing scratch registers after reload, you must define **SECONDARY_INPUT_RELOAD_CLASS** and perhaps also **SECONDARY_OUTPUT_RELOAD_CLASS** to detect them, and provide patterns 'reload_in*m*' or 'reload_out*m*' to handle them. See Section 17.6 [Register Classes], page 420.

The global variable `no_new_pseudos` can be used to determine if it is unsafe to create new pseudo registers. If this variable is nonzero, then it is unsafe to call `gen_reg_rtx` to allocate a new pseudo.

The constraints on a 'mov*m*' must permit moving any hard register to any other hard register provided that `HARD_REGNO_MODE_OK` permits mode *m* in both registers and `REGISTER_MOVE_COST` applied to their classes returns a value of 2.

It is obligatory to support floating point 'mov*m*' instructions into and out of any registers that can hold fixed point values, because unions and structures (which have modes `SImode` or `DImode`) can be in those registers and they may have floating point members.

There may also be a need to support fixed point 'mov*m*' instructions in and out of floating point registers. Unfortunately, I have forgotten why this was so, and I don't know whether it is still true. If `HARD_REGNO_MODE_OK` rejects fixed point values in floating point registers, then the constraints of the fixed point 'mov*m*' instructions must be designed to avoid ever trying to reload into a floating point register.

'`reload_in`*m*'
'`reload_out`*m*'

> Like 'mov*m*', but used when a scratch register is required to move between operand 0 and operand 1. Operand 2 describes the scratch register. See the discussion of the `SECONDARY_RELOAD_CLASS` macro in see Section 17.6 [Register Classes], page 420.

'`movstrict`*m*'

> Like 'mov*m*' except that if operand 0 is a `subreg` with mode *m* of a register whose natural mode is wider, the 'movstrict*m*' instruction is guaranteed not to alter any of the register except the part which belongs to mode *m*.

'`load_multiple`'

> Load several consecutive memory locations into consecutive registers. Operand 0 is the first of the consecutive registers, operand 1 is the first memory location, and operand 2 is a constant: the number of consecutive registers.

> Define this only if the target machine really has such an instruction; do not define this if the most efficient way of loading consecutive registers from memory is to do them one at a time.

> On some machines, there are restrictions as to which consecutive registers can be stored into memory, such as particular starting or ending register numbers or only a range of valid counts. For those machines, use a `define_expand` (see Section 16.13 [Expander Definitions], page 374) and make the pattern fail if the restrictions are not met.

Write the generated insn as a **parallel** with elements being a **set** of one register from the appropriate memory location (you may also need **use** or **clobber** elements). Use a **match_parallel** (see Section 16.3 [RTL Template], page 328) to recognize the insn. See 'a29k.md' and 'rs6000.md' for examples of the use of this insn pattern.

'store_multiple'

Similar to 'load_multiple', but store several consecutive registers into consecutive memory locations. Operand 0 is the first of the consecutive memory locations, operand 1 is the first register, and operand 2 is a constant: the number of consecutive registers.

'add*m*3'   Add operand 2 and operand 1, storing the result in operand 0. All operands must have mode *m*. This can be used even on two-address machines, by means of constraints requiring operands 1 and 0 to be the same location.

'sub*m*3', 'mul*m*3'
'div*m*3', 'udiv*m*3', 'mod*m*3', 'umod*m*3'
'smin*m*3', 'smax*m*3', 'umin*m*3', 'umax*m*3'
'and*m*3', 'ior*m*3', 'xor*m*3'

Similar, for other arithmetic operations.

'mulhisi3'

Multiply operands 1 and 2, which have mode **HImode**, and store a **SImode** product in operand 0.

'mulqihi3', 'mulsidi3'

Similar widening-multiplication instructions of other widths.

'umulqihi3', 'umulhisi3', 'umulsidi3'

Similar widening-multiplication instructions that do unsigned multiplication.

'mul*m*3_highpart'

Perform a signed multiplication of operands 1 and 2, which have mode *m*, and store the most significant half of the product in operand 0. The least significant half of the product is discarded.

'umul*m*3_highpart'

Similar, but the multiplication is unsigned.

'divmod*m*4'

Signed division that produces both a quotient and a remainder. Operand 1 is divided by operand 2 to produce a quotient stored in operand 0 and a remainder stored in operand 3.

For machines with an instruction that produces both a quotient and a remainder, provide a pattern for 'divmod*m*4' but do not provide patterns for 'div*m*3' and 'mod*m*3'. This allows optimization in the relatively common case when both the quotient and remainder are computed.

If an instruction that just produces a quotient or just a remainder exists and is more efficient than the instruction that produces both, write the output routine of 'divmod*m*4' to call `find_reg_note` and look for a `REG_UNUSED` note on the quotient or remainder and generate the appropriate instruction.

'udivmod*m*4'
> Similar, but does unsigned division.

'ashl*m*3' Arithmetic-shift operand 1 left by a number of bits specified by operand 2, and store the result in operand 0. Here *m* is the mode of operand 0 and operand 1; operand 2's mode is specified by the instruction pattern, and the compiler will convert the operand to that mode before generating the instruction.

'ashr*m*3', 'lshr*m*3', 'rotl*m*3', 'rotr*m*3'
> Other shift and rotate instructions, analogous to the `ashl`*m*3 instructions.

'neg*m*2' Negate operand 1 and store the result in operand 0.

'abs*m*2' Store the absolute value of operand 1 into operand 0.

'sqrt*m*2' Store the square root of operand 1 into operand 0.

> The `sqrt` built-in function of C always uses the mode which corresponds to the C data type `double`.

'ffs*m*2' Store into operand 0 one plus the index of the least significant 1-bit of operand 1. If operand 1 is zero, store zero. *m* is the mode of operand 0; operand 1's mode is specified by the instruction pattern, and the compiler will convert the operand to that mode before generating the instruction.

> The `ffs` built-in function of C always uses the mode which corresponds to the C data type `int`.

'one_cmpl*m*2'
> Store the bitwise-complement of operand 1 into operand 0.

'cmp*m*' Compare operand 0 and operand 1, and set the condition codes. The RTL pattern should look like this:

```
(set (cc0) (compare (match_operand:m 0 ...)
                    (match_operand:m 1 ...)))
```

'tst*m*' Compare operand 0 against zero, and set the condition codes. The RTL pattern should look like this:

```
(set (cc0) (match_operand:m 0 ...))
```

'tst*m*' patterns should not be defined for machines that do not use (cc0). Doing so would confuse the optimizer since it would no longer be clear which **set** operations were comparisons. The 'cmp*m*' patterns should be used instead.

'movstr*m*' Block move instruction. The addresses of the destination and source strings are the first two operands, and both are in mode **Pmode**.

The number of bytes to move is the third operand, in mode *m*. Usually, you specify **word_mode** for *m*. However, if you can generate better code knowing the range of valid lengths is smaller than those representable in a full word, you should provide a pattern with a mode corresponding to the range of values you can handle efficiently (e.g., **QImode** for values in the range 0–127; note we avoid numbers that appear negative) and also a pattern with **word_mode**.

The fourth operand is the known shared alignment of the source and destination, in the form of a **const_int** rtx. Thus, if the compiler knows that both source and destination are word-aligned, it may provide the value 4 for this operand.

Descriptions of multiple **movstr***m* patterns can only be beneficial if the patterns for smaller modes have fewer restrictions on their first, second and fourth operands. Note that the mode *m* in **movstr***m* does not impose any restriction on the mode of individually moved data units in the block.

These patterns need not give special consideration to the possibility that the source and destination strings might overlap.

'clrstr*m*' Block clear instruction. The addresses of the destination string is the first operand, in mode **Pmode**. The number of bytes to clear is the second operand, in mode *m*. See 'movstr*m*' for a discussion of the choice of mode.

The third operand is the known alignment of the destination, in the form of a **const_int** rtx. Thus, if the compiler knows that the destination is word-aligned, it may provide the value 4 for this operand.

The use for multiple **clrstr***m* is as for **movstr***m*.

'cmpstr*m*' Block compare instruction, with five operands. Operand 0 is the output; it has mode *m*. The remaining four operands are like the operands of 'movstr*m*'. The two memory blocks specified are compared byte by byte in lexicographic order. The effect of the instruction is to store a value in operand 0 whose sign indicates the result of the comparison.

'strlen*m*' Compute the length of a string, with three operands. Operand 0 is the result (of mode *m*), operand 1 is a **mem** referring to the first character of the string, operand 2 is the character to search for (normally zero), and operand 3 is a constant describing the known alignment of the beginning of the string.

'float*mn*2'
Convert signed integer operand 1 (valid for fixed point mode m) to floating point mode n and store in operand 0 (which has mode n).

'floatuns*mn*2'
Convert unsigned integer operand 1 (valid for fixed point mode m) to floating point mode n and store in operand 0 (which has mode n).

'fix*mn*2'   Convert operand 1 (valid for floating point mode m) to fixed point mode n as a signed number and store in operand 0 (which has mode n). This instruction's result is defined only when the value of operand 1 is an integer.

'fixuns*mn*2'
Convert operand 1 (valid for floating point mode m) to fixed point mode n as an unsigned number and store in operand 0 (which has mode n). This instruction's result is defined only when the value of operand 1 is an integer.

'ftrunc*m*2'
Convert operand 1 (valid for floating point mode m) to an integer value, still represented in floating point mode m, and store it in operand 0 (valid for floating point mode m).

'fix_trunc*mn*2'
Like 'fix*mn*2' but works for any floating point value of mode m by converting the value to an integer.

'fixuns_trunc*mn*2'
Like 'fixuns*mn*2' but works for any floating point value of mode m by converting the value to an integer.

'trunc*mn*2'
Truncate operand 1 (valid for mode m) to mode n and store in operand 0 (which has mode n). Both modes must be fixed point or both floating point.

'extend*mn*2'
Sign-extend operand 1 (valid for mode m) to mode n and store in operand 0 (which has mode n). Both modes must be fixed point or both floating point.

'zero_extend*mn*2'
Zero-extend operand 1 (valid for mode m) to mode n and store in operand 0 (which has mode n). Both modes must be fixed point.

'extv'   Extract a bit field from operand 1 (a register or memory
               operand), where operand 2 specifies the width in bits and
               operand 3 the starting bit, and store it in operand 0. Operand 0
               must have mode `word_mode`. Operand 1 may have mode `byte_mode` or `word_mode`; often `word_mode` is allowed only for registers. Operands 2 and 3 must be valid for `word_mode`.

               The RTL generation pass generates this instruction only with
               constants for operands 2 and 3.

               The bit-field value is sign-extended to a full word integer before
               it is stored in operand 0.

'extzv'   Like 'extv' except that the bit-field value is zero-extended.

'insv'   Store operand 3 (which must be valid for `word_mode`) into a
               bit field in operand 0, where operand 1 specifies the width in
               bits and operand 2 the starting bit. Operand 0 may have mode
               `byte_mode` or `word_mode`; often `word_mode` is allowed only for
               registers. Operands 1 and 2 must be valid for `word_mode`.

               The RTL generation pass generates this instruction only with
               constants for operands 1 and 2.

'mov*mode*cc'
               Conditionally move operand 2 or operand 3 into operand 0 according to the comparison in operand 1. If the comparison is
               true, operand 2 is moved into operand 0, otherwise operand 3 is
               moved.

               The mode of the operands being compared need not be the same
               as the operands being moved. Some machines, sparc64 for example, have instructions that conditionally move an integer value
               based on the floating point condition codes and vice versa.

               If the machine does not have conditional move instructions, do
               not define these patterns.

's*cond*'   Store zero or nonzero in the operand according to the condition
               codes. Value stored is nonzero iff the condition *cond* is true.
               cond is the name of a comparison operation expression code,
               such as `eq`, `lt` or `leu`.

               You specify the mode that the operand must have when you
               write the `match_operand` expression. The compiler automatically sees which mode you have used and supplies an operand of
               that mode.

               The value stored for a true condition must have 1 as its low
               bit, or else must be negative. Otherwise the instruction is not
               suitable and you should omit it from the machine description.
               You describe to the compiler exactly which value is stored by
               defining the macro `STORE_FLAG_VALUE` (see Section 17.19 [Misc],

page 511). If a description cannot be found that can be used for all the 'scond' patterns, you should omit those operations from the machine description.

These operations may fail, but should do so only in relatively uncommon cases; if they would fail for common cases involving integer comparisons, it is best to omit these patterns.

If these operations are omitted, the compiler will usually generate code that copies the constant one to the target and branches around an assignment of zero to the target. If this code is more efficient than the potential instructions used for the 'scond' pattern followed by those required to convert the result into a 1 or a zero in SImode, you should omit the 'scond' operations from the machine description.

'bcond'   Conditional branch instruction. Operand 0 is a `label_ref` that refers to the label to jump to. Jump if the condition codes meet condition *cond*.

Some machines do not follow the model assumed here where a comparison instruction is followed by a conditional branch instruction. In that case, the 'cmp*m*' (and 'tst*m*') patterns should simply store the operands away and generate all the required insns in a `define_expand` (see Section 16.13 [Expander Definitions], page 374) for the conditional branch operations. All calls to expand 'bcond' patterns are immediately preceded by calls to expand either a 'cmp*m*' pattern or a 'tst*m*' pattern.

Machines that use a pseudo register for the condition code value, or where the mode used for the comparison depends on the condition being tested, should also use the above mechanism. See Section 16.10 [Jump Patterns], page 367.

The above discussion also applies to the 'mov*mode*cc' and 'scond' patterns.

'call'   Subroutine call instruction returning no value. Operand 0 is the function to call; operand 1 is the number of bytes of arguments pushed as a `const_int`; operand 2 is the number of registers used as operands.

On most machines, operand 2 is not actually stored into the RTL pattern. It is supplied for the sake of some RISC machines which need to put this information into the assembler code; they can put it in the RTL instead of operand 1.

Operand 0 should be a `mem` RTX whose address is the address of the function. Note, however, that this address can be a `symbol_ref` expression even if it would not be a legitimate memory address on the target machine. If it is also not a valid argument for a call instruction, the pattern for this operation should be a `define_expand` (see Section 16.13 [Expander Definitions], page 374) that places the address into a register and uses that register in the call instruction.

'`call_value`'

Subroutine call instruction returning a value. Operand 0 is the hard register in which the value is returned. There are three more operands, the same as the three operands of the '`call`' instruction (but with numbers increased by one).

Subroutines that return `BLKmode` objects use the '`call`' insn.

'`call_pop`', '`call_value_pop`'

Similar to '`call`' and '`call_value`', except used if defined and if `RETURN_POPS_ARGS` is non-zero. They should emit a `parallel` that contains both the function call and a `set` to indicate the adjustment made to the frame pointer.

For machines where `RETURN_POPS_ARGS` can be non-zero, the use of these patterns increases the number of functions for which the frame pointer can be eliminated, if desired.

'`untyped_call`'

Subroutine call instruction returning a value of any type. Operand 0 is the function to call; operand 1 is a memory location where the result of calling the function is to be stored; operand 2 is a `parallel` expression where each element is a `set` expression that indicates the saving of a function return value into the result block.

This instruction pattern should be defined to support `__builtin_apply` on machines where special instructions are needed to call a subroutine with arbitrary arguments or to save the value returned. This instruction pattern is required on machines that have multiple registers that can hold a return value (i.e. `FUNCTION_VALUE_REGNO_P` is true for more than one register).

'`return`'   Subroutine return instruction. This instruction pattern name should be defined only if a single instruction can do all the work of returning from a function.

Like the '`mov`*m*' patterns, this pattern is also used after the RTL generation phase. In this case it is to support machines where multiple instructions are usually needed to return from a function, but some class of functions only requires one instruction to implement a return. Normally, the applicable functions are those which do not need to save any registers or allocate stack space.

For such machines, the condition specified in this pattern should only be true when `reload_completed` is non-zero and the function's epilogue would only be a single instruction. For machines with register windows, the routine `leaf_function_p` may be used to determine if a register window push is required.

Machines that have conditional return instructions should define patterns such as

```
(define_insn ""
  [(set (pc)
        (if_then_else (match_operator
                        0 "comparison_operator"
                        [(cc0) (const_int 0)])
                      (return)
                      (pc)))]
  "condition"
  "...")
```

where *condition* would normally be the same condition specified on the named 'return' pattern.

'untyped_return'
:   Untyped subroutine return instruction. This instruction pattern should be defined to support `__builtin_return` on machines where special instructions are needed to return a value of any type.

    Operand 0 is a memory location where the result of calling a function with `__builtin_apply` is stored; operand 1 is a `parallel` expression where each element is a `set` expression that indicates the restoring of a function return value from the result block.

'nop'
:   No-op instruction. This instruction pattern name should always be defined to output a no-op in assembler code. (`const_int 0`) will do as an RTL pattern.

'indirect_jump'
:   An instruction to jump to an address which is operand zero. This pattern name is mandatory on all machines.

'casesi'
:   Instruction to jump through a dispatch table, including bounds checking. This instruction takes five operands:

    1. The index to dispatch on, which has mode `SImode`.

    2. The lower bound for indices in the table, an integer constant.

    3. The total range of indices in the table—the largest index minus the smallest one (both inclusive).

    4. A label that precedes the table itself.

    5. A label to jump to if the index has a value outside the bounds. (If the machine-description macro `CASE_DROPS_THROUGH` is defined, then an out-of-bounds index drops

through to the code following the jump table instead of jumping to this label. In that case, this label is not actually used by the 'casesi' instruction, but it is always provided as an operand.)

The table is a addr_vec or addr_diff_vec inside of a jump_insn. The number of elements in the table is one plus the difference between the upper bound and the lower bound.

'tablejump'

Instruction to jump to a variable address. This is a low-level capability which can be used to implement a dispatch table when there is no 'casesi' pattern.

This pattern requires two operands: the address or offset, and a label which should immediately precede the jump table. If the macro CASE_VECTOR_PC_RELATIVE evaluates to a nonzero value then the first operand is an offset which counts from the address of the table; otherwise, it is an absolute address to jump to. In either case, the first operand has mode Pmode.

The 'tablejump' insn is always the last insn before the jump table it uses. Its assembler code normally has no need to use the second operand, but you should incorporate it in the RTL pattern so that the jump optimizer will not delete the table as unreachable code.

'canonicalize_funcptr_for_compare'

Canonicalize the function pointer in operand 1 and store the result into operand 0.

Operand 0 is always a reg and has mode Pmode; operand 1 may be a reg, mem, symbol_ref, const_int, etc and also has mode Pmode.

Canonicalization of a function pointer usually involves computing the address of the function which would be called if the function pointer were used in an indirect call.

Only define this pattern if function pointers on the target machine can have different values but still call the same function when used in an indirect call.

'save_stack_block'
'save_stack_function'
'save_stack_nonlocal'
'restore_stack_block'
'restore_stack_function'
'restore_stack_nonlocal'

Most machines save and restore the stack pointer by copying it to or from an object of mode Pmode. Do not define these patterns on such machines.

Some machines require special handling for stack pointer saves
and restores. On those machines, define the patterns corresponding to the non-standard cases by using a `define_expand`
(see Section 16.13 [Expander Definitions], page 374) that produces the required insns. The three types of saves and restores
are:

1. 'save_stack_block' saves the stack pointer at the start
   of a block that allocates a variable-sized object, and
   'restore_stack_block' restores the stack pointer when
   the block is exited.

2. 'save_stack_function' and 'restore_stack_function'
   do a similar job for the outermost block of a function and
   are used when the function allocates variable-sized objects
   or calls `alloca`. Only the epilogue uses the restored stack
   pointer, allowing a simpler save or restore sequence on some
   machines.

3. 'save_stack_nonlocal' is used in functions that contain
   labels branched to by nested functions. It saves the stack
   pointer in such a way that the inner function can use
   'restore_stack_nonlocal' to restore the stack pointer.
   The compiler generates code to restore the frame and argument pointer registers, but some machines require saving
   and restoring additional data such as register window information or stack backchains. Place insns in these patterns
   to save and restore any such required data.

When saving the stack pointer, operand 0 is the save area
and operand 1 is the stack pointer. The mode used to allocate the save area defaults to `Pmode` but you can override that
choice by defining the `STACK_SAVEAREA_MODE` macro (see Section 17.3 [Storage Layout], page 403). You must specify an
integral mode, or `VOIDmode` if no save area is needed for a particular type of save (either because no save is needed or because
a machine-specific save area can be used). Operand 0 is the
stack pointer and operand 1 is the save area for restore operations. If 'save_stack_block' is defined, operand 0 must not be
`VOIDmode` since these saves can be arbitrarily nested.

A save area is a `mem` that is at a constant offset from `virtual_`
`stack_vars_rtx` when the stack pointer is saved for use by non-
local gotos and a `reg` in the other two cases.

'allocate_stack'

Subtract (or add if `STACK_GROWS_DOWNWARD` is undefined)
operand 1 from the stack pointer to create space for dynamically allocated data.

Store the resultant pointer to this space into operand 0. If you are allocating space from the main stack, do this by emitting a move insn to copy `virtual_stack_dynamic_rtx` to operand 0. If you are allocating the space elsewhere, generate code to copy the location of the space to operand 0. In the latter case, you must ensure this space gets freed when the corresponding space on the main stack is free.

Do not define this pattern if all that must be done is the subtraction. Some machines require other operations such as stack probes or maintaining the back chain. Define this pattern to emit those operations in addition to updating the stack pointer.

'probe'   Some machines require instructions to be executed after space is allocated from the stack, for example to generate a reference at the bottom of the stack.

If you need to emit instructions before the stack has been adjusted, put them into the 'allocate_stack' pattern. Otherwise, define this pattern to emit the required instructions.

No operands are provided.

'check_stack'
             If stack checking cannot be done on your system by probing the stack with a load or store instruction (see Section 17.7.2 [Stack Checking], page 430), define this pattern to perform the needed check and signaling an error if the stack has overflowed. The single operand is the location in the stack furthest from the current stack pointer that you need to validate. Normally, on machines where this pattern is needed, you would obtain the stack limit from a global or thread-specific variable or register.

'nonlocal_goto'
             Emit code to generate a non-local goto, e.g., a jump from one function to a label in an outer function. This pattern has four arguments, each representing a value to be used in the jump. The first argument is to be loaded into the frame pointer, the second is the address to branch to (code to dispatch to the actual label), the third is the address of a location where the stack is saved, and the last is the address of the label, to be placed in the location for the incoming static chain.

On most machines you need not define this pattern, since GNU CC will already generate the correct code, which is to load the frame pointer and static chain, restore the stack (using the 'restore_stack_nonlocal' pattern, if defined), and jump indirectly to the dispatcher. You need only define this pattern if this code will not work on your machine.

`nonlocal_goto_receiver`

> This pattern, if defined, contains code needed at the target of a nonlocal goto after the code already generated by GNU CC. You will not normally need to define this pattern. A typical reason why you might need this pattern is if some value, such as a pointer to a global table, must be restored when the frame pointer is restored. Note that a nonlocal goto only ocurrs within a unit-of-translation, so a global table pointer that is shared by all functions of a given module need not be restored. There are no arguments.

`exception_receiver`

> This pattern, if defined, contains code needed at the site of an exception handler that isn't needed at the site of a nonlocal goto. You will not normally need to define this pattern. A typical reason why you might need this pattern is if some value, such as a pointer to a global table, must be restored after control flow is branched to the handler of an exception. There are no arguments.

`builtin_setjmp_setup`

> This pattern, if defined, contains additional code needed to initialize the `jmp_buf`. You will not normally need to define this pattern. A typical reason why you might need this pattern is if some value, such as a pointer to a global table, must be restored. Though it is preferred that the pointer value be recalculated if possible (given the address of a label for instance). The single argument is a pointer to the `jmp_buf`. Note that the buffer is five words long and that the first three are normally used by the generic mechanism.

`builtin_setjmp_receiver`

> This pattern, if defined, contains code needed at the site of an builtin setjmp that isn't needed at the site of a nonlocal goto. You will not normally need to define this pattern. A typical reason why you might need this pattern is if some value, such as a pointer to a global table, must be restored. It takes one argument, which is the label to which builtin_longjmp transfered control; this pattern may be emitted at a small offset from that label.

`builtin_longjmp`

> This pattern, if defined, performs the entire action of the longjmp. You will not normally need to define this pattern unless you also define `builtin_setjmp_setup`. The single argument is a pointer to the `jmp_buf`.

'eh_epilogue'
> This pattern, if defined, affects the way **__builtin_eh_return**, and thence **__throw** are built. It is intended to allow communication between the exception handling machinery and the normal epilogue code for the target.
>
> The pattern takes three arguments. The first is the exception context pointer. This will have already been copied to the function return register appropriate for a pointer; normally this can be ignored. The second argument is an offset to be added to the stack pointer. It will have been copied to some arbitrary call-clobbered hard reg so that it will survive until after reload to when the normal epilogue is generated. The final argument is the address of the exception handler to which the function should return. This will normally need to copied by the pattern to some special register.
>
> This pattern must be defined if **RETURN_ADDR_RTX** does not yield something that can be reliably and permanently modified, i.e. a fixed hard register or a stack memory reference.

'prologue'
> This pattern, if defined, emits RTL for entry to a function. The function entry is resposible for setting up the stack frame, initializing the frame pointer register, saving callee saved registers, etc.
>
> Using a prologue pattern is generally preferred over defining **FUNCTION_PROLOGUE** to emit assembly code for the prologue.
>
> The **prologue** pattern is particularly useful for targets which perform instruction scheduling.

'epilogue'
> This pattern, if defined, emits RTL for exit from a function. The function exit is resposible for deallocating the stack frame, restoring callee saved registers and emitting the return instruction.
>
> Using an epilogue pattern is generally preferred over defining **FUNCTION_EPILOGUE** to emit assembly code for the prologue.
>
> The **epilogue** pattern is particularly useful for targets which perform instruction scheduling or which have delay slots for their return instruction.

'sibcall_epilogue'
> This pattern, if defined, emits RTL for exit from a function without the final branch back to the calling function. This pattern will be emitted before any sibling call (aka tail call) sites.
>
> The **sibcall_epilogue** pattern must not clobber any arguments used for parameter passing or any stack slots for arguments passed to the current function.

16.8 When the Order of Patterns Matters

Sometimes an insn can match more than one instruction pattern. Then the pattern that appears first in the machine description is the one used. Therefore, more specific patterns (patterns that will match fewer things) and faster instructions (those that will produce better code when they do match) should usually go first in the description.

In some cases the effect of ordering the patterns can be used to hide a pattern when it is not valid. For example, the 68000 has an instruction for converting a fullword to floating point and another for converting a byte to floating point. An instruction converting an integer to floating point could match either one. We put the pattern to convert the fullword first to make sure that one will be used rather than the other. (Otherwise a large integer might be generated as a single-byte immediate quantity, which would not work.) Instead of using this pattern ordering it would be possible to make the pattern for convert-a-byte smart enough to deal properly with any constant value.

16.9 Interdependence of Patterns

Every machine description must have a named pattern for each of the conditional branch names 'b*cond*'. The recognition template must always have the form

```
(set (pc)
     (if_then_else (cond (cc0) (const_int 0))
                   (label_ref (match_operand 0 "" ""))
                   (pc)))
```

In addition, every machine description must have an anonymous pattern for each of the possible reverse-conditional branches. Their templates look like

```
(set (pc)
     (if_then_else (cond (cc0) (const_int 0))
                   (pc)
                   (label_ref (match_operand 0 "" ""))))
```

They are necessary because jump optimization can turn direct-conditional branches into reverse-conditional branches.

It is often convenient to use the `match_operator` construct to reduce the number of patterns that must be specified for branches. For example,

```
(define_insn ""
  [(set (pc)
        (if_then_else (match_operator 0 "comparison_operator"
                                      [(cc0) (const_int 0)])
                      (pc)
                      (label_ref (match_operand 1 "" ""))))]
  "condition"
```

```
"...")
```

In some cases machines support instructions identical except for the machine mode of one or more operands. For example, there may be "sign-extend halfword" and "sign-extend byte" instructions whose patterns are

```
(set (match_operand:SI 0 ...)
     (extend:SI (match_operand:HI 1 ...)))
```

```
(set (match_operand:SI 0 ...)
     (extend:SI (match_operand:QI 1 ...)))
```

Constant integers do not specify a machine mode, so an instruction to extend a constant value could match either pattern. The pattern it actually will match is the one that appears first in the file. For correct results, this must be the one for the widest possible mode (`HImode`, here). If the pattern matches the `QImode` instruction, the results will be incorrect if the constant value does not actually fit that mode.

Such instructions to extend constants are rarely generated because they are optimized away, but they do occasionally happen in nonoptimized compilations.

If a constraint in a pattern allows a constant, the reload pass may replace a register with a constant permitted by the constraint in some cases. Similarly for memory references. Because of this substitution, you should not provide separate patterns for increment and decrement instructions. Instead, they should be generated from the same pattern that supports register-register add insns by examining the operands and generating the appropriate machine instruction.

16.10 Defining Jump Instruction Patterns

For most machines, GNU CC assumes that the machine has a condition code. A comparison insn sets the condition code, recording the results of both signed and unsigned comparison of the given operands. A separate branch insn tests the condition code and branches or not according its value. The branch insns come in distinct signed and unsigned flavors. Many common machines, such as the Vax, the 68000 and the 32000, work this way.

Some machines have distinct signed and unsigned compare instructions, and only one set of conditional branch instructions. The easiest way to handle these machines is to treat them just like the others until the final stage where assembly code is written. At this time, when outputting code for the compare instruction, peek ahead at the following branch using `next_cc0_user (insn)`. (The variable `insn` refers to the insn being output, in the output-writing code in an instruction pattern.) If the RTL says that is an unsigned branch, output an unsigned compare; otherwise output a signed compare. When the branch itself is output, you can treat signed and unsigned branches identically.

The reason you can do this is that GNU CC always generates a pair of consecutive RTL insns, possibly separated by `note` insns, one to set the condition code and one to test it, and keeps the pair inviolate until the end.

To go with this technique, you must define the machine-description macro `NOTICE_UPDATE_CC` to do `CC_STATUS_INIT`; in other words, no compare instruction is superfluous.

Some machines have compare-and-branch instructions and no condition code. A similar technique works for them. When it is time to "output" a compare instruction, record its operands in two static variables. When outputting the branch-on-condition-code instruction that follows, actually output a compare-and-branch instruction that uses the remembered operands.

It also works to define patterns for compare-and-branch instructions. In optimizing compilation, the pair of compare and branch instructions will be combined according to these patterns. But this does not happen if optimization is not requested. So you must use one of the solutions above in addition to any special patterns you define.

In many RISC machines, most instructions do not affect the condition code and there may not even be a separate condition code register. On these machines, the restriction that the definition and use of the condition code be adjacent insns is not necessary and can prevent important optimizations. For example, on the IBM RS/6000, there is a delay for taken branches unless the condition code register is set three instructions earlier than the conditional branch. The instruction scheduler cannot perform this optimization if it is not permitted to separate the definition and use of the condition code register.

On these machines, do not use `(cc0)`, but instead use a register to represent the condition code. If there is a specific condition code register in the machine, use a hard register. If the condition code or comparison result can be placed in any general register, or if there are multiple condition registers, use a pseudo register.

On some machines, the type of branch instruction generated may depend on the way the condition code was produced; for example, on the 68k and Sparc, setting the condition code directly from an add or subtract instruction does not clear the overflow bit the way that a test instruction does, so a different branch instruction must be used for some conditional branches. For machines that use `(cc0)`, the set and use of the condition code must be adjacent (separated only by `note` insns) allowing flags in `cc_status` to be used. (See Section 17.12 [Condition Code], page 466.) Also, the comparison and branch insns can be located from each other by using the functions `prev_cc0_setter` and `next_cc0_user`.

However, this is not true on machines that do not use `(cc0)`. On those machines, no assumptions can be made about the adjacency of the compare and branch insns and the above methods cannot be used. Instead, we use the machine mode of the condition code register to record different formats of the condition code register.

Registers used to store the condition code value should have a mode that is in class `MODE_CC`. Normally, it will be `CCmode`. If additional modes are required (as for the add example mentioned above in the Sparc), define the macro `EXTRA_CC_MODES` to list the additional modes required (see Section 17.12 [Condition Code], page 466). Also define `EXTRA_CC_NAMES` to list the names of those modes and `SELECT_CC_MODE` to choose a mode given an operand of a compare.

If it is known during RTL generation that a different mode will be required (for example, if the machine has separate compare instructions for signed and unsigned quantities, like most IBM processors), they can be specified at that time.

If the cases that require different modes would be made by instruction combination, the macro `SELECT_CC_MODE` determines which machine mode should be used for the comparison result. The patterns should be written using that mode. To support the case of the add on the Sparc discussed above, we have the pattern

```
(define_insn ""
  [(set (reg:CC_NOOV 0)
        (compare:CC_NOOV
          (plus:SI (match_operand:SI 0 "register_operand" "%r")
                   (match_operand:SI 1 "arith_operand" "rI"))
          (const_int 0)))]
  ""
  "...")
```

The `SELECT_CC_MODE` macro on the Sparc returns `CC_NOOVmode` for comparisons whose argument is a `plus`.

16.11 Canonicalization of Instructions

There are often cases where multiple RTL expressions could represent an operation performed by a single machine instruction. This situation is most commonly encountered with logical, branch, and multiply-accumulate instructions. In such cases, the compiler attempts to convert these multiple RTL expressions into a single canonical form to reduce the number of insn patterns required.

In addition to algebraic simplifications, following canonicalizations are performed:

- For commutative and comparison operators, a constant is always made the second operand. If a machine only supports a constant as the second operand, only patterns that match a constant in the second operand need be supplied.

  For these operators, if only one operand is a `neg`, `not`, `mult`, `plus`, or `minus` expression, it will be the first operand.

- For the `compare` operator, a constant is always the second operand on machines where `cc0` is used (see Section 16.10 [Jump Patterns], page 367). On other machines, there are rare cases where the compiler might want to construct a `compare` with a constant as the first operand. However, these cases are not common enough for it to be worthwhile to provide a pattern matching a constant as the first operand unless the machine actually has such an instruction.

  An operand of `neg`, `not`, `mult`, `plus`, or `minus` is made the first operand under the same conditions as above.

- (`minus` x (`const_int` n)) is converted to (`plus` x (`const_int` -n)).

- Within address computations (i.e., inside `mem`), a left shift is converted into the appropriate multiplication by a power of two.

- De'Morgan's Law is used to move bitwise negation inside a bitwise logical-and or logical-or operation. If this results in only one operand being a `not` expression, it will be the first one.

  A machine that has an instruction that performs a bitwise logical-and of one operand with the bitwise negation of the other should specify the pattern for that instruction as

  ```
  (define_insn ""
    [(set (match_operand:m 0 ...)
          (and:m (not:m (match_operand:m 1 ...))
                 (match_operand:m 2 ...)))]
    "..."
    "...")
  ```

  Similarly, a pattern for a "NAND" instruction should be written

  ```
  (define_insn ""
    [(set (match_operand:m 0 ...)
          (ior:m (not:m (match_operand:m 1 ...))
                 (not:m (match_operand:m 2 ...))))]
    "..."
    "...")
  ```

  In both cases, it is not necessary to include patterns for the many logically equivalent RTL expressions.

- The only possible RTL expressions involving both bitwise exclusive-or and bitwise negation are (`xor:`m x y) and (`not:`m (`xor:`m x y)).

- The sum of three items, one of which is a constant, will only appear in the form

  (`plus:`m (`plus:`m x y) *constant*)

- On machines that do not use `cc0`, (`compare` x (`const_int` 0)) will be converted to x.

- Equality comparisons of a group of bits (usually a single bit) with zero will be written using `zero_extract` rather than the equivalent `and` or `sign_extract` operations.

16.12 Machine-Specific Peephole Optimizers

In addition to instruction patterns the 'md' file may contain definitions of machine-specific peephole optimizations.

The combiner does not notice certain peephole optimizations when the data flow in the program does not suggest that it should try them. For example, sometimes two consecutive insns related in purpose can be combined even though the second one does not appear to use a register computed in the first one. A machine-specific peephole optimizer can detect such opportunities.

A definition looks like this:

```
(define_peephole
  [insn-pattern-1
   insn-pattern-2
   ...]
  "condition"
  "template"
  "optional insn-attributes")
```

The last string operand may be omitted if you are not using any machine-specific information in this machine description. If present, it must obey the same rules as in a `define_insn`.

In this skeleton, *insn-pattern-1* and so on are patterns to match consecutive insns. The optimization applies to a sequence of insns when *insn-pattern-1* matches the first one, *insn-pattern-2* matches the next, and so on.

Each of the insns matched by a peephole must also match a `define_insn`. Peepholes are checked only at the last stage just before code generation, and only optionally. Therefore, any insn which would match a peephole but no `define_insn` will cause a crash in code generation in an unoptimized compilation, or at various optimization stages.

The operands of the insns are matched with `match_operands`, `match_operator`, and `match_dup`, as usual. What is not usual is that the operand numbers apply to all the insn patterns in the definition. So, you can check for identical operands in two insns by using `match_operand` in one insn and `match_dup` in the other.

The operand constraints used in `match_operand` patterns do not have any direct effect on the applicability of the peephole, but they will be validated afterward, so make sure your constraints are general enough to apply whenever the peephole matches. If the peephole matches but the constraints are not satisfied, the compiler will crash.

It is safe to omit constraints in all the operands of the peephole; or you can write constraints which serve as a double-check on the criteria previously tested.

Once a sequence of insns matches the patterns, the *condition* is checked. This is a C expression which makes the final decision whether to perform the optimization (we do so if the expression is nonzero). If *condition* is omitted (in other words, the string is empty) then the optimization is applied to every sequence of insns that matches the patterns.

The defined peephole optimizations are applied after register allocation is complete. Therefore, the peephole definition can check which operands have ended up in which kinds of registers, just by looking at the operands.

The way to refer to the operands in *condition* is to write `operands[i]` for operand number *i* (as matched by (`match_operand` *i* ...)). Use the variable `insn` to refer to the last of the insns being matched; use `prev_active_insn` to find the preceding insns.

When optimizing computations with intermediate results, you can use *condition* to match only when the intermediate results are not used elsewhere. Use the C expression `dead_or_set_p (`*insn, op*`)`, where *insn* is the insn in which you expect the value to be used for the last time (from the value of `insn`, together with use of `prev_nonnote_insn`), and *op* is the intermediate value (from `operands[i]`).

Applying the optimization means replacing the sequence of insns with one new insn. The *template* controls ultimate output of assembler code for this combined insn. It works exactly like the template of a `define_insn`. Operand numbers in this template are the same ones used in matching the original sequence of insns.

The result of a defined peephole optimizer does not need to match any of the insn patterns in the machine description; it does not even have an opportunity to match them. The peephole optimizer definition itself serves as the insn pattern to control how the insn is output.

Defined peephole optimizers are run as assembler code is being output, so the insns they produce are never combined or rearranged in any way.

Here is an example, taken from the 68000 machine description:

```
(define_peephole
  [(set (reg:SI 15) (plus:SI (reg:SI 15) (const_int 4)))
   (set (match_operand:DF 0 "register_operand" "=f")
        (match_operand:DF 1 "register_operand" "ad"))]
  "FP_REG_P (operands[0]) && ! FP_REG_P (operands[1])"
  "*
{
  rtx xoperands[2];
  xoperands[1] = gen_rtx (REG, SImode, REGNO (operands[1]) + 1);
#ifdef MOTOROLA
  output_asm_insn (\"move.l %1,(sp)\", xoperands);
  output_asm_insn (\"move.l %1,-(sp)\", operands);
  return \"fmove.d (sp)+,%0\";
#else
```

```
    output_asm_insn (\"movel %1,sp@\", xoperands);
    output_asm_insn (\"movel %1,sp@-\", operands);
    return \"fmoved sp@+,%0\";
  #endif
  }
  ")
```

The effect of this optimization is to change

```
    jbsr _foobar
    addql #4,sp
    movel d1,sp@-
    movel d0,sp@-
    fmoved sp@+,fp0
```

into

```
    jbsr _foobar
    movel d1,sp@
    movel d0,sp@-
    fmoved sp@+,fp0
```

insn-pattern-1 and so on look *almost* like the second operand of `define_insn`. There is one important difference: the second operand of `define_insn` consists of one or more RTX's enclosed in square brackets. Usually, there is only one: then the same action can be written as an element of a `define_peephole`. But when there are multiple actions in a `define_insn`, they are implicitly enclosed in a `parallel`. Then you must explicitly write the `parallel`, and the square brackets within it, in the `define_peephole`. Thus, if an insn pattern looks like this,

```
(define_insn "divmodsi4"
  [(set (match_operand:SI 0 "general_operand" "=d")
        (div:SI (match_operand:SI 1 "general_operand" "0")
                (match_operand:SI 2 "general_operand" "dmsK")))
   (set (match_operand:SI 3 "general_operand" "=d")
        (mod:SI (match_dup 1) (match_dup 2)))]
  "TARGET_68020"
  "divsl%.1 %2,%3:%0")
```

then the way to mention this insn in a peephole is as follows:

```
(define_peephole
  [...
   (parallel
    [(set (match_operand:SI 0 "general_operand" "=d")
          (div:SI (match_operand:SI 1 "general_operand" "0")
                  (match_operand:SI 2 "general_operand" "dmsK")))
     (set (match_operand:SI 3 "general_operand" "=d")
          (mod:SI (match_dup 1) (match_dup 2)))])
   ...]
```

. . .)

16.13 Defining RTL Sequences for Code Generation

On some target machines, some standard pattern names for RTL generation cannot be handled with single insn, but a sequence of RTL insns can represent them. For these target machines, you can write a `define_expand` to specify how to generate the sequence of RTL.

A `define_expand` is an RTL expression that looks almost like a `define_insn`; but, unlike the latter, a `define_expand` is used only for RTL generation and it can produce more than one RTL insn.

A `define_expand` RTX has four operands:

- The name. Each `define_expand` must have a name, since the only use for it is to refer to it by name.

- The RTL template. This is just like the RTL template for a `define_peephole` in that it is a vector of RTL expressions each being one insn.

- The condition, a string containing a C expression. This expression is used to express how the availability of this pattern depends on subclasses of target machine, selected by command-line options when GNU CC is run. This is just like the condition of a `define_insn` that has a standard name. Therefore, the condition (if present) may not depend on the data in the insn being matched, but only the target-machine-type flags. The compiler needs to test these conditions during initialization in order to learn exactly which named instructions are available in a particular run.

- The preparation statements, a string containing zero or more C statements which are to be executed before RTL code is generated from the RTL template.

  Usually these statements prepare temporary registers for use as internal operands in the RTL template, but they can also generate RTL insns directly by calling routines such as `emit_insn`, etc. Any such insns precede the ones that come from the RTL template.

Every RTL insn emitted by a `define_expand` must match some `define_insn` in the machine description. Otherwise, the compiler will crash when trying to generate code for the insn or trying to optimize it.

The RTL template, in addition to controlling generation of RTL insns, also describes the operands that need to be specified when this pattern is used. In particular, it gives a predicate for each operand.

A true operand, which needs to be specified in order to generate RTL from the pattern, should be described with a `match_operand` in its first occurrence in the RTL template. This enters information on the operand's predicate into the tables that record such things. GNU CC uses the information to preload the operand into a register if that is required for valid RTL code. If the operand is referred to more than once, subsequent references should use `match_dup`.

The RTL template may also refer to internal "operands" which are temporary registers or labels used only within the sequence made by the `define_expand`. Internal operands are substituted into the RTL template with `match_dup`, never with `match_operand`. The values of the internal operands are not passed in as arguments by the compiler when it requests use of this pattern. Instead, they are computed within the pattern, in the preparation statements. These statements compute the values and store them into the appropriate elements of `operands` so that `match_dup` can find them.

There are two special macros defined for use in the preparation statements: `DONE` and `FAIL`. Use them with a following semicolon, as a statement.

DONE   Use the `DONE` macro to end RTL generation for the pattern. The only RTL insns resulting from the pattern on this occasion will be those already emitted by explicit calls to `emit_insn` within the preparation statements; the RTL template will not be generated.

FAIL   Make the pattern fail on this occasion. When a pattern fails, it means that the pattern was not truly available. The calling routines in the compiler will try other strategies for code generation using other patterns.

            Failure is currently supported only for binary (addition, multiplication, shifting, etc.) and bitfield (`extv`, `extzv`, and `insv`) operations.

Here is an example, the definition of left-shift for the SPUR chip:

```
(define_expand "ashlsi3"
  [(set (match_operand:SI 0 "register_operand" "")
        (ashift:SI
          (match_operand:SI 1 "register_operand" "")
          (match_operand:SI 2 "nonmemory_operand" "")))]
  ""
  "
  {
    if (GET_CODE (operands[2]) != CONST_INT
        || (unsigned) INTVAL (operands[2]) > 3)
      FAIL;
  }")
```

This example uses `define_expand` so that it can generate an RTL insn for shifting when the shift-count is in the supported range of 0 to 3 but fail in other cases where machine insns aren't available. When it fails, the compiler tries another strategy using different patterns (such as, a library call).

If the compiler were able to handle nontrivial condition-strings in patterns with names, then it would be possible to use a `define_insn` in that case. Here is another case (zero-extension on the 68000) which makes more use of the power of `define_expand`:

```
(define_expand "zero_extendhisi2"
  [(set (match_operand:SI 0 "general_operand" "")
        (const_int 0))
   (set (strict_low_part
          (subreg:HI
            (match_dup 0)
            0))
        (match_operand:HI 1 "general_operand" ""))]
  ""
  "operands[1] = make_safe_from (operands[1], operands[0]);")
```

Here two RTL insns are generated, one to clear the entire output operand and the other to copy the input operand into its low half. This sequence is incorrect if the input operand refers to [the old value of] the output operand, so the preparation statement makes sure this isn't so. The function `make_safe_from` copies the `operands[1]` into a temporary register if it refers to `operands[0]`. It does this by emitting another RTL insn.

Finally, a third example shows the use of an internal operand. Zero-extension on the SPUR chip is done by and-ing the result against a halfword mask. But this mask cannot be represented by a `const_int` because the constant value is too large to be legitimate on this machine. So it must be copied into a register with `force_reg` and then the register used in the `and`.

```
(define_expand "zero_extendhisi2"
  [(set (match_operand:SI 0 "register_operand" "")
        (and:SI (subreg:SI
                  (match_operand:HI 1 "register_operand" "")
                  0)
                (match_dup 2)))]
  ""
  "operands[2]
     = force_reg (SImode, GEN_INT (65535)); ")
```

Note: If the `define_expand` is used to serve a standard binary or unary arithmetic operation or a bitfield operation, then the last insn it generates must not be a `code_label`, `barrier` or `note`. It must be an insn, `jump_insn` or `call_insn`. If you don't need a real insn at the end, emit an insn to copy the result of the operation into itself. Such an insn will generate no code, but it can avoid problems in the compiler.

16.14 Defining How to Split Instructions

There are two cases where you should specify how to split a pattern into multiple insns. On machines that have instructions requiring delay slots (see Section 16.15.7 [Delay Slots], page 388) or that have instructions whose output is not available for multiple cycles (see Section 16.15.8 [Function Units], page 389), the compiler phases that optimize these cases need to be able to move insns into one-instruction delay slots. However, some insns may generate more than one machine instruction. These insns cannot be placed into a delay slot.

Often you can rewrite the single insn as a list of individual insns, each corresponding to one machine instruction. The disadvantage of doing so is that it will cause the compilation to be slower and require more space. If the resulting insns are too complex, it may also suppress some optimizations. The compiler splits the insn if there is a reason to believe that it might improve instruction or delay slot scheduling.

The insn combiner phase also splits putative insns. If three insns are merged into one insn with a complex expression that cannot be matched by some `define_insn` pattern, the combiner phase attempts to split the complex pattern into two insns that are recognized. Usually it can break the complex pattern into two patterns by splitting out some subexpression. However, in some other cases, such as performing an addition of a large constant in two insns on a RISC machine, the way to split the addition into two insns is machine-dependent.

The `define_split` definition tells the compiler how to split a complex insn into several simpler insns. It looks like this:

```
(define_split
  [insn-pattern]
  "condition"
  [new-insn-pattern-1
   new-insn-pattern-2
   ...]
  "preparation statements")
```

insn-pattern is a pattern that needs to be split and *condition* is the final condition to be tested, as in a `define_insn`. When an insn matching *insn-pattern* and satisfying *condition* is found, it is replaced in the insn list with the insns given by *new-insn-pattern-1*, *new-insn-pattern-2*, etc.

The *preparation statements* are similar to those statements that are specified for `define_expand` (see Section 16.13 [Expander Definitions], page 374) and are executed before the new RTL is generated to prepare for the generated code or emit some insns whose pattern is not fixed. Unlike those in `define_expand`, however, these statements must not generate any new pseudo-registers. Once reload has completed, they also must not allocate any space in the stack frame.

Patterns are matched against *insn-pattern* in two different circumstances. If an insn needs to be split for delay slot scheduling or insn scheduling, the insn is already known to be valid, which means that it must have been matched by some `define_insn` and, if `reload_completed` is non-zero, is known to satisfy the constraints of that `define_insn`. In that case, the new insn patterns must also be insns that are matched by some `define_insn` and, if `reload_completed` is non-zero, must also satisfy the constraints of those definitions.

As an example of this usage of `define_split`, consider the following example from 'a29k.md', which splits a `sign_extend` from HImode to SImode into a pair of shift insns:

```
(define_split
  [(set (match_operand:SI 0 "gen_reg_operand" "")
        (sign_extend:SI (match_operand:HI 1 "gen_reg_operand" "")))]
  ""
  [(set (match_dup 0)
        (ashift:SI (match_dup 1)
                   (const_int 16)))
   (set (match_dup 0)
        (ashiftrt:SI (match_dup 0)
                     (const_int 16)))]
  "
  { operands[1] = gen_lowpart (SImode, operands[1]); }")
```

When the combiner phase tries to split an insn pattern, it is always the case that the pattern is *not* matched by any `define_insn`. The combiner pass first tries to split a single `set` expression and then the same `set` expression inside a `parallel`, but followed by a `clobber` of a pseudo-reg to use as a scratch register. In these cases, the combiner expects exactly two new insn patterns to be generated. It will verify that these patterns match some `define_insn` definitions, so you need not do this test in the `define_split` (of course, there is no point in writing a `define_split` that will never produce insns that match).

Here is an example of this use of `define_split`, taken from 'rs6000.md':

```
(define_split
  [(set (match_operand:SI 0 "gen_reg_operand" "")
        (plus:SI (match_operand:SI 1 "gen_reg_operand" "")
                 (match_operand:SI 2 "non_add_cint_operand" "")))]
  ""
  [(set (match_dup 0) (plus:SI (match_dup 1) (match_dup 3)))
   (set (match_dup 0) (plus:SI (match_dup 0) (match_dup 4)))]
  "
{
  int low = INTVAL (operands[2]) & 0xffff;
  int high = (unsigned) INTVAL (operands[2]) >> 16;
```

```
    if (low & 0x8000)
      high++, low |= 0xffff0000;

    operands[3] = GEN_INT (high << 16);
    operands[4] = GEN_INT (low);
  }")
```

Here the predicate `non_add_cint_operand` matches any `const_int` that is *not* a valid operand of a single add insn. The add with the smaller displacement is written so that it can be substituted into the address of a subsequent operation.

An example that uses a scratch register, from the same file, generates an equality comparison of a register and a large constant:

```
(define_split
  [(set (match_operand:CC 0 "cc_reg_operand" "")
        (compare:CC (match_operand:SI 1 "gen_reg_operand" "")
                    (match_operand:SI 2 "non_short_cint_operand" "")))
   (clobber (match_operand:SI 3 "gen_reg_operand" ""))]
  "find_single_use (operands[0], insn, 0)
   && (GET_CODE (*find_single_use (operands[0], insn, 0)) == EQ
       || GET_CODE (*find_single_use (operands[0], insn, 0)) == NE)"
  [(set (match_dup 3) (xor:SI (match_dup 1) (match_dup 4)))
   (set (match_dup 0) (compare:CC (match_dup 3) (match_dup 5)))]
  "
{
  /* Get the constant we are comparing against, C, and see what it
     looks like sign-extended to 16 bits.  Then see what constant
     could be XOR'ed with C to get the sign-extended value.  */

  int c = INTVAL (operands[2]);
  int sextc = (c << 16) >> 16;
  int xorv = c ^ sextc;

  operands[4] = GEN_INT (xorv);
  operands[5] = GEN_INT (sextc);
}")
```

To avoid confusion, don't write a single `define_split` that accepts some insns that match some `define_insn` as well as some insns that don't. Instead, write two separate `define_split` definitions, one for the insns that are valid and one for the insns that are not valid.

16.15 Instruction Attributes

In addition to describing the instruction supported by the target machine, the 'md' file also defines a group of *attributes* and a set of values for each. Every generated insn is assigned a value for each attribute. One possible attribute would be the effect that the insn has on the machine's condition code. This attribute can then be used by NOTICE_UPDATE_CC to track the condition codes.

16.15.1 Defining Attributes and their Values

The define_attr expression is used to define each attribute required by the target machine. It looks like:

    (define_attr *name list-of-values default*)

name is a string specifying the name of the attribute being defined.

list-of-values is either a string that specifies a comma-separated list of values that can be assigned to the attribute, or a null string to indicate that the attribute takes numeric values.

default is an attribute expression that gives the value of this attribute for insns that match patterns whose definition does not include an explicit value for this attribute. See Section 16.15.4 [Attr Example], page 385, for more information on the handling of defaults. See Section 16.15.6 [Constant Attributes], page 388, for information on attributes that do not depend on any particular insn.

For each defined attribute, a number of definitions are written to the 'insn-attr.h' file. For cases where an explicit set of values is specified for an attribute, the following are defined:

- A '#define' is written for the symbol 'HAVE_ATTR_*name*'.

- An enumeral class is defined for 'attr_*name*' with elements of the form '*upper-name_upper-value*' where the attribute name and value are first converted to upper case.

- A function 'get_attr_*name*' is defined that is passed an insn and returns the attribute value for that insn.

For example, if the following is present in the 'md' file:

    (define_attr "type" "branch,fp,load,store,arith" ...)

the following lines will be written to the file 'insn-attr.h'.

    #define HAVE_ATTR_type
    enum attr_type {TYPE_BRANCH, TYPE_FP, TYPE_LOAD,
                    TYPE_STORE, TYPE_ARITH};
    extern enum attr_type get_attr_type ();

If the attribute takes numeric values, no **enum** type will be defined and the function to obtain the attribute's value will return **int**.

16.15.2 Attribute Expressions

RTL expressions used to define attributes use the codes described above plus a few specific to attribute definitions, to be discussed below. Attribute value expressions must have one of the following forms:

(const_int *i*)

> The integer *i* specifies the value of a numeric attribute. *i* must be non-negative.
>
> The value of a numeric attribute can be specified either with a const_int, or as an integer represented as a string in const_string, eq_attr (see below), attr, symbol_ref, simple arithmetic expressions, and set_attr overrides on specific instructions (see Section 16.15.3 [Tagging Insns], page 383).

(const_string *value*)

> The string *value* specifies a constant attribute value. If *value* is specified as '"*"', it means that the default value of the attribute is to be used for the insn containing this expression. '"*"' obviously cannot be used in the *default* expression of a define_attr.
>
> If the attribute whose value is being specified is numeric, *value* must be a string containing a non-negative integer (normally const_int would be used in this case). Otherwise, it must contain one of the valid values for the attribute.

(if_then_else *test true-value false-value*)

> *test* specifies an attribute test, whose format is defined below. The value of this expression is *true-value* if *test* is true, otherwise it is *false-value*.

(cond [*test1 value1* ...] *default*)

> The first operand of this expression is a vector containing an even number of expressions and consisting of pairs of *test* and *value* expressions. The value of the cond expression is that of the *value* corresponding to the first true *test* expression. If none of the *test* expressions are true, the value of the cond expression is that of the *default* expression.

test expressions can have one of the following forms:

(const_int *i*)

> This test is true if *i* is non-zero and false otherwise.

(not *test*)
(ior *test1 test2*)
(and *test1 test2*)

> These tests are true if the indicated logical function is true.

(`match_operand:`*m n pred constraints*)

> This test is true if operand *n* of the insn whose attribute value
> is being determined has mode *m* (this part of the test is ignored
> if *m* is `VOIDmode`) and the function specified by the string *pred*
> returns a non-zero value when passed operand *n* and mode *m*
> (this part of the test is ignored if *pred* is the null string).
>
> The *constraints* operand is ignored and should be the null string.

(`le` *arith1 arith2*)
(`leu` *arith1 arith2*)
(`lt` *arith1 arith2*)
(`ltu` *arith1 arith2*)
(`gt` *arith1 arith2*)
(`gtu` *arith1 arith2*)
(`ge` *arith1 arith2*)
(`geu` *arith1 arith2*)
(`ne` *arith1 arith2*)
(`eq` *arith1 arith2*)

> These tests are true if the indicated comparison of the two arith-
> metic expressions is true. Arithmetic expressions are formed
> with `plus`, `minus`, `mult`, `div`, `mod`, `abs`, `neg`, `and`, `ior`, `xor`, `not`,
> `ashift`, `lshiftrt`, and `ashiftrt` expressions.
>
> `const_int` and `symbol_ref` are always valid terms (see Sec-
> tion 16.15.5 [Insn Lengths], page 386, for additional forms).
> `symbol_ref` is a string denoting a C expression that yields an
> `int` when evaluated by the 'get_attr_...' routine. It should
> normally be a global variable.

(`eq_attr` *name value*)

> *name* is a string specifying the name of an attribute.
>
> *value* is a string that is either a valid value for attribute *name*, a
> comma-separated list of values, or '!' followed by a value or list.
> If *value* does not begin with a '!', this test is true if the value of
> the *name* attribute of the current insn is in the list specified by
> *value*. If *value* begins with a '!', this test is true if the attribute's
> value is *not* in the specified list.
>
> For example,
>
>   (eq_attr "type" "load,store")
>
> is equivalent to
>
>   (ior (eq_attr "type" "load") (eq_attr "type" "store"))
>
> If *name* specifies an attribute of 'alternative', it refers to the
> value of the compiler variable `which_alternative` (see Sec-
> tion 16.5 [Output Statement], page 335) and the values must
> be small integers. For example,
>
>   (eq_attr "alternative" "2,3")

is equivalent to

```
(ior (eq (symbol_ref "which_alternative") (const_int 2))
     (eq (symbol_ref "which_alternative") (const_int 3)))
```

Note that, for most attributes, an `eq_attr` test is simplified in cases where the value of the attribute being tested is known for all insns matching a particular pattern. This is by far the most common case.

`(attr_flag` *name*`)`

>The value of an `attr_flag` expression is true if the flag specified by *name* is true for the `insn` currently being scheduled.

>*name* is a string specifying one of a fixed set of flags to test. Test the flags `forward` and `backward` to determine the direction of a conditional branch. Test the flags `very_likely`, `likely`, `very_unlikely`, and `unlikely` to determine if a conditional branch is expected to be taken.

>If the `very_likely` flag is true, then the `likely` flag is also true. Likewise for the `very_unlikely` and `unlikely` flags.

>This example describes a conditional branch delay slot which can be nullified for forward branches that are taken (annul-true) or for backward branches which are not taken (annul-false).

```
(define_delay (eq_attr "type" "cbranch")
  [(eq_attr "in_branch_delay" "true")
   (and (eq_attr "in_branch_delay" "true")
        (attr_flag "forward"))
   (and (eq_attr "in_branch_delay" "true")
        (attr_flag "backward"))])
```

>The `forward` and `backward` flags are false if the current `insn` being scheduled is not a conditional branch.

>The `very_likely` and `likely` flags are true if the `insn` being scheduled is not a conditional branch. The `very_unlikely` and `unlikely` flags are false if the `insn` being scheduled is not a conditional branch.

>`attr_flag` is only used during delay slot scheduling and has no meaning to other passes of the compiler.

`(attr` *name*`)`

>The value of another attribute is returned. This is most useful for numeric attributes, as `eq_attr` and `attr_flag` produce more efficient code for non-numeric attributes.

16.15.3 Assigning Attribute Values to Insns

The value assigned to an attribute of an insn is primarily determined by which pattern is matched by that insn (or which `define_peephole` generated it). Every `define_insn` and `define_peephole` can have an optional last argument to specify the values of attributes for matching insns. The value of any attribute not specified in a particular insn is set to the default value for that attribute, as specified in its `define_attr`. Extensive use of default values for attributes permits the specification of the values for only one or two attributes in the definition of most insn patterns, as seen in the example in the next section.

The optional last argument of `define_insn` and `define_peephole` is a vector of expressions, each of which defines the value for a single attribute. The most general way of assigning an attribute's value is to use a `set` expression whose first operand is an `attr` expression giving the name of the attribute being set. The second operand of the `set` is an attribute expression (see Section 16.15.2 [Expressions], page 381) giving the value of the attribute.

When the attribute value depends on the 'alternative' attribute (i.e., which is the applicable alternative in the constraint of the insn), the `set_attr_alternative` expression can be used. It allows the specification of a vector of attribute expressions, one for each alternative.

When the generality of arbitrary attribute expressions is not required, the simpler `set_attr` expression can be used, which allows specifying a string giving either a single attribute value or a list of attribute values, one for each alternative.

The form of each of the above specifications is shown below. In each case, *name* is a string specifying the attribute to be set.

(`set_attr` *name value-string*)

> *value-string* is either a string giving the desired attribute value, or a string containing a comma-separated list giving the values for succeeding alternatives. The number of elements must match the number of alternatives in the constraint of the insn pattern.
>
> Note that it may be useful to specify '*' for some alternative, in which case the attribute will assume its default value for insns matching that alternative.

(`set_attr_alternative` *name* [*value1 value2* ...])

> Depending on the alternative of the insn, the value will be one of the specified values. This is a shorthand for using a `cond` with tests on the 'alternative' attribute.

(`set` (`attr` *name*) *value*)

> The first operand of this `set` must be the special RTL expression `attr`, whose sole operand is a string giving the name of the attribute being set. *value* is the value of the attribute.

The following shows three different ways of representing the same attribute value specification:

```
(set_attr "type" "load,store,arith")
```

```
(set_attr_alternative "type"
                      [(const_string "load") (const_string "store")
                      (const_string "arith")])

(set (attr "type")
     (cond [(eq_attr "alternative" "1") (const_string "load")
            (eq_attr "alternative" "2") (const_string "store")]
           (const_string "arith")))
```

The `define_asm_attributes` expression provides a mechanism to specify the attributes assigned to insns produced from an `asm` statement. It has the form:

```
(define_asm_attributes [attr-sets])
```

where *attr-sets* is specified the same as for both the `define_insn` and the `define_peephole` expressions.

These values will typically be the "worst case" attribute values. For example, they might indicate that the condition code will be clobbered.

A specification for a `length` attribute is handled specially. The way to compute the length of an `asm` insn is to multiply the length specified in the expression `define_asm_attributes` by the number of machine instructions specified in the `asm` statement, determined by counting the number of semicolons and newlines in the string. Therefore, the value of the `length` attribute specified in a `define_asm_attributes` should be the maximum possible length of a single machine instruction.

16.15.4 Example of Attribute Specifications

The judicious use of defaulting is important in the efficient use of insn attributes. Typically, insns are divided into *types* and an attribute, customarily called `type`, is used to represent this value. This attribute is normally used only to define the default value for other attributes. An example will clarify this usage.

Assume we have a RISC machine with a condition code and in which only full-word operations are performed in registers. Let us assume that we can divide all insns into loads, stores, (integer) arithmetic operations, floating point operations, and branches.

Here we will concern ourselves with determining the effect of an insn on the condition code and will limit ourselves to the following possible effects: The condition code can be set unpredictably (clobbered), not be changed, be set to agree with the results of the operation, or only changed if the item previously set into the condition code has been modified.

Here is part of a sample 'md' file for such a machine:

```
(define_attr "type" "load,store,arith,fp,branch" (const_string "arith"))
```

```
(define_attr "cc" "clobber,unchanged,set,change0"
            (cond [(eq_attr "type" "load")
                        (const_string "change0")
                   (eq_attr "type" "store,branch")
                        (const_string "unchanged")
                   (eq_attr "type" "arith")
                        (if_then_else (match_operand:SI 0 "" "")
                                      (const_string "set")
                                      (const_string "clobber"))]
                  (const_string "clobber")))


(define_insn ""
  [(set (match_operand:SI 0 "general_operand" "=r,r,m")
        (match_operand:SI 1 "general_operand" "r,m,r"))]
  ""
  "@
   move %0,%1
   load %0,%1
   store %0,%1"
  [(set_attr "type" "arith,load,store")])
```

Note that we assume in the above example that arithmetic operations
performed on quantities smaller than a machine word clobber the condition
code since they will set the condition code to a value corresponding to the
full-word result.

16.15.5 Computing the Length of an Insn

For many machines, multiple types of branch instructions are provided,
each for different length branch displacements. In most cases, the assembler
will choose the correct instruction to use. However, when the assembler
cannot do so, GCC can when a special attribute, the 'length' attribute, is
defined. This attribute must be defined to have numeric values by specifying
a null string in its `define_attr`.

In the case of the 'length' attribute, two additional forms of arithmetic
terms are allowed in test expressions:

`(match_dup n)`
> This refers to the address of operand n of the current insn, which
> must be a `label_ref`.

`(pc)`
> This refers to the address of the *current* insn. It might have
> been more consistent with other usage to make this the address
> of the *next* insn but this would be confusing because the length
> of the current insn is to be computed.

For normal insns, the length will be determined by value of the 'length' attribute. In the case of **addr_vec** and **addr_diff_vec** insn patterns, the length is computed as the number of vectors multiplied by the size of each vector.

Lengths are measured in addressable storage units (bytes).

The following macros can be used to refine the length computation:

FIRST_INSN_ADDRESS

> When the **length** insn attribute is used, this macro specifies the value to be assigned to the address of the first insn in a function. If not specified, 0 is used.

ADJUST_INSN_LENGTH (*insn*, *length*)

> If defined, modifies the length assigned to instruction *insn* as a function of the context in which it is used. *length* is an lvalue that contains the initially computed length of the insn and should be updated with the correct length of the insn.

> This macro will normally not be required. A case in which it is required is the ROMP. On this machine, the size of an **addr_vec** insn must be increased by two to compensate for the fact that alignment may be required.

The routine that returns **get_attr_length** (the value of the **length** attribute) can be used by the output routine to determine the form of the branch instruction to be written, as the example below illustrates.

As an example of the specification of variable-length branches, consider the IBM 360. If we adopt the convention that a register will be set to the starting address of a function, we can jump to labels within 4k of the start using a four-byte instruction. Otherwise, we need a six-byte sequence to load the address from memory and then branch to it.

On such a machine, a pattern for a branch instruction might be specified as follows:

```
(define_insn "jump"
  [(set (pc)
        (label_ref (match_operand 0 "" "")))]
  ""
  "*
{
  return (get_attr_length (insn) == 4
          ? \"b %l0\" : \"l r15,=a(%l0); br r15\");
}"
  [(set (attr "length") (if_then_else (lt (match_dup 0) (const_int 4096))
                                      (const_int 4)
                                      (const_int 6)))])
```

16.15.6 Constant Attributes

A special form of `define_attr`, where the expression for the default value
is a `const` expression, indicates an attribute that is constant for a given run
of the compiler. Constant attributes may be used to specify which variety
of processor is used. For example,

```
(define_attr "cpu" "m88100,m88110,m88000"
 (const
  (cond [(symbol_ref "TARGET_88100") (const_string "m88100")
         (symbol_ref "TARGET_88110") (const_string "m88110")]
        (const_string "m88000"))))


(define_attr "memory" "fast,slow"
 (const
  (if_then_else (symbol_ref "TARGET_FAST_MEM")
                (const_string "fast")
                (const_string "slow"))))
```

The routine generated for constant attributes has no parameters as it
does not depend on any particular insn. RTL expressions used to define the
value of a constant attribute may use the `symbol_ref` form, but may not use
either the `match_operand` form or `eq_attr` forms involving insn attributes.

16.15.7 Delay Slot Scheduling

The insn attribute mechanism can be used to specify the requirements
for delay slots, if any, on a target machine. An instruction is said to require
a *delay slot* if some instructions that are physically after the instruction are
executed as if they were located before it. Classic examples are branch and
call instructions, which often execute the following instruction before the
branch or call is performed.

On some machines, conditional branch instructions can optionally *annul*
instructions in the delay slot. This means that the instruction will not be
executed for certain branch outcomes. Both instructions that annul if the
branch is true and instructions that annul if the branch is false are supported.

Delay slot scheduling differs from instruction scheduling in that determining whether an instruction needs a delay slot is dependent only on the
type of instruction being generated, not on data flow between the instructions. See the next section for a discussion of data-dependent instruction
scheduling.

The requirement of an insn needing one or more delay slots is indicated
via the `define_delay` expression. It has the following form:

```
(define_delay test
              [delay-1 annul-true-1 annul-false-1
               delay-2 annul-true-2 annul-false-2
```

```
                        ...])
```

test is an attribute test that indicates whether this `define_delay` applies
to a particular insn. If so, the number of required delay slots is determined
by the length of the vector specified as the second argument. An insn placed
in delay slot *n* must satisfy attribute test *delay-n*. *annul-true-n* is an attribute test that specifies which insns may be annulled if the branch is true.
Similarly, *annul-false-n* specifies which insns in the delay slot may be annulled if the branch is false. If annulling is not supported for that delay slot,
(nil) should be coded.

For example, in the common case where branch and call insns require a
single delay slot, which may contain any insn other than a branch or call,
the following would be placed in the 'md' file:

```
(define_delay (eq_attr "type" "branch,call")
              [(eq_attr "type" "!branch,call") (nil) (nil)])
```

Multiple `define_delay` expressions may be specified. In this case, each
such expression specifies different delay slot requirements and there must be
no insn for which tests in two `define_delay` expressions are both true.

For example, if we have a machine that requires one delay slot for branches
but two for calls, no delay slot can contain a branch or call insn, and any
valid insn in the delay slot for the branch can be annulled if the branch is
true, we might represent this as follows:

```
(define_delay (eq_attr "type" "branch")
   [(eq_attr "type" "!branch,call")
    (eq_attr "type" "!branch,call")
    (nil)])


(define_delay (eq_attr "type" "call")
              [(eq_attr "type" "!branch,call") (nil) (nil)
               (eq_attr "type" "!branch,call") (nil) (nil)])
```

16.15.8 Specifying Function Units

On most RISC machines, there are instructions whose results are not
available for a specific number of cycles. Common cases are instructions
that load data from memory. On many machines, a pipeline stall will result
if the data is referenced too soon after the load instruction.

In addition, many newer microprocessors have multiple function units,
usually one for integer and one for floating point, and often will incur pipeline
stalls when a result that is needed is not yet ready.

The descriptions in this section allow the specification of how much time
must elapse between the execution of an instruction and the time when
its result is used. It also allows specification of when the execution of an
instruction will delay execution of similar instructions due to function unit
conflicts.

For the purposes of the specifications in this section, a machine is divided into *function units*, each of which execute a specific class of instructions in first-in-first-out order. Function units that accept one instruction each cycle and allow a result to be used in the succeeding instruction (usually via forwarding) need not be specified. Classic RISC microprocessors will normally have a single function unit, which we can call 'memory'. The newer "superscalar" processors will often have function units for floating point operations, usually at least a floating point adder and multiplier.

Each usage of a function units by a class of insns is specified with a `define_function_unit` expression, which looks like this:

```
(define_function_unit name multiplicity simultaneity
                      test ready-delay issue-delay
                      [conflict-list])
```

name is a string giving the name of the function unit.

multiplicity is an integer specifying the number of identical units in the processor. If more than one unit is specified, they will be scheduled independently. Only truly independent units should be counted; a pipelined unit should be specified as a single unit. (The only common example of a machine that has multiple function units for a single instruction class that are truly independent and not pipelined are the two multiply and two increment units of the CDC 6600.)

simultaneity specifies the maximum number of insns that can be executing in each instance of the function unit simultaneously or zero if the unit is pipelined and has no limit.

All `define_function_unit` definitions referring to function unit *name* must have the same name and values for *multiplicity* and *simultaneity*.

test is an attribute test that selects the insns we are describing in this definition. Note that an insn may use more than one function unit and a function unit may be specified in more than one `define_function_unit`.

ready-delay is an integer that specifies the number of cycles after which the result of the instruction can be used without introducing any stalls.

issue-delay is an integer that specifies the number of cycles after the instruction matching the *test* expression begins using this unit until a subsequent instruction can begin. A cost of *N* indicates an *N-1* cycle delay. A subsequent instruction may also be delayed if an earlier instruction has a longer *ready-delay* value. This blocking effect is computed using the *simultaneity, ready-delay, issue-delay,* and *conflict-list* terms. For a normal non-pipelined function unit, *simultaneity* is one, the unit is taken to block for the *ready-delay* cycles of the executing insn, and smaller values of *issue-delay* are ignored.

conflict-list is an optional list giving detailed conflict costs for this unit. If specified, it is a list of condition test expressions to be applied to insns chosen to execute in *name* following the particular insn matching *test* that is already executing in *name*. For each insn in the list, *issue-delay* specifies the conflict cost; for insns not in the list, the cost is zero. If not specified, *conflict-list* defaults to all instructions that use the function unit.

Typical uses of this vector are where a floating point function unit can pipeline either single- or double-precision operations, but not both, or where a memory unit can pipeline loads, but not stores, etc.

As an example, consider a classic RISC machine where the result of a load instruction is not available for two cycles (a single "delay" instruction is required) and where only one load instruction can be executed simultaneously. This would be specified as:

```
(define_function_unit "memory" 1 1 (eq_attr "type" "load") 2 0)
```

For the case of a floating point function unit that can pipeline either single or double precision, but not both, the following could be specified:

```
(define_function_unit
  "fp" 1 0 (eq_attr "type" "sp_fp") 4 4 [(eq_attr "type" "dp_fp")])
(define_function_unit
  "fp" 1 0 (eq_attr "type" "dp_fp") 4 4 [(eq_attr "type" "sp_fp")])
```

Note: The scheduler attempts to avoid function unit conflicts and uses all the specifications in the `define_function_unit` expression. It has recently come to our attention that these specifications may not allow modeling of some of the newer "superscalar" processors that have insns using multiple pipelined units. These insns will cause a potential conflict for the second unit used during their execution and there is no way of representing that conflict. We welcome any examples of how function unit conflicts work in such processors and suggestions for their representation.

17 Target Description Macros

In addition to the file 'machine.md', a machine description includes a C header file conventionally given the name 'machine.h'. This header file defines numerous macros that convey the information about the target machine that does not fit into the scheme of the '.md' file. The file 'tm.h' should be a link to 'machine.h'. The header file 'config.h' includes 'tm.h' and most compiler source files include 'config.h'.

17.1 Controlling the Compilation Driver, 'gcc'

You can control the compilation driver.

SWITCH_TAKES_ARG (*char*)

> A C expression which determines whether the option '-*char*' takes arguments. The value should be the number of arguments that option takes–zero, for many options.
>
> By default, this macro is defined as DEFAULT_SWITCH_TAKES_ ARG, which handles the standard options properly. You need not define SWITCH_TAKES_ARG unless you wish to add additional options which take arguments. Any redefinition should call DEFAULT_SWITCH_TAKES_ARG and then check for additional options.

WORD_SWITCH_TAKES_ARG (*name*)

> A C expression which determines whether the option '-*name*' takes arguments. The value should be the number of arguments that option takes–zero, for many options. This macro rather than SWITCH_TAKES_ARG is used for multi-character option names.
>
> By default, this macro is defined as DEFAULT_WORD_SWITCH_ TAKES_ARG, which handles the standard options properly. You need not define WORD_SWITCH_TAKES_ARG unless you wish to add additional options which take arguments. Any redefinition should call DEFAULT_WORD_SWITCH_TAKES_ARG and then check for additional options.

SWITCH_CURTAILS_COMPILATION (*char*)

> A C expression which determines whether the option '-*char*' stops compilation before the generation of an executable. The value is boolean, non-zero if the option does stop an executable from being generated, zero otherwise.
>
> By default, this macro is defined as DEFAULT_SWITCH_CURTAILS_ COMPILATION, which handles the standard options properly. You need not define SWITCH_CURTAILS_COMPILATION unless you wish to add additional options which affect the generation of

an executable. Any redefinition should call `DEFAULT_SWITCH_CURTAILS_COMPILATION` and then check for additional options.

`SWITCHES_NEED_SPACES`

A string-valued C expression which enumerates the options for which the linker needs a space between the option and its argument.

If this macro is not defined, the default value is `""`.

`CPP_SPEC` A C string constant that tells the GNU CC driver program options to pass to CPP. It can also specify how to translate options you give to GNU CC into options for GNU CC to pass to the CPP.

Do not define this macro if it does not need to do anything.

`NO_BUILTIN_SIZE_TYPE`

If this macro is defined, the preprocessor will not define the builtin macro `__SIZE_TYPE__`. The macro `__SIZE_TYPE__` must then be defined by `CPP_SPEC` instead.

This should be defined if `SIZE_TYPE` depends on target dependent flags which are not accessible to the preprocessor. Otherwise, it should not be defined.

`NO_BUILTIN_PTRDIFF_TYPE`

If this macro is defined, the preprocessor will not define the builtin macro `__PTRDIFF_TYPE__`. The macro `__PTRDIFF_TYPE__` must then be defined by `CPP_SPEC` instead.

This should be defined if `PTRDIFF_TYPE` depends on target dependent flags which are not accessible to the preprocessor. Otherwise, it should not be defined.

`SIGNED_CHAR_SPEC`

A C string constant that tells the GNU CC driver program options to pass to CPP. By default, this macro is defined to pass the option '`-D__CHAR_UNSIGNED__`' to CPP if `char` will be treated as `unsigned char` by `cc1`.

Do not define this macro unless you need to override the default definition.

`CC1_SPEC` A C string constant that tells the GNU CC driver program options to pass to `cc1`. It can also specify how to translate options you give to GNU CC into options for GNU CC to pass to the `cc1`.

Do not define this macro if it does not need to do anything.

`CC1PLUS_SPEC`

A C string constant that tells the GNU CC driver program options to pass to `cc1plus`. It can also specify how to translate

options you give to GNU CC into options for GNU CC to pass
to the `cc1plus`.

Do not define this macro if it does not need to do anything.

ASM_SPEC   A C string constant that tells the GNU CC driver program op-
            tions to pass to the assembler. It can also specify how to trans-
            late options you give to GNU CC into options for GNU CC to
            pass to the assembler. See the file 'sun3.h' for an example of
            this.

            Do not define this macro if it does not need to do anything.

ASM_FINAL_SPEC
            A C string constant that tells the GNU CC driver program how
            to run any programs which cleanup after the normal assembler.
            Normally, this is not needed. See the file 'mips.h' for an example
            of this.

            Do not define this macro if it does not need to do anything.

LINK_SPEC
            A C string constant that tells the GNU CC driver program op-
            tions to pass to the linker. It can also specify how to translate
            options you give to GNU CC into options for GNU CC to pass
            to the linker.

            Do not define this macro if it does not need to do anything.

LIB_SPEC   Another C string constant used much like LINK_SPEC. The dif-
            ference between the two is that LIB_SPEC is used at the end of
            the command given to the linker.

            If this macro is not defined, a default is provided that loads the
            standard C library from the usual place. See 'gcc.c'.

LIBGCC_SPEC
            Another C string constant that tells the GNU CC driver program
            how and when to place a reference to 'libgcc.a' into the linker
            command line. This constant is placed both before and after the
            value of LIB_SPEC.

            If this macro is not defined, the GNU CC driver provides a
            default that passes the string '-lgcc' to the linker unless the
            '-shared' option is specified.

STARTFILE_SPEC
            Another C string constant used much like LINK_SPEC. The dif-
            ference between the two is that STARTFILE_SPEC is used at the
            very beginning of the command given to the linker.

            If this macro is not defined, a default is provided that loads the
            standard C startup file from the usual place. See 'gcc.c'.

ENDFILE_SPEC

> Another C string constant used much like LINK_SPEC. The difference between the two is that ENDFILE_SPEC is used at the very end of the command given to the linker.
>
> Do not define this macro if it does not need to do anything.

EXTRA_SPECS

> Define this macro to provide additional specifications to put in the 'specs' file that can be used in various specifications like CC1_SPEC.
>
> The definition should be an initializer for an array of structures, containing a string constant, that defines the specification name, and a string constant that provides the specification.
>
> Do not define this macro if it does not need to do anything.
>
> EXTRA_SPECS is useful when an architecture contains several related targets, which have various ..._SPECS which are similar to each other, and the maintainer would like one central place to keep these definitions.
>
> For example, the PowerPC System V.4 targets use EXTRA_SPECS to define either _CALL_SYSV when the System V calling sequence is used or _CALL_AIX when the older AIX-based calling sequence is used.
>
> The 'config/rs6000/rs6000.h' target file defines:
>
> ```
> #define EXTRA_SPECS \
>   { "cpp_sysv_default", CPP_SYSV_DEFAULT },
> ```
>
> ```
> #define CPP_SYS_DEFAULT ""
> ```
>
> The 'config/rs6000/sysv.h' target file defines:
>
> ```
> #undef CPP_SPEC
> #define CPP_SPEC \
> "%{posix: -D_POSIX_SOURCE } \
> %{mcall-sysv: -D_CALL_SYSV } %{mcall-aix: -D_CALL_AIX } \
> %{!mcall-sysv: %{!mcall-aix: %(cpp_sysv_default) }} \
> %{msoft-float: -D_SOFT_FLOAT} %{mcpu=403: -D_SOFT_FLOAT}"
> ```
>
> ```
> #undef CPP_SYSV_DEFAULT
> #define CPP_SYSV_DEFAULT "-D_CALL_SYSV"
> ```
>
> while the 'config/rs6000/eabiaix.h' target file defines CPP_SYSV_DEFAULT as:
>
> ```
> #undef CPP_SYSV_DEFAULT
> #define CPP_SYSV_DEFAULT "-D_CALL_AIX"
> ```

LINK_LIBGCC_SPECIAL

> Define this macro if the driver program should find the library 'libgcc.a' itself and should not pass '-L' options to the linker.

If you do not define this macro, the driver program will pass the argument '-lgcc' to tell the linker to do the search and will pass '-L' options to it.

LINK_LIBGCC_SPECIAL_1

Define this macro if the driver program should find the library 'libgcc.a'. If you do not define this macro, the driver program will pass the argument '-lgcc' to tell the linker to do the search. This macro is similar to LINK_LIBGCC_SPECIAL, except that it does not affect '-L' options.

LINK_COMMAND_SPEC

A C string constant giving the complete command line need to execute the linker. When you do this, you will need to update your port each time a change is made to the link command line within 'gcc.c'. Therefore, define this macro only if you need to completely redefine the command line for invoking the linker and there is no other way to accomplish the effect you need.

MULTILIB_DEFAULTS

Define this macro as a C expression for the initializer of an array of string to tell the driver program which options are defaults for this target and thus do not need to be handled specially when using MULTILIB_OPTIONS.

Do not define this macro if MULTILIB_OPTIONS is not defined in the target makefile fragment or if none of the options listed in MULTILIB_OPTIONS are set by default. See Section 19.1 [Target Fragment], page 527.

RELATIVE_PREFIX_NOT_LINKDIR

Define this macro to tell gcc that it should only translate a '-B' prefix into a '-L' linker option if the prefix indicates an absolute file name.

STANDARD_EXEC_PREFIX

Define this macro as a C string constant if you wish to override the standard choice of '/usr/local/lib/gcc-lib/' as the default prefix to try when searching for the executable files of the compiler.

MD_EXEC_PREFIX

If defined, this macro is an additional prefix to try after STANDARD_EXEC_PREFIX. MD_EXEC_PREFIX is not searched when the '-b' option is used, or the compiler is built as a cross compiler. If you define MD_EXEC_PREFIX, then be sure to add it to the list of directories used to find the assembler in 'configure.in'.

STANDARD_STARTFILE_PREFIX

>Define this macro as a C string constant if you wish to override the standard choice of '/usr/local/lib/' as the default prefix to try when searching for startup files such as 'crt0.o'.

MD_STARTFILE_PREFIX

>If defined, this macro supplies an additional prefix to try after the standard prefixes. MD_EXEC_PREFIX is not searched when the '-b' option is used, or when the compiler is built as a cross compiler.

MD_STARTFILE_PREFIX_1

>If defined, this macro supplies yet another prefix to try after the standard prefixes. It is not searched when the '-b' option is used, or when the compiler is built as a cross compiler.

INIT_ENVIRONMENT

>Define this macro as a C string constant if you wish to set environment variables for programs called by the driver, such as the assembler and loader. The driver passes the value of this macro to putenv to initialize the necessary environment variables.

LOCAL_INCLUDE_DIR

>Define this macro as a C string constant if you wish to override the standard choice of '/usr/local/include' as the default prefix to try when searching for local header files. LOCAL_INCLUDE_DIR comes before SYSTEM_INCLUDE_DIR in the search order.

>Cross compilers do not use this macro and do not search either '/usr/local/include' or its replacement.

SYSTEM_INCLUDE_DIR

>Define this macro as a C string constant if you wish to specify a system-specific directory to search for header files before the standard directory. SYSTEM_INCLUDE_DIR comes before STANDARD_INCLUDE_DIR in the search order.

>Cross compilers do not use this macro and do not search the directory specified.

STANDARD_INCLUDE_DIR

>Define this macro as a C string constant if you wish to override the standard choice of '/usr/include' as the default prefix to try when searching for header files.

>Cross compilers do not use this macro and do not search either '/usr/include' or its replacement.

STANDARD_INCLUDE_COMPONENT

>The "component" corresponding to STANDARD_INCLUDE_DIR. See INCLUDE_DEFAULTS, below, for the description of components. If you do not define this macro, no component is used.

INCLUDE_DEFAULTS

> Define this macro if you wish to override the entire default search path for include files. For a native compiler, the default search path usually consists of GCC_INCLUDE_DIR, LOCAL_INCLUDE_DIR, SYSTEM_INCLUDE_DIR, GPLUSPLUS_INCLUDE_DIR, and STANDARD_INCLUDE_DIR. In addition, GPLUSPLUS_INCLUDE_DIR and GCC_INCLUDE_DIR are defined automatically by 'Makefile', and specify private search areas for GCC. The directory GPLUSPLUS_INCLUDE_DIR is used only for C++ programs.
>
> The definition should be an initializer for an array of structures. Each array element should have four elements: the directory name (a string constant), the component name, and flag for C++-only directories, and a flag showing that the includes in the directory don't need to be wrapped in **extern 'C'** when compiling C++. Mark the end of the array with a null element.
>
> The component name denotes what GNU package the include file is part of, if any, in all upper-case letters. For example, it might be 'GCC' or 'BINUTILS'. If the package is part of the a vendor-supplied operating system, code the component name as '0'.
>
> For example, here is the definition used for VAX/VMS:
>
> ```
> #define INCLUDE_DEFAULTS \
> {                                            \
>   { "GNU_GXX_INCLUDE:", "G++", 1, 1},        \
>   { "GNU_CC_INCLUDE:", "GCC", 0, 0},         \
>   { "SYS$SYSROOT:[SYSLIB.]", 0, 0, 0},       \
>   { ".", 0, 0, 0},                           \
>   { 0, 0, 0, 0}                              \
> }
> ```

Here is the order of prefixes tried for exec files:

1. Any prefixes specified by the user with '-B'.
2. The environment variable GCC_EXEC_PREFIX, if any.
3. The directories specified by the environment variable COMPILER_PATH.
4. The macro STANDARD_EXEC_PREFIX.
5. '/usr/lib/gcc/'.
6. The macro MD_EXEC_PREFIX, if any.

Here is the order of prefixes tried for startfiles:

1. Any prefixes specified by the user with '-B'.
2. The environment variable GCC_EXEC_PREFIX, if any.
3. The directories specified by the environment variable LIBRARY_PATH (native only, cross compilers do not use this).

4. The macro `STANDARD_EXEC_PREFIX`.

5. '`/usr/lib/gcc/`'.

6. The macro `MD_EXEC_PREFIX`, if any.

7. The macro `MD_STARTFILE_PREFIX`, if any.

8. The macro `STANDARD_STARTFILE_PREFIX`.

9. '`/lib/`'.

10. '`/usr/lib/`'.

17.2 Run-time Target Specification

Here are run-time target specifications.

`CPP_PREDEFINES`

Define this to be a string constant containing '`-D`' options to define the predefined macros that identify this machine and system. These macros will be predefined unless the '`-ansi`' option is specified.

In addition, a parallel set of macros are predefined, whose names are made by appending '`__`' at the beginning and at the end. These '`__`' macros are permitted by the ANSI standard, so they are predefined regardless of whether '`-ansi`' is specified.

For example, on the Sun, one can use the following value:

```
"-Dmc68000 -Dsun -Dunix"
```

The result is to define the macros `__mc68000__`, `__sun__` and `__unix__` unconditionally, and the macros `mc68000`, `sun` and `unix` provided '`-ansi`' is not specified.

`extern int target_flags;`

This declaration should be present.

`TARGET_...`

This series of macros is to allow compiler command arguments to enable or disable the use of optional features of the target machine. For example, one machine description serves both the 68000 and the 68020; a command argument tells the compiler whether it should use 68020-only instructions or not. This command argument works by means of a macro `TARGET_68020` that tests a bit in `target_flags`.

Define a macro `TARGET_`*featurename* for each such option. Its definition should test a bit in `target_flags`; for example:

```
#define TARGET_68020 (target_flags & 1)
```

One place where these macros are used is in the condition-expressions of instruction patterns. Note how `TARGET_68020` appears frequently in the 68000 machine description file, '`m68k.md`'.

Another place they are used is in the definitions of the other macros in the 'machine.h' file.

TARGET_SWITCHES

This macro defines names of command options to set and clear bits in `target_flags`. Its definition is an initializer with a sub-grouping for each command option.

Each subgrouping contains a string constant, that defines the option name, a number, which contains the bits to set in `target_flags`, and a second string which is the description displayed by –help. If the number is negative then the bits specified by the number are cleared instead of being set. If the description string is present but empty, then no help information will be displayed for that option, but it will not count as an undocumented option. The actual option name is made by appending '-m' to the specified name.

One of the subgroupings should have a null string. The number in this grouping is the default value for `target_flags`. Any target options act starting with that value.

Here is an example which defines '-m68000' and '-m68020' with opposite meanings, and picks the latter as the default:

```
#define TARGET_SWITCHES \
  { { "68020", 1, "" },           \
    { "68000", -1, "Compile for the 68000" }, \
    { "", 1, "" }}
```

TARGET_OPTIONS

This macro is similar to TARGET_SWITCHES but defines names of command options that have values. Its definition is an initializer with a subgrouping for each command option.

Each subgrouping contains a string constant, that defines the fixed part of the option name, the address of a variable, and a description string. The variable, type `char *`, is set to the variable part of the given option if the fixed part matches. The actual option name is made by appending '-m' to the specified name.

Here is an example which defines '-mshort-data-*number*'. If the given option is '-mshort-data-512', the variable `m88k_short_data` will be set to the string `"512"`.

```
extern char *m88k_short_data;
#define TARGET_OPTIONS \
  { { "short-data-", &m88k_short_data, "Specify the size of the \
      short data section" } }
```

TARGET_VERSION

This macro is a C statement to print on `stderr` a string describing the particular machine description choice. Every machine description should define TARGET_VERSION. For example:

```
#ifdef MOTOROLA
#define TARGET_VERSION \
  fprintf (stderr, " (68k, Motorola syntax)");
#else
#define TARGET_VERSION \
  fprintf (stderr, " (68k, MIT syntax)");
#endif
```

OVERRIDE_OPTIONS

Sometimes certain combinations of command options do not make sense on a particular target machine. You can define a macro OVERRIDE_OPTIONS to take account of this. This macro, if defined, is executed once just after all the command options have been parsed.

Don't use this macro to turn on various extra optimizations for '-O'. That is what OPTIMIZATION_OPTIONS is for.

OPTIMIZATION_OPTIONS (*level*, *size*)

Some machines may desire to change what optimizations are performed for various optimization levels. This macro, if defined, is executed once just after the optimization level is determined and before the remainder of the command options have been parsed. Values set in this macro are used as the default values for the other command line options.

level is the optimization level specified; 2 if '-O2' is specified, 1 if '-O' is specified, and 0 if neither is specified.

size is non-zero if '-Os' is specified and zero otherwise.

You should not use this macro to change options that are not machine-specific. These should uniformly selected by the same optimization level on all supported machines. Use this macro to enable machine-specific optimizations.

Do not examine `write_symbols` in this macro! The debugging options are not supposed to alter the generated code.

CAN_DEBUG_WITHOUT_FP

Define this macro if debugging can be performed even without a frame pointer. If this macro is defined, GNU CC will turn on the '-fomit-frame-pointer' option whenever '-O' is specified.

17.3 Storage Layout

Note that the definitions of the macros in this table which are sizes or alignments measured in bits do not need to be constant. They can be C expressions that refer to static variables, such as the `target_flags`. See Section 17.2 [Run-time Target], page 400.

BITS_BIG_ENDIAN

> Define this macro to have the value 1 if the most significant bit in a byte has the lowest number; otherwise define it to have the value zero. This means that bit-field instructions count from the most significant bit. If the machine has no bit-field instructions, then this must still be defined, but it doesn't matter which value it is defined to. This macro need not be a constant.

> This macro does not affect the way structure fields are packed into bytes or words; that is controlled by `BYTES_BIG_ENDIAN`.

BYTES_BIG_ENDIAN

> Define this macro to have the value 1 if the most significant byte in a word has the lowest number. This macro need not be a constant.

WORDS_BIG_ENDIAN

> Define this macro to have the value 1 if, in a multiword object, the most significant word has the lowest number. This applies to both memory locations and registers; GNU CC fundamentally assumes that the order of words in memory is the same as the order in registers. This macro need not be a constant.

LIBGCC2_WORDS_BIG_ENDIAN

> Define this macro if WORDS_BIG_ENDIAN is not constant. This must be a constant value with the same meaning as WORDS_BIG_ENDIAN, which will be used only when compiling libgcc2.c. Typically the value will be set based on preprocessor defines.

FLOAT_WORDS_BIG_ENDIAN

> Define this macro to have the value 1 if `DFmode`, `XFmode` or `TFmode` floating point numbers are stored in memory with the word containing the sign bit at the lowest address; otherwise define it to have the value 0. This macro need not be a constant.

> You need not define this macro if the ordering is the same as for multi-word integers.

BITS_PER_UNIT

> Define this macro to be the number of bits in an addressable storage unit (byte); normally 8.

BITS_PER_WORD

> Number of bits in a word; normally 32.

MAX_BITS_PER_WORD

Maximum number of bits in a word. If this is undefined, the default is BITS_PER_WORD. Otherwise, it is the constant value that is the largest value that BITS_PER_WORD can have at run-time.

UNITS_PER_WORD

Number of storage units in a word; normally 4.

MIN_UNITS_PER_WORD

Minimum number of units in a word. If this is undefined, the default is UNITS_PER_WORD. Otherwise, it is the constant value that is the smallest value that UNITS_PER_WORD can have at run-time.

POINTER_SIZE

Width of a pointer, in bits. You must specify a value no wider than the width of Pmode. If it is not equal to the width of Pmode, you must define POINTERS_EXTEND_UNSIGNED.

POINTERS_EXTEND_UNSIGNED

A C expression whose value is nonzero if pointers that need to be extended from being POINTER_SIZE bits wide to Pmode are to be zero-extended and zero if they are to be sign-extended.

You need not define this macro if the POINTER_SIZE is equal to the width of Pmode.

PROMOTE_MODE (*m*, *unsignedp*, *type*)

A macro to update *m* and *unsignedp* when an object whose type is *type* and which has the specified mode and signedness is to be stored in a register. This macro is only called when *type* is a scalar type.

On most RISC machines, which only have operations that operate on a full register, define this macro to set *m* to word_mode if *m* is an integer mode narrower than BITS_PER_WORD. In most cases, only integer modes should be widened because wider-precision floating-point operations are usually more expensive than their narrower counterparts.

For most machines, the macro definition does not change *unsignedp*. However, some machines, have instructions that preferentially handle either signed or unsigned quantities of certain modes. For example, on the DEC Alpha, 32-bit loads from memory and 32-bit add instructions sign-extend the result to 64 bits. On such machines, set *unsignedp* according to which kind of extension is more efficient.

Do not define this macro if it would never modify *m*.

PROMOTE_FUNCTION_ARGS

> Define this macro if the promotion described by PROMOTE_MODE should also be done for outgoing function arguments.

PROMOTE_FUNCTION_RETURN

> Define this macro if the promotion described by PROMOTE_MODE should also be done for the return value of functions.
>
> If this macro is defined, FUNCTION_VALUE must perform the same promotions done by PROMOTE_MODE.

PROMOTE_FOR_CALL_ONLY

> Define this macro if the promotion described by PROMOTE_MODE should *only* be performed for outgoing function arguments or function return values, as specified by PROMOTE_FUNCTION_ARGS and PROMOTE_FUNCTION_RETURN, respectively.

PARM_BOUNDARY

> Normal alignment required for function parameters on the stack, in bits. All stack parameters receive at least this much alignment regardless of data type. On most machines, this is the same as the size of an integer.

STACK_BOUNDARY

> Define this macro if there is a guaranteed alignment for the stack pointer on this machine. The definition is a C expression for the desired alignment (measured in bits). This value is used as a default if PREFERRED_STACK_BOUNDARY is not defined.

PREFERRED_STACK_BOUNDARY

> Define this macro if you wish to preserve a certain alignment for the stack pointer. The definition is a C expression for the desired alignment (measured in bits). If STACK_BOUNDARY is also defined, this macro must evaluate to a value equal to or larger than STACK_BOUNDARY.
>
> If PUSH_ROUNDING is not defined, the stack will always be aligned to the specified boundary. If PUSH_ROUNDING is defined and specifies a less strict alignment than PREFERRED_STACK_BOUNDARY, the stack may be momentarily unaligned while pushing arguments.

FUNCTION_BOUNDARY

> Alignment required for a function entry point, in bits.

BIGGEST_ALIGNMENT

> Biggest alignment that any data type can require on this machine, in bits.

MINIMUM_ATOMIC_ALIGNMENT

> If defined, the smallest alignment, in bits, that can be given to an object that can be referenced in one operation, without

disturbing any nearby object. Normally, this is `BITS_PER_UNIT`, but may be larger on machines that don't have byte or half-word store operations.

`BIGGEST_FIELD_ALIGNMENT`

Biggest alignment that any structure field can require on this machine, in bits. If defined, this overrides `BIGGEST_ALIGNMENT` for structure fields only.

`ADJUST_FIELD_ALIGN` (*field*, *computed*)

An expression for the alignment of a structure field *field* if the alignment computed in the usual way is *computed*. GNU CC uses this value instead of the value in `BIGGEST_ALIGNMENT` or `BIGGEST_FIELD_ALIGNMENT`, if defined, for structure fields only.

`MAX_OFILE_ALIGNMENT`

Biggest alignment supported by the object file format of this machine. Use this macro to limit the alignment which can be specified using the `__attribute__` ((aligned (n))) construct. If not defined, the default value is `BIGGEST_ALIGNMENT`.

`DATA_ALIGNMENT` (*type*, *basic-align*)

If defined, a C expression to compute the alignment for a variables in the static store. *type* is the data type, and *basic-align* is the alignment that the object would ordinarily have. The value of this macro is used instead of that alignment to align the object.

If this macro is not defined, then *basic-align* is used.

One use of this macro is to increase alignment of medium-size data to make it all fit in fewer cache lines. Another is to cause character arrays to be word-aligned so that `strcpy` calls that copy constants to character arrays can be done inline.

`CONSTANT_ALIGNMENT` (*constant*, *basic-align*)

If defined, a C expression to compute the alignment given to a constant that is being placed in memory. *constant* is the constant and *basic-align* is the alignment that the object would ordinarily have. The value of this macro is used instead of that alignment to align the object.

If this macro is not defined, then *basic-align* is used.

The typical use of this macro is to increase alignment for string constants to be word aligned so that `strcpy` calls that copy constants can be done inline.

`LOCAL_ALIGNMENT` (*type*, *basic-align*)

If defined, a C expression to compute the alignment for a variables in the local store. *type* is the data type, and *basic-align* is the alignment that the object would ordinarily have. The value of this macro is used instead of that alignment to align the object.

If this macro is not defined, then *basic-align* is used.

One use of this macro is to increase alignment of medium-size data to make it all fit in fewer cache lines.

EMPTY_FIELD_BOUNDARY

Alignment in bits to be given to a structure bit field that follows an empty field such as `int : 0;`.

Note that `PCC_BITFIELD_TYPE_MATTERS` also affects the alignment that results from an empty field.

STRUCTURE_SIZE_BOUNDARY

Number of bits which any structure or union's size must be a multiple of. Each structure or union's size is rounded up to a multiple of this.

If you do not define this macro, the default is the same as `BITS_PER_UNIT`.

STRICT_ALIGNMENT

Define this macro to be the value 1 if instructions will fail to work if given data not on the nominal alignment. If instructions will merely go slower in that case, define this macro as 0.

PCC_BITFIELD_TYPE_MATTERS

Define this if you wish to imitate the way many other C compilers handle alignment of bitfields and the structures that contain them.

The behavior is that the type written for a bitfield (`int`, `short`, or other integer type) imposes an alignment for the entire structure, as if the structure really did contain an ordinary field of that type. In addition, the bitfield is placed within the structure so that it would fit within such a field, not crossing a boundary for it.

Thus, on most machines, a bitfield whose type is written as `int` would not cross a four-byte boundary, and would force four-byte alignment for the whole structure. (The alignment used may not be four bytes; it is controlled by the other alignment parameters.)

If the macro is defined, its definition should be a C expression; a nonzero value for the expression enables this behavior.

Note that if this macro is not defined, or its value is zero, some bitfields may cross more than one alignment boundary. The compiler can support such references if there are 'insv', 'extv', and 'extzv' insns that can directly reference memory.

The other known way of making bitfields work is to define
`STRUCTURE_SIZE_BOUNDARY` as large as `BIGGEST_ALIGNMENT`.
Then every structure can be accessed with fullwords.

Unless the machine has bitfield instructions or you define
`STRUCTURE_SIZE_BOUNDARY` that way, you must define `PCC_`
`BITFIELD_TYPE_MATTERS` to have a nonzero value.

If your aim is to make GNU CC use the same conventions for
laying out bitfields as are used by another compiler, here is how
to investigate what the other compiler does. Compile and run
this program:

```
struct foo1
{
  char x;
  char :0;
  char y;
};

struct foo2
{
  char x;
  int :0;
  char y;
};

main ()
{
  printf ("Size of foo1 is %d\n",
          sizeof (struct foo1));
  printf ("Size of foo2 is %d\n",
          sizeof (struct foo2));
  exit (0);
}
```

If this prints 2 and 5, then the compiler's behavior is what you
would get from `PCC_BITFIELD_TYPE_MATTERS`.

`BITFIELD_NBYTES_LIMITED`

> Like PCC_BITFIELD_TYPE_MATTERS except that its effect
> is limited to aligning a bitfield within the structure.

`ROUND_TYPE_SIZE` (*type, computed, specified*)

> Define this macro as an expression for the overall size of a type
> (given by *type* as a tree node) when the size computed in the
> usual way is *computed* and the alignment is *specified*.

> The default is to round *computed* up to a multiple of *specified*.

`ROUND_TYPE_ALIGN` (*type, computed, specified*)

Define this macro as an expression for the alignment of a type (given by *type* as a tree node) if the alignment computed in the usual way is *computed* and the alignment explicitly specified was *specified*.

The default is to use *specified* if it is larger; otherwise, use the smaller of *computed* and `BIGGEST_ALIGNMENT`

`MAX_FIXED_MODE_SIZE`

An integer expression for the size in bits of the largest integer machine mode that should actually be used. All integer machine modes of this size or smaller can be used for structures and unions with the appropriate sizes. If this macro is undefined, `GET_MODE_BITSIZE` (`DImode`) is assumed.

`STACK_SAVEAREA_MODE` (*save_level*)

If defined, an expression of type **enum machine_mode** that specifies the mode of the save area operand of a `save_stack_`*level* named pattern (see Section 16.7 [Standard Names], page 350). *save_level* is one of `SAVE_BLOCK`, `SAVE_FUNCTION`, or `SAVE_NONLOCAL` and selects which of the three named patterns is having its mode specified.

You need not define this macro if it always returns `Pmode`. You would most commonly define this macro if the `save_stack_`*level* patterns need to support both a 32- and a 64-bit mode.

`STACK_SIZE_MODE`

If defined, an expression of type **enum machine_mode** that specifies the mode of the size increment operand of an `allocate_stack` named pattern (see Section 16.7 [Standard Names], page 350).

You need not define this macro if it always returns `word_mode`. You would most commonly define this macro if the `allocate_stack` pattern needs to support both a 32- and a 64-bit mode.

`CHECK_FLOAT_VALUE` (*mode, value, overflow*)

A C statement to validate the value *value* (of type **double**) for mode *mode*. This means that you check whether *value* fits within the possible range of values for mode *mode* on this target machine. The mode *mode* is always a mode of class `MODE_FLOAT`. *overflow* is nonzero if the value is already known to be out of range.

If *value* is not valid or if *overflow* is nonzero, you should set *overflow* to 1 and then assign some valid value to *value*. Allowing an invalid value to go through the compiler can produce incorrect assembler code which may even cause Unix assemblers to crash.

This macro need not be defined if there is no work for it to do.

TARGET_FLOAT_FORMAT

A code distinguishing the floating point format of the target machine. There are three defined values:

IEEE_FLOAT_FORMAT

This code indicates IEEE floating point. It is the default; there is no need to define this macro when the format is IEEE.

VAX_FLOAT_FORMAT

This code indicates the peculiar format used on the Vax.

UNKNOWN_FLOAT_FORMAT

This code indicates any other format.

The value of this macro is compared with HOST_FLOAT_FORMAT (see Chapter 18 [Config], page 523) to determine whether the target machine has the same format as the host machine. If any other formats are actually in use on supported machines, new codes should be defined for them.

The ordering of the component words of floating point values stored in memory is controlled by FLOAT_WORDS_BIG_ENDIAN for the target machine and HOST_FLOAT_WORDS_BIG_ENDIAN for the host.

DEFAULT_VTABLE_THUNKS

GNU CC supports two ways of implementing C++ vtables: traditional or with so-called "thunks". The flag '-fvtable-thunk' chooses between them. Define this macro to be a C expression for the default value of that flag. If DEFAULT_VTABLE_THUNKS is 0, GNU CC uses the traditional implementation by default. The "thunk" implementation is more efficient (especially if you have provided an implementation of ASM_OUTPUT_MI_THUNK, see Section 17.7.10 [Function Entry], page 446), but is not binary compatible with code compiled using the traditional implementation. If you are writing a new ports, define DEFAULT_VTABLE_THUNKS to 1.

If you do not define this macro, the default for '-fvtable-thunk' is 0.

17.4 Layout of Source Language Data Types

These macros define the sizes and other characteristics of the standard basic data types used in programs being compiled. Unlike the macros in the previous section, these apply to specific features of C and related languages, rather than to fundamental aspects of storage layout.

INT_TYPE_SIZE

A C expression for the size in bits of the type **int** on the target machine. If you don't define this, the default is one word.

MAX_INT_TYPE_SIZE

Maximum number for the size in bits of the type **int** on the target machine. If this is undefined, the default is `INT_TYPE_SIZE`. Otherwise, it is the constant value that is the largest value that `INT_TYPE_SIZE` can have at run-time. This is used in **cpp**.

SHORT_TYPE_SIZE

A C expression for the size in bits of the type **short** on the target machine. If you don't define this, the default is half a word. (If this would be less than one storage unit, it is rounded up to one unit.)

LONG_TYPE_SIZE

A C expression for the size in bits of the type **long** on the target machine. If you don't define this, the default is one word.

MAX_LONG_TYPE_SIZE

Maximum number for the size in bits of the type **long** on the target machine. If this is undefined, the default is `LONG_TYPE_SIZE`. Otherwise, it is the constant value that is the largest value that `LONG_TYPE_SIZE` can have at run-time. This is used in **cpp**.

LONG_LONG_TYPE_SIZE

A C expression for the size in bits of the type **long long** on the target machine. If you don't define this, the default is two words. If you want to support GNU Ada on your machine, the value of macro must be at least 64.

CHAR_TYPE_SIZE

A C expression for the size in bits of the type **char** on the target machine. If you don't define this, the default is one quarter of a word. (If this would be less than one storage unit, it is rounded up to one unit.)

MAX_CHAR_TYPE_SIZE

Maximum number for the size in bits of the type **char** on the target machine. If this is undefined, the default is `CHAR_TYPE_SIZE`. Otherwise, it is the constant value that is the largest value that `CHAR_TYPE_SIZE` can have at run-time. This is used in **cpp**.

FLOAT_TYPE_SIZE

A C expression for the size in bits of the type **float** on the target machine. If you don't define this, the default is one word.

DOUBLE_TYPE_SIZE

A C expression for the size in bits of the type **double** on the target machine. If you don't define this, the default is two words.

LONG_DOUBLE_TYPE_SIZE

> A C expression for the size in bits of the type `long double` on the target machine. If you don't define this, the default is two words.

WIDEST_HARDWARE_FP_SIZE

> A C expression for the size in bits of the widest floating-point format supported by the hardware. If you define this macro, you must specify a value less than or equal to the value of LONG_DOUBLE_TYPE_SIZE. If you do not define this macro, the value of LONG_DOUBLE_TYPE_SIZE is the default.

DEFAULT_SIGNED_CHAR

> An expression whose value is 1 or 0, according to whether the type `char` should be signed or unsigned by default. The user can always override this default with the options '-fsigned-char' and '-funsigned-char'.

DEFAULT_SHORT_ENUMS

> A C expression to determine whether to give an `enum` type only as many bytes as it takes to represent the range of possible values of that type. A nonzero value means to do that; a zero value means all `enum` types should be allocated like `int`.
>
> If you don't define the macro, the default is 0.

SIZE_TYPE

> A C expression for a string describing the name of the data type to use for size values. The typedef name `size_t` is defined using the contents of the string.
>
> The string can contain more than one keyword. If so, separate them with spaces, and write first any length keyword, then `unsigned` if appropriate, and finally `int`. The string must exactly match one of the data type names defined in the function `init_decl_processing` in the file 'c-decl.c'. You may not omit `int` or change the order—that would cause the compiler to crash on startup.
>
> If you don't define this macro, the default is `"long unsigned int"`.

PTRDIFF_TYPE

> A C expression for a string describing the name of the data type to use for the result of subtracting two pointers. The typedef name `ptrdiff_t` is defined using the contents of the string. See SIZE_TYPE above for more information.
>
> If you don't define this macro, the default is `"long int"`.

WCHAR_TYPE

> A C expression for a string describing the name of the data type to use for wide characters. The typedef name `wchar_t` is defined

using the contents of the string. See `SIZE_TYPE` above for more information.

If you don't define this macro, the default is `"int"`.

`WCHAR_TYPE_SIZE`

A C expression for the size in bits of the data type for wide characters. This is used in `cpp`, which cannot make use of `WCHAR_TYPE`.

`MAX_WCHAR_TYPE_SIZE`

Maximum number for the size in bits of the data type for wide characters. If this is undefined, the default is `WCHAR_TYPE_SIZE`. Otherwise, it is the constant value that is the largest value that `WCHAR_TYPE_SIZE` can have at run-time. This is used in `cpp`.

`OBJC_INT_SELECTORS`

Define this macro if the type of Objective C selectors should be `int`.

If this macro is not defined, then selectors should have the type `struct objc_selector *`.

`OBJC_SELECTORS_WITHOUT_LABELS`

Define this macro if the compiler can group all the selectors together into a vector and use just one label at the beginning of the vector. Otherwise, the compiler must give each selector its own assembler label.

On certain machines, it is important to have a separate label for each selector because this enables the linker to eliminate duplicate selectors.

`TARGET_BELL`

A C constant expression for the integer value for escape sequence '`\a`'.

`TARGET_BS`
`TARGET_TAB`
`TARGET_NEWLINE`

C constant expressions for the integer values for escape sequences '`\b`', '`\t`' and '`\n`'.

`TARGET_VT`
`TARGET_FF`
`TARGET_CR`

C constant expressions for the integer values for escape sequences '`\v`', '`\f`' and '`\r`'.

17.5 Register Usage

This section explains how to describe what registers the target machine has, and how (in general) they can be used.

The description of which registers a specific instruction can use is done with register classes; see Section 17.6 [Register Classes], page 420. For information on using registers to access a stack frame, see Section 17.7.3 [Frame Registers], page 432. For passing values in registers, see Section 17.7.6 [Register Arguments], page 438. For returning values in registers, see Section 17.7.7 [Scalar Return], page 442.

17.5.1 Basic Characteristics of Registers

Registers have various characteristics.

FIRST_PSEUDO_REGISTER

>Number of hardware registers known to the compiler. They receive numbers 0 through FIRST_PSEUDO_REGISTER-1; thus, the first pseudo register's number really is assigned the number FIRST_PSEUDO_REGISTER.

FIXED_REGISTERS

>An initializer that says which registers are used for fixed purposes all throughout the compiled code and are therefore not available for general allocation. These would include the stack pointer, the frame pointer (except on machines where that can be used as a general register when no frame pointer is needed), the program counter on machines where that is considered one of the addressable registers, and any other numbered register with a standard use.

>This information is expressed as a sequence of numbers, separated by commas and surrounded by braces. The nth number is 1 if register n is fixed, 0 otherwise.

>The table initialized from this macro, and the table initialized by the following one, may be overridden at run time either automatically, by the actions of the macro CONDITIONAL_REGISTER_USAGE, or by the user with the command options '-ffixed-reg', '-fcall-used-reg' and '-fcall-saved-reg'.

CALL_USED_REGISTERS

>Like FIXED_REGISTERS but has 1 for each register that is clobbered (in general) by function calls as well as for fixed registers. This macro therefore identifies the registers that are not available for general allocation of values that must live across function calls.

>If a register has 0 in CALL_USED_REGISTERS, the compiler automatically saves it on function entry and restores it on function exit, if the register is used within the function.

HARD_REGNO_CALL_PART_CLOBBERED (regno, mode)

>A C expression that is non-zero if it is not permissible to store a value of mode mode in hard register number regno across a call

without some part of it being clobbered. For most machines this macro need not be defined. It is only required for machines that do not preserve the entire contents of a register across a call.

`CONDITIONAL_REGISTER_USAGE`

Zero or more C statements that may conditionally modify four variables `fixed_regs`, `call_used_regs`, `global_regs` (these three are of type `char []`) and `reg_class_contents` (of type `HARD_REG_SET`). Before the macro is called `fixed_regs`, `call_used_regs` and `reg_class_contents` have been initialized from `FIXED_REGISTERS`, `CALL_USED_REGISTERS` and `REG_CLASS_CONTENTS`, respectively, `global_regs` has been cleared, and any '`-ffixed-`*reg*', '`-fcall-used-`*reg*' and '`-fcall-saved-`*reg*' command options have been applied.

This is necessary in case the fixed or call-clobbered registers depend on target flags.

You need not define this macro if it has no work to do.

If the usage of an entire class of registers depends on the target flags, you may indicate this to GCC by using this macro to modify `fixed_regs` and `call_used_regs` to 1 for each of the registers in the classes which should not be used by GCC. Also define the macro `REG_CLASS_FROM_LETTER` to return `NO_REGS` if it is called with a letter for a class that shouldn't be used.

(However, if this class is not included in `GENERAL_REGS` and all of the insn patterns whose constraints permit this class are controlled by target switches, then GCC will automatically avoid using these registers when the target switches are opposed to them.)

`NON_SAVING_SETJMP`

If this macro is defined and has a nonzero value, it means that `setjmp` and related functions fail to save the registers, or that `longjmp` fails to restore them. To compensate, the compiler avoids putting variables in registers in functions that use `setjmp`.

`INCOMING_REGNO` (*out*)

Define this macro if the target machine has register windows. This C expression returns the register number as seen by the called function corresponding to the register number *out* as seen by the calling function. Return *out* if register number *out* is not an outbound register.

`OUTGOING_REGNO` (*in*)

Define this macro if the target machine has register windows. This C expression returns the register number as seen by the calling function corresponding to the register number *in* as seen by the called function. Return *in* if register number *in* is not an inbound register.

17.5.2 Order of Allocation of Registers

Registers are allocated in order.

REG_ALLOC_ORDER

> If defined, an initializer for a vector of integers, containing the numbers of hard registers in the order in which GNU CC should prefer to use them (from most preferred to least).
>
> If this macro is not defined, registers are used lowest numbered first (all else being equal).
>
> One use of this macro is on machines where the highest numbered registers must always be saved and the save-multiple-registers instruction supports only sequences of consecutive registers. On such machines, define REG_ALLOC_ORDER to be an initializer that lists the highest numbered allocable register first.

ORDER_REGS_FOR_LOCAL_ALLOC

> A C statement (sans semicolon) to choose the order in which to allocate hard registers for pseudo-registers local to a basic block.
>
> Store the desired register order in the array reg_alloc_order. Element 0 should be the register to allocate first; element 1, the next register; and so on.
>
> The macro body should not assume anything about the contents of reg_alloc_order before execution of the macro.
>
> On most machines, it is not necessary to define this macro.

17.5.3 How Values Fit in Registers

This section discusses the macros that describe which kinds of values (specifically, which machine modes) each register can hold, and how many consecutive registers are needed for a given mode.

HARD_REGNO_NREGS (regno, mode)

> A C expression for the number of consecutive hard registers, starting at register number regno, required to hold a value of mode mode.
>
> On a machine where all registers are exactly one word, a suitable definition of this macro is

```
#define HARD_REGNO_NREGS(REGNO, MODE)            \
  ((GET_MODE_SIZE (MODE) + UNITS_PER_WORD - 1)  \
   / UNITS_PER_WORD))
```

ALTER_HARD_SUBREG (tgt_mode, word, src_mode, regno)

> A C expression that returns an adjusted hard register number for

> (subreg:*tgt_mode* (reg:*src_mode regno*) *word*)

This may be needed if the target machine has mixed sized big-endian registers, like Sparc v9.

HARD_REGNO_MODE_OK (*regno*, *mode*)

> A C expression that is nonzero if it is permissible to store a value of mode *mode* in hard register number *regno* (or in several registers starting with that one). For a machine where all registers are equivalent, a suitable definition is

```
#define HARD_REGNO_MODE_OK(REGNO, MODE) 1
```

> You need not include code to check for the numbers of fixed registers, because the allocation mechanism considers them to be always occupied.

> On some machines, double-precision values must be kept in even/odd register pairs. You can implement that by defining this macro to reject odd register numbers for such modes.

> The minimum requirement for a mode to be OK in a register is that the 'mov*mode*' instruction pattern support moves between the register and other hard register in the same class and that moving a value into the register and back out not alter it.

> Since the same instruction used to move **word_mode** will work for all narrower integer modes, it is not necessary on any machine for **HARD_REGNO_MODE_OK** to distinguish between these modes, provided you define patterns 'movhi', etc., to take advantage of this. This is useful because of the interaction between **HARD_REGNO_MODE_OK** and **MODES_TIEABLE_P**; it is very desirable for all integer modes to be tieable.

> Many machines have special registers for floating point arithmetic. Often people assume that floating point machine modes are allowed only in floating point registers. This is not true. Any registers that can hold integers can safely *hold* a floating point machine mode, whether or not floating arithmetic can be done on it in those registers. Integer move instructions can be used to move the values.

> On some machines, though, the converse is true: fixed-point machine modes may not go in floating registers. This is true if the floating registers normalize any value stored in them, because storing a non-floating value there would garble it. In this case, **HARD_REGNO_MODE_OK** should reject fixed-point machine modes in floating registers. But if the floating registers do not automatically normalize, if you can store any bit pattern in one and retrieve it unchanged without a trap, then any machine mode may go in a floating register, so you can define this macro to say so.

The primary significance of special floating registers is rather that they are the registers acceptable in floating point arithmetic instructions. However, this is of no concern to `HARD_REGNO_MODE_OK`. You handle it by writing the proper constraints for those instructions.

On some machines, the floating registers are especially slow to access, so that it is better to store a value in a stack frame than in such a register if floating point arithmetic is not being done. As long as the floating registers are not in class `GENERAL_REGS`, they will not be used unless some pattern's constraint asks for one.

`MODES_TIEABLE_P` (*mode1*, *mode2*)

A C expression that is nonzero if a value of mode *mode1* is accessible in mode *mode2* without copying.

If `HARD_REGNO_MODE_OK` (*r*, *mode1*) and `HARD_REGNO_MODE_OK` (*r*, *mode2*) are always the same for any *r*, then `MODES_TIEABLE_P` (*mode1*, *mode2*) should be nonzero. If they differ for any *r*, you should define this macro to return zero unless some other mechanism ensures the accessibility of the value in a narrower mode.

You should define this macro to return nonzero in as many cases as possible since doing so will allow GNU CC to perform better register allocation.

`AVOID_CCMODE_COPIES`

Define this macro if the compiler should avoid copies to/from `CCmode` registers. You should only define this macro if support fo copying to/from `CCmode` is incomplete.

17.5.4 Handling Leaf Functions

On some machines, a leaf function (i.e., one which makes no calls) can run more efficiently if it does not make its own register window. Often this means it is required to receive its arguments in the registers where they are passed by the caller, instead of the registers where they would normally arrive.

The special treatment for leaf functions generally applies only when other conditions are met; for example, often they may use only those registers for its own variables and temporaries. We use the term "leaf function" to mean a function that is suitable for this special handling, so that functions with no calls are not necessarily "leaf functions".

GNU CC assigns register numbers before it knows whether the function is suitable for leaf function treatment. So it needs to renumber the registers in order to output a leaf function. The following macros accomplish this.

LEAF_REGISTERS

A C initializer for a vector, indexed by hard register number, which contains 1 for a register that is allowable in a candidate for leaf function treatment.

If leaf function treatment involves renumbering the registers, then the registers marked here should be the ones before renumbering—those that GNU CC would ordinarily allocate. The registers which will actually be used in the assembler code, after renumbering, should not be marked with 1 in this vector.

Define this macro only if the target machine offers a way to optimize the treatment of leaf functions.

LEAF_REG_REMAP (*regno*)

A C expression whose value is the register number to which *regno* should be renumbered, when a function is treated as a leaf function.

If *regno* is a register number which should not appear in a leaf function before renumbering, then the expression should yield -1, which will cause the compiler to abort.

Define this macro only if the target machine offers a way to optimize the treatment of leaf functions, and registers need to be renumbered to do this.

Normally, `FUNCTION_PROLOGUE` and `FUNCTION_EPILOGUE` must treat leaf functions specially. They can test the C variable `current_function_is_leaf` which is nonzero for leaf functions. `current_function_is_leaf` is set prior to local register allocation and is valid for the remaining compiler passes. They can also test the C variable `current_function_uses_only_leaf_regs` which is nonzero for leaf functions which only use leaf registers. `current_function_uses_only_leaf_regs` is valid after reload and is only useful if `LEAF_REGISTERS` is defined.

17.5.5 Registers That Form a Stack

There are special features to handle computers where some of the "registers" form a stack, as in the 80387 coprocessor for the 80386. Stack registers are normally written by pushing onto the stack, and are numbered relative to the top of the stack.

Currently, GNU CC can only handle one group of stack-like registers, and they must be consecutively numbered.

STACK_REGS

Define this if the machine has any stack-like registers.

FIRST_STACK_REG

The number of the first stack-like register. This one is the top of the stack.

LAST_STACK_REG
> The number of the last stack-like register. This one is the bottom of the stack.

17.5.6 Obsolete Macros for Controlling Register Usage

These features do not work very well. They exist because they used to be required to generate correct code for the 80387 coprocessor of the 80386. They are no longer used by that machine description and may be removed in a later version of the compiler. Don't use them!

OVERLAPPING_REGNO_P (*regno*)
> If defined, this is a C expression whose value is nonzero if hard register number *regno* is an overlapping register. This means a hard register which overlaps a hard register with a different number. (Such overlap is undesirable, but occasionally it allows a machine to be supported which otherwise could not be.) This macro must return nonzero for *all* the registers which overlap each other. GNU CC can use an overlapping register only in certain limited ways. It can be used for allocation within a basic block, and may be spilled for reloading; that is all.
>
> If this macro is not defined, it means that none of the hard registers overlap each other. This is the usual situation.

INSN_CLOBBERS_REGNO_P (*insn, regno*)
> If defined, this is a C expression whose value should be nonzero if the insn *insn* has the effect of mysteriously clobbering the contents of hard register number *regno*. By "mysterious" we mean that the insn's RTL expression doesn't describe such an effect.
>
> If this macro is not defined, it means that no insn clobbers registers mysteriously. This is the usual situation; all else being equal, it is best for the RTL expression to show all the activity.

17.6 Register Classes

On many machines, the numbered registers are not all equivalent. For example, certain registers may not be allowed for indexed addressing; certain registers may not be allowed in some instructions. These machine restrictions are described to the compiler using *register classes*.

You define a number of register classes, giving each one a name and saying which of the registers belong to it. Then you can specify register classes that are allowed as operands to particular instruction patterns.

In general, each register will belong to several classes. In fact, one class must be named ALL_REGS and contain all the registers. Another class must be named NO_REGS and contain no registers. Often the union of two classes will be another class; however, this is not required.

One of the classes must be named GENERAL_REGS. There is nothing terribly special about the name, but the operand constraint letters 'r' and 'g' specify this class. If GENERAL_REGS is the same as ALL_REGS, just define it as a macro which expands to ALL_REGS.

Order the classes so that if class *x* is contained in class *y* then *x* has a lower class number than *y*.

The way classes other than GENERAL_REGS are specified in operand constraints is through machine-dependent operand constraint letters. You can define such letters to correspond to various classes, then use them in operand constraints.

You should define a class for the union of two classes whenever some instruction allows both classes. For example, if an instruction allows either a floating point (coprocessor) register or a general register for a certain operand, you should define a class FLOAT_OR_GENERAL_REGS which includes both of them. Otherwise you will get suboptimal code.

You must also specify certain redundant information about the register classes: for each class, which classes contain it and which ones are contained in it; for each pair of classes, the largest class contained in their union.

When a value occupying several consecutive registers is expected in a certain class, all the registers used must belong to that class. Therefore, register classes cannot be used to enforce a requirement for a register pair to start with an even-numbered register. The way to specify this requirement is with HARD_REGNO_MODE_OK.

Register classes used for input-operands of bitwise-and or shift instructions have a special requirement: each such class must have, for each fixed-point machine mode, a subclass whose registers can transfer that mode to or from memory. For example, on some machines, the operations for single-byte values (QImode) are limited to certain registers. When this is so, each register class that is used in a bitwise-and or shift instruction must have a subclass consisting of registers from which single-byte values can be loaded or stored. This is so that PREFERRED_RELOAD_CLASS can always have a possible value to return.

enum reg_class

An enumeral type that must be defined with all the register class names as enumeral values. NO_REGS must be first. ALL_REGS must be the last register class, followed by one more enumeral value, LIM_REG_CLASSES, which is not a register class but rather tells how many classes there are.

Each register class has a number, which is the value of casting the class name to type int. The number serves as an index in many of the tables described below.

`N_REG_CLASSES`

> The number of distinct register classes, defined as follows:
>
> `#define N_REG_CLASSES (int) LIM_REG_CLASSES`

`REG_CLASS_NAMES`

> An initializer containing the names of the register classes as C string constants. These names are used in writing some of the debugging dumps.

`REG_CLASS_CONTENTS`

> An initializer containing the contents of the register classes, as integers which are bit masks. The nth integer specifies the contents of class n. The way the integer *mask* is interpreted is that register r is in the class if *mask* `& (1 << r)` is 1.
>
> When the machine has more than 32 registers, an integer does not suffice. Then the integers are replaced by sub-initializers, braced groupings containing several integers. Each sub-initializer must be suitable as an initializer for the type `HARD_REG_SET` which is defined in 'hard-reg-set.h'.

`REGNO_REG_CLASS` (*regno*)

> A C expression whose value is a register class containing hard register *regno*. In general there is more than one such class; choose a class which is *minimal*, meaning that no smaller class also contains the register.

`BASE_REG_CLASS`

> A macro whose definition is the name of the class to which a valid base register must belong. A base register is one used in an address which is the register value plus a displacement.

`INDEX_REG_CLASS`

> A macro whose definition is the name of the class to which a valid index register must belong. An index register is one used in an address where its value is either multiplied by a scale factor or added to another register (as well as added to a displacement).

`REG_CLASS_FROM_LETTER` (*char*)

> A C expression which defines the machine-dependent operand constraint letters for register classes. If *char* is such a letter, the value should be the register class corresponding to it. Otherwise, the value should be `NO_REGS`. The register letter 'r', corresponding to class `GENERAL_REGS`, will not be passed to this macro; you do not need to handle it.

`REGNO_OK_FOR_BASE_P` (*num*)

> A C expression which is nonzero if register number *num* is suitable for use as a base register in operand addresses. It may be either a suitable hard register or a pseudo register that has been allocated such a hard register.

REGNO_MODE_OK_FOR_BASE_P (*num*, *mode*)

> A C expression that is just like REGNO_OK_FOR_BASE_P, except that that expression may examine the mode of the memory reference in *mode*. You should define this macro if the mode of the memory reference affects whether a register may be used as a base register. If you define this macro, the compiler will use it instead of REGNO_OK_FOR_BASE_P.

REGNO_OK_FOR_INDEX_P (*num*)

> A C expression which is nonzero if register number *num* is suitable for use as an index register in operand addresses. It may be either a suitable hard register or a pseudo register that has been allocated such a hard register.

> The difference between an index register and a base register is that the index register may be scaled. If an address involves the sum of two registers, neither one of them scaled, then either one may be labeled the "base" and the other the "index"; but whichever labeling is used must fit the machine's constraints of which registers may serve in each capacity. The compiler will try both labelings, looking for one that is valid, and will reload one or both registers only if neither labeling works.

PREFERRED_RELOAD_CLASS (*x*, *class*)

> A C expression that places additional restrictions on the register class to use when it is necessary to copy value *x* into a register in class *class*. The value is a register class; perhaps *class*, or perhaps another, smaller class. On many machines, the following definition is safe:

> #### #define PREFERRED_RELOAD_CLASS(X,CLASS) CLASS

> Sometimes returning a more restrictive class makes better code. For example, on the 68000, when *x* is an integer constant that is in range for a 'moveq' instruction, the value of this macro is always DATA_REGS as long as *class* includes the data registers. Requiring a data register guarantees that a 'moveq' will be used.

> If *x* is a const_double, by returning NO_REGS you can force *x* into a memory constant. This is useful on certain machines where immediate floating values cannot be loaded into certain kinds of registers.

PREFERRED_OUTPUT_RELOAD_CLASS (*x*, *class*)

> Like PREFERRED_RELOAD_CLASS, but for output reloads instead of input reloads. If you don't define this macro, the default is to use *class*, unchanged.

LIMIT_RELOAD_CLASS (*mode*, *class*)

> A C expression that places additional restrictions on the register class to use when it is necessary to be able to hold a value

of mode *mode* in a reload register for which class *class* would ordinarily be used.

Unlike `PREFERRED_RELOAD_CLASS`, this macro should be used when there are certain modes that simply can't go in certain reload classes.

The value is a register class; perhaps *class*, or perhaps another, smaller class.

Don't define this macro unless the target machine has limitations which require the macro to do something nontrivial.

`SECONDARY_RELOAD_CLASS` (*class*, *mode*, *x*)
`SECONDARY_INPUT_RELOAD_CLASS` (*class*, *mode*, *x*)
`SECONDARY_OUTPUT_RELOAD_CLASS` (*class*, *mode*, *x*)

Many machines have some registers that cannot be copied directly to or from memory or even from other types of registers. An example is the 'MQ' register, which on most machines, can only be copied to or from general registers, but not memory. Some machines allow copying all registers to and from memory, but require a scratch register for stores to some memory locations (e.g., those with symbolic address on the RT, and those with certain symbolic address on the Sparc when compiling PIC). In some cases, both an intermediate and a scratch register are required.

You should define these macros to indicate to the reload phase that it may need to allocate at least one register for a reload in addition to the register to contain the data. Specifically, if copying *x* to a register *class* in *mode* requires an intermediate register, you should define `SECONDARY_INPUT_RELOAD_CLASS` to return the largest register class all of whose registers can be used as intermediate registers or scratch registers.

If copying a register *class* in *mode* to *x* requires an intermediate or scratch register, `SECONDARY_OUTPUT_RELOAD_CLASS` should be defined to return the largest register class required. If the requirements for input and output reloads are the same, the macro `SECONDARY_RELOAD_CLASS` should be used instead of defining both macros identically.

The values returned by these macros are often `GENERAL_REGS`. Return `NO_REGS` if no spare register is needed; i.e., if *x* can be directly copied to or from a register of *class* in *mode* without requiring a scratch register. Do not define this macro if it would always return `NO_REGS`.

If a scratch register is required (either with or without an intermediate register), you should define patterns for '`reload_in`*m*' or '`reload_out`*m*', as required (see Section 16.7 [Standard Names], page 350. These patterns, which will normally be implemented with a **define_expand**, should be similar to the 'mov$m$' patterns, except that operand 2 is the scratch register.

Define constraints for the reload register and scratch register that contain a single register class. If the original reload register (whose class is *class*) can meet the constraint given in the pattern, the value returned by these macros is used for the class of the scratch register. Otherwise, two additional reload registers are required. Their classes are obtained from the constraints in the insn pattern.

x might be a pseudo-register or a **subreg** of a pseudo-register, which could either be in a hard register or in memory. Use **true_regnum** to find out; it will return -1 if the pseudo is in memory and the hard register number if it is in a register.

These macros should not be used in the case where a particular class of registers can only be copied to memory and not to another class of registers. In that case, secondary reload registers are not needed and would not be helpful. Instead, a stack location must be used to perform the copy and the mov$m$ pattern should use memory as a intermediate storage. This case often occurs between floating-point and general registers.

SECONDARY_MEMORY_NEEDED (*class1*, *class2*, *m*)

Certain machines have the property that some registers cannot be copied to some other registers without using memory. Define this macro on those machines to be a C expression that is nonzero if objects of mode m in registers of *class1* can only be copied to registers of class *class2* by storing a register of *class1* into memory and loading that memory location into a register of *class2*.

Do not define this macro if its value would always be zero.

SECONDARY_MEMORY_NEEDED_RTX (*mode*)

Normally when **SECONDARY_MEMORY_NEEDED** is defined, the compiler allocates a stack slot for a memory location needed for register copies. If this macro is defined, the compiler instead uses the memory location defined by this macro.

Do not define this macro if you do not define **SECONDARY_MEMORY_NEEDED**.

SECONDARY_MEMORY_NEEDED_MODE (*mode*)

When the compiler needs a secondary memory location to copy between two registers of mode *mode*, it normally allocates sufficient memory to hold a quantity of **BITS_PER_WORD** bits and performs the store and load operations in a mode that many bits wide and whose class is the same as that of *mode*.

This is right thing to do on most machines because it ensures that all bits of the register are copied and prevents accesses to the registers in a narrower mode, which some machines prohibit for floating-point registers.

However, this default behavior is not correct on some machines, such as the DEC Alpha, that store short integers in floating-point registers differently than in integer registers. On those machines, the default widening will not work correctly and you must define this macro to suppress that widening in some cases. See the file 'alpha.h' for details.

Do not define this macro if you do not define SECONDARY_MEMORY_NEEDED or if widening *mode* to a mode that is BITS_PER_WORD bits wide is correct for your machine.

SMALL_REGISTER_CLASSES

On some machines, it is risky to let hard registers live across arbitrary insns. Typically, these machines have instructions that require values to be in specific registers (like an accumulator), and reload will fail if the required hard register is used for another purpose across such an insn.

Define SMALL_REGISTER_CLASSES to be an expression with a non-zero value on these machines. When this macro has a non-zero value, the compiler will try to minimize the lifetime of hard registers.

It is always safe to define this macro with a non-zero value, but if you unnecessarily define it, you will reduce the amount of optimizations that can be performed in some cases. If you do not define this macro with a non-zero value when it is required, the compiler will run out of spill registers and print a fatal error message. For most machines, you should not define this macro at all.

CLASS_LIKELY_SPILLED_P (*class*)

A C expression whose value is nonzero if pseudos that have been assigned to registers of class *class* would likely be spilled because registers of *class* are needed for spill registers.

The default value of this macro returns 1 if *class* has exactly one register and zero otherwise. On most machines, this default should be used. Only define this macro to some other expression if pseudos allocated by 'local-alloc.c' end up in memory because their hard registers were needed for spill registers. If this macro returns nonzero for those classes, those pseudos will only be allocated by 'global.c', which knows how to reallocate the pseudo to another register. If there would not be another register available for reallocation, you should not change the definition of this macro since the only effect of such a definition would be to slow down register allocation.

CLASS_MAX_NREGS (*class*, *mode*)

> A C expression for the maximum number of consecutive registers of class *class* needed to hold a value of mode *mode*.

> This is closely related to the macro HARD_REGNO_NREGS. In fact, the value of the macro CLASS_MAX_NREGS (*class*, *mode*) should be the maximum value of HARD_REGNO_NREGS (*regno*, *mode*) for all *regno* values in the class *class*.

> This macro helps control the handling of multiple-word values in the reload pass.

CLASS_CANNOT_CHANGE_SIZE

> If defined, a C expression for a class that contains registers which the compiler must always access in a mode that is the same size as the mode in which it loaded the register.

> For the example, loading 32-bit integer or floating-point objects into floating-point registers on the Alpha extends them to 64-bits. Therefore loading a 64-bit object and then storing it as a 32-bit object does not store the low-order 32-bits, as would be the case for a normal register. Therefore, 'alpha.h' defines this macro as FLOAT_REGS.

Three other special macros describe which operands fit which constraint letters.

CONST_OK_FOR_LETTER_P (*value*, *c*)

> A C expression that defines the machine-dependent operand constraint letters ('I', 'J', 'K', ... 'P') that specify particular ranges of integer values. If *c* is one of those letters, the expression should check that *value*, an integer, is in the appropriate range and return 1 if so, 0 otherwise. If *c* is not one of those letters, the value should be 0 regardless of *value*.

CONST_DOUBLE_OK_FOR_LETTER_P (*value*, *c*)

> A C expression that defines the machine-dependent operand constraint letters that specify particular ranges of const_double values ('G' or 'H').

> If *c* is one of those letters, the expression should check that *value*, an RTX of code const_double, is in the appropriate range and return 1 if so, 0 otherwise. If *c* is not one of those letters, the value should be 0 regardless of *value*.

> const_double is used for all floating-point constants and for DImode fixed-point constants. A given letter can accept either or both kinds of values. It can use GET_MODE to distinguish between these kinds.

EXTRA_CONSTRAINT (*value*, *c*)

> A C expression that defines the optional machine-dependent constraint letters ('Q', 'R', 'S', 'T', 'U') that can be used to segregate

specific types of operands, usually memory references, for the target machine. Normally this macro will not be defined. If it is required for a particular target machine, it should return 1 if *value* corresponds to the operand type represented by the constraint letter *c*. If *c* is not defined as an extra constraint, the value returned should be 0 regardless of *value*.

For example, on the ROMP, load instructions cannot have their output in r0 if the memory reference contains a symbolic address. Constraint letter '`Q`' is defined as representing a memory address that does *not* contain a symbolic address. An alternative is specified with a '`Q`' constraint on the input and '`r`' on the output. The next alternative specifies '`m`' on the input and a register class that does not include r0 on the output.

17.7 Stack Layout and Calling Conventions

This describes the stack layout and calling conventions.

17.7.1 Basic Stack Layout

Here is the basic stack layout.

STACK_GROWS_DOWNWARD

> Define this macro if pushing a word onto the stack moves the stack pointer to a smaller address.
>
> When we say, "define this macro if ...," it means that the compiler checks this macro only with `#ifdef` so the precise definition used does not matter.

FRAME_GROWS_DOWNWARD

> Define this macro if the addresses of local variable slots are at negative offsets from the frame pointer.

ARGS_GROW_DOWNWARD

> Define this macro if successive arguments to a function occupy decreasing addresses on the stack.

STARTING_FRAME_OFFSET

> Offset from the frame pointer to the first local variable slot to be allocated.
>
> If FRAME_GROWS_DOWNWARD, find the next slot's offset by subtracting the first slot's length from STARTING_FRAME_OFFSET. Otherwise, it is found by adding the length of the first slot to the value STARTING_FRAME_OFFSET.

STACK_POINTER_OFFSET

> Offset from the stack pointer register to the first location at which outgoing arguments are placed. If not specified, the de-

fault value of zero is used. This is the proper value for most machines.

If `ARGS_GROW_DOWNWARD`, this is the offset to the location above the first location at which outgoing arguments are placed.

`FIRST_PARM_OFFSET` (*fundecl*)

Offset from the argument pointer register to the first argument's address. On some machines it may depend on the data type of the function.

If `ARGS_GROW_DOWNWARD`, this is the offset to the location above the first argument's address.

`STACK_DYNAMIC_OFFSET` (*fundecl*)

Offset from the stack pointer register to an item dynamically allocated on the stack, e.g., by `alloca`.

The default value for this macro is `STACK_POINTER_OFFSET` plus the length of the outgoing arguments. The default is correct for most machines. See 'function.c' for details.

`DYNAMIC_CHAIN_ADDRESS` (*frameaddr*)

A C expression whose value is RTL representing the address in a stack frame where the pointer to the caller's frame is stored. Assume that *frameaddr* is an RTL expression for the address of the stack frame itself.

If you don't define this macro, the default is to return the value of *frameaddr*—that is, the stack frame address is also the address of the stack word that points to the previous frame.

`SETUP_FRAME_ADDRESSES`

If defined, a C expression that produces the machine-specific code to setup the stack so that arbitrary frames can be accessed. For example, on the Sparc, we must flush all of the register windows to the stack before we can access arbitrary stack frames. You will seldom need to define this macro.

`BUILTIN_SETJMP_FRAME_VALUE`

If defined, a C expression that contains an rtx that is used to store the address of the current frame into the built in `setjmp` buffer. The default value, `virtual_stack_vars_rtx`, is correct for most machines. One reason you may need to define this macro is if `hard_frame_pointer_rtx` is the appropriate value on your machine.

`RETURN_ADDR_RTX` (*count, frameaddr*)

A C expression whose value is RTL representing the value of the return address for the frame *count* steps up from the current frame, after the prologue. *frameaddr* is the frame pointer of the *count* frame, or the frame pointer of the *count* − 1 frame if `RETURN_ADDR_IN_PREVIOUS_FRAME` is defined.

The value of the expression must always be the correct address when *count* is zero, but may be `NULL_RTX` if there is not way to determine the return address of other frames.

`RETURN_ADDR_IN_PREVIOUS_FRAME`

Define this if the return address of a particular stack frame is accessed from the frame pointer of the previous stack frame.

`INCOMING_RETURN_ADDR_RTX`

A C expression whose value is RTL representing the location of the incoming return address at the beginning of any function, before the prologue. This RTL is either a `REG`, indicating that the return value is saved in 'REG', or a `MEM` representing a location in the stack.

You only need to define this macro if you want to support call frame debugging information like that provided by DWARF 2.

`INCOMING_FRAME_SP_OFFSET`

A C expression whose value is an integer giving the offset, in bytes, from the value of the stack pointer register to the top of the stack frame at the beginning of any function, before the prologue. The top of the frame is defined to be the value of the stack pointer in the previous frame, just before the call instruction.

You only need to define this macro if you want to support call frame debugging information like that provided by DWARF 2.

`ARG_POINTER_CFA_OFFSET`

A C expression whose value is an integer giving the offset, in bytes, from the argument pointer to the canonical frame address (cfa). The final value should coincide with that calculated by `INCOMING_FRAME_SP_OFFSET`. Which is unfortunately not usable during virtual register instantiation.

You only need to define this macro if you want to support call frame debugging information like that provided by DWARF 2.

17.7.2 Specifying How Stack Checking is Done

GNU CC will check that stack references are within the boundaries of the stack, if the '-fstack-check' is specified, in one of three ways:

1. If the value of the `STACK_CHECK_BUILTIN` macro is nonzero, GNU CC will assume that you have arranged for stack checking to be done at appropriate places in the configuration files, e.g., in `FUNCTION_PROLOGUE`. GNU CC will do not other special processing.

2. If `STACK_CHECK_BUILTIN` is zero and you defined a named pattern called `check_stack` in your 'md' file, GNU CC will call that pattern with one argument which is the address to compare the stack value against. You must arrange for this pattern to report an error if the stack pointer is out of range.

3. If neither of the above are true, GNU CC will generate code to period-
ically "probe" the stack pointer using the values of the macros defined
below.

Normally, you will use the default values of these macros, so GNU CC
will use the third approach.

STACK_CHECK_BUILTIN

> A nonzero value if stack checking is done by the configuration
> files in a machine-dependent manner. You should define this
> macro if stack checking is require by the ABI of your machine or
> if you would like to have to stack checking in some more efficient
> way than GNU CC's portable approach. The default value of
> this macro is zero.

STACK_CHECK_PROBE_INTERVAL

> An integer representing the interval at which GNU CC must
> generate stack probe instructions. You will normally define this
> macro to be no larger than the size of the "guard pages" at the
> end of a stack area. The default value of 4096 is suitable for
> most systems.

STACK_CHECK_PROBE_LOAD

> A integer which is nonzero if GNU CC should perform the stack
> probe as a load instruction and zero if GNU CC should use a
> store instruction. The default is zero, which is the most efficient
> choice on most systems.

STACK_CHECK_PROTECT

> The number of bytes of stack needed to recover from a stack
> overflow, for languages where such a recovery is supported. The
> default value of 75 words should be adequate for most machines.

STACK_CHECK_MAX_FRAME_SIZE

> The maximum size of a stack frame, in bytes. GNU CC will
> generate probe instructions in non-leaf functions to ensure at
> least this many bytes of stack are available. If a stack frame
> is larger than this size, stack checking will not be reliable and
> GNU CC will issue a warning. The default is chosen so that
> GNU CC only generates one instruction on most systems. You
> should normally not change the default value of this macro.

STACK_CHECK_FIXED_FRAME_SIZE

> GNU CC uses this value to generate the above warning message.
> It represents the amount of fixed frame used by a function, not
> including space for any callee-saved registers, temporaries and
> user variables. You need only specify an upper bound for this
> amount and will normally use the default of four words.

STACK_CHECK_MAX_VAR_SIZE

The maximum size, in bytes, of an object that GNU CC will place in the fixed area of the stack frame when the user specifies '-fstack-check'. GNU CC computed the default from the values of the above macros and you will normally not need to override that default.

17.7.3 Registers That Address the Stack Frame

This discusses registers that address the stack frame.

STACK_POINTER_REGNUM

The register number of the stack pointer register, which must also be a fixed register according to FIXED_REGISTERS. On most machines, the hardware determines which register this is.

FRAME_POINTER_REGNUM

The register number of the frame pointer register, which is used to access automatic variables in the stack frame. On some machines, the hardware determines which register this is. On other machines, you can choose any register you wish for this purpose.

HARD_FRAME_POINTER_REGNUM

On some machines the offset between the frame pointer and starting offset of the automatic variables is not known until after register allocation has been done (for example, because the saved registers are between these two locations). On those machines, define FRAME_POINTER_REGNUM the number of a special, fixed register to be used internally until the offset is known, and define HARD_FRAME_POINTER_REGNUM to be the actual hard register number used for the frame pointer.

You should define this macro only in the very rare circumstances when it is not possible to calculate the offset between the frame pointer and the automatic variables until after register allocation has been completed. When this macro is defined, you must also indicate in your definition of ELIMINABLE_REGS how to eliminate FRAME_POINTER_REGNUM into either HARD_FRAME_POINTER_REGNUM or STACK_POINTER_REGNUM.

Do not define this macro if it would be the same as FRAME_POINTER_REGNUM.

ARG_POINTER_REGNUM

The register number of the arg pointer register, which is used to access the function's argument list. On some machines, this is the same as the frame pointer register. On some machines, the hardware determines which register this is. On other machines, you can choose any register you wish for this purpose. If this is not the same register as the frame pointer register, then you must mark it as a fixed register according to `FIXED_REGISTERS`, or arrange to be able to eliminate it (see Section 17.7.4 [Elimination], page 433).

`RETURN_ADDRESS_POINTER_REGNUM`

> The register number of the return address pointer register, which is used to access the current function's return address from the stack. On some machines, the return address is not at a fixed offset from the frame pointer or stack pointer or argument pointer. This register can be defined to point to the return address on the stack, and then be converted by `ELIMINABLE_REGS` into either the frame pointer or stack pointer.
>
> Do not define this macro unless there is no other way to get the return address from the stack.

`STATIC_CHAIN_REGNUM`
`STATIC_CHAIN_INCOMING_REGNUM`

> Register numbers used for passing a function's static chain pointer. If register windows are used, the register number as seen by the called function is `STATIC_CHAIN_INCOMING_REGNUM`, while the register number as seen by the calling function is `STATIC_CHAIN_REGNUM`. If these registers are the same, `STATIC_CHAIN_INCOMING_REGNUM` need not be defined.
>
> The static chain register need not be a fixed register.
>
> If the static chain is passed in memory, these macros should not be defined; instead, the next two macros should be defined.

`STATIC_CHAIN`
`STATIC_CHAIN_INCOMING`

> If the static chain is passed in memory, these macros provide rtx giving `mem` expressions that denote where they are stored. `STATIC_CHAIN` and `STATIC_CHAIN_INCOMING` give the locations as seen by the calling and called functions, respectively. Often the former will be at an offset from the stack pointer and the latter at an offset from the frame pointer.
>
> The variables `stack_pointer_rtx`, `frame_pointer_rtx`, and `arg_pointer_rtx` will have been initialized prior to the use of these macros and should be used to refer to those items.
>
> If the static chain is passed in a register, the two previous macros should be defined instead.

17.7.4 Eliminating Frame Pointer and Arg Pointer

This is about eliminating the frame pointer and arg pointer.

FRAME_POINTER_REQUIRED

A C expression which is nonzero if a function must have and use a frame pointer. This expression is evaluated in the reload pass. If its value is nonzero the function will have a frame pointer.

The expression can in principle examine the current function and decide according to the facts, but on most machines the constant 0 or the constant 1 suffices. Use 0 when the machine allows code to be generated with no frame pointer, and doing so saves some time or space. Use 1 when there is no possible advantage to avoiding a frame pointer.

In certain cases, the compiler does not know how to produce valid code without a frame pointer. The compiler recognizes those cases and automatically gives the function a frame pointer regardless of what **FRAME_POINTER_REQUIRED** says. You don't need to worry about them.

In a function that does not require a frame pointer, the frame pointer register can be allocated for ordinary usage, unless you mark it as a fixed register. See **FIXED_REGISTERS** for more information.

INITIAL_FRAME_POINTER_OFFSET (*depth-var*)

A C statement to store in the variable *depth-var* the difference between the frame pointer and the stack pointer values immediately after the function prologue. The value would be computed from information such as the result of **get_frame_size** () and the tables of registers **regs_ever_live** and **call_used_regs**.

If **ELIMINABLE_REGS** is defined, this macro will be not be used and need not be defined. Otherwise, it must be defined even if **FRAME_POINTER_REQUIRED** is defined to always be true; in that case, you may set *depth-var* to anything.

ELIMINABLE_REGS

If defined, this macro specifies a table of register pairs used to eliminate unneeded registers that point into the stack frame. If it is not defined, the only elimination attempted by the compiler is to replace references to the frame pointer with references to the stack pointer.

The definition of this macro is a list of structure initializations, each of which specifies an original and replacement register.

On some machines, the position of the argument pointer is not known until the compilation is completed. In such a case, a separate hard register must be used for the argument pointer. This register can be eliminated by replacing it with either the frame pointer or the argument pointer, depending on whether or not the frame pointer has been eliminated.

In this case, you might specify:

```
#define ELIMINABLE_REGS  \
{{ARG_POINTER_REGNUM, STACK_POINTER_REGNUM}, \
 {ARG_POINTER_REGNUM, FRAME_POINTER_REGNUM}, \
 {FRAME_POINTER_REGNUM, STACK_POINTER_REGNUM}}
```

Note that the elimination of the argument pointer with the stack pointer is specified first since that is the preferred elimination.

CAN_ELIMINATE (*from-reg*, *to-reg*)

A C expression that returns non-zero if the compiler is allowed to try to replace register number *from-reg* with register number *to-reg*. This macro need only be defined if `ELIMINABLE_REGS` is defined, and will usually be the constant 1, since most of the cases preventing register elimination are things that the compiler already knows about.

INITIAL_ELIMINATION_OFFSET (*from-reg*, *to-reg*, *offset-var*)

This macro is similar to `INITIAL_FRAME_POINTER_OFFSET`. It specifies the initial difference between the specified pair of registers. This macro must be defined if `ELIMINABLE_REGS` is defined.

LONGJMP_RESTORE_FROM_STACK

Define this macro if the `longjmp` function restores registers from the stack frames, rather than from those saved specifically by `setjmp`. Certain quantities must not be kept in registers across a call to `setjmp` on such machines.

17.7.5 Passing Function Arguments on the Stack

The macros in this section control how arguments are passed on the stack. See the following section for other macros that control passing certain arguments in registers.

PROMOTE_PROTOTYPES

Define this macro if an argument declared in a prototype as an integral type smaller than `int` should actually be passed as an `int`. In addition to avoiding errors in certain cases of mismatch, it also makes for better code on certain machines.

PUSH_ROUNDING (*npushed*)

A C expression that is the number of bytes actually pushed onto the stack when an instruction attempts to push *npushed* bytes.

If the target machine does not have a push instruction, do not define this macro. That directs GNU CC to use an alternate strategy: to allocate the entire argument block and then store the arguments into it.

On some machines, the definition

```
#define PUSH_ROUNDING(BYTES) (BYTES)
```

will suffice. But on other machines, instructions that appear to push one byte actually push two bytes in an attempt to maintain alignment. Then the definition should be

```
#define PUSH_ROUNDING(BYTES) (((BYTES) + 1) & ~1)
```

ACCUMULATE_OUTGOING_ARGS

If defined, the maximum amount of space required for outgoing arguments will be computed and placed into the variable `current_function_outgoing_args_size`. No space will be pushed onto the stack for each call; instead, the function prologue should increase the stack frame size by this amount.

Defining both `PUSH_ROUNDING` and `ACCUMULATE_OUTGOING_ARGS` is not proper.

REG_PARM_STACK_SPACE (*fndecl*)

Define this macro if functions should assume that stack space has been allocated for arguments even when their values are passed in registers.

The value of this macro is the size, in bytes, of the area reserved for arguments passed in registers for the function represented by *fndecl*, which can be zero if GNU CC is calling a library function.

This space can be allocated by the caller, or be a part of the machine-dependent stack frame: `OUTGOING_REG_PARM_STACK_SPACE` says which.

MAYBE_REG_PARM_STACK_SPACE
FINAL_REG_PARM_STACK_SPACE (*const_size, var_size*)

Define these macros in addition to the one above if functions might allocate stack space for arguments even when their values are passed in registers. These should be used when the stack space allocated for arguments in registers is not a simple constant independent of the function declaration.

The value of the first macro is the size, in bytes, of the area that we should initially assume would be reserved for arguments passed in registers.

The value of the second macro is the actual size, in bytes, of the area that will be reserved for arguments passed in registers. This takes two arguments: an integer representing the number of bytes of fixed sized arguments on the stack, and a tree representing the number of bytes of variable sized arguments on the stack.

When these macros are defined, `REG_PARM_STACK_SPACE` will only be called for libcall functions, the current function, or for a function being called when it is known that such stack space must be allocated. In each case this value can be easily computed.

When deciding whether a called function needs such stack space, and how much space to reserve, GNU CC uses these two macros instead of REG_PARM_STACK_SPACE.

OUTGOING_REG_PARM_STACK_SPACE
Define this if it is the responsibility of the caller to allocate the area reserved for arguments passed in registers.

If ACCUMULATE_OUTGOING_ARGS is defined, this macro controls whether the space for these arguments counts in the value of current_function_outgoing_args_size.

STACK_PARMS_IN_REG_PARM_AREA
Define this macro if REG_PARM_STACK_SPACE is defined, but the stack parameters don't skip the area specified by it.

Normally, when a parameter is not passed in registers, it is placed on the stack beyond the REG_PARM_STACK_SPACE area. Defining this macro suppresses this behavior and causes the parameter to be passed on the stack in its natural location.

RETURN_POPS_ARGS (*fundecl*, *funtype*, *stack-size*)
A C expression that should indicate the number of bytes of its own arguments that a function pops on returning, or 0 if the function pops no arguments and the caller must therefore pop them all after the function returns.

fundecl is a C variable whose value is a tree node that describes the function in question. Normally it is a node of type FUNCTION_DECL that describes the declaration of the function. From this you can obtain the DECL_MACHINE_ATTRIBUTES of the function.

funtype is a C variable whose value is a tree node that describes the function in question. Normally it is a node of type FUNCTION_TYPE that describes the data type of the function. From this it is possible to obtain the data types of the value and arguments (if known).

When a call to a library function is being considered, *fundecl* will contain an identifier node for the library function. Thus, if you need to distinguish among various library functions, you can do so by their names. Note that "library function" in this context means a function used to perform arithmetic, whose name is known specially in the compiler and was not mentioned in the C code being compiled.

stack-size is the number of bytes of arguments passed on the stack. If a variable number of bytes is passed, it is zero, and argument popping will always be the responsibility of the calling function.

On the Vax, all functions always pop their arguments, so the definition of this macro is *stack-size*. On the 68000, using the standard calling convention, no functions pop their arguments, so the value of the macro is always 0 in this case. But an alternative calling convention is available in which functions that take a fixed number of arguments pop them but other functions (such as `printf`) pop nothing (the caller pops all). When this convention is in use, *funtype* is examined to determine whether a function takes a fixed number of arguments.

17.7.6 Passing Arguments in Registers

This section describes the macros which let you control how various types of arguments are passed in registers or how they are arranged in the stack.

FUNCTION_ARG (*cum, mode, type, named*)

A C expression that controls whether a function argument is passed in a register, and which register.

The arguments are *cum*, which summarizes all the previous arguments; *mode*, the machine mode of the argument; *type*, the data type of the argument as a tree node or 0 if that is not known (which happens for C support library functions); and *named*, which is 1 for an ordinary argument and 0 for nameless arguments that correspond to '...' in the called function's prototype.

The value of the expression is usually either a `reg` RTX for the hard register in which to pass the argument, or zero to pass the argument on the stack.

For machines like the Vax and 68000, where normally all arguments are pushed, zero suffices as a definition.

The value of the expression can also be a `parallel` RTX. This is used when an argument is passed in multiple locations. The mode of the of the `parallel` should be the mode of the entire argument. The `parallel` holds any number of `expr_list` pairs; each one describes where part of the argument is passed. In each `expr_list` the first operand must be a `reg` RTX for the hard register in which to pass this part of the argument, and the mode of the register RTX indicates how large this part of the argument is. The second operand of the `expr_list` is a `const_int` which gives the offset in bytes into the entire argument of where this part starts. As a special exception the first `expr_list` in the `parallel` RTX may have a first operand of zero. This indicates that the bytes starting from the second operand of that `expr_list` are stored on the stack and not held in a register.

The usual way to make the ANSI library 'stdarg.h' work on a machine where some arguments are usually passed in registers, is to cause nameless arguments to be passed on the stack instead. This is done by making `FUNCTION_ARG` return 0 whenever *named* is 0.

You may use the macro `MUST_PASS_IN_STACK` (*mode, type*) in the definition of this macro to determine if this argument is of a type that must be passed in the stack. If `REG_PARM_STACK_SPACE` is not defined and `FUNCTION_ARG` returns non-zero for such an argument, the compiler will abort. If `REG_PARM_STACK_SPACE` is defined, the argument will be computed in the stack and then loaded into a register.

`MUST_PASS_IN_STACK` (*mode, type*)

Define as a C expression that evaluates to nonzero if we do not know how to pass TYPE solely in registers. The file 'expr.h' defines a definition that is usually appropriate, refer to 'expr.h' for additional documentation.

`FUNCTION_INCOMING_ARG` (*cum, mode, type, named*)

Define this macro if the target machine has "register windows", so that the register in which a function sees an arguments is not necessarily the same as the one in which the caller passed the argument.

For such machines, `FUNCTION_ARG` computes the register in which the caller passes the value, and `FUNCTION_INCOMING_ARG` should be defined in a similar fashion to tell the function being called where the arguments will arrive.

If `FUNCTION_INCOMING_ARG` is not defined, `FUNCTION_ARG` serves both purposes.

`FUNCTION_ARG_PARTIAL_NREGS` (*cum, mode, type, named*)

A C expression for the number of words, at the beginning of an argument, must be put in registers. The value must be zero for arguments that are passed entirely in registers or that are entirely pushed on the stack.

On some machines, certain arguments must be passed partially in registers and partially in memory. On these machines, typically the first *n* words of arguments are passed in registers, and the rest on the stack. If a multi-word argument (a **double** or a structure) crosses that boundary, its first few words must be passed in registers and the rest must be pushed. This macro tells the compiler when this occurs, and how many of the words should go in registers.

`FUNCTION_ARG` for these arguments should return the first register to be used by the caller for this argument; likewise `FUNCTION_INCOMING_ARG`, for the called function.

FUNCTION_ARG_PASS_BY_REFERENCE (*cum*, *mode*, *type*, *named*)

A C expression that indicates when an argument must be passed by reference. If nonzero for an argument, a copy of that argument is made in memory and a pointer to the argument is passed instead of the argument itself. The pointer is passed in whatever way is appropriate for passing a pointer to that type.

On machines where **REG_PARM_STACK_SPACE** is not defined, a suitable definition of this macro might be

```
#define FUNCTION_ARG_PASS_BY_REFERENCE\
(CUM, MODE, TYPE, NAMED)  \
  MUST_PASS_IN_STACK (MODE, TYPE)
```

FUNCTION_ARG_CALLEE_COPIES (*cum*, *mode*, *type*, *named*)

If defined, a C expression that indicates when it is the called function's responsibility to make a copy of arguments passed by invisible reference. Normally, the caller makes a copy and passes the address of the copy to the routine being called. When FUNCTION_ARG_CALLEE_COPIES is defined and is nonzero, the caller does not make a copy. Instead, it passes a pointer to the "live" value. The called function must not modify this value. If it can be determined that the value won't be modified, it need not make a copy; otherwise a copy must be made.

CUMULATIVE_ARGS

A C type for declaring a variable that is used as the first argument of **FUNCTION_ARG** and other related values. For some target machines, the type **int** suffices and can hold the number of bytes of argument so far.

There is no need to record in **CUMULATIVE_ARGS** anything about the arguments that have been passed on the stack. The compiler has other variables to keep track of that. For target machines on which all arguments are passed on the stack, there is no need to store anything in **CUMULATIVE_ARGS**; however, the data structure must exist and should not be empty, so use **int**.

INIT_CUMULATIVE_ARGS (*cum*, *fntype*, *libname*, *indirect*)

A C statement (sans semicolon) for initializing the variable *cum* for the state at the beginning of the argument list. The variable has type **CUMULATIVE_ARGS**. The value of *fntype* is the tree node for the data type of the function which will receive the args, or 0 if the args are to a compiler support library function. The value of *indirect* is nonzero when processing an indirect call, for example a call through a function pointer. The value of *indirect* is zero for a call to an explicitly named function, a library function call, or when **INIT_CUMULATIVE_ARGS** is used to find arguments for the function being compiled.

When processing a call to a compiler support library function, *libname* identifies which one. It is a `symbol_ref` rtx which contains the name of the function, as a string. *libname* is 0 when an ordinary C function call is being processed. Thus, each time this macro is called, either *libname* or *fntype* is nonzero, but never both of them at once.

`INIT_CUMULATIVE_INCOMING_ARGS` (*cum, fntype, libname*)

Like `INIT_CUMULATIVE_ARGS` but overrides it for the purposes of finding the arguments for the function being compiled. If this macro is undefined, `INIT_CUMULATIVE_ARGS` is used instead.

The value passed for *libname* is always 0, since library routines with special calling conventions are never compiled with GNU CC. The argument *libname* exists for symmetry with `INIT_CUMULATIVE_ARGS`.

`FUNCTION_ARG_ADVANCE` (*cum, mode, type, named*)

A C statement (sans semicolon) to update the summarizer variable *cum* to advance past an argument in the argument list. The values *mode, type* and *named* describe that argument. Once this is done, the variable *cum* is suitable for analyzing the *following* argument with `FUNCTION_ARG`, etc.

This macro need not do anything if the argument in question was passed on the stack. The compiler knows how to track the amount of stack space used for arguments without any special help.

`FUNCTION_ARG_PADDING` (*mode, type*)

If defined, a C expression which determines whether, and in which direction, to pad out an argument with extra space. The value should be of type `enum direction`: either `upward` to pad above the argument, `downward` to pad below, or `none` to inhibit padding.

The *amount* of padding is always just enough to reach the next multiple of `FUNCTION_ARG_BOUNDARY`; this macro does not control it.

This macro has a default definition which is right for most systems. For little-endian machines, the default is to pad upward. For big-endian machines, the default is to pad downward for an argument of constant size shorter than an `int`, and upward otherwise.

`FUNCTION_ARG_BOUNDARY` (*mode, type*)

If defined, a C expression that gives the alignment boundary, in bits, of an argument with the specified mode and type. If it is not defined, `PARM_BOUNDARY` is used for all arguments.

FUNCTION_ARG_REGNO_P (*regno*)

> A C expression that is nonzero if *regno* is the number of a hard register in which function arguments are sometimes passed. This does *not* include implicit arguments such as the static chain and the structure-value address. On many machines, no registers can be used for this purpose since all function arguments are pushed on the stack.

LOAD_ARGS_REVERSED

> If defined, the order in which arguments are loaded into their respective argument registers is reversed so that the last argument is loaded first. This macro only effects arguments passed in registers.

17.7.7 How Scalar Function Values Are Returned

This section discusses the macros that control returning scalars as values—values that can fit in registers.

TRADITIONAL_RETURN_FLOAT

> Define this macro if '`-traditional`' should not cause functions declared to return `float` to convert the value to `double`.

FUNCTION_VALUE (*valtype*, *func*)

> A C expression to create an RTX representing the place where a function returns a value of data type *valtype*. *valtype* is a tree node representing a data type. Write TYPE_MODE (*valtype*) to get the machine mode used to represent that type. On many machines, only the mode is relevant. (Actually, on most machines, scalar values are returned in the same place regardless of mode).
>
> The value of the expression is usually a **reg** RTX for the hard register where the return value is stored. The value can also be a **parallel** RTX, if the return value is in multiple places. See FUNCTION_ARG for an explanation of the **parallel** form.
>
> If PROMOTE_FUNCTION_RETURN is defined, you must apply the same promotion rules specified in PROMOTE_MODE if *valtype* is a scalar type.
>
> If the precise function being called is known, *func* is a tree node (FUNCTION_DECL) for it; otherwise, *func* is a null pointer. This makes it possible to use a different value-returning convention for specific functions when all their calls are known.
>
> FUNCTION_VALUE is not used for return vales with aggregate data types, because these are returned in another way. See STRUCT_VALUE_REGNUM and related macros, below.

`FUNCTION_OUTGOING_VALUE` (*valtype*, *func*)

> Define this macro if the target machine has "register windows" so that the register in which a function returns its value is not the same as the one in which the caller sees the value.
>
> For such machines, `FUNCTION_VALUE` computes the register in which the caller will see the value. `FUNCTION_OUTGOING_VALUE` should be defined in a similar fashion to tell the function where to put the value.
>
> If `FUNCTION_OUTGOING_VALUE` is not defined, `FUNCTION_VALUE` serves both purposes.
>
> `FUNCTION_OUTGOING_VALUE` is not used for return vales with aggregate data types, because these are returned in another way. See `STRUCT_VALUE_REGNUM` and related macros, below.

`LIBCALL_VALUE` (*mode*)

> A C expression to create an RTX representing the place where a library function returns a value of mode *mode*. If the precise function being called is known, *func* is a tree node (`FUNCTION_DECL`) for it; otherwise, *func* is a null pointer. This makes it possible to use a different value-returning convention for specific functions when all their calls are known.
>
> Note that "library function" in this context means a compiler support routine, used to perform arithmetic, whose name is known specially by the compiler and was not mentioned in the C code being compiled.
>
> The definition of **LIBRARY_VALUE** need not be concerned aggregate data types, because none of the library functions returns such types.

`FUNCTION_VALUE_REGNO_P` (*regno*)

> A C expression that is nonzero if *regno* is the number of a hard register in which the values of called function may come back.
>
> A register whose use for returning values is limited to serving as the second of a pair (for a value of type **double**, say) need not be recognized by this macro. So for most machines, this definition suffices:
>
> ```
> #define FUNCTION_VALUE_REGNO_P(N) ((N) == 0)
> ```
>
> If the machine has register windows, so that the caller and the called function use different registers for the return value, this macro should recognize only the caller's register numbers.

`APPLY_RESULT_SIZE`

> Define this macro if 'untyped_call' and 'untyped_return' need more space than is implied by `FUNCTION_VALUE_REGNO_P` for saving and restoring an arbitrary return value.

17.7.8 How Large Values Are Returned

When a function value's mode is `BLKmode` (and in some other cases), the value is not returned according to `FUNCTION_VALUE` (see Section 17.7.7 [Scalar Return], page 442). Instead, the caller passes the address of a block of memory in which the value should be stored. This address is called the *structure value address*.

This section describes how to control returning structure values in memory.

RETURN_IN_MEMORY (*type*)

> A C expression which can inhibit the returning of certain function values in registers, based on the type of value. A nonzero value says to return the function value in memory, just as large structures are always returned. Here *type* will be a C expression of type `tree`, representing the data type of the value.
>
> Note that values of mode `BLKmode` must be explicitly handled by this macro. Also, the option '-fpcc-struct-return' takes effect regardless of this macro. On most systems, it is possible to leave the macro undefined; this causes a default definition to be used, whose value is the constant 1 for `BLKmode` values, and 0 otherwise.
>
> Do not use this macro to indicate that structures and unions should always be returned in memory. You should instead use `DEFAULT_PCC_STRUCT_RETURN` to indicate this.

DEFAULT_PCC_STRUCT_RETURN

> Define this macro to be 1 if all structure and union return values must be in memory. Since this results in slower code, this should be defined only if needed for compatibility with other compilers or with an ABI. If you define this macro to be 0, then the conventions used for structure and union return values are decided by the `RETURN_IN_MEMORY` macro.
>
> If not defined, this defaults to the value 1.

STRUCT_VALUE_REGNUM

> If the structure value address is passed in a register, then `STRUCT_VALUE_REGNUM` should be the number of that register.

STRUCT_VALUE

> If the structure value address is not passed in a register, define `STRUCT_VALUE` as an expression returning an RTX for the place where the address is passed. If it returns 0, the address is passed as an "invisible" first argument.

STRUCT_VALUE_INCOMING_REGNUM

> On some architectures the place where the structure value address is found by the called function is not the same place that

the caller put it. This can be due to register windows, or it could be because the function prologue moves it to a different place.

If the incoming location of the structure value address is in a register, define this macro as the register number.

STRUCT_VALUE_INCOMING

> If the incoming location is not a register, then you should define STRUCT_VALUE_INCOMING as an expression for an RTX for where the called function should find the value. If it should find the value on the stack, define this to create a mem which refers to the frame pointer. A definition of 0 means that the address is passed as an "invisible" first argument.

PCC_STATIC_STRUCT_RETURN

> Define this macro if the usual system convention on the target machine for returning structures and unions is for the called function to return the address of a static variable containing the value.

> Do not define this if the usual system convention is for the caller to pass an address to the subroutine.

> This macro has effect in '-fpcc-struct-return' mode, but it does nothing when you use '-freg-struct-return' mode.

17.7.9 Caller-Saves Register Allocation

If you enable it, GNU CC can save registers around function calls. This makes it possible to use call-clobbered registers to hold variables that must live across calls.

DEFAULT_CALLER_SAVES

> Define this macro if function calls on the target machine do not preserve any registers; in other words, if CALL_USED_REGISTERS has 1 for all registers. When defined, this macro enables '-fcaller-saves' by default for all optimization levels. It has no effect for optimization levels 2 and higher, where '-fcaller-saves' is the default.

CALLER_SAVE_PROFITABLE (refs, calls)

> A C expression to determine whether it is worthwhile to consider placing a pseudo-register in a call-clobbered hard register and saving and restoring it around each function call. The expression should be 1 when this is worth doing, and 0 otherwise.

> If you don't define this macro, a default is used which is good on most machines: 4 * calls < refs.

HARD_REGNO_CALLER_SAVE_MODE (regno, nregs)

> A C expression specifying which mode is required for saving nregs of a pseudo-register in call-clobbered hard register regno.

If *regno* is unsuitable for caller save, `VOIDmode` should be returned. For most machines this macro need not be defined since GCC will select the smallest suitable mode.

17.7.10 Function Entry and Exit

This section describes the macros that output function entry (*prologue*) and exit (*epilogue*) code.

`FUNCTION_PROLOGUE` (*file, size*)

> A C compound statement that outputs the assembler code for entry to a function. The prologue is responsible for setting up the stack frame, initializing the frame pointer register, saving registers that must be saved, and allocating *size* additional bytes of storage for the local variables. *size* is an integer. *file* is a stdio stream to which the assembler code should be output.
>
> The label for the beginning of the function need not be output by this macro. That has already been done when the macro is run.
>
> To determine which registers to save, the macro can refer to the array `regs_ever_live`: element *r* is nonzero if hard register *r* is used anywhere within the function. This implies the function prologue should save register *r*, provided it is not one of the call-used registers. (`FUNCTION_EPILOGUE` must likewise use `regs_ever_live`.)
>
> On machines that have "register windows", the function entry code does not save on the stack the registers that are in the windows, even if they are supposed to be preserved by function calls; instead it takes appropriate steps to "push" the register stack, if any non-call-used registers are used in the function.
>
> On machines where functions may or may not have frame-pointers, the function entry code must vary accordingly; it must set up the frame pointer if one is wanted, and not otherwise. To determine whether a frame pointer is in wanted, the macro can refer to the variable `frame_pointer_needed`. The variable's value will be 1 at run time in a function that needs a frame pointer. See Section 17.7.4 [Elimination], page 433.
>
> The function entry code is responsible for allocating any stack space required for the function. This stack space consists of the regions listed below. In most cases, these regions are allocated in the order listed, with the last listed region closest to the top of the stack (the lowest address if `STACK_GROWS_DOWNWARD` is defined, and the highest address if it is not defined). You can use a different order for a machine if doing so is more convenient or required for compatibility reasons. Except in cases where

required by standard or by a debugger, there is no reason why the stack layout used by GCC need agree with that used by other compilers for a machine.

- A region of `current_function_pretend_args_size` bytes of uninitialized space just underneath the first argument arriving on the stack. (This may not be at the very start of the allocated stack region if the calling sequence has pushed anything else since pushing the stack arguments. But usually, on such machines, nothing else has been pushed yet, because the function prologue itself does all the pushing.) This region is used on machines where an argument may be passed partly in registers and partly in memory, and, in some cases to support the features in 'varargs.h' and 'stdargs.h'.

- An area of memory used to save certain registers used by the function. The size of this area, which may also include space for such things as the return address and pointers to previous stack frames, is machine-specific and usually depends on which registers have been used in the function. Machines with register windows often do not require a save area.

- A region of at least *size* bytes, possibly rounded up to an allocation boundary, to contain the local variables of the function. On some machines, this region and the save area may occur in the opposite order, with the save area closer to the top of the stack.

- Optionally, when `ACCUMULATE_OUTGOING_ARGS` is defined, a region of `current_function_outgoing_args_size` bytes to be used for outgoing argument lists of the function. See Section 17.7.5 [Stack Arguments], page 435.

Normally, it is necessary for the macros `FUNCTION_PROLOGUE` and `FUNCTION_EPILOGUE` to treat leaf functions specially. The C variable `current_function_is_leaf` is nonzero for such a function.

`EXIT_IGNORE_STACK`

Define this macro as a C expression that is nonzero if the return instruction or the function epilogue ignores the value of the stack pointer; in other words, if it is safe to delete an instruction to adjust the stack pointer before a return from the function.

Note that this macro's value is relevant only for functions for which frame pointers are maintained. It is never safe to delete a final stack adjustment in a function that has no frame pointer, and the compiler knows this regardless of `EXIT_IGNORE_STACK`.

EPILOGUE_USES (*regno*)

>Define this macro as a C expression that is nonzero for registers are used by the epilogue or the 'return' pattern. The stack and frame pointer registers are already be assumed to be used as needed.

FUNCTION_EPILOGUE (*file, size*)

>A C compound statement that outputs the assembler code for exit from a function. The epilogue is responsible for restoring the saved registers and stack pointer to their values when the function was called, and returning control to the caller. This macro takes the same arguments as the macro FUNCTION_PROLOGUE, and the registers to restore are determined from regs_ever_live and CALL_USED_REGISTERS in the same way.

>On some machines, there is a single instruction that does all the work of returning from the function. On these machines, give that instruction the name 'return' and do not define the macro FUNCTION_EPILOGUE at all.

>Do not define a pattern named 'return' if you want the FUNCTION_EPILOGUE to be used. If you want the target switches to control whether return instructions or epilogues are used, define a 'return' pattern with a validity condition that tests the target switches appropriately. If the 'return' pattern's validity condition is false, epilogues will be used.

>On machines where functions may or may not have frame-pointers, the function exit code must vary accordingly. Sometimes the code for these two cases is completely different. To determine whether a frame pointer is wanted, the macro can refer to the variable frame_pointer_needed. The variable's value will be 1 when compiling a function that needs a frame pointer.

>Normally, FUNCTION_PROLOGUE and FUNCTION_EPILOGUE must treat leaf functions specially. The C variable current_function_is_leaf is nonzero for such a function. See Section 17.5.4 [Leaf Functions], page 418.

>On some machines, some functions pop their arguments on exit while others leave that for the caller to do. For example, the 68020 when given '-mrtd' pops arguments in functions that take a fixed number of arguments.

>Your definition of the macro RETURN_POPS_ARGS decides which functions pop their own arguments. FUNCTION_EPILOGUE needs to know what was decided. The variable that is called current_function_pops_args is the number of bytes of its arguments that a function should pop. See Section 17.7.7 [Scalar Return], page 442.

DELAY_SLOTS_FOR_EPILOGUE

Define this macro if the function epilogue contains delay slots to which instructions from the rest of the function can be "moved". The definition should be a C expression whose value is an integer representing the number of delay slots there.

ELIGIBLE_FOR_EPILOGUE_DELAY (*insn*, *n*)

A C expression that returns 1 if *insn* can be placed in delay slot number *n* of the epilogue.

The argument *n* is an integer which identifies the delay slot now being considered (since different slots may have different rules of eligibility). It is never negative and is always less than the number of epilogue delay slots (what **DELAY_SLOTS_FOR_EPILOGUE** returns). If you reject a particular insn for a given delay slot, in principle, it may be reconsidered for a subsequent delay slot. Also, other insns may (at least in principle) be considered for the so far unfilled delay slot.

The insns accepted to fill the epilogue delay slots are put in an RTL list made with **insn_list** objects, stored in the variable **current_function_epilogue_delay_list**. The insn for the first delay slot comes first in the list. Your definition of the macro **FUNCTION_EPILOGUE** should fill the delay slots by outputting the insns in this list, usually by calling **final_scan_insn**.

You need not define this macro if you did not define **DELAY_SLOTS_FOR_EPILOGUE**.

ASM_OUTPUT_MI_THUNK (*file*, *thunk_fndecl*, *delta*, *function*)

A C compound statement that outputs the assembler code for a thunk function, used to implement C++ virtual function calls with multiple inheritance. The thunk acts as a wrapper around a virtual function, adjusting the implicit object parameter before handing control off to the real function.

First, emit code to add the integer *delta* to the location that contains the incoming first argument. Assume that this argument contains a pointer, and is the one used to pass the **this** pointer in C++. This is the incoming argument *before* the function prologue, e.g. '%o0' on a sparc. The addition must preserve the values of all other incoming arguments.

After the addition, emit code to jump to *function*, which is a **FUNCTION_DECL**. This is a direct pure jump, not a call, and does not touch the return address. Hence returning from *FUNCTION* will return to whoever called the current 'thunk'.

The effect must be as if *function* had been called directly with the adjusted first argument. This macro is responsible for emitting all of the code for a thunk function; `FUNCTION_PROLOGUE` and `FUNCTION_EPILOGUE` are not invoked.

The *thunk_fndecl* is redundant. (*delta* and *function* have already been extracted from it.) It might possibly be useful on some targets, but probably not.

If you do not define this macro, the target-independent code in the C++ frontend will generate a less efficient heavyweight thunk that calls *function* instead of jumping to it. The generic approach does not support varargs.

17.7.11 Generating Code for Profiling

These macros will help you generate code for profiling.

FUNCTION_PROFILER (*file*, *labelno*)

A C statement or compound statement to output to *file* some assembler code to call the profiling subroutine `mcount`. Before calling, the assembler code must load the address of a counter variable into a register where `mcount` expects to find the address. The name of this variable is 'LP' followed by the number *labelno*, so you would generate the name using 'LP%d' in a `fprintf`.

The details of how the address should be passed to `mcount` are determined by your operating system environment, not by GNU CC. To figure them out, compile a small program for profiling using the system's installed C compiler and look at the assembler code that results.

PROFILE_BEFORE_PROLOGUE

Define this macro if the code for function profiling should come before the function prologue. Normally, the profiling code comes after.

FUNCTION_BLOCK_PROFILER (*file*, *labelno*)

A C statement or compound statement to output to *file* some assembler code to initialize basic-block profiling for the current object module. The global compile flag `profile_block_flag` distinguishes two profile modes.

`profile_block_flag != 2`

Output code to call the subroutine `__bb_init_func` once per object module, passing it as its sole argument the address of a block allocated in the object module.

The name of the block is a local symbol made with this statement:

```
ASM_GENERATE_INTERNAL_LABEL (buffer, "LPBX", 0);
```

Of course, since you are writing the definition of
`ASM_GENERATE_INTERNAL_LABEL` as well as that of
this macro, you can take a short cut in the definition
of this macro and use the name that you know will
result.

The first word of this block is a flag which will
be nonzero if the object module has already
been initialized. So test this word first, and do
not call `__bb_init_func` if the flag is nonzero.
BLOCK_OR_LABEL contains a unique number
which may be used to generate a label as a branch
destination when `__bb_init_func` will not be
called.

Described in assembler language, the code to be output looks like:

```
cmp (LPBX0),0
bne local_label
parameter1 <- LPBX0
call __bb_init_func
local_label:
```

`profile_block_flag == 2`

Output code to call the subroutine `__bb_init_`
`trace_func` and pass two parameters to it. The
first parameter is the same as for `__bb_init_`
`func`. The second parameter is the number of
the first basic block of the function as given
by BLOCK_OR_LABEL. Note that `__bb_init_`
`trace_func` has to be called, even if the object
module has been initialized already.

Described in assembler language, the code to be output looks like:

```
parameter1 <- LPBX0
parameter2 <- BLOCK_OR_LABEL
call __bb_init_trace_func
```

`BLOCK_PROFILER` (file, blockno)

A C statement or compound statement to output to file some
assembler code to increment the count associated with the basic
block number blockno. The global compile flag `profile_block_`
`flag` distinguishes two profile modes.

`profile_block_flag != 2`

Output code to increment the counter directly. Basic blocks are numbered separately from zero within
each compilation. The count associated with block

number *blockno* is at index *blockno* in a vector of
words; the name of this array is a local symbol made
with this statement:

```
ASM_GENERATE_INTERNAL_LABEL (buffer, "LPBX", 2);
```

Of course, since you are writing the definition of
`ASM_GENERATE_INTERNAL_LABEL` as well as that of
this macro, you can take a short cut in the definition
of this macro and use the name that you know will
result.

Described in assembler language, the code to be output looks like:

```
inc (LPBX2+4*BLOCKNO)
```

`profile_block_flag == 2`

Output code to initialize the global structure `__bb`
and call the function `__bb_trace_func`, which will
increment the counter.

`__bb` consists of two words. In the first word, the
current basic block number, as given by BLOCKNO,
has to be stored. In the second word, the address
of a block allocated in the object module has to be
stored. The address is given by the label created
with this statement:

```
ASM_GENERATE_INTERNAL_LABEL (buffer, "LPBX", 0);
```

Described in assembler language, the code to be output looks like:

```
move BLOCKNO -> (__bb)
move LPBX0 -> (__bb+4)
call __bb_trace_func
```

`FUNCTION_BLOCK_PROFILER_EXIT` (*file*)

A C statement or compound statement to output to *file* assembler code to call function `__bb_trace_ret`. The assembler
code should only be output if the global compile flag `profile_block_flag == 2`. This macro has to be used at every place
where code for returning from a function is generated (e.g.
`FUNCTION_EPILOGUE`). Although you have to write the definition
of `FUNCTION_EPILOGUE` as well, you have to define this macro to
tell the compiler, that the proper call to `__bb_trace_ret` is
produced.

`MACHINE_STATE_SAVE` (*id*)

A C statement or compound statement to save all registers,
which may be clobbered by a function call, including condition
codes. The `asm` statement will be mostly likely needed to handle

this task. Local labels in the assembler code can be concatenated
with the string *id*, to obtain a unique lable name.

Registers or condition codes clobbered by `FUNCTION_PROLOGUE`
or `FUNCTION_EPILOGUE` must be saved in the macros `FUNCTION_`
`BLOCK_PROFILER`, `FUNCTION_BLOCK_PROFILER_EXIT` and `BLOCK_`
`PROFILER` prior calling `__bb_init_trace_func`, `__bb_trace_`
`ret` and `__bb_trace_func` respectively.

`MACHINE_STATE_RESTORE` (*id*)

A C statement or compound statement to restore all registers,
including condition codes, saved by `MACHINE_STATE_SAVE`.

Registers or condition codes clobbered by `FUNCTION_PROLOGUE`
or `FUNCTION_EPILOGUE` must be restored in the macros
`FUNCTION_BLOCK_PROFILER`, `FUNCTION_BLOCK_PROFILER_EXIT`
and `BLOCK_PROFILER` after calling `__bb_init_trace_func`, `__`
`bb_trace_ret` and `__bb_trace_func` respectively.

`BLOCK_PROFILER_CODE`

A C function or functions which are needed in the library to
support block profiling.

17.8 Implementing the Varargs Macros

GNU CC comes with an implementation of '`varargs.h`' and '`stdarg.h`'
that work without change on machines that pass arguments on the stack.
Other machines require their own implementations of varargs, and the two
machine independent header files must have conditionals to include it.

ANSI '`stdarg.h`' differs from traditional '`varargs.h`' mainly in the calling convention for `va_start`. The traditional implementation takes just one
argument, which is the variable in which to store the argument pointer. The
ANSI implementation of `va_start` takes an additional second argument.
The user is supposed to write the last named argument of the function here.

However, `va_start` should not use this argument. The way to find the
end of the named arguments is with the built-in functions described below.

`__builtin_saveregs` ()

Use this built-in function to save the argument registers in memory so that the varargs mechanism can access them. Both
ANSI and traditional versions of `va_start` must use `__builtin_`
`saveregs`, unless you use `SETUP_INCOMING_VARARGS` (see below)
instead.

On some machines, `__builtin_saveregs` is open-coded under
the control of the macro `EXPAND_BUILTIN_SAVEREGS`. On other
machines, it calls a routine written in assembler language, found
in '`libgcc2.c`'.

Code generated for the call to `__builtin_saveregs` appears at the beginning of the function, as opposed to where the call to `__builtin_saveregs` is written, regardless of what the code is. This is because the registers must be saved before the function starts to use them for its own purposes.

`__builtin_args_info` (*category*)

Use this built-in function to find the first anonymous arguments in registers.

In general, a machine may have several categories of registers used for arguments, each for a particular category of data types. (For example, on some machines, floating-point registers are used for floating-point arguments while other arguments are passed in the general registers.) To make non-varargs functions use the proper calling convention, you have defined the `CUMULATIVE_ARGS` data type to record how many registers in each category have been used so far

`__builtin_args_info` accesses the same data structure of type `CUMULATIVE_ARGS` after the ordinary argument layout is finished with it, with *category* specifying which word to access. Thus, the value indicates the first unused register in a given category.

Normally, you would use `__builtin_args_info` in the implementation of `va_start`, accessing each category just once and storing the value in the `va_list` object. This is because `va_list` will have to update the values, and there is no way to alter the values accessed by `__builtin_args_info`.

`__builtin_next_arg` (*lastarg*)

This is the equivalent of `__builtin_args_info`, for stack arguments. It returns the address of the first anonymous stack argument, as type `void *`. If `ARGS_GROW_DOWNWARD`, it returns the address of the location above the first anonymous stack argument. Use it in `va_start` to initialize the pointer for fetching arguments from the stack. Also use it in `va_start` to verify that the second parameter *lastarg* is the last named argument of the current function.

`__builtin_classify_type` (*object*)

Since each machine has its own conventions for which data types are passed in which kind of register, your implementation of `va_arg` has to embody these conventions. The easiest way to categorize the specified data type is to use `__builtin_classify_type` together with `sizeof` and `__alignof__`.

`__builtin_classify_type` ignores the value of *object*, considering only its data type. It returns an integer describing what kind of type that is—integer, floating, pointer, structure, and so on.

The file 'typeclass.h' defines an enumeration that you can use to interpret the values of __builtin_classify_type.

These machine description macros help implement varargs:

EXPAND_BUILTIN_SAVEREGS (*args*)

If defined, is a C expression that produces the machine-specific code for a call to __builtin_saveregs. This code will be moved to the very beginning of the function, before any parameter access are made. The return value of this function should be an RTX that contains the value to use as the return of __builtin_saveregs.

The argument *args* is a tree_list containing the arguments that were passed to __builtin_saveregs.

If this macro is not defined, the compiler will output an ordinary call to the library function '__builtin_saveregs'.

SETUP_INCOMING_VARARGS (*args_so_far*, *mode*, *type*, *pretend_args_size*, *second_time*)

This macro offers an alternative to using __builtin_saveregs and defining the macro EXPAND_BUILTIN_SAVEREGS. Use it to store the anonymous register arguments into the stack so that all the arguments appear to have been passed consecutively on the stack. Once this is done, you can use the standard implementation of varargs that works for machines that pass all their arguments on the stack.

The argument *args_so_far* is the CUMULATIVE_ARGS data structure, containing the values that obtain after processing of the named arguments. The arguments *mode* and *type* describe the last named argument—its machine mode and its data type as a tree node.

The macro implementation should do two things: first, push onto the stack all the argument registers *not* used for the named arguments, and second, store the size of the data thus pushed into the int-valued variable whose name is supplied as the argument *pretend_args_size*. The value that you store here will serve as additional offset for setting up the stack frame.

Because you must generate code to push the anonymous arguments at compile time without knowing their data types, SETUP_INCOMING_VARARGS is only useful on machines that have just a single category of argument register and use it uniformly for all data types.

If the argument *second_time* is nonzero, it means that the arguments of the function are being analyzed for the second time. This happens for an inline function, which is not actually compiled until the end of the source file. The macro `SETUP_INCOMING_VARARGS` should not generate any instructions in this case.

`STRICT_ARGUMENT_NAMING`

Define this macro to be a nonzero value if the location where a function argument is passed depends on whether or not it is a named argument.

This macro controls how the *named* argument to `FUNCTION_ARG` is set for varargs and stdarg functions. If this macro returns a nonzero value, the *named* argument is always true for named arguments, and false for unnamed arguments. If it returns a value of zero, but `SETUP_INCOMING_VARARGS` is defined, then all arguments are treated as named. Otherwise, all named arguments except the last are treated as named.

You need not define this macro if it always returns zero.

`PRETEND_OUTGOING_VARARGS_NAMED`

If you need to conditionally change ABIs so that one works with `SETUP_INCOMING_VARARGS`, but the other works like neither `SETUP_INCOMING_VARARGS` nor `STRICT_ARGUMENT_NAMING` was defined, then define this macro to return nonzero if `SETUP_INCOMING_VARARGS` is used, zero otherwise. Otherwise, you should not define this macro.

17.9 Trampolines for Nested Functions

A *trampoline* is a small piece of code that is created at run time when the address of a nested function is taken. It normally resides on the stack, in the stack frame of the containing function. These macros tell GNU CC how to generate code to allocate and initialize a trampoline.

The instructions in the trampoline must do two things: load a constant address into the static chain register, and jump to the real address of the nested function. On CISC machines such as the m68k, this requires two instructions, a move immediate and a jump. Then the two addresses exist in the trampoline as word-long immediate operands. On RISC machines, it is often necessary to load each address into a register in two parts. Then pieces of each address form separate immediate operands.

The code generated to initialize the trampoline must store the variable parts—the static chain value and the function address—into the immediate operands of the instructions. On a CISC machine, this is simply a matter of copying each address to a memory reference at the proper offset from the start of the trampoline. On a RISC machine, it may be necessary to take out pieces of the address and store them separately.

TRAMPOLINE_TEMPLATE (file)
> A C statement to output, on the stream file, assembler code for a block of data that contains the constant parts of a trampoline. This code should not include a label—the label is taken care of automatically.
>
> If you do not define this macro, it means no template is needed for the target. Do not define this macro on systems where the block move code to copy the trampoline into place would be larger than the code to generate it on the spot.

TRAMPOLINE_SECTION
> The name of a subroutine to switch to the section in which the trampoline template is to be placed (see Section 17.14 [Sections], page 474). The default is a value of 'readonly_data_section', which places the trampoline in the section containing read-only data.

TRAMPOLINE_SIZE
> A C expression for the size in bytes of the trampoline, as an integer.

TRAMPOLINE_ALIGNMENT
> Alignment required for trampolines, in bits.
>
> If you don't define this macro, the value of BIGGEST_ALIGNMENT is used for aligning trampolines.

INITIALIZE_TRAMPOLINE (addr, fnaddr, static_chain)
> A C statement to initialize the variable parts of a trampoline. addr is an RTX for the address of the trampoline; fnaddr is an RTX for the address of the nested function; static_chain is an RTX for the static chain value that should be passed to the function when it is called.

ALLOCATE_TRAMPOLINE (fp)
> A C expression to allocate run-time space for a trampoline. The expression value should be an RTX representing a memory reference to the space for the trampoline.
>
> If this macro is not defined, by default the trampoline is allocated as a stack slot. This default is right for most machines. The exceptions are machines where it is impossible to execute instructions in the stack area. On such machines, you may have to implement a separate stack, using this macro in conjunction with FUNCTION_PROLOGUE and FUNCTION_EPILOGUE.
>
> fp points to a data structure, a struct function, which describes the compilation status of the immediate containing function of the function which the trampoline is for. Normally (when ALLOCATE_TRAMPOLINE is not defined), the stack slot for the trampoline is in the stack frame of this containing function.

Other allocation strategies probably must do something analogous with this information.

Implementing trampolines is difficult on many machines because they have separate instruction and data caches. Writing into a stack location fails to clear the memory in the instruction cache, so when the program jumps to that location, it executes the old contents.

Here are two possible solutions. One is to clear the relevant parts of the instruction cache whenever a trampoline is set up. The other is to make all trampolines identical, by having them jump to a standard subroutine. The former technique makes trampoline execution faster; the latter makes initialization faster.

To clear the instruction cache when a trampoline is initialized, define the following macros which describe the shape of the cache.

INSN_CACHE_SIZE

    The total size in bytes of the cache.

INSN_CACHE_LINE_WIDTH

    The length in bytes of each cache line. The cache is divided into cache lines which are disjoint slots, each holding a contiguous chunk of data fetched from memory. Each time data is brought into the cache, an entire line is read at once. The data loaded into a cache line is always aligned on a boundary equal to the line size.

INSN_CACHE_DEPTH

    The number of alternative cache lines that can hold any particular memory location.

Alternatively, if the machine has system calls or instructions to clear the instruction cache directly, you can define the following macro.

CLEAR_INSN_CACHE (*BEG, END*)

    If defined, expands to a C expression clearing the *instruction cache* in the specified interval. If it is not defined, and the macro INSN_CACHE_SIZE is defined, some generic code is generated to clear the cache. The definition of this macro would typically be a series of **asm** statements. Both *BEG* and *END* are both pointer expressions.

To use a standard subroutine, define the following macro. In addition, you must make sure that the instructions in a trampoline fill an entire cache line with identical instructions, or else ensure that the beginning of the trampoline code is always aligned at the same point in its cache line. Look in 'm68k.h' as a guide.

TRANSFER_FROM_TRAMPOLINE

    Define this macro if trampolines need a special subroutine to do their work. The macro should expand to a series of **asm** statements which will be compiled with GNU CC. They go in a library function named `__transfer_from_trampoline`.

If you need to avoid executing the ordinary prologue code of a compiled C function when you jump to the subroutine, you can do so by placing a special label of your own in the assembler code. Use one `asm` statement to generate an assembler label, and another to make the label global. Then trampolines can use that label to jump directly to your special assembler code.

17.10 Implicit Calls to Library Routines

Here is an explanation of implicit calls to library routines.

MULSI3_LIBCALL

>   A C string constant giving the name of the function to call for multiplication of one signed full-word by another. If you do not define this macro, the default name is used, which is `__mulsi3`, a function defined in 'libgcc.a'.

DIVSI3_LIBCALL

>   A C string constant giving the name of the function to call for division of one signed full-word by another. If you do not define this macro, the default name is used, which is `__divsi3`, a function defined in 'libgcc.a'.

UDIVSI3_LIBCALL

>   A C string constant giving the name of the function to call for division of one unsigned full-word by another. If you do not define this macro, the default name is used, which is `__udivsi3`, a function defined in 'libgcc.a'.

MODSI3_LIBCALL

>   A C string constant giving the name of the function to call for the remainder in division of one signed full-word by another. If you do not define this macro, the default name is used, which is `__modsi3`, a function defined in 'libgcc.a'.

UMODSI3_LIBCALL

>   A C string constant giving the name of the function to call for the remainder in division of one unsigned full-word by another. If you do not define this macro, the default name is used, which is `__umodsi3`, a function defined in 'libgcc.a'.

MULDI3_LIBCALL

>   A C string constant giving the name of the function to call for multiplication of one signed double-word by another. If you do not define this macro, the default name is used, which is `__muldi3`, a function defined in 'libgcc.a'.

DIVDI3_LIBCALL

> A C string constant giving the name of the function to call for division of one signed double-word by another. If you do not define this macro, the default name is used, which is `__divdi3`, a function defined in 'libgcc.a'.

UDIVDI3_LIBCALL

> A C string constant giving the name of the function to call for division of one unsigned full-word by another. If you do not define this macro, the default name is used, which is `__udivdi3`, a function defined in 'libgcc.a'.

MODDI3_LIBCALL

> A C string constant giving the name of the function to call for the remainder in division of one signed double-word by another. If you do not define this macro, the default name is used, which is `__moddi3`, a function defined in 'libgcc.a'.

UMODDI3_LIBCALL

> A C string constant giving the name of the function to call for the remainder in division of one unsigned full-word by another. If you do not define this macro, the default name is used, which is `__umoddi3`, a function defined in 'libgcc.a'.

INIT_TARGET_OPTABS

> Define this macro as a C statement that declares additional library routines renames existing ones. `init_optabs` calls this macro after initializing all the normal library routines.

TARGET_EDOM

> The value of `EDOM` on the target machine, as a C integer constant expression. If you don't define this macro, GNU CC does not attempt to deposit the value of `EDOM` into `errno` directly. Look in '/usr/include/errno.h' to find the value of `EDOM` on your system.
>
> If you do not define `TARGET_EDOM`, then compiled code reports domain errors by calling the library function and letting it report the error. If mathematical functions on your system use `matherr` when there is an error, then you should leave `TARGET_EDOM` undefined so that `matherr` is used normally.

GEN_ERRNO_RTX

> Define this macro as a C expression to create an rtl expression that refers to the global "variable" `errno`. (On certain systems, `errno` may not actually be a variable.) If you don't define this macro, a reasonable default is used.

TARGET_MEM_FUNCTIONS

>Define this macro if GNU CC should generate calls to the System V (and ANSI C) library functions `memcpy` and `memset` rather than the BSD functions `bcopy` and `bzero`.

LIBGCC_NEEDS_DOUBLE

>Define this macro if only `float` arguments cannot be passed to library routines (so they must be converted to `double`). This macro affects both how library calls are generated and how the library routines in 'libgcc1.c' accept their arguments. It is useful on machines where floating and fixed point arguments are passed differently, such as the i860.

FLOAT_ARG_TYPE

>Define this macro to override the type used by the library routines to pick up arguments of type `float`. (By default, they use a union of `float` and `int`.)

>The obvious choice would be `float`—but that won't work with traditional C compilers that expect all arguments declared as `float` to arrive as `double`. To avoid this conversion, the library routines ask for the value as some other type and then treat it as a `float`.

>On some systems, no other type will work for this. For these systems, you must use `LIBGCC_NEEDS_DOUBLE` instead, to force conversion of the values `double` before they are passed.

FLOATIFY (*passed-value*)

>Define this macro to override the way library routines redesignate a `float` argument as a `float` instead of the type it was passed as. The default is an expression which takes the `float` field of the union.

FLOAT_VALUE_TYPE

>Define this macro to override the type used by the library routines to return values that ought to have type `float`. (By default, they use `int`.)

>The obvious choice would be `float`—but that won't work with traditional C compilers gratuitously convert values declared as `float` into `double`.

INTIFY (*float-value*)

>Define this macro to override the way the value of a `float`-returning library routine should be packaged in order to return it. These functions are actually declared to return type `FLOAT_VALUE_TYPE` (normally `int`).

>These values can't be returned as type `float` because traditional C compilers would gratuitously convert the value to a `double`.

A local variable named `intify` is always available when the macro `INTIFY` is used. It is a union of a `float` field named `f` and a field named `i` whose type is `FLOAT_VALUE_TYPE` or `int`.

If you don't define this macro, the default definition works by copying the value through that union.

`nongcc_SI_type`

Define this macro as the name of the data type corresponding to `SImode` in the system's own C compiler.

You need not define this macro if that type is `long int`, as it usually is.

`nongcc_word_type`

Define this macro as the name of the data type corresponding to the word_mode in the system's own C compiler.

You need not define this macro if that type is `long int`, as it usually is.

`perform_...`

Define these macros to supply explicit C statements to carry out various arithmetic operations on types `float` and `double` in the library routines in 'libgcc1.c'. See that file for a full list of these macros and their arguments.

On most machines, you don't need to define any of these macros, because the C compiler that comes with the system takes care of doing them.

`NEXT_OBJC_RUNTIME`

Define this macro to generate code for Objective C message sending using the calling convention of the NeXT system. This calling convention involves passing the object, the selector and the method arguments all at once to the method-lookup library function.

The default calling convention passes just the object and the selector to the lookup function, which returns a pointer to the method.

17.11 Addressing Modes

This is about addressing modes.

`HAVE_POST_INCREMENT`

A C expression that is nonzero the machine supports post-increment addressing.

HAVE_PRE_INCREMENT
HAVE_POST_DECREMENT
HAVE_PRE_DECREMENT
> Similar for other kinds of addressing.

CONSTANT_ADDRESS_P (x)
> A C expression that is 1 if the RTX x is a constant which is a valid address. On most machines, this can be defined as CONSTANT_P (x), but a few machines are more restrictive in which constant addresses are supported.
>
> CONSTANT_P accepts integer-values expressions whose values are not explicitly known, such as symbol_ref, label_ref, and high expressions and const arithmetic expressions, in addition to const_int and const_double expressions.

MAX_REGS_PER_ADDRESS
> A number, the maximum number of registers that can appear in a valid memory address. Note that it is up to you to specify a value equal to the maximum number that GO_IF_LEGITIMATE_ADDRESS would ever accept.

GO_IF_LEGITIMATE_ADDRESS (mode, x, label)
> A C compound statement with a conditional goto label; executed if x (an RTX) is a legitimate memory address on the target machine for a memory operand of mode mode.
>
> It usually pays to define several simpler macros to serve as subroutines for this one. Otherwise it may be too complicated to understand.
>
> This macro must exist in two variants: a strict variant and a non-strict one. The strict variant is used in the reload pass. It must be defined so that any pseudo-register that has not been allocated a hard register is considered a memory reference. In contexts where some kind of register is required, a pseudo-register with no hard register must be rejected.
>
> The non-strict variant is used in other passes. It must be defined to accept all pseudo-registers in every context where some kind of register is required.
>
> Compiler source files that want to use the strict variant of this macro define the macro REG_OK_STRICT. You should use an #ifdef REG_OK_STRICT conditional to define the strict variant in that case and the non-strict variant otherwise.
>
> Subroutines to check for acceptable registers for various purposes (one for base registers, one for index registers, and so on) are typically among the subroutines used to define GO_IF_LEGITIMATE_ADDRESS. Then only these subroutine macros need have two variants; the higher levels of macros may be the same whether strict or not.

Normally, constant addresses which are the sum of a `symbol_`
`ref` and an integer are stored inside a `const` RTX to mark them
as constant. Therefore, there is no need to recognize such sums
specifically as legitimate addresses. Normally you would simply
recognize any `const` as legitimate.

Usually `PRINT_OPERAND_ADDRESS` is not prepared to handle constant sums that are not marked with `const`. It assumes that a
naked `plus` indicates indexing. If so, then you *must* reject such
naked constant sums as illegitimate addresses, so that none of
them will be given to `PRINT_OPERAND_ADDRESS`.

On some machines, whether a symbolic address is legitimate
depends on the section that the address refers to. On these
machines, define the macro `ENCODE_SECTION_INFO` to store the
information into the `symbol_ref`, and then check for it here.
When you see a `const`, you will have to look inside it to find the
`symbol_ref` in order to determine the section. See Section 17.16
[Assembler Format], page 478.

The best way to modify the name string is by adding text to the
beginning, with suitable punctuation to prevent any ambiguity.
Allocate the new name in `saveable_obstack`. You will have to
modify `ASM_OUTPUT_LABELREF` to remove and decode the added
text and output the name accordingly, and define `STRIP_NAME_`
`ENCODING` to access the original name string.

You can check the information stored here into the `symbol_`
`ref` in the definitions of the macros `GO_IF_LEGITIMATE_ADDRESS`
and `PRINT_OPERAND_ADDRESS`.

REG_OK_FOR_BASE_P (*x*)

A C expression that is nonzero if *x* (assumed to be a `reg` RTX)
is valid for use as a base register. For hard registers, it should
always accept those which the hardware permits and reject the
others. Whether the macro accepts or rejects pseudo registers
must be controlled by `REG_OK_STRICT` as described above. This
usually requires two variant definitions, of which `REG_OK_STRICT`
controls the one actually used.

REG_MODE_OK_FOR_BASE_P (*x*, *mode*)

A C expression that is just like `REG_OK_FOR_BASE_P`, except that
that expression may examine the mode of the memory reference
in *mode*. You should define this macro if the mode of the memory reference affects whether a register may be used as a base
register. If you define this macro, the compiler will use it instead
of `REG_OK_FOR_BASE_P`.

REG_OK_FOR_INDEX_P (*x*)

A C expression that is nonzero if *x* (assumed to be a `reg` RTX)
is valid for use as an index register.

The difference between an index register and a base register is that the index register may be scaled. If an address involves the sum of two registers, neither one of them scaled, then either one may be labeled the "base" and the other the "index"; but whichever labeling is used must fit the machine's constraints of which registers may serve in each capacity. The compiler will try both labelings, looking for one that is valid, and will reload one or both registers only if neither labeling works.

LEGITIMIZE_ADDRESS (x, oldx, mode, win)

A C compound statement that attempts to replace x with a valid memory address for an operand of mode mode. win will be a C statement label elsewhere in the code; the macro definition may use

GO_IF_LEGITIMATE_ADDRESS (mode, x, win);

to avoid further processing if the address has become legitimate.

x will always be the result of a call to break_out_memory_refs, and oldx will be the operand that was given to that function to produce x.

The code generated by this macro should not alter the substructure of x. If it transforms x into a more legitimate form, it should assign x (which will always be a C variable) a new value.

It is not necessary for this macro to come up with a legitimate address. The compiler has standard ways of doing so in all cases. In fact, it is safe for this macro to do nothing. But often a machine-dependent strategy can generate better code.

LEGITIMIZE_RELOAD_ADDRESS (x, mode, opnum, type, ind_levels, win)

A C compound statement that attempts to replace x, which is an address that needs reloading, with a valid memory address for an operand of mode mode. win will be a C statement label elsewhere in the code. It is not necessary to define this macro, but it might be useful for performance reasons.

For example, on the i386, it is sometimes possible to use a single reload register instead of two by reloading a sum of two pseudo registers into a register. On the other hand, for number of RISC processors offsets are limited so that often an intermediate address needs to be generated in order to address a stack slot. By defining LEGITIMIZE_RELOAD_ADDRESS appropriately, the intermediate addresses generated for adjacent some stack slots can be made identical, and thus be shared.

Note: This macro should be used with caution. It is necessary to know something of how reload works in order to effectively use this, and it is quite easy to produce macros that build in too much knowledge of reload internals.

Note: This macro must be able to reload an address created by a previous invocation of this macro. If it fails to handle such addresses then the compiler may generate incorrect code or abort.

The macro definition should use `push_reload` to indicate parts that need reloading; *opnum*, *type* and *ind_levels* are usually suitable to be passed unaltered to `push_reload`.

The code generated by this macro must not alter the substructure of *x*. If it transforms *x* into a more legitimate form, it should assign *x* (which will always be a C variable) a new value. This also applies to parts that you change indirectly by calling `push_reload`.

The macro definition may use `strict_memory_address_p` to test if the address has become legitimate.

If you want to change only a part of *x*, one standard way of doing this is to use `copy_rtx`. Note, however, that is unshares only a single level of rtl. Thus, if the part to be changed is not at the top level, you'll need to replace first the top leve It is not necessary for this macro to come up with a legitimate address; but often a machine-dependent strategy can generate better code.

`GO_IF_MODE_DEPENDENT_ADDRESS` (*addr*, *label*)

A C statement or compound statement with a conditional `goto` *label*; executed if memory address *x* (an RTX) can have different meanings depending on the machine mode of the memory reference it is used for or if the address is valid for some modes but not others.

Autoincrement and autodecrement addresses typically have mode-dependent effects because the amount of the increment or decrement is the size of the operand being addressed. Some machines have other mode-dependent addresses. Many RISC machines have no mode-dependent addresses.

You may assume that *addr* is a valid address for the machine.

`LEGITIMATE_CONSTANT_P` (*x*)

A C expression that is nonzero if *x* is a legitimate constant for an immediate operand on the target machine. You can assume that *x* satisfies `CONSTANT_P`, so you need not check this. In fact, '1' is a suitable definition for this macro on machines where anything `CONSTANT_P` is valid.

17.12 Condition Code Status

This describes the condition code status.

The file 'conditions.h' defines a variable cc_status to describe how the condition code was computed (in case the interpretation of the condition code depends on the instruction that it was set by). This variable contains the RTL expressions on which the condition code is currently based, and several standard flags.

Sometimes additional machine-specific flags must be defined in the machine description header file. It can also add additional machine-specific information by defining CC_STATUS_MDEP.

CC_STATUS_MDEP

> C code for a data type which is used for declaring the mdep component of cc_status. It defaults to int.
>
> This macro is not used on machines that do not use cc0.

CC_STATUS_MDEP_INIT

> A C expression to initialize the mdep field to "empty". The default definition does nothing, since most machines don't use the field anyway. If you want to use the field, you should probably define this macro to initialize it.
>
> This macro is not used on machines that do not use cc0.

NOTICE_UPDATE_CC (exp, insn)

> A C compound statement to set the components of cc_status appropriately for an insn insn whose body is exp. It is this macro's responsibility to recognize insns that set the condition code as a byproduct of other activity as well as those that explicitly set (cc0).
>
> This macro is not used on machines that do not use cc0.
>
> If there are insns that do not set the condition code but do alter other machine registers, this macro must check to see whether they invalidate the expressions that the condition code is recorded as reflecting. For example, on the 68000, insns that store in address registers do not set the condition code, which means that usually NOTICE_UPDATE_CC can leave cc_status unaltered for such insns. But suppose that the previous insn set the condition code based on location 'a4@(102)' and the current insn stores a new value in 'a4'. Although the condition code is not changed by this, it will no longer be true that it reflects the contents of 'a4@(102)'. Therefore, NOTICE_UPDATE_CC must alter cc_status in this case to say that nothing is known about the condition code value.
>
> The definition of NOTICE_UPDATE_CC must be prepared to deal with the results of peephole optimization: insns whose patterns are parallel RTXs containing various reg, mem or constants which are just the operands. The RTL structure of these insns is not sufficient to indicate what the insns actually do. What

`NOTICE_UPDATE_CC` should do when it sees one is just to run `CC_STATUS_INIT`.

A possible definition of `NOTICE_UPDATE_CC` is to call a function that looks at an attribute (see Section 16.15 [Insn Attributes], page 380) named, for example, 'cc'. This avoids having detailed information about patterns in two places, the 'md' file and in `NOTICE_UPDATE_CC`.

`EXTRA_CC_MODES`

A list of names to be used for additional modes for condition code values in registers (see Section 16.10 [Jump Patterns], page 367). These names are added to `enum machine_mode` and all have class `MODE_CC`. By convention, they should start with 'CC' and end with 'mode'.

You should only define this macro if your machine does not use cc0 and only if additional modes are required.

`EXTRA_CC_NAMES`

A list of C strings giving the names for the modes listed in `EXTRA_CC_MODES`. For example, the Sparc defines this macro and `EXTRA_CC_MODES` as

```
#define EXTRA_CC_MODES CC_NOOVmode, CCFPmode, CCFPEmode
#define EXTRA_CC_NAMES "CC_NOOV", "CCFP", "CCFPE"
```

This macro is not required if `EXTRA_CC_MODES` is not defined.

`SELECT_CC_MODE` (*op*, *x*, *y*)

Returns a mode from class `MODE_CC` to be used when comparison operation code *op* is applied to rtx *x* and *y*. For example, on the Sparc, `SELECT_CC_MODE` is defined as (see see Section 16.10 [Jump Patterns], page 367 for a description of the reason for this definition)

```
#define SELECT_CC_MODE(OP,X,Y) \
  (GET_MODE_CLASS (GET_MODE (X)) == MODE_FLOAT          \
   ? ((OP == EQ || OP == NE) ? CCFPmode : CCFPEmode)    \
   : ((GET_CODE (X) == PLUS || GET_CODE (X) == MINUS    \
       || GET_CODE (X) == NEG) \
      ? CC_NOOVmode : CCmode))
```

You need not define this macro if `EXTRA_CC_MODES` is not defined.

`CANONICALIZE_COMPARISON` (*code*, *op0*, *op1*)

One some machines not all possible comparisons are defined, but you can convert an invalid comparison into a valid one. For example, the Alpha does not have a `GT` comparison, but you can use an `LT` comparison instead and swap the order of the operands.

On such machines, define this macro to be a C statement to do any required conversions. *code* is the initial comparison code and *op0* and *op1* are the left and right operands of the comparison, respectively. You should modify *code*, *op0*, and *op1* as required. GNU CC will not assume that the comparison resulting from this macro is valid but will see if the resulting insn matches a pattern in the 'md' file.

You need not define this macro if it would never change the comparison code or operands.

REVERSIBLE_CC_MODE (*mode*)

A C expression whose value is one if it is always safe to reverse a comparison whose mode is *mode*. If SELECT_CC_MODE can ever return *mode* for a floating-point inequality comparison, then REVERSIBLE_CC_MODE (*mode*) must be zero.

You need not define this macro if it would always returns zero or if the floating-point format is anything other than IEEE_FLOAT_FORMAT. For example, here is the definition used on the Sparc, where floating-point inequality comparisons are always given CCFPEmode:

```
#define REVERSIBLE_CC_MODE(MODE)  ((MODE) != CCFPEmode)
```

17.13 Describing Relative Costs of Operations

These macros let you describe the relative speed of various operations on the target machine.

CONST_COSTS (*x*, *code*, *outer_code*)

A part of a C `switch` statement that describes the relative costs of constant RTL expressions. It must contain `case` labels for expression codes `const_int`, `const`, `symbol_ref`, `label_ref` and `const_double`. Each case must ultimately reach a `return` statement to return the relative cost of the use of that kind of constant value in an expression. The cost may depend on the precise value of the constant, which is available for examination in *x*, and the rtx code of the expression in which it is contained, found in *outer_code*.

code is the expression code—redundant, since it can be obtained with GET_CODE (*x*).

RTX_COSTS (*x*, *code*, *outer_code*)

Like CONST_COSTS but applies to nonconstant RTL expressions. This can be used, for example, to indicate how costly a multiply instruction is. In writing this macro, you can use the construct COSTS_N_INSNS (*n*) to specify a cost equal to *n* fast instructions. *outer_code* is the code of the expression in which *x* is contained.

This macro is optional; do not define it if the default cost assumptions are adequate for the target machine.

DEFAULT_RTX_COSTS (x, *code*, *outer_code*)

This macro, if defined, is called for any case not handled by the RTX_COSTS or CONST_COSTS macros. This eliminates the need to put case labels into the macro, but the code, or any functions it calls, must assume that the RTL in x could be of any type that has not already been handled. The arguments are the same as for RTX_COSTS, and the macro should execute a return statement giving the cost of any RTL expressions that it can handle. The default cost calculation is used for any RTL for which this macro does not return a value.

This macro is optional; do not define it if the default cost assumptions are adequate for the target machine.

ADDRESS_COST (*address*)

An expression giving the cost of an addressing mode that contains *address*. If not defined, the cost is computed from the *address* expression and the CONST_COSTS values.

For most CISC machines, the default cost is a good approximation of the true cost of the addressing mode. However, on RISC machines, all instructions normally have the same length and execution time. Hence all addresses will have equal costs.

In cases where more than one form of an address is known, the form with the lowest cost will be used. If multiple forms have the same, lowest, cost, the one that is the most complex will be used.

For example, suppose an address that is equal to the sum of a register and a constant is used twice in the same basic block. When this macro is not defined, the address will be computed in a register and memory references will be indirect through that register. On machines where the cost of the addressing mode containing the sum is no higher than that of a simple indirect reference, this will produce an additional instruction and possibly require an additional register. Proper specification of this macro eliminates this overhead for such machines.

Similar use of this macro is made in strength reduction of loops.

address need not be valid as an address. In such a case, the cost is not relevant and can be any value; invalid addresses need not be assigned a different cost.

On machines where an address involving more than one register is as cheap as an address computation involving only one register, defining ADDRESS_COST to reflect this can cause two registers to be live over a region of code where only one would have been if ADDRESS_COST were not defined in that manner. This effect should be considered in the definition of this macro. Equivalent costs should probably only be given to addresses with different numbers of registers on machines with lots of registers.

This macro will normally either not be defined or be defined as a constant.

REGISTER_MOVE_COST (*from*, *to*)

A C expression for the cost of moving data from a register in class *from* to one in class *to*. The classes are expressed using the enumeration values such as GENERAL_REGS. A value of 2 is the default; other values are interpreted relative to that.

It is not required that the cost always equal 2 when *from* is the same as *to*; on some machines it is expensive to move between registers if they are not general registers.

If reload sees an insn consisting of a single set between two hard registers, and if REGISTER_MOVE_COST applied to their classes returns a value of 2, reload does not check to ensure that the constraints of the insn are met. Setting a cost of other than 2 will allow reload to verify that the constraints are met. You should do this if the 'mov*m*' pattern's constraints do not allow such copying.

MEMORY_MOVE_COST (*mode*, *class*, *in*)

A C expression for the cost of moving data of mode *mode* between a register of class *class* and memory; *in* is zero if the value is to be written to memory, non-zero if it is to be read in. This cost is relative to those in REGISTER_MOVE_COST. If moving between registers and memory is more expensive than between two registers, you should define this macro to express the relative cost.

If you do not define this macro, GNU CC uses a default cost of 4 plus the cost of copying via a secondary reload register, if one is needed. If your machine requires a secondary reload register to copy between memory and a register of *class* but the reload mechanism is more complex than copying via an intermediate, define this macro to reflect the actual cost of the move.

GNU CC defines the function memory_move_secondary_cost if secondary reloads are needed. It computes the costs due to copying via a secondary register. If your machine copies from memory using a secondary register in the conventional way but the default base value of 4 is not correct for your machine, define this macro to add some other value to the result of that function. The arguments to that function are the same as to this macro.

BRANCH_COST

A C expression for the cost of a branch instruction. A value of 1 is the default; other values are interpreted relative to that.

Here are additional macros which do not specify precise relative costs, but only that certain actions are more expensive than GNU CC would ordinarily expect.

SLOW_BYTE_ACCESS

> Define this macro as a C expression which is nonzero if accessing less than a word of memory (i.e. a `char` or a `short`) is no faster than accessing a word of memory, i.e., if such access require more than one instruction or if there is no difference in cost between byte and (aligned) word loads.

> When this macro is not defined, the compiler will access a field by finding the smallest containing object; when it is defined, a fullword load will be used if alignment permits. Unless bytes accesses are faster than word accesses, using word accesses is preferable since it may eliminate subsequent memory access if subsequent accesses occur to other fields in the same word of the structure, but to different bytes.

SLOW_ZERO_EXTEND

> Define this macro if zero-extension (of a `char` or `short` to an `int`) can be done faster if the destination is a register that is known to be zero.

> If you define this macro, you must have instruction patterns that recognize RTL structures like this:

> ```
> (set (strict_low_part (subreg:QI (reg:SI ...) 0)) ...)
> ```
> and likewise for `HImode`.

SLOW_UNALIGNED_ACCESS

> Define this macro to be the value 1 if unaligned accesses have a cost many times greater than aligned accesses, for example if they are emulated in a trap handler.

> When this macro is non-zero, the compiler will act as if STRICT_ ALIGNMENT were non-zero when generating code for block moves. This can cause significantly more instructions to be produced. Therefore, do not set this macro non-zero if unaligned accesses only add a cycle or two to the time for a memory access.

> If the value of this macro is always zero, it need not be defined.

DONT_REDUCE_ADDR

> Define this macro to inhibit strength reduction of memory addresses. (On some machines, such strength reduction seems to do harm rather than good.)

MOVE_RATIO

> The threshold of number of scalar memory-to-memory move insns, *below* which a sequence of insns should be generated instead of a string move insn or a library call. Increasing the value will

always make code faster, but eventually incurs high cost in increased code size.

Note that on machines with no memory-to-memory move insns, this macro denotes the corresponding number of memory-to-memory *sequences*.

If you don't define this, a reasonable default is used.

MOVE_BY_PIECES_P (*size, alignment*)

A C expression used to determine whether `move_by_pieces` will be used to copy a chunk of memory, or whether some other block move mechanism will be used. Defaults to 1 if `move_by_pieces_ninsns` returns less than `MOVE_RATIO`.

MOVE_MAX_PIECES

A C expression used by `move_by_pieces` to determine the largest unit a load or store used to copy memory is. Defaults to `MOVE_MAX`.

USE_LOAD_POST_INCREMENT (*mode*)

A C expression used to determine whether a load postincrement is a good thing to use for a given mode. Defaults to the value of `HAVE_POST_INCREMENT`.

USE_LOAD_POST_DECREMENT (*mode*)

A C expression used to determine whether a load postdecrement is a good thing to use for a given mode. Defaults to the value of `HAVE_POST_DECREMENT`.

USE_LOAD_PRE_INCREMENT (*mode*)

A C expression used to determine whether a load preincrement is a good thing to use for a given mode. Defaults to the value of `HAVE_PRE_INCREMENT`.

USE_LOAD_PRE_DECREMENT (*mode*)

A C expression used to determine whether a load predecrement is a good thing to use for a given mode. Defaults to the value of `HAVE_PRE_DECREMENT`.

USE_STORE_POST_INCREMENT (*mode*)

A C expression used to determine whether a store postincrement is a good thing to use for a given mode. Defaults to the value of `HAVE_POST_INCREMENT`.

USE_STORE_POST_DECREMENT (*mode*)

A C expression used to determine whether a store postdeccrement is a good thing to use for a given mode. Defaults to the value of `HAVE_POST_DECREMENT`.

USE_STORE_PRE_INCREMENT (*mode*)

> This macro is used to determine whether a store preincrement is a good thing to use for a given mode. Defaults to the value of HAVE_PRE_INCREMENT.

USE_STORE_PRE_DECREMENT (*mode*)

> This macro is used to determine whether a store predecrement is a good thing to use for a given mode. Defaults to the value of HAVE_PRE_DECREMENT.

NO_FUNCTION_CSE

> Define this macro if it is as good or better to call a constant function address than to call an address kept in a register.

NO_RECURSIVE_FUNCTION_CSE

> Define this macro if it is as good or better for a function to call itself with an explicit address than to call an address kept in a register.

ADJUST_COST (*insn*, *link*, *dep_insn*, *cost*)

> A C statement (sans semicolon) to update the integer variable *cost* based on the relationship between *insn* that is dependent on *dep_insn* through the dependence *link*. The default is to make no adjustment to *cost*. This can be used for example to specify to the scheduler that an output- or anti-dependence does not incur the same cost as a data-dependence.

ADJUST_PRIORITY (*insn*)

> A C statement (sans semicolon) to update the integer scheduling priority INSN_PRIORITY(*insn*). Reduce the priority to execute the *insn* earlier, increase the priority to execute *insn* later. Do not define this macro if you do not need to adjust the scheduling priorities of insns.

17.14 Dividing the Output into Sections (Texts, Data, . . .)

An object file is divided into sections containing different types of data. In the most common case, there are three sections: the *text section*, which holds instructions and read-only data; the *data section*, which holds initialized writable data; and the *bss section*, which holds uninitialized data. Some systems have other kinds of sections.

The compiler must tell the assembler when to switch sections. These macros control what commands to output to tell the assembler this. You can also define additional sections.

TEXT_SECTION_ASM_OP

>A C expression whose value is a string containing the assembler operation that should precede instructions and read-only data. Normally `".text"` is right.

DATA_SECTION_ASM_OP

>A C expression whose value is a string containing the assembler operation to identify the following data as writable initialized data. Normally `".data"` is right.

SHARED_SECTION_ASM_OP

>If defined, a C expression whose value is a string containing the assembler operation to identify the following data as shared data. If not defined, `DATA_SECTION_ASM_OP` will be used.

BSS_SECTION_ASM_OP

>If defined, a C expression whose value is a string containing the assembler operation to identify the following data as uninitialized global data. If not defined, and neither `ASM_OUTPUT_BSS` nor `ASM_OUTPUT_ALIGNED_BSS` are defined, uninitialized global data will be output in the data section if '`-fno-common`' is passed, otherwise `ASM_OUTPUT_COMMON` will be used.

SHARED_BSS_SECTION_ASM_OP

>If defined, a C expression whose value is a string containing the assembler operation to identify the following data as uninitialized global shared data. If not defined, and `BSS_SECTION_ASM_OP` is, the latter will be used.

INIT_SECTION_ASM_OP

>If defined, a C expression whose value is a string containing the assembler operation to identify the following data as initialization code. If not defined, GNU CC will assume such a section does not exist.

EXTRA_SECTIONS

>A list of names for sections other than the standard two, which are `in_text` and `in_data`. You need not define this macro on a system with no other sections (that GCC needs to use).

EXTRA_SECTION_FUNCTIONS

>One or more functions to be defined in '`varasm.c`'. These functions should do jobs analogous to those of `text_section` and `data_section`, for your additional sections. Do not define this macro if you do not define `EXTRA_SECTIONS`.

READONLY_DATA_SECTION

>On most machines, read-only variables, constants, and jump tables are placed in the text section. If this is not the case on your machine, this macro should be defined to be the name of a

function (either `data_section` or a function defined in `EXTRA_SECTIONS`) that switches to the section to be used for read-only items.

If these items should be placed in the text section, this macro should not be defined.

SELECT_SECTION (*exp*, *reloc*)

> A C statement or statements to switch to the appropriate section for output of *exp*. You can assume that *exp* is either a `VAR_DECL` node or a constant of some sort. *reloc* indicates whether the initial value of *exp* requires link-time relocations. Select the section by calling `text_section` or one of the alternatives for other sections.

> Do not define this macro if you put all read-only variables and constants in the read-only data section (usually the text section).

SELECT_RTX_SECTION (*mode*, *rtx*)

> A C statement or statements to switch to the appropriate section for output of *rtx* in mode *mode*. You can assume that *rtx* is some kind of constant in RTL. The argument *mode* is redundant except in the case of a `const_int` rtx. Select the section by calling `text_section` or one of the alternatives for other sections.

> Do not define this macro if you put all constants in the read-only data section.

JUMP_TABLES_IN_TEXT_SECTION

> Define this macro to be an expression with a non-zero value if jump tables (for `tablejump` insns) should be output in the text section, along with the assembler instructions. Otherwise, the readonly data section is used.

> This macro is irrelevant if there is no separate readonly data section.

ENCODE_SECTION_INFO (*decl*)

> Define this macro if references to a symbol must be treated differently depending on something about the variable or function named by the symbol (such as what section it is in).

> The macro definition, if any, is executed immediately after the rtl for *decl* has been created and stored in `DECL_RTL` (*decl*). The value of the rtl will be a `mem` whose address is a `symbol_ref`.

> The usual thing for this macro to do is to record a flag in the `symbol_ref` (such as SYMBOL_REF_FLAG) or to store a modified name string in the `symbol_ref` (if one bit is not enough information).

STRIP_NAME_ENCODING (*var*, *sym_name*)

> Decode *sym_name* and store the real name part in *var*, sans
> the characters that encode section info. Define this macro if
> ENCODE_SECTION_INFO alters the symbol's name string.

UNIQUE_SECTION_P (*decl*)

> A C expression which evaluates to true if *decl* should be placed
> into a unique section for some target-specific reason. If you do
> not define this macro, the default is '0'. Note that the flag
> '-ffunction-sections' will also cause functions to be placed
> into unique sections.

UNIQUE_SECTION (*decl*, *reloc*)

> A C statement to build up a unique section name, expressed
> as a STRING_CST node, and assign it to 'DECL_SECTION_NAME
> (*decl*)'. *reloc* indicates whether the initial value of *exp* requires
> link-time relocations. If you do not define this macro, GNU CC
> will use the symbol name prefixed by '.' as the section name.

17.15 Position Independent Code

This section describes macros that help implement generation of position
independent code. Simply defining these macros is not enough to generate
valid PIC; you must also add support to the macros GO_IF_LEGITIMATE_
ADDRESS and PRINT_OPERAND_ADDRESS, as well as LEGITIMIZE_ADDRESS.
You must modify the definition of 'movsi' to do something appropriate when
the source operand contains a symbolic address. You may also need to alter
the handling of switch statements so that they use relative addresses.

PIC_OFFSET_TABLE_REGNUM

> The register number of the register used to address a table of
> static data addresses in memory. In some cases this register is
> defined by a processor's "application binary interface" (ABI).
> When this macro is defined, RTL is generated for this register
> once, as with the stack pointer and frame pointer registers. If
> this macro is not defined, it is up to the machine-dependent files
> to allocate such a register (if necessary).

PIC_OFFSET_TABLE_REG_CALL_CLOBBERED

> Define this macro if the register defined by PIC_OFFSET_TABLE_
> REGNUM is clobbered by calls. Do not define this macro if PIC_
> OFFSET_TABLE_REGNUM is not defined.

FINALIZE_PIC

> By generating position-independent code, when two different
> programs (A and B) share a common library (libC.a), the text
> of the library can be shared whether or not the library is linked

at the same address for both programs. In some of these environments, position-independent code requires not only the use of different addressing modes, but also special code to enable the use of these addressing modes.

The `FINALIZE_PIC` macro serves as a hook to emit these special codes once the function is being compiled into assembly code, but not before. (It is not done before, because in the case of compiling an inline function, it would lead to multiple PIC prologues being included in functions which used inline functions and were compiled to assembly language.)

`LEGITIMATE_PIC_OPERAND_P` (x)

A C expression that is nonzero if x is a legitimate immediate operand on the target machine when generating position independent code. You can assume that x satisfies `CONSTANT_P`, so you need not check this. You can also assume *flag_pic* is true, so you need not check it either. You need not define this macro if all constants (including `SYMBOL_REF`) can be immediate operands when generating position independent code.

17.16 Defining the Output Assembler Language

This section describes macros whose principal purpose is to describe how to write instructions in assembler language–rather than what the instructions do.

17.16.1 The Overall Framework of an Assembler File

This describes the overall framework of an assembler file.

`ASM_FILE_START` (*stream*)

A C expression which outputs to the stdio stream *stream* some appropriate text to go at the start of an assembler file.

Normally this macro is defined to output a line containing '`#NO_APP`', which is a comment that has no effect on most assemblers but tells the GNU assembler that it can save time by not checking for certain assembler constructs.

On systems that use SDB, it is necessary to output certain commands; see '`attasm.h`'.

`ASM_FILE_END` (*stream*)

A C expression which outputs to the stdio stream *stream* some appropriate text to go at the end of an assembler file.

If this macro is not defined, the default is to output nothing special at the end of the file. Most systems don't require any definition.

On systems that use SDB, it is necessary to output certain commands; see 'attasm.h'.

ASM_IDENTIFY_GCC (file)

A C statement to output assembler commands which will identify the object file as having been compiled with GNU CC (or another GNU compiler).

If you don't define this macro, the string 'gcc_compiled.:' is output. This string is calculated to define a symbol which, on BSD systems, will never be defined for any other reason. GDB checks for the presence of this symbol when reading the symbol table of an executable.

On non-BSD systems, you must arrange communication with GDB in some other fashion. If GDB is not used on your system, you can define this macro with an empty body.

ASM_COMMENT_START

A C string constant describing how to begin a comment in the target assembler language. The compiler assumes that the comment will end at the end of the line.

ASM_APP_ON

A C string constant for text to be output before each asm statement or group of consecutive ones. Normally this is "#APP", which is a comment that has no effect on most assemblers but tells the GNU assembler that it must check the lines that follow for all valid assembler constructs.

ASM_APP_OFF

A C string constant for text to be output after each asm statement or group of consecutive ones. Normally this is "#NO_APP", which tells the GNU assembler to resume making the time-saving assumptions that are valid for ordinary compiler output.

ASM_OUTPUT_SOURCE_FILENAME (stream, name)

A C statement to output COFF information or DWARF debugging information which indicates that filename name is the current source file to the stdio stream stream.

This macro need not be defined if the standard form of output for the file format in use is appropriate.

OUTPUT_QUOTED_STRING (stream, name)

A C statement to output the string string to the stdio stream stream. If you do not call the function output_quoted_string in your config files, GNU CC will only call it to output filenames to the assembler source. So you can use it to canonicalize the format of the filename using this macro.

ASM_OUTPUT_SOURCE_LINE (*stream*, *line*)

> A C statement to output DBX or SDB debugging information before code for line number *line* of the current source file to the stdio stream *stream*.

> This macro need not be defined if the standard form of debugging information for the debugger in use is appropriate.

ASM_OUTPUT_IDENT (*stream*, *string*)

> A C statement to output something to the assembler file to handle a '#ident' directive containing the text *string*. If this macro is not defined, nothing is output for a '#ident' directive.

ASM_OUTPUT_SECTION_NAME (*stream*, *decl*, *name*, *reloc*)

> A C statement to output something to the assembler file to switch to section *name* for object *decl* which is either a FUNCTION_DECL, a VAR_DECL or NULL_TREE. *reloc* indicates whether the initial value of *exp* requires link-time relocations. Some target formats do not support arbitrary sections. Do not define this macro in such cases.

> At present this macro is only used to support section attributes. When this macro is undefined, section attributes are disabled.

OBJC_PROLOGUE

> A C statement to output any assembler statements which are required to precede any Objective C object definitions or message sending. The statement is executed only when compiling an Objective C program.

17.16.2 Output of Data

This describes data output.

ASM_OUTPUT_LONG_DOUBLE (*stream*, *value*)
ASM_OUTPUT_DOUBLE (*stream*, *value*)
ASM_OUTPUT_FLOAT (*stream*, *value*)
ASM_OUTPUT_THREE_QUARTER_FLOAT (*stream*, *value*)
ASM_OUTPUT_SHORT_FLOAT (*stream*, *value*)
ASM_OUTPUT_BYTE_FLOAT (*stream*, *value*)

> A C statement to output to the stdio stream *stream* an assembler instruction to assemble a floating-point constant of TFmode, DFmode, SFmode, TQFmode, HFmode, or QFmode, respectively, whose value is *value*. *value* will be a C expression of type REAL_VALUE_TYPE. Macros such as REAL_VALUE_TO_TARGET_DOUBLE are useful for writing these definitions.

ASM_OUTPUT_QUADRUPLE_INT (*stream*, *exp*)
ASM_OUTPUT_DOUBLE_INT (*stream*, *exp*)
ASM_OUTPUT_INT (*stream*, *exp*)
ASM_OUTPUT_SHORT (*stream*, *exp*)
ASM_OUTPUT_CHAR (*stream*, *exp*)

> A C statement to output to the stdio stream *stream* an assembler instruction to assemble an integer of 16, 8, 4, 2 or 1 bytes, respectively, whose value is *value*. The argument *exp* will be an RTL expression which represents a constant value. Use 'output_addr_const (*stream*, *exp*)' to output this value as an assembler expression.
>
> For sizes larger than UNITS_PER_WORD, if the action of a macro would be identical to repeatedly calling the macro corresponding to a size of UNITS_PER_WORD, once for each word, you need not define the macro.

ASM_OUTPUT_BYTE (*stream*, *value*)

> A C statement to output to the stdio stream *stream* an assembler instruction to assemble a single byte containing the number *value*.

ASM_BYTE_OP

> A C string constant giving the pseudo-op to use for a sequence of single-byte constants. If this macro is not defined, the default is "byte".

ASM_OUTPUT_ASCII (*stream*, *ptr*, *len*)

> A C statement to output to the stdio stream *stream* an assembler instruction to assemble a string constant containing the *len* bytes at *ptr*. *ptr* will be a C expression of type char * and *len* a C expression of type int.
>
> If the assembler has a .ascii pseudo-op as found in the Berkeley Unix assembler, do not define the macro ASM_OUTPUT_ASCII.

CONSTANT_POOL_BEFORE_FUNCTION

> You may define this macro as a C expression. You should define the expression to have a non-zero value if GNU CC should output the constant pool for a function before the code for the function, or a zero value if GNU CC should output the constant pool after the function. If you do not define this macro, the usual case, GNU CC will output the constant pool before the function.

ASM_OUTPUT_POOL_PROLOGUE (*file funname fundecl size*)

> A C statement to output assembler commands to define the start of the constant pool for a function. *funname* is a string giving the name of the function. Should the return type of the function be required, it can be obtained via *fundecl*. *size* is the size, in

bytes, of the constant pool that will be written immediately after this call.

If no constant-pool prefix is required, the usual case, this macro need not be defined.

ASM_OUTPUT_SPECIAL_POOL_ENTRY (*file*, *x*, *mode*, *align*, *labelno*, *jumpto*)

A C statement (with or without semicolon) to output a constant in the constant pool, if it needs special treatment. (This macro need not do anything for RTL expressions that can be output normally.)

The argument *file* is the standard I/O stream to output the assembler code on. *x* is the RTL expression for the constant to output, and *mode* is the machine mode (in case *x* is a 'const_int'). *align* is the required alignment for the value *x*; you should output an assembler directive to force this much alignment.

The argument *labelno* is a number to use in an internal label for the address of this pool entry. The definition of this macro is responsible for outputting the label definition at the proper place. Here is how to do this:

ASM_OUTPUT_INTERNAL_LABEL (*file*, "LC", *labelno*);

When you output a pool entry specially, you should end with a `goto` to the label *jumpto*. This will prevent the same pool entry from being output a second time in the usual manner.

You need not define this macro if it would do nothing.

CONSTANT_AFTER_FUNCTION_P (*exp*)

Define this macro as a C expression which is nonzero if the constant *exp*, of type `tree`, should be output after the code for a function. The compiler will normally output all constants before the function; you need not define this macro if this is OK.

ASM_OUTPUT_POOL_EPILOGUE (*file funname fundecl size*)

A C statement to output assembler commands to at the end of the constant pool for a function. *funname* is a string giving the name of the function. Should the return type of the function be required, you can obtain it via *fundecl*. *size* is the size, in bytes, of the constant pool that GNU CC wrote immediately before this call.

If no constant-pool epilogue is required, the usual case, you need not define this macro.

IS_ASM_LOGICAL_LINE_SEPARATOR (*C*)

Define this macro as a C expression which is nonzero if *C* is used as a logical line separator by the assembler.

If you do not define this macro, the default is that only the character ';' is treated as a logical line separator.

ASM_OPEN_PAREN
ASM_CLOSE_PAREN
>These macros are defined as C string constant, describing the syntax in the assembler for grouping arithmetic expressions. The following definitions are correct for most assemblers:

```
#define ASM_OPEN_PAREN "("
#define ASM_CLOSE_PAREN ")"
```

These macros are provided by 'real.h' for writing the definitions of ASM_OUTPUT_DOUBLE and the like:

REAL_VALUE_TO_TARGET_SINGLE (*x*, *l*)
REAL_VALUE_TO_TARGET_DOUBLE (*x*, *l*)
REAL_VALUE_TO_TARGET_LONG_DOUBLE (*x*, *l*)
>These translate *x*, of type REAL_VALUE_TYPE, to the target's floating point representation, and store its bit pattern in the array of long int whose address is *l*. The number of elements in the output array is determined by the size of the desired target floating point data type: 32 bits of it go in each long int array element. Each array element holds 32 bits of the result, even if long int is wider than 32 bits on the host machine.
>
>The array element values are designed so that you can print them out using fprintf in the order they should appear in the target machine's memory.

REAL_VALUE_TO_DECIMAL (*x*, *format*, *string*)
>This macro converts *x*, of type REAL_VALUE_TYPE, to a decimal number and stores it as a string into *string*. You must pass, as *string*, the address of a long enough block of space to hold the result.
>
>The argument *format* is a printf-specification that serves as a suggestion for how to format the output string.

17.16.3 Output of Uninitialized Variables

Each of the macros in this section is used to do the whole job of outputting a single uninitialized variable.

ASM_OUTPUT_COMMON (*stream*, *name*, *size*, *rounded*)
>A C statement (sans semicolon) to output to the stdio stream *stream* the assembler definition of a common-label named *name* whose size is *size* bytes. The variable *rounded* is the size rounded up to whatever alignment the caller wants.
>
>Use the expression assemble_name (*stream*, *name*) to output the name itself; before and after that, output the additional assembler syntax for defining the name, and a newline.

This macro controls how the assembler definitions of uninitialized common global variables are output.

ASM_OUTPUT_ALIGNED_COMMON (*stream, name, size, alignment*)

Like ASM_OUTPUT_COMMON except takes the required alignment as a separate, explicit argument. If you define this macro, it is used in place of ASM_OUTPUT_COMMON, and gives you more flexibility in handling the required alignment of the variable. The alignment is specified as the number of bits.

ASM_OUTPUT_ALIGNED_DECL_COMMON (*stream, decl, name, size, alignment*)

Like ASM_OUTPUT_ALIGNED_COMMON except that *decl* of the variable to be output, if there is one, or NULL_TREE if there is not corresponding variable. If you define this macro, GNU CC wil use it in place of both ASM_OUTPUT_COMMON and ASM_OUTPUT_ALIGNED_COMMON. Define this macro when you need to see the variable's decl in order to chose what to output.

ASM_OUTPUT_SHARED_COMMON (*stream, name, size, rounded*)

If defined, it is similar to ASM_OUTPUT_COMMON, except that it is used when *name* is shared. If not defined, ASM_OUTPUT_COMMON will be used.

ASM_OUTPUT_BSS (*stream, decl, name, size, rounded*)

A C statement (sans semicolon) to output to the stdio stream *stream* the assembler definition of uninitialized global *decl* named *name* whose size is *size* bytes. The variable *rounded* is the size rounded up to whatever alignment the caller wants.

Try to use function asm_output_bss defined in 'varasm.c' when defining this macro. If unable, use the expression assemble_name (*stream, name*) to output the name itself; before and after that, output the additional assembler syntax for defining the name, and a newline.

This macro controls how the assembler definitions of uninitialized global variables are output. This macro exists to properly support languages like c++ which do not have common data. However, this macro currently is not defined for all targets. If this macro and ASM_OUTPUT_ALIGNED_BSS are not defined then ASM_OUTPUT_COMMON or ASM_OUTPUT_ALIGNED_COMMON or ASM_OUTPUT_ALIGNED_DECL_COMMON is used.

ASM_OUTPUT_ALIGNED_BSS (*stream, decl, name, size, alignment*)

Like ASM_OUTPUT_BSS except takes the required alignment as a separate, explicit argument. If you define this macro, it is used in place of ASM_OUTPUT_BSS, and gives you more flexibility in handling the required alignment of the variable. The alignment is specified as the number of bits.

Try to use function `asm_output_aligned_bss` defined in file
'`varasm.c`' when defining this macro.

`ASM_OUTPUT_SHARED_BSS` (*stream, decl, name, size, rounded*)

If defined, it is similar to `ASM_OUTPUT_BSS`, except that it is used
when *name* is shared. If not defined, `ASM_OUTPUT_BSS` will be
used.

`ASM_OUTPUT_LOCAL` (*stream, name, size, rounded*)

A C statement (sans semicolon) to output to the stdio stream
stream the assembler definition of a local-common-label named
name whose size is *size* bytes. The variable *rounded* is the size
rounded up to whatever alignment the caller wants.

Use the expression `assemble_name` (*stream, name*) to output
the name itself; before and after that, output the additional
assembler syntax for defining the name, and a newline.

This macro controls how the assembler definitions of uninitialized static variables are output.

`ASM_OUTPUT_ALIGNED_LOCAL` (*stream, name, size, alignment*)

Like `ASM_OUTPUT_LOCAL` except takes the required alignment as
a separate, explicit argument. If you define this macro, it is used
in place of `ASM_OUTPUT_LOCAL`, and gives you more flexibility in
handling the required alignment of the variable. The alignment
is specified as the number of bits.

`ASM_OUTPUT_ALIGNED_DECL_LOCAL` (*stream, decl, name, size, alignment*)

Like `ASM_OUTPUT_ALIGNED_DECL` except that *decl* of the variable
to be output, if there is one, or `NULL_TREE` if there is not corresponding variable. If you define this macro, GNU CC wil use it
in place of both `ASM_OUTPUT_DECL` and `ASM_OUTPUT_ALIGNED_`
`DECL`. Define this macro when you need to see the variable's decl
in order to chose what to output.

`ASM_OUTPUT_SHARED_LOCAL` (*stream, name, size, rounded*)

If defined, it is similar to `ASM_OUTPUT_LOCAL`, except that it is
used when *name* is shared. If not defined, `ASM_OUTPUT_LOCAL`
will be used.

17.16.4 Output and Generation of Labels

This is about outputting labels.

`ASM_OUTPUT_LABEL` (*stream, name*)

A C statement (sans semicolon) to output to the stdio stream
stream the assembler definition of a label named *name*. Use the
expression `assemble_name` (*stream, name*) to output the name
itself; before and after that, output the additional assembler
syntax for defining the name, and a newline.

ASM_DECLARE_FUNCTION_NAME (*stream*, *name*, *decl*)

A C statement (sans semicolon) to output to the stdio stream *stream* any text necessary for declaring the name *name* of a function which is being defined. This macro is responsible for outputting the label definition (perhaps using **ASM_OUTPUT_LABEL**). The argument *decl* is the **FUNCTION_DECL** tree node representing the function.

If this macro is not defined, then the function name is defined in the usual manner as a label (by means of **ASM_OUTPUT_LABEL**).

ASM_DECLARE_FUNCTION_SIZE (*stream*, *name*, *decl*)

A C statement (sans semicolon) to output to the stdio stream *stream* any text necessary for declaring the size of a function which is being defined. The argument *name* is the name of the function. The argument *decl* is the **FUNCTION_DECL** tree node representing the function.

If this macro is not defined, then the function size is not defined.

ASM_DECLARE_OBJECT_NAME (*stream*, *name*, *decl*)

A C statement (sans semicolon) to output to the stdio stream *stream* any text necessary for declaring the name *name* of an initialized variable which is being defined. This macro must output the label definition (perhaps using **ASM_OUTPUT_LABEL**). The argument *decl* is the **VAR_DECL** tree node representing the variable.

If this macro is not defined, then the variable name is defined in the usual manner as a label (by means of **ASM_OUTPUT_LABEL**).

ASM_FINISH_DECLARE_OBJECT (*stream*, *decl*, *toplevel*, *atend*)

A C statement (sans semicolon) to finish up declaring a variable name once the compiler has processed its initializer fully and thus has had a chance to determine the size of an array when controlled by an initializer. This is used on systems where it's necessary to declare something about the size of the object.

If you don't define this macro, that is equivalent to defining it to do nothing.

ASM_GLOBALIZE_LABEL (*stream*, *name*)

A C statement (sans semicolon) to output to the stdio stream *stream* some commands that will make the label *name* global; that is, available for reference from other files. Use the expression **assemble_name** (*stream*, *name*) to output the name itself; before and after that, output the additional assembler syntax for making that name global, and a newline.

ASM_WEAKEN_LABEL

A C statement (sans semicolon) to output to the stdio stream *stream* some commands that will make the label *name* weak;

that is, available for reference from other files but only used if no other definition is available. Use the expression `assemble_name` (*stream, name*) to output the name itself; before and after that, output the additional assembler syntax for making that name weak, and a newline.

If you don't define this macro, GNU CC will not support weak symbols and you should not define the `SUPPORTS_WEAK` macro.

`SUPPORTS_WEAK`

A C expression which evaluates to true if the target supports weak symbols.

If you don't define this macro, 'defaults.h' provides a default definition. If `ASM_WEAKEN_LABEL` is defined, the default definition is '1'; otherwise, it is '0'. Define this macro if you want to control weak symbol support with a compiler flag such as '-melf'.

`MAKE_DECL_ONE_ONLY`

A C statement (sans semicolon) to mark *decl* to be emitted as a public symbol such that extra copies in multiple translation units will be discarded by the linker. Define this macro if your object file format provides support for this concept, such as the 'COMDAT' section flags in the Microsoft Windows PE/COFF format, and this support requires changes to *decl*, such as putting it in a separate section.

`SUPPORTS_ONE_ONLY`

A C expression which evaluates to true if the target supports one-only semantics.

If you don't define this macro, 'varasm.c' provides a default definition. If `MAKE_DECL_ONE_ONLY` is defined, the default definition is '1'; otherwise, it is '0'. Define this macro if you want to control one-only symbol support with a compiler flag, or if setting the `DECL_ONE_ONLY` flag is enough to mark a declaration to be emitted as one-only.

`ASM_OUTPUT_EXTERNAL` (*stream, decl, name*)

A C statement (sans semicolon) to output to the stdio stream *stream* any text necessary for declaring the name of an external symbol named *name* which is referenced in this compilation but not defined. The value of *decl* is the tree node for the declaration.

This macro need not be defined if it does not need to output anything. The GNU assembler and most Unix assemblers don't require anything.

ASM_OUTPUT_EXTERNAL_LIBCALL (*stream, symref*)

> A C statement (sans semicolon) to output on *stream* an assembler pseudo-op to declare a library function name external. The name of the library function is given by *symref*, which has type **rtx** and is a **symbol_ref**.
>
> This macro need not be defined if it does not need to output anything. The GNU assembler and most Unix assemblers don't require anything.

ASM_OUTPUT_LABELREF (*stream, name*)

> A C statement (sans semicolon) to output to the stdio stream *stream* a reference in assembler syntax to a label named *name*. This should add '_' to the front of the name, if that is customary on your operating system, as it is in most Berkeley Unix systems. This macro is used in **assemble_name**.

ASM_OUTPUT_INTERNAL_LABEL (*stream, prefix, num*)

> A C statement to output to the stdio stream *stream* a label whose name is made from the string *prefix* and the number *num*.
>
> It is absolutely essential that these labels be distinct from the labels used for user-level functions and variables. Otherwise, certain programs will have name conflicts with internal labels.
>
> It is desirable to exclude internal labels from the symbol table of the object file. Most assemblers have a naming convention for labels that should be excluded; on many systems, the letter 'L' at the beginning of a label has this effect. You should find out what convention your system uses, and follow it.
>
> The usual definition of this macro is as follows:
>
>   fprintf (*stream*, "L%s%d:\n", *prefix, num*)

ASM_GENERATE_INTERNAL_LABEL (*string, prefix, num*)

> A C statement to store into the string *string* a label whose name is made from the string *prefix* and the number *num*.
>
> This string, when output subsequently by **assemble_name**, should produce the output that **ASM_OUTPUT_INTERNAL_LABEL** would produce with the same *prefix* and *num*.
>
> If the string begins with '*', then **assemble_name** will output the rest of the string unchanged. It is often convenient for **ASM_GENERATE_INTERNAL_LABEL** to use '*' in this way. If the string doesn't start with '*', then **ASM_OUTPUT_LABELREF** gets to output the string, and may change it. (Of course, **ASM_OUTPUT_LABELREF** is also part of your machine description, so you should know what it does on your machine.)

ASM_FORMAT_PRIVATE_NAME (*outvar, name, number*)

A C expression to assign to *outvar* (which is a variable of type `char *`) a newly allocated string made from the string *name* and the number *number*, with some suitable punctuation added. Use `alloca` to get space for the string.

The string will be used as an argument to `ASM_OUTPUT_LABELREF` to produce an assembler label for an internal static variable whose name is *name*. Therefore, the string must be such as to result in valid assembler code. The argument *number* is different each time this macro is executed; it prevents conflicts between similarly-named internal static variables in different scopes.

Ideally this string should not be a valid C identifier, to prevent any conflict with the user's own symbols. Most assemblers allow periods or percent signs in assembler symbols; putting at least one of these between the name and the number will suffice.

ASM_OUTPUT_DEF (*stream, name, value*)

A C statement to output to the stdio stream *stream* assembler code which defines (equates) the symbol *name* to have the value *value*.

If SET_ASM_OP is defined, a default definition is provided which is correct for most systems.

ASM_OUTPUT_DEFINE_LABEL_DIFFERENCE_SYMBOL (*stream, symbol, high, low*)

A C statement to output to the stdio stream *stream* assembler code which defines (equates) the symbol *symbol* to have a value equal to the difference of the two symbols *high* and *low*, i.e. *high* minus *low*. GNU CC guarantees that the symbols *high* and *low* are already known by the assembler so that the difference resolves into a constant.

If SET_ASM_OP is defined, a default definition is provided which is correct for most systems.

ASM_OUTPUT_WEAK_ALIAS (*stream, name, value*)

A C statement to output to the stdio stream *stream* assembler code which defines (equates) the weak symbol *name* to have the value *value*.

Define this macro if the target only supports weak aliases; define ASM_OUTPUT_DEF instead if possible.

OBJC_GEN_METHOD_LABEL (*buf, is_inst, class_name, cat_name, sel_name*)

Define this macro to override the default assembler names used for Objective C methods.

The default name is a unique method number followed by the name of the class (e.g. '`_1_Foo`'). For methods in categories, the name of the category is also included in the assembler name (e.g. '_1_Foo_Bar').

These names are safe on most systems, but make debugging difficult since the method's selector is not present in the name. Therefore, particular systems define other ways of computing names.

buf is an expression of type `char *` which gives you a buffer in which to store the name; its length is as long as *class_name*, *cat_name* and *sel_name* put together, plus 50 characters extra.

The argument *is_inst* specifies whether the method is an instance method or a class method; *class_name* is the name of the class; *cat_name* is the name of the category (or NULL if the method is not in a category); and *sel_name* is the name of the selector.

On systems where the assembler can handle quoted names, you can use this macro to provide more human-readable names.

17.16.5 How Initialization Functions Are Handled

The compiled code for certain languages includes *constructors* (also called *initialization routines*)—functions to initialize data in the program when the program is started. These functions need to be called before the program is "started"—that is to say, before `main` is called.

Compiling some languages generates *destructors* (also called *termination routines*) that should be called when the program terminates.

To make the initialization and termination functions work, the compiler must output something in the assembler code to cause those functions to be called at the appropriate time. When you port the compiler to a new system, you need to specify how to do this.

There are two major ways that GCC currently supports the execution of initialization and termination functions. Each way has two variants. Much of the structure is common to all four variations.

The linker must build two lists of these functions—a list of initialization functions, called `__CTOR_LIST__`, and a list of termination functions, called `__DTOR_LIST__`.

Each list always begins with an ignored function pointer (which may hold 0, -1, or a count of the function pointers after it, depending on the environment). This is followed by a series of zero or more function pointers to constructors (or destructors), followed by a function pointer containing zero.

Depending on the operating system and its executable file format, either 'crtstuff.c' or 'libgcc2.c' traverses these lists at startup time and exit time. Constructors are called in reverse order of the list; destructors in forward order.

The best way to handle static constructors works only for object file formats which provide arbitrarily-named sections. A section is set aside for a list of constructors, and another for a list of destructors. Traditionally these are called '.ctors' and '.dtors'. Each object file that defines an initialization function also puts a word in the constructor section to point to that function. The linker accumulates all these words into one contiguous '.ctors' section. Termination functions are handled similarly.

To use this method, you need appropriate definitions of the macros ASM_OUTPUT_CONSTRUCTOR and ASM_OUTPUT_DESTRUCTOR. Usually you can get them by including 'svr4.h'.

When arbitrary sections are available, there are two variants, depending upon how the code in 'crtstuff.c' is called. On systems that support an *init* section which is executed at program startup, parts of 'crtstuff.c' are compiled into that section. The program is linked by the gcc driver like this:

```
ld -o output_file crtbegin.o ... crtend.o -lgcc
```

The head of a function (__do_global_ctors) appears in the init section of 'crtbegin.o'; the remainder of the function appears in the init section of 'crtend.o'. The linker will pull these two parts of the section together, making a whole function. If any of the user's object files linked into the middle of it contribute code, then that code will be executed as part of the body of __do_global_ctors.

To use this variant, you must define the INIT_SECTION_ASM_OP macro properly.

If no init section is available, do not define INIT_SECTION_ASM_OP. Then __do_global_ctors is built into the text section like all other functions, and resides in 'libgcc.a'. When GCC compiles any function called main, it inserts a procedure call to __main as the first executable code after the function prologue. The __main function, also defined in 'libgcc2.c', simply calls '__do_global_ctors'.

In file formats that don't support arbitrary sections, there are again two variants. In the simplest variant, the GNU linker (GNU ld) and an 'a.out' format must be used. In this case, ASM_OUTPUT_CONSTRUCTOR is defined to produce a .stabs entry of type 'N_SETT', referencing the name __CTOR_LIST__, and with the address of the void function containing the initialization code as its value. The GNU linker recognizes this as a request to add the value to a "set"; the values are accumulated, and are eventually placed in the executable as a vector in the format described above, with a leading (ignored) count and a trailing zero element. ASM_OUTPUT_DESTRUCTOR is handled similarly. Since no init section is available, the absence of INIT_SECTION_ASM_OP causes the compilation of main to call __main as above, starting the initialization process.

The last variant uses neither arbitrary sections nor the GNU linker. This is preferable when you want to do dynamic linking and when using file formats which the GNU linker does not support, such as 'ECOFF'. In this case, `ASM_OUTPUT_CONSTRUCTOR` does not produce an `N_SETT` symbol; initialization and termination functions are recognized simply by their names. This requires an extra program in the linkage step, called `collect2`. This program pretends to be the linker, for use with GNU CC; it does its job by running the ordinary linker, but also arranges to include the vectors of initialization and termination functions. These functions are called via `__main` as described above.

Choosing among these configuration options has been simplified by a set of operating-system-dependent files in the 'config' subdirectory. These files define all of the relevant parameters. Usually it is sufficient to include one into your specific machine-dependent configuration file. These files are:

'`aoutos.h`'
:   For operating systems using the 'a.out' format.

'`next.h`'   For operating systems using the 'MachO' format.

'`svr3.h`'   For System V Release 3 and similar systems using 'COFF' format.

'`svr4.h`'   For System V Release 4 and similar systems using 'ELF' format.

'`vms.h`'   For the VMS operating system.

17.16.6 Macros Controlling Initialization Routines

Here are the macros that control how the compiler handles initialization and termination functions:

`INIT_SECTION_ASM_OP`
:   If defined, a C string constant for the assembler operation to identify the following data as initialization code. If not defined, GNU CC will assume such a section does not exist. When you are using special sections for initialization and termination functions, this macro also controls how 'crtstuff.c' and 'libgcc2.c' arrange to run the initialization functions.

`HAS_INIT_SECTION`
:   If defined, `main` will not call `__main` as described above. This macro should be defined for systems that control the contents of the init section on a symbol-by-symbol basis, such as OSF/1, and should not be defined explicitly for systems that support `INIT_SECTION_ASM_OP`.

`LD_INIT_SWITCH`
:   If defined, a C string constant for a switch that tells the linker that the following symbol is an initialization routine.

`LD_FINI_SWITCH`
:   If defined, a C string constant for a switch that tells the linker that the following symbol is a finalization routine.

`INVOKE__main`

> If defined, `main` will call `__main` despite the presence of `INIT_`
> `SECTION_ASM_OP`. This macro should be defined for systems
> where the init section is not actually run automatically, but is
> still useful for collecting the lists of constructors and destructors.

`ASM_OUTPUT_CONSTRUCTOR` (*stream, name*)

> Define this macro as a C statement to output on the stream
> *stream* the assembler code to arrange to call the function named
> *name* at initialization time.

> Assume that *name* is the name of a C function generated au-
> tomatically by the compiler. This function takes no arguments.
> Use the function `assemble_name` to output the name *name*; this
> performs any system-specific syntactic transformations such as
> adding an underscore.

> If you don't define this macro, nothing special is output to ar-
> range to call the function. This is correct when the function
> will be called in some other manner—for example, by means of
> the `collect2` program, which looks through the symbol table
> to find these functions by their names.

`ASM_OUTPUT_DESTRUCTOR` (*stream, name*)

> This is like `ASM_OUTPUT_CONSTRUCTOR` but used for termination
> functions rather than initialization functions.

> When `ASM_OUTPUT_CONSTRUCTOR` and `ASM_OUTPUT_DESTRUCTOR`
> are defined, the initializaiton routine generated for the generated
> object file will have static linkage.

If your system uses `collect2` as the means of processing constructors,
then that program normally uses `nm` to scan an object file for constructor
functions to be called. On such systems you must not define `ASM_OUTPUT_`
`CONSTRUCTOR` and `ASM_OUTPUT_DESTRUCTOR` as the object file's initialization
routine must have global scope.

On certain kinds of systems, you can define these macros to make
`collect2` work faster (and, in some cases, make it work at all):

`OBJECT_FORMAT_COFF`

> Define this macro if the system uses COFF (Common Ob-
> ject File Format) object files, so that `collect2` can assume
> this format and scan object files directly for dynamic construc-
> tor/destructor functions.

`OBJECT_FORMAT_ROSE`

> Define this macro if the system uses ROSE format object files,
> so that `collect2` can assume this format and scan object files
> directly for dynamic constructor/destructor functions.

> These macros are effective only in a native compiler; `collect2`
> as part of a cross compiler always uses `nm` for the target machine.

REAL_NM_FILE_NAME

> Define this macro as a C string constant containing the file name to use to execute **nm**. The default is to search the path normally for **nm**.
>
> If your system supports shared libraries and has a program to list the dynamic dependencies of a given library or executable, you can define these macros to enable support for running initialization and termination functions in shared libraries:

LDD_SUFFIX

> Define this macro to a C string constant containing the name of the program which lists dynamic dependencies, like **"ldd"** under SunOS 4.

PARSE_LDD_OUTPUT (*PTR*)

> Define this macro to be C code that extracts filenames from the output of the program denoted by **LDD_SUFFIX**. *PTR* is a variable of type **char *** that points to the beginning of a line of output from **LDD_SUFFIX**. If the line lists a dynamic dependency, the code must advance *PTR* to the beginning of the filename on that line. Otherwise, it must set *PTR* to **NULL**.

17.16.7 Output of Assembler Instructions

This describes assembler instruction output.

REGISTER_NAMES

> A C initializer containing the assembler's names for the machine registers, each one as a C string constant. This is what translates register numbers in the compiler into assembler language.

ADDITIONAL_REGISTER_NAMES

> If defined, a C initializer for an array of structures containing a name and a register number. This macro defines additional names for hard registers, thus allowing the **asm** option in declarations to refer to registers using alternate names.

ASM_OUTPUT_OPCODE (*stream, ptr*)

> Define this macro if you are using an unusual assembler that requires different names for the machine instructions.
>
> The definition is a C statement or statements which output an assembler instruction opcode to the stdio stream *stream*. The macro-operand *ptr* is a variable of type **char *** which points to the opcode name in its "internal" form—the form that is written in the machine description. The definition should output the opcode name to *stream*, performing any translation you desire, and increment the variable *ptr* to point at the end of the opcode so that it will not be output twice.

In fact, your macro definition may process less than the entire opcode name, or more than the opcode name; but if you want to process text that includes '%'-sequences to substitute operands, you must take care of the substitution yourself. Just be sure to increment *ptr* over whatever text should not be output normally.

If you need to look at the operand values, they can be found as the elements of `recog_operand`.

If the macro definition does nothing, the instruction is output in the usual way.

FINAL_PRESCAN_INSN (*insn*, *opvec*, *noperands*)

> If defined, a C statement to be executed just prior to the output of assembler code for *insn*, to modify the extracted operands so they will be output differently.
>
> Here the argument *opvec* is the vector containing the operands extracted from *insn*, and *noperands* is the number of elements of the vector which contain meaningful data for this insn. The contents of this vector are what will be used to convert the insn template into assembler code, so you can change the assembler output by changing the contents of the vector.
>
> This macro is useful when various assembler syntaxes share a single file of instruction patterns; by defining this macro differently, you can cause a large class of instructions to be output differently (such as with rearranged operands). Naturally, variations in assembler syntax affecting individual insn patterns ought to be handled by writing conditional output routines in those patterns.
>
> If this macro is not defined, it is equivalent to a null statement.

FINAL_PRESCAN_LABEL

> If defined, FINAL_PRESCAN_INSN will be called on each CODE_LABEL. In that case, *opvec* will be a null pointer and *noperands* will be zero.

PRINT_OPERAND (*stream*, *x*, *code*)

> A C compound statement to output to stdio stream *stream* the assembler syntax for an instruction operand *x*. *x* is an RTL expression.
>
> *code* is a value that can be used to specify one of several ways of printing the operand. It is used when identical operands must be printed differently depending on the context. *code* comes from the '%' specification that was used to request printing of the operand. If the specification was just '%*digit*' then *code* is 0; if the specification was '%*ltr digit*' then *code* is the ASCII code for *ltr*.

If *x* is a register, this macro should print the register's name. The names can be found in an array `reg_names` whose type is `char *[]`. `reg_names` is initialized from `REGISTER_NAMES`.

When the machine description has a specification '%*punct*' (a '%' followed by a punctuation character), this macro is called with a null pointer for *x* and the punctuation character for *code*.

PRINT_OPERAND_PUNCT_VALID_P (*code*)

A C expression which evaluates to true if *code* is a valid punctuation character for use in the `PRINT_OPERAND` macro. If `PRINT_OPERAND_PUNCT_VALID_P` is not defined, it means that no punctuation characters (except for the standard one, '%') are used in this way.

PRINT_OPERAND_ADDRESS (*stream*, *x*)

A C compound statement to output to stdio stream *stream* the assembler syntax for an instruction operand that is a memory reference whose address is *x*. *x* is an RTL expression.

On some machines, the syntax for a symbolic address depends on the section that the address refers to. On these machines, define the macro `ENCODE_SECTION_INFO` to store the information into the `symbol_ref`, and then check for it here. See Section 17.16 [Assembler Format], page 478.

DBR_OUTPUT_SEQEND(*file*)

A C statement, to be executed after all slot-filler instructions have been output. If necessary, call `dbr_sequence_length` to determine the number of slots filled in a sequence (zero if not currently outputting a sequence), to decide how many no-ops to output, or whatever.

Don't define this macro if it has nothing to do, but it is helpful in reading assembly output if the extent of the delay sequence is made explicit (e.g. with white space).

Note that output routines for instructions with delay slots must be prepared to deal with not being output as part of a sequence (i.e. when the scheduling pass is not run, or when no slot fillers could be found.) The variable `final_sequence` is null when not processing a sequence, otherwise it contains the `sequence` rtx being output.

REGISTER_PREFIX
LOCAL_LABEL_PREFIX
USER_LABEL_PREFIX
IMMEDIATE_PREFIX

If defined, C string expressions to be used for the '%R', '%L', '%U', and '%I' options of `asm_fprintf` (see 'final.c'). These are useful when a single 'md' file must support multiple assembler formats. In that case, the various 'tm.h' files can define these macros differently.

ASSEMBLER_DIALECT

If your target supports multiple dialects of assembler language (such as different opcodes), define this macro as a C expression that gives the numeric index of the assembler language dialect to use, with zero as the first variant.

If this macro is defined, you may use constructs of the form '{option0|option1|option2...}' in the output templates of patterns (see Section 16.4 [Output Template], page 334) or in the first argument of asm_fprintf. This construct outputs 'option0', 'option1' or 'option2', etc., if the value of ASSEMBLER_DIALECT is zero, one or two, etc. Any special characters within these strings retain their usual meaning.

If you do not define this macro, the characters '{', '|' and '}' do not have any special meaning when used in templates or operands to asm_fprintf.

Define the macros REGISTER_PREFIX, LOCAL_LABEL_PREFIX, USER_LABEL_PREFIX and IMMEDIATE_PREFIX if you can express the variations in assembler language syntax with that mechanism. Define ASSEMBLER_DIALECT and use the '{option0|option1}' syntax if the syntax variant are larger and involve such things as different opcodes or operand order.

ASM_OUTPUT_REG_PUSH (*stream*, *regno*)

A C expression to output to *stream* some assembler code which will push hard register number *regno* onto the stack. The code need not be optimal, since this macro is used only when profiling.

ASM_OUTPUT_REG_POP (*stream*, *regno*)

A C expression to output to *stream* some assembler code which will pop hard register number *regno* off of the stack. The code need not be optimal, since this macro is used only when profiling.

17.16.8 Output of Dispatch Tables

This concerns dispatch tables.

ASM_OUTPUT_ADDR_DIFF_ELT (*stream*, *body*, *value*, *rel*)

A C statement to output to the stdio stream *stream* an assembler pseudo-instruction to generate a difference between two labels. *value* and *rel* are the numbers of two internal labels. The definitions of these labels are output using ASM_OUTPUT_INTERNAL_LABEL, and they must be printed in the same way here. For example,

> fprintf (*stream*, "\t.word L%d-L%d\n",
>   *value*, *rel*)

You must provide this macro on machines where the addresses in a dispatch table are relative to the table's own address. If defined, GNU CC will also use this macro on all machines when producing PIC. *body* is the body of the ADDR_DIFF_VEC; it is provided so that the mode and flags can be read.

`ASM_OUTPUT_ADDR_VEC_ELT` (*stream*, *value*)

This macro should be provided on machines where the addresses in a dispatch table are absolute.

The definition should be a C statement to output to the stdio stream *stream* an assembler pseudo-instruction to generate a reference to a label. *value* is the number of an internal label whose definition is output using `ASM_OUTPUT_INTERNAL_LABEL`. For example,

> fprintf (*stream*, "\t.word L%d\n", *value*)

`ASM_OUTPUT_CASE_LABEL` (*stream*, *prefix*, *num*, *table*)

Define this if the label before a jump-table needs to be output specially. The first three arguments are the same as for `ASM_OUTPUT_INTERNAL_LABEL`; the fourth argument is the jump-table which follows (a `jump_insn` containing an `addr_vec` or `addr_diff_vec`).

This feature is used on system V to output a `swbeg` statement for the table.

If this macro is not defined, these labels are output with `ASM_OUTPUT_INTERNAL_LABEL`.

`ASM_OUTPUT_CASE_END` (*stream*, *num*, *table*)

Define this if something special must be output at the end of a jump-table. The definition should be a C statement to be executed after the assembler code for the table is written. It should write the appropriate code to stdio stream *stream*. The argument *table* is the jump-table insn, and *num* is the label-number of the preceding label.

If this macro is not defined, nothing special is output at the end of the jump-table.

17.16.9 Assembler Commands for Exception Regions

This describes commands marking the start and the end of an exception region.

`ASM_OUTPUT_EH_REGION_BEG` ()

A C expression to output text to mark the start of an exception region.

This macro need not be defined on most platforms.

ASM_OUTPUT_EH_REGION_END ()

A C expression to output text to mark the end of an exception region.

This macro need not be defined on most platforms.

EXCEPTION_SECTION ()

A C expression to switch to the section in which the main exception table is to be placed (see Section 17.14 [Sections], page 474). The default is a section named `.gcc_except_table` on machines that support named sections via `ASM_OUTPUT_SECTION_NAME`, otherwise if '-fpic' or '-fPIC' is in effect, the `data_section`, otherwise the `readonly_data_section`.

EH_FRAME_SECTION_ASM_OP

If defined, a C string constant for the assembler operation to switch to the section for exception handling frame unwind information. If not defined, GNU CC will provide a default definition if the target supports named sections. 'crtstuff.c' uses this macro to switch to the appropriate section.

You should define this symbol if your target supports DWARF 2 frame unwind information and the default definition does not work.

OMIT_EH_TABLE ()

A C expression that is nonzero if the normal exception table output should be omitted.

This macro need not be defined on most platforms.

EH_TABLE_LOOKUP ()

Alternate runtime support for looking up an exception at runtime and finding the associated handler, if the default method won't work.

This macro need not be defined on most platforms.

DOESNT_NEED_UNWINDER

A C expression that decides whether or not the current function needs to have a function unwinder generated for it. See the file `except.c` for details on when to define this, and how.

MASK_RETURN_ADDR

An rtx used to mask the return address found via RETURN_ADDR_RTX, so that it does not contain any extraneous set bits in it.

DWARF2_UNWIND_INFO

Define this macro to 0 if your target supports DWARF 2 frame unwind information, but it does not yet work with exception handling. Otherwise, if your target supports this information (if it defines 'INCOMING_RETURN_ADDR_RTX' and either 'UNALIGNED_INT_ASM_OP' or 'OBJECT_FORMAT_ELF'), GCC will provide a default definition of 1.

If this macro is defined to 1, the DWARF 2 unwinder will be the default exception handling mechanism; otherwise, setjmp/longjmp will be used by default.

If this macro is defined to anything, the DWARF 2 unwinder will be used instead of inline unwinders and __unwind_function in the non-setjmp case.

17.16.10 Assembler Commands for Alignment

This describes commands for alignment.

LABEL_ALIGN_AFTER_BARRIER (*label*)
> The alignment (log base 2) to put in front of *label*, which follows a BARRIER.
>
> This macro need not be defined if you don't want any special alignment to be done at such a time. Most machine descriptions do not currently define the macro.

LOOP_ALIGN (*label*)
> The alignment (log base 2) to put in front of *label*, which follows a NOTE_INSN_LOOP_BEG note.
>
> This macro need not be defined if you don't want any special alignment to be done at such a time. Most machine descriptions do not currently define the macro.

LABEL_ALIGN (*label*)
> The alignment (log base 2) to put in front of *label*. If LABEL_ALIGN_AFTER_BARRIER / LOOP_ALIGN specify a different alignment, the maximum of the specified values is used.

ASM_OUTPUT_SKIP (*stream, nbytes*)
> A C statement to output to the stdio stream *stream* an assembler instruction to advance the location counter by *nbytes* bytes. Those bytes should be zero when loaded. *nbytes* will be a C expression of type int.

ASM_NO_SKIP_IN_TEXT
> Define this macro if ASM_OUTPUT_SKIP should not be used in the text section because it fails to put zeros in the bytes that are skipped. This is true on many Unix systems, where the pseudo-op to skip bytes produces no-op instructions rather than zeros when used in the text section.

ASM_OUTPUT_ALIGN (*stream*, *power*)

> A C statement to output to the stdio stream *stream* an assembler command to advance the location counter to a multiple of 2 to the *power* bytes. *power* will be a C expression of type `int`.

ASM_OUTPUT_MAX_SKIP_ALIGN (*stream*, *power*, *max_skip*)

> A C statement to output to the stdio stream *stream* an assembler command to advance the location counter to a multiple of 2 to the *power* bytes, but only if *max_skip* or fewer bytes are needed to satisfy the alignment request. *power* and *max_skip* will be a C expression of type `int`.

17.17 Controlling Debugging Information Format

This describes how to specify debugging information.

17.17.1 Macros Affecting All Debugging Formats

These macros affect all debugging formats.

DBX_REGISTER_NUMBER (*regno*)

> A C expression that returns the DBX register number for the compiler register number *regno*. In simple cases, the value of this expression may be *regno* itself. But sometimes there are some registers that the compiler knows about and DBX does not, or vice versa. In such cases, some register may need to have one number in the compiler and another for DBX.
>
> If two registers have consecutive numbers inside GNU CC, and they can be used as a pair to hold a multiword value, then they *must* have consecutive numbers after renumbering with `DBX_REGISTER_NUMBER`. Otherwise, debuggers will be unable to access such a pair, because they expect register pairs to be consecutive in their own numbering scheme.
>
> If you find yourself defining `DBX_REGISTER_NUMBER` in way that does not preserve register pairs, then what you must do instead is redefine the actual register numbering scheme.

DEBUGGER_AUTO_OFFSET (*x*)

> A C expression that returns the integer offset value for an automatic variable having address *x* (an RTL expression). The default computation assumes that *x* is based on the frame-pointer and gives the offset from the frame-pointer. This is required for targets that produce debugging output for DBX or COFF-style debugging output for SDB and allow the frame-pointer to be eliminated when the '-g' options is used.

DEBUGGER_ARG_OFFSET (*offset*, *x*)

A C expression that returns the integer offset value for an argument having address *x* (an RTL expression). The nominal offset is *offset*.

PREFERRED_DEBUGGING_TYPE

A C expression that returns the type of debugging output GNU CC should produce when the user specifies just '-g'. Define this if you have arranged for GNU CC to support more than one format of debugging output. Currently, the allowable values are DBX_DEBUG, SDB_DEBUG, DWARF_DEBUG, DWARF2_DEBUG, and XCOFF_DEBUG.

When the user specifies '-ggdb', GNU CC normally also uses the value of this macro to select the debugging output format, but with two exceptions. If DWARF2_DEBUGGING_INFO is defined and LINKER_DOES_NOT_WORK_WITH_DWARF2 is not defined, GNU CC uses the value DWARF2_DEBUG. Otherwise, if DBX_DEBUGGING_INFO is defined, GNU CC uses DBX_DEBUG.

The value of this macro only affects the default debugging output; the user can always get a specific type of output by using '-gstabs', '-gcoff', '-gdwarf-1', '-gdwarf-2', or '-gxcoff'.

17.17.2 Specific Options for DBX Output

These are specific options for DBX output.

DBX_DEBUGGING_INFO

Define this macro if GNU CC should produce debugging output for DBX in response to the '-g' option.

XCOFF_DEBUGGING_INFO

Define this macro if GNU CC should produce XCOFF format debugging output in response to the '-g' option. This is a variant of DBX format.

DEFAULT_GDB_EXTENSIONS

Define this macro to control whether GNU CC should by default generate GDB's extended version of DBX debugging information (assuming DBX-format debugging information is enabled at all). If you don't define the macro, the default is 1: always generate the extended information if there is any occasion to.

DEBUG_SYMS_TEXT

Define this macro if all .stabs commands should be output while in the text section.

ASM_STABS_OP

A C string constant naming the assembler pseudo op to use instead of .stabs to define an ordinary debugging symbol. If you don't define this macro, `.stabs` is used. This macro applies only to DBX debugging information format.

ASM_STABD_OP

A C string constant naming the assembler pseudo op to use instead of `.stabd` to define a debugging symbol whose value is the current location. If you don't define this macro, `.stabd` is used. This macro applies only to DBX debugging information format.

ASM_STABN_OP

A C string constant naming the assembler pseudo op to use instead of `.stabn` to define a debugging symbol with no name. If you don't define this macro, `.stabn` is used. This macro applies only to DBX debugging information format.

DBX_NO_XREFS

Define this macro if DBX on your system does not support the construct 'xs*tagname*'. On some systems, this construct is used to describe a forward reference to a structure named *tagname*. On other systems, this construct is not supported at all.

DBX_CONTIN_LENGTH

A symbol name in DBX-format debugging information is normally continued (split into two separate `.stabs` directives) when it exceeds a certain length (by default, 80 characters). On some operating systems, DBX requires this splitting; on others, splitting must not be done. You can inhibit splitting by defining this macro with the value zero. You can override the default splitting-length by defining this macro as an expression for the length you desire.

DBX_CONTIN_CHAR

Normally continuation is indicated by adding a '\' character to the end of a `.stabs` string when a continuation follows. To use a different character instead, define this macro as a character constant for the character you want to use. Do not define this macro if backslash is correct for your system.

DBX_STATIC_STAB_DATA_SECTION

Define this macro if it is necessary to go to the data section before outputting the '`.stabs`' pseudo-op for a non-global static variable.

DBX_TYPE_DECL_STABS_CODE

The value to use in the "code" field of the `.stabs` directive for a typedef. The default is `N_LSYM`.

DBX_STATIC_CONST_VAR_CODE

> The value to use in the "code" field of the `.stabs` directive for a static variable located in the text section. DBX format does not provide any "right" way to do this. The default is `N_FUN`.

DBX_REGPARM_STABS_CODE

> The value to use in the "code" field of the `.stabs` directive for a parameter passed in registers. DBX format does not provide any "right" way to do this. The default is `N_RSYM`.

DBX_REGPARM_STABS_LETTER

> The letter to use in DBX symbol data to identify a symbol as a parameter passed in registers. DBX format does not customarily provide any way to do this. The default is `'P'`.

DBX_MEMPARM_STABS_LETTER

> The letter to use in DBX symbol data to identify a symbol as a stack parameter. The default is `'p'`.

DBX_FUNCTION_FIRST

> Define this macro if the DBX information for a function and its arguments should precede the assembler code for the function. Normally, in DBX format, the debugging information entirely follows the assembler code.

DBX_LBRAC_FIRST

> Define this macro if the `N_LBRAC` symbol for a block should precede the debugging information for variables and functions defined in that block. Normally, in DBX format, the `N_LBRAC` symbol comes first.

DBX_BLOCKS_FUNCTION_RELATIVE

> Define this macro if the value of a symbol describing the scope of a block (`N_LBRAC` or `N_RBRAC`) should be relative to the start of the enclosing function. Normally, GNU C uses an absolute address.

DBX_USE_BINCL

> Define this macro if GNU C should generate `N_BINCL` and `N_EINCL` stabs for included header files, as on Sun systems. This macro also directs GNU C to output a type number as a pair of a file number and a type number within the file. Normally, GNU C does not generate `N_BINCL` or `N_EINCL` stabs, and it outputs a single number for a type number.

17.17.3 Open-Ended Hooks for DBX Format

These are hooks for DBX format.

`DBX_OUTPUT_LBRAC` (*stream*, *name*)

> Define this macro to say how to output to *stream* the debugging information for the start of a scope level for variable names. The argument *name* is the name of an assembler symbol (for use with `assemble_name`) whose value is the address where the scope begins.

`DBX_OUTPUT_RBRAC` (*stream*, *name*)

> Like `DBX_OUTPUT_LBRAC`, but for the end of a scope level.

`DBX_OUTPUT_ENUM` (*stream*, *type*)

> Define this macro if the target machine requires special handling to output an enumeration type. The definition should be a C statement (sans semicolon) to output the appropriate information to *stream* for the type *type*.

`DBX_OUTPUT_FUNCTION_END` (*stream*, *function*)

> Define this macro if the target machine requires special output at the end of the debugging information for a function. The definition should be a C statement (sans semicolon) to output the appropriate information to *stream*. *function* is the `FUNCTION_DECL` node for the function.

`DBX_OUTPUT_STANDARD_TYPES` (*syms*)

> Define this macro if you need to control the order of output of the standard data types at the beginning of compilation. The argument *syms* is a `tree` which is a chain of all the predefined global symbols, including names of data types.
>
> Normally, DBX output starts with definitions of the types for integers and characters, followed by all the other predefined types of the particular language in no particular order.
>
> On some machines, it is necessary to output different particular types first. To do this, define `DBX_OUTPUT_STANDARD_TYPES` to output those symbols in the necessary order. Any predefined types that you don't explicitly output will be output afterward in no particular order.
>
> Be careful not to define this macro so that it works only for C. There are no global variables to access most of the built-in types, because another language may have another set of types. The way to output a particular type is to look through *syms* to see if you can find it. Here is an example:
>
> ```
> {
>   tree decl;
>   for (decl = syms; decl; decl = TREE_CHAIN (decl))
>     if (!strcmp (IDENTIFIER_POINTER (DECL_NAME (decl)),
>                  "long int"))
>       dbxout_symbol (decl);
> ```

```
        . . .
    }
```

This does nothing if the expected type does not exist.

See the function `init_decl_processing` in 'c-decl.c' to find the names to use for all the built-in C types.

Here is another way of finding a particular type:

```
    {
      tree decl;
      for (decl = syms; decl; decl = TREE_CHAIN (decl))
        if (TREE_CODE (decl) == TYPE_DECL
            && (TREE_CODE (TREE_TYPE (decl))
                == INTEGER_CST)
            && TYPE_PRECISION (TREE_TYPE (decl)) == 16
            && TYPE_UNSIGNED (TREE_TYPE (decl)))
          /* This must be unsigned short. */
          dbxout_symbol (decl);
        . . .
    }
```

`NO_DBX_FUNCTION_END`

Some stabs encapsulation formats (in particular ECOFF), cannot handle the `.stabs "",N_FUN,,0,0,Lscope-function-1` gdb dbx extention construct. On those machines, define this macro to turn this feature off without disturbing the rest of the gdb extensions.

17.17.4 File Names in DBX Format

This describes file names in DBX format.

`DBX_WORKING_DIRECTORY`

Define this if DBX wants to have the current directory recorded in each object file.

Note that the working directory is always recorded if GDB extensions are enabled.

`DBX_OUTPUT_MAIN_SOURCE_FILENAME` (*stream, name*)

A C statement to output DBX debugging information to the stdio stream *stream* which indicates that file *name* is the main source file—the file specified as the input file for compilation. This macro is called only once, at the beginning of compilation.

This macro need not be defined if the standard form of output for DBX debugging information is appropriate.

DBX_OUTPUT_MAIN_SOURCE_DIRECTORY (*stream*, *name*)

>A C statement to output DBX debugging information to the stdio stream *stream* which indicates that the current directory during compilation is named *name*.
>
>This macro need not be defined if the standard form of output for DBX debugging information is appropriate.

DBX_OUTPUT_MAIN_SOURCE_FILE_END (*stream*, *name*)

>A C statement to output DBX debugging information at the end of compilation of the main source file *name*.
>
>If you don't define this macro, nothing special is output at the end of compilation, which is correct for most machines.

DBX_OUTPUT_SOURCE_FILENAME (*stream*, *name*)

>A C statement to output DBX debugging information to the stdio stream *stream* which indicates that file *name* is the current source file. This output is generated each time input shifts to a different source file as a result of '#include', the end of an included file, or a '#line' command.
>
>This macro need not be defined if the standard form of output for DBX debugging information is appropriate.

17.17.5 Macros for SDB and DWARF Output

Here are macros for SDB and DWARF output.

SDB_DEBUGGING_INFO

>Define this macro if GNU CC should produce COFF-style debugging output for SDB in response to the '-g' option.

DWARF_DEBUGGING_INFO

>Define this macro if GNU CC should produce dwarf format debugging output in response to the '-g' option.

DWARF2_DEBUGGING_INFO

>Define this macro if GNU CC should produce dwarf version 2 format debugging output in response to the '-g' option.
>
>To support optional call frame debugging information, you must also define INCOMING_RETURN_ADDR_RTX and either set RTX_FRAME_RELATED_P on the prologue insns if you use RTL for the prologue, or call dwarf2out_def_cfa and dwarf2out_reg_save as appropriate from FUNCTION_PROLOGUE if you don't.

DWARF2_FRAME_INFO

>Define this macro to a nonzero value if GNU CC should always output Dwarf 2 frame information. If DWARF2_UNWIND_INFO (see Section 17.16.9 [Exception Region Output], page 498 is nonzero, GNU CC will output this information not matter how you define DWARF2_FRAME_INFO.

`LINKER_DOES_NOT_WORK_WITH_DWARF2`
> Define this macro if the linker does not work with Dwarf version 2. Normally, if the user specifies only '`-ggdb`' GNU CC will use Dwarf version 2 if available; this macro disables this. See the description of the `PREFERRED_DEBUGGING_TYPE` macro for more details.

`PUT_SDB_`...
> Define these macros to override the assembler syntax for the special SDB assembler directives. See '`sdbout.c`' for a list of these macros and their arguments. If the standard syntax is used, you need not define them yourself.

`SDB_DELIM`
> Some assemblers do not support a semicolon as a delimiter, even between SDB assembler directives. In that case, define this macro to be the delimiter to use (usually '`\n`'). It is not necessary to define a new set of `PUT_SDB_`*op* macros if this is the only change required.

`SDB_GENERATE_FAKE`
> Define this macro to override the usual method of constructing a dummy name for anonymous structure and union types. See '`sdbout.c`' for more information.

`SDB_ALLOW_UNKNOWN_REFERENCES`
> Define this macro to allow references to unknown structure, union, or enumeration tags to be emitted. Standard COFF does not allow handling of unknown references, MIPS ECOFF has support for it.

`SDB_ALLOW_FORWARD_REFERENCES`
> Define this macro to allow references to structure, union, or enumeration tags that have not yet been seen to be handled. Some assemblers choke if forward tags are used, while some require it.

17.18 Cross Compilation and Floating Point

While all modern machines use 2's complement representation for integers, there are a variety of representations for floating point numbers. This means that in a cross-compiler the representation of floating point numbers in the compiled program may be different from that used in the machine doing the compilation.

Because different representation systems may offer different amounts of range and precision, the cross compiler cannot safely use the host machine's floating point arithmetic. Therefore, floating point constants must be represented in the target machine's format. This means that the cross compiler cannot use `atof` to parse a floating point constant; it must have its own special routine to use instead. Also, constant folding must emulate the target machine's arithmetic (or must not be done at all).

The macros in the following table should be defined only if you are cross compiling between different floating point formats.

Otherwise, don't define them. Then default definitions will be set up which use `double` as the data type, `==` to test for equality, etc.

You don't need to worry about how many times you use an operand of any of these macros. The compiler never uses operands which have side effects.

REAL_VALUE_TYPE

> A macro for the C data type to be used to hold a floating point value in the target machine's format. Typically this would be a `struct` containing an array of `int`.

REAL_VALUES_EQUAL (x, y)

> A macro for a C expression which compares for equality the two values, x and y, both of type REAL_VALUE_TYPE.

REAL_VALUES_LESS (x, y)

> A macro for a C expression which tests whether x is less than y, both values being of type REAL_VALUE_TYPE and interpreted as floating point numbers in the target machine's representation.

REAL_VALUE_LDEXP (x, *scale*)

> A macro for a C expression which performs the standard library function `ldexp`, but using the target machine's floating point representation. Both x and the value of the expression have type REAL_VALUE_TYPE. The second argument, *scale*, is an integer.

REAL_VALUE_FIX (x)

> A macro whose definition is a C expression to convert the target-machine floating point value x to a signed integer. x has type REAL_VALUE_TYPE.

REAL_VALUE_UNSIGNED_FIX (x)

> A macro whose definition is a C expression to convert the target-machine floating point value x to an unsigned integer. x has type REAL_VALUE_TYPE.

REAL_VALUE_RNDZINT (x)

> A macro whose definition is a C expression to round the target-machine floating point value x towards zero to an integer value (but still as a floating point number). x has type REAL_VALUE_TYPE, and so does the value.

REAL_VALUE_UNSIGNED_RNDZINT (x)

> A macro whose definition is a C expression to round the target-machine floating point value x towards zero to an unsigned in-

teger value (but still represented as a floating point number). x has type `REAL_VALUE_TYPE`, and so does the value.

`REAL_VALUE_ATOF` (*string, mode*)

A macro for a C expression which converts *string*, an expression of type `char *`, into a floating point number in the target machine's representation for mode *mode*. The value has type `REAL_VALUE_TYPE`.

`REAL_INFINITY`

Define this macro if infinity is a possible floating point value, and therefore division by 0 is legitimate.

`REAL_VALUE_ISINF` (x)

A macro for a C expression which determines whether x, a floating point value, is infinity. The value has type `int`. By default, this is defined to call `isinf`.

`REAL_VALUE_ISNAN` (x)

A macro for a C expression which determines whether x, a floating point value, is a "nan" (not-a-number). The value has type `int`. By default, this is defined to call `isnan`.

Define the following additional macros if you want to make floating point constant folding work while cross compiling. If you don't define them, cross compilation is still possible, but constant folding will not happen for floating point values.

`REAL_ARITHMETIC` (*output, code, x, y*)

A macro for a C statement which calculates an arithmetic operation of the two floating point values x and y, both of type `REAL_VALUE_TYPE` in the target machine's representation, to produce a result of the same type and representation which is stored in *output* (which will be a variable).

The operation to be performed is specified by *code*, a tree code which will always be one of the following: `PLUS_EXPR`, `MINUS_EXPR`, `MULT_EXPR`, `RDIV_EXPR`, `MAX_EXPR`, `MIN_EXPR`.

The expansion of this macro is responsible for checking for overflow. If overflow happens, the macro expansion should execute the statement `return 0;`, which indicates the inability to perform the arithmetic operation requested.

`REAL_VALUE_NEGATE` (x)

A macro for a C expression which returns the negative of the floating point value x. Both x and the value of the expression have type `REAL_VALUE_TYPE` and are in the target machine's floating point representation.

There is no way for this macro to report overflow, since overflow can't happen in the negation operation.

REAL_VALUE_TRUNCATE (*mode*, *x*)

> A macro for a C expression which converts the floating point value *x* to mode *mode*.
>
> Both *x* and the value of the expression are in the target machine's floating point representation and have type REAL_VALUE_TYPE. However, the value should have an appropriate bit pattern to be output properly as a floating constant whose precision accords with mode *mode*.
>
> There is no way for this macro to report overflow.

REAL_VALUE_TO_INT (*low*, *high*, *x*)

> A macro for a C expression which converts a floating point value *x* into a double-precision integer which is then stored into *low* and *high*, two variables of type *int*.

REAL_VALUE_FROM_INT (*x*, *low*, *high*, *mode*)

> A macro for a C expression which converts a double-precision integer found in *low* and *high*, two variables of type *int*, into a floating point value which is then stored into *x*. The value is in the target machine's representation for mode *mode* and has the type REAL_VALUE_TYPE.

17.19 Miscellaneous Parameters

Here are several miscellaneous parameters.

PREDICATE_CODES

> Define this if you have defined special-purpose predicates in the file '*machine*.c'. This macro is called within an initializer of an array of structures. The first field in the structure is the name of a predicate and the second field is an array of rtl codes. For each predicate, list all rtl codes that can be in expressions matched by the predicate. The list should have a trailing comma. Here is an example of two entries in the list for a typical RISC machine:
>
> ```
> #define PREDICATE_CODES \
>   {"gen_reg_rtx_operand", {SUBREG, REG}},  \
>   {"reg_or_short_cint_operand", {SUBREG, REG, CONST_INT}},
> ```
>
> Defining this macro does not affect the generated code (however, incorrect definitions that omit an rtl code that may be matched by the predicate can cause the compiler to malfunction). Instead, it allows the table built by 'genrecog' to be more compact and efficient, thus speeding up the compiler. The most important predicates to include in the list specified by this macro are those used in the most insn patterns.

CASE_VECTOR_MODE

> An alias for a machine mode name. This is the machine mode that elements of a jump-table should have.

CASE_VECTOR_SHORTEN_MODE (*min_offset*, *max_offset*, *body*)

> Optional: return the preferred mode for an `addr_diff_vec` when the minimum and maximum offset are known. If you define this, it enables extra code in branch shortening to deal with `addr_diff_vec`. To make this work, you also have to define INSN_ALIGN and make the alignment for `addr_diff_vec` explicit. The *body* argument is provided so that the offset_unsigned and scale flags can be updated.

CASE_VECTOR_PC_RELATIVE

> Define this macro to be a C expression to indicate when jump-tables should contain relative addresses. If jump-tables never contain relative addresses, then you need not define this macro.

CASE_DROPS_THROUGH

> Define this if control falls through a `case` insn when the index value is out of range. This means the specified default-label is actually ignored by the `case` insn proper.

CASE_VALUES_THRESHOLD

> Define this to be the smallest number of different values for which it is best to use a jump-table instead of a tree of conditional branches. The default is four for machines with a `casesi` instruction and five otherwise. This is best for most machines.

WORD_REGISTER_OPERATIONS

> Define this macro if operations between registers with integral mode smaller than a word are always performed on the entire register. Most RISC machines have this property and most CISC machines do not.

LOAD_EXTEND_OP (*mode*)

> Define this macro to be a C expression indicating when insns that read memory in *mode*, an integral mode narrower than a word, set the bits outside of *mode* to be either the sign-extension or the zero-extension of the data read. Return `SIGN_EXTEND` for values of *mode* for which the insn sign-extends, `ZERO_EXTEND` for which it zero-extends, and `NIL` for other modes.
>
> This macro is not called with *mode* non-integral or with a width greater than or equal to `BITS_PER_WORD`, so you may return any value in this case. Do not define this macro if it would always return `NIL`. On machines where this macro is defined, you will normally define it as the constant `SIGN_EXTEND` or `ZERO_EXTEND`.

SHORT_IMMEDIATES_SIGN_EXTEND

> Define this macro if loading short immediate values into registers sign extends.

IMPLICIT_FIX_EXPR

> An alias for a tree code that should be used by default for conversion of floating point values to fixed point. Normally, FIX_ROUND_EXPR is used.

FIXUNS_TRUNC_LIKE_FIX_TRUNC

> Define this macro if the same instructions that convert a floating point number to a signed fixed point number also convert validly to an unsigned one.

EASY_DIV_EXPR

> An alias for a tree code that is the easiest kind of division to compile code for in the general case. It may be TRUNC_DIV_EXPR, FLOOR_DIV_EXPR, CEIL_DIV_EXPR or ROUND_DIV_EXPR. These four division operators differ in how they round the result to an integer. EASY_DIV_EXPR is used when it is permissible to use any of those kinds of division and the choice should be made on the basis of efficiency.

MOVE_MAX   The maximum number of bytes that a single instruction can move quickly between memory and registers or between two memory locations.

MAX_MOVE_MAX

> The maximum number of bytes that a single instruction can move quickly between memory and registers or between two memory locations. If this is undefined, the default is MOVE_MAX. Otherwise, it is the constant value that is the largest value that MOVE_MAX can have at run-time.

SHIFT_COUNT_TRUNCATED

> A C expression that is nonzero if on this machine the number of bits actually used for the count of a shift operation is equal to the number of bits needed to represent the size of the object being shifted. When this macro is non-zero, the compiler will assume that it is safe to omit a sign-extend, zero-extend, and certain bitwise 'and' instructions that truncates the count of a shift operation. On machines that have instructions that act on bitfields at variable positions, which may include 'bit test' instructions, a nonzero SHIFT_COUNT_TRUNCATED also enables deletion of truncations of the values that serve as arguments to bitfield instructions.

> If both types of instructions truncate the count (for shifts) and position (for bitfield operations), or if no variable-position bitfield instructions exist, you should define this macro.

However, on some machines, such as the 80386 and the 680x0, truncation only applies to shift operations and not the (real or pretended) bitfield operations. Define `SHIFT_COUNT_TRUNCATED` to be zero on such machines. Instead, add patterns to the 'md' file that include the implied truncation of the shift instructions.

You need not define this macro if it would always have the value of zero.

`TRULY_NOOP_TRUNCATION` (*outprec*, *inprec*)

A C expression which is nonzero if on this machine it is safe to "convert" an integer of *inprec* bits to one of *outprec* bits (where *outprec* is smaller than *inprec*) by merely operating on it as if it had only *outprec* bits.

On many machines, this expression can be 1.

When `TRULY_NOOP_TRUNCATION` returns 1 for a pair of sizes for modes for which `MODES_TIEABLE_P` is 0, suboptimal code can result. If this is the case, making `TRULY_NOOP_TRUNCATION` return 0 in such cases may improve things.

`STORE_FLAG_VALUE`

A C expression describing the value returned by a comparison operator with an integral mode and stored by a store-flag instruction ('s*cond*') when the condition is true. This description must apply to *all* the 's*cond*' patterns and all the comparison operators whose results have a `MODE_INT` mode.

A value of 1 or -1 means that the instruction implementing the comparison operator returns exactly 1 or -1 when the comparison is true and 0 when the comparison is false. Otherwise, the value indicates which bits of the result are guaranteed to be 1 when the comparison is true. This value is interpreted in the mode of the comparison operation, which is given by the mode of the first operand in the 's*cond*' pattern. Either the low bit or the sign bit of `STORE_FLAG_VALUE` be on. Presently, only those bits are used by the compiler.

If `STORE_FLAG_VALUE` is neither 1 or -1, the compiler will generate code that depends only on the specified bits. It can also replace comparison operators with equivalent operations if they cause the required bits to be set, even if the remaining bits are undefined. For example, on a machine whose comparison operators return an `SImode` value and where `STORE_FLAG_VALUE` is defined as '0x80000000', saying that just the sign bit is relevant, the expression

        (ne:SI (and:SI x (const_int *power-of-2*)) (const_int 0))

can be converted to

        (ashift:SI x (const_int *n*))

where n is the appropriate shift count to move the bit being tested into the sign bit.

There is no way to describe a machine that always sets the low-order bit for a true value, but does not guarantee the value of any other bits, but we do not know of any machine that has such an instruction. If you are trying to port GNU CC to such a machine, include an instruction to perform a logical-and of the result with 1 in the pattern for the comparison operators and let us know. (see Section 8.3 [How to Report Bugs], page 252).

Often, a machine will have multiple instructions that obtain a value from a comparison (or the condition codes). Here are rules to guide the choice of value for `STORE_FLAG_VALUE`, and hence the instructions to be used:

- Use the shortest sequence that yields a valid definition for `STORE_FLAG_VALUE`. It is more efficient for the compiler to "normalize" the value (convert it to, e.g., 1 or 0) than for the comparison operators to do so because there may be opportunities to combine the normalization with other operations.

- For equal-length sequences, use a value of 1 or -1, with -1 being slightly preferred on machines with expensive jumps and 1 preferred on other machines.

- As a second choice, choose a value of '0x80000001' if instructions exist that set both the sign and low-order bits but do not define the others.

- Otherwise, use a value of '0x80000000'.

Many machines can produce both the value chosen for `STORE_FLAG_VALUE` and its negation in the same number of instructions. On those machines, you should also define a pattern for those cases, e.g., one matching

```
(set A (neg:m (ne:m B C)))
```

Some machines can also perform **and** or **plus** operations on condition code values with less instructions than the corresponding '*scond*' insn followed by **and** or **plus**. On those machines, define the appropriate patterns. Use the names `incscc` and `decscc`, respectively, for the patterns which perform **plus** or **minus** operations on condition code values. See '`rs6000.md`' for some examples. The GNU Superoptizer can be used to find such instruction sequences on other machines.

You need not define `STORE_FLAG_VALUE` if the machine has no store-flag instructions.

FLOAT_STORE_FLAG_VALUE

A C expression that gives a non-zero floating point value that is returned when comparison operators with floating-point results are true. Define this macro on machine that have comparison operations that return floating-point values. If there are no such operations, do not define this macro.

Pmode

An alias for the machine mode for pointers. On most machines, define this to be the integer mode corresponding to the width of a hardware pointer; `SImode` on 32-bit machine or `DImode` on 64-bit machines. On some machines you must define this to be one of the partial integer modes, such as `PSImode`.

The width of `Pmode` must be at least as large as the value of `POINTER_SIZE`. If it is not equal, you must define the macro `POINTERS_EXTEND_UNSIGNED` to specify how pointers are extended to `Pmode`.

FUNCTION_MODE

An alias for the machine mode used for memory references to functions being called, in `call` RTL expressions. On most machines this should be `QImode`.

INTEGRATE_THRESHOLD (*decl*)

A C expression for the maximum number of instructions above which the function *decl* should not be inlined. *decl* is a `FUNCTION_DECL` node.

The default definition of this macro is 64 plus 8 times the number of arguments that the function accepts. Some people think a larger threshold should be used on RISC machines.

SCCS_DIRECTIVE

Define this if the preprocessor should ignore `#sccs` directives and print no error message.

NO_IMPLICIT_EXTERN_C

Define this macro if the system header files support C++ as well as C. This macro inhibits the usual method of using system header files in C++, which is to pretend that the file's contents are enclosed in '`extern "C" {...}`'.

HANDLE_PRAGMA (*getc, ungetc, name*)

Define this macro if you want to implement any pragmas. If defined, it is a C expression whose value is 1 if the pragma was handled by the macro, zero otherwise. The argument *getc* is a function of type '`int (*)(void)`' which will return the next character in the input stream, or EOF if no characters are left. The argument *ungetc* is a function of type '`void (*)(int)`' which will push a character back into the input stream. The argument *name* is the word following #pragma in the input stream.

The input stream pointer will be pointing just beyond the end of this word. The input stream should be left undistrubed if the expression returns zero, otherwise it should be pointing at the next character after the end of the pragma. Any characters remaining on the line will be ignored.

It is generally a bad idea to implement new uses of `#pragma`. The only reason to define this macro is for compatibility with other compilers that do support `#pragma` for the sake of any user programs which already use it.

If the pragma can be implemented by atttributes then the macro 'INSERT_ATTRIBUTES' might be a useful one to define as well.

Note: older versions of this macro only had two arguments: *stream* and *token*. The macro was changed in order to allow it to work when gcc is built both with and without a cpp library.

HANDLE_SYSV_PRAGMA

Define this macro (to a value of 1) if you want the System V style pragmas '`#pragma pack(<n>)`' and '`#pragma weak <name> [=<value>]`' to be supported by gcc.

The pack pragma specifies the maximum alignment (in bytes) of fields within a structure, in much the same way as the '`__aligned__`' and '`__packed__`' `__attribute__`s do. A pack value of zero resets the behaviour to the default.

The weak pragma only works if `SUPPORTS_WEAK` and `ASM_WEAKEN_LABEL` are defined. If enabled it allows the creation of specifically named weak labels, optionally with a value.

HANDLE_PRAGMA_PACK_PUSH_POP

Define this macro (to a value of 1) if you want to support the Win32 style pragmas '`#pragma pack(push,<n>)`' and '`#pragma pack(pop)`'. The pack(push,<n>) pragma specifies the maximum alignment (in bytes) of fields within a structure, in much the same way as the '`__aligned__`' and '`__packed__`' `__attribute__`s do. A pack value of zero resets the behaviour to the default. Successive invocations of this pragma cause the previous values to be stacked, so that invocations of '`#pragma pack(pop)`' will return to the previous value.

VALID_MACHINE_DECL_ATTRIBUTE (*decl, attributes, identifier, args*)

If defined, a C expression whose value is nonzero if *identifier* with arguments *args* is a valid machine specific attribute for *decl*. The attributes in *attributes* have previously been assigned to *decl*.

VALID_MACHINE_TYPE_ATTRIBUTE (*type, attributes, identifier, args*)

If defined, a C expression whose value is nonzero if *identifier* with arguments *args* is a valid machine specific attribute for *type*. The attributes in *attributes* have previously been assigned to *type*.

COMP_TYPE_ATTRIBUTES (*type1*, *type2*)

If defined, a C expression whose value is zero if the attributes on *type1* and *type2* are incompatible, one if they are compatible, and two if they are nearly compatible (which causes a warning to be generated).

SET_DEFAULT_TYPE_ATTRIBUTES (*type*)

If defined, a C statement that assigns default attributes to newly defined *type*.

MERGE_MACHINE_TYPE_ATTRIBUTES (*type1*, *type2*)

Define this macro if the merging of type attributes needs special handling. If defined, the result is a list of the combined TYPE_ATTRIBUTES of *type1* and *type2*. It is assumed that comptypes has already been called and returned 1.

MERGE_MACHINE_DECL_ATTRIBUTES (*olddecl*, *newdecl*)

Define this macro if the merging of decl attributes needs special handling. If defined, the result is a list of the combined DECL_MACHINE_ATTRIBUTES of *olddecl* and *newdecl*. *newdecl* is a duplicate declaration of *olddecl*. Examples of when this is needed are when one attribute overrides another, or when an attribute is nullified by a subsequent definition.

INSERT_ATTRIBUTES (*node*, *attr_ptr*, *prefix_ptr*)

Define this macro if you want to be able to add attributes to a decl when it is being created. This is normally useful for backends which wish to implement a pragma by using the attributes which correspond to the pragma's effect. The *node* argument is the decl which is being created. The *attr_ptr* argument is a pointer to the attribute list for this decl. The *prefix_ptr* is a pointer to the list of attributes that have appeared after the specifiers and modifiers of the declaration, but before the declaration proper.

SET_DEFAULT_DECL_ATTRIBUTES (*decl*, *attributes*)

If defined, a C statement that assigns default attributes to newly defined *decl*.

DOLLARS_IN_IDENTIFIERS

Define this macro to control use of the character '$' in identifier names. 0 means '$' is not allowed by default; 1 means it is allowed. 1 is the default; there is no need to define this macro in that case. This macro controls the compiler proper; it does not affect the preprocessor.

NO_DOLLAR_IN_LABEL

> Define this macro if the assembler does not accept the character '$' in label names. By default constructors and destructors in G++ have '$' in the identifiers. If this macro is defined, '.' is used instead.

NO_DOT_IN_LABEL

> Define this macro if the assembler does not accept the character '.' in label names. By default constructors and destructors in G++ have names that use '.'. If this macro is defined, these names are rewritten to avoid '.'.

DEFAULT_MAIN_RETURN

> Define this macro if the target system expects every program's main function to return a standard "success" value by default (if no other value is explicitly returned).

> The definition should be a C statement (sans semicolon) to generate the appropriate rtl instructions. It is used only when compiling the end of main.

HAVE_ATEXIT

> Define this if the target system supports the function atexit from the ANSI C standard. If this is not defined, and INIT_SECTION_ASM_OP is not defined, a default exit function will be provided to support C++.

EXIT_BODY

> Define this if your exit function needs to do something besides calling an external function _cleanup before terminating with _exit. The EXIT_BODY macro is only needed if neither HAVE_ATEXIT nor INIT_SECTION_ASM_OP are defined.

INSN_SETS_ARE_DELAYED (*insn*)

> Define this macro as a C expression that is nonzero if it is safe for the delay slot scheduler to place instructions in the delay slot of *insn*, even if they appear to use a resource set or clobbered in *insn*. *insn* is always a jump_insn or an insn; GNU CC knows that every call_insn has this behavior. On machines where some insn or jump_insn is really a function call and hence has this behavior, you should define this macro.

> You need not define this macro if it would always return zero.

INSN_REFERENCES_ARE_DELAYED (*insn*)

> Define this macro as a C expression that is nonzero if it is safe for the delay slot scheduler to place instructions in the delay slot of *insn*, even if they appear to set or clobber a resource referenced in *insn*. *insn* is always a jump_insn or an insn. On machines where some insn or jump_insn is really a function call and its operands are registers whose use is actually in the subroutine it

calls, you should define this macro. Doing so allows the delay slot scheduler to move instructions which copy arguments into the argument registers into the delay slot of *insn*.

You need not define this macro if it would always return zero.

MACHINE_DEPENDENT_REORG (*insn*)

In rare cases, correct code generation requires extra machine dependent processing between the second jump optimization pass and delayed branch scheduling. On those machines, define this macro as a C statement to act on the code starting at *insn*.

MULTIPLE_SYMBOL_SPACES

Define this macro if in some cases global symbols from one translation unit may not be bound to undefined symbols in another translation unit without user intervention. For instance, under Microsoft Windows symbols must be explicitly imported from shared libraries (DLLs).

ISSUE_RATE

A C expression that returns how many instructions can be issued at the same time if the machine is a superscalar machine. This is only used by the 'Haifa' scheduler, and not the traditional scheduler.

MD_SCHED_INIT (*file, verbose*)

A C statement which is executed by the 'Haifa' scheduler at the beginning of each block of instructions that are to be scheduled. *file* is either a null pointer, or a stdio stream to write any debug output to. *verbose* is the verbose level provided by '-fsched-verbose-'*n*.

MD_SCHED_REORDER (*file, verbose, ready, n_ready*)

A C statement which is executed by the 'Haifa' scheduler after it has scheduled the ready list to allow the machine description to reorder it (for example to combine two small instructions together on 'VLIW' machines). *file* is either a null pointer, or a stdio stream to write any debug output to. *verbose* is the verbose level provided by '-fsched-verbose-'*n*. *ready* is a pointer to the ready list of instructions that are ready to be scheduled. *n_ready* is the number of elements in the ready list. The scheduler reads the ready list in reverse order, starting with *ready*[*n_ready*-1] and going to *ready*[0].

MD_SCHED_VARIABLE_ISSUE (*file, verbose, insn, more*)

A C statement which is executed by the 'Haifa' scheduler after it has scheduled an insn from the ready list. *file* is either a null pointer, or a stdio stream to write any debug output to. *verbose* is the verbose level provided by '-fsched-verbose-'*n*. *insn* is the instruction that was scheduled. *more* is the number

of instructions that can be issued in the current cycle. The
'MD_SCHED_VARIABLE_ISSUE' macro is responsible for updating
the value of *more* (typically by *more–*).

MAX_INTEGER_COMPUTATION_MODE

Define this to the largest integer machine mode which can be
used for operations other than load, store and copy operations.

You need only define this macro if the target holds values larger
than word_mode in general purpose registers. Most targets
should not define this macro.

MATH_LIBRARY

Define this macro as a C string constant for the linker argument
to link in the system math library, or '""' if the target does not
have a separate math library.

You need only define this macro if the default of '"-lm"' is wrong.

18 The Configuration File

The configuration file 'xm-*machine*.h' contains macro definitions that describe the machine and system on which the compiler is running, unlike the definitions in '*machine*.h', which describe the machine for which the compiler is producing output. Most of the values in 'xm-*machine*.h' are actually the same on all machines that GCC runs on, so large parts of all configuration files are identical. But there are some macros that vary:

USG   Define this macro if the host system is System V.

VMS   Define this macro if the host system is VMS.

FATAL_EXIT_CODE
           A C expression for the status code to be returned when the compiler exits after serious errors.

SUCCESS_EXIT_CODE
           A C expression for the status code to be returned when the compiler exits without serious errors.

HOST_WORDS_BIG_ENDIAN
           Defined if the host machine stores words of multi-word values in big-endian order. (GCC does not depend on the host byte ordering within a word.)

HOST_FLOAT_WORDS_BIG_ENDIAN
           Define this macro to be 1 if the host machine stores DFmode, XFmode or TFmode floating point numbers in memory with the word containing the sign bit at the lowest address; otherwise, define it to be zero.

           This macro need not be defined if the ordering is the same as for multi-word integers.

HOST_FLOAT_FORMAT
           A numeric code distinguishing the floating point format for the host machine. See TARGET_FLOAT_FORMAT in Section 17.3 [Storage Layout], page 403 for the alternatives and default.

HOST_BITS_PER_CHAR
           A C expression for the number of bits in char on the host machine.

HOST_BITS_PER_SHORT
           A C expression for the number of bits in short on the host machine.

HOST_BITS_PER_INT
           A C expression for the number of bits in int on the host machine.

HOST_BITS_PER_LONG
> A C expression for the number of bits in **long** on the host machine.

ONLY_INT_FIELDS
> Define this macro to indicate that the host compiler only supports **int** bit fields, rather than other integral types, including **enum**, as do most C compilers.

OBSTACK_CHUNK_SIZE
> A C expression for the size of ordinary obstack chunks. If you don't define this, a usually-reasonable default is used.

OBSTACK_CHUNK_ALLOC
> The function used to allocate obstack chunks. If you don't define this, **xmalloc** is used.

OBSTACK_CHUNK_FREE
> The function used to free obstack chunks. If you don't define this, **free** is used.

USE_C_ALLOCA
> Define this macro to indicate that the compiler is running with the **alloca** implemented in C. This version of **alloca** can be found in the file 'alloca.c'; to use it, you must also alter the 'Makefile' variable ALLOCA. (This is done automatically for the systems on which we know it is needed.)
>
> If you do define this macro, you should probably do it as follows:
>
> ```
> #ifndef __GNUC__
> #define USE_C_ALLOCA
> #else
> #define alloca __builtin_alloca
> #endif
> ```
>
> so that when the compiler is compiled with GCC it uses the more efficient built-in **alloca** function.

FUNCTION_CONVERSION_BUG
> Define this macro to indicate that the host compiler does not properly handle converting a function value to a pointer-to-function when it is used in an expression.

MULTIBYTE_CHARS
> Define this macro to enable support for multibyte characters in the input to GCC. This requires that the host system support the ANSI C library functions for converting multibyte characters to wide characters.

POSIX   Define this if your system is POSIX.1 compliant.

NO_SYS_SIGLIST

> Define this if your system *does not* provide the variable `sys_siglist`.
>
> Some systems do provide this variable, but with a different name such as `_sys_siglist`. On these systems, you can define `sys_siglist` as a macro which expands into the name actually provided.
>
> Autoconf normally defines `SYS_SIGLIST_DECLARED` when it finds a declaration of `sys_siglist` in the system header files. However, when you define `sys_siglist` to a different name autoconf will not automatically define `SYS_SIGLIST_DECLARED`. Therefore, if you define `sys_siglist`, you should also define `SYS_SIGLIST_DECLARED`.

USE_PROTOTYPES

> Define this to be 1 if you know that the host compiler supports prototypes, even if it doesn't define `__STDC__`, or define it to be 0 if you do not want any prototypes used in compiling GCC. If 'USE_PROTOTYPES' is not defined, it will be determined automatically whether your compiler supports prototypes by checking if '`__STDC__`' is defined.

NO_MD_PROTOTYPES

> Define this if you wish suppression of prototypes generated from the machine description file, but to use other prototypes within GCC. If 'USE_PROTOTYPES' is defined to be 0, or the host compiler does not support prototypes, this macro has no effect.

MD_CALL_PROTOTYPES

> Define this if you wish to generate prototypes for the `gen_call` or `gen_call_value` functions generated from the machine description file. If 'USE_PROTOTYPES' is defined to be 0, or the host compiler does not support prototypes, or 'NO_MD_PROTOTYPES' is defined, this macro has no effect. As soon as all of the machine descriptions are modified to have the appropriate number of arguments, this macro will be removed.

PATH_SEPARATOR

> Define this macro to be a C character constant representing the character used to separate components in paths. The default value is the colon character

DIR_SEPARATOR

> If your system uses some character other than slash to separate directory names within a file specification, define this macro to be a C character constant specifying that character. When GCC displays file names, the character you specify will be used. GCC will test for both slash and the character you specify when parsing filenames.

OBJECT_SUFFIX

> Define this macro to be a C string representing the suffix for object files on your machine. If you do not define this macro, GCC will use '.o' as the suffix for object files.

EXECUTABLE_SUFFIX

> Define this macro to be a C string representing the suffix for executable files on your machine. If you do not define this macro, GCC will use the null string as the suffix for object files.

COLLECT_EXPORT_LIST

> If defined, `collect2` will scan the individual object files specified on its command line and create an export list for the linker. Define this macro for systems like AIX, where the linker discards object files that are not referenced from `main` and uses export lists.

In addition, configuration files for system V define `bcopy`, `bzero` and `bcmp` as aliases. Some files define `alloca` as a macro when compiled with GCC, in order to take advantage of the benefit of GCC's built-in `alloca`.

19 Makefile Fragments

When you configure GCC using the 'configure' script (see Chapter 3 [Installation], page 121), it will construct the file 'Makefile' from the template file 'Makefile.in'. When it does this, it will incorporate makefile fragment files from the 'config' directory, named 't-*target*' and 'x-*host*'. If these files do not exist, it means nothing needs to be added for a given target or host.

19.1 The Target Makefile Fragment

The target makefile fragment, 't-*target*', defines special target dependent variables and targets used in the 'Makefile':

LIBGCC1   The rule to use to build 'libgcc1.a'. If your target does not need to use the functions in 'libgcc1.a', set this to empty. See Chapter 13 [Interface], page 271.

CROSS_LIBGCC1

The rule to use to build 'libgcc1.a' when building a cross compiler. If your target does not need to use the functions in 'libgcc1.a', set this to empty. See Section 3.4.4 [Cross Runtime], page 151.

LIBGCC2_CFLAGS

Compiler flags to use when compiling 'libgcc2.c'.

LIB2FUNCS_EXTRA

A list of source file names to be compiled or assembled and inserted into 'libgcc.a'.

CRTSTUFF_T_CFLAGS

Special flags used when compiling 'crtstuff.c'. See Section 17.16.5 [Initialization], page 490.

CRTSTUFF_T_CFLAGS_S

Special flags used when compiling 'crtstuff.c' for shared linking. Used if you use 'crtbeginS.o' and 'crtendS.o' in EXTRA-PARTS. See Section 17.16.5 [Initialization], page 490.

MULTILIB_OPTIONS

For some targets, invoking GCC in different ways produces objects that can not be linked together. For example, for some targets GCC produces both big and little endian code. For these targets, you must arrange for multiple versions of 'libgcc.a' to be compiled, one for each set of incompatible options. When GCC invokes the linker, it arranges to link in the right version of 'libgcc.a', based on the command line options used.

The `MULTILIB_OPTIONS` macro lists the set of options for which special versions of 'libgcc.a' must be built. Write options that are mutually incompatible side by side, separated by a slash. Write options that may be used together separated by a space. The build procedure will build all combinations of compatible options.

For example, if you set `MULTILIB_OPTIONS` to 'm68000/m68020 msoft-float', 'Makefile' will build special versions of 'libgcc.a' using the following sets of options: '-m68000', '-m68020', '-msoft-float', '-m68000 -msoft-float', and '-m68020 -msoft-float'.

`MULTILIB_DIRNAMES`

If `MULTILIB_OPTIONS` is used, this variable specifies the directory names that should be used to hold the various libraries. Write one element in `MULTILIB_DIRNAMES` for each element in `MULTILIB_OPTIONS`. If `MULTILIB_DIRNAMES` is not used, the default value will be `MULTILIB_OPTIONS`, with all slashes treated as spaces.

For example, if `MULTILIB_OPTIONS` is set to 'm68000/m68020 msoft-float', then the default value of `MULTILIB_DIRNAMES` is 'm68000 m68020 msoft-float'. You may specify a different value if you desire a different set of directory names.

`MULTILIB_MATCHES`

Sometimes the same option may be written in two different ways. If an option is listed in `MULTILIB_OPTIONS`, GCC needs to know about any synonyms. In that case, set `MULTILIB_MATCHES` to a list of items of the form 'option=option' to describe all relevant synonyms. For example, 'm68000=mc68000 m68020=mc68020'.

`MULTILIB_EXCEPTIONS`

Sometimes when there are multiple sets of `MULTILIB_OPTIONS` being specified, there are combinations that should not be built. In that case, set `MULTILIB_EXCEPTIONS` to be all of the switch exceptions in shell case syntax that should not be built.

For example, in the PowerPC embedded ABI support, it was not desirable to build libraries that compiled with the '-mcall-aixdesc' option and either of the '-mcall-aixdesc' or '-mlittle' options at the same time, and therefore `MULTILIB_EXCEPTIONS` is set to *mrelocatable/*mcall-aixdesc* *mlittle/*mcall-aixdesc*.

`MULTILIB_EXTRA_OPTS`

Sometimes it is desirable that when building multiple versions of 'libgcc.a' certain options should always be passed on to the compiler. In that case, set `MULTILIB_EXTRA_OPTS` to be the list of options to be used for all builds.

19.2 The Host Makefile Fragment

The host makefile fragment, 'x-*host*', defines special host dependent variables and targets used in the 'Makefile':

CC   The compiler to use when building the first stage.

CLIB   Additional host libraries to link with.

OLDCC   The compiler to use when building 'libgcc1.a' for a native compilation.

OLDAR   The version of **ar** to use when building 'libgcc1.a' for a native compilation.

INSTALL   The install program to use.

Funding Free Software

If you want to have more free software a few years from now, it makes sense for you to help encourage people to contribute funds for its development. The most effective approach known is to encourage commercial redistributors to donate.

Users of free software systems can boost the pace of development by encouraging for-a-fee distributors to donate part of their selling price to free software developers—the Free Software Foundation, and others.

The way to convince distributors to do this is to demand it and expect it from them. So when you compare distributors, judge them partly by how much they give to free software development. Show distributors they must compete to be the one who gives the most.

To make this approach work, you must insist on numbers that you can compare, such as, "We will donate ten dollars to the Frobnitz project for each disk sold." Don't be satisfied with a vague promise, such as "A portion of the profits are donated," since it doesn't give a basis for comparison.

Even a precise fraction "of the profits from this disk" is not very meaningful, since creative accounting and unrelated business decisions can greatly alter what fraction of the sales price counts as profit. If the price you pay is $50, ten percent of the profit is probably less than a dollar; it might be a few cents, or nothing at all.

Some redistributors do development work themselves. This is useful too; but to keep everyone honest, you need to inquire how much they do, and what kind. Some kinds of development make much more long-term difference than others. For example, maintaining a separate version of a program contributes very little; maintaining the standard version of a program for the whole community contributes much. Easy new ports contribute little, since someone else would surely do them; difficult ports such as adding a new CPU to the GNU Compiler Collection contribute more; major new features or packages contribute the most.

By establishing the idea that supporting further development is "the proper thing to do" when distributing free software for a fee, we can assure a steady flow of resources into making more free software.

Linux and the GNU Project

Many computer users run a modified version of the GNU system every day, without realizing it. Through a peculiar turn of events, the version of GNU which is widely used today is more often known as "Linux", and many users are not aware of the extent of its connection with the GNU Project.

There really is a Linux; it is a kernel, and these people are using it. But you can't use a kernel by itself; a kernel is useful only as part of a whole system. The system in which Linux is typically used is a modified variant of the GNU system—in other words, a Linux-based GNU system.

Many users are not fully aware of the distinction between the kernel, which is Linux, and the whole system, which they also call "Linux". The ambiguous use of the name doesn't promote understanding.

Programmers generally know that Linux is a kernel. But since they have generally heard the whole system called "Linux" as well, they often envisage a history which fits that name. For example, many believe that once Linus Torvalds finished writing the kernel, his friends looked around for other free software, and for no particular reason most everything necessary to make a Unix-like system was already available.

What they found was no accident—it was the GNU system. The available free software added up to a complete system because the GNU Project had been working since 1984 to make one. The GNU Manifesto had set forth the goal of developing a free Unix-like system, called GNU. By the time Linux was written, the system was almost finished.

Most free software projects have the goal of developing a particular program for a particular job. For example, Linus Torvalds set out to write a Unix-like kernel (Linux); Donald Knuth set out to write a text formatter (TeX); Bob Scheifler set out to develop a window system (X Windows). It's natural to measure the contribution of this kind of project by specific programs that came from the project.

If we tried to measure the GNU Project's contribution in this way, what would we conclude? One CD-ROM vendor found that in their "Linux distribution", GNU software was the largest single contingent, around 28% of the total source code, and this included some of the essential major components without which there could be no system. Linux itself was about 3%. So if you were going to pick a name for the system based on who wrote the programs in the system, the most appropriate single choice would be "GNU".

But we don't think that is the right way to consider the question. The GNU Project was not, is not, a project to develop specific software packages. It was not a project to develop a C compiler, although we did. It was not a project to develop a text editor, although we developed one. The GNU Project's aim was to develop *a complete free Unix-like system*.

Many people have made major contributions to the free software in the system, and they all deserve credit. But the reason it is *a system*—and not just a collection of useful programs—is because the GNU Project set out to make it one. We wrote the programs that were needed to make a *complete* free system. We wrote essential but unexciting major components, such as the assembler and linker, because you can't have a system without them. A complete system needs more than just programming tools, so we wrote other components as well, such as the Bourne Again SHell, the PostScript interpreter Ghostscript, and the GNU C library.

By the early 90s we had put together the whole system aside from the kernel (and we were also working on a kernel, the GNU Hurd, which runs on top of Mach). Developing this kernel has been a lot harder than we expected, and we are still working on finishing it.

Fortunately, you don't have to wait for it, because Linux is working now. When Linus Torvalds wrote Linux, he filled the last major gap. People could then put Linux together with the GNU system to make a complete free system: a Linux-based GNU system (or GNU/Linux system, for short).

Putting them together sounds simple, but it was not a trivial job. The GNU C library (called glibc for short) needed substantial changes. Integrating a complete system as a distribution that would work "out of the box" was a big job, too. It required addressing the issue of how to install and boot the system—a problem we had not tackled, because we hadn't yet reached that point. The people who developed the various system distributions made a substantial contribution.

The GNU Project supports GNU/Linux systems as well as *the* GNU system—even with funds. We funded the rewriting of the Linux-related extensions to the GNU C library, so that now they are well integrated, and the newest GNU/Linux systems use the current library release with no changes. We also funded an early stage of the development of Debian GNU/Linux.

We use Linux-based GNU systems today for most of our work, and we hope you use them too. But please don't confuse the public by using the name "Linux" ambiguously. Linux is the kernel, one of the essential major components of the system. The system as a whole is more or less the GNU system.

GNU GENERAL PUBLIC LICENSE

Version 2, June 1991

Copyright © 1989, 1991 Free Software Foundation, Inc.
59 Temple Place - Suite 330, Boston, MA 02111-1307, USA

Preamble

The licenses for most software are designed to take away your freedom to share and change it. By contrast, the GNU General Public License is intended to guarantee your freedom to share and change free software—to make sure the software is free for all its users. This General Public License applies to most of the Free Software Foundation's software and to any other program whose authors commit to using it. (Some other Free Software Foundation software is covered by the GNU Library General Public License instead.) You can apply it to your programs, too.

When we speak of free software, we are referring to freedom, not price. Our General Public Licenses are designed to make sure that you have the freedom to distribute copies of free software (and charge for this service if you wish), that you receive source code or can get it if you want it, that you can change the software or use pieces of it in new free programs; and that you know you can do these things.

To protect your rights, we need to make restrictions that forbid anyone to deny you these rights or to ask you to surrender the rights. These restrictions translate to certain responsibilities for you if you distribute copies of the software, or if you modify it.

For example, if you distribute copies of such a program, whether gratis or for a fee, you must give the recipients all the rights that you have. You must make sure that they, too, receive or can get the source code. And you must show them these terms so they know their rights.

We protect your rights with two steps: (1) copyright the software, and (2) offer you this license which gives you legal permission to copy, distribute and/or modify the software.

Also, for each author's protection and ours, we want to make certain that everyone understands that there is no warranty for this free software. If the software is modified by someone else and passed on, we want its recipients to know that what they have is not the original, so that any problems introduced by others will not reflect on the original authors' reputations.

Finally, any free program is threatened constantly by software patents. We wish to avoid the danger that redistributors of a free program will individually obtain patent licenses, in effect making the program proprietary.

To prevent this, we have made it clear that any patent must be licensed for everyone's free use or not licensed at all.

The precise terms and conditions for copying, distribution and modification follow.

TERMS AND CONDITIONS FOR COPYING, DISTRIBUTION AND MODIFICATION

0. This License applies to any program or other work which contains a notice placed by the copyright holder saying it may be distributed under the terms of this General Public License. The "Program", below, refers to any such program or work, and a "work based on the Program" means either the Program or any derivative work under copyright law: that is to say, a work containing the Program or a portion of it, either verbatim or with modifications and/or translated into another language. (Hereinafter, translation is included without limitation in the term "modification".) Each licensee is addressed as "you".

   Activities other than copying, distribution and modification are not covered by this License; they are outside its scope. The act of running the Program is not restricted, and the output from the Program is covered only if its contents constitute a work based on the Program (independent of having been made by running the Program). Whether that is true depends on what the Program does.

1. You may copy and distribute verbatim copies of the Program's source code as you receive it, in any medium, provided that you conspicuously and appropriately publish on each copy an appropriate copyright notice and disclaimer of warranty; keep intact all the notices that refer to this License and to the absence of any warranty; and give any other recipients of the Program a copy of this License along with the Program.

   You may charge a fee for the physical act of transferring a copy, and you may at your option offer warranty protection in exchange for a fee.

2. You may modify your copy or copies of the Program or any portion of it, thus forming a work based on the Program, and copy and distribute such modifications or work under the terms of Section 1 above, provided that you also meet all of these conditions:

   a. You must cause the modified files to carry prominent notices stating that you changed the files and the date of any change.

   b. You must cause any work that you distribute or publish, that in whole or in part contains or is derived from the Program or any part thereof, to be licensed as a whole at no charge to all third parties under the terms of this License.

   c. If the modified program normally reads commands interactively when run, you must cause it, when started running for such interactive use in the most ordinary way, to print or display an announcement including an appropriate copyright notice and a notice that there is no warranty (or else, saying that you provide a warranty) and that users may redistribute the program under these conditions, and telling the user how to view a copy of this License. (Exception: if the Program itself is interactive but does not normally print such an announcement, your work based on the Program is not required to print an announcement.)

These requirements apply to the modified work as a whole. If identifiable sections of that work are not derived from the Program, and can be reasonably considered independent and separate works in themselves, then this License, and its terms, do not apply to those sections when you distribute them as separate works. But when you distribute the same sections as part of a whole which is a work based on the Program, the distribution of the whole must be on the terms of this License, whose permissions for other licensees extend to the entire whole, and thus to each and every part regardless of who wrote it.

Thus, it is not the intent of this section to claim rights or contest your rights to work written entirely by you; rather, the intent is to exercise the right to control the distribution of derivative or collective works based on the Program.

In addition, mere aggregation of another work not based on the Program with the Program (or with a work based on the Program) on a volume of a storage or distribution medium does not bring the other work under the scope of this License.

3. You may copy and distribute the Program (or a work based on it, under Section 2) in object code or executable form under the terms of Sections 1 and 2 above provided that you also do one of the following:

   a. Accompany it with the complete corresponding machine-readable source code, which must be distributed under the terms of Sections 1 and 2 above on a medium customarily used for software interchange; or,

   b. Accompany it with a written offer, valid for at least three years, to give any third party, for a charge no more than your cost of physically performing source distribution, a complete machine-readable copy of the corresponding source code, to be distributed under the terms of Sections 1 and 2 above on a medium customarily used for software interchange; or,

   c. Accompany it with the information you received as to the offer to distribute corresponding source code. (This alternative is allowed only for noncommercial distribution and only if you received the program in object code or executable form with such an offer, in accord with Subsection b above.)

The source code for a work means the preferred form of the work for making modifications to it. For an executable work, complete source code means all the source code for all modules it contains, plus any associated interface definition files, plus the scripts used to control compilation and installation of the executable. However, as a special exception, the source code distributed need not include anything that is normally distributed (in either source or binary form) with the major components (compiler, kernel, and so on) of the operating system on which the executable runs, unless that component itself accompanies the executable.

If distribution of executable or object code is made by offering access to copy from a designated place, then offering equivalent access to copy the source code from the same place counts as distribution of the source code, even though third parties are not compelled to copy the source along with the object code.

4. You may not copy, modify, sublicense, or distribute the Program except as expressly provided under this License. Any attempt otherwise to copy, modify, sublicense or distribute the Program is void, and will automatically terminate your rights under this License. However, parties who have received copies, or rights, from you under this License will not have their licenses terminated so long as such parties remain in full compliance.

5. You are not required to accept this License, since you have not signed it. However, nothing else grants you permission to modify or distribute the Program or its derivative works. These actions are prohibited by law if you do not accept this License. Therefore, by modifying or distributing the Program (or any work based on the Program), you indicate your acceptance of this License to do so, and all its terms and conditions for copying, distributing or modifying the Program or works based on it.

6. Each time you redistribute the Program (or any work based on the Program), the recipient automatically receives a license from the original licensor to copy, distribute or modify the Program subject to these terms and conditions. You may not impose any further restrictions on the recipients' exercise of the rights granted herein. You are not responsible for enforcing compliance by third parties to this License.

7. If, as a consequence of a court judgment or allegation of patent infringement or for any other reason (not limited to patent issues), conditions are imposed on you (whether by court order, agreement or otherwise) that contradict the conditions of this License, they do not excuse you from the conditions of this License. If you cannot distribute so as to satisfy simultaneously your obligations under this License and any other pertinent obligations, then as a consequence you may not distribute the Program at all. For example, if a patent license would not permit royalty-free redistribution of the Program by all those who receive copies directly or indirectly through you, then the only way you could satisfy both it and this License would be to refrain entirely from distribution of the Program.

If any portion of this section is held invalid or unenforceable under any particular circumstance, the balance of the section is intended to apply and the section as a whole is intended to apply in other circumstances.

It is not the purpose of this section to induce you to infringe any patents or other property right claims or to contest validity of any such claims; this section has the sole purpose of protecting the integrity of the free software distribution system, which is implemented by public license practices. Many people have made generous contributions to the wide range of software distributed through that system in reliance on consistent application of that system; it is up to the author/donor to decide if he or she is willing to distribute software through any other system and a licensee cannot impose that choice.

This section is intended to make thoroughly clear what is believed to be a consequence of the rest of this License.

8. If the distribution and/or use of the Program is restricted in certain countries either by patents or by copyrighted interfaces, the original copyright holder who places the Program under this License may add an explicit geographical distribution limitation excluding those countries, so that distribution is permitted only in or among countries not thus excluded. In such case, this License incorporates the limitation as if written in the body of this License.

9. The Free Software Foundation may publish revised and/or new versions of the General Public License from time to time. Such new versions will be similar in spirit to the present version, but may differ in detail to address new problems or concerns.

Each version is given a distinguishing version number. If the Program specifies a version number of this License which applies to it and "any later version", you have the option of following the terms and conditions either of that version or of any later version published by the Free Software Foundation. If the Program does not specify a version number of this License, you may choose any version ever published by the Free Software Foundation.

10. If you wish to incorporate parts of the Program into other free programs whose distribution conditions are different, write to the author to ask for permission. For software which is copyrighted by the Free Software Foundation, write to the Free Software Foundation; we sometimes make exceptions for this. Our decision will be guided by the two goals of preserving the free status of all derivatives of our free software and of promoting the sharing and reuse of software generally.

NO WARRANTY

11. BECAUSE THE PROGRAM IS LICENSED FREE OF CHARGE, THERE IS NO WARRANTY FOR THE PROGRAM, TO THE EXTENT PERMITTED BY APPLICABLE LAW. EXCEPT WHEN

OTHERWISE STATED IN WRITING THE COPYRIGHT HOLDERS AND/OR OTHER PARTIES PROVIDE THE PROGRAM "AS IS" WITHOUT WARRANTY OF ANY KIND, EITHER EXPRESSED OR IMPLIED, INCLUDING, BUT NOT LIMITED TO, THE IMPLIED WARRANTIES OF MERCHANTABILITY AND FITNESS FOR A PARTICULAR PURPOSE. THE ENTIRE RISK AS TO THE QUALITY AND PERFORMANCE OF THE PROGRAM IS WITH YOU. SHOULD THE PROGRAM PROVE DEFECTIVE, YOU ASSUME THE COST OF ALL NECESSARY SERVICING, REPAIR OR CORRECTION.

12. IN NO EVENT UNLESS REQUIRED BY APPLICABLE LAW OR AGREED TO IN WRITING WILL ANY COPYRIGHT HOLDER, OR ANY OTHER PARTY WHO MAY MODIFY AND/OR REDISTRIBUTE THE PROGRAM AS PERMITTED ABOVE, BE LIABLE TO YOU FOR DAMAGES, INCLUDING ANY GENERAL, SPECIAL, INCIDENTAL OR CONSEQUENTIAL DAMAGES ARISING OUT OF THE USE OR INABILITY TO USE THE PROGRAM (INCLUDING BUT NOT LIMITED TO LOSS OF DATA OR DATA BEING RENDERED INACCURATE OR LOSSES SUSTAINED BY YOU OR THIRD PARTIES OR A FAILURE OF THE PROGRAM TO OPERATE WITH ANY OTHER PROGRAMS), EVEN IF SUCH HOLDER OR OTHER PARTY HAS BEEN ADVISED OF THE POSSIBILITY OF SUCH DAMAGES.

END OF TERMS AND CONDITIONS

How to Apply These Terms to Your New Programs

If you develop a new program, and you want it to be of the greatest possible use to the public, the best way to achieve this is to make it free software which everyone can redistribute and change under these terms.

To do so, attach the following notices to the program. It is safest to attach them to the start of each source file to most effectively convey the exclusion of warranty; and each file should have at least the "copyright" line and a pointer to where the full notice is found.

> *one line to give the program's name and a brief idea of what it does.*
> Copyright (C) *yyyy   name of author*
>
> This program is free software; you can redistribute it and/or modify
> it under the terms of the GNU General Public License as published by
> the Free Software Foundation; either version 2 of the License, or
> (at your option) any later version.
>
> This program is distributed in the hope that it will be useful,
> but WITHOUT ANY WARRANTY; without even the implied warranty of
> MERCHANTABILITY or FITNESS FOR A PARTICULAR PURPOSE. See the
> GNU General Public License for more details.
>
> You should have received a copy of the GNU General Public License
> along with this program; if not, write to the Free Software
> Foundation, Inc., 59 Temple Place - Suite 330, Boston, MA 02111-1307, USA.

Also add information on how to contact you by electronic and paper mail.

If the program is interactive, make it output a short notice like this when it starts in an interactive mode:

> Gnomovision version 69, Copyright (C) *yyyy name of author*
> Gnomovision comes with ABSOLUTELY NO WARRANTY; for details
> type 'show w'.
> This is free software, and you are welcome to redistribute it
> under certain conditions; type 'show c' for details.

The hypothetical commands 'show w' and 'show c' should show the appropriate parts of the General Public License. Of course, the commands you use may be called something other than 'show w' and 'show c'; they could even be mouse-clicks or menu items—whatever suits your program.

You should also get your employer (if you work as a programmer) or your school, if any, to sign a "copyright disclaimer" for the program, if necessary. Here is a sample; alter the names:

> Yoyodyne, Inc., hereby disclaims all copyright interest in the program
> 'Gnomovision' (which makes passes at compilers) written by James Hacker.

signature of Ty Coon, 1 April 1989

Ty Coon, President of Vice

This General Public License does not permit incorporating your program into proprietary programs. If your program is a subroutine library, you may consider it more useful to permit linking proprietary applications with the library. If this is what you want to do, use the GNU Library General Public License instead of this License.

Contributors to GCC

In addition to Richard Stallman, several people have written parts of GCC.

- The idea of using RTL and some of the optimization ideas came from the program PO written at the University of Arizona by Jack Davidson and Christopher Fraser. See "Register Allocation and Exhaustive Peephole Optimization", Software Practice and Experience 14 (9), Sept. 1984, 857-866.

- Paul Rubin wrote most of the preprocessor.

- Leonard Tower wrote parts of the parser, RTL generator, and RTL definitions, and of the Vax machine description.

- Ted Lemon wrote parts of the RTL reader and printer.

- Jim Wilson implemented loop strength reduction and some other loop optimizations.

- Nobuyuki Hikichi of Software Research Associates, Tokyo, contributed the support for the Sony NEWS machine.

- Charles LaBrec contributed the support for the Integrated Solutions 68020 system.

- Michael Tiemann of Cygnus Support wrote the front end for C++, as well as the support for inline functions and instruction scheduling. Also the descriptions of the National Semiconductor 32000 series cpu, the SPARC cpu and part of the Motorola 88000 cpu.

- Gerald Baumgartner added the signature extension to the C++ front-end.

- Jan Stein of the Chalmers Computer Society provided support for Genix, as well as part of the 32000 machine description.

- Randy Smith finished the Sun FPA support.

- Robert Brown implemented the support for Encore 32000 systems.

- David Kashtan of SRI adapted GCC to VMS.

- Alex Crain provided changes for the 3b1.

- Greg Satz and Chris Hanson assisted in making GCC work on HP-UX for the 9000 series 300.

- William Schelter did most of the work on the Intel 80386 support.

- Christopher Smith did the port for Convex machines.

- Paul Petersen wrote the machine description for the Alliant FX/8.

- Dario Dariol contributed the four varieties of sample programs that print a copy of their source.

- Alain Lichnewsky ported GCC to the Mips cpu.

- Devon Bowen, Dale Wiles and Kevin Zachmann ported GCC to the Tahoe.

- Jonathan Stone wrote the machine description for the Pyramid computer.

- Gary Miller ported GCC to Charles River Data Systems machines.

- Richard Kenner of the New York University Ultracomputer Research Laboratory wrote the machine descriptions for the AMD 29000, the DEC Alpha, the IBM RT PC, and the IBM RS/6000 as well as the support for instruction attributes. He also made changes to better support RISC processors including changes to common subexpression elimination, strength reduction, function calling sequence handling, and condition code support, in addition to generalizing the code for frame pointer elimination.

- Richard Kenner and Michael Tiemann jointly developed reorg.c, the delay slot scheduler.

- Mike Meissner and Tom Wood of Data General finished the port to the Motorola 88000.

- Masanobu Yuhara of Fujitsu Laboratories implemented the machine description for the Tron architecture (specifically, the Gmicro).

- NeXT, Inc. donated the front end that supports the Objective C language.

- James van Artsdalen wrote the code that makes efficient use of the Intel 80387 register stack.

- Mike Meissner at the Open Software Foundation finished the port to the MIPS cpu, including adding ECOFF debug support, and worked on the Intel port for the Intel 80386 cpu. Later at Cygnus Support, he worked on the rs6000 and PowerPC ports.

- Ron Guilmette implemented the `protoize` and `unprotoize` tools, the support for Dwarf symbolic debugging information, and much of the support for System V Release 4. He has also worked heavily on the Intel 386 and 860 support.

- Torbjorn Granlund implemented multiply- and divide-by-constant optimization, improved long long support, and improved leaf function register allocation.

- Mike Stump implemented the support for Elxsi 64 bit CPU.

- John Wehle added the machine description for the Western Electric 32000 processor used in several 3b series machines (no relation to the National Semiconductor 32000 processor).

- Holger Teutsch provided the support for the Clipper cpu.

- Kresten Krab Thorup wrote the run time support for the Objective C language.

- Stephen Moshier contributed the floating point emulator that assists in cross-compilation and permits support for floating point numbers wider than 64 bits.

- David Edelsohn contributed the changes to RS/6000 port to make it support the PowerPC and POWER2 architectures.
- Steve Chamberlain wrote the support for the Hitachi SH processor.
- Peter Schauer wrote the code to allow debugging to work on the Alpha.
- Oliver M. Kellogg of Deutsche Aerospace contributed the port to the MIL-STD-1750A.
- Michael K. Gschwind contributed the port to the PDP-11.
- David Reese of Sun Microsystems contributed to the Solaris on PowerPC port.

Index

!

#

$

%

&

,

(

*

-

.

/

=

?

_

B

G

H

I

J

K

L

M

N

O

P

Q

R

S

V

W

X

Z

Available from the Free Software Foundation...

This is a list of items available from the Free Software Foundation as of the publication of this manual. New items may not yet appear on this list. Please consult our web site at http://www.gnu.org/order/orders.html for current information and pricing, or call our distribution office at +1-617-542-5942.

BOOKS:

- **GNU Emacs Manual** - Using Emacs for editing. 518 pp. $30
- **GNU Emacs Lisp Reference Manual** - over 950 pp. $60
- **Programming in Emacs Lisp: An Introduction** - 257 pp. $20
- **Using and Porting GNU CC** - Compiler for C and more. 574 pp. $50
- **Debugging with GDB** - How to use the GNU Debugger. 201 pp. $20
- **GNU Make** - Extensions, writing makefiles, reference. 158 pp. $20
- **Bison Manual** - YACC-compatible parser generator. 104 pp. $20
- **GAWK: GNU Awk User's Guide** - Easy text processing. 324 pp. $25
- **Texinfo** - Producing printed and online documentation. 256 pp. $25
- **C Library Reference Manual** - Revised for V.2. 2 vol., 1080 pp. $50
- **Flex: The Lexical Scanner Generator** - An improved lex. 120 pp. $20
- **Termcap Manual** - Display terminal data base library. 64 pp. $15
- **Calc Manual** - Numeric math and algebra in GNU Emacs. 572 pp. $50

OTHER ITEMS:

- **GNU Source Code CD-ROM** All the GNU project source code - 3 discs.
- **GNU Compiler Tools Binaries CD-ROM** Directly installable compiler executables for several operating systems (see *http://www.gnu.org*).
- **GNU Software for MS-Windows and MS-DOS and Compatible Systems** - the GNU compiler, tools, and utilities for various Microsoft OSes and compatible systems. This CD-ROM comes with a printed guide to installation.
- **Reference cards** - available for Emacs, Calc, GDB, Flex, and Bison.
- **GNU t-shirts**

All purchases made from the FSF help support the development of more free software and documentation. The Free Software Foundation is a 501 (c) 3 not-for-profit corporation, and donations are tax-deductible in the U.S.

Free Software Foundation, 59 Temple Place, Suite 330, Boston, MA 02111
+1-617-542-5942 Fax: +1-617-542-2652 gnu@gnu.org http://www.gnu.org